The Institutions of Advanced Societies

*

THE INSTITUTIONS OF ADVANCED SOCIETIES

*

EDITED BY ARNOLD M. ROSE

*

UNIVERSITY OF MINNESOTA PRESS, MINNEAPOLIS

*

PREFACE

*

The idea for this volume came to me as I was participating in a meeting in Paris called by UNESCO, in June 1952, to discuss "The Teaching of Sociology." Professor Morris Ginsberg of the London School of Economics, one of the wisest sociologists of our times, pointed out that there were very few adequate teaching materials in comparative sociology. In fact, he might have added, contemporary sociologists have seriously neglected the *research* possibilities in the comparative study of institutions in the so-called advanced societies. Some anthropologists have made brilliant scientific studies by comparing specific aspects of a wide range of the so-called primitive societies. Some of them, with the aid of a few psychiatrists and psychologists, have attempted to study the advanced societies with the holistic approach characteristic of anthropology, and have developed such challenging concepts as "basic personality," "cultural themes," "national character," and even the methodological "culture at a distance." But contemporary sociologists have done very little work on the comparative study of society.

The challenge to sociologists is even greater than is implied above. One of the core fields of sociology, in theory, is the study of social organization or social institutions. But since the 1930s—when the works of Ballard, Chapin, Hertzler, and Panunzio appeared—there has been no textbook published in this field in the United States. In their worship of constantly new idols which they hope will turn out to be golden, sociologists neglect their tried and true gods. There are significant exceptions, of course: The study of the family has remained a constant in sociological history, and there has been a steady increase in the number of studies of industrial institutions. The popular structural-functionalist school has constantly called attention to the central role of social organization, although its primary object has been to expound a certain point of view. There have been a few studies of communities, though nowhere near the number that appeared during the 1930s, which have reported on institutions and have implied a comparative approach. American sociologists, working with a variety of other social scientists, have made penetrating analyses of the social structure of one society other than their own, the Soviet Union. But all this, I submit, is not enough.

Human behavior occurs within a social structure. However much we study various aspects of human behavior, in whatever settings, we cannot proceed beyond a certain point unless we understand the organizational framework for the behavior. We can best grasp the role of a given institutional structure by comparing it with others. By common agreement, teachers of the introductory course in sociology find it necessary to explain cultural relativism, and for this they almost invariably use anthropological materials on primitive societies. But apparently this means little to their students or to themselves and their colleagues—the family system of the Manus or the economic system of the Trobriand Islanders seems too remote, too "primitive," for pointing up the institutional framework of our own society. Not only would a description and analysis of the role of the French mistress or the German trade union be more pedagogically sound for the beginning American student, but it might also restrain some of our advanced researchers from making generalizations about "human behavior" from a study of thirty small groups of high school seniors in a typical midwestern city.

To what classroom use can a book on the *comparative* institutions of advanced societies be put? In the first place, as already suggested, it ought to be basic reading for the course on Social Organization or Social Institutions. Second, it could provide a sound approach for the developing general studies courses usually called Introduction to Social Science. Not only could it be used to provide a meaningful introduction to several social sciences, but it might also give a realistic basis for the international understanding which everyone seems so earnestly to desire. Even those who do not consider themselves students may find this value in the book. Third, the book might be used in some of the "area studies" courses now developing at many universities, although it is likely that these courses are too specialized to make central use of a book that covers so wide a ground.

The societies chosen for description in this volume represent a very broad geographic and cultural range. Invidious distinctions are inevitably implied when one uses the term "advanced" societies, but the intention was to indicate the limitation to societies which use writing, make formal education available to at least a sizable proportion of their younger citizens, and employ "modern" machinery in a significant part of their economic production.* It may come as a surprise to a number of our readers that some of the societies included in this volume properly fall under this definition. Obviously not all the societies falling under the definition could be reported on in this volume. A selection had to be made which was partly arbitrary, so as to keep within a reasonable length and still cover a great geographic and cultural range. Some exclusions were not arbitrary in the sense that no qualified scholar was available from those societies who could freely and objectively report on the structure of his society. I particularly regret the absence from the volume of an Asian society—if we ignore the purely geographic fact that Israel is in Asia—but it was not possible to gain the cooperation of an Asian sociologist.

Almost all the authors of the chapters of this volume are permanent native residents of the societies they are describing.† This gives them an access to materials of scholarship‡ and personal experience which few non-natives could have. It gives comparative sociology a participant quality that comparative anthropology can rarely have. At the same time, all the authors have the cultural perspective achieved by a significant period of residence and study abroad (mostly in the United States). Thus, they can take the point of view of the foreign reader in perceiving the exotic in what personally may seem commonplace. The authors are inevitably biased by being members of the societies they are describing, but no more so than sociologists generally are. In a few cases there is additional bias from perceived political pressures, but the reader can readily take account of these. There is also the bias involved in presenting one's own culture to a foreign audience.

While it is necessary to call the reader's attention to these possible

---

*Perhaps better ways to state this last criterion are to use the phrases "high energy society" (Fred Cottrell) and "society with a low proportion of its population in primary occupations" (Colin Clark). See Fred Cottrell, *Energy and Society* (New York: McGraw-Hill, 1955); Colin Clark, *The Conditions of Economic Progress* (London: Macmillan, 1940), pp. 337–373.

†The only exceptions are Professors Eisenstadt, Koty, and Willems who came to their societies as children or as young men (Professor Willems also is now on a permanent teaching appointment in the United States).

‡There was one disadvantage to this advantage: Not all of the contributors were meticulous in citing sources and where the sources were not available in standard American libraries, I had no way of checking and correcting them. Thus a few of the references are not complete and may not be reliable.

biases, it also seems proper to call attention to the honesty and courage of some of the authors who are subject to strong political pressures and yet have tried to depict their country's institutions objectively. Their courage might well point a lesson for the others of us who live under minimal political pressures and yet sometimes succumb to these, for the sake of personal advancement at the price of complete scientific honesty and objectivity.

The authors for all the societies but one—Australia—are primarily sociologists. The absence of sociologists in Australia led me to invite a psychologist and an economist to team up in an account of their society, and the quality of their product more than justifies the exception. Some of the authors are more than academic sociologists: Jan Szczepanski is a university president and Oleg Mandich is a professor of law.

I provided an outline so that the authors would produce comparable chapters. I was also accorded the privilege of rewriting and cutting, without changing the meaning or altering the point of view and interpretations, so that the style of presentation would not be too far out of harmony with good English usage and the chapters more in harmony with each other. Otherwise each author was an independent judge of what to include in the limited space assigned him. It is a sign of the growing maturity of sociology that comparable frameworks for selection of materials are evident throughout the chapters. Naturally each author felt constrained by the space limitation of fifty or seventy-five pages which were accorded to authors from "small" and "large" countries, respectively. Because at least half of the authors had difficulty in expressing themselves in the English language (only the French contribution had to be translated into English), the work of the editor was often difficult, laborious, and sometimes creative.

In the Introduction, I have attempted to draw a few generalizations directly from the concrete materials presented in the rest of the volume, but this basic task of comparative sociology is left far from complete. The main purpose of the Introduction is to examine the theoretical and methodological problems in the comparative study of modern societies. Ultimately we may look forward to systematic correlations of cultures and social environments, using specific societies or subsocieties as units. This book attempts to stimulate such studies, but does not attempt to carry them out. A single example of the research possibilities stimulated by the volume may be given by way of illustration: Several of the authors attempt to explain the failure of their societies to develop a large variety and number of voluntary associations in terms of their particular national histories. Yet a reading of the several contributions which make this type of analysis lead one to suspect that broader social forces—independent of specific national history—are also at work, and that a rigorous comparison of the social structures of the societies which have a significant development of voluntary associations with those that do not would point to such international forces as technological development, the class system, general social structure, and world ideologies.

I wish to take this opportunity to express my appreciation to the authors for their cooperation and their reasonable compliance with the many pressures and restrictions I felt it necessary to place on them in order to produce a coordinated volume. I am most indebted to my wife, Caroline Baer Rose, who shared the editorial responsibilities. I wish also to thank Helen Clapesattle, former director of the University of Minnesota Press, and Malcolm M. Willey, vice-president of the University of Minnesota, for their vision in perceiving the potential importance of this volume and encouraging its publication.

ARNOLD M. ROSE

June 1957
University of Minnesota

*

CONTENTS

*

ARNOLD M. ROSE, Professor of Sociology at the University of Minnesota, is the author of *The Negro's Morale: Group Identification and Protest* (1949), *Union Solidarity: The Internal Cohesion of a Labor Union* (1952), and *Theory and Method in the Social Sciences* (1954). He has taught and carried on research in France and Italy.

ANTHONY H. RICHMOND, Lecturer in Social Theory at the University of Edinburgh and visiting Professor of Sociology at Fisk University in 1957–58, is the author of *Colour Prejudice in Britain* (1954), *The Colour Problem* (1955), and has published articles on the sociology of industrial, social, and international relations.

RONALD TAFT, Senior Lecturer in Psychology at the University of Western Australia, took his Ph.D. degree at the University of California. He has published articles in the fields of social psychology, personality assessment, and personnel psychology. KENNETH F. WALKER, Professor and Head of the Department of Psychology at the University of Western Australia, took his Ph.D. degree at Harvard University. He was for ten years associated with the Australian Department of Labor, conducting research in personnel and industrial relations. He is the author of *Industrial Relations in Australia* (1956), and has published articles on general, experimental, and industrial psychology.

HEIKKI WARIS is Professor of Social Policy and Acting Professor of Sociology at the University of Helsinki. He undertook post-doctoral studies on a Rockefeller Foundation fellowship at the University of Chicago in 1934–35 and carried on research at several American universities in 1952–53. He has written numerous articles and studies, both in Finnish and English.

JAN SZCZEPANSKI, Professor of Sociology and Rector of the University of Lódź, has published several studies in Polish, including *The Techniques of Social Research*

(1951), *Sociological Theories of the Nineteenth and Twentieth Centuries* (1953), and two monographs, *The Philosophy and Sociology of Auguste Comte* (1952) and *The Problems of Social Research as Seen by Marx and Engels* (1952).

YUGOSLAVIA 274

OLEG MANDICH, Professor on the Faculty of Law at the University of Zagreb, is a specialist in sociology as related to law, politics, and religion. He has published a great number of articles pertaining to these three associated fields.

GREECE 330

JOHN KOTY, Professor of Sociology at the Institute of Social Sciences at the American College, Athens, lectured at Boston University and Ohio State University in 1950–51 as a Fulbright visiting professor. He has published a number of books and articles in Greek, including *Law in Primitive Communism* (1950) and *Social Stratification in Greece: The Role of the Middle Class* (1956).

ISRAEL 384

S. N. EISENSTADT, Head of the Department of Sociology at the Hebrew University, Jerusalem, held a fellowship at the Center for Advanced Study in the Behavioral Sciences at Stanford University in 1955–56. He has published *The Absorption of Immigrants* (1954), *From Generation to Generation: Age Groups and Social Structure* (1956), and several papers on communication, reference group behavior, and comparative political structures.

FRANCE 444

FRANÇOIS BOURRICAUD, Agrégé de l'Université (philosophy) and Maître de Conferences de Sociologie à la Faculté des Lettres de Bordeaux, has studied at Harvard University and has published several articles and a translation of a selection of Parsons' essays, *Elements pour une Sociologie de l'Action* (1955). He has written a study of Peruvian Sierra culture, *Peru: Essai de sociologie Andine*, to be published by the *Cahiers de la Fondation des Sciences Politiques*.

BRAZIL 525

EMILIO WILLEMS, Professor of Anthropology at Vanderbilt University, studied at the universities of Cologne, Paris, and Berlin (Ph.D.). He was Professor of Anthropology at the University of São Paulo, Brazil, from 1941 to 1949. He has written several studies of Brazilian culture, including *Buzios Island: A Caiçara Community in Southern Brazil* (1952).

THE UNITED STATES 592

JESSIE BERNARD, Professor of Sociology at Pennsylvania State University, is the co-author, with L. L. Bernard, of *Origins of American Sociology* (1942) and has published *American Family Behavior* (1942), *American Community Behavior* (1949), *Remarriage* (1956), and *Social Problems at Mid-Century* (1957).

INDEX 677

The Institutions of Advanced Societies

*

Arnold M. Rose

THE COMPARATIVE STUDY
OF INSTITUTIONS

*

Invidious Comparisons and Cultural Relativity

THE observation of differences between peoples seems to have fascinated men since ancient times. An invidious quality frequently characterized these observations, in modern times as well as ancient: the behavior of another people was described to indicate its inferiority to that of the society to which the writer belonged. The reasons used to explain the differences might be religious, biological, geographic, or historical. The ancient Hebrews attributed their particular qualities to God's selection of them as the "chosen people." The ancient Greeks used a wider range of explanations, but they were equally derogatory to the outsiders, or "barbarians."

The early social scientists did not immediately forgo the easy tendency to evaluate their own societies as better than others. Most of the nineteenth-century anthropologists were imbued with the concept of "evolution," in which societies—like animal species—were held to have developed to different stages. Future development would inevitably bring to other societies the qualities already achieved by their own society, but then their own society would have progressed considerably further. The school of "folk psychology," dominant in Germany for a period, did not even envisage societies as developing along parallel paths. Societies—like individuals—had different biological inheritances, and some of these are obviously and inevitably better than others.

Several social science discoveries of the past century have given us a new perspective for observing the differences among peoples. In the first place, there is a recognition that a society has a cultural heritage—a vast

3

number of learned behaviors which are transmitted (and modified) from generation to generation. Many types of influences gave rise to these cultural elements at their inception, and many types of influences have modified them in their course to the present. Geographic forces have set some limitations on these cultural elements, and individual psychology has set other limitations. Purely biological forces are now given less deterministic weight than they once were—for research has demonstrated that any large group of people is likely to have approximately the same distribution of inherited capacities as any other group, although there are significant individual differences within the group. Behaviors are no longer thought of as determined purely by inherited motivations (the discarded theory of human instincts), but by a number of forces in which biological inheritance offers potentialities and limitations just as do a number of other factors, such as climate and the degree of affection manifested by the mother for the child. Certain characteristics of the culture itself—like its technology and the structure of its institutions—help to shape its development. A certain role must also be assigned to what are called "historical accidents"—those intrinsically minor events that happen to occur at such a significant time and place that their influence becomes profound.

Cultural behaviors—with the meanings and values that interpret and guide them—have a certain persistency, largely because they are practically the only behaviors an individual perceives and is taught. It is impossible for an individual to invent, or even to modify, more than a small proportion of all the behaviors he must act out in order to be an effective member of his society and a functioning organism. But it would be erroneous to think of culture as static: there are constant accretions, deteriorations, and other modifications. A description of any culture can at best have the reality of a photograph: it depicts merely a slice of reality at one given moment of time. The discovery of a learned, changing culture as a dominant influence on the behavior of man represents the most important discovery of modern social science.

A second discovery, of the late nineteenth century, related to the considerable variety of human cultures. Anthropologists, historians, and archeologists led in this discovery, but sociologists contributed with their descriptions of ethnic minorities and class variations. An increasingly accurate description and a more sympathetic interpretation of this variation challenged the age-old evaluation that "our culture is best." The concept of "cultural relativism" offered several chastening insights to the modern educated man. One was that the interpretation of one's own culture as superior was not subject to empirical verification but represented a value judgment. Second, such an interpretation was seen to be most often born of ignorance of the satisfactions provided by other cultures (a type of ignorance given the specialized name of "ethnocentrism"). Mannheim and other social scientists were later able to show that all perceptions were conditioned by individual and group experiences, so that "truth" could only be grasped from the "standpoint" of the perceiver.[1] Third, it was recognized that a given cultural element fitted in best with its own culture complex, and often made no sense or was a source of individual dissatisfaction when thrust into an alien culture. (The truth of this simple observation of cultural functionalism was sometimes glorified by a school of "functionalists" into the major or sole principle of interpretation of culture.)

The discovery of cultural relativism had the effect of a cleansing on the minds of social scientists: It wiped away ancient prejudices and blinding conceits. It counteracted the naive "idea of progress" so dominant in the nineteenth century.[2] But it was not sufficient for understanding certain aspects of cultural difference and cultural change. Certain aspects of culture, at least, were cumulative and "progressive" within the framework of that aspect of culture. The most evident example was science. New discoveries were partly based on old ones, and each verification of a hypothesis gave additional support to the whole theory from which the hypothesis was drawn. Science could be thought of as a continually growing structure, never complete, but in which each brick made possible the addition of other bricks, and consisting of functional sections that could be used for a surprising number of purposes. Science was, and is, so highly valued by Westerners that the question was seldom raised whether an "advance" in scientific knowledge is "good," especially when it was realized that "primitive" peoples used magical procedures where "advanced" peoples used scientific ones. Some modern scientists are beginning to raise questions about knowledge that can be put to practical use in such a way as to harm mankind. It may be supposed that Alfred Nobel's establishment of a peace prize expressed his moral qualms after discovering dynamite. And the invention of the atomic bomb in the 1940's made many scientists wonder about the desirability of their research in nuclear fission. But within the framework of science itself, it was obvious that science was functionally cumulative, so that one society could be said to be scientifically advanced and another scientifically backward.

5

Somewhat the same view holds for technology and the practical arts, although here there is more controversy. Each invention made possible further inventions, and a society having certain technological equipment was better able to use most other technological equipment.[3] Thus, within the framework of technology itself, there could be little question that it was functionally cumulative, and that one society could be described as technologically advanced whereas another was technologically backward. There is more question, however, about the value of technological advance, although the question relates to the use of technology rather than to its discovery or existence. Whereas an advanced technology permits greater speed, efficiency, and quantity of production, it does not permit the workman to be close to his materials or work on his product from beginning to end. This "alienation" from work—which students of industry from Marx to Mayo have described—might be considered by some people as compensating, or more than compensating, for the increments in consumption which technology provides. On the other hand, modern technology can make work more pleasant by eliminating many of the heavy, difficult, and disagreeable tasks, and modern personnel practices compensate somewhat for the separation from work by providing more time and opportunity for workers to associate with each other.

Modern anthropology, probably as a result of its recent interaction with psychiatry, has come to recognize yet another qualification to relativism. It starts with a recognition of the fact that different societies have differing proportions of mentally ill persons among their members, and that mental health seems to be a fairly universal value. The question is then raised whether cultures may not be ranked according to the extent of mental disturbance (not only the extreme forms of mental disease) associated with them. Having gone so far, some social scientists are willing to look for other universal values as measures of the quality of societies,[4] and at least one philosophic anthropologist[5] has proposed that a systematic, scientific study be made of the universality of values which would lead to a scale to measure the worth or degree of advancement of societies. The eminent anthropologist Clyde Kluckhohn has expressed one way in which most anthropologists have moved away from a "naive relativism." After pointing out that a recognition of cultural relativity does not prevent one from setting up moral absolutes, he says: "Cultural relativity means, on the contrary, that the appropriateness of any positive or negative custom must be evaluated with regard to how this habit fits in with other group habits."[6]

While contemporary social scientists are thus willing to distinguish between "backward" and "advanced" societies and cultures in many respects, they have retained the relativist principles that their own societies are not necessarily the most advanced and that there are many diverse forms of a desirable culture and social organization. The combined insights —that some cultures are more intrinsically desirable than others in some respects and that desirable cultures are organized in many different ways —have restored the scientific respectability of another old concept, that of "national character." This term was also associated, in the nineteenth century, with the effort to prove the racial and cultural superiority of the writer who happened to be using the term. Today this tendentious motivation has been eliminated, and social scientists have found the concept to be highly useful and, indeed, necessary for a complete description of a culture in relation to the personality of the individuals who practice the culture.

The Study of National Character

Much of the recent discussion of national character has taken the form of analyzing modal personality characteristics in terms of typical cultural patterns of child-rearing.[7] The hypothesis is that the child-rearing patterns of a culture, functionally formed by and adapted to the entire structure of the culture, activate certain psychological mechanisms in such a way that the child grows up with a certain type of personality, and that this type of personality in turn functionally supports the structure of the culture that gives rise to it. The psychological mechanisms are predominantly those hypothesized by Freud. This general hypothesis has stimulated a considerable number of concrete studies, by both anthropologists and analytical psychiatrists, on both nonliterate and advanced cultures.[8]

Without attempting to evaluate this hypothesis or the studies using its framework, I should like to describe another approach to the study of national character to which the sociologist can make a special contribution. The hypothesis behind the studies cited is that the institutions of a culture require certain behaviors—often structured into roles—which give a characteristic cast to the personality. This influence is exerted throughout the life of the individual and not only in childhood, so that the modal personality may be considerably different in old age from what it is in young adulthood. The question may be raised—as it is by Inkeles and Levinson[9] —whether it is worthwhile to consider the behaviors formed in this manner

7

as personality traits, whether it is not sufficient to speak merely of culture rather than national character. After all, culture consists in the acting out by the individual of certain behaviors expected by the society, and it is well known that cultures differ from society to society. Using the hypothesis of institution-personality just enunciated, we see two values in the concept of national character:

First, the institutions of a society offer a framework of meanings and values which is all that the individual has available for making choices in all aspects of his life; he does not have unlimited understanding or free choice of values, but his behavior is guided by what is *available* in the culture. We must abandon the mistaken conception—explicitly enunciated by Freud and implicitly accepted by practically all psychologists—that culture is solely a repressive or molding force which is imposed upon some of the behavior of the independently developing individual personality. In one aspect and to a certain degree, the individual *incorporates* the culture into his behavior and mental processes so that, in this aspect and degree, his personality *is* the culture.

Second, in another aspect and to a certain degree, the individual personality does develop from biological and psychological mechanisms independently of the culture. But even here, culture sets some of the limitations and provides some of the specific content, and this influence is exerted throughout life. For example, a certain individual with a high biological potential for intelligent behavior cannot rationally think through certain problems which a person of lesser biological intelligence can adequately handle, because the former has grown up with an ideology which provides a dogmatic answer to the problem and no alternatives are tolerated. It has been widely observed that otherwise "intelligent" Communists and other people with an overwhelming faith are "stupid" in certain matters. Another kind of example is that provided by personality traits such as aggressiveness. Any person may feel an impulse to be aggressive, but the particular observable manifestation of this aggressiveness will range from crude spontaneous violence to subtle "biting" humor, depending on what is approved in the individual's society, his class, his peer group, his sex, his occupational group, and so on.

It would be advantageous at this point to provide an example of each of these two kinds of relationships between social institutions and national character, using concrete data and more rigorous analysis. To provide an example of the first kind, I shall attempt to demonstrate a causal relationship between the relative absence of voluntary associations of the social influence type in France and the allegedly typical French tendency to be individualistic.[10] Both of these characteristics are relative to what exists in other societies—that is, it may be that a Burmese would find an unusually large number of Frenchmen participating in voluntary associations, and a Tibetan would find little individualism in France. It is therefore specified that these two characteristics are seen as typical of France when viewed by an American, an Englishman, a Scandinavian, or a Swiss, as well as by a Frenchman. There is no implication in the hypothesis that the only cause of individualism is the degree of development of voluntary associations in the society, or that the only way for France to reduce the amount of individualism among its people is to encourage the founding of voluntary associations. The hypothesis is thus limited by the usual *caeteris paribus,* and therefore by the particular circumstances of modern French history.

France, like other Western countries that have gone through the Commercial and Industrial revolutions and the rise of liberal democracy, has experienced a certain decline of its religious and extended family institutions and of local community cohesiveness relative to what existed in the Middle Ages, when France was no more individualistic than other Western countries. These changes tended to develop individualism in all Western countries; but by the eighteenth century certain counteracting forces emerged which began to limit individualism. One of the most important of these was a type of institution which is relatively unique to modern Western culture—the deliberate and free association of several persons for the accomplishment of purposes other than expressiveness or personal gain (this is the definition here of the voluntary association for social influence purposes). Such associations ranged from certain kinds of trade unions to the private charity, and included the parents' associations that were formed to promote the welfare and education of children. There was a marked outcropping of all sorts of associations of this type in all Western countries after the late eighteenth century, and while there has been an extraordinarily high death rate among them, outside of France the birth rate exceeded the death rate, and some of them achieved "permanent" stability. In France, beginning in 1791 and extending throughout the nineteenth century, there was a series of laws and court decisions which prohibited the formation of voluntary associations and punished those who led in their formation. Thousands of associations were formed—including such "innocent" ones as organizations for the promotion of literature and student

9

activities—but the authorities repressed them. Most Frenchmen learned to avoid forming or joining such groups, and practically no Frenchmen obtained experience with the achievements or satisfactions that could be had through them. Even when the French parliament passed a law for the "freedom of associations" in 1901, it hedged them about with such restrictions that they could not function effectively (with the possible exception of the associations for economic purposes). Thus Frenchmen have never had much opportunity to cooperate with each other (except in nuclear families, political parties under democratic regimes, and relatively recently in economic associations and such expressive associations as sports groups).

This alone would make Frenchmen individualistic, but the national character trait has been strengthened by an expressed ideology—in the nature of a group rationalization—that "Frenchmen are individualistic," which serves to justify failures of cooperation and inhibit motives to attempt cooperation. The death rate of cooperative and associative ventures is high in every country, but only where the expressed ideology—in itself almost an intellectual institution—exists does the failure enhance the individual's proclivity to individualism. It is as if every time a child tries a certain game or sport and fails to perform satisfactorily, he is told that the failure constitutes proof of his incapacity to perform. The probable result is that he will give up his efforts and never learn to perform the particular action. This analysis is obviously oversimplified in many respects, but perhaps it offers a basically correct interpretation the outlines of which could be utilized in gaining a better understanding of other "national character" traits.

The second relationship—that between institutions and deep-seated psychological traits activated by basic psychological mechanisms—will be illustrated by the relationship between certain aspects of family life and interpersonal relations in France and the United States and the trait of masculinity-femininity. Many psychologists and psychiatrists have considered masculinity-femininity as a major personality trait determined completely independently of cultural forces. Yet there have been innumerable references to different degrees of masculinity shown by men and the different degrees of femininity shown by women in different societies. Data on the marriage and birth rates suggest that Indian males are not biologically different in primary sex characteristics than are the more masculine-appearing Turkish males (that is, masculine-appearing to an American or Turk). Nor has any convincing evidence been adduced to account for national differences in the appearance of masculinity in purely psychological terms, although there is good evidence that the feminine-looking boy in such a society as the American can be best understood in terms of psychological or physiological mechanisms.

In Western society the nation frequently held to produce the largest number of feminine-appearing males is France. My effort to explain this will be based on general observation and mere conjecture, offered tentatively because no relevant study of any kind is available. The first observation is that some of this appearance of femininity is based solely on certain French manners and styles of dress. But there is more than this, for few French popular heroes (in the comic strips, movies, and so on) appear to be what Americans call "he-man types"; Frenchmen seem less likely than Americans to emphasize nonsexual behaviors which distinguish them as masculine; Frenchmen seem to be less disturbed when they are put in a passive, dependent role (as when they are supported by their wives). Assuming that these observations are accurate—they have by no means been demonstrated—we can ask what aspects of social structure differentiate the role of a male in France from the role of a male in the United States. Here we are obliged to introduce an intervening concept between the social structure and the modal personality trait: role identification (or role definition).

In the French family and society generally, the child is given to understand that he is either male or female, and that this is immutable no matter what his behavior. The little boy seems never to be called a "sissy" or the little girl a "tomboy" no matter how he or she behaves. It is not insisted that the boy be a "boy" or a "little man" as distinguished from a little girl. Little boys are more likely to be kept longer in "Little Lord Fauntleroy" clothing and in curls than is common in the United States. A large proportion of women are gainfully employed in France, many women earn more than do their husbands, and many women manage the family finances, but seldom is the wife said to be "wearing the pants in the family." It is usually assumed that a man is a man by virtue of his biological characteristics, whereas in the United States it is often said that a "male must prove that he is a man." Only recently in the United States has it been possible for a man to show himself engaged in women's household tasks, and even now he must add a "typically masculine gesture" when he is discovered working at them. In the United States it is considered very important for a man to be taller and stronger than his wife; in France this does not seem to be a

11

necessary factor in mate selection, whereas the size of the wife's dowry and her abilities as a cook are considered important. The result of all this is that the French male is more likely to exhibit "feminine" behavior than is an American male, but is much less concerned about his identification as a male.

In the less abundant French economy (due, incidentally, to poor technology and industrial organization rather than to lack of natural resources), two members of a family have to work to keep up "middle-class" standards of living. More women work in France than in the United States, and more of them work because they are obliged to economically than because they want to. Thus an economic factor reduces sex role differentiation. The low sex ratio in France puts men at a relative premium (as compared with the high sex ratio of the United States—especially in the West, where women have been at a premium and men have had to prove their masculinity in other ways than by having a family). Frenchmen find they are sought after by women and can even be dependent on women. Thus a demographic factor affects the role definition of men. Historically, the super-husky man was less necessary in France, as compared with the United States (where a man had to fell trees, engage in other extremely arduous tasks, and physically protect his family from human and animal marauders). Thus, the lack of a "frontier history" in France made an extreme masculine physique less necessary than in the United States, and there was no need for a man to emphasize his physical prowess and masculine physique to himself or others.

This highly conjectural, undocumented account of social factors contributing to a modal personality trait is presented solely to suggest a type of analysis in which sociologists may make a contribution to knowledge about national character. In this type of analysis it is important to understand the entire structure and folkways of a society. It assumes that a causal relationship is possible between the particular institutions and patterns of a culture and the modal behaviors and traits of its people, even as they carry on their life activities outside of those particular institutions or patterns. For example, it would be held that a certain kind of capitalistic economic institution would be likely to promote the personality trait of orderliness and passion for efficiency in any sphere of life, whereas a feudal economy would more probably result in more permissive and passive relations in all behaviors. A related requirement for such analysis would be an understanding of the history of the particular society.

While one can logically take the viewpoint of Kurt Lewin and say that an individual's behavior can be understood completely in terms of all the forces operating on him at a given moment,[11] it is highly unlikely that we can understand or even discern all the forces acting on an individual at one moment unless we learn a good deal not only about his individual life history but also about the history of his society. History creates culture, including the all-important institutions within the framework of which individuals must carry on their behavior, and comparative history is thus the most important source of hypotheses concerning the forces which operate on an individual at any one time. This is true also because an individual's behavior is molded and motivated by his elders, and theirs by their elders, so that a knowledge of a society's history is essential for understanding an individual member's behavior at any one time. This point of view could, of course, lead to a highly static and conservative analysis, but this can be tempered by the recognition that a society is capable of undergoing rapid and even cataclysmic social change at almost any time, so that its history of even a decade earlier is relatively unimportant (this is probably true for children growing up in the revolutionary France of the 1790's and possibly even for children growing up in the depression-ridden society of the 1930's). But even social cataclysms can best be understood as part of history.

A final methodological suggestion is that history itself can best be understood in comparative terms. The historian does this, often unwillingly, by observing a single society at different epochs, but his understanding would be enhanced if he made his comparison explicit and if he extended the range of the comparison by bringing to the analysis some knowledge of other societies.

The Internal Unity of a Society: Functionalism

The question we shall next examine is the extent to which a society may be expected to have internal consistency, unity, or "character." Those anthropologists of the last generation, led by Boas, who reacted against all biological determinism on culture—who rejected the notion that a society went through certain stages in its evolution and hence always had the internal consistency of institutions, beliefs, and practices characteristic of the stage—rejected the question. They concerned themselves primarily with a thoroughgoing description of societies, and considered as biasing any assumption of necessary internal consistency, although they were willing to

13

correlate the various aspects of a society once the description was complete.

Two other modern schools of anthropology—led respectively by Malinowski and by Radcliffe-Brown—which also rejected theories of societal evolution but in a different way, held that each society was characterized by a strong internal coherence of its structural parts, and that an adequate description of a society required that the bases of this coherence be searched for and demonstrated. Malinowski believed that the general reason for this was that societies consisted of individuals with biological needs and limitations, which required adjustment to the physical environment and to surrounding societies, and hence that all the institutions and ideologies of a society had the common and consistent focus given to it by its particular adjustment. Radcliffe-Brown, partly influenced by Durkheim, was more inclined to find the internal consistency in more purely social variables or in an assumed tendency of man to be consistent within himself. Both of these modern schools of anthropology call themselves "functionalists" to suggest that each part-structure of a society has to take a given form to be consistent with and to support all the other part-structures: each has a "function" in providing this support or in aiding the adjustment of people to their own biology or to the external environment. Thus, while avoiding the doctrine of societal evolution, they also reject what they considered to be the "pure descriptiveness" or the agnosticism concerning purpose and integration characteristic of the Boas tradition.[12]

The functional anthropologists have strongly justified their assumption of functionalism by their seminal researches and stimulating interpretations of specific cultures. Even the skeptics of the Boas tradition have recognized some of the merits of the functional approach, although they wisely caution against premature theorizing about the basis of functional unity within any given society. The sociologist would want to raise further warnings to the anthropologist who wishes to study what we are calling an "advanced society."

First, a literate society with advanced technology is likely to be made up of several heterogeneous subcultures, often with different historical traditions. This is the case because the advanced society usually has to be defined partly in political terms—in terms of the power of a given government to exercise hegemony over a large number of people—rather than in terms of a more or less socially isolated kinship group. Second, an advanced society is always in the process of undergoing rapid social change, and the various part-structures cannot remain in harmony very long even if they may once have been so aligned. "Cultural lags," or even more violent discontinuities and unharmonious relationships between the various parts of a society, are just as natural a fact about advanced societies as any tendency toward internal unity that they may have. Third, the economy of an advanced society usually requires a highly developed division of labor by locality rather than a relatively homogeneous means of livelihood prevailing among most of the family groups within the society. Typically, the advanced society has both an urban and a rural population; some of its cities find their economic base in manufacturing, while others find it in trade, finance, or administration. Fourth, the advanced society has so many people that direct communication among them is less important than communication by means of the mass media and through instrumentalities of government and industry. Fifth, the advanced society has a technology with which it can control its environment to a certain extent, and there is no necessity for perfect "adaptation" to the immediate environment. This is even more true when the society can and does produce an economic surplus.

For these and allied reasons, there is less justification for expecting a single dominant basis of internal coherence in an advanced society than there would be in a nonliterate, technologically undeveloped society which did not have these traits. Hence, the anthropologist who attempts the study of an advanced society should be extremely cautious about postulating functional relationships between the part-structures of such a society, unless he limits himself to a fairly small, homogeneous section of the society.

The above survey of preliminary considerations applies to an *anthropologist* whose major task it is to characterize a society or a subsociety as a whole. It is much more questionable for a *sociologist* to use the assumptions of functionalism, because his major task is not to describe the modal behavior of a society or subsociety but rather to account for variations in behavior. For example, while the anthropologist might be justified in studying the relation between the "class system" of a given advanced society and its political organization, the sociologist is typically more interested in such matters as the relationships between the factors conferring status; the varying degree of class rigidity, consciousness, and conflict; the changes in class over time and space within the society. For research on the latter kinds of problems, a functionalist orientation is not only irrelevant but actually positively misleading. It tends to pose the wrong research questions, to blind the investigator to the most important variables, and to

15

give him a systematic bias in all his observations. In their concrete researches, functional sociologists have certainly not yet demonstrated the value of their theoretical orientation as have functional anthropologists, except possibly when they are behaving as anthropologists and are solely intent on interpreting some subsociety within the larger advanced society. It is highly questionable whether even the functional anthropologists use functional assumptions when studying sociological problems *within* a given nonliterate society.

Functionalism has two sources, but they have now so blended in sociological theory that it is extremely difficult to separate them. Functionalism first arose out of certain observations—by Durkheim,[13] for example—of how one institution of a given society had a certain peculiar form that seemed specially adapted to other institutions of that society, and how social change directly affecting one institution seemed to be transmitted gradually to other institutions so that they regained their mutually adaptive character. A second origin was in the biological concept of homeostasis, which had a steady development in the science of physiology and reached a brilliant culmination with the publication in 1932 of Walter B. Cannon's *The Wisdom of the Body*.[14] Cannon's theory was simply that many continuing and seemingly static physiological states are in fact the product of a constant opposition of forces—an addition being compensated for by a subtraction and vice versa—and that with some of these, when there is a deviation from the balance, that deviation sets in operation processes which (other conditions being constant) restore the balance.

Cannon's theory had an enormous body of long-accumulated evidence in physiology to support it. But the theory was shortly extended to psychology and sociology, in which disciplines the evidence supporting it was either dubious or altogether lacking. Analogies from the older, well-established sciences have often tempted certain followers of the newer, less secure human sciences, and this seems to be especially true of notions of equilibrium—as witnessed by the stultifying conceptions of certain economists.[15] As a matter of fact, the theory is not found to be wholly satisfactory by contemporary physiologists. Dickinson W. Richards of Columbia University, for example, holds that nature provides almost as many examples of nonhomeostatic change in physiological processes as of homeostatic ones.[16] I shall not here be concerned with the controversy among psychologists as to whether the concept of homeostasis has value for the understanding of individual mental processes.[17] My hypothesis is that it

16

has little value in the study of social or cultural processes or institutions, and that insofar as it underlies contemporary functionalist theories in sociology it renders those theories at least partially invalid.

Let us first consider some concrete examples of the use of functionalist theory in sociology; these are not intended to be representative samples since my purpose is not to demonstrate that functionalist theory is completely invalid, but rather to demonstrate that there are pitfalls into which functionalist theory tends to slip. After citing these examples I shall attempt a more systematic theoretical evaluation of functionalist theory.

Durkheim, father of so many seminal ideas in sociology and anthropology, was an originator of contemporary functionalism—if we ignore the earlier speculations of Jaques Novicow, Paul von Lilienfeld, and Albert Schaeffle, whose organismic conceptions of society apparently influenced few or none of the later sociologists. While several of Durkheim's analyses of social phenomena have held up through several generations of later research and criticism, his functionalist interpretation of crime and punishment seems bizarre and has been followed by no latter-day criminologist.[18] While stressing man's characteristic effort to maintain social bonds, he raised the question as to why crime exists when crime seems to involve such a sharp disruption of social bonds. His functionalist answer was that social bonds tend to wear down and gradually become meaningless unless and until they are renewed by experiences which bring sharp realization of their value. As social bonds wear down, crime increases. The criminals are the ones least socially integrated while others are better able to see the value of social bonds and the need for restoring them. And so the others react by punishing the criminals; the assignments of punishment are ritual acts which restore the original strength of the social bond. Thus the "function" of punishment is to restore society to its "proper" state.

To this interpretation could be opposed a different but equally functionalist interpretation of punishment which comes out of east European Yiddish folklore: "Thanks be to God," the thief reflected, "for jailing and punishing thieves and pickpockets. If it weren't for that, my profession would be so overcrowded that a poor thief like me could never earn a living."[19] While contemporary criminologists are far from agreed in their interpretations of crime, they can point to such research findings as the following to discredit Durkheim's hypothesis: (1) The strengthening of law enforcement and the heightening of punishment are alone seldom effective in decreasing crime or in reducing alienation throughout the society at large.

(2) Punishment is differentially applied to law violators of the different social classes, and the desires of middle and upper income people to punish lower class criminals are seldom accompanied by equally strong desires to punish criminals of their own class.[20] (3) The laws specifying punishment typically reflect attitudes concerning the seriousness of crimes prevalent in earlier generations rather than what contemporary people regard as appropriate punishments.[21] (4) While weakening of social bonds might be one cause of crime, there is strong evidence that two other factors— loyalty to and learning of standards of behavior from certain subgroups in the society and certain patterns of personality development—are more important factors.[22]

The most highly esteemed contemporary functional sociologist is Talcott Parsons. While his work consists mainly of theoretical formulations, he has occasionally provided interpretations of observable social phenomena. In one instance he has undertaken to explain the numerical predominance of unmarried women among elementary schoolteachers in the United States.[23] This he attributes primarily to the family structure of the country in which mothers rather than fathers control the upbringing of children and yet boys are expected to emancipate themselves from their mothers and gradually assume what are defined as masculine roles in the society. In order to take the first steps toward emancipation and yet not experience too drastic a rupture from their mothers, boys are transferred to the control of persons like their mothers (other women) who have one major characteristic different from their mothers (they are unmarried). Thus this society selects as its elementary schoolteachers unmarried women who can serve a special function in relation to the family and the development of independent male roles.

The more usual explanation of the numerical prevalence of unmarried women among elementary schoolteachers runs something like this: Until recently, teaching was one of the few occupations that both had moderately high status and was open to women. The middle class has steadily produced a certain proportion of women who did not marry, who needed to earn a steady living, and who sought to retain their social "respectability." Until recently these jobs were scarce, relative to the number of applicants, and many people felt that married women "needed" them less than did unmarried women because the latter had no other source of income. Also married teachers were found to have higher absentee and turnover rates than unmarried ones, and hence were less reliable on the average.

Finally, men could always compete for many other kinds of respectable occupations that paid more and were less overcrowded. This explanation can be extended to account for the changing situation during the 1940's and 1950's, for as the economic demand for schoolteachers sharply increased married women and men were rapidly welcomed into the ranks of teachers, and unmarried women no longer preponderate.

Parsons has also attempted to explain the rapid increase in the use of hospital facilities for the care of the sick.[24] He attributes this to the weakening of family ties and the growth of obligations of women outside the family. Since the family (or at least the women in the family) are less "willing" to take care of the sick, the hospital (including its specialized women who attend the sick as an occupation—the nurses) has expanded to perform that "function." The more typical explanation of the expansion of hospital facilities relies on this reasoning: The care of the sick now more typically requires special equipment and a rigorous regimen which can only be provided in the hospital (for nonwealthy persons). The doctors' professional association has succeeded in reducing the proportion of doctors in the population, so that doctors have less time to spend per case, and they can perform their necessary functions much more rapidly in a hospital than they can by going to patients' homes. Social movements to expand the availability of medical care have succeeded in creating hospitalization insurance programs which make hospitalization less costly to the insured.

Functionalist interpretations of social phenomena in technologically advanced countries have the characteristics of being simpler and more straightforward than nonfunctionalist interpretations; being only one of several conceivable alternative functionalist interpretations (usually selecting the family rather than the political, the economic, or the associational institutions to require "adjustment" to); ignoring the heterogeneity and rapid social change characteristic of those societies. Whether these are defects inherent in functionalism or mere accidents, it is difficult to say. Until more theoretically satisfying and empirically valid functional explanations of specific social phenomena are forthcoming, I will hold the view that current sociological functionalism, based on the concept of homeostasis, has certain inherent deficiencies as a theoretical framework for explaining social phenomena. My reasons are the following:

1. A functionalist explanation tends to be teleological, although it need not logically have this characteristic. With every situation having the "pur-

pose" of maintaining its equilibrium or restoring itself to equilibrium, the "effect" is implicit in the "cause" rather than consequent to it. A functionalist interpretation also tends to be naive and simplistic: any preceding condition is said to be the "cause" of the succeeding condition simply because it is a preceding condition (and also happens to fit a specific functionalist hypothesis).

2. A functionalist explanation is much less susceptible to the application of accepted canons of scientific proof than is the usual "if cause then effect, holding constant extraneous variables" type of explanation. This is because there is no known way of randomizing or otherwise holding constant extraneous variables with a functionalist hypothesis, since everything is dependent on everything else.

3. A functionalist explanation cannot explain certain kinds of heterogeneity in a society (that induced by the coming together of bearers of different cultural traditions), and can account for the initiation of social change only by positing influences extraneous to the society. Ginsberg has made this point in a special context:

Functionalist theories are generally nonhistorical, and their application to history would present great difficulties. Admittedly development is not unilinear. There are different traditions, each to a large extent following its own line. But they never have been completely independent, and radical changes have frequently been due to contacts, friendly or otherwise, between them. The effects of contact must differ greatly in different spheres of culture, leading to genuine assimilation in some and to mere syncretism in others. Thus at one time any society will contain elements borrowed from others which it has integrated into its own, and also other elements which have not been and never may be fully absorbed.[25]

4. There seems to be a hidden assumption in functionalism of *necessary,* not merely actual or probable, interdependence of parts and automaticity of process. This perhaps comes from the analogy of society and the biological organism. All analogies should be suspect, but this one especially because the order of biological and social phenomena are on different "levels," in Schneirla's sense.[26] More particularly, the parts of a body necessarily have to hang together, and therefore there is a greater presumption that they function together than in the case of a society in which the several segments can physically and symbolically go off in different directions and have great physical or symbolic separation from each other. It is possible for two societies to inhabit the same geographic space and physical facilities without having any more than economic contacts with each

other (this has actually happened). It is also a matter of fact that while Cannon's physiological homeostasis starts from a premise of instability, Parsons' sociological homeostasis starts from a premise of stability.[27] There is no automatic mechanism in society which gets it moving in an efficient direction, as breathing is increased when a person steps up his energy consumption. Some societies continue to act indefinitely in an inefficient manner in the face of all sorts of external stimuli to change, and some societies even "die" when a simple change would keep them active.[28]

5. Functionalism is not a theory from which verifiable hypotheses and predictions can be deduced. It is rather a point of view—a way of analyzing social phenomena (and then perhaps formulating specific theories within the framework). It seems questionable whether the addition of philosophic frameworks—beyond those already considered to be the basis of all science—are useful in social science.

6. Both structure and "function" of an institution are partly a matter of inference and definition. Social reality consists of unmarked variations. Can a functionalist interpretation handle this? For example, a married couple without children "function" as a family in some respects but not in others. If a functional explanation is offered for some aspect of family behavior that depends on the role of ●hildren, does this mean that the childless couple are not covered by the explanation? What happens when there are children, but they are temporarily away from home, or when the children in the home are grandchildren? What are the limits of inference regarding a function? For example, it can be inferred—because French Canada has a disconcertingly high birth rate and outside stairways that become slippery in winter—that the function of the outside stairways is to cause pregnant women to fall and have miscarriages (which they do). The concept of function is too easy to use to be scientifically helpful. In this respect it is like the concept of "instinct," which was originally also transferred by analogy from biology to social science, and which was also used in social science to explain too much too easily. What is useful as a descriptive label is misleading as an explanation. While the modifying concept of "functional alternatives" has been developed to compensate for some of these deficiencies in original sociological functionalism,[29] in practice there is a tendency to ignore the concept, as Schwartz points out.[30]

7. The "function" of an institution depends on the role one plays in relation to the institution. For example, the function of a radio program for the sponsor is to provide a vehicle for advertising; for the listener it is to

provide entertainment. The British anthropologist Firth[31] provides a better example: the trade union has the function of providing security and a proportionate share of the productive wealth to its members, but it is also disruptive from the standpoint of industrial organization. If these are regarded as different orders of functions, can a single functionalist explanation account for the whole institution?

8. Anthropology and history have provided much evidence that a given social structure has engaged in a wide variety of different "functions," and that a given social activity is accomplished by a wide variety of different social structures. Would not a functionalist interpretation be able to explain this only by a complete description of the society in which a given activity is associated with a given structure—indicating that when one or the other changes the rest of the society must also be changing? Such a cumbersome explanation becomes history rather than sociology. To avoid becoming history, functional explanations oversimplify or distort the facts.

Avoidance of functionalist interpretation of social phenomena based on homeostasis would not preclude use of the concept of "function." An institution's functions could be defined as the opposite of the consequences of removal of the institution. (An institution might be removed by historical circumstances, by deliberate experiment, or possibly imaginatively by logical inference.) It might even be discovered by this means that some minor institution has no function, that it exists as a vestige—a traditional pattern of habits—of an older institution which once did have a function. A function in this sense is a datum which is empirically ascertainable and verifiable (at least conceivably so, even if verification is not feasible). No assumptions concerning the required degree of integration of the society or the required relation among institutions or the required "strain and tension" to change the society are necessary. But hypotheses concerning these matters can be formulated if it is deemed desirable on observational and theoretical grounds. Such hypotheses would have to be tested empirically by the usual canons of science, in order to be maintained beyond the initial theorizing stage. The concept "function" would be useful in calling attention to what might be hidden in a culture, to suggest hypothetical explanations for what might appear superficially to be irrational, as when "latent functions" are suggested.[32] When a concept of "function" is used, it should be given all the qualifications and limitations implied in the above list of criticisms of functionalism.[33]

The use in biology of the word "function" is illustrated in the following sentence: "The function of the lungs is to transfer oxygen from the air to the blood stream, by which it can be distributed throughout the body to oxidize other chemicals so as to release energy." Both the nonorganic oxygen and the organic lungs are described as having functions necessary to the maintenance of life in the above sentence. The biologist does not imply that equivalents for them are impossible in other organisms, but merely that in the evolutionary process of genetic variation, natural selection, and fixation, the oxygen-lungs-energy cycle is the only possible one for mammals. If the concept of function is to be borrowed from biology by the social sciences we need to do more than merely analogize; we must also rigorously describe concrete processes of cultural variation, structural selection, and natural history for each institution or equivalent. The more specific requirements, which are highly complex, are explicitly set forth by Ernest Nagel[34] and by Jules Henry.[35] Nagel points out that functional statements are "appropriate in connection with systems possessing self-maintaining mechanisms for certain of their traits, but seem pointless and even misleading when used with reference to systems lacking such self-regulatory devices." Sociologists who use the concept of function must be willing to accept the implications of the phrase "the wisdom of social systems" in the same way that physiologists accept the implications of Cannon's phrase "the wisdom of the body."

The Internal Unity of a Society: Cultural Postulates and Themes

If a functionalist interpretation of social phenomena is rejected, on what basis can we explain the often-observed harmony or internal coherence of the various institutions of a given society? Alternatives to functionalism are not only possible, but some of them face fewer of the objections that have been raised against functionalism.

Before launching into specific positive suggestions, it would be well to indicate some features of all social science theories so that functionalism as a special theory is not confused with the general nature of all social science theory. Some students have slipped into this confusion, and hence have, on the one hand, credited functionalism with traits it shares with all theories and, on the other, failed to credit functionalism with its specific traits. First, all scientific theories assume that if everything is known about all the pertinent elements of a situation, an accurate prediction can be made about that situation if it continues to develop as it has been developing or if an outside force does not impinge on the situation (this is the premise of "determinism"). Functionalist theory is more specific about the nature of social change. Second, it is a general scientific and historical maxim that everything influences everything else, directly or indirectly (although not all influences are perceptible or significant). Functionalist theory is more specific about the mutual influence of the "parts" of a society.

The alternative theoretical orientation I shall use to explain the internal coherence of a culture owes much to the anthropologists, who have developed a simpler and better factually based functionalism. For this discussion I shall use the equivalent[36] anthropological terms of covert culture elements (Clyde Kluckhohn), cultural themes (Morris E. Opler), and cultural postulates (E. Adamson Hoebel).[37] These may be defined as general assumptions underlying the cultural aspects of behavior. They are either meanings (definitional assumptions) or values (directional or motivating assumptions), but are distinguished from other meanings and values of the culture by being quite general and more or less hidden in everyday behavior. There are a quite limited number of them in any culture, but one or more of them are expressed in all the diverse behaviors found in the culture. Hence common threads run through the diverse aspects of a given culture. While two or more cultures may have some of the same assumptions, each culture has its own particular total combination of them. Hence each culture has its own distinctive character.

The limited number of covert culture elements which run through the diverse manifestations of the overt culture are not all that give a culture its coherence. There is also a tendency to logical consistency among these postulates, a strain toward consistency possibly grounded in man's tendency to think of himself as consistent or logical, despite the apparent inconsistency in the overt culture. Here we find it useful to think of two categories of postulates. First, there are those which are covert only in the sense that members of the society have not thought of them but are quite willing to acknowledge them when the postulates are brought to the members' attention. They are often not thought of because they are so general, and few but social scientists (and possibly priests and politicians) think in a general way about their society. Second, there are covert culture elements which are repressed in such a way that any effort to bring them to the attention of members of the society are strongly resisted.[38] Covert culture elements of the first type are often logically inconsistent, and their expression in overt behavior manifests itself in the often-observed inconsistencies of daily behavior. Yet man thinks of himself as consistent and

24

logical, and when two of his cultural behaviors are apparently inconsistent he uses some camouflaged reference to covert culture postulates of the second type, which logically make the covert culture postulates of the first type really consistent.

Let us consider an example. In the traditional caste system of the American South, there occur the following two covert culture elements of the first type which are inconsistent with each other: (1) Negroes are innately inferior to whites and therefore cannot successfully compete with them; (2) if given equal social opportunities and allowed to mingle socially with whites, Negroes—even though in the numerical minority[39]—would dominate the South. Seemingly these two postulates of the white South—which underlie much of the concrete behavior toward Negroes, which cover a large portion of public abstract thinking in the South, and which give the unity to southern culture which we see in prejudice and oppression—are inconsistent with each other. How, then, can the caste system be considered coherent and integrated?

When an outsider presses the southerner for explanations of his behavior or belief in regard to Negroes, which in specific instances is often contrary to easily observable facts, he gets various explanations and rationalizations. The ultimate answer, considered by southerners to be the major real explanation, is usually expressed as some variation of "Would you want your daughter to marry a Negro?" This phrase, because of its use as the ultimate explanation, should be regarded as of crucial significance by the sociologist. It obviously does not refer to the interlocutor, since he usually does not have the same caste-supportive feelings as the southerner, otherwise he would not be raising the question of why there are caste behavior and beliefs. It obviously refers to the southerner himself, and it says that, if there were no caste behaviors or beliefs, the daughter would accept the hand of a Negro in marriage. She would do this because of some great attractiveness on the part of the Negro. This can be interpreted as a sexual and "human" attractiveness, since the lore of the South accords great sexual powers to the Negro and such qualities as humor, earthiness, and kindliness, but practically no other positive qualities. The postulate that, if the choice were free and all other things were equal, the white daughter would choose a Negro husband to a white one is the covert culture element (of the second type) that logically reconciles the two other postulates of the culture. Whereas these other two appeared mutually contradictory, the third postulate makes them quite consistent. But, for obvious reasons,

25

white southerners "reject" the third postulate even while they believe it; hence it becomes covert and manifests itself only in the expression "Would you want your daughter to marry a Negro?"

In sum, the internal coherence of a culture is given by the existence of a limited number of postulates—basic, generalized beliefs—that run through all the cultural behaviors and attitudes. Where the overt behaviors and attitudes or even some of the covert postulates (of the first type) appear to be mutually contradictory, they are reconciled by other covert postulates (of the second type) which are too shocking to be openly recognized and admitted but which are believed nevertheless. Thus a given culture tends to have an internal consistency and harmony. This tendency, however, should not be exaggerated: In many respects our advanced cultures are not internally consistent and harmonious. They are composed of too many subgroups, often with divergent and conflicting interests, and relations among them are often so indirect and segmentalized that coherence in culture is impossible. Even where the society is sufficiently homogeneous so that one can find a large area of common culture, a great variety of diverse behaviors and attitudes can reflect the same basic cultural postulates.

The Beginnings of a World Culture

We may call the approach to the study of a society outlined above *a postulational approach*. Anthropologists like Kluckhohn, Opler, and Redfield are using it for some relatively advanced societies as well as for the primitive ones.[40] While the approach is a most appropriate and fruitful one for all societies, it needs to be supplemented by a historical approach, especially when studying the advanced societies. The advanced societies are characterized by rapid social change, and some specific dimensions of that change need to be studied in order to understand the institutions or "character" of these societies. A world culture affecting all advanced societies has been developing for the past four centuries or so; hence there is a *common* history that is important for all advanced societies. The source and heart of this common culture lies in world trade and industrialization and their immediate consequences in urbanization, specialization, secularization, and the opening of possibilities for social mobility, universal education, and improvement in the material standard of living.

At the considerable risk of exaggeration I shall essay to outline some of the major characteristics of the "world culture" that is thus developing in all advanced societies. There is no doubt that considerable, perhaps even fundamental, differences underlie the modern development of such diverse nations as Japan, the Soviet Union, and the United States. And when I imply that India, Yugoslavia, and the Gold Coast are beginning to follow the same path, the purists will have even more justification for charging me with intellectual barbarism. Yet I believe that the Commercial and Industrial revolutions which have come to all these societies, and are continuing to influence them, are having profound effects on many basic traditional values and are causing these diverse societies to become similar to one another in certain significant respects. If this is so, we may properly speak of a world culture.[41] There is a tendency to regard this world culture as "Western"—that is, as emanating from Western Europe. This, I hold, is true only in the limited sense that the Commercial and Industrial revolutions developed first in Western Europe, and were copied from and stimulated by that region. Certain specific values characteristic of Western culture probably were diffused along with trade and industry, but the more important aspects of world culture were those imminent in the Commercial and Industrial revolutions. An obvious part of this culture—directly necessary for world trade and industry—are such important economic institutions as the factory, the port, and the bank. A secondary effect—*indirectly* necessary for sustaining industrialism—may be seen in such institutions as the specialized training school, the modern police system (as sharply distinguished from the army), and the shift from the extended family to the nuclear family. Each of these (and others of their type) requires a monograph in itself, and yet I shall move hastily on to consider a tertiary set of consequences of world trade and industry—possibly not *necessary* for sustaining them but highly likely to *follow* them. The tertiary aspects of world culture are on the level of fundamental meanings and values, and concerning them I shall be frankly speculative.

The extension of the market, the increased division of labor, and the use of machines greatly raise productivity. The new wealth may be appropriated by the government (for war, for the personal luxuries of the rulers, for capital investment) or it may be distributed among some or all of the people. In any case, the people see the new wealth they are producing or they see how *other* people are producing great wealth with what appears to be a small amount of labor, and it is likely that they rapidly raise their material aspirations. Desire and hope for a raised material standard of living is thus one of the first value characteristics of the world culture to appear. Perhaps after initial resistance by government and by private holders of great capital, the masses of the people do acquire some of this new wealth for their own use. Technological development abets the raised income as it offers new kinds of equipment for the home and other consumer use. Of course, increased length of life dissipates the new wealth until the birth rate is lowered, but increased length of life is also one of the new values achievable through the new technology.

The demand for experts and other trained workers couples with the new aspirations of the masses to produce a new value of social mobility. More and more people want to and do move out of the peasant and *lumpen*-proletariat classes. Mobility on the one hand tends to bring demands for universal education and what are popularly conceived of, rightly or wrongly, as the more desirable and hitherto restricted aspects of the culture—namely, the arts. Mobility on the other hand, and for the same reason, brings the demand for the material luxuries, conspicuous consumption, and the striving to keep up with and surpass one's neighbors.

Trade and industry bring another kind of mobility—geographic relocation—as workers must be physically distributed to where they can be more productive under the new production system. The social consequences of extensive migration of individuals and families, mostly to cities, are enormous. These consequences have been extensively described by sociologists,[42] and here I can but draw attention to only a few of them. The breakdown of attachment to local community and extended family tends to weaken all traditional values, and tends to shift people from sacred to secular behavior. The breakdown of the protection against life crises afforded by the local community and the extended family brings demands for various forms of "social security" by the state. Life in the large, changing city promotes "individualism" in all sorts of ways. The integrated society tends to be transformed into a mass or audience, and a large proportion of people become partially "alienated" from their culture.[43]

The aspirations stimulated by the possibilities for vertical mobility and the anonymity and secularization consequent to geographic mobility combine to create a general desire for political and social freedom. Liberty and equality have been associated with the particular value systems of Western Europe and their branches in other parts of the world (perhaps especially in the United States). But I predict that future historians will see them as aspirations characteristic of world culture, emanating from the Commercial and Industrial revolutions. The French and American political revolulutions, especially their slogans, have become models for other advanced peoples, but the stimulation to use these models stems from more general and basic social and economic forces. It is not merely a case of diffusion. And the aspirations are present, whether non-Western peoples can achieve them or not, because of the restricting power of their governments or upper classes, or because of such inhibiting forces as over-population.

Another important model has been the Leninist political revolution,[44] particularly as it developed in the Soviet Union. The Leninist revolution has been at once a revolt against feudalistic barriers to industrialization (in this way little different from the "bourgeois" political revolution) and a promise that the masses would share immediately in the benefits of industrialization. The economically backward nations want to take a short cut to industrialization and all its good effects, rather than follow the slower American and Western European model. It remains to be seen whether the faster model is truly speedier and surer in the long run, and whether a more democratic and liberal phase must not be attained even in the Leninist state before it can reach its goal. The reader of the chapter on Yugoslavia in this book will note the trend toward economic decentralization in that Leninist state.

Western European social structure—including that of the United States—provides one model for the underdeveloped countries, and Soviet social structure provides another. Still others may develop. The important thing, however, is that most nations of the world are now developing something of a common culture based largely on world trade and industrialization. To state this is not to deny the overwhelming divergencies and consequences which each country's development will have. The history and tradition of each society will make its absorption of world trade and industrialization, and the institutions and values consequent to them, unique. Many institutions and values of the society will not be significantly affected by the changes described here. Further, each society will develop its own form of political structure to facilitate and control these changes. One should not predict uniformity for all the world's societies in the future. But these obvious and important facts should not prevent us from observing that a common world culture is now beginning to develop. This can be seen in the fact that the Soviet Union and the United States have several significant convergences despite their vastly different histories and political-economic systems. The reader of the present book will note how the societies described, vastly different though they are, have certain convergences and that these arise out of a common concern with the fact and the consequences of becoming economically "modern."

Concepts for the Study of Modern Society

The social scientist who studies a modern society, as well as the reader who would understand a modern society, needs a body of concepts as one of the basic tools of this undertaking. Sociologists have been developing such a body of concepts, and while these no doubt will have to be greatly modified as the study develops, it will be useful to review them at this time before going on to the descriptions and analyses of specific societies. I shall limit myself to those concepts which refer to the institutions of a society.

The common meanings and values making up the culture of a society do not exist in the minds of the members of the society independent of one another, but rather often form interrelated clusters, where one element has a high degree of dependency on the others in the same cluster. Since each meaning or value indicates what members of the society may or should do, each cluster may be thought of as an interrelated group of guides and directions for complex behavior patterns. Such clusters, or groups of complex behavior patterns within the culture, and the interrelations among them, make up a large part of the social structure of the society. If one of these clusters has a high degree of specificity and internal cohesiveness, it is generally spoken of by social scientists as an *institution*, although the popular meaning of "institution" is usually not quite so broad.

Not all of social structure is made up of the institutions of a society, because deliberately excluded from institutions are structures of common meanings and values governing the behavior of such groupings of persons as socioeconomic categories or ethnic groups. Socioeconomic categories may be organized into classes, and minority groups may be organized into castes, and both classes and castes are a part of social structure that are not as internally cohesive and specific as institutions.

Sociologists have been divided in their use of the term "institution." Some have used it to refer to interrelated clusters of meanings and values, as I have defined it above, while others have used it to refer to a number of people in organized interaction. The French sociologist Maurice Hauriou[45] distinguished between the "institution as object" and the "institution as group" to refer to these two definitions.[46] This distinction need not bother us if we recognize the limited sense in which the concept of "group" is used when considered to be an institution. It is not merely a number of people, or a category of people, or such a special mode of relationship linking a number of people as the crowd or audience. In the context of social structure a group is to be narrowly considered as an "integrated group" which is defined as a number of *socialized* persons who have already had some history of interaction with each other. They have learned to predict each other's behavior fairly accurately so that they can adjust to each other. This is made possible through common meanings and values, occasionally devised out of the communication between the members of the group, but much more often transmitted to them from long-past communications through the process of socialization.

Considered in this limited sense, an "institution as group" *is* an "institution as object" when attention is focused on the interacting members rather than on the meanings and values on the basis of which the members interact. Keeping in mind that we shall use the word "group" in this limited "integrated group" sense of the term, we can thus use the terms "group" and "institution" interchangeably. We can now also understand why the institution continues when a unit of its individual members leave or die out. The interrelated cluster of common meanings and values which constitute the family continues even when the father and mother die and the children are dispersed, for the children form almost identical family units based upon most of the same common meanings and values.

Groups can be classified in a very large number of different ways; the merit of a classification depends on the use one has for it. Since my purpose at this point is to note variation, I shall adopt the lengthy classification of groups proposed by Georges Gurvitch.[47] The list of types of groups should not be thought of as complete, but merely as helpful in social research and in understanding social variation.

Groups can be thought of in terms of the number of functions they serve. Some groups exist entirely for one purpose, many have one dominant purpose and several lesser ones, others have several coordinate purposes. Functions can be classified in many different ways, perhaps most easily in these terms: child-rearing, friendship, economic, educational, scientific, political, social welfare, military, religious, occupational, recreational, aesthetic, communicative, and so on. A group can carry on its activities with a great deal of vigor and fervor, or it can operate slowly and lackadaisically. A group can be composed of only two persons or it can be as large as a nation. The number of members helps to determine the nature of the contacts between them: intimate and frequent (primary contacts) or segmentalized and occasional and often made through intermediaries (secondary contacts). Individuals are born into certain types of groups (families, nations, religious denominations), membership in other groups is imposed on them later (schools, armies), while still other groups they join more or less voluntarily. Groups that one joins voluntarily may be open to everyone, may be limited to certain specified categories of the population, or may be open to everyone who will go through certain ceremonies. Groups may be deliberately organized or they may take form slowly and without intention (these are Sumner's *enacted* and *crescive* types of institutions).[48] Groups may be formal or informal, highly structured or practically unstructured, related to other groups or unattached, open to outside influences or highly resistant to outside influences, unified or composed of subgroups, highly directive of the behavior of its members or permissive toward them, in conflict with the outside society or accommodated to it. In other words, the common meanings and values which govern the organized group can vary in many respects.

Some of the specific interests of a sociologist making a study of an institution would be these: the social situation out of which the institution arose, the process of growth of the institution, the external structure of the institution, the means by which the institution is perpetuated, the means by which the institution will meet an unexpected crisis, the manner in which new members and functionaries are brought into the institution, the relation of the institution to other institutions and to the general community, the spheres of life in which the institution operates, the extent and manner of control over the members, the expansion of function or structure of the institution, the functions of the institution and the relation of function to location, and the career of an individual in the institution. In short, an institution is studied as a means whereby a number of people act collectively on the basis of common understandings that have a high degree of persistency.

While each institution contains within itself many values, it can be itself regarded as a means whereby individuals who perform the behaviors it prescribes can attain certain more inclusive or "higher" values. This instrumental character of the institution is often spoken of as its "function."[49] An institution typically has more than one function:

The real component units of culture which have a considerable degree of permanence, universality, and independence are the organized systems of human activities called institutions. Every institution centers around a fundamental need, permanently unites a group of people in a cooperative

32

task and has its particular body of doctrine and its technique or craft. Institutions are not correlated simply and directly to their functions; one need does not receive one satisfaction in one institution. But institutions show a pronounced amalgamation of functions and have a synthetic character.[50]

Durkheim originally, and more recently Chapin[51] and Merton,[52] have distinguished the "latent functions" from the "manifest functions" of institutions.[53] The latter are what appear to be, and are deliberately intended to be, the functions of institutions. The former are the regular but unanticipated consequences of the activities of institutions. The latent functions are often not perceived by those who participate in an institution, but are discernible only to objective outsiders who look at the recurring effects of group activity and not only at the expressed intentions. Even when participants understand the latent functions of their institution, they usually do not discuss them. Thus latent functions can be considered to be among the covert elements of culture.[54] In studying an institution it is important to discover its latent as well as its manifest functions.

It is also important to recognize that an institution can change its functions and that the same function can be performed by several institutions. Certain functions are performed by elaborate systems of interconnected institutions. The traditional doctor's office, which once served as clinic, medical school, surgery, and laboratory, is today but one among many institutions concerned with healing. In addition to those already named there are hospitals for various kinds of people and various ailments, the schools and professional associations of various auxiliary occupations, the associations and examining boards of special branches of medicine, as well as the governmental, philanthropic, and private institutions for distributing medical care and protecting the health of the public. To say that the function of any one of these institutions is healing, without specifying its particular function in the whole healing system, would be a truism without meaning.[55]

The meanings and values which constitute an institution do not, of course, exist in themselves. They are the rules or prescriptions for behavior of individuals, and they manifest themselves in the regularity and consistency of that behavior. One observes the behavior; the meanings and values can only be inferred from the consistency of the behavior. Institutions tend to use organized sanctions, in Radcliffe-Brown's sense of the term; the rules are explicit and generally recognized: only the proper officers may perform the various procedures expected in an institution.

Reference to the regularity and consistency of behavior does not mean

33

that every person who is a member of an institution is expected to have the same behavior. In the first place, much of a member's life lies outside the institution, and few people in society have exactly the same rounds of institutions and activities. Secondly, within the institution he plays a *role* which is never the same for all members of the institution. Each institution has a *division of labor* among its participants: there are several roles, and each fits into the other to make the institution operate.

Some of the roles are especially important in the institution and are filled by a small number of the group members. These are called the *offices* of an institution, and those who fill them are called the *officers* or *functionaries*. They derive a certain *authority* by virtue of their office and thus have influence over the behavior of other members. Since their roles are generally fairly well prescribed by the meanings and values relevant to their offices, their behavior is largely sociogenic in the institutional setting. Still, each officer is also a person with a complete personality, and thus his behavior is also individualized and never completely in accord with his institutional role.[56] In other words, no two officers are exactly alike, even though they fill the same office. Different offices permit different degrees of individual initiative, just as different individuals are ready to assume different degrees of initiative. Thus there are often special qualifications for offices.

Institutions vary in the degree of specialization expected of persons, and this is often related to the degree of control the institution has over the life of its members. The more specialized and segmentalized the relation of a given member to an institution, the less is its control over him. The teacher is associated with the school only in his occupational life, whereas the nun is associated with the church in most aspects of her life. Even within the same institution this holds true: the religious leader (rabbi, priest, minister) has a less specialized relation to his church than does the average member, and his life is much more controlled by the institution. To the extent that an individual's life is controlled by one institution, he must have fewer relationships with other institutions. A priest, for example, must even withdraw from family life.

Durkheim[57] distinguished two types of societies, which should be thought of as end-points of a continuum rather than as merely two distinctive categories. He was interested in what holds the society together, on what basis there is a mutual adjustment of roles. The first type is a society in which there are not many different roles, and most individuals have therefore to play only one or two of a limited number of roles: this he called a society with *mechanical solidarity*. The second type is a society with many different roles, and each individual plays several different roles which are not likely to be the same for all individuals: this he called a society with *organic solidarity*. In a society with mechanical solidarity it is similarity of role of individuals that holds the society together. In a society with organic solidarity it is mutual dependence of roles that holds the society together. From our knowledge that mutual dependence of roles is characteristic of institutions, we can deduce that a society with many and complicated institutions is a society held together in organic solidarity.

Durkheim implied, somewhat incorrectly, that the preliterate societies have mechanical solidarity and that the literate societies have organic solidarity. Actually our better knowledge of anthropology today shows us that some preliterate societies have a huge number of complicated institutions with a great deal of dependence of role. In fact some of these preliterate societies have more organic solidarity than many societies possessing knowledge of writing. What is valuable in Durkheim's analysis, however, is his recognition that "advanced societies"—within the meaning of this book—are held together largely by mutual interdependence of roles, that the existence of many institutions and high division of labor within and between institutions make us highly dependent on one another. The cohesiveness or solidarity of our society is thus based on our "awareness" of the many diverse roles played in the many diverse institutions of our society, and our "willingness" to adjust our role to the others in a division of labor.

An institution usually has characteristics other than the roles of the people who carry on its activity. Some of these are meanings and values which specify or clarify the manifest functions of the institution; others are meanings and values attributed to the tools or instruments which aid the members in performing the functions (both manifest and latent) of the institution. Chapin has classified the constituent elements of an institution into four "type parts":

The four main type parts that combine to produce the configuration or cultural concretion known as the social institution are:

First, common reciprocating attitudes of individuals and their conventionalized behavior patterns.

Second, cultural objects of symbolic value; that is, objects charged with sentimental meaning to which human behavior has been conditioned.

Third, cultural objects possessing utilitarian value; that is, material objects that satisfy creature wants and through conditioned response and habit attach the other parts of the pattern to a specific location: objects called property.

Fourth, oral or written language symbols that preserve the descriptions and specifications of the patterns of interrelationship among the other three parts—attitudes, symbolic culture traits, and utilitarian culture traits or real property. When the formulation is compactly organized it is called a code.[58]

The extent to which the manifest functions of an institution and the techniques for performing them are overtly specified—to that extent it may be called a *formal* institution. "A statement of purpose" or preamble to the constitution of a voluntary association would be a most obvious example of meanings and values specifying the manifest functions of a formal institution. The remainder of the constitution of a voluntary association, or the administrative regulations set by a school board to govern a school, would be obvious examples of the "code" specifying the expected attitudes, symbols, and tools used in accomplishing the manifest functions of a formal institution (the tools or utilitarian objects themselves are, of course, to be distinguished from the written specifications for them). In the case of the family the manifest functions and some of the means for achieving them are specified in law in our society, and also in the words with which a marriage ceremony is performed. In France, where the law is modeled after ancient Roman law, the manifest function, expected attitudes, and tools of nearly all institutions are specified in law or the administrative regulations of the state, so that in France practically all institutions are formal.

Ceremonies are rules of behavior that govern the members of an institution on special occasions, usually when they come together and celebrate some recurring event important for the functioning of the institutions. Ceremonies often accompany the change of role or assumption of a new role by a member of the group. In the family, for example, ceremonies accompany the christening or circumcision (for Christians and Jews, respectively) of new members. Transition from childhood to adulthood is marked by puberty rites in many societies, by confirmation in our own society.[59] The ceremony of marriage accompanies the creation of a new family unit. In many organized groups ceremonies accompany the inauguration of a leader. Initiation ceremonies are performed when new members enter some voluntary association, and graduation ceremonies are performed when qualified members leave the institution of a school. Sometimes ceremonies accompany the entrance of a new tool into the institution, if the tool is important enough, such as a building (such a ceremony is spoken of as a "dedication").

Another category of ceremonies is that involved in the commemoration of events in the past which have been crucially important to the group. Holiday ceremonies are used principally by nations and religious denominations, but families celebrate anniversaries and birthdays in a similar manner. The important functions of ceremonies, if there are any, must be latent, since overtly they merely call attention to what every member should know anyway. Sociologists have generally hypothesized that the function of ceremonies is to re-cement the group by recalling attention to its fundamental values. Since the values are always old ones, ceremony is a conservative force that discourages change. The conservatism of ceremonies suggests another latent function: since ceremonies so often occur at critical stages in the lives of members of the institution, it may be that a function of ceremonies is to help the members over these crises and so keep them attached to the institution.

A crisis in the life of an individual is not necessarily a crisis for an institution in which he participates. Indeed, one of the most common of institutional functions is provision for crises in the lives of individuals. To the individual, his marriage, illnesses, sins, and fear of death are unique and critical. To the church these crises are recurrent, and there is a way of dealing with each. Institutions, so long as they can meet the crises of the individual, are not themselves in a critical state. When, however, some new type of situation, not provided for by the existing institutions, becomes chronic and widespread, the institutions themselves are in a parlous state.[60]

Rituals are often parts of ceremonies, but may be used more frequently in nonceremonial settings. A ritual is a prescribed set of words and acts, used practically without variation, that is believed to have symbolic powers to produce certain desired results. Ritual sometimes loses its meaning and is repeated merely out of respect for tradition. If its meaning, that it produces a certain result, is believed, it is a form of magic.[61]

Some institutions have *formal symbols* which are simple physical objects that are intended to convey the meaning of the major manifest function of the institution as a whole. A common example of a formal symbol is a flag. The flag of the United States not only symbolizes the nation, but also its function of uniting all the separate states. The flag of the Union of Soviet Socialist Republics not only symbolizes that nation as a whole, but also the collaboration of manual workers and peasants (hammer and sickle) in "red" revolution. The flag of the Red Cross symbolizes not only that voluntary association, but also its major manifest function of bringing aid to those in distress. Religious institutions usually have symbols also representing what is conceived to be the major manifest function of the religion. The Christian cross, for example, symbolizes the death of Jesus, which is believed to have made possible the salvation of sinful man. Salvation is intended to be the major manifest function of the Christian church. The statue of Buddha, seated cross-legged, symbolizes the aim of Buddhism to encourage the contemplative life as a means of achieving what is good. Some sports groups or youth groups may use a live animal as a symbol ("mascot") of what are conceived to be the desirable virtues for members of the group. All such formal symbols represent the unity of the institution as a whole. When they also obviously represent the major manifest function of the group, it is understood that this function is an ideal, not always achieved in practice.

Other physical appurtenances of an institution usually belong to its "tool" side. There are physical objects which aid the members in the performance of their various roles in the institution. A school has a building with rooms of a certain type, stocked with books, blackboards, desks, laboratory equipment, and all the other physical implements that help the members to perform their roles, not only in relation with each other, but also in furtherance of the functions described earlier. Quite often the building which implements the functioning of the institution is taken to stand for the institution as a whole, and thus it becomes the symbol of the institution.

While it is quite likely that an institution will acquire physical appurtenances to aid its functioning, just as a person does, the absence of these does not mean that there is no institution. Among the ancient Greeks there were some schools—on what we today would call the "university level"—which apparently had no physical appurtenances whatsoever; a teacher would meet his students at prearranged times and places, and they would sit or walk together while he gave them instruction. This arrangement was still an institution, and deserves the name of school because of its functions and the specialized roles which the persons played toward each other. It is to be considered, however, as a very informal institution. Not only were there no physical appurtenances, but there were no symbols, no written specification of the functions, no written specification as to how a person acquired or lost a certain role.

THE COMPARATIVE STUDY OF INSTITUTIONS

We have considered, in a general manner, the characteristics associated with institutions. However, not all institutions have all of these characteristics: the minimum essentials of an institution are that a number of persons play certain roles toward each other, in a regularized division of labor, for the purpose of accomplishing certain functions.

These few concepts, the theoretical framework, the world cultural perspective, have been presented as devices for aiding the understanding and analysis of the following descriptions of the institutions of certain selected advanced societies. What has been offered is very general; each author of the following sections will have his own explanations and interpretations for the concrete phenomena he describes. If there is to be comparative analysis, however, a more general framework must be sought. The theory and methodology offered here may be quite inadequate: these efforts are presented tentatively as a first step in the formulation of theory and method for the comparative study of advanced societies. The next steps are obvious: With data presented in this volume and elsewhere, specific hypotheses within the framework must be tested and modified; new data must be collected that will be more directly pertinent to this and other theoretical frameworks; more comprehensive theoretical frameworks must be devised. This volume, then, attempts to offer only a challenge to the comparative study of advanced societies.

Notes

[1] Karl Mannheim, *Ideology and Utopia* (New York: Harcourt, Brace, 1936).

[2] J. B. Bury, *The Idea of Progress* (London: Macmillan, 1921).

[3] No one has brought this out so well as William F. Ogburn, *Social Change* (New York: B. W. Huebsch, 1922).

[4] Probably the contemporary sociologists Foote and Cottrell have gone furthest in this direction by adopting a definite set of top-level values which they assume to be universal (although possibly interpreted in somewhat different ways in different societies). Their list — health, intelligence, empathy, autonomy, judgment, and creativity — is reminiscent of that of a pioneer American sociologist, Albion W. Small, thereby recognizing that the relativist trend in social science after Small went to excess in rejecting him and like-minded social scientists. See Nelson Foote and Leonard S. Cottrell, Jr., *Identity and Interpersonal Competence* (Chicago: University of Chicago Press, 1955), pp. 41–43.

[5] F. S. C. Northrup, *The Logic of the Sciences and the Humanities* (New York: Macmillan, 1947).

[6] Clyde Kluckhohn, *Mirror for Man* (New York: McGraw-Hill, 1949), p. 41.

[7] Abram Kardiner and Ralph Linton, *The Individual and His Society* (New York: Columbia University Press, 1939); Margaret Mead, *And Keep Your Powder Dry* (New York: Morrow, 1942); Ruth Benedict, *The Chrysanthemum and the Sword* (Boston: Houghton Mifflin, 1946).

[8] See, for example, the symposium in the *Journal of Social Issues,* 11 (No. 2, 1955), 3–56.

[9] Alex Inkeles and Daniel J. Levinson, "National Character: The Study of Modal Personality and Socio-cultural Systems," in G. Lindzey (ed.), *Handbook of Social Psychology* (Cambridge, Mass.: Addison-Wesley Publishing Co., 1954).

[10] This analysis is a theoretically slightly extended and factually greatly abbreviated statement of my "Voluntary Associations in France," Chapter 4 of *Theory and Method in the Social Sciences* (Minneapolis: University of Minnesota Press, 1954). For documentation the reader is referred to this source.

[11] "The Conflict between Aristotelian and Galileian Modes of Thought in Contemporary Psychology," *Journal of General Psychology* 5 (1931), 141–177. Reprinted in Lewin's *A Dynamic Theory of Personality* (New York: McGraw-Hill, 1935).

[12] Actually, it is not quite accurate to say that Boas believed that the part-structures of a society were unrelated. It is rather that he would search empirically for the relationship between any two part-structures rather than assume a priori that there must be a relationship.

[13] Radcliffe-Brown gives credit to Durkheim's *Regles de la Methode Sociologique,* 1895. A. R. Radcliffe-Brown, "Concept of Function in Social Science," *American Anthropologist,* 37 (July–Sept. 1935), 394–402.

[14] Walter B. Cannon, *The Wisdom of the Body* (London: Kegan Paul, 1932).

[15] Myrdal has reviewed the literature on notions of stable equilibrium in economics and has provided a devastating critique of them. See Gunnar Myrdal, *The Political Element in the Development of Economic Theory,* translated from the German by Paul Streeten (Cambridge, Mass.: Harvard University Press, 1954).

[16] "Homeostasis Versus Hyperexis," *Scientific Monthly,* 77 (December 1953), 289–294. On page 291, Richards says, "Take the process of fibrosis, scar tissue formation. This heals wounds, disposes of infections – surely a homeostatic mechanism. But is it always so? What about scar tissue in rheumatoid arthritis, ending in frozen immobile joints, scar tissue in the kidneys, ending in glomerular nephritis, scar tissue in the liver, ending in cirrhosis, scar tissue in the lungs, choking the breathing process into asphyxia? In trying to be homeostatic in one direction, the body finds that it has been most un-homeostatic in another."

[17] For statements on both sides, see E. W. Dempsey, "Homeostatis," in S. S. Stevens (ed.), *Handbook of Experimental Psychology* (New York: Wiley, 1951), pp. 209–235; Ross Stagner, "Homeostasis as a Unifying Concept in Personality Theory," *Psychological Review,* 58 (No. 1, 1951), 5–17; J. R. Maze, "On Some Corruptions of the Doctrine of Homeostasis," *Psychological Review,* 60 (No. 6, 1953), 405–412; Ross Stagner, "Homeostasis: Corruptions or Misconceptions? A Reply," *Psychological Review,* 61 (No. 3, 1954), 205–208. Some psychiatrists have also made use of the concept of homeostasis. For example: Lawrence Kubie in *Psychosomatic Medicine,* 10 (1948), 15ff; G. Engel in R. Grinker (ed.), *Mid-Century Psychiatry* (Springfield, Ill.: Thomas, 1953), pp. 33ff; D. Orr in *Psychoanalytic Quarterly,* 11 (1942), 322ff.

[18] Emile Durkheim, *Rules of Sociological Method,* translated from the French by S. A. Solovay and S. H. Mueller (Chicago: University of Chicago Press, 1938; 1st edition, 1895), p. 67.

[19] Nathan Ausubel (ed.), *A Treasury of Jewish Folklore* (New York: Crown, 1948), p. 372.

[20] Edwin A. Sutherland, *White Collar Crime* (New York: Dryden, 1949). Austin L. Porterfield, *Youth in Trouble* (Austin, Texas: Leo Potishman Foundation, 1946).

[21] Arnold M. Rose and Arthur E. Prell, "Does the Punishment Fit the Crime? A Study in Social Valuation," *American Journal of Sociology,* 61 (November 1955), 247–259.

[22] E. A. Sutherland and D. R. Cressey, *Principle of Criminology* (Philadelphia: Lippincott, 5th edition, 1955); William Healy, *New Light on Delinquency and Its Treatment* (New Haven, Conn.: Yale University Press, 1936); Paul W. Tappan,

Juvenile Delinquency (New York: McGraw-Hill, 1949); S. R. Hathaway and E. D. Monachesi, "The Minnesota Multiphasic Personality Inventory in the Study of Juvenile Delinquents," *American Sociological Review,* 17 (December 1952), 704–710.

[23] *The Social System* (Glencoe, Ill.: The Free Press, 1951), pp. 240–242.

[24] *Ibid.,* pp. 428–479.

[25] Morris Ginsberg, *The Idea of Progress: A Revaluation* (London: Methuen, 1953), p. 58. Also see Alexander Lesser, "Functionalism in Social Anthropology," *American Anthropologist,* 37 (July–Sept. 1935), 386–393.

[26] T. C. Schneirla, Chapter 4 of John H. Rohrer and Muzafer Sherif (eds.), *Social Psychology at the Crossroads* (New York: Harper, 1951).

[27] Cannon, *op. cit.,* pp. 286–288; Parsons, *The Social System,* pp. 482–483.

[28] Jules Henry, "Homeostasis, Society, and Evolution: A Critique," *Scientific Monthly,* 81 (December 1955), 300–309, esp. p. 306.

[29] Robert K. Merton, *Social Theory and Social Structure* (Glencoe, Ill.: The Free Press, 1949), pp. 34–37, 52–53.

[30] Richard D. Schwartz, "Functional Alternatives to Inequality," *American Sociological Review,* 20 (August 1955), 424–430.

[31] Raymond Firth, "Function," *Yearbook of Anthropology* (New York: Wenner-Gren Foundation, 1955), pp. 237–258.

[32] Merton, *op. cit.*

[33] It is legitimate also to use the term "function" in a common-sense way, as "instinct" is used in everyday speech to refer to spontaneous human behavior. In this sense, function usually means how a thing operates. There is no implication in such usage that an explanation is being offered of the behavior referred to.

[34] In "A Formalization of Functionalism," unpublished PPAT Document No. 112, October 1953.

[35] *Op. cit.,* pp. 300–302.

[36] At least two of the three authors referred to have acknowledged the equivalency of the terms, and I have had no occasion to discuss the matter with the third (Opler).

[37] Clyde Kluckhohn, "Patterning as Exemplified in Navaho Culture," in L. Spier, A. I. Hallowell, and S. S. Newman (eds.), *Language Culture and Personality* (Menasha, Wisc.: Sapir Memorial Publication Fund, 1941), pp. 109–128; Morris E. Opler, "Themes as Dynamic Forces in Culture," *American Journal of Sociology,* 51 (1945), 198–206; Opler, "An Application of the Theory of Themes in Culture," *Journal of the Washington Academy of Sciences,* 36 (1946), 137–166; E. Adamson Hoebel, *The Law of Primitive Man* (Cambridge, Mass.: Harvard University Press, 1954).

[38] I have limited my own previous discussion of "covert culture elements" to this second category, and while I have referred to Kluckhohn's discussion, I have not until recently recognized that my use of the term was narrower than his. See Arnold M. Rose, "Popular Logic in the Study of Covert Culture," in *Theory and Method in the Social Sciences,* Chapter 21; Bernard Bowron, Leo Marx, and Arnold M. Rose, "Literature in the Study of Covert Culture," to be published in *American Quarterly.*

[39] Negroes have never been in the numerical majority in the South as a whole, and —since 1890, when the caste system crystallized in its pure form—there have never been more than two states with a majority of Negroes. Since 1940 there have been no states with a Negro majority.

[40] Kluckhohn includes the Mormons, Texans, and Spanish-Americans in his "values project" in New Mexico, while Opler and Redfield have started to study India.

[41] I am obviously not speaking here of man's common biological heritage, of human nature, or of the "psychic unity of mankind"; but rather of a common culture arising out of exposure to similar forces of trade and industrialization and out of intercommunication as a result of these forces.

[42] To mention just a few: Simmel, Toennies, Durkheim, Cooley, Thomas, Park, Becker, and Blumer.

[43] Arnold M. Rose, *Theory and Method in the Social Sciences*, Chapter 2.

[44] I use the label Leninist rather than socialist because a good number of socialist leaders—especially in Great Britain and Scandinavia—have deliberately rejected Leninism and even some of the teachings of Marx. Democratic socialism in the Western countries has been a refinement and stepping up of certain equalitarian tendencies already developing under capitalism.

[45] *La science sociale traditionelle* (Paris: La Larose, 1896), *L'Institution et le droit statutaire* (Paris: La Larose, 1906). See also Florian Znaniecki, "Social Organization and Institutions," in G. Gurvitch and W. E. Moore, *Twentieth Century Sociology* (New York: Philosophical Library, 1945), pp. 187 ff.

[46] MacIver distinguishes between these two by calling them, respectively, institution and association. (Robert M. MacIver, *Society: Its Structure and Changes* (New York: Ray Long & Richard R. Smith, 1932), Chapter 2.) Similarly, Chapin distinguishes between diffused-symbolic institutions and nucleated institutions. (F. Stuart Chapin, *Contemporary Social Institutions* (New York: Harper, 1935), p. 13.)

[47] "Groupement social et classe sociale," *Cahiers Internationaux de Sociologie*, 7 (1949), 1–33.

[48] William Graham Sumner, *Folkways* (Boston: Ginn, 1906), p. 54.

[49] Sumner defined an institution as consisting of a concept and a structure. In our terminology, the "concept" of an institution is its function; its structure is the cluster of meanings and values which specify behavior within it and in relation to it. (Sumner, *op. cit.*, Chapter 1.)

[50] B. Malinowski, "Culture," *Encyclopedia of the Social Sciences* (New York: Macmillan, 1931), vol. 4, pp. 621–646; quotation at p. 626.

[51] F. Stuart Chapin, "Latent Culture Patterns of the Unseen World of Social Reality," *American Journal of Sociology*, 40 (July 1934), 61–68; *Contemporary Social Institutions*, pp. 21 ff.

[52] Robert K. Merton, *op. cit.*, pp. 21–81.

[53] Sumner considered institutions to be consciously utilitarian; hence by implication he would not have considered them to have latent functioning.

[54] See the third section of this chapter, "The Internal Unity of a Society: Functionalism."

[55] Everett C. Hughes, "Institutions," in Alfred McClung Lee (ed.), *New Outline of the Principles of Sociology* (New York: Barnes & Noble, 1946), p. 231.

[56] Everett C. Hughes, "Institutional Office and the Person," *American Journal of Sociology*, 42 (1937), 404–413.

[57] Emile Durkheim, *The Division of Labor in Society* (Glencoe, Ill.: The Free Press, 1947; 1st edition, 1893).

[58] F. Stuart Chapin, *Contemporary Social Institutions*, p. 15.

[59] A term by Arnold van Gennep has come to be used to refer to these ceremonies of transition from childhood to adulthood—*rites de passage*. See his *Les Rites de passage* (Paris, 1909).

[60] Everett C. Hughes, "Institutions," *op. cit.*, p. 236.

[61] For a discussion of how magic underlies ritual see Ruth Benedict, *Patterns of Culture* (Boston: Houghton Mifflin, 1934).

*

Anthony H. Richmond

THE UNITED KINGDOM

*

THE outstanding features of the social structure, institutions, and culture of the United Kingdom are a consequence of their uninterrupted development over a long period. Britain has been free from foreign invasion or military occupation for nine hundred years. Except for the strife which led to the establishment of the Republic of Eire, the country has not experienced a violent revolution since the seventeenth century. Its insularity enabled it to escape the turmoils that ravaged the continent of Europe, and the British people long enjoyed the stability and security so essential to the emergence of democratic values and institutions.

It was not until the invention of the airplane, which destroyed the protection afforded by the English Channel, that Britain became vulnerable from a military aspect. With the spread of mass media of communication the country also became vulnerable from a cultural point of view. While Britain has not succumbed to military force, it has responded to the peaceful penetration of other outside influences, among which the effects in the twentieth century of American culture, mediated through the cinema, have been the most powerful. Every British child plays "Cowboys and Indians," and the American cultural influence persists throughout life.

Unlike the United States, the United Kingdom has no written constitution. Its basic social and political values are deeply embedded in custom and convention. With the exception of the Magna Carta (1215), the Bill of Rights (1689), and the Parliament Act (1911), the fundamental rights and freedoms—the basic tenets, ideals, and values to which the people in the United Kingdom subscribe—are nowhere set down in constitutional form. As far as the actual machinery of government is concerned, this has the advantage of providing flexibility and ease of adaptation to changed

43

circumstances and ideas. In relation to fundamental democratic values, however, it has the disadvantage—whenever a divergence arises between these cultural values and institutional practice—of lacking an instrument, such as that provided by the Supreme Court in the United States, through which a remedy may be sought.

A moral philosopher examining the values and ideals implicit in the culture pattern of the United Kingdom would describe the society as united in a common loyalty to the British way of life, yet tolerant of minorities and those who do not entirely conform; fundamentally egalitarian in spirit, orderly, law-abiding, promoting freedom and individuality; democratic in its form of government and pursuing world peace in a spirit of realism and compromise that is based on experience and a respect for the rights of other nations; a society in which the members are governed by a personal morality and a social ethic derived from the Christian-humanist tradition; concerned to promote the welfare of its citizens, who, in their turn, are restrained and unaggressive, with a love of home and family life, possessing a deep respect for the contribution which education can make to the improvement of material and moral conditions in the future generations.

By way of contrast a cynical realist, determined to expose other aspects of life in the United Kingdom, would paint a very different picture. He would describe a society divided by local nationalist sentiments, religious animosities, inequalities of wealth, class consciousness, and ethnocentrism; torn by a struggle for power between capitalist monopolies on the one hand and trade unions on the other, both engaging in restrictive practices for their own ends; governed by a political minority put into power by an ignorant and apathetic electorate; preparing for war and pursuing power politics abroad, turning a blind eye to tyranny and racial intolerance in the colonies, and undermining individual responsibility at home through the machinery of the welfare state. He would describe a society whose people are given to petty crime and dishonesty; their personal morality governed by puritanism and hypocrisy; their aggression turned against outgroups; their family life threatened by sexual maladjustment and the incidence of divorce; a society in which an outdated educational system makes the rising generation singularly unfitted to meet its responsibilities.

Neither the idealist nor the cynical realist would be correct in his diagnosis, yet both would have described an aspect of the truth. A key to this apparent paradox may be found in a consideration of the outstanding differences between a primitive society and one with an advanced culture.

The social institutions of an advanced culture may be distinguished from those of a less advanced by their greater diversity, by their propensity to change, and by the probability that there will be a greater divergence between manifest values and actual behavior. A static, relatively unchanging society, bound by custom and tradition, revering its ancestors and determined to preserve its past, may succeed in molding the personalities and behavior of its members into conformity with its norms and ideals. To deviate from these would be to threaten the stability of the whole society; therefore conformity is enforced by collective sanctions, reinforced by fears of supernatural forces. The reverse is the case in a society in which, far from trying to preserve the traditions of the past, the members are dedicated to the pursuit of "progress." The ideal of "progress," unlike that of "perfection" as understood, for example, in Hindu or Buddhist philosophy, necessarily implies change.

There has been a reaction against the naive belief in the inevitability of progress which was characteristic of the nineteenth century. But it is still an implicit assumption of the British way of life that technological advancement and improved social welfare are desirable, practicable, and necessary aims. But social change cannot take place without generating conflicts. Toynbee has shown that a society only survives when it meets each challenge by a response which exposes it to a further challenge. It is often out of the tensions created in a conflict situation that the energy is created which carries a society on to the next level of partial equilibrium.

An outstanding challenge facing the United Kingdom today is the evident discrepancy between cultural ideals and reality. Studies of the social psychology of democracy, in contrast with that of dictatorship, emphasize that recognition of a dualism between the transcendental ideal and the immanent empirical social order is one of the main sources of tolerance. "Living within the frame of high ideals, and being aware of their unrealizable character and at the same time measuring one's action against these ideals, leads in the long run to a strong feeling of self-limitation and humility. This feeling, applied to human relationships, promotes understanding for and tolerance towards one's fellow men."[1]

The United Kingdom is not unique in exhibiting an inherent contradiction between the values to which lip-service is paid and those which govern actual behavior. Such inconsistencies are to be found in all advanced cultures and democratic societies, not least in the United States where Myrdal drew attention to an outstanding American dilemma. The nature of its ideals largely determines the direction of change in a society even though movement in that direction may be faltering. A comparison between the present economic, political, and social organization of the United Kingdom and the situation a hundred or even fifty years ago shows that the degree of inconsistency has been reduced enormously.

Demography and Social Structure

POPULATION TRENDS

The population of the United Kingdom is approximately 51 million persons.[2] Its present distribution and that at the time of the census of 1951 are shown in Table 1. The over-all density is approximately 533 persons per square mile, which is almost the highest in the world.

Table 2 illustrates the distribution of births. The net reproduction rate for the United Kingdom as a whole is only very slightly above unity. The crude birth rate is 15.8 per thousand of the population, of which 4.8 per cent are illegitimate. The low illegitimacy rate in Northern Ireland is partly explained by the fact that some unmarried mothers go to England to have their babies. There are no available statistics concerning the number of legitimate births per thousand women aged 16–44 years in Northern Ireland in 1951. The latest available figure, 197.6, is for the year 1937 when the birth rate per thousand women aged 15–44 years in Northern Ireland was 85.2 compared with 91.1 today.

All mortality rates, including those for infants, have been reduced considerably in the course of the last fifty years. One in twenty-five infants in Scotland and one in thirty in England and Wales die before the age of one year. The crude death rate for the population is approximately twelve per thousand and is slightly higher for men than for women, so that the ratio of women to men increases with age. Death rates are influenced by the age distribution of the population, shown in Table 3. Expectation of life is now 66.5 years for men and 71.5 years for women. Various forms of cancer and heart disease are the most frequent causes of mortality. The incidence of tuberculosis as a cause of mortality is declining rapidly.

The age group 0–4 in Table 3 represents infants of preschool age; the group 5–14 represents the school population with the exception of those who remain at school beyond the minimum school-leaving age of fifteen years. Men and women of working age are represented in groups 15–64 and 15–59 respectively. Most men but only slightly under half the women in these age groups are occupied, the remaining women being housewives

Table 1. Population of the United Kingdom in 1951 and 1955

Section	1951	1955
England	41,147,938	*44,441,000**
Wales and Monmouthshire	2,596,986	
Scotland	5,096,415	5,133,000
Northern Ireland	1,370,921	1,394,000

Source: General Register Office.

*Including Wales and Monmouthshire.

Table 2. Births in the United Kingdom in 1951

Item	United Kingdom	England and Wales	Scotland	Northern Ireland
Total live births	797,000	678,000	90,600	28,500
Males	410,000	349,000	46,700	14,600
Females	387,000	329,000	43,900	13,800
Males per thousand females	1,060	1,060	1,063	1,058
Legitimate births	758,000	645,000	86,000	27,600
Illegitimate births	38,000	33,000	4,600	1,000
Percentage of illegitimate births	4.8%	4.8%	5.1%	3.1%
Total live births per thousand population .	15.8	15.5	17.7	20.7
Total live births per thousand women, 15–44 years	73.0	71.5	80.2	91.1
Legitimate births per thousand married women, 16–44 years	. . .	105.2	132.2	. . .
Still births	. . .	16,000	2,500	. . .
Rate of still births per thousand births .	. . .	23	27	. . .

Source: General Register Office.

Table 3. Age Distribution of Population in the United Kingdom in 1955 (in thousands)

Sex and Age	Number	Percentage
Males		
0–4	1,973	8
5–14	4,011	16
15–64	16,482	67
Over 65	2,307	9
Total	24,773	100
Females		
0–4	1,878	7
5–14	3,838	14
15–59	15,855	62
Over 60	4,876	17
Total	26,447	100
Both sexes		
0–4	3,851	7
5–14	7,849	15
15–64 (15–59 for females)	32,337	65
Over 65 (over 60 for females)	7,183	13
Total	51,221	100

Source: Central Statistical Office.

47

not in employment. The balance, aged over 65 for men and over 60 for women, are mainly retired persons.

In the course of the next thirty years the proportion of the population over retiring age will increase from approximately 13 to 20 per cent. This will throw an increasing burden on the working population and upon the social services which are concerned with the health and social welfare of old people. The problems connected with Britain's aging population have been considered by social welfare workers, natural scientists, social scientists, politicians, and administrators. Some attempt is being made to encourage older people to remain in employment after normal retiring age, to assist in their adjustment to new and less onerous occupations, and to ease the economic problems of retired people.

The population of the United Kingdom has been affected by external and internal migration. Since the beginning of the nineteenth century about 25 million persons born in the British Isles have settled in the United States or in Commonwealth countries. Emigration has been proportionately greater from Scotland, Ireland, and Wales than from England. Against the loss by emigration must be set the European immigrants who have settled in Britain since the latter part of the nineteenth century. Compared with immigration to the United States, the number has been very small. Nevertheless, the net loss by migration from the present area of the United Kingdom has been reduced to about 3.5 million since 1871. For a short period after World War II the net balance was inward. In 1948 the highest figure of 64,000 alien immigrants was recorded. However, if we take the postwar period as a whole, the net balance of migration has been outward, owing to the fact that some 85,000 persons emigrate annually to Commonwealth countries, particularly Australia and Canada.

Internal migration is probably on a smaller scale than in the United States. In one inquiry it was found that half the population had lived in the same house for more than ten years and 16 per cent for more than twenty years. Possibly because of the housing shortage in Britain, once a person is married and settled in his own home he is unlikely to migrate. Nevertheless, an investigation in 1948–49 showed that 20 per cent of the population were involved in moves between local authority areas but slightly less than half these moves were under forty miles. The age and sex distribution of the migrants moving in and out of an area appeared to be approximately the same. There was a predominance of the young adult group between twenty and twenty-nine years of age among the migrants, but after this age people are more likely to settle down to a steady job. Furthermore, a person who leaves an area in which he has lived for some time not only has to find other accommodation, but loses any priority that he may have for rehousing by the local authority. However strong the financial inducements may be to find work elsewhere, the housing shortage is a powerful influence restricting occupational and geographical mobility.

During the last hundred years there has been considerable rural depopulation throughout the United Kingdom, and this situation has been particularly acute in Scotland. The trend is no longer so marked, although, on balance, migration still favors the towns. At the same time net changes in the population of urban and rural areas are less than 5 per cent of the gross movement in and out of those areas. Compared with the United States the United Kingdom is more urbanized, as is evident from Table 4. The figures for England and Wales are slightly misleading insofar as the rural population includes an increasing number of people who work in the cities but reside on the outskirts of an urban area which at present falls in a rural district for administrative purposes. A notable feature is the concentration of two fifths of the population in conurbations. These have grown up as a consequence of the spread of towns and cities in certain industrial areas to such an extent that they have absorbed the rural areas

Table 4. Distribution of Urban and Rural Population in the United Kingdom in 1951 (in thousands)

Section	Urban		Rural	
	Number	Percentage	Number	Percentage
England and Wales	35,322	81	8,423	19
Scotland	4,227	83	870	17
Northern Ireland	728	53	643	47

Source: Census, 1951.

Table 5. Population of Largest Conurbations in Britain in 1951

Conurbation	Number
Greater London	8,346,000
West Midlands (Birmingham)	2,237,000
West Yorkshire	1,692,000
South-East Lancashire	2,421,000
Merseyside	1,382,000
Tyneside and Wearside	1,320,000
Clydeside	1,758,000

Source: Census, 1951.

that once separated them. Table 5 shows the populations of the largest conurbations in 1951.

Reference will be made below to certain differences within the United Kingdom that are associated with regional subcultures and socioeconomic status. From the demographic point of view these differences are reflected in the higher birth rates in Scotland and Northern Ireland, partly explained by a slightly higher proportion of Roman Catholics in these countries than in England and Wales. Scotland and Northern Ireland also exhibit higher morbidity and mortality rates than England and Wales. Within England and Wales the southeast tends to have lower morbidity and mortality rates than the rest of the country.

The size of family and the incidence of births, prenuptial conceptions, illegitimate births, stillbirths, neonatal deaths, prematurity, infant and adult morbidity, and infant and adult mortality are all greater at the lower ends of the socioeconomic status scale compared with the upper, although these differences have shown some tendency to decline since World War II.

ETHNIC AND REGIONAL SUBCULTURES

The fact that immigration has been on a comparatively small scale in the last hundred years means that the United Kingdom is relatively homogeneous from the ethnic point of view, in contrast with the United States. There are nearly two million people resident in the United Kingdom who were born elsewhere, but this does not mean that they are either culturally or politically alien. Table 6 indicates the numbers resident in Britain but born outside the United Kingdom, according to the census of 1951.

The position of those born in the Republic of Eire was changed by the British Nationality Act of 1948. Those born before the act are entitled to retain their British nationality but those born since are regarded as aliens, although there is no restriction on their movement to and from the United Kingdom. Any person—of whatever race—born in a dominion or colony automatically receives British nationality; but those born in a British protectorate acquire British citizenship by registration unless their parents were British.

The largest groups of aliens by country of birth are represented in Table 7. Between 1941 and 1950 approximately 14,000 Germans, 8,000 Austrians, and 8,000 Poles were granted certificates of naturalization. Many other immigrants have made a permanent home in Britain, although they have not acquired British nationality. Since the end of World War II,

Table 6. British Residents Born Outside the United Kingdom

Item	Number
British born in Eire	527,700
British born in Commonwealth territories	375,000
British born in foreign territories	114,600
British by naturalization, registration, or marriage	191,800
Nationality not stated	268,700
Aliens	405,700
Total	1,883,500

Source: Census, 1951.

Table 7. Aliens Resident in Britain in 1951

Country of Birth	Number
Poland	140,800
Russia	55,200
Germany	45,800
United States	38,000
Italy	24,400
Other countries	101,500

Source: Census, 1951.

100,000 members of the Polish forces have been absorbed into the building, agricultural, and coal-mining industries. Other immigrants came to Britain under the European Volunteer Worker programs from Germany, Austria, Denmark, and Italy. The male volunteers filled vacancies in agriculture and coal mining while the women entered domestic service, textiles, and nursing. The absorption of these immigrants was not always without difficulties. There was, for example, opposition to the employment of Italians in coal mines in certain areas.

The socially significant ethnic minorities may be defined by nationality, country of origin, religion, race, or any combination of these factors. The ethnic "visibility" of the individual is greater when two or more of these characteristics are combined, as when an immigrant has a distinctive race or religion which—combined with differences of language or custom— causes conspicuousness. The religious minorities include Roman Catholics, Jews, Greek Orthodox adherents, Moslems, Hindus, and Buddhists in that order of numerical importance. As defined by race the main minorities (apart from eastern, central, and Mediterranean Europeans) are Africans, and others of Negro descent, and Asians. Some of the latter are of Mongoloid appearance. Although, statistically regarded, the colored im-

51

migrants and their descendents are a small group not exceeding 100,000 in all, their sociological significance is considerable. Because the majority are British subjects, their exact numbers are unknown. (Most of those enumerated in the census as born in Commonwealth or colonial territories are of European origin.) Largely because of their color, non-Europeans have greater difficulty in assimilating than immigrants from Europe or America.

Although color prejudice and anti-Semitism are widespread, there is no institutionalized discrimination against, or segregation of, ethnic minorities. As might be expected the immigrants tend to congregate in particular localities, but in course of time some dispersal takes place. With the exception of some colored immigrants, most of the immigrant ethnic minorities appear to have been successfully absorbed into the social structure. Jewish, Moslem, and Chinese immigrants appear to have been absorbed into the social structure as separate ethnic groups. Negro immigrants, particularly West Indians, aspire to assimilation as individuals, but that hope is largely precluded by prejudice and noninstitutionalized discrimination. The fact that discrimination is not institutionalized, and similarly that there is no institutionalized machinery for dealing with it when it does occur, must be attributed to the relatively small size of the ethnic minorities concerned.

The Jewish population of Britain is the largest minority, but it is an indication of the ethnic homogeneity of the country as a whole that it numbers only about 450,000, which is less than 1 per cent of the total population. There is some difficulty in defining the Jewish population, since a number who have lived in Britain for several generations have been assimilated to an extent by becoming Christian, or by professing agnosticism and playing no part in Jewish religious observances.

The Jewish population was expelled from Britain in 1290 and readmitted in 1656. The earliest settlers after that date were the *Sephardi*, mainly Portuguese speaking, and the *Ashkenazi*, or Jews from Germany and eastern Europe. The gradual Anglicization of the two communities led to their closer association in the nineteenth century. In the present day it is usual to distinguish between the orthodox, the reformed, and the liberal branches of the Jewish faith.

The importance of the synagogue as a focal point in religious and social life has meant that there has always been a tendency for the Jewish population to constitute an ecological community without necessarily being confined to ghettos. On arrival in Britain Jewish immigrants tended to congregate in poorer districts, such as the East End of London, and moved to other localities as they became more prosperous. There are, for example, parts of north London which are recognized Jewish localities even though the actual proportion of Jews in those districts may be comparatively small.

The complete assimilation of individual Jews is possible only when they cease to conform to the requirements of the Jewish faith, although this does not prevent the acceptance of those who are acculturated in the sense that their education, speech, and mannerisms are entirely English. Generally speaking, the Jewish population is an integral part of the social structure of the United Kingdom while retaining its identity as a separate ethnic minority. British social life adjusts in many ways to the needs and interests of its Jewish participants, in part by permitting the operation of Kosher kitchens, restaurants, and slaughterhouses; by allowing shopkeepers to close on Saturday and open on Sunday; and by granting Jewish school children and employees the time to observe their Sabbath and various festivals. But however accommodating the social structure may be, this tolerance is paralleled by the maintenance on both sides of a certain social distance. Intermarriage, while it takes place, is not encouraged; on the whole, Jews are respected more for their adherence to Jewish custom than for too strenuous an effort to become assimilated.

In many respects regional subcultures are of greater significance than ethnic differences resulting from immigration. The social structures, institutions, and culture of Scotland, Wales, and Northern Ireland differ from one another so much that they almost warrant separate treatment, but that is not possible here. Wales is administered integrally with England, although a minister for Welsh affairs has recently been appointed. Scotland and Northern Ireland have their own administrations. Both send representatives to Westminster, but Northern Ireland also has its own parliament. Scotland has its own judicial and legal system as well as its own civil service, centered in Edinburgh. Furthermore, the three Celtic countries are each distinguished by a cultural and political nationalist movement, supported by a minority.

There are also important differences between urban and rural areas. The social life of an English village differs enormously from the social life of a mining town in the North or a manufacturing town in the Midlands. Similarly rural Wales differs profoundly from urban Wales; the same applies to rural Ireland and rural Scotland. In a few paragraphs it is possible to touch upon only a few of these subcultural differences.

Kinship and family relationships will be dealt with in a later section, but it may be mentioned here that there are significant regional differences in the importance of the extended family, in the domestic roles of husband and wife, and in the frequency with which married women go out to work. Other regional differences are connected with specialized local industries and occupations, such as the pottery industry in Staffordshire, mining in South Wales, or shipbuilding on the Clyde in Scotland, all of which tend to create regional subcultural characteristics. Other differences may be observed in connection with housing, home life, and the preparation of food, which vary regionally and locally.

Differences in language and accent are of considerable importance and probably correlate with many other subcultural variations. Although the use of Gaelic in Scotland and Northern Ireland has practically disappeared, it is still spoken by about 2 per cent of the population in the remoter rural areas. The use of Welsh has also declined, but the language is still spoken and understood by about 700,000 people—29 per cent of the population of Wales—the majority of whom also speak English. Then, too, English itself is spoken with a variety of characteristic regional accents. Anyone with an acute ear and a knowledge of accents can place, within a few miles, the locality in which a man or woman has grown up. Higher education and, to some extent, the influence of "standard English" as used by the British Broadcasting Corporation have reduced the differences, but they are by no means eliminated. No regional accent except Scots is acceptable in professional and upper-class circles. The acquisition of the accent and speech mannerisms acquired at expensive boarding schools is a necessary precondition of acceptance by the elite.

SOCIAL CLASS AND STATUS MOBILITY

Heredity, income, education, accent, mannerisms, occupation, household, domestic habits, and leisure-time pursuits are the principal criteria, in the United Kingdom, that define an individual's social status. Heredity, income, and education, of course, are the prime determinants from which the remaining criteria are largely derived.

At the top of the social scale heredity and family connection count for a great deal. The prestige associated with the royal family and the traditional aristocracy is considerable. Many new peerages have been created in the twentieth century, but ancient peerages and baronetcies are more highly regarded, even when—as is often the case—the successor to a title of ancient lineage is relatively impoverished by death duties on his estate. Many wealthy businessmen do not feel that they have "arrived" in high society until they have acquired a country estate and been rewarded for their generosity to voluntary social services or party political funds with a seat in the House of Lords. Among the well-to-do there is competition to have an eligible daughter presented at court, although presentation is not the highly ritualized affair that it was a generation ago. Today a debutante need not be so heavily subsidized by her parents, nor is it unknown for a "deb" to be currently acting in a London play or earning her living as a fashion model.

Under the impact of progressive taxation the traditional "upper" class is rapidly disappearing, but only to be increasingly assimilated by the "upper middle" class. It is significant that in a public opinion poll conducted in 1952 only 1 per cent described themselves as "upper" class, while 49 per cent assigned themselves to one or another division of the "middle" class, and 46 per cent to the "working" class. On this basis half the population regard themselves as members of the middle classes. Only 4 per cent did not place themselves at all.

The extent of redistribution of incomes is reflected in Table 8. As a result of high progressive taxation it has been estimated that the ratio of the

Table 8. Distribution of Personal Incomes in the United Kingdom
before and after Tax in 1954

	Before Tax			After Tax		
Range of Income per year	No. of Incomes (in thousands)	%	Range of Income per year	No. of Incomes (in thousands)	%	Percentage of Income Retained
Under £250	8,540	32	Under £250	8,750	33	99.4
£251–£500	8,690	33	£251–£500	9,420	36	95.5
£501–£750	5,900	22	£501–£750	5,780	22	93.4
£751–£1,000	1,750	7	£751–£1,000	1,315	5	88.8
£1,001–£1,500	700		£1,001–£2,000	701		76.9
£1,501–£2,000	210		£2,001–£4,000	127.4	4†	50.8
£2,001–£3,000	161		£4,001–£6,000	6.41		22.5
£3,001–£5,000	96	6*	Over £6,000	0.19		8.3
£5,001–£10,000	41					
£10,001–£20,000	10		Total	26,100	100	89.6
Over £20,000	2					
Total	26,100	100				

Source: Central Statistical Office.
*This percentage is for incomes before tax from £1,001 to over £20,000.
†This percentage is for incomes after tax from £1,001 to over £6,000.

available income of a high ranking business executive to the available income of one of his unskilled employees is only about 7 to 1 compared with 25 to 1 in the United States. There are fewer than two hundred people in the United Kingdom with net incomes of more than £6,000 per annum after taxes.

After allowing for taxes, approximately 10 per cent of all earners receive a quarter of total personal incomes, while 33 per cent of the earners receive 13 per cent. Approximately 66 per cent of total personal income is earned as wages, salaries, or fees, while 34 per cent is income from property. The distribution of property is more uneven. In 1946–47, 2 to 3 per cent of persons over twenty-five years of age held 60 to 65 per cent of personal capital and 40 per cent held 96 per cent of personal capital. Although 95 per cent of shareholders are individual persons, about a third of the large holdings of shares in public companies are in the hands of banks, insurance companies, investment trusts, and nominee companies.

Differences in the educational experience of the adult population of Britain are shown in Table 9. Boarding schools are those carrying the highest status, and they consist mainly of those institutions whose headmasters are invited to attend the so-called Headmasters' Conference. Although paradoxically known as "public" schools, they are in fact socially exclusive and, moreover, independent of the state or public schools run by the local educational authorities.

The majority of adults who attended what are now called secondary modern schools (formerly senior elementary schools) finished their education at the age of fourteen. They proceeded to the lower paid occupations. Those who went to a grammar school usually left at sixteen or seventeen, although a few went on to a university, as did many of those who had gone to boarding schools. About 6.5 per cent of the total population received some kind of further education leading to a professional qualification, but only about 3 per cent attended a university. The proportion of

Table 9. Percentage of Students Attending Three Types
of Secondary Schools in England and Wales

Sex	Modern School	Grammar School	Boarding School
Boys	85.4%	12.7%	1.9%
Girls	85.9	11.6	2.5
Both sexes	85.6	12.1	2.3

Source: D. V. Glass, ed., *Social Mobility in Britain.*

the total population receiving a grammar-school education has not materially increased since the Education Act of 1944, but a larger proportion of children from poorer homes, who could not previously afford to go to a grammar school or university, are now able to do so.

Recent investigations have shown that although secondary grammar-school education is now free, there are still some working-class parents who are not particularly anxious for their children to enter a grammar school rather than a modern school. It has been found that if children of similar intelligence are compared, those from small families and middle-class homes stand a better chance of passing the examination to the grammar school than those from large families and / or working-class homes. If we compare performance at school and participation in extracurricular activities, middle-class boys tend to be rated higher by their teachers than working-class boys of similar intelligence. These findings reflect the fact that differences in home background, in terms of physical living conditions and the attitudes of parents toward their children's achievements at school, have an influence on children which tends to perpetuate existing social-status differences in the community.

Attempts to raise the prestige of the secondary modern school in the eyes of parents who are middle-class, or have middle-class aspirations for their children, have not been successful. It has been suggested that this will continue to be the case so long as a particular kind of education, namely that provided in the secondary grammar school, is seen to be the only avenue—apart from boarding schools—to the professions and other occupations carrying middle-class status. However, experiments are proceeding in the provision of "multilateral" or comprehensive schools which will house under one roof children receiving grammar, modern, and technical types of secondary education. It is hoped that by mixing different intellectual types and social classes in extracurricular activities, such as sports, and by having all pupils wear a school uniform, differences in social status will be minimized. But it is still too soon to judge the effects of these experiments.

Today a university education is available to an increasing number of working-class children of ability, so that income and occupation are no longer a sure guide to social origin. It is therefore significant that there should appear to be an increase in intellectual snobbishness and a renewed concern with social etiquette and the nuances of grammar, vocabulary, pronunciation, and accent.[3] This is not a new phenomenon in England, but its revival may be interpreted as a rear-guard action on the part of those who have received an expensive education at a school of high prestige, which may or may not have been followed by a period at a university. The characteristic mode of speech and the other mannerisms acquired at home and in expensive schools are the last remaining criteria that distinguish the "polished" person of "good breeding," if not from the *nouveaux riches,* at any rate from those whose higher socioeconomic status has been achieved at the expense of the state.

The registrar general ranks occupations in Great Britain into five social classes, as shown in Table 10. This classification is arbitrary, and there is no positive evidence to show that it corresponds with the prestige value of the occupations. A slightly more elaborate classification into seven categories has been devised which does appear to correspond with prestige

Table 10. Registrar General's Ranking of Social Classes in Great Britain, with Percentage Distribution of Householders and Occupied and Retired Men in 1951

Class	Householders	Occupied and Retired Men
1. Higher administrative, professional, and managerial workers, including employers	3.3%	3.3%
2. Intermediate administrative, professional, and managerial workers, including farmers, teachers, shopkeepers, and small employers	18.3	14.8
3. Shop assistants, clerical workers, foremen and supervisors, personal services and skilled workers ..	49.5	52.5
4. Semiskilled workers, agricultural laborers	16.5	16.4
5. Unskilled workers	12.4	13.0

Source: Census, 1951.

Table 11. Ranking of Occupations for England and Wales by Prestige Value, with Percentage Distribution of Random Sample of Men

Class	Percentage of Random Sample of Men
1. Professional and higher administrative	2.9%
2. Managerial and executive	4.5
3. Inspectional, supervisory, and others nonmanual (higher)	9.8
4. Inspectional, supervisory, and others nonmanual (lower)	12.7
5. Skilled manual and routine grades nonmanual	41.2
6. Semiskilled manual	16.5
7. Unskilled manual	12.4

Source: D. V. Glass, ed., *Social Mobility in Britain.*

ratings. The seven categories and the percentage distribution of a random sample of the male population of England and Wales, according to occupation, are given in Table 11.

Closely connected with income and occupation as criteria for determining social status is the type of house occupied, its size, locality, the way in which it is furnished, and the domestic arrangements of the household. There is real significance in the old adage that "an Englishman's home is his castle." Social distance is maintained by a process of voluntary segregation, in which the members of each social class put barriers between themselves and those who are much lower or much higher on the scale. Easy informality in social relations between members at the two extremes of the socioeconomic status scale is unheard of. Servants and tradesmen calling at an upper-class home go to the back door and are received in the kitchen, while an upper- or middle-class person calling on a working-class home is ushered into the "parlor" rather than the living room or kitchen.

In an attempt to break down barriers of social distance and encourage the emergence of local community leaders who are in touch with the inhabitants, theorists concerned with town planning, and to some extent official policy-makers, have advocated that different social classes should be encouraged to live in the same neighborhood. But actually, when people are given a free choice they prefer neighborhoods that are relatively homogeneous in social status. Studies of migration, and of the motives for moving from a present locality, tend to confirm the view that the people most dissatisfied with the neighborhood in which they live are those who have status aspirations that lead them to identify with people of a higher social status than those who live near them. The decision by a local authority to build a subsidized housing estate near a private estate carrying higher status results in a number of families removing from the private estate and a fall in property values in that district. This may become a vicious downward spiral as more people decide to leave before they lose the whole of the capital tied up in a house. Only the gross housing shortage prevents the downward movement in property values from being more marked than it is in such circumstances. The reverse process can also take place—if a neighborhood becomes fashionable rapidly adapted "mews" flats and other old properties may fetch prices out of all proportion to their intrinsic value.

Blocks of tenements are much more common in Scotland than in England or Wales, but in both countries the detached or semidetached house with a small garden is preferred. Some degree of privacy is valued by all social classes, although it is not always obtainable in overcrowded working-class areas in towns, or even in the jerry-built flats and attached houses, in suburban areas, where sounds carry through party walls. In England and Wales between the two world wars, however, there was a great improvement in housing conditions; many slums created by the Industrial Revolution were abolished. Nevertheless, the shortage of houses still remains the outstanding social problem of the postwar world throughout the United Kingdom, a situation aggravated by the decay of old property as well as by the destruction of old and new alike during the war. The situation is even worse in Scotland, where housing conditions and standards are markedly lower than in England and less satisfactory progress has been made in remedying the situation, with consequent effects on morbidity and mortality from pulmonary tuberculosis and similar diseases.

Table 12 draws attention to the fact that Scottish houses tend to be smaller than those in England and Wales. Only 37.4 per cent of Scottish houses have more than three rooms compared with 84.7 per cent in England and Wales. In 1951, 15.5 per cent of the Scottish population lived with more than two persons to a room, compared with 2.2 per cent in England and Wales; 43.6 per cent of the households lacked a fixed bath in Scotland, compared with 36.8 per cent in England and Wales; and 5 per cent in Scotland compared with 2 per cent in England lacked a cooking stove. As many as 11 per cent of the households in Scotland lacked the exclusive use of a cooking stove, and a similar proportion did not have exclusive use of piped water or a kitchen sink.

Investigations similar to those undertaken by Chapin in the United States have shown that the interior furnishing and pattern of usage in houses also corresponds to variations in socioeconomic status and sub-

Table 12. Size of Dwellings in England and Wales and in Scotland in 1951, as Indicated by Percentage of Houses with One to Six or More Rooms

Number of Rooms	England and Wales	Scotland
1	0.8%	5.7%
2	3.6	26.3
3	10.9	30.6
4	28.2	21.2
5	35.5	7.6
6 or more	21.0	8.6

Source: Census, 1951.

culture. Utilitarian or functional considerations of the performance value of an item of furniture tend to take second place to its "display" or prestige-bearing qualities. Compared with expenditure on the bedroom and lounge, provision of kitchen equipment tends to be neglected. By American standards the majority of British housewives, even in the higher socioeconomic status groups, are drudges. The absence of climatic extremes has resulted in the perpetuation of the open hearth, with its coal fire, and central heating is rare. The high cost and inefficiency of using an open fire for space heating means that in many working-class houses one or two rooms are used constantly and bedrooms are unheated.

Once they have passed the stage of infancy, children find that their physical, social, and psychological needs are often overlooked. In one inquiry it was found that 22 per cent of the children in summer, and 41 per cent in winter (when a separate room would have to be heated), had no access to a room apart from the rest of the household where they could have proper conditions for private study or for play.

In many working-class homes one room, known as the parlor, is often set aside and used for the display of prestige-bearing articles, family heirlooms, and photographs or portraits. This room is reserved for ritual occasions, family gatherings for births, marriages, and funerals, and as a reception room for visitors, such as a clergyman or schoolteacher, whose higher status does not permit them to be admitted to the intimacy and disorder of the living room.

An interesting feature of British postwar housing policy is that local authorities have rehoused large numbers of working-class families in subsidized dwellings. This means that the rent paid for the accommodation is considerably below the economic rent. Sometimes the rent paid is on a sliding scale according to income; but since there is a traditional dislike of the "means test" in the United Kingdom, most local authorities charge the same subsidized rent for each dwelling irrespective of total family income. In contrast many lower-middle-class people—who do not qualify for, or for prestige reasons would not accept, a "council house"—prefer to purchase a house by means of a mortgage. As a result their expenditure on housing consumes a very much higher proportion of their income than is true of tenants in either local authority houses or privately let older dwellings, whose rents are restricted by statute. It follows that many working-class families are able to afford prestige-bearing articles, such as washing machines, television sets, and motorcars, which lower-middle-class families cannot afford. The latter gain compensatory status from the location of the house and the fact that they are owners and not tenants.

Leisure-time pursuits and interests are another sphere in which social-status differences are clearly apparent. Yachting and regattas, polo, the breeding of race horses, fox or stag hunting, deerstalking, and the shooting of grouse are the exclusive preserves of the rich, while darts, attendance at greyhound races, skittles, the breeding of racing pigeons, and the trapping of rabbits and other small animals are confined to the lower income groups. In Scotland golf is universal, but in England it is mainly confined to the wealthy. Membership in clubs of various kinds is characteristic of all social classes, but the kind of club immediately determines a man's status. There is no comparison between an aristocratic club in Pall Mall, a professional or university club in a provincial town, and a workingman's club in the Midlands or the North.

Between those activities which are exclusively confined to the extreme ends of the socioeconomic scale is a wide range of leisure pursuits, such as watching horse racing, football, or cricket, and attendance at cinemas, which are enjoyed by a wide cross section of the population. Nevertheless, class distinctions are maintained in these circumstances by the operation of the price mechanism. According to the price paid, people are segregated and provided with different standards of comfort in which to view the sport or entertainment. The price mechanism similarly operates to segregate members of different social classes from one another when they eat in public. Most large factories have three or more canteens for different grades of employee. A working-class person eats fish and chips, at the counter or (wrapped in a newspaper) in the street, and follows the meal with a glass of beer; a middle-class person eats his fish more delicately served in a large restaurant, and follows it with coffee; while an upper-class person has caviar and champagne in a secluded corner of an exclusive hotel or club.

Sociologists normally distinguish between the concept of "class" as a subjective reference group, seen through the eyes of an individual member of a society, and "class" as a more or less objectively determined phenomenon, related to the socioeconomic structure of society. In the United Kingdom these two concepts of social class do not always closely correspond with one another.

Subjective experience of social class in Britain varies according to a variety of economic and cultural factors. It has been suggested that although, for example, a wood polisher in the East End of London and a civil servant (bureaucrat) in north London are both members of the larger society of the United Kingdom, they really live in different worlds, with totally different experiences of life in general and the class system in particular.

In the lower income groups men—more often than women—tended, in the past, to view the class structure of society in terms of relative power, whereas the middle and upper income groups were more inclined to view the situation in terms of relative prestige. The ordinary working-class man was inclined to regard himself and his "mates" as ranged against the "bosses," who—though a minority—wielded most of the power. For this reason loyalty to his "mates" was of the utmost importance, because it was only by sticking together that they could hope to protect their interests against the exploiters. This fact goes a long way to explain why, in Britain, status competition and social-mobility aspirations have been confined to the middle class and the border line that separates it from the working class. If advancement meant alienation from his workmates and neighbors, the ordinary workingman often preferred to stay where he was. Recent studies have shown that even when higher wages were earned after the war, as in the case of miners who vastly improved their incomes relative to other occupations, there were only minor changes in the traditional standard of living and way of life. This does not mean that the ordinary workingman did not dream of achieving a higher standard of living. In fact he did, and some dreamed of little else. But it was success in terms of luck—winning a fortune in some form of gambling—that he yearned for. Competition for jobs, for promotion, for higher pay and prestige were middle-class preoccupations, and were strongly disapproved by many working-class people. The myth of the self-made man, which appeared to act as a stimulus in the United States, had little appeal in Britain where a more realistic view of the individual's life chances was taken.

Part of the explanation for this attitude toward the class structure may be found in studies of social mobility in Britain. Using the seven status categories based upon the prestige value of occupations, listed in Table 11, a study was made of the degree of social-status mobility in Britain in relation to a hypothetical model of "perfect mobility." The degree of association between the occupations of fathers and sons was examined. The closest association (that is to say, the least mobility) was found in the professional and higher administrative category. The skilled manual and the routine nonmanual categories showed the smallest association—meaning the greatest degree of social-status mobility—as measured by changes of occupation from father to son. The greatest rigidity appeared at the two extremes of the scale, with varying degrees of mobility in between. Although the general picture in the first half of the twentieth century was one of a stable social structure, it was by no means rigid. The evidence suggests that the degree of mobility in Britain is greater than in France or Italy and probably about the same as in the United States. For example, among men born between 1900 and 1909 it appears that 46 per cent of those whose fathers had been in categories 1 and 2 fell in social status; while of those men whose fathers had been semiskilled or unskilled manual workers, 53 per cent achieved a higher social status than that of their fathers. These findings are partly accounted for by changes in the economic structure of the society as a whole; since the turn of the century, for example, there has been an increasing number of occupations in the middle ranges of prestige. Combined with the unchanging rigidity at the extremes, this means that the amount of mobility which can be attributed to individual effort is small.

As the present period is one of transition, it is not surprising that some of the old attitudes toward social classes as power rather than prestige groups should still persist, especially among the older generation. Attitudes toward social mobility in the future are likely to be influenced by the Education Act of 1944. This act abolished fees in all state schools in England and established an entrance examination, based on tests of intelligence and educational attainment, as the sole means of entry to grammar schools. As time goes on the number of intelligent working-class children unable to go to a grammar school or obtain a university education is likely to diminish. At the same time there will be an increasing number of middle-class children who fail to pass the entrance examination for the grammar school, and whose parents cannot afford to pay the high fees demanded by an exclusive boarding school.

Inequality of opportunity in the past resulted in a large number of able and intelligent men and women remaining in the ranks of the working class, providing the backbone of the Workers Educational Association, assuming positions of leadership and responsibility in the trade-union movement, the Labour party, other voluntary organizations, and local government. These able men and women will be lost to the working class and the labor movement in the future because they will have the opportunity, early in their careers, to receive a higher education and take their places in the ranks of the professional and technical elite. At the same time those who do not achieve a higher education will be more than ever conscious that they are the failures, the ones who score low marks, who have not been endowed with what is required for success in a competitive world. Whether, as has been suggested, they will react by adopting a "sour grapes" attitude, regarding success as the result of sycophancy, cheating, or chance, and become even more jealous of those with higher incomes, remains to be seen. Certainly there is no guarantee that increased social mobility will narrow differences between social classes. The conflict between those who fail and those who succeed may be aggravated when failure can no longer be blamed on the system.

Economic Organization and Social Welfare

BASIC CHARACTERISTICS OF THE ECONOMY

The high density of population in the United Kingdom and the relative deficiency of natural resources mean that Britain is overwhelmingly dependent upon external trade. It must import half the food consumed and most essential raw materials such as cotton, rubber, jute, aluminum, lead, copper, tin, zinc, iron, wood, and wool. In return it must sell abroad machinery, vehicles, aircraft, electrical goods, textiles, pottery, chemicals, whisky, and many other manufactured goods.

Before World War II a high proportion of the essential imports were paid for in "invisible" exports consisting mainly of the returns on overseas investments and various commercial services which did not figure in the visible trade statistics. Most overseas investments were sold in order to pay for war supplies, and as a consequence of this and other unavoidable economic circumstances, Britain in the postwar world has been faced with a constant problem of how to balance its overseas payments. Periodic crises have led to a drain upon gold and dollar reserves and threatened the position of sterling on the world money market. In 1955, for example, there was an adverse balance of visible trade of £352 million, with a consequent fall of nearly $1,000 million in reserves and a depreciation of the value of sterling. The future position will depend upon the success of British exports in competition with those of Germany, Japan, and other countries.

Table 13 shows the distribution of the working population, according to the census of 1951, in terms of their status as employers, managers, employees, and self-employed persons working on their own account. Some

Table 13. Working Population of Britain in 1951 (in thousands)

Status	Men No.	Men %	Women No.	Women %	Total No.	Total %
Employers	405.9	2.6	54.0	0.8	459.9	2.1
Managers	637.1	4.1	111.1	1.7	748.2	3.4
Employees	13,405.7	87.5	6,394.9	94.1	19,800.6	89.3
Self-employed	887.4	5.8	237.2	3.5	1,124.6	5.1
Total	15,336.1	100.0	6,797.2	100.0	22,133.3	100.0

Source: Central Statistical Office.

Table 14. Distribution of Manpower in Industries of Britain and the United States

Industry	United States (1940) %	Britain (1951) %	Britain (1951) No.
Agriculture, forestry, and fishing	18.8	5.0	1,139,000
Mining and quarrying	2.0	3.8	856,000
Manufacturing	23.4	37.6	8,736,000
Public utilities	1.2	1.7	362,000
Building and construction	4.6	6.2	1,449,000
Services including transport	48.5	45.7	9,672,000
Total in civil employment	100.0	100.0	22,214,000

Source: U.S. Census, 1940, and British Census, 1951.

employers are small, and it is difficult to distinguish them from those working on their own account among whom some professional workers must be included.

When a comparison is made between the economic structures of the United Kingdom and the United States, there are a number of points of similarity and contrast. Table 14 shows the distribution of manpower by industry. The main difference in industrial structure is the much higher proportion engaged in agriculture in the United States and in mining and manufacturing in Britain.

An important difference between Britain and America is the intensity of capital investment—in relation to manpower—as measured by the amount of horsepower available per worker. There are wide variations among different industries, and although any one industry tends to have the same relative degree of mechanization in both countries, over-all horsepower per worker is about three times as high in the United States. Consequently American productivity per man hour is much higher. It has been estimated that the value of an hour's work is about half as much again in

66

the United States as in the United Kingdom. When labor was cheap relative to capital, increased mechanization was not necessarily the most economically efficient means of production. Now that labor is scarce in Britain there must be more mechanization and automation, involving heavy investment in plant and machinery. In the United Kingdom output per man year rose by 23 per cent between 1948 and 1955, an average of 3 per cent per annum.

Increased productivity does not depend on investment alone. There must also be efficient organization of production by management and a willingness on the part of employees to cooperate. Administrative overheads are increasing in Britain, as in America, and are not always accompanied by a corresponding increase in efficiency. It is frequently alleged that the American worker appreciates the connection between productivity and a high level of wages more than his British counterpart, who tends to think in terms of squeezing profits for higher wages. This is probably less true now than formerly, but one important cultural difference remains. In America there is a much stronger pressure to increase earnings in order that the individual may improve his material standards. In Britain this competitive tendency is less in evidence. This is partly because—in the postwar world—consumer goods have not always been readily available, and partly because some British workers value a less intensive effort at work and an increase in leisure time more than higher purchasing power. Furthermore, inflationary tendencies in the postwar period have meant that sometimes it has been necessary to work harder and longer merely to keep pace with the rising cost of living, without much possibility of raising the standard. Nevertheless, there has been a marked change in the patterns of consumption in Britain compared with the prewar period.

Before the war the consumer market in Britain was divided between some 800,000 people at the upper end of the income scale who consumed 20 per cent of the nation's net personal income, and 20,000,000 at the lower end who consumed 60 per cent. Between these two extremes fell some 2,500,000 middle-class white-collar workers who, after meeting expenses for housing, health, and education had little left over. In the postwar period progressive taxation has reduced the advantage of the higher income groups, and full employment has improved the position of the large majority of workers. In the calculation of a new cost-of-living index, which came into use at the beginning of 1956, two groups of householders were left out of account as untypical. They were the 3.5 per cent with incomes over £20 per week and the 6.5 per cent who were dependent upon national insurance or assistance benefits. This leaves a large group of working- and middle-class families who provide a growing market for consumer goods.

It is illuminating to consider the percentage of households in Britain buying or owning various durable goods in 1955. Thirty-one per cent of households owned their house or were buying it on a mortgage. The percentage of households owning certain goods is shown below:[4]

```
Television set . . . . . . . . . . . . . . . . . . . . . . . . .34%
Washing machine . . . . . . . . . . . . . . . . . . . . .22
Car. . . . . . . . . . . . . . . . . . . . . . . . . . . . . . . . .18
Telephone  . . . . . . . . . . . . . . . . . . . . . . . . . .15
Refrigerator  . . . . . . . . . . . . . . . . . . . . . . . . . 8
```

In Britain in 1955 there was one car to every fourteen persons, compared with one to three persons in the United States. Refrigerators are not such essential items in Britain as in parts of the United States, but it is evident that the level of consumption of durable goods is still well below American standards.

As in America, a large proportion of durable goods of this character are bought on a hire purchase system or under some other form of consumer credit. It has been estimated that outstanding consumer installment credit at the end of 1955 amounted to some £550 million. The worst abuses of the hire purchase system, which enabled finance companies to take advantage of temporary financial disability and repossess the goods even though most of the debt had been paid, are now prevented by legislation. Nevertheless, there appears to be a growing tendency for itinerant traders and others to impose unwanted goods on housewives, irrespective of their capacity to pay, and for the quality of some goods bought on hire purchase to be poor. From time to time the government has found it necessary to place restrictions on hire purchase by raising minimum deposits and shortening the period of credit in an attempt to combat the inflationary consequences of a rapid increase in credit trading.

Professor Sargent-Florence has summed up the main differences and similarities between the British and American industrial structures.[5] He mentions differences in area and climate, in the scope of agriculture and the degree of mechanization in industry, but—with one important exception—he found striking similarities in the structure and government of British and American industries. Similarities were evident in selling costs, patterns of location, integration, prevailing size of plant and firm, staff ratios, frequency and distribution of incorporation, the unequal distribution of shareholdings, the existence of holding companies and interlocking directorates, the concentration of control over the output of certain products, and the relations between industrial firms and trade unions on the one hand and consumers on the other. The most significant difference between the two countries concerned the role of the state in the economy.

ECONOMIC CONTROLS AND THE WELFARE STATE

In the United Kingdom the nineteenth-century ideal of *laisser-faire* has long been abandoned. It is now universally accepted that the community, through its representatives in government, should exercise such powers of control and direction as are considered necessary to achieve certain fundamental objectives for the welfare of the community as a whole. This is accepted by all political parties, who differ not on the fundamental objectives but on the way in which they should be achieved. The Labour party advocates an extension of nationalization and public ownership together with the use of direct economic controls involving the allocation of scarce raw materials, price limitation, and other measures which were found effective in planning the economy in wartime. The Conservative party, while not opposed to the nationalization of certain basic industries, prefers to use financial measures—such as the annual budget and variations in the bank rate—and to rely upon the voluntary cooperation of industry in combating inflation and other economic difficulties.

The fundamental objectives of public economic policy, upon which almost everyone in Britain agrees, are as follows:

1. That the state should ensure that priority be given to organization and production for defense.

2. That the state should take such steps as are necessary to combat inflationary or deflationary tendencies in the economy and to maintain *full employment*.

3. That extremes of wealth and poverty should be prevented and *incomes redistributed* through progressive taxation and other measures to the advantage of the lower income groups, and that the state, in collaboration with voluntary agencies, should take steps to promote the health and welfare of the population through an extensive system of *social services*.

4. That the state should ensure—by *nationalization* and public ownership, if necessary—that basic industries and services upon which the wel-

fare of the community depend should be run efficiently and in the public interest, particularly those where private owners lack either the will or the capacity to do so.

It is one of the ironic characteristics of contemporary societies with advanced cultures that while unanimous in proclaiming their peaceful intentions toward other countries, they are at the same time devoting a high proportion of their economic resources to what is euphemistically described as "defense." In the absence of an integrating ideology, economic interdependence of the nations of the world has brought about a state of anomie rather than organic solidarity.

The United Kingdom devotes approximately £1,600 million annually to preparation for war. This represents approximately 11.3 per cent of the gross national product, 27 per cent of all public expenditure, and 37 per cent of the central government's budget. The figure compares with 14.7 per cent of the gross national product of the United States similarly devoted to defense and, as far as it is possible to calculate it, 20 per cent of that of the U.S.S.R. Of the population of the United Kingdom, 1.8 per cent—compared with 2.1 per cent of the United States and 2.4 per cent of the U.S.S.R. —are full-time members of the armed forces. In Britain all physically fit men aged eighteen must do two years of national service unless they are given deferment for higher education, exempted because they are already employed in work of national importance, or allowed to register as conscientious objectors, in which case it is usual to undertake some alternative service not in the armed forces. Only a small fraction register as conscientious objectors. It is frequently alleged that the period of national service is too long, that the men called up are not fully occupied, that national service has a disturbing effect on vocational adjustment, and that it should be abolished. But the majority of young men appear to have accepted a period of military service as a necessary if somewhat irksome duty.

The large proportion of the nation's resources devoted to defense has had two important consequences. On the one hand, the defense program has contributed to the maintenance of full employment in the postwar period by providing a constant stimulus to consumption and investment, making it unnecessary to act upon the elaborate plans which were drawn up for combating deflation. On the other hand, the defense program has had a seriously retarding effect on the production of consumer goods and the investment in improved roads or new plants and machinery, which would in the long run have contributed to an improvement in the standard of living. Furthermore, the defense program has added to the inflationary tendencies inherent in full employment by increasing the pressure of rising incomes upon the prices of relatively scarce consumer goods. This is overlooked in a recent white paper on the economic implications of full employment.

Whereas in the prewar period unemployment in the United Kingdom averaged 10 per cent and was sometimes higher, since the war it has averaged only 2 per cent and declined in 1955 to 1 per cent. There are pockets of greater unemployment, notably in Northern Ireland, but active steps are being taken to eliminate them by stimulating industrial development in the areas concerned.

After current defense expenditures and charges on the national debt, largely incurred in previous wars, the most important item of government expenditure is the social services, as Table 15 indicates.

The social services of the United Kingdom have developed gradually since the almsgiving of the monasteries and the Elizabethan Poor Law Act of 1601. In the present day there is a similar combination of statutory and voluntary provision. The scope of the social service has been extended considerably in the course of the twentieth century. The Minority Report of the Royal Commission on the Poor Laws in 1909 (largely inspired by Beatrice Webb, a Fabian socialist reformer) foreshadowed many of the measures which culminated in the implementation of the Beveridge Report after World War II. Beveridge considered it the responsibility of the community to combat five main social evils: want, disease, ignorance, squalor, and idleness. It has been the aim of the welfare state in Britain to remove or reduce the incidence of each of these. The problem of idleness has so far solved itself, although it may in the future require positive state action.

The attempt to abolish poverty and extreme want in Britain in the post-

Table 15. The United Kingdom Government Budget for 1954–55
(in millions of pounds sterling)

Revenue Source	Amount	Expenditure	Amount
Taxes on income and capital ...	£2,328	Defense	£1,668
Taxes on spending	1,915	National debt charges	606
Non-tax revenue	290	Social services and subsidies	1,737
		Other services.................	512
Total	£4,533	Surplus	10
		Total	£4,533

Source: H.M. Stationery Office.

war world has been largely successful, although the lot of those old-age pensioners and others entirely dependent upon social security benefits is not an easy one. Investigations in York before the war showed that 17.7 per cent of the total population had an income which was less than sufficient to meet basic human needs as defined on a rigorous standard. By 1950 a combination of better wages, full employment, and improved social services had reduced this figure to 1.7 per cent; most of these were old-age pensioners. Since that date the rate of retirement pensions has been increased, but those dependent solely on national insurance and assistance are still the poorest in the community.

The circumstances in which an individual or family is most likely to fall below the poverty line and become most in need of social security benefits arise (1) during periods of normal earning capacity when a man with a family may be at a disadvantage relative to other wage earners without family responsibilities, and (2) during periods when normal earning capacity is interrupted. In the first contingency, as part of the policy to encourage the birth rate and ensure proper care of children, the Family Allowances Act of 1945 makes a small cash grant, paid out of general taxation, to all parents on the birth of their second and each subsequent child. The government also provides additional income tax allowances. To relieve the second condition, the National Insurance Act of 1946 provides a comprehensive scheme of social security benefits for periods of unemployment or sickness and for retirement—together with widows' pensions and special grants toward maternity or burial expenses. The National Insurance (Industrial Injuries) Act of 1946 makes special provision for compensation in the case of accidents at work, independent of claims that may be made at common law or against employers' liability in the case of negligence. National insurance benefits are financed from three sources: weekly contributions by employees, contributions by employers, and from the state through general taxation. The total cost of the national insurance scheme is about £660 million annually of which £248 million is contributed by employers, £284 million by employees, £79 million from taxation, and £49 million from interest on the National Insurance Fund. The scheme is compulsory and comprehensive, covering the whole population irrespective of individual means.

In addition the National Assistance Act of 1948 provides benefits for any destitute person, whatever his nationality and whether or not he has made an insurance contribution. It supplements the amount of national insurance benefits in cases where these are inadequate to meet genuine needs and the applicant has no other source of income. Through the local authorities the National Assistance Board provides emergency accommodation for persons who are otherwise without a home, and is responsible for special welfare services for the blind, deaf, crippled, and other disabled persons.

The financial assistance provided by social security and other benefits can be supplemented by private insurance, by membership in Friendly Societies, and by the efforts of voluntary case-work agencies concerned with family welfare, although the scope of the latter has tended to change since the extension of national insurance. Voluntary agencies are now increasingly concerned with the social and psychological aspects of family welfare rather than the economic.

The welfare state in Britain attacks the social evil of disease by means of a comprehensive and almost free health service for all inhabitants. Four fifths of the cost, or £430 million, comes from the general exchequer grant — with a small contribution from the insurance fund — and nominal charges for surgical appliances, spectacles, dentures, and the dispensing of medical prescriptions. These charges are a fraction of the actual cost. Although the incidence of most diseases — cancer and chronic heart diseases excepted — has been falling steadily in the course of the twentieth century, prewar studies showed that only about 14 per cent of the population were positively healthy in the sense of being completely free from any major or minor disorder. The medical profession was conscious of the fact that many people were barred from receiving proper medical attention because of expense, and favored some kind of national health service which would be more comprehensive than the limited scheme of national health insurance then in operation.

The National Health Service Act of 1948 provides for the services of a general practitioner, a hospital specialist, and certain auxiliaries. It encourages the setting up of new medical practices in the densely populated areas of the country rather than in less populated but previously more remunerative areas. General practitioners or "family doctors" are an institution in Britain. They receive a basic salary plus an additional sum for every patient on their list up to a maximum of 3,500 patients. In fact there are about 23,000 general practitioners, with an average of 2,400 patients each. Patients are free to choose their own doctor and to change if they wish. Doctors are free to remain outside the service (about a thousand have done so) or to take a limited number of private fee-paying patients in addition to those on the health service. There are also general dental and ophthalmic services.

Hospital and specialist services are provided without charge. It is possible for the poorest person to have the most expensive specialist treatment, including surgery and modern drugs, without incurring any personal expense. There are special maternity and child welfare services, tuberculosis clinics and sanatoriums, psychiatric clinics and mental hospitals, convalescent homes and other special medical and welfare services, including the provision of domestic service or "home helps" during maternity confinement or illness. The latter is particularly valuable since the decline in supply—and therefore the high cost—of domestic servants. Medical and psychiatric social workers are attached to hospitals and clinics.

The Children Act of 1948 makes special provision for the welfare of children who are orphans, illegitimate, exposed to moral danger, or for any other reason deprived of a normal home life. Local authorities have set up children's departments that arrange for both the boarding out of children in foster homes and adoptions. They also supervise the care of children in institutions and, in collaboration with the probation service, the after-care of children from approved (i.e, reform) schools. A good deal of child welfare work is undertaken by voluntary agencies that work in conjunction with the statutory departments.

Voluntary social service organizations may employ voluntary workers, but the majority employ full-time paid workers who have been properly trained. These organizations are mainly financed from voluntary contributions but are often dependent upon direct or indirect subsidies from local or central government. Examples are old people's welfare, club and community-center work for youth and adults, case-work agencies, citizens' advice bureaus, and marriage guidance councils. There are several reasons why voluntary social service agencies in Britain are more frequently in financial difficulties than those in the United States. In the first place, there is not the same tradition of giving regular sums to charitable bodies, particularly since—unlike the American practice—these cannot be deducted for income-tax purposes. In the second place, steep progressive taxation leaves a much smaller margin to the wealthier person than before the war, and there is not the pressure—apparent in America—to win the esteem of others in the community by conspicuous donations to charity.

The consequences of a comprehensive system of social services, aiding the citizen from the cradle to the grave, will be observed in succeeding generations. There are cynics and pessimists who predict that the benefit to material welfare and physical health will be negated by a diminution in responsibility and an increasingly dependent attitude of mind. They are afraid that people will lose initiative and look to the state to meet every need and solve every problem which they could easily deal with themselves. At present this question can only be a matter for speculation, since concrete factual evidence does not exist and probably could not be collected for another generation.

The remaining aspect of the welfare state, the question of public ownership of certain industries, will be dealt with in the next section.

ORGANIZATION OF AGRICULTURE, INDUSTRY, AND COMMERCE

Britain has a mixed economy which combines a large sector of private enterprise with a smaller sector of public ownership. It falls between the completely socialist system of the U.S.S.R. and the private capitalist system of the United States. Even in America there are certain types of enterprise which—in the public interest—are exempt from capitalistic control and independent of commercial principles. They include educational institutions, museums, libraries, hospitals, recreation parks, and most roads or highways. In Britain this idea of public ownership and control has been extended further, although it does not always mean that nationalized industries and services are exempt from the obligation to make a profit. It does mean, however, that whether they make a profit or not, they must continue to operate. It is notable that the Conservative party was not opposed to the nationalization of railways and coal mines, which were having difficulty in making a profit; whereas it denationalized road transport and the steel manufacturing industries, which the Labour government had brought into public ownership, and which were profitable. In the view of the Labour party, failure to run efficiently at a profit is not the sole justification for nationalization; it is also advocated for those basic industries upon which the welfare of the community depends, as well as those where there is evidence of monopolistic exploitation by private enterprise.

Approximately 22.5 per cent of the total number of persons in civil employment are in the public sector of the economy and the remainder in private enterprise. In manufacturing and building, private enterprise accounts for 96 per cent of the persons engaged in these industries, but for only 30 per cent of those working in public utilities such as gas, electricity, water, and transport. All nationalization acts make use of the device of the public corporation, similar in its conception to the organization of the Tennessee Valley Authority in the United States. The public corporation is free from direct executive control by ministers of the government, but must submit annual reports to Parliament and is subject to its direction on matters of policy. The pattern of organization and administration varies, for each industry, from a completely unified structure to the use of the public corporation as a holding company.

Although nationalization of the land has been suggested, agricultural production is almost entirely in the hands of private enterprise. The Forestry Commission is the only public corporation concerned with production, but there are producers' marketing boards—subject to Parliamentary control—for milk, potatoes, hops, wool, and bacon pigs. Present agricultural policy in the United Kingdom is based upon the Agriculture Act of 1947, under which the government provides certain guarantees regarding quantities and prices and in return demands a minimum level of efficiency from farmers, who may be dispossessed if they persistently fall below this standard. There are about 535,000 farms in the country, of which three fifths are less than fifty acres in size. About eight million acres are devoted to cereals; three million acres to potatoes, sugar beets, and fodder crops; one million acres to fruits or vegetables and other crops; about 19 million acres to grass and 17 million to rough grazing.

The other main extractive industry is coal mining, which was nationalized in 1947. The National Coal Board is responsible for nine hundred collieries, grouped into fifty areas and employing 786,000 men. Although it has been estimated that there are supplies of coal sufficient for the next hundred years, the most easily worked seams have been exhausted and it is a constant struggle to maintain productivity. Since nationalization, total output (225 million tons a year) has risen, as well as output per manshift. There has been considerable improvement in working conditions for miners and in their remuneration. Were it not for the Board's primary obligation to pay interest on the compensation to previous owners, and the loss which it bears on the resale of imported coal, it would run at a profit. Overall policy and planning is in the hands of the Ministry of Fuel and Power, which has plans to supplement coal production in the future with atomic energy and by tapping supplies of oil and natural gas.

Reference has been made to the fact that the principal public utilities are subject to state control. Local authorities control the supply of water in most cases, while the supply of electricity is controlled by the British Electricity Authority, established in 1948. Gas production is now the responsibility of the Gas Council with twelve area boards. Public transport of passengers and goods has been subject to a vacillating policy, following the Conservative government's reversal of the schemes instituted under the Labour government by the Transport Act of 1947. This act provided for the nationalization and central control of railways and of public transport on roads. The Transport Act of 1953 denationalized road haulage, and — while keeping them under public ownership — arranged for some decentralization of control of the railways and encouraged competition between road and rail transport. Internal and external airways are under the control of public corporations (BEA and BOAC). Merchant shipping, however, is still in the hands of private enterprise, but the majority of canals, docks, and harbors are subject to some form of public control. The use of casual labor on the docks has been abolished by the institution of a National Dock Labour Board and a guaranteed minimum wage.

Before the war, steel firms had not shown the degree of enterprise and efficiency that should be expected of such an important industry. During the war it remained in the hands of private enterprise, subject to close supervision by the government. After the war, schemes of modernization were instituted which raised steel production from twelve to eighteen million tons annually. After nationalization in 1951, the industry remained under public ownership for two years and was then returned to private enterprise, subject to the supervision of an Iron and Steel Board. The Board was charged with the task of securing efficient, economic, and adequate supplies of iron and steel under competitive conditions. The Board also has powers in relation to the development and procurement of raw materials, and sets maximum prices for finished products.

The remaining branches of manufacturing industry in the United Kingdom are in the hands of private enterprise, as is almost all commerce. During the war a Ministry of Food was responsible for bulk buying and distribution of food, but since the abolition of rationing, wholesale and retail trading has returned to private enterprise. The central Bank of England is a nationalized concern but the remaining banks are not; nor are the insurance companies and building societies, which are among the wealthiest institutions in the country. Retail distribution is in the hands of over a million traders, with a total turnover of £6,500 million; 58.5 per cent of the business is done by small independent organizations, while 29 per cent is done by multiple shops and department stores, with annual sales of over £1 million each. Mention should be made of the part played in retail distribution by cooperative societies, who handle 12.5 per cent of the total national expenditure on consumer goods and services and 25 per cent of that spent on food. Cooperative societies are run by their members — numbered at eleven million — and profits are distributed among members in the form of a dividend and by means of educational and similar joint activities. Like other democratic institutions, only a small proportion of the total membership takes any active part in the control of the movement. The cooperatives are affiliated with the Co-operative Wholesale Society, which engages in manufacturing, packing, and similar activities.

Concern has been expressed in recent years at the extent to which manufacturers and distributors — operating through their respective trade associations — engage in restrictive practices and enforce retail price maintenance through economic sanctions upon traders. A commission was set up in 1948 to investigate this question and produced reports concerning a wide variety of products, ranging from dental goods, electrical appliances, pneumatic tires, and copper alloys to sand and gravel. The commission had no power to enforce remedies. The Restrictive Trade Practices Act of 1956 requires the registration of all restrictive practices. These practices are investigated by a committee which will decide whether they are contrary to public interest and what action should be taken. The procedure is cumbersome and unlikely to be effective in preventing monopolistic exploitation. Comparisons between Britain and America suggest that the tendency toward monopoly is evident in the same type of industry. It appears to be related to the physical, technological, and distributional characteristics of the industry and to the inelasticity of supply and demand for its products. An important difference between the two countries is in the attitude of the public toward monopolies. In Britain concentration and control does not justify interference if it can be shown that the organization has not abused its power, and is providing consumers with their requirements at a reasonable price. Nevertheless, it is evident that an increasing tendency for production and distribution to be controlled by semimonopolistic concerns could introduce serious abuses. Reference has been made to the potential power exercised by economic pressure groups in the form of large trade associations. It is doubtful if they would continue to exercise restraint if they considered that their interests were seriously threatened in any way.

THE UNITED KINGDOM

ORGANIZATION OF LABOR AND WAGE DETERMINATION

Hardly less powerful than commercial and industrial organizations in the postwar period of full employment are the trade unions. Nearly ten million workers are organized into 690 separate unions, but 67 per cent of all trade unionists are in seventeen large unions. The majority of trade unions are affiliated with the Trades Unions Congress, but this body has no executive power. Power is vested in the individual union. The basis of trade union membership is voluntary, but in an increasing number of industries the unions collaborate with employers in the enforcement of a "closed shop" so that nonunion members are not employed. There are isolated employers who will not permit unions to be organized among their employees, and there are a few "company unions"—at one time a familiar type in the United States—which are designed to forestall an effective combination of the workers, but these are extraordinary situations.

A distinction is usually made between the "craft" unions based upon the nature of a man's skill and the "industrial" unions which bring together a variety of different occupations associated with the same industry. An example of the former is the Amalgamated Engineering Union (756,000 members). Although this organization now includes some semiskilled and unskilled workers, it is actually a multiple-craft type of union, covering fitters, turners, planers, borers, pattern makers, and similar trades. In contrast the National Union of Mineworkers (600,000 members) is a union of the industrial type, covering every conceivable kind of employee in the mining industry. Sometimes there are rivalries between unions of different types in the same place of employment, which are usually resolved by the Trades Unions Congress. The largest general union covering many different industries and occupations is the Transport and General Workers Union, with over a million members. The most serious difficulty encountered by such a large union is that it develops all the characteristics of a large bureaucratic organization; as a consequence, it tends to lose touch with the rank-and-file members. This accounts for the increasing number of unofficial ("wildcat") strikes, not supported by the union.

Although democratic in their constitution, many unions tend to exhibit oligarchical tendencies—owing mainly to the failure of members to maintain an active interest in union affairs except in times of crisis. Attendance at branch meetings ranges between 2 and 30 per cent of the membership. The annual or biennial conferences, which most unions hold, help to keep the paid official and the executive in touch with the prevailing mood of the members, but it is doubtful if a conference of this kind can exercise effective control over an executive handling complex affairs. Another weakness of trade-union organization is the lack of effective coordination between the branch with its secretary (based upon a geographical area and possibly covering several firms) and the workshop where an employee is appointed shop steward and acts as a representative of union members.

Many unions will shortly have to face a problem in the remuneration of headquarters officials. Many general Secretaries at present in office have grown up with the trade-union movement as it has gathered strength in the last fifty years. They have given their lives to the movement because they had faith in its ideals. In return they have received salaries which average £800 to £1,200 a year; the best paid general secretaryship is worth only £2,000 a year. These salaries are small compared with those received by union officials holding similar positions in the United States or even in comparison with what they might earn if their administrative talents were put to other use.

In Britain wages and salaries are mainly determined by collective bargaining through voluntary agreements—often reached on a national level—between the representatives of the trade union concerned and the equivalent employers' federation. It is often necessary to adjust piece rates and other details at the local level, but in most cases national minimums are in operation. When an agreement cannot be reached, voluntary conciliation and arbitration may be resorted to, or in extreme cases the dispute may be referred by the Ministry of Labour to the national Industrial Disputes Tribunal. Since 1951 no legal action may be taken against people for not observing the Tribunal's awards, but in most disputes these are accepted by the parties concerned.

Officially the trade-union movement disapproves of the strike weapon except as a last resort, but there is a tendency for dissatisfied members to call unofficial strikes if satisfactory agreements regarding disputes are not reached without delay. During 1954, 2,457 working days were lost in official and unofficial strikes and lockouts, affecting 448,000 workers.

In some forty-eight branches of industry such as agriculture and the catering trades, where union organization has always been weak and wages low, the government has set up wages councils which periodically review wages and working conditions and set standards that must be adhered to throughout the country. They are enforced by statute, whereas wages determined by collective bargaining depend upon voluntary agreement.

Wages councils are responsible for determining the wages of approximately three million workers. Wages and salaries in the United Kingdom are determined by a variety of factors. It is not surprising that in the absence of any unifying wage policy (except that of restraint, which has been urged by successive chancellors of the exchequer faced with growing inflation), there are many anomalies in and little logic behind wage differentials. For example, until recently the salaries of schoolteachers in state schools were periodically reviewed and fixed by a standing committee, established for that purpose, so that in the postwar period schoolteachers were able to obtain several increases in salary to keep pace with the rising cost of living. In contrast, university teachers have had no standing machinery for determining their salaries, which have therefore lagged far behind rising prices.

National wage policy endeavors to ensure that aggregate increases in wages are compatible with the general economic situation, that wage differentials are such that industries short of labor are able to attract workers by higher pay, that special talents, skills, and training are recognized, and that adequate incentives to increase productivity are offered where appropriate. At the present time none of these objectives has been effectively achieved. There is a tendency for differentials between wage rates for skilled and unskilled workers to be narrow. Whereas in the United States a skilled man often earns two to three times as much as the unskilled, in the United Kingdom an unskilled man's wage rate is on the average 83.4 per cent of that of the skilled man. In contrast certain professionals, such as doctors and lawyers, earn far more than can be explained in terms of a return on the investment in their training. Doctors, for example, have been able to use their monopolistic position to exact high salaries from the National Health Service, and in universities medically qualified research workers are paid at a higher rate than colleagues whose academic qualifications may be higher but whose degrees are not in medicine.

The tendency at the present time is for all groups of workers—whether industrial or professional—to be concerned with the preservation of traditional wage and salary differentials, irrespective of whether they have any rational justification. Another anomaly has arisen as a consequence of heavy progressive taxation. Many employers endeavor to supplement the incomes of their managerial staff and other employees by providing houses, cars, and generous expense accounts.

There appears to be a fundamental conflict of values in the determination of incomes in contemporary societies, and this is clearly seen in the United Kingdom. In the early days trade unions were governed by a concern for social justice and an essentially egalitarian philosophy which has since been replaced by a concern to maintain and enhance a relative advantage over those whose power to extort increases from employers is not as strong. The result, as one writer has put it, is typical of an acquisitive, competitive, hierarchical, envious society.

HUMAN RELATIONS IN INDUSTRY

Since the end of the nineteenth century the state has legislated minimum standards regarding working conditions and health or safety of employees, in factories and elsewhere. Trade unions have obtained additional privileges and safeguards for the welfare of workers. The twentieth century has been characterized by a growing recognition from employers that good working conditions and harmonious relations between the managerial and production branches of industry contribute to productivity. Many firms appoint personnel managers and welfare officers, and the need for improved communication and consultation among all levels in a large industrial organization is recognized. There is still a marked dichotomy between "management" and "workers," even though the majority of managerial staff are as much employees of the organization as those engaged in production. The difficulties of maintaining effective cooperation among the various branches increase with the size of the firm. Table 16 shows the number of firms of different sizes. Comparisons with the United States suggest no great differences.

The syndicalist movement for workers' control of industry, which has had some support on the Continent, has never succeeded in Britain. However, considerable lip-service is paid to the idea of "industrial democracy,"

Table 16. Size of Manufacturing Firms in Great Britain in 1954

Number of Employees	Establishments	Employees (in thousands)
Total	*56,207*	*7,427*
11–24	16,521	285
25–99	25,225	1,258
100–499	11,902	2,487
500–999	1,510	1,034
1,000–1,999	685	941
2,000 or more	364	1,422

Source: Central Statistical Office.

although there is no clear definition of the concept. The two world wars encouraged some diminution of the traditional antagonism between trade unions and employers, and between managers and workers. These groups were prepared to sink their differences in a common "war effort" to increase production. In many industries formal consultative machinery was set up by means of joint production committees and works' councils. This machinery extended in some industries from the factory floor to the national level and has largely been retained in the postwar period. Consultative procedures of this kind are separate from the existing machinery for collective bargaining. Most works councils are expressly excluded from considering wages or other matters traditionally dealt with by trade unions; instead they concern themselves mainly with questions of production and welfare. The majority of studies of joint consultation in the United Kingdom conclude that even if formal consultative machinery has been of value in some cases, the introduction of such machinery does not necessarily lead to an improvement in human relations in the factory and has sometimes had the reverse effect. Such machinery is usually successful where there is a measure of good will among the various levels of the organization and informal consultation already exists.

Those who emphasize the importance of democratic participation by workers in industrial organization tend to underestimate the significance of institutional conflict. Copartnership and profit sharing, measures suggested by the Liberal party, have won some support among employers. In a period of full employment it seems reasonable that employees should receive a share in the profits they have helped to earn and that there should be "partnership" between management and production workers in an effort to increase output. Successive reports of committees that have visited the United States under the auspices of the Anglo-American Productivity Council have noted that this attitude is more widespread in the United States than in the United Kingdom. It overlooks the fact that in a system of free enterprise and capitalist production the interests of employers and employees are not always identical, as would be seen in a period of trade depression. The conscious or unconscious recognition of this fact makes trade unionists cling to traditional attitudes of suspicion toward management and retain the restrictive practices which, however mistakenly, they believe are necessary to protect their interests.

The problem is more complicated when relationships in a nationalized industry are considered. In these industries employees cannot argue that further effort on their part increases the private profits of the employer. They may consider, however, that the community through its representatives on the board of the nationalized industry does not have the welfare of the employees in that industry sufficiently in mind. Before World War II, when coal miners desired the nationalization of the mines they imagined that this would end the old "boss" system and begin a new era of self-government by the miners. Then under nationalization there was disillusionment when many of the original owners and managers were retained as officials on the newly constituted National Coal Board. Thus innovations under nationalization that were intended to increase efficiency and improve the miners' conditions were sometimes greeted with the same mistrust accorded in the past to similar attempts made by private employers, which were suspected of being efforts to get more work out of the men for less pay.

There has been considerable controversy within the trade-union movement concerning the appointment of trade-union officials to the boards of nationalized industries. Some think this is desirable as a means of providing a measure of "workers' control," while others argue that this undermines the independence of the trade unions, who must negotiate with the nationalized board—when determining salaries and conditions of work—in the same way as with any other employer. In most cases a compromise has been reached whereby trade unionists so appointed relinquish any official connection with the movement and sit as independent members, but with the workers' interests in mind. An exception is the participation of trade unions on the National Dock Labour Board which has produced considerable confusion among dock workers, who sometimes feel that their interests are in direct conflict with those of the Board on which their own representatives sit. This situation is partly responsible for frequent unofficial strikes among dock workers in Britain.

HOURS OF WORK AND THE USE OF LEISURE

The average number of hours worked per week in Britain in 1951 was 48 for adult men and 42 for women. The details for selected industries are set forth in Table 17.

During full employment the actual number of hours worked tends to exceed the standard hours established in wage agreements. Reduction in standard hours is as much designed to increase real earnings as it is to provide employees with more leisure, because overtime rates are paid for addi-

Table 17. Average Hours Worked Weekly by Men, Women, and Juveniles in the United Kingdom in 1951 (for Selected Industries)

Industry	April 1951	October 1951
Transport	49.9	49.3
Mining and quarrying	47.8	48.1
Metal manufacture	47.1	47.5
National and local government	44.8	44.8
Clothing	41.9	40.4
All industries	46.3	46.1

Source: Central Statistical Office.

tional hours worked. A five-and-a-half-day working week applies in most industries, although in some industries and commercial establishments a five-day week has been adopted. The Trades Union Congress would like to see a forty-hour, five-day week in all industries. One week's holiday with pay is now usual in most industries together with six statutory days known as bank holidays, spread through the year. The majority of other workers have a fortnight's holiday, while civil servants, local government officers, and school and university teachers have longer. An annual visit to the seaside is a British institution enjoyed by about half the population regularly.

Reference has been made to the influence of social class on leisure-time pursuits, but there are many activities, of course, which are more or less universal. The British are noted for their interest in sports of all kinds, but far more people watch sports, especially association football (soccer), than take an active part. About one in three men and one in ten women regularly watch football. A still larger proportion of the population gamble on the results of football matches; as many as 50 per cent of the men and 28 per cent of the women risk an average of five shillings per week on football pools. Gambling on horse racing is equally widespread, but much larger sums are wagered. Dog racing is less popular than football and horse racing, but also attracts a following of betters. All told, more than £800 million are spent annually on legalized gambling. Street betting, gaming, and lotteries are illegal, but proposals have been put forward to legalize charitable lotteries.

The provision of public entertainment is a major industry on which consumers spent £187 million in 1954. Radio is found in almost all homes, and television has penetrated to about half. Although 75 per cent of the population visit a cinema at least once a month, attendance has declined considerably with the increased popularity of television. However, the live theater is still popular among the more sophisticated and—unlike America —is not virtually confined to the metropolis since good professional repertory companies exist in the provinces. Drama is not normally taught at the universities, although Bristol is a recent exception.

The "public house" or bar for the sale of alcoholic liquor (with hours of opening regulated by law) is a familiar British institution. As commonly applied to different kinds of drinking places, the terms "public," "saloon," and "private" suggest a distinction of types on a class basis. In addition there are also licensed private clubs. Patrons for these places are drawn from the three fourths of the population who drink beer, wines, or spirits. Of this large nonabstaining proportion, in a typical fortnight 41 per cent have a drink in a public house, 20 per cent at home, and 9 per cent in a club; far more men than women visit public houses or clubs. As the most popular drink, beer is consumed at an average of three fourths of a pint a day per head. Wine and spirits, however, are not as regularly consumed. It is estimated that consumers spent £842 million on alcoholic drinks in 1954.

Despite recent findings concerning the relation between smoking and carcinoma of the lung, 80 per cent of the men and 40 per cent of the women in Britain smoke regularly, mainly cigarettes. An average of fifteen to twenty cigarettes a day is normal for a man. Approximately 240 million pounds of tobacco were consumed in 1954, on which £855 million were spent.

It may provide some insight into current scales of values in the United Kingdom if it is pointed out that approximately £1 per week per head of the total population—or £170 per annum per household—is spent on alcohol, smoking, and gambling. This is roughly equal to the amount spent on housing, fuel, and clothing combined. It must, of course, be remembered that alcohol, tobacco, and gambling are subject to heavy taxation and duty charges. At factor cost, expenditure is approximately 11s. 6d. per head per week, or £100 per household per annum. This is about equal to the expenditure on clothing and fuel.

Social Control: Law, Politics, and Religion

LAW

It is sometimes suggested that the British are among the most orderly and law-abiding peoples in the world. A superficial consideration of the statistics of crime appears to confirm this. In 1954 the total number of persons found guilty of crimes and offenses of all kinds in England and Wales was 725,578, of whom 106,731 were found guilty of crimes (indictable offenses), 618,565 of less serious (nonindictable) offenses, and 642 of offenses against the defense regulations. This gives an over-all rate of 16.5 per thousand of the total population. While the majority of nonindictable offenses brought to the attention of the police are cleared up, about 50 per cent of indictable offenses known to the police remain undetected. The rate of known crimes per thousand of the population over eight years of age is approximately 11.25, as shown in Table 18. The rate for crimes of violence against the person is 0.195 per thousand. About 50 per cent of the nonindictable offenses are against highway and traffic acts.

Unfortunately, there has been a considerable increase in the more serious types of crime as well as a deterioration in the general level of public honesty since the prewar period. The incidence of violent assault and injuries is almost four times as high as in the prewar period; the incidence of rape four times as high; burglary and larceny twice as high. Malicious damage to property is ten times as frequent. Care must be taken in the interpretation of these statistics, as in certain instances the higher figures

Table 18. Crimes (Indictable Offenses) Known to Police in England and Wales
(per million of population over eight years of age)

Crime	Annual Average		
	1930–39	1940–49	1954
Murder	3.6	4.4	3.8
Attempted murder	2.6	4.4	6.2
Manslaughter, infanticide	5.3	5.0	4.3
Wounding	46.1	77.2	167.7
Other violent crimes	8.0	14.0	12.5
Unnatural offenses and attempts	25.8	59.4	164.7
Rape and other offenses against females	77.1	139.0	242.2
Bigamy	9.0	24.2	10.1
Burglary, housebreaking, etc.	1,085.5	2,208.0	1,965.9
Robbery and extortion	9.0	23.9	23.7
Aggravated larcenies	446.8	1,013.0	992.4
Other larcenies	3,993.8	6,832.9	6,395.5
Obtaining by false pretenses	342.4	338.3	430.6
Other frauds	89.6	71.9	249.8
Receiving stolen goods	82.7	223.7	167.6
Malicious injuries to property	13.1	55.1	136.0
Forgery, coining	42.9	111.1	127.0
Attempted suicide	89.1	85.0	125.5
Other indictable offenses	18.1	15.9	25.6
Total	6,390.6	11,306.4	11,251.1

Source: Home Office.

may represent increased vigilance on the part of the police or they may mean that certain offenses are being treated more seriously than before the war. Nevertheless, the general picture is one of a marked deterioration. The over-all incidence of indictable offenses is almost twice as high as in the period 1930–39.

Although there is little difference in the over-all figures of the incidence of nonindictable offenses, shown in Table 19, certain items have increased considerably. Offenses connected with prostitution are between four and five times as frequent, although to a limited extent this too may be a result of increased police activity. A part of the increase in indictable offenses must be attributed to the growth of juvenile crime, which is 50 per cent higher than in 1938. This is indicated in Table 20. The peak age for boys and girls is fourteen years, but the rate for boys is ten times as high as that for girls. Of the offenses committed by juveniles, 98 per cent are against property. Crimes of violence are only a small proportion but they are increasing, as are the rates for sexual offenses, drunkenness, disorderly behavior, and attempted suicide of youths between seventeen and twenty. The incidence of nonindictable offenses by juveniles has decreased since

Table 19. Persons Proceeded against for Minor (Nonindictable) Offenses in England and Wales (per million of population over eight years of age)

Offense	Annual Average		
	1930–39	1940–49	1954
Assaults	555.9	483.6	450.2
Brothel-keeping and living off			
prostitutes' earnings	12.2	19.5	22.9
Offenses by prostitutes	59.0	85.1	315.0
Indecent exposure	45.4	44.5	67.0
Cruelty to children	24.5	33.9	22.2
Malicious damage	297.2	315.6	237.7
Prevention of crimes acts	4.5	1.4	9.5
Unlawful possession	14.7	34.9	15.0
Frequenting enclosed premises	124.0	57.8	72.5
Betting and gaming	366.4	210.8	330.3
Highways and traffic offenses	10,380.0	5,907.4	10,357.1
Intoxicating liquor offenses	1,481.1	861.5	1,476.9
Local regulations	1,187.2	567.5	629.2
Revenue laws	904.9	661.0	533.2
Sunday trading	600.6	2.6	6.1
Vagrancy acts	346.9	159.3	115.6
Other nonindictable offenses................	1,649.2	1,584.8	2,223.1
Total.............................	18,053.5	11,031.2	16,883.5

Source: Home Office.

Table 20. Juvenile Crime in England and Wales (Number of Young Persons 8–17 Years Found Guilty of Indictable Offenses per 100,000 of the Population of the Age Group)

Age in Years	Boys		Girls	
	1954	1938	1954	1938
8	291	220	12	9
9	599	451	47	27
10	854	703	58	37
11	1,090	931	88	62
12	1,411	1,111	133	66
13	1,794	1,315	177	73
14	1,975	1,141	197	84
15	1,404	1,145	179	97
16	1,271	1,110	188	91
17	1,179	867	185	99

Source: Home Office.

1938, although juvenile crimes and offenses reached a peak in 1950–51; since then, however, there has been a slight decline.

Comparisons between England and Wales and the rest of the United Kingdom are difficult because of differences in the judicial system, the classification of crime, and general procedures. However, Northern Ireland and Scotland both show increases in crime since the prewar period; although Scotland had the highest crime rate before the war, its rate of increase has been smaller than that of England and Wales so that there is less difference today. Since 1938 both Scotland and Northern Ireland have exhibited a phenomenal decline in the incidence of drunkenness, largely owing to the high price and scarcity of whisky. There also appears to be a decline in offenses connected with prostitution in Northern Ireland, but this may be a consequence of diminished police activity in this area. The rates for all indictable offenses—especially those connected with town life, such as housebreaking and violence—are much lower in Northern Ireland, reflecting its predominantly rural character.

Table 21 presents some comparable statistics of crimes and offenses for England and Wales and for Scotland. These are based upon categories which the Home Office and the Scottish Home Department believe to be as nearly equivalent as possible, although in certain respects the comparison is still arbitrary and must be interpreted with care.[6] Certain differences between Scotland, on the one hand, and England and Wales, on the other, emerge clearly. England and Wales have significantly higher rates of murder, embezzlement, revenue offenses, railway offenses, brothel-keeping,

Table 21. Comparison of Selected Criminal Statistics for England-Wales and Scotland in 1952

	England and Wales				Scotland		
Description of Offense	Persons Found Guilty	Crimes Known to Police	Rate per Million of Population*	Description of Offense	Persons against Whom Charges Were Proved†	Crimes Known to Police	Rate per Million of Population*
Serious offenses				*Serious offenses*			
Murder	41	146	3.8	Murder	3.0	13	3
Attempt to murder	28	155	4.0	Attempt to murder, etc.	1.6	7	...
Felonious wounding, malicious wounding, assault	3,792	5,980	154.2	Assaults	141.0	608	354
Robbery and assaults with intent to rob	456	1,002	24.0	Robbery and assaults with intent to rob	20.0	304	78
Housebreaking, attempts; sacrilege, burglary	21,838	97,941	2,559.7	Housebreaking	6,535.6	28,103	5,822
Embezzlement, frauds, falsifying accounts	1,966	8,782	225.2	Breach of trust and embezzlement	83.7	360	151
Larceny, stealing, obtaining goods by false pretenses, other frauds, forgery	90,448	367,444	9,421.6	Theft, falsehood, and willful imposition, post office offenses, forgery	9,409.7	41,322	13,280
Less serious offenses				*Less serious offenses*			
Disorderly behavior, assaults, attempted suicide	25,214	...	646.5	Breach of peace	3,990.5	...	17,159
Brothel-keeping	258	...	6.6	Brothel-keeping	2.3	...	10
Prostitutes, offenses by and abetting	10,390	...	265.4	Prostitution	22.1	...	95
Drunkenness, simple and aggravated	51,488	...	1,320.2	Drunkenness, drunk and incapable, drunk and disorderly, drunk in charge of child, etc.	2,232.4	...	9,621
Railway offenses	18,604	...	477.0	Railways	241.2	...	1,037
Revenue offenses, including dog licenses	25,228	...	846.9	Revenue laws including dog licenses	269.8	...	1,160

Source: Home Office and Scottish Home Department.

*Over eight years of age. In the case of serious offenses these are rates of offenses known to the police; in the case of less serious offenses

90

and prostitution. Scotland has significantly higher rates of robbery, house-breaking, disorderly behavior, and drunkenness.

Apart from the incidence of crime there is other evidence of a decline in standards of public morality since the prewar period. Many people did not regard minor breaches of rationing regulations (now abolished) as offenses, and a similar attitude exists today with regard to traffic regulations. The majority of people are not above a certain amount of "fiddling" —a term widely accepted as a euphemism for offenses the commission of which does not generate any marked feelings of guilt. They may include tax evasion by overcharging on expense accounts and by other means, malingering, pilfering from railways or place of employment, and similar activities. One inquiry found that in England two thirds of the sample investigated admitted to some kind of fiddling. The large number of petty crimes which remain undetected bears witness to this. The situation is not confined to England, however. One observer noted the rapid growth of undetected crimes of a minor character in Scotland, and suggested that "the moral deterioration that this implies may be a worse omen for Scotland than would a period of outbreak of a smaller number of much more serious crimes."[7]

Full employment has indirectly contributed to the problem by reducing the number of police below establishment, by necessitating the employment in commerce and industry of men with bad records in positions of responsibility, and by tying the hands of employers who, faced with a shortage of workers, must turn a blind eye to dishonesty among their employees for fear of precipitating labor troubles.

Despite the evidence of declining moral standards and increased rates of crime, the incidence of law-breaking and violence is still very much lower in the United Kingdom than in the United States and other countries. In this connection the role of the British police and judicial systems may be considered.

The present strength of the regular police force in Britain is approximately 72,000 men and 2,000 women. Whereas in many countries the police are treated with fear or contempt, the British police, despite occasional lapses, are almost universally admired for their honesty, reliability, courtesy, and kindness. Their essential characteristics may be described as follows: (1) they are a civilian force, recruited from a wide cross section of the population on a basis of good character and educational qualifications which are high enough to ensure the appointment of men and women of good intelligence but not so high as to alienate them from the ordinary citizen. (2) Although uniformed, they are a civilian force and not regimented or segregated in barracks. (3) They are armed only with a truncheon and—except in unusual circumstances—are not issued firearms. (4) Apart from the Metropolitan police in London and the Royal Ulster Constabulary in Northern Ireland, the police forces are not responsible to the state but rather to local government authorities. (5) Any complaint against the police is publicly investigated, and the highest standards of honesty are enforced. (6) The prime duty of the police is to "maintain the peace," and the apprehension of criminals is secondary to the prevention of crime.

The British judicial system is also noted for its integrity and impartiality. At one time there was "one law for the poor and another for the rich," but the institution of legal aid for those who cannot afford the full cost of pursuing or defending a case in any civil or criminal court has done much to reduce this discrepancy, although the cost of litigation is still high. Important features are the independence of the judiciary, the absence of political interference with the course of justice or with the appointment of judges, who hold their position for life. Courts of summary jurisdiction may be presided over by one or more justices of the peace or a full-time stipendiary magistrate. There are separate courts for juveniles.

The treatment of criminals has undergone progressive reform since the beginning of the nineteenth century, when the English penal code (known as the "bloody code") imposed the death penalty for some 220 offenses, including the theft of an article worth more than five shillings. At the present time hanging is applicable only in cases of wartime treason and murder. A high proportion of murders are subsequently reprieved on the ground of insanity or for other reasons, but the narrow legal interpretation given to the term "insanity" means that some who go to the gallows are undoubtedly insane by modern psychiatric standards. About twelve persons a year are hanged. In 1956 a private member's bill for the abolition of the death penalty was passed on a free vote in the House of Commons but rejected in the Lords. Subsequently, the government introduced a bill limiting the death penalty to murder in special circumstances, e.g., the murder of a policeman.

Conditions in prisons, though not ideal, have improved in recent years. There are experimental prisons "without bars," and useful forms of employment are now usual in all prisons. The aim of imprisonment, as of any punishment, is deterrent and reformative, but the reforming influence of imprisonment is not as evident as it might be. Of the 33,722 persons admitted to prison in England and Wales in 1951, 17,869 had previous sentences; more than 5,500 had four or more prison sentences; and nearly 2,000, ten or more. In Scotland, out of 8,762 admissions in 1951, 5,476 had previous sentences; over 2,000, more than four; and 792, over ten.

Persons found guilty of crimes or offenses are dealt with as follows: imprisonment, 20 per cent; absolute discharge, 3 per cent; conditional discharge, 12 per cent; probation orders, 10 per cent; fines, 52 per cent; otherwise disposed of, 3 per cent. Children and young persons under twenty-one years of age may be discharged, put on probation, sent to an approved school, or — if over eighteen — to a Borstal training establishment. The large majority of juveniles appearing before the court are first offenders and do not reappear. The hard core of persistent offenders who are sent to approved schools after failing to respond to probation are usually suffering from severe emotional disturbance, frequently connected with home background and family relationships. Approximately 5 per cent of all juvenile offenders are sent to approved schools or Borstals.

It is characteristic of societies with advanced cultures that law tends to replace custom as an agent of social control and is concerned less with the suppression of crime than with the enforcement of contract. As Durkheim has pointed out, this tendency is a consequence of increasing role-differentiation in urban societies. He made it the basis of his distinction between mechanical and organic solidarity, which corresponds closely to the distinction that Toennies made between *Gemeinschaft* and *Gesellschaft* and that Maine made between societies in which relationships are governed by status and those in which they are governed by contract. In recent years the growth of public and administrative law has involved a partial reversal of this trend. Theoretically, a legal contract is a freely established agreement between individuals. However, the extension of the welfare state, the institution of collective bargaining, and the standardization of contracts of various kinds for purposes of efficiency have resulted in some diminution of individual freedom in the interests of the community at large.

The movement from status to contract and back to status has proceeded to extremes in totalitarian states where the freedom and autonomy of individuals and groups has been destroyed by the state in return for security and protection. Some fear that this will be the ultimate consequence of the extension of public control under the welfare state in Britain. A detailed examination of this question cannot be undertaken in the present context. But it may be noted that at least one eminent exponent of the sociology of law has come to the conclusion that freedom and the rule of law—as traditionally understood in Britain—are not incompatible with the growth of public control, and that "the incompatibility of planning with the rule of law is a myth sustainable only by prejudice or ignorance."[8]

GOVERNMENT AND POLITICS

One of the most important differences between the British and American legal and political systems is the supremacy of Parliament in the former. There are no separate constitutional laws, defined and interpreted by a supreme court. British courts interpret the common law, established by precedent, and the statutes passed by Parliament. But Parliament is free to legislate what it pleases, and no court can declare an act unconstitutional. In fact it has been suggested that the American presidency "is a much more monarchical institution than the modern English kingship and that, by its acceptance of the unlimited power of sovereign people, the English parliamentary system is more republican than the elaborately divided system of the United States."[9]

The institution of the monarchy in the United Kingdom fulfills an integrative function in the social and political life of the country. Unlike the United States, where the president as the head of the state is associated with party political controversy, the monarchy is able to provide stability and continuity precisely because the queen is above such controversy. Effective power is in the hands of the prime minister, and the queen cannot act except on the advice of her ministers. It has been pointed out that the very powerlessness of the monarchy is the source of its strength. Ambivalent attitudes toward authority can be more satisfactorily resolved when mutually antagonistic sentiments can be directed onto separate objects. Hostility toward authority tends to be displaced from the monarchy onto the heads of the government and opposition. Aggressive impulses normally channeled into politics are modified by sentiments of loyalty to the crown.

The coronation of Queen Elizabeth II was an occasion for national rejoicing and expressions of unity and loyalty to the crown (despite the demonstrations of certain Scottish nationalists). Yet it is an exaggeration to say that "the Coronation provided at one time and for practically the entire society such an intensive contact with the sacred" that it constituted a "great act of national communion."[10] This view underestimates the extent to which the occasion was treated simply as an excuse for a national holiday, and overlooks class and other conflicts which divide the country. Nevertheless, it is true that since the reign of Queen Victoria the royal family has been regarded by many people as a symbol of correct behavior and conformity to middle-class ideals of conduct.

Although there is no written constitution, there are certain well-established conventions which make the smooth working of parliamentary government possible. For instance the queen appoints as prime minister the man who leads the party with a majority in the House of Commons; he then nominates M.P.'s of his own party whom the queen appoints as ministers, i.e., political heads of the various departments of state. The more important departments are represented in the Cabinet. In this way a strong executive is created with the guaranteed support of a majority of the legislature.

Another important convention is that the leader of the second largest party in the House of Commons becomes "Leader of Her Majesty's Opposition," which is a salaried post similar to that of a minister. This institutionalization of the role of the opposition party in the House of Commons is a unique feature of the British constitution and has contributed much to its stability. The leader of the Opposition is recognized as a potential prime minister, and he forms a "shadow cabinet," ready to take office if his party should win the next election. This means that while the Opposition's criticisms of government policy are rarely lacking in fervor, it must always be responsible criticism. The policy of the Opposition must be a practical one which could be effectively implemented if the party is returned to office.

The Cabinet shares collective responsibility for government policy, and each minister is responsible for everything that happens in his department. The permanent heads of departments are civil servants, appointed for life on the basis of competitive examination, and—like all civil servants—remain in office no matter what changes there may be in the government. They may advise the minister on the basis of their expert knowledge, but in the last resort it is the minister and not the permanent head who is responsible for the decisions reached—even on minor matters over which he has never been consulted. This responsibility is enforced largely through the institution of questions which may be asked in Parliament regarding any activities of the civil service. One reason why the civil service is sometimes accused of being unduly bound with "red tape" is that a permanent record must be kept of its activities in order that proper explanations can be given if a question is asked in Parliament. Unless it can be shown that an individual civil servant has been guilty of a gross breach of duty or has not lived up to the high standards of honesty and integrity that are demanded, he cannot be removed.

Some modification of traditional practice in this respect has recently been made necessary in dealing with Communists or others of doubtful loyalty in positions of responsibility. With considerable reluctance, the government felt it necessary to introduce regulations enabling the removal of persons known or suspected of Communist sympathies from any position where their activities might constitute a security risk. This reluctance in the face of the acknowledged need to prevent Communists from having access to secret information stems from the fact that to make such a policy effective involves delving into the private lives of civil servants, innocent and guilty alike. That such an intrusion of authority is repugnant to British traditions of liberty illustrates an interesting difference in attitude between Britain and America in this respect.

In contrast to American traditions the British way of life has evolved slowly in the course of the last thousand years. Because it is so deeply embedded, institutionally and psychologically, deviation from its norms can be tolerated with greater equanimity. Behavior which is "not quite British" is regarded as a source of amusement rather than indignation. For this reason religious and political minorities—including the Communist party—have been able to survive in an atmosphere of condescending tolerance because they are not taken quite seriously. It is only since direct evidence of disloyalty among individual civil servants and others has been revealed that the government has felt compelled to follow the American example and remove any person of whom there is any suspicion. Nevertheless, McCarthy-like witch hunts are inconceivable in the United Kingdom, and even those removed from their positions in the Foreign Office or Defence Ministries are found other employment elsewhere.

It is one of the characteristics of the British political system that there are normally two major parties distinguished from one another, primarily by degrees of conservatism or radicalism in relation to current economic, social, and political issues. There have always been minority parties in the House of Commons, but they have seldom exercised influence unless they held the balance between the two main parties. At the present time numerical support for the Conservative (Tory) and Labour (Socialist) parties is fairly evenly divided throughout the country, and at each election it requires only a small swing in the number of votes for either party to reverse the power position in the House of Commons. The electoral system in Britain does not exactly reflect the distribution of support for the two parties in the country, but exaggerates any swing. Thus in 1951 it was possible for the Conservative party to obtain a majority of seats in the House, although the Labour party polled more votes. The Labour party requires roughly 250,000 more votes than the Conservatives to secure any given number of seats. This is due to the concentration and consequent wastage of Labour votes in industrial areas.

Psephologists (students of electoral behavior) have paid special attention to the "floating voter" in the United Kingdom. Eighty per cent of voters are loyal to one party most of their lives, but those who change their allegiance appear to be spread evenly among all social classes. Although there appears to be a connection between social class and support for either the Conservative or Labour party, the relationship is not perfect. Approximately 80 per cent of those who call themselves upper or upper middle class vote Conservative, and approximately 60 per cent of those describing themselves as working class vote Labour. It is evident therefore that a considerable number of people vote contrary to class interests in the light of the Marxist position, as interpreted by Centers under the explanation of voting behavior. Furthermore, the working-class supporters of each of the political parties are relatively more conservative in their social attitudes than the middle-class members of the same political party. Similarly, working-class supporters of each party tend to be slightly more authoritarian or "tough-minded" in their attitudes than the middle-class supporters of the same party.

It is important to distinguish between the parliamentary Conservative and Labour parties, which consist of the members of Parliament, and the supporting Conservative and Labour parties outside the House. The parliamentary parties are more or less autonomous and in no way responsible to their supporters, although they must, naturally, be sensitive to their opinions. A member of Parliament represents the whole of his constituency, and not merely his supporters.

Although elections are conducted in a way which suggests that a rational appeal is being made to the elector on the basis of the election issues and the record of the respective parties, it appears that the rationality of the voter is something of a myth. The comparative stability of the electorate and their loyalty to one party have already been mentioned. Election issues, the character of the candidate, and the efficiency of local party machinery in canvassing electors and conducting public meetings bears remarkably little relation to the outcome of the election; only a small minority are influenced by these factors. The fact that the electoral system exaggerates a swing in votes may be a virtue rather than a fault of the system. At least it prevents political stagnation in the House of Commons, and means that neither party is so remote from office that it feels impelled to seek extreme methods of gaining power. At the same time, the opposing interests and conflicts that have become a traditional part of the national and party "mythology" help to keep both parties active.

Between national elections, when an average of 75 per cent of the electorate votes, the majority of the people are politically apathetic. Only a small proportion of the electorate are actually subscribing members of a political party, and only a minority of the subscribing members take any part in regular constituency party meetings or even interest themselves in the nomination of their candidate. Although the Labour party receives considerable financial support from trade unions, few of their members take any interest in the political activities of the union. Similarly, a fairly large number of the Conservative party supporters in the constituencies, especially women, are more interested in their local quasi-political social gatherings than in national or international politics.

Despite superficial differences in organization, the distribution of power in the two main parties is not substantially different and is centered on the parliamentary "front bench" of government and opposition. This does not mean that the business interests that support the Conservatives, or the trade unions that support the Labour party, are without influence; but they cannot bring direct pressure to bear through the party machinery.

It is interesting to examine the social composition of the members of Parliament for the two main parties. Among the Conservative members of the House of Commons in the postwar period the professions are well represented. The legal profession is the most heavily represented, followed by former officers of the armed services and businessmen. Employers and managers constitute one third of the Conservative party and one tenth of the Labour party. The occupations most frequently represented among Labour M.P.'s are trade-union officials, teachers, journalists, and lawyers. As would be expected, there are significant differences in education. The majority (83 per cent) of Conservative M.P.'s have been to one or another of the highly esteemed and exclusive public schools. Of these Eton is the school most frequently represented. Of Labour M.P.'s, 51 per cent have attended a state elementary school, leaving school at fourteen years of age; 26 per cent, a state secondary school; and 23 per cent, public schools, but rarely Eton or Harrow. Of Conservative M.P.'s, 63 per cent, and of Labour M.P.'s, 38 per cent have attended a university. Of the university-educated Conservatives, 79 per cent—compared with 40 per cent of the university-educated Labour members—have gone either to Oxford or Cambridge University.

Members of Parliament in Britain receive a relatively small salary (£1,000 a year) and very little in the way of expense allowances; only a few M.P.'s can afford a full-time secretary whom they would have to pay out of their own pocket. This means that the majority of members have to supplement their incomes, either by continuing part time in their profession or business, or if this is not possible, by journalism, broadcasting, and similar activities. This is a result of the tradition that M.P.'s were supposed to be persons of independent means, and that politics was not a career or full-time occupation. But this has long since ceased to be a reality; nowadays, when the two parties are evenly balanced, full-time attendance at the House of Commons is essential—and often incompatible with the maintenance of outside interests. Some M.P.'s receive a retaining fee from industrial or commercial concerns in return for their services as political advisers or as members of a board of directors, while certain Labour M.P.'s retain their trade-union office and salary.

The British Parliament, by means of the Cabinet system which ensures a strong executive, is a more powerful body than the American Congress, and it does not have to share its powers with a president or a court. At the same time, M.P.'s are less important individually than congressmen, and are sometimes compelled to subordinate their personal views on a political issue to the interests of the party machinery. Failure to "toe the party line" on an important issue may result in temporary or permanent expulsion from the party. Expulsion means that the member stands little chance of re-election to Parliament at the next poll, because—since the abolition of university seats—the chances of an independent being elected are negligible. The first qualification of a prospective M.P. is his ability to contribute a substantial sum to party funds in the district for which he stands, although he is not required to live in that district. This is particularly true of a Labour candidate unless he has the financial backing of the trade-union movement, for his party is more in need of funds than the Conservatives. Once an election has been declared, the amount which may be spent in campaigning by a candidate is governed by legislation and must be officially accounted for.

No reference has been made to the composition of the second chamber, the House of Lords, which is an integral part of Parliament. The House of Lords must first approve every measure that is passed, before the queen may give her assent. However, its power is limited by the fact that it cannot delay a "money" bill more than a month, and other bills for more than a year. Nevertheless, it performs a valuable revising function and a check on hasty legislation, although its influence invariably favors the Conservative party. At one time there was considerable discussion of reforming the House of Lords, but this is no longer advocated even by the Labour party. Although in theory the majority of peers (eight hundred in all, including all hereditary peers of England and Wales, sixteen hereditary peers of Scotland, and five of Ireland) are entitled to sit in the House of Lords, in practice only a limited number exercise this right; and those who take seats are often men of exceptional knowledge and experience in public affairs. Princes of royal blood, by convention, do not take any part in the proceedings. The remaining members are the law lords and the senior bishops of the Church of England (whose positions are not hereditary). In recent years an increasing number of trade unionists and members of the Labour party have accepted peerages as a reward for their long service to the country. As in the case of Earl Attlee, the institution of the House of Lords provides a useful means by which a man who wishes to retire from the strenuous life of party struggle in the House of Commons can still render valuable service to the country from his seat in the House of Lords. Some would argue that the hereditary principle should be dispensed with, and peers created for life only. However, it is typical that so long as those hereditary peers who have no claim to public distinction refrain from exercising their right to take part in the proceedings of the House, most people are prepared to let sleeping dogs lie.

It would not be appropriate to close the discussion of government and politics without referring to local government. At one time national party politics were of little significance in local government, but this is no longer the case. There is much less public interest in local elections than in national ones, but the same division between Conservative and Labour supporters tends to be observed. As in central government, the daily routine of local government in the counties and towns is in the hands of permanent officials, headed by the town clerk, who are independent of political changes. Town and county authorities are responsible for such varied matters as education, housing and planning, public health, highways, and police. Councilors are elected every three years and they elect a mayor annually, to preside over the council. Special committees deal with each of the main departments of local government. The council and its committees are responsible for formulating policies which are implemented by permanent local government officials, as in the civil service.

It is often suggested that participation in local government is a valuable experience in democratic self-government, but the apathy which the majority of people exhibit concerning local affairs does not support this contention. Nevertheless, 25 per cent of the Conservative M.P.'s and 55 per cent of the Labour M.P.'s have had previous experience on local or county councils.

The powers of local authorities have tended to diminish, relative to the central government. Local authorities cannot finance their services entirely from rates on property, and are dependent upon the national exchequer for about 60 per cent of their income. Financial assistance is accompanied by administrative control, which is also exercised in a number of other ways. A recent study of local government and central control, in five counties in the West Midland region of England, expresses concern at the effects of centralization in reducing the responsibility vested in local authorities and the decline of interest and enthusiasm of the electorate in local affairs.[11] Mention is also made of the tendency for local councilors to regard themselves as having a watching brief for the special interests of industrialists, trade unions, landowners, builders, and the like, rather than as democratic representatives of the community at large. While the influence of diverse interests and pressure groups is not confined to local government alone, the fact that it exists on the local level is another indication of public apathy and lack of official responsibility.

PUBLIC OPINION, THE PRESS, AND PRESSURE GROUPS

The term "public opinion" is used by sociologists in several different senses. There is, first of all, the control which is exercised over behavior by the desire to elicit the approval of others. In this sense public opinion exercises a powerful sanction, promoting conformity to each individual's conception of the approved norm of behavior. In Britain the majority of people are particularly sensitive to the attitudes and opinions of their neighbors and friends. "What would the neighbors think!" is a frequent response to any proposal involving a deviation from customary behavior. Fear of differing from the norm suggests an essentially extra-punitive attitude on many matters where the moral sanction has not been internalized. Conformity is ensured by sensitivity to public opinion.

A second sense in which the term "public opinion" is used derives from the activities of those who apply the technique of random sampling in order to gauge the state of opinion on a given subject. The "measurement" of attitudes has been reduced to a fine art by those employing social-survey techniques for market research, predicting election results, and studying attitudes to various subjects of social and political interest. In Britain, in addition to a number of commercial market-research organizations, the government has its own social survey—a department of the Central Office of Information—which uses sampling techniques in the collection of factual data and information on the public's attitude toward subjects of importance and interest to the government.

The British Institute of Public Opinion conducts polls on questions of social and political interest in domestic and foreign affairs. From these inquiries it is evident that a very large proportion of the public is ignorant of the facts concerning many important events of the day, especially in foreign affairs. It is possible to divide the population into three groups of roughly equal size: (1) those who are completely ignorant of the issues involved; (2) those who are aware of the question, but ill informed; (3) those who are reasonably well informed on the subject and ready to give an opinion. The proportion answering "Don't know" to questions concerning foreign affairs in a recent poll varied between 17 per cent and 79 per cent, and averaged 40 per cent of the sample.

An attempt has been made to assess the degree to which people are exposed to different "channels of communication," including primary groups and mass media, and its relation to age, sex, social status, and similar criteria. Based on investigations carried out in the Midland city of Derby, an "index of intercommunication" has been calculated which enables the different communication situations to be weighed and related to each individual's customary behavior.[12] The index ranges from 0 to 100. In Derby, which is probably typical of most of the country, the distribution of scores appears to follow a normal bimodal pattern, probably reflecting the fact that women had consistently lower scores than men, although the range and distribution were similar. Scores decreased with age and correlated with occupational status and with education, taken separately and together. Radio-listening and newspaper-reading were the only communicative activities widely dispersed throughout the population.

Used in a third sense, the term "public opinion" is connected with the sensitivity of politicians and administrators to the attitudes and opinions— including the prejudices—of a comparatively few influential persons. While susceptibility to an influence of this kind applies to foreign policy as well, it is particularly characteristic of domestic affairs—our immediate concern here. In a democratic society it is assumed that public opinion will have considerable influence upon the activities of politicians and those in positions of governmental authority and power. At least once in five years the British public has the opportunity of putting into power a government that will be elected on the basis of one man, one vote. But the voice of the people cannot be consulted in the detailed decisions that the government must make from day to day, because a considerable proportion of the population is not in a position to know the facts of the situation and probably could not understand them if it did. At the same time there is a limit to the margin of discretion which any politician has in a democratic society; he must have public approval for his decisions if he is to be returned at the next election. But he must particularly avoid doing anything that will bring disrepute upon himself or his party among the more responsible and better informed members of the public who are in a position to influence others.

Among these influential persons the proprietors, editors, subeditors, and leader writers of the principal newspapers rank high. The question whether the press merely reflects public opinion or actually creates it is really unanswerable. Certainly the relationship between a newspaper and its readers is a symbiotic one. The attitudes and opinions of the readers will undoubtedly be influenced by the content of newspapers; at the same time the policy and presentation of the newspaper must be responsive to the interests and views of its readers if its circulation and, therefore, its revenue —including that from advertising—are to be maintained.

There are a number of significant differences between newspapers in Britain and America. The majority of newspapers in the United Kingdom have a national coverage and consequently much larger circulations than their American counterparts. The paper with the largest circulation in the world is the Sunday *News of the World*, which has a circulation of over eight million copies. It specializes in reporting the sordid details of violent or sexual crimes and circumstantial accounts of divorce actions. The *Daily*

Mirror, with a circulation of four and a half million, and the *Daily Express*, with over four million, are the most popular dailies. In contrast the London *Times*, which is the most serious and intellectual daily paper in Britain, has only a circulation of just over 200,000 throughout Britain compared with the *New York Times* which has twice that sale, mainly in the New York area. In Britain 611 copies of daily newspapers are sold per 1,000 of population, compared with 353 in the United States. But American papers are much larger than British. For example, the *New York Times* has nearly 100 pages to the 16–24 of the London *Times*. However, a larger proportion (75 per cent) of newspaper content in America is devoted to advertising; in Britain the proportion is only 33 per cent. The report of a Royal Commission on the Press, published in 1949, concluded that there was no evidence that advertisers influenced the policies of the press; the policies expressed were those of the owners. Ownership is concentrated in five large press groups, each of which owns several newspapers. But the five "press lords" rival each other, and there is no monopoly. On the recommendation of the Commission, a General Council of the Press was set up to raise and maintain high standards of journalism. The mass-circulation papers devote a great deal of space to features designed to provide entertainment rather than enlightenment. When they endeavor to exercise an influence on the political opinions of their readers they are not always successful. This is evidenced by the overwhelming success of the Labour party in the 1945 election despite a press which was more than 75 per cent hostile.

At least as important as newspapers in the dissemination of news in Britain are radio and television, which are very different from the American equivalents. The British Broadcasting Corporation is a public body with a monopoly on sound broadcasting in the United Kingdom. It had a monopoly on television broadcasting until 1954, when the Independent Television Authority was established with power to provide television services from revenues provided by advertising. The revenues of the BBC are obtained from taxation through wireless licenses, and no advertising is allowed. The ITA works through program contractors, and time is sold to advertisers but they do not directly sponsor particular programs. The ITA is also subsidized by the state. The news programs of both the BBC and the ITA are strictly neutral and factual in content. Equal time is allotted to the main political parties for "party political broadcasts" (about one a month at the most). Controversial discussion on questions of political and social interest may be broadcast, so long as an opportunity is provided for all sides of a question to be presented and there is no breach of the "seven-day rule." The latter prevents any reference other than statements of fact to be made to a subject due to be debated in the House of Commons within seven days. (There is at present a "fourteen-day rule," but a "seven-day rule" has been recommended by a special committee.) News broadcasts and political discussions are a small part of the radio and television programs, the majority of which are devoted to entertainment.

The other media of mass communication influencing public opinion and attitudes are films, books, and magazines. Although all three are primarily sources of entertainment rather than information or education, documentary films are occasionally shown, some magazines feature current events or problems, and approximately 20 per cent of books read are nonfiction — mainly history, biography, and travel. An inquiry in 1950 showed that 55 per cent of the population were currently reading a book, compared with 21 per cent in the United States. In Britain book-reading is more popular with men than women, with the middle class than the working class, and with those under forty-five years than with older persons. This brief summary reflects, at least in part, the general pattern of exposure to communication activities.

Reference has been made to the fact that the majority of people in the United Kingdom, as in other countries, are relatively uninformed and comparatively apathetic with regard to political questions. It would be wrong to draw from this the conclusion that public opinion does not make itself felt in government circles. It does mean that this influence is exercised through the operation of special interest and pressure groups. The idea of pressure groups having power to influence government sometimes carries a sinister connotation, but this need not be the case if the means adopted to present the point of view of a particular group are entirely constitutional. Furthermore, not all pressure groups are selfishly pursuing their own interests. Some are concerned with the promotion of reforms, the prevention of injustice, and other humanitarian objectives from which the participants obtain no benefit. Among this type of pressure group must be included the many organizations that spontaneously take form to promote some currently popular cause, and seek to arouse public opinion and influence the government in the suppression of obscene publications and "horror comics"; in the prevention of racial discrimination, including opposition to the Central African Federation; and in the abolition of capital punishment. Less ephemeral organizations are those which are concerned with the prevention of cruelty to children and animals, the promotion of penal reform, the preservation of civil liberties, and similar causes.

Among the more powerful pressure groups directly promoting the interests of their members are those associated with industry and commerce, on the one hand, and with professional organizations, on the other. Most employers belong to the Federation of British Industries, which is the largest body of its kind, and/or the National Union of Manufacturers, the Association of British Chambers of Commerce, or the National Farmers' Union. The most powerful professional associations are those of the medical, legal, accountancy, and teaching professions. Most other employees belong to trade unions which in their turn are affiliated with the Trades Union Congress. The organization of industry, commerce, and labor has been discussed. In addition to providing advisory and other services to their members, all these organizations regard it as part of their responsibility to make representations from time to time to the government. It should be noted that neither the employers' organizations nor the Trades Union Congress is directly connected with any political party, although their constituent members may be. Nevertheless, it is not surprising that the views and policies of the Federation of British Industries, for example, normally coincide with those of the Conservative party while those of the Trades Union Congress are usually in agreement with the Labour party.

Concern is sometimes expressed at the actual or potential power of private capital in Britain and in other Western countries. Studies of the operation of pressure groups representing private-capital interests in the United Kingdom suggest that while the potential power of private capital—for example, to sabotage a nationalization scheme implemented by the Labour party—is considerable, its actual practical influence in the past has been restrained and limited. There is no evidence of bribery or corruption on any scale, and such pressure as has been exercised on governments in the past has been constitutional in character. While a democratically elected government can, if it wishes, impose its policies on an industry—however opposed that industry may be to them—and while there is always a reasonable chance of a change of government in the future, private-capital interests find it expedient to operate through constitutional channels. However, it must be recognized that a combination of wealth and effective organization enables private capital to influence public opinion by propaganda, and parliamentary action by its close association with the Conservative party.

CHRISTIANITY AND OTHER BELIEFS

In most societies religion is an important agent of social control. Britain is nominally a Christian country, but only a small proportion of the population regularly participates in the ritual observances of institutionalized Christianity. It has been estimated that 58 per cent of the total population of the United States are actual members of a religious denomination. The equivalent is 17 per cent for England and Wales, 45 per cent for Scotland, and 60 per cent for Northern Ireland. These figures are misleading because they exclude people who attend a place of worship without becoming members of any denomination. Furthermore, church membership and attendance is best related to the adult rather than the total population. Full membership of the main denominational groupings in the United Kingdom is shown in Table 22. If we abstracted the figure for Wales alone, it would show a considerably higher percentage membership than that for England.

Although only 23 per cent of the adult population of England claim to be full members of religious denominations, 75 per cent are nominally attached to one of the churches; only 7 per cent do not attend church, even for weddings or funerals. The number calling themselves "Church of Eng-

Table 22. Membership of Religious Denominations in the United Kingdom (estimated)

Denomination	England and Wales*	Scotland*	Northern Ireland†
Church of England (Episcopal or Anglican) ...	3,161,500	56,400	337,000
Presbyterian	229,300	1,309,100	410,000
Methodist	730,600	13,000	
Baptist	313,000	20,000	
Congregational	230,000	35,000	*85,000*‡
Unitarian	20,000	1,000	
Other free churches	484,700	76,700	
All Protestant	5,169,100	1,511,200	899,000
Roman Catholic	2,034,600	505,200	471,000
Jewish	430,000	20,000	....
Total	7,633,700	2,036,400	1,370,000

Source: The author acknowledges with thanks permission to use statistics in this table referring to Christian church membership in Scotland and in England and Wales, which are based upon material collected by Dr. John Highet and published in *The Scottish Economy*, edited by A. K. Cairncross (Cambridge: The University Press, 1954).

*Full or "communicating" members excluding nominal adherents or occasional worshipers.

†All, including nominal adherents (Census, 1951).

‡This figure is the total for five groups: Methodist, Baptist, Congregational, Unitarian, and other free churches.

land" has been variously estimated at between 50 and 60 per cent. The Church of England has a unique position in relation to the community and the state, as it is "by law established" in England but not in the rest of the United Kingdom. The Presbyterian Church of Scotland is "established" in Scotland. There is no established church in Wales or Northern Ireland. The "establishment" of the Church of England means that there is a close connection between the state and the Church, although the state pays nothing to the Church, nor are the Anglican clergy state servants. The prime minister (who may be of any denomination) appoints the bishops, and certain ecclesiastical officers are appointed by other secular officials. The archbishops and twenty-six senior bishops sit in the House of Lords. The Prayer Book, which is the approved liturgical form of worship, is subject to the approval of Parliament, and an attempt to revise the Prayer Book in 1928 was rejected by the House of Commons. Nevertheless, the report of a church-appointed commission on church-state relations in 1952 was opposed to disestablishment and was unanimously accepted by the Church Assembly, which is the governing body of the Church of England.

After the Church of England the largest denominational group in England are the Methodists, who constitute 10 per cent of all those claiming some religious adherence. They are followed by Roman Catholics (8 per cent), and by a large number of smaller nonconformist sects (3 per cent), including Baptists and Congregationalists, while Jews account for less than 1 per cent. Regular churchgoers (once a week or more) constitute about 15 per cent of the population, and attendance is more frequent among women, among rural dwellers, among older people, and among single and widowed rather than married people. In one inquiry just over half the parents studied sent their children to Sunday school, but few people in Britain believe in hell or the devil, and only about half consider that there is any kind of life after death.

For many people in Britain, religion is ceasing to be a matter of ritual observance and is becoming a vague affirmation of Christian ethical principles. It is a matter of controversy whether these principles can be instilled in the rising generation without reference to the religious faith which has provided their foundation in the past. Among intellectuals there is an increasing tendency to embrace an agnostic humanism and to reject theism. Many middle- and working-class people refrain from participation in public worship except for certain rituals such as baptism, weddings, and funerals, which carry with them a strong social sanction in addition to their religious implications. About a third of the population falls into this category.

At the same time there is evidence of a widespread spiritual uneasiness and psychological insecurity. In 1943 it was correctly asserted that there was then no demand in England for the old-fashioned, hell-fire, fundamentalist preacher of the type still popular in parts of America. Yet in 1954 it was possible for an American evangelist to sweep through Britain in a campaign of religious revivalism which made an immediate impact on all social classes. His public meetings were a subject of discussion and controversy from the factory bench to the senior common rooms of the universities. But the impact was not lasting; many rejected his biblical fundamentalism while others responded mainly to his personal magnetism.

Psychological insecurity is evident in the frequency with which many people admit to superstitious beliefs and practices. One investigation revealed that about 80 per cent of women and 60 per cent of men read horoscopes, and that 33 per cent of women and 18 per cent of men apparently took them seriously and followed their advice. It appeared that those most inclined to accept a magical view of the universe—implied by fortunetelling of various kinds—were also the most fervent in their practice of religion, while those who were skeptical about fortunetelling were the least religious in belief and practice. The only exception to this appeared to be in the use of wartime mascots which were owned by a considerable number of servicemen irrespective of their religious or magical beliefs.

There are a number of pseudoreligious organizations, some of a semisecret nature, which provide a source of security and social solidarity for certain people. Among them the Freemasons are probably the largest group. Their activities and ritual observances have been the object of attack and criticism by some of the clergy, but are defended by others who are themselves Freemasons.

Institutionalized religion in England has ceased to perform a socially integrating function. To a lesser extent this also applies to Scotland, Wales, and Northern Ireland. No secular belief or political ideology has replaced religion, as in totalitarian countries. The result is a widespread malaise, the symptoms of which closely resemble *anomie.* The problem of maladjustment and its treatment has become important in twentieth-century Britain, as it has in other societies with advanced cultures.

Family, Socialization, and Personality

REGULATION OF SEX RELATIONS

From infancy onward the social roles of male and female are clearly differentiated, although — as in American and other societies with advanced cultures — the emancipation of women at the beginning of the twentieth century has meant a narrowing of the role and status differences between the sexes. Nevertheless, throughout life distinctive clothing is worn, and transvestism is frowned upon in women and regarded as a criminal offense for men. Male homosexuality is also a serious criminal offense which arouses considerable moral indignation in the minds of many people. At the same time, some feel that the law concerning homosexuality in the United Kingdom is too harsh in its attitude toward a behavior which is increasingly understood to have its origins in biopsychological disturbances requiring medical rather than penal treatment. The home secretary has appointed an expert committee to examine the question.

Apparently, a clear demarcation of the sexual roles is deeply embedded in the normal personality. At the same time, the popularity in Britain of male and female impersonators, the traditional reversal of the male and female roles in theatrical pantomime, and the interest of the popular press in cases of homosexuality and transvestism, suggest that there are unconscious tendencies toward bisexualism. Effeminate tendencies in men and masculinity in women are strongly disapproved. Women are expected to be the more decorative sex, wearing bright colors and using cosmetics, which are taboo for the male. Men's clothes are dull in color and standardized in style. The physical appearance of a man is of less importance than his social standing, but an ideal man is one who exhibits some athletic prowess.

The role and status of men and women in relation to one another have undergone considerable modification, and the ideal of the Victorian middle-class paterfamilias with his meek, submissive wife has completely disappeared. At the same time the feminine character today shows signs of an incomplete adjustment. Women tend to be torn between a desire to establish a home and have children and a desire to compete on equal terms with men in the economic system. This is particularly true of women who have received a higher education or training for a profession before marriage. The shortage of domestic servants also adds to the difficulty of combining the roles of career woman and housewife.

Marriage is the principal social institution concerned with the regulation

110

of sex relations. Legally, in the United Kingdom, it need only be ratified by the civil authorities, but convention demands that in the large majority of cases a religious ceremony should also be held. The ideal pattern of sexual behavior, from which there is considerable deviation, requires premarital chastity and postmarital fidelity from men and women alike. Table 23 shows the marital status of the population.

As in all societies, the incest taboo is rigidly enforced; but there are no other exogamous rules apart from the relics of ecclesiastical prohibitions. However, there is a marked endogamous tendency in that a person is encouraged to marry within his own race, nationality, religion, education, social status, and age group. There are no absolute barriers to marriage outside these limits, but disapproval may be strongly expressed, especially against interracial marriages. The partners to and children of a mixed racial marriage are likely to experience manifestations of severe prejudice from members of their own family and community.

At the two extremes of the socioeconomic status scale there is little social-status mobility by marriage, but in intermediate groups—especially among skilled manual workers—there is less rigidity. More women than men marry upwards in the social scale, but in 71.6 per cent of the marriages the level of education of husband and wife is the same. There is some evidence that in Scotland women who are upwardly mobile in social status are more physically fit, have fewer complications in pregnancy, and have heavier babies.

The relationships of husband and wife are governed by certain legal minimum requirements, and failure to fulfill these obligations may provide grounds for nullity or divorce. Beyond the legal minimums the pattern of sexual and domestic behavior of the couple after marriage varies considerably according to social status and subculture. Studies of marriage and the family have been neglected in Britain, and existing information tends to be unreliable or applicable only to particular groups who may not be

Table 23. Marital Status of the Population in the United Kingdom (in thousands)

Status	England and Wales (1951)		Scotland (1951)		Northern Ireland (1937)	
	Men	Women	Men	Women	Men	Women
Single	9,168	9,222	1,225	1,265	389	387
Married	11,002	11,112	1,111	1,132	209	215
Widowed or divorced	809	2,432	102	261	25	54

Source: Royal Commission on Marriage and Divorce, Cmd. 9678.

typical. Various studies draw attention to the frequency of sexual maladjustment between husband and wife, emphasizing the failure among wives of all social classes to achieve a satisfying orgasmic experience. Birth-control measures are taken by more than half of all married couples, although a much smaller proportion use the contraceptive method recommended by the medical profession. As a consequence more than 50 per cent of the children born are unplanned, although not necessarily unwanted.

The domestic roles and relationships of husband and wife are influenced by social status, region or locality, and individual personality factors. The evidence from one inquiry suggests that in the South of England husbands tend to look for desirable qualities of personality in their wives, while in the North domestic skill is more often mentioned as a virtue. There are some households where the husband does no domestic work whatsoever, even if his wife is also employed outside the home, and others where there is an equal division of household labor. About 60 per cent of women remain in employment after marriage until the birth of the first child; less than 10 per cent are at work before their second confinement.

There are certain differences between the laws relating to marriage and divorce in England and Scotland. In Scotland a person may marry without parents' consent or the authority of a magistrate's court if both parties are over sixteen, whereas the consent of parents or a court is required in England up to the age of twenty-one. This sometimes leads to elopements by young English couples who cross the border into Scotland to get married. There are also minor differences in the law concerning nullity and divorce, but these are likely to be removed in the near future.

Subject to certain provisions regarding knowledge of the facts by the petitioner before the marriage, in England and Wales a marriage may be declared null and void if a proper ceremony has not been performed; if either party is under sixteen years of age; if the parties are within certain prohibited degrees of relationship by blood or affinity; if either party has been married before and that marriage is valid and still subsisting; if either party is insane at the time of the marriage or mentally defective; if there is true lack of consent by reason of duress or mistake; if there is willful refusal to consummate the marriage; if the respondent was suffering from communicable venereal disease or was pregnant by another man at the time of the marriage.

The only ground for divorce in the United Kingdom is the commission of a "matrimonial offense" without the collusion of the applicant. Offenses include adultery, cruelty, desertion for three years or more, insanity, and sodomy or bestiality. A recent Royal Commission on Marriage and Divorce suggested minor amendments in the law but rejected any alteration in principle. It would not consider recommending the option of either party —after either a period of separation or the complete breakdown of the marriage—without the commission of one of the above offenses, as sufficient ground for divorce. It was pointed out to the Commission that trumped-up evidence of adultery is sometimes produced in a deliberate attempt to deceive the court when husband and wife both desire to end the marriage relationship. However, the Royal Commission reasoned that the frequency with which collusion takes place is exaggerated, and it persisted in its refusal to countenance any proposal that might make divorce easier.

The incidence of divorce petitions in the United Kingdom is shown in Table 24. Prior to the Matrimonial Causes Act of 1939 it was not possible to obtain a divorce in Northern Ireland. The incidence of divorce in England and Wales increased from 0.1 per thousand of the total population in 1935 to 0.67 in 1953. In the same period in Scotland divorce increased from 0.1 per thousand of the total population to 0.46. Before the war 1.5 per cent of marriages ended in divorce, whereas today the figure is nearer 6.7 per cent in England and Wales and 4.9 per cent in Scotland. These figures partly reflect changes in legislation and the availability of legal aid. At the same time they parallel the increase in divorce rates in America and other countries in the postwar period.

In 1953 the highest divorce rate in England and Wales—56.6 per thousand married women—was that for women under the age of 25 who had been married between seven and ten years. This compared with 4.5 per

Table 24. Incidence of Divorce Petitions in the United Kingdom in 1950

Item	England and Wales	Scotland	Northern Ireland
Married Population	22,034,000	2,247,000	258,000*
Petitions filed	29,096	2,216	154
Petitions filed per 10,000 of married population	13.21	9.86	6.0
Percentage of increase in 1937–50 period			
Married population	18	18	...
Petitions filed	406	245	...
Rate per 10,000 married population	329	193	...

Source: Royal Commission on Marriage and Divorce, Cmd. 9678.
*Estimated.

thousand for women aged between 30 and 34 years, married for the same length of time. The equivalent rates for Scotland were 43.5 per thousand and 3.2 per thousand. Apparently the higher rate for younger women reflects the combined risks of an early marriage and marriage in wartime.

Concern with the postwar increase in divorce is centered mainly on the detrimental effects of divorce upon the welfare of children, but the fact that an unhappy home can also lead to maladjustment in the children is sometimes overlooked.

In an attempt to prevent marriage failure a number of voluntary organizations provide marriage guidance, and offer both education for marriage and advice when difficulty occurs afterwards. Probation officers of local courts also undertake reconciliation work. It should be mentioned that in Britain it is possible for a wife to obtain a legal separation order together with an order for maintenance if she is judged the innocent party, but a legal separation does not permit either party to remarry. In England and Wales the rate of legal separation is approximately 0.2 per thousand of the population.

The incidence of divorce is not the only evidence of deviation from the ideal cultural norm. Although no investigation as comprehensive as that of Kinsey in the United States has been undertaken in the United Kingdom, the information at present available suggests that approximately 50 per cent of men and 30–40 per cent of women experience premarital sex relations. Whether in all cases this experience involves actual intercourse is not entirely clear. As in America, there is some evidence that intense petting not involving a technical break of virginity is practiced among middle- and upper-class youth. That in many cases sexual intercourse does take place is proved by the incidence of premarital conceptions and illegitimacy. The over-all rate of illegitimacy has remained more or less constant at about 5 per cent of all births, but since 1949 there has been an increase in the proportion of illegitimacy among girls under twenty years of age. The stigma attached to an unmarried mother is such that every endeavor is made to bring about marriage with the putative father. As a consequence, about a third of all girls marrying under the age of twenty are pregnant at the time. Studies of attitudes toward premarital sex relations show that many people who have such experience feel guilty and regret their behavior afterwards. Nevertheless, in one inquiry half of those questioned approved premarital sex experience for men and a third approved it for women.

The double standard of morality which condones premarital sex relations for men but not for women still exists, although it appears to be declining. Its existence provides part of the explanation for the fact that female prostitution flourishes. Other contributory factors appear to be the anonymity of town life which enables unmarried men, men separated from their wives, and those whose marital relations are unsatisfactory to obtain sexual gratification in circumstances which have no emotional involvement. Female prostitution, as such, is not illegal in the United Kingdom, although in certain cities soliciting in the street is prohibited by bylaws and may incur a maximum penalty of £2. The streetwalker is the lowest in the status hierarchy of prostitutes. Among the higher ranks are those who pay an annual rent of £1,000 for a flat in the West End of London and have a regular clientele among the wealthier men in the metropolis. One property owner is known to draw an income of £30,000 a year from one block of flats let to prostitutes. Keeping a brothel and "living off immoral earnings" are offenses, but letting a self-contained flat to a prostitute is an ordinary business transaction which incurs no penalty in law. It has been estimated that there are some sixty to seventy thousand professional prostitutes in Britain, including some ten thousand in London. Although economic gain provides one motive for entering prostitution, it appears that—apart from a minority who are brought up in the trade by their mothers—many prostitutes are psychologically disturbed or suffering from a glandular imbalance which creates abnormal sexual desires. Others have been forced into prostitution after being rejected by their families and by society as a consequence of having an illegitimate child.

The gap between accepted ideals of premarital chastity and postmarital fidelity and actual practice creates guilt feelings, and the problem is aggravated by the prudery which still surrounds the free discussion of sexual questions. Efforts to ensure proper sex education in schools and youth clubs are gaining wider currency, but few parents are willing to assume the responsibility of giving proper advice and instruction. As a result many young people obtain their knowledge from undesirable sources and enter marriage inadequately prepared.

KINSHIP, COMMUNITY, AND THE HOME

As in other societies with advanced cultures, the wider kinship system does not have the social significance that it has in less complex cultures. Many functions of the family and the kinship group in primitive societies are now performed by other social institutions, such has the formal education system and the elaborate economic and political institutions that have been described. In both the United Kingdom and the United States, the family may be described as an open, multilineal conjugal system. In many cases the British family shares with its American counterpart the isolation of the conjugal unit which results from a separate household being established—sometimes geographically at a distance—apart from the parental home and the homes of other members of the extended family. Nevertheless, recent investigations have drawn attention to the fact that in rural areas, in certain long-established working-class neighborhoods in London, and in industrial areas in the Midlands and the North the extended kinship system is of considerable social and even economic significance in the lives of its members. The tie between mother and daughter appears to be particularly strong, and there is a tendency toward matrilocalism. Consequently old people in such neighborhoods are not so isolated as they may be elsewhere. They frequently perform services for their children, especially in connection with the care of grandchildren. Thus they have the satisfactions of companionship and communication with the various members of their family, and many receive financial assistance if needed. When poorer working-class neighborhoods in urban areas are broken up in the course of official rehousing programs the consequent problems of adjustment are sometimes serious.

Apart from relationships with members of the kinship group, interaction between people living in the same urban area depends upon several factors, among which the social stratification and ethnic composition of the locality are the most important. Immigrants, whether from another part of the United Kingdom or from overseas, tend to withdraw into their own social groups, thereby retaining barriers to communication and reinforcing existing unfavorable stereotypes and prejudices. This applies most acutely to Jewish and colored immigrants. In neighborhoods of relative ethnic homogeneity social-status differences are of greater significance. In a suburban district inhabited mainly by middle-class people there is a minimum of overt interaction between neighbors, although there may be underlying good will which manifests itself in emergencies. In neighborhoods where different social classes are mixed, a distinction frequently arises between housewives who are constantly "popping in and out" of their neighbors' houses and those who "keep themselves to themselves." The latter often have higher status aspirations and look down upon the more gre-

116

garious, who, in their turn, tend to scorn the "snobbishness" of the reserved.

Although more evidence is required before the hypothesis is finally established, an interesting connection has been suggested pertaining to conjugal role-differentiation between husband and wife in the home and the character of their social relationships outside the home. Studies in various parts of London appear to support the view that when the domestic roles of husband and wife are clearly segregated, so that neither will undertake or assist the other in duties that are held to be individual responsibilities, it is probable that they will move socially within a narrow circle, most of whose members are acquainted with one another. In contrast, when husband and wife share domestic responsibilities to a greater extent, they have a wider circle, including acquaintances who are not connected with one another. This association appears to be only indirectly related to social status. Families with tightly connected networks of friends and acquaintances are likely to be in the working class because it is only in long-established working-class areas that there is a concentration of people with similar occupational background and little physical or social mobility. But not all working-class families—and very few in the professional classes —concern themselves with belonging to any widely extended network.

Attempts in Britain to promote artificially a sense of community by planning urban neighborhoods as self-contained units have not proved successful. The setting up of a community center with facilities for communal recreation is no guarantee that the center will be used. Much depends upon the age distribution and social status of the inhabitants. Clubs and community centers are appreciated by the young and the old, but married couples with families have little time for communal activities. The most successful adult clubs are the workingmen's clubs in the older established urban districts in the Midlands and the North. These are primarily regarded as alternatives to the public house, as places for a drink and a game of billiards or darts. On weekends popular entertainment is offered, and on these occasions wives are admitted. The planning of neighborhood units in new housing areas has benefited from studies of the convenience of location in terms of traveling time and distance, but the preoccupation of postwar town planning in Britain with a sentimental notion of communities and neighborhoods has proved somewhat abortive. This appears to have been due to an idealized impression of rural village life which emphasized social solidarity to the exclusion of conflict and tension.

SOCIALIZATION AND EDUCATION OF CHILDREN

Reference has been made to the extensive social services available in the field of child welfare, which are used by a wide cross section of the population. Doctors and clinics give advice on the care of infants, although there is a tendency for mothers to be confused by the changing fashions and views of the medical profession on questions such as toilet training and weaning. The majority of parents consider that toilet training should start before the child is one year of age, and more than half suggest within six months of birth. Poorer working-class families tend to be less strict.

The father is generally the prime source of discipline in the home, although his absence during a large part of the day means that this responsibility is frequently delegated to the mother. In some cases the mother may shirk this responsibility and "You wait until your father comes home" is not an uncommon threat. There is little belief in childish innocence, and it is generally considered that children are wild and that their unruly tendencies must be curbed in their own interests and those of others. The view that children should be encouraged to give free expression to their feelings — that more harm than good will result from suppressing antisocial tendencies — has little support among parents in the United Kingdom. Most parents consider that children require more rather than less discipline, and are anxious to eradicate the aggressive impulses for which children find expression in the destruction of property, cruelty to animals or other children, and any inclination to defy their parents. In middle- and upper-class homes parental discipline tends to be reasonably consistent and in accord with the standards inculcated at school. But among poorer working-class families discipline tends to be more erratic, and the standards demanded at home may conflict with the stricter demands of the school.

There are some significant differences in attitudes toward discipline — particularly regarding appropriate methods of punishment — between the South of England and the North. The contrast is even more marked if England is compared with Scotland. In the South of England there is widespread objection by parents to all forms of corporal punishment for boys or girls, although caning is disapproved less than other forms of physical punishment. In English schools the use of corporal punishment has by no means disappeared, but in state schools its use is closely regulated and infrequent. By contrast, in Scotland corporal punishment does not appear to be opposed by parents, and its use in schools is almost universal. A Scottish schoolteacher nearly always carries a "tawse" or leather strap in the hand which is used on children of all ages and both sexes for disciplinary purposes and occasionally for bad work. The majority of schoolteachers in England consider that corporal punishment should be retained, but that its use should be restricted to occasions when other forms of discipline have failed. In Scotland the majority of teachers consider that the use of the tawse is an essential prerequisite of order in the classroom.

In a study of the childhood experiences and subsequent personality development of a group of children from a London slum compared with a number of children of very wealthy parents, attention was drawn to the fact that American subcultural differences do not correspond with findings in England.[13] For example, one American investigation revealed that a middle-class group compared with a white working-class group completed bladder training earlier, weaned later, and required children to help in the house later. Another American inquiry came to the conclusion that children in an underprivileged group received more consistent discipline and were more secure than the overprivileged. A third study suggested that emotional problems are relatively more prominent in the upper classes, and that an upper-class environment is especially hard on a boy and a lower-class environment on a girl. On all these points reverse conclusions were reached in the study of "deprived" and "privileged" children in England.

An experience of indulgence in infancy followed by comparative neglect and emotional rejection when the child reaches the "toddler" stage, or on the arrival of another infant, is not uncommon among poorer working-class families. In overcrowded urban slums a child who constantly cries is a source of irritation to husband and neighbors, and must be pacified at all costs. As the child gets older it becomes more of a nuisance in the house, and is soon encouraged to play with other small children in the street. At this stage the child probably begins to feel distinctly unwanted by the mother, and this feeling of rejection may have important consequences on subsequent behavioral and personality adjustment. One reaction to the ambivalent attitudes toward parents appears to be a tendency to create idealized parent images and project hostility onto a convenient outgroup.

A traumatic experience of separation and rejection also appears to be common among children of families at the opposite end of the socioeconomic status scale, although this rejection is usually experienced when the child is older. Children of the upper and upper middle classes, often cared for in infancy by a professional "nanny," are similar to deprived working-class children in that they do not grow up in an atmosphere of emotional warmth. Positive feelings of rejection are not likely to occur until the child is sent to a residential preparatory school, often at the age of eight years. Neither the "deprived" nor the "privileged" groups can be regarded as numerically typical of the population at large. In the majority of working-class and middle-class homes a child is less likely to experience a markedly traumatic experience of rejection, although toilet training and other disciplinary measures, necessary as the child grows older, will generate ambivalent feelings toward the parents.

The strain involved in the relationships between one generation and another is aggravated by rapid social change, and results in the internalization of conflicting norms and values. It is one manifestation of a lack of integration in the social system and inconsistencies in the culture pattern. Adolescence, in particular, tends to be a critical period in the adjustment of the individual to his social environment in most advanced cultures. A number of writers have drawn attention to the existence in the United States of a characteristic adolescent subculture that emphasizes independence of—and antagonism to—adult expectations and authority, compulsive conformity to the peer group, and excessive romanticism. Some doubt has been thrown upon the universality of this pattern, even in the United States. In one American suburban town studied, the children of upper-middle-class parents appeared to exhibit less rejection and a greater internalization of adult values than has previously been regarded as typical. The pattern in all social classes in the United Kingdom appears to correspond closely with the latter findings. Compared with American youth there is less pressure on the adolescent to revolt against the older generation and more pressure to conform to it. Marked rebellion is typical of a delinquent minority but should not be regarded as a norm. Young people are expected to, and usually do, pay attention to the demands and opinions of their elders. The Victorian adage that a child should be seen and not heard, is no longer rigidly enforced, but respect for elders and conformity to their wishes is still regarded as a virtue.

Despite the fact that adolescence appears to be less a period of "storm and stress" in Britain than in the United States, there is nevertheless evidence that adjustment at this age is not always satisfactory. For boys, the period from their leaving school until some time after national service is completed appears to be a difficult one, particularly with regard to vocational adjustment. The same applies to girls during the period between leaving school and marriage. Restlessness and apathy are traits frequently noted among boys and girls at this age. Reference has been made to the growth of juvenile delinquency and crime. Equally disturbing is the increase in suicides and attempted suicides under twenty years of age. In 1953–54 the rate was two-thirds higher for girls and four times higher for boys than in 1938, being 2.2 and 4.0 per 10,000 respectively.

An investigation carried out in London among eighteen-year-old boys immediately before their period of national service showed that although the majority were physically fit, many exhibited emotional insecurity and appeared to derive little satisfaction from their work or leisure activities. The least well adjusted conveyed an impression of passively accepting the world around them, and exhibited anxiety with regard to their relationships at home and at work. Although there are many exceptions to these generalizations, the over-all picture is confirmed in studies of other cities.

Reference has been made in a previous section to the relation between formal education and the class structure in England and Wales. Although the pattern has been modified to some extent by the Education Act of 1944, it is still true to say that the education experience of the average child is likely to be markedly different from that of a child whose parents are sufficiently wealthy to enable them to purchase the type of education provided by expensive boarding schools. The outstanding features of the latter type of school are their exclusive character and the homogeneity of their pupils from the point of view of parental social status; the smallness of the classes and consequent possibility of individual instruction; their residential character so that the children experience communal corporate life at an early age; the segregation of the sexes; the emphasis upon the classics in education, and until very recently, a comparative neglect of science; the large amount of time devoted to participation in sports of various kinds, and the importance placed upon success in this field as a factor in molding character and developing qualities of leadership and "team spirit"; the organization of the school into "houses" which are competitive in sports and other activities; the institution of a prefect system whereby senior pupils are largely responsible for maintaining discipline, sometimes with the aid of corporal punishment; and finally the stamp which the school leaves on the personality of its pupils, and the sense of loyalty to "the old school tie" which is carried into later business and professional life. Less than 3 per cent of the population receive this type of education. Many of the pupils from these schools proceed to either Oxford or Cambridge

University and complete their education when about twenty-two years old.

In contrast to the experience of the privileged minority about 85 per cent of the population attend a state primary school, followed by what is now called a secondary modern school, and complete their education at fifteen years. These schools are free and nonresidential; some are coeducational; and pupils are representative of a wide cross section of working- and middle-class parents. Classrooms tend to be overcrowded and the schools understaffed and poorly equipped, although in recent years a number of new schools have been built which are up to the highest standards. Those who proceed to a secondary modern school are of average and below average intelligence. The boys among them later take up occupations, classified as skilled, semiskilled, or unskilled, which are mainly manual rather than professional or administrative, while the girls enter clerical or manual work of some kind.

At the best modern schools real efforts are made to provide a curriculum which is both interesting and useful in later life, but many fail to achieve this aim. As a result the last years at school are often burdensome to the pupil who is anxious to leave and begin earning a living. Largely because of lack of equipment or playing fields, sports—with the possible exception of association football for boys and net-ball or hockey for girls—do not play a very important part in school life, and there is not the same corporate feeling of identification with the school that is found in boarding schools.

Between the boarding and the secondary modern schools are the free state secondary grammar schools which are attended by approximately 12 per cent of the population. At the age of eleven, pupils in the primary schools are given an examination which selects—on the basis of intelligence and educational attainment—those who may enter a secondary grammar school. In certain respects state grammar schools have consciously imitated the boarding schools in their bias, now less pronounced than formerly, toward the classics, the use of house and prefect systems, and the encouragement given to sports. Only a few are coeducational. They differ from the boarding schools in not being residential; in the wider variety of social status and background of the parents; and in the smaller proportion of staff to pupils. In recent years they have devoted more time to the teaching of science subjects. This particular development has been limited, however, by the existence of secondary art and technical schools which draw a minority of children having good intelligence but a definite bias toward practical rather than academic interests. Some children leave grammar school at the minimum age of fifteen, but the majority remain to take a general certificate of education at sixteen years. Since the institution of national service a larger proportion now remain for a further two years to take a higher certificate.

Between 3 and 4 per cent of the population receive a university education, and these are almost exclusively drawn from the ranks of those who take a higher certificate of education at a secondary grammar school or who come from one of the boarding schools. Through adult education, at evening classes run by the local authority, and through private study men or women who have attended a secondary modern school occasionally succeed in winning a place in a university, but this is unusual. As we have seen, it will be even more unusual in the future, since as a result of the Education Act of 1944, fewer working-class children are now deprived of a grammar school education because their parents cannot afford it. A high academic standard is demanded of all those attending a university, and a stiff entrance examination must be passed by all students whether they are winners of scholarships and grants or whether they pay fees. In fact about 80 per cent of the students in English and Welsh universities receive some assistance toward fees and maintenance from a local authority or other source, compared with 57 per cent in Scotland. Some students take jobs during the vacation period, but only a few work their way through a university in the American fashion.

There are a number of other differences between the educational system of Scotland and that of England and Wales. Not all state-provided education in Scotland is free. Apart from Edinburgh, which is an exception, a smaller proportion of Scottish pupils attend schools outside the state system. A larger proportion of pupils leave school at the minimum school-leaving age of fifteen. However, of those who remain at school a higher proportion probably proceed to a university because the proportion of university students is higher in Scotland. But since some Scottish students go to England and some English students go to Scotland, this conclusion cannot be regarded as definite.

Universities in Britain may be divided into two categories. There are the ancient universities of Oxford and Cambridge, based upon the college system and with a high proportion of students resident in college, i.e., in American terminology, resident on a campus. In Scotland all the universities are of ancient origin. The remaining English and Welsh universities are of the civic variety. Established in the later nineteenth or early twentieth century, they have little attraction for the products of the boarding schools and are more dependent upon the grammar schools for pupils. Some students are drawn from the immediate locality and continue to live with their families, while others obtain lodgings in the town. As a consequence the corporate life of the university is much less conspicuous, and there is no equivalent of the American "Greek letter" societies. Such extracurricular activities as exist tend to be connected with special interests, particularly sports, hobbies, academic subjects, or politics.

The universities in Britain are increasingly dependent upon the state for financial support, although they have private endowments. In order to preserve the independence of the universities and to minimize state control or interference, the sum granted by the Treasury for universities is allocated by a special University Grants Committee on which the universities have majority representation. The universities are singularly free from outside control or interference in any form, being largely governed by the academic staff and the graduates of the university in a democratic fashion. They are jealous of their privileges and the fact that they are the upholders of a long tradition of academic and political freedom.

Full-time attendance at a university is not the only avenue to a higher education or vocational training. Although only 3 or 4 per cent go to a university, twice this number have some kind of professional or technical qualification. The University of London has a system whereby a student can take an "external" degree by studying at home or attending evening classes. The standards of the London external examinations for degree are as high as those of the internal examinations. Furthermore, the majority of teachers in primary schools do not go to a university but attend a teachers' training college for two years, usually after taking a higher school-leaving certificate at a grammar school. Qualifications for such professions as law, accountancy, architecture, engineering, and commerce can be obtained in a university, or by means of "articles." This is the professional equivalent of the skilled tradesman's apprenticeship by which practical experience in an office is combined with private study or attendance at part-time courses, and the passing of qualifying examinations set by the professional association concerned. This is sometimes to be preferred to university training, which may be unduly academic and often has to be followed by practical experience before final qualification.

Local education authorities provide technical courses which students attend in the evening; some employers release their young apprentices for a period each week to attend day courses in technical subjects. It has been estimated that 75 per cent of boys and 45 per cent of girls leaving school at fifteen in 1954 continued their education in full or part-time classes for the first year or two but that the proportion falls rapidly after the age of eighteen. Some vocational training is provided for boys during national service.

Finally, the Workers' Educational Association and the universities cooperate in providing extramural courses in nonvocational subjects. Although attended by people of different social backgrounds, these courses are most popular in the present day among middle-aged teachers and housewives who already have some higher education.

NATIONAL CHARACTER AND PERSONALITY IN RELATION TO SUBCULTURE

The large and heterogeneous population of an advanced culture is such that it is almost impossible to find any characteristics of personality and behavior which can be properly regarded as "national." The above account of the socialization and education of children has drawn attention to a few of the marked subcultural differences in the upbringing of children in Britain. It is hardly surprising to find considerable diversity of character when parental attitudes toward discipline and child care vary so much and children at school are deliberately differentiated and segregated on a basis of age, sex, intelligence, vocational interest, and the social status of their parents. It is likely that a more fruitful approach would be in terms of subculture rather than over-all national character. Unfortunately, inquiries that have been undertaken have not been sufficiently detailed to enable the formulation of any reliable generalizations. No systematic studies have been made, for example, of the undoubted differences among the English, Welsh, Irish, and Scots.

On the basis of an investigation of two deviant minorities, the deprived and the privileged, Spinley concluded that there were sufficient characteristics in common between the personalities of the members of these two subcultures to justify the postulate of a "basic personality type." [14] However, there were also wide divergences on certain points, and there is some reason to believe that some of the similarities may be accidental rather than a consequence of common elements in the culture. Two points of similarity may warrant further consideration.

125

First of all, it is evident that the differences in personality between the sexes are more marked than differences due to subcultural environmental influences. There was a marked sex typing, with boys showing greater spontaneity and girls greater constriction in response to Rorschach tests.

Secondly, it appears that both the deprived and the privileged groups attempted to keep a tight hold on themselves, only occasionally allowing emotion to break through their self-control. This is a point which is emphasized by Gorer in a recent study of English national character.[15] The control of aggression is central to any study of personality adjustment, and various studies of other cultures and subcultures have considered the ways in which aggression is controlled and channeled by the cultural process. In the eighteenth and early nineteenth century the English were an extremely aggressive people, disorderly and violent, indulging in cruel sports and upholding a vicious penal code which prescribed the death penalty for over two hundred offenses; men could be hanged and children deported for minor crimes like stealing a handkerchief. In contrast it is evident that in the present day the English are relatively law-abiding, generally humanitarian, and anxious to suppress aggressive impulses in their children.

What has happened to the expressions of aggression which were characteristic of the English a hundred and fifty years ago? Gorer's hypothesis is that the institution of the English police force in 1829, with its characteristic policy of recruitment and training, provided a model for all the qualities of the ideal male character, "self-controlled, possessing more strength than he ever has to call into use except in the gravest emergency, fair and impartial, serving the abstractions of Peace and Justice, rather than any personal allegiance or sectional advantage." The existence of this model, it is argued, has led to the progressive modification of English national character until it corresponds closely to these ideals.

But only an oversimplified analysis would ignore the fact that aggression (while not the only possible response to—nor caused only by—frustration) is a very frequent consequence of a restrictive, depriving, insecure, frustrating environment such as characterized the squalid lives of the majority of the inhabitants of England, and of the United Kingdom as a whole, in the eighteenth and nineteenth centuries. Since then tremendous strides have been made in the provision of better housing, working conditions, and standards of living; advancements in education and a wider variety of opportunities for self-expression, leisure occupations, and entertainment have been secured. These advantages have certainly reduced the potentiality of aggression that is consequent upon frustration. In addition, the consumption of beer has fallen to a half—and of alcoholic spirits to a tenth—of what it was a hundred years ago. Alcohol has the effect of lowering self-control and releasing aggression; and it is notable that the underprivileged 5 per cent in Britain today are also the heaviest drinkers and the most aggressive.

Until further research has been undertaken it will not be possible to describe a basic personality type or national character for the inhabitants of the United Kingdom. Indeed it is doubtful if one exists. If it does, however, the rate of social change owing to technological advance and internal social mobility is likely to modify that character so that what may be true in this generation may be false in the next.

Conclusion

To the sociologist, the geographical boundaries of a society must appear to be somewhat arbitrary. The behavior of the inhabitants of the United Kingdom is not governed simply by the cultural norms that have grown up within the institutional framework described in this paper. There is constant interaction at the economic, political, and social levels with the inhabitants of other countries. The close ties between the United Kingdom, the Republic of Eire, the continents of Europe and America, and all the territories of the Commonwealth, whether self-governing or dependent, are of considerable importance. Equally influential in determining the behavior of people in Britain are their fears of other major world powers, suspected of being ultimately hostile. A large part of the economy of the country is affected by defense preparations consequent upon fear of a third world war.

Democratic values and institutions only survive in an atmosphere of stability and security. Internal or external threats or conflicts generate fear and insecurity which lead to a rigid social organization and concentration of power, characteristic of totalitarian societies. The continued existence of world tensions is a serious threat to democracy and freedom throughout the world.

The relationships between the people of the United Kingdom and the non-self-governing peoples of the Commonwealth are also critical. In all the colonies, protectorates, and trust territories for which Britain is responsible, some advance is being made toward the establishment of free, independent, democratic states. But progress is uneven. In the territories in which very few Europeans have made their permanent homes, increasing responsibility is being assumed by the indigenous populations for self-determination. Social, educational, and economic development is proceeding concurrently with political advancement. Unfortunately, the same cannot be said of many of the territories in which a dominant white minority maintains its supremacy.

In the dependent colonial territories the divergence between the ideals of the British way of life and actual behavior is very much greater than in the United Kingdom itself. Hellenic democracy ignored the position of its slaves; American democracy sometimes overlooks the Negro population; British democracy all too frequently leaves out of account the colored colonial peoples who are directly subject to the United Kingdom Parliament. Racial intolerance, economic inequality, and political domination are evident in the colonies, while cruelty and oppression are not entirely absent. The way in which the people of the United Kingdom respond to the pressing demands from their colonial subjects for freedom and equality may be as important for the future as the consequences of the conflict between communism and anticommunism.

Notes

[1] Z. Barbu, *Democracy and Dictatorship* (London: Routledge, 1956), p. 66.

[2] Care should be taken in the interpretation of statistics to distinguish between the United Kingdom as a whole and Great Britain, which consists of England, Wales, and Scotland but excludes Northern Ireland. The Isle of Man and the Channel Islands are also excluded since they have a measure of autonomy and are not strictly part of the United Kingdom.

[3] N. Mitford, (ed.), *Noblesse Oblige* (London: Hamish Hamilton, 1956).

[4] Mark Abrams, *Manchester Guardian Survey of Industry.*

[5] P. Sargent-Florence, *The Logic of British and American Industry* (London: Routledge, 1953).

[6] U.K. Home Office and Scottish Home Department, "Comparison of the Criminal Statistics of England and Wales and Scotland," mimeographed (London: Home Office, 1954).

[7] J. Mack, "Crime," in A. K. Cairncross (ed.), *The Scottish Economy* (Cambridge: Cambridge University Press, 1954), p. 243.

[8] W. Friedmann, *Law and Social Change in Contemporary Britain* (London: Stevens, 1951), p. 310.

[9] D. Brogan, *The English People* (London: Hamish Hamilton, 1943), p. 60.

[10] E. Shils and M. Young, "The Meaning of the Coronation," *Sociological Review* (New Series, December 1953), 63–81.

[11] W. Martineau, *et al., Local Government and Central Control* (West Midland Group) (London: Routledge, 1956).

[12] T. Cauter and J. S. Downham, *The Communication of Ideas* (London: Chatto, 1954).

[13] B. M. Spinley, *The Deprived and the Privileged* (London: Routledge, 1953).

[14] *Ibid.*

[15] G. Gorer, *Exploring English Character* (London: Cresset, 1955).

THE UNITED KINGDOM
Supplementary References

GENERAL WORKS

Ginsberg, M., *The Idea of Progress: A Re-valuation* (London: Methuen, 1953).

Smellie, K. B., *The British Way of Life* (London: Heinemann, 1955).

United Kingdom, Central Office of Information, *Britain: An Official Handbook* (London: H.M. Stationery Office, 1955).

United Kingdom, Central Statistical Office, *Annual Abstract of Statistics,* No. 91 (London: H.M. Stationery Office, 1955).

DEMOGRAPHY AND SOCIAL STRUCTURE

Cole, G. D. H., *Studies in Class Structure* (London: Routledge, 1955).

Freedman, M. (ed.), *A Minority in Britain* (the Jewish community in Britain) (London: Vallentine, Mitchell, 1955).

Glass, D. V. (ed.), *Social Mobility in Britain* (London: Routledge, 1954).

United Kingdom, *Royal Commission on Population,* Cmd. 7695 (London: H.M. Stationery Office, 1949).

United Kingdom, General Register Office, *Census, 1951: One per cent Sample Tables,* 2 vols. (London: H.M. Stationery Office, 1952).

ECONOMIC ORGANIZATION AND SOCIAL WELFARE

Allen, G. C., *British Industries and their Organization* (London: Longmans, 1951).

Carter, C. F., and A. D. Roy, *British Economic Statistics* (Cambridge: Cambridge University Press, 1954).

Chester, D. N., *The Nationalized Industries* (London: Allen and Unwin, 1951).

Flanders, A., and H. Clegg, *The System of Industrial Relations in Great Britain* (London: Blackwell, 1954).

Hall, P., *English Social Services* (revised edition; London: Routledge, 1955).

Political and Economic Planning, *British Trade Unionism* (revised edition; London: Political and Economic Planning, 1949).

Rowntree, B. S., and G. R. Lavers, *Poverty and the Welfare State* (London: Longmans, 1951).

United Kingdom, Central Statistical Office, *National Income and Expenditure, 1955* (London: H.M. Stationery Office, 1955).

Wootten, B., *The Social Foundations of Wage Policy* (London: Allen and Unwin, 1955).

Zweig, F., *The British Worker* (Harmondsworth: Penguin Books, 1952).

SOCIAL CONTROL

Butler, D. E., *The Electoral System in Britain, 1918–1951* (London: Oxford University Press, 1953).

Cairncross, A. K. (ed.), *The Scottish Economy* (Cambridge: Cambridge University Press, 1954).

Chester, D. N., *Central and Local Government* (London: Macmillan, 1951).

Finer, S. E., "The Political Power of Private Capital," *Sociological Review* (New Series), Vol. 3, No. 2 and Vol. 4, No. 1 (1955–56).

Jennings, I., *The Queen's Government* (Harmondsworth: Penguin Books, 1954).

McKenzie, R. T., *British Political Parties* (London: Heinemann, 1955).

Robson, W. A. (ed.), *The Civil Service in Britain and France* (London: Hogarth, 1956).

United Kingdom, *Royal Commission on the Press,* Cmd. 7700 (London: H.M. Stationery Office, 1949).

129

United Kingdom, Home Office, *Criminal Statistics, England and Wales, 1954,* Cmd. 9574 (London: H.M. Stationery Office, 1955).

FAMILY, SOCIALIZATION, AND PERSONALITY

Chapman, D., *The Home and Social Status* (London: Routledge, 1955).
Lowndes, G. A. N., *The British Educational System* (London: Hutchinson, 1955).
Slater, E. T. O., and M. Woodside, *Patterns of Marriage* (London: Cassell, 1951).
United Kingdom, *Royal Commission on Marriage and Divorce,* Cmd. 9678 (London: H.M. Stationery Office, 1956).

CONCLUSION

Richmond, A. H., *The Colour Problem* (Harmondsworth: Penguin Books, 1955).

*

Ronald Taft and Kenneth F. Walker

AUSTRALIA

*

THE Commonwealth of Australia is a transplanted version of British culture ten thousand miles from its source. Lying on the periphery of the subcontinent of Southeast Asia, it is an independent member of the British Commonwealth of Nations and recognizes the British monarch as its sovereign. With its European background, advanced economic organization, high standard of living, and equalitarian democracy, it contrasts with its Asian neighbors, and the nine million well-fed and comparatively carefree Australians orient themselves almost entirely toward their British "parents" and American "cousins" rather than toward Asia. Like most of the New World residents, Australians are possessed of a sense of independent destiny.

Geographic Factors

Geographically, Australia is an island continent elliptical in shape and lying astride the Tropic of Capricorn. Although its area is almost three million square miles, equal to that of the United States, four fifths of the continent is arid or semi-arid land suitable only for sparse grazing. The possibilities of river irrigation are extremely limited by meager rainfall and unfavorable topography, and extensive prairie grasslands are lacking. Artesian well water not suitable for human consumption is plentiful in some districts but there are only 100,000 square miles of land in which intensive cultivation is possible. Thus farms tend to be large and dependent on mechanical appliances for economic operation. Over the five years up to June 1954, the agricultural, pastoral, and dairying industries, which employed 13 per cent of the occupied population, contributed 40 per cent of the total recorded production.[1] Primary products account for about four

131

fifths of Australia's export income, which plays a vital and strategic role in its prosperity.

The Urban Bias

The sparseness of population in Australia is one of the important sociological consequences of the geographical features. The average density is three persons per square mile, the lowest of any country in the world. However, this low density is accompanied by one of the highest rates of urbanization for any country; even as early as 1880 more than one half of the Australian population was urban, and today the proportion is four fifths.

The feature of urban distribution of special interest to the sociologist is the centralization of the population in the few large seaports that constitute the capital cities of the states. The two largest, Sydney and Melbourne, contain between them 38 per cent of the total population, and over half of the nine million Australians live in the capital cities of the five largest states. Fifty-four per cent of the Australian people live in large cities (population over 250,000), 21 per cent in farms or "hamlets," and only 15 per cent in small towns (1,000–20,000) and 10 per cent in small cities (20,000–250,000). The small proportion in the last two categories contrasts with the population distribution in other advanced countries. Recent efforts by state governments to build up towns and cities outside the metropolitan areas through the planned development of industry and ports have failed. Although Australia can show outstanding examples of rural pioneers and agricultural experimenters, farming is commonly regarded as a business rather than a way of life. Sociologically, Australia must be viewed mainly as a nation of metropolis dwellers, with all that this implies for political, social, family, and moral life, in the absence of local and national tradition. Furthermore, Australia never was a land of peasant farmers, nor has it been peopled by uprooted peasants. Consequently it has been spared the social disintegration that has accompanied the urbanization of peasants in other countries.

We should temper this emphasis on urbanization by pointing out that the Australian city dwellers are not as far removed from rural life as urban residents in other countries. In the first place, the mode of living in Australian cities is suburban rather than urban. Apartment houses and tenements are comparatively few and the residential areas consist mainly of well-dispersed suburban villas, each with its own garden plot and many with vegetable gardens and poultry pens—81 per cent of the residents of the five large cities live in detached single-family dwellings, with an average of just over 3.5 persons per dwelling. In the second place, an important part of urban commercial activities is still concerned with processing farm products and, more especially, trading in these products.

This partial economic dependence probably underlies the willingness of city dwellers to accord certain respect and privileges to the rural population. Examples of this attitude are reflected in their evaluating farming as an occupation of high prestige, in granting extra weight to rural votes in elections, in "glamorizing" rural life in literature, cinema, and the theater, and in extending certain economic privileges to rural industries.

Living Standards

Like other mixed economies, Australia has experienced cyclical fluctuations in prosperity that have generally corresponded to international cycles, the principal dynamic factor in the Australian cycles being export prices. Since the world depression of 1929–34, the repercussions of export price fluctuations have been dampened to some extent by the countermeasures of Australian governments.

International comparisons of living standards put Australia among the richest eight or nine countries in the world.[2] Such comparisons are admittedly rough, and do not include consideration of a number of aspects of the general social welfare of the population. In health, for example, most of the available statistics show Australia in a favorable light; the death rate (adjusted for age distribution) is third lowest in the world, as is the infant mortality rate, although the maternal mortality rate is only ninth lowest. The expectation of life at birth is the fourth highest. Diet, housing, and working conditions, although showing scope for improvement, are of a reasonably high standard. For example, 63 per cent of dwellings are owned completely or are being purchased by the occupiers, and there is an average of over 1.4 rooms per person in all residences. Social services — once in the vanguard of the world — are today not as highly developed as those in Britain or Scandinavia, but they are more comprehensive than those in the United States. The total benefits received from social services equal about 8 per cent of the typical wage earner's income.

The distribution of Australian personal incomes appears to have been one of the most equalitarian in the world during this century, although equality has decreased recently. Labor's share in the national income has remained relatively stable in the last fifty years, at 55 to 60 per cent. This fact, and the relatively equal income distribution, reflect in part the early success of trade unionism, but suggest that the early gains have not been greatly extended.

The People

IMMIGRATION

In 1788 Australia was inhabited only by technologically primitive aborigines who presented no serious barrier to the free expansion of white settlement. The first immigrants—convicts, soldiers, and officials—arrived in Sydney from England, and in the intervening years the population has been built up by periodic waves of immigrants. These waves were largest in the periods 1851–59 (associated with the discovery of gold), 1881–88, 1910–14, 1920–29, and from 1948 to the present. From 1948 to 1954, an average of 120,000 immigrants arrived each year, over one half of whom were non-British Europeans. The immigrants can be classified into three types: (1) convicts, (2) unassisted settlers, and (3) government-assisted immigrants.

Transported convicts totaled some 165,000, nearly all before 1852. Despite some popular myths to the contrary, convict ancestry is neither genealogically nor sociologically important to modern Australia. "The facts go to prove that they [the convicts] handed down no heritage of moral obliquity, industrial incapacity or helpless and immediate poverty."[3]

The early unassisted settlers were often former military officers and men of penal guard units already in the colony, but free settlers began to arrive in steady numbers in the first half of the nineteenth century, mainly with the hope of making quick money in sheep grazing or commerce. With similar materialistic motives, free immigrants flocked to the gold fields in the 1850s. Since that time immigrants have arrived (and quite a few departed) at a rate that has fluctuated with economic, political, and military events in Australia and in Britain, so that at times the emigrants have even exceeded the immigrants. In line with other countries, immigration visas were first instituted in 1924, and the main requirements today for free immigrants are European racial origin, sound health, good character, and good financial prospects. Requirements tend to be flexible, and officers of the Immigration Department can exercise a certain amount of discretion according to the current policy.

Migration sponsored and assisted by the government has provided Australia with almost half of her new arrivals, for the hazards of a new country and the long and expensive journey made Australia a poor competitor without subsidies for much-needed laborers, skilled craftsmen, and women for domestic work and matrimony. This government-subsidized immigration is a necessary requirement for any planned development of the Australian nation, but it has usually been suspended in times of depression. (Australia's immigrant intake-absorption cycle has been likened to the digestive process of a boa constrictor.[4] Since 1947 the shortage of labor and the nation's feeling of military weakness have been so acute that government assistance to both non-British and British immigrants has reached record levels, frequently by agreement with the governments of the countries of emigration. There is a long tradition of officially receiving and aiding immigrants on their arrival, and today provision is made for temporary housing, employment guidance (and sometimes, direction), and English-language training for the new immigrants.

The governments have mostly carried out their immigration schemes as a matter of state policy, with little regard for public prejudices. For example, the Labor government in 1949–50 admitted large numbers of European displaced persons through I.R.O. despite strong opposition from many of the trade unions.

The economic and political background of the immigrants, both free and assisted, is significant for the development of Australia. The typical immigrant has been a young, comparatively enlightened urban resident (usually British) seeking to improve his economic or political lot; for example, among new male arrivals in 1950 only 17 per cent of those gainfully employed were in rural occupations, while 36 per cent were craftsmen. In 1947, 62 per cent of foreign-born Australians lived in metropolitan areas, compared with 50 per cent of the native-born. While most of the immigrants have come to Australia for materialistic motives, many groups have included political refugees and deportees, namely Irish rebels, German Lutherans, and English Chartists in the middle ninteenth century, and refugees from totalitarianism in the middle twentieth. Few of the assisted immigrants have been paupers, and they have tended to be more sophisticated regarding democracy and better educated than the remainder of the population in the countries from which they came. These characteristics of the immigrants have almost certainly had a considerable effect on the pattern of Australian democracy. The absence of large numbers of uneducated, economically dispossessed immigrants of rural origin distinguishes the Australian immigration process quite markedly from that of the United

States and, in fact, from most new countries. Frontier exploitation of the nation's wealth, achieved in the United States largely by a combination of private enterprise and economically underprivileged immigrants, is today being achieved in Australia largely by a combination of government-sponsored enterprise and immigrants working under well-paid contracts.

NATURAL INCREASE

The rate of natural increase of the Australian population since 1861 is shown in Table 1. The downward trend from 1860 to 1940 reflects a fall in fertility comparable to that experienced in most countries of Western culture. As in other such countries, this fall in fertility has been accompanied by a great reduction in death rates; the crude Australian death rate has fallen by 40 per cent since 1881, and even the death rate adjusted for age distribution has fallen by 25 per cent. The net reproduction rate fell smoothly from 1.88 in 1881 to 0.86 in 1932, and although it had recovered to 1.04 by 1940 and reached 1.71 in 1951, the recovery up to 1946 was entirely attributable to a rise in the marriage rate; it is only since then that fertility itself has been rising. It is too early yet to be sure whether this rise in fertility results from an increase in the average family size of two to three children, or merely from a fall in the number of childless marriages. Whatever its basis, however, the Australian rise in fertility parallels that experienced in the same period by countries such as the United States, England and Wales, Scandinavia, Switzerland, and New Zealand.

Australian fertility has also varied among income groups and between the urban and rural populations, following a pattern similar to that in other countries of Western culture. In general, richer people tend to have fewer children than the poor, although the highest income groups have recently tended toward slightly larger families than the middle classes, and the

Table 1. Rate of Natural Increase of Australian
Population, 1861–1953

Period	Rate*	Period	Rate*
1861–1870	24.31	1921–1930	12.97
1871–1880	20.45	1931–1940	7.92
1881–1890	19.96	1941–1950	12.05
1891–1900	16.91	1951	13.23
1901–1910	15.29	1952	13.89
1911–1920	15.77	1953	13.82

Source: Commonwealth Demography Bulletin, No. 71, 1953.
*Excess of births over deaths per 1,000 of mean population.

differential birth rate is offset to some extent by the higher rate of infant mortality among the urban poor. Furthermore, country dwellers tend to have larger families than city dwellers.

Australia has shown the same short-term demographic reactions to economic fluctuations as have other industrialized countries, depressions causing postponement of marriage and lower fertility, and prosperity favoring upward trends. Demographically, Australia presents a sharp contrast with her neighbors, who are faced with the problems inherent to high fertility and high mortality rates.

AGE AND SEX COMPOSITION

The long-term fall in fertility has had the effect of raising the proportion of older people in the Australian population. The average expectation of life at birth in the decade 1891–1900 was 51 years for a male and nearly 55 for a female; in 1946–48, it was 66 years and 70 years respectively. In 1921, only 3.9 per cent of the population was over 65, but by 1954 the proportion was 7.5 per cent. In general, the age distribution of the Australian population is comparable with that of other countries of Western culture, and contrasts with her Asian neighbors.

In common with other "countries of immigration" such as Canada, South Africa, and New Zealand, Australia has more men than women, although there is a surplus of women in the large cities. The ratio of men to women in the total population has fallen from 110.55 in 1900 to 102.4 in 1954; but in the important age group 15–49 the ratio is 105, much higher than the corresponding rates in the United States or Britain.

ETHNIC COMPOSITION

One of the important sociological features of Australia's population in the past has been its homogeneity, although certain minor regional differences in ethnic background have arisen. Australia's social institutions obviously owe a great deal to their common British source. In 1947 the proportion of the population born in Australia of almost entirely British ancestry[5] was 90 per cent, and of those born in other British countries 8 per cent, leaving only 2 per cent non-British. By 1955 the non-British proportion had risen to 7 per cent, while the native-born percentage had declined to 85. Almost 8 per cent of the present population are post–World War II immigrants—mainly English, Italian, Dutch, German, and Polish, in that order—and the proportion is still increasing. Using present religious

137

groups as a rough guide, we find perhaps one fifth of the present Australian people are of Irish descent, and one tenth of Scottish. The only other non-English groups that have ever immigrated in significant numbers are Germans (mainly 1850–90) and Chinese; the latter numbered 40,000 in 1860, about 3.5 per cent of the total population at that time. The Chinese group probably made its greatest impact on Australia in a negative fashion, by tightening the resolve of Australian workers to retain high standards of wages and working conditions through the institution of a policy to keep Australia "white." As a result of this policy, other immigration from neighboring Asian countries has been negligible and the Chinese population has greatly diminished through repatriation or death without issue.

The Australian aborigines numbered some 300,000 at the end of the eighteenth century. Today they stand reduced to approximately 75,000, mainly through the ravages of disease and loss of tribal lands, but perhaps also through the loss of *élan vital* due to social disorganization.[6] Their numbers are now increasing again, but they have little impact either socially or economically on the institutions of white Australia except in a few sparsely populated pastoral regions where they provide much-needed labor, sometimes of a skilled type. (An influence on current artistic expression is mentioned below.) Fewer than 10,000 aborigines live in urban areas, and only a quarter of adult Australians claim to have had any association at all with them.[7] The typical way in which Australians express their prejudice is to ignore the existence of these aborigines rather than shun or spurn them, but in some outlying areas they are economically exploited. The official government policy on aborigines is assimilation, but few steps are taken toward this end and no real attempt has been made to prepare the public for the social implications of that policy; however, segregation has developed no rigid formulation equivalent to "Jim Crowism," but is better described as "pre–Jim Crow."

Some degree of education is provided for many of the aborigines through special government or mission schools, but standards of education are invariably low and it is extremely rare for an aboriginal to engage in an occupation that requires literacy.

ETHNIC ATTITUDES AND ASSIMILATION

It is only in the past few years that public-opinion studies have provided objective evidence on ethnic attitudes, but there is ample documentary evidence of fluctuating attitudes in the past. The groups to whom Australians have been most opposed as immigrants are those whose cultural distance is greatest, and who are therefore believed to be the most difficult to assimilate. There is some evidence for the existence of the traditional Anglo-Saxon preference for northwestern Europeans, followed by southern and eastern Europeans, and then, by Asians and Africans. Australian ethnic preferences (as determined in unpublished studies conducted by Ronald Taft) seem very similar in rank order to recently reported American results. Possible differences might be that Australians are relatively more favorable toward Chinese and less toward southern Europeans than are Americans, but the various studies are not sufficiently parallel to enable one to draw definite conclusions. Since World War II there has been ample evidence of considerable hostility and prejudice of Australians toward the Japanese, who are still regarded by a large majority as constituting a threat to Australian safety.[8]

While the hierarchy of ethnic preferences tends to remain constant, the actual behavior toward non-Australian groups seems to vary wtih situational factors, mostly related to apparent or real threats. Thus the "white Australia" policy of excluding non-Europeans, instituted on a nationwide basis in 1901, stemmed from a long-standing fear that immigrants from nearby Asia—particularly Chinese—would subvert the Australian "way of life" as an outpost of European culture. (Actually, there is no real evidence that large numbers of Asians ever regarded Australia as a possible new permanent home.) More specifically the implementation of the policy was precipitated by the employment of cheap Melanesian labor in Queensland, which increased the concern of labor leaders that employers would use colored labor more widely to undermine working and living standards. The achievement of the total-exclusion policy was accompanied by prejudiced statements of the most primitive nature against the Chinese, and yet, as we have seen, today there is comparatively little prejudice against Chinese. However, the attempted Japanese invasion of Australia strengthened the feeling that the "white Australia" policy was necessary in order to avoid a potential fifth column in a possible future war.

What are the typical Australian attitudes toward assimilation, and what is the effect of these attitudes on the actual assimilation process? Although we know of no careful studies of the Australian frame of reference toward assimilation,[9] we do not think that many Australians would support cultural pluralism. Australia has long tolerated a small semiclosed rural community of German immigrants, but today, with universal education of a standard type, comparatively little social discrimination, and well-developed communication facilities, the enduring existence of this or any other closed ethnic community seems unlikely. Small "ghettos" of first-generation immigrants do exist, however, in a few Australian cities.

Except in wartime, legislation has provided for European aliens who have been admitted as immigrants rights in most matters equal to those of the native-born; for example, they receive child-endowment payments, and naturalization is comparatively easy after a five-years' residence. At present there is some public consideration being given to the possibility that the interaction of old and new Australians may lead to cultural modifications on both sides, but we cannot determine—on the evidence available—to what degree this "interactionist" orientation [10] toward assimilation prevails in comparison with the monistic assumption that the migrant must conform to the Australian "way of life." There are already signs, however, that European influences have broadened the range of acceptable preferences in clothes, food, and entertainment among Australians.

Studies of assimilation in Australia [11] suggest that there are distinct barriers to ready assimilation even for British immigrants. Conscious efforts have been made by successive Australian governments and by private voluntary bodies to assist the assimilation process, but the outcome of such efforts is dependent on subsequent economic and political trends that are difficult to predict. The present immigration to Australia is unique in that a large group of the immigrants cannot return to their countries of origin, and in the face of discrimination and prejudice they would have to stage their self-defense *in situ*.

The assimilation problems of Australia may resemble in some superficial respects those in the United States of the early twentieth century, but the situation is probably profoundly different. The most important of these differences are the relative sophistication of the immigrants, the orientation of both majority and minority groups toward problems of assimilation, government concern with the problem, and the present prosperous economic position that offers opportunities for immigrants at all levels.

Social Stratification

The existence of social strata can be approached from a number of viewpoints: the "objective" viewpoint (e.g., economic or occupational groupings); the social ranking accorded groups and persons by the population; the sociometric viewpoint (social intimacy and distance); and the "subjective" viewpoint (self-ascribed status). In each of these respects, themselves interrelated, the stratification in Australia probably follows lines similar to those in the United States.[12] By similarity we imply that most people will agree on the existence of three classes, "upper," "middle," and "working," into one of which they can place themselves, most of their acquaintances, and persons in various occupational groups. The social distance between individuals is influenced by their ascribed social status, although barriers may be surmounted to some extent by individual achievements, for example, by becoming a champion in some highly regarded sport or an outstanding entertainment figure. By and large, the same interrelated criteria can be applied to class in both Australia and the United States, for example, power, occupation, social attitudes, way of life (values, mores, and etiquette), income and wealth, intelligence and level of education, family membership, and ethnic and religious background. As in the United States, the external symbols of class are not clear-cut and the differences in speech, manners, dress, and possessions between upper and working class are not as great as they are, say, in Britain. In one Australian public-opinion study[13] the correlation was only 0.50 between the social status which the subjects ascribed to themselves and the status assigned to them by their interviewers, using such external signs as "clothes, speech, neighborhood and apparent affluence." Occupational status is probably the most potent of the interrelated criteria of class described above, and Australian workers and middle class agree closely on the occupational hierarchy.[14] This hierarchy is similar to the hierarchy in Britain and the United States. However, Australian upper classes probably place less emphasis on family background than the upper classes in these other countries.

Research data on the status hierarchy in Australia are very limited, but from the available studies[15] and observers' comments the following differences seem to distinguish the strata in Australia from those in the United States:

1. The differential between the lowest and the highest incomes is low in Australia. Within any commercial or industrial organization the salary of the second-highest-level executives is usually not more than three times that of the lowest paid adult male employee (before income tax, which levels the incomes considerably more).

2. The upper class in Australia is probably less exclusive in its behavior than in other countries. This could partly be explained by the compara-

tively short history of "old" families and the fact that these families had to share the hardships and the risks of developing a new country with the "lesser orders." Australian governments have firmly rejected suggestions that they should adopt the British practice of bestowing hereditary peerages, and even British and European immigrants who might legitimately retain aristocratic titles are rarely known to use them.

3. The high proportion of the Australian population living in large cities tends to reduce the importance of family as a determinant of social class; in fact, it might well reduce the significance of class itself as a determinant of social behavior, compared with countries where a larger part of the population live in small cities.

4. "Money" is regarded as a more important determinant of class by Australian workers than by American workers.[16] "Belief" is considered unimportant as a determinant by the Australian respondents while "beliefs and attitudes" is regarded as the most important by the American sample.

5. Slightly more Australians than Americans describe themselves as "middle class." The percentages are 50 and 42 respectively. The corresponding percentage in Britain is 35.[17]

6. The self-ascribed status of Australians is particularly realistic if we use occupation as the criterion of their "real" class.[18] Compared with American and other countries, the Australian middle and upper classes are much less inclined to describe themselves as belonging to the "working class." This results from the stress in Australia on class consciousness and identification which stemmed from the polarization of classes in the nineteenth century. This polarization, manifested in the trade union and in the political solidarity of the working class in the 1880s and 1890s, paralleled a realization by the landless masses that there were few opportunities for them as entrepreneurs either in primary or secondary production. Thus to identify oneself as a "worker" often implies a defiant aggression against the owner class in society. The resentment of workers against the "upper" class in Australia, shown clearly by Oeser and Hammond,[19] is particularly high for a country where communism is comparatively unimportant.

VERTICAL MOBILITY

It is usually assumed that the opportunities offered by the open frontiers of a relatively virgin continent tend rapidly to break down class differentials imported from abroad. This has not been the case in Australia in the past, nor is it notably so today, although the influence of accidental factors —finding gold, weather conditions, export prices of primary products, and even the speed of a race horse—cannot be ignored. Generally speaking, the relative status of families has tended to remain somewhat stable from one generation to the next. Thus, in Oeser's study[20] a correlation of + .63 was found between the present occupation level of 121 urban breadwinners and that of their fathers. Some downward mobility was present at all levels, and there was very little upward mobility among the semiskilled and skilled groups; only half of the expected proportion of the white-collar and proprietor groups were sons of semiskilled or skilled fathers.[21] A comparison between these Australian data and data on social mobility from the United States and certain western European countries[22] suggests that there is much less mobility from manual to nonmanual occupations in Australia than in the others.

The downward mobility of the nonmanual groups is partly due to a constant reduction in the number of small proprietors (including farmers), but the reasons for the low upward mobility of persons of lower economic status are more complicated. Partly, they suffer from handicaps in obtaining promotion in competition with age peers from higher class families; the latter have the advantages of being related to the proprietors or at least having easier access to them. But this is not the full explanation; education and special training could compensate to some extent for these social disabilities since the required educational levels for white-collar, executive, and proprietor positions are comparatively low. According to Oeser's study, only 9 per cent of white-collar workers and 13 per cent of proprietors have a formal education beyond the tenth year. The main bar to upward mobility in the working class is probably the lack of motivation which results from the high degree of class identification mentioned above. In general an Australian tends both to pursue his occupation and to live his social life within those spheres that he conceives appropriate to his class; trifling but significant instances are his choice of drinking-place, swimming beach, restaurant, or seat in a sports arena. Even in middle-class circles there is a tendency to check and even to hide personal ambition rather than risk the loss of peer approval. Australian and American workers seem to differ in their attitudes toward the value of "success," in the social and economic sense. There is little acceptance by the Australian worker of the proposition that the road to happiness lies through effort, study, and the acquiring of the techniques and social skills necessary for socioeconomic mobility. He places more value than the American on class solidarity in order to obtain the companionship, economic security, and comfortable living conditions which he seeks.

Key National Values and Traits

In this section we shall concentrate on the unique aspects of the Australian value system. Most of the social institutions derive from the Britain of the nineteenth century, but evolution in a different social setting, and a calculated rejection of the British ruling classes, have wrought important changes. In the second half of the nineteenth century, the key values of the Australian culture were being formulated and publicized in a self-conscious manner by writers and politicians. These values are summed up by the term "aggressive democracy," implying a demand for political and social equality, economic security and equality of opportunity, material comfort, and national independence; if necessary these rights were to be secured by government action. The sense of destiny which played such a fundamental role in the formulation of these ideals seems to have been weakened today by a great deal of cynicism, but to some extent the nineteenth-century attitudes are still valued.

We have already suggested some of the values and beliefs that operate as "keys" to the understanding of present-day Australian social institutions. Perhaps the most important of all are the underlying class attitudes: *militant equalitarian social attitudes* on the part of the workers, set in the background of *politico-economic class consciousness* that we have already described. These equalitarian attitudes have taken the form of militant attempts to eliminate the material and prestige liabilities of the working class, and are not so much reflected by any personal efforts to enter a more privileged class. Thus a high value is placed on activities aimed at protecting and promoting the standing of the "underdog" by abusing privileged or would-be privileged persons, by collective action such as strikes, and by purposively seeking the support of legislative and government agencies.

Although, as we have seen, middle-class Australians avoid identifying themselves as workers, they nonetheless typically share this militant equalitarianism against authority or prestige figures and tend to be indulgent, if not encouraging, toward the aggressions of workers. Thus the middle class, by and large, supports the welfare state, maintains the right of workers to strike and to look after their own interests, and eschews the servility associated with certain necessary occupational roles. Australians are poor at providing personal service and are reluctant to demand it.

A number of factors have combined to keep violence down to a minimum despite the widespread acceptance of the class struggle and the readiness to revolt against authority. British traditions, comparative lack of poverty, homogeneity of background, and a comradeship deriving from participation in the common task of taming a continent have together saved the country from any prolonged strife that might have left a scar of bitterness, ready to react to any slight irritation. Public patience was notable when, in the years following World War II, public services (e.g., light and transport) were frequently curtailed or suspended because of strikes. Perhaps another reason for lack of civic strife is a widespread *suspicion of abstract slogans*. As Crawford has pointed out there has been "a readiness to experiment by adaptation to circumstances rather than by the wholesale imposition of doctrinaire systems."[23] Australians do not readily join or support abstract movements, whether political or spiritual, and pragmatic slogans such as "give him a fair go" or "live and let live" are much more apt to be heard than "Peace, Democracy, Liberty, and Communism."

We have dwelt on the values of the working and middle classes at length, but we should also mention the small but influential minority who regard themselves as "upper class," and constitute perhaps 2 per cent of the population.[24] These people tend to look to their fellow "uppers" abroad as their comrades rather than to their fellow Australians. Australia has always had a small minority of this class who regard her as a potential, even though difficult, source for quickly increasing their wealth so that they can then live, in an appropriate manner with their own class, in more "civilized" countries. By "civilized" they presumably mean a country where personal service and an attitude of respect can be purchased, where luxuries are readily available, and possibly also where government interference with their lives will be minimal.

Counterposed to this minority attitude—that of the British exile—is a *militant and smug parochialism* on the part of the majority. This parochialism took the form of a blatant nationalism in the late nineteenth century when the expression "offensively Australian" was coined as a term of approval. Although such excesses have given way under the pressure of World War II, postwar immigration, and a general increase in overseas communication, much of this early attitude still remains. Typical signs are exaggerated ideas of the standing of Australia in the world and of the repute of some of her outstanding achievements, the tendency to ignore her nearby Asian neighbors, and feelings against foreign-born immigrants (including British). The story, doubtless apocryphal, is told of the Australian tourist who visited Europe and was amazed by the number of "New Australians" (the current term for European immigrants) he found wherever he looked.

A further important aspect of Australian values is a *strong reliance on government control and initiative.* Whether we speak of immigration, farm development, communications, industrial development, or social welfare, government initiative has almost always been the main prompter, and government itself often an active participant. The nature of the country, the mode of colonization, and the small population made government enterprise the most appropriate method of developing the economy in many respects, for example, the telegraph and railways. Government control has also played its part in furthering justice and equality from the earliest days of Australia's history by repressing the excesses of private enterprise. Even non-Labor governments have incurred the wrath of the "upper" class by imposing restrictions for the "public good." Despite the Australian reliance on government action to maintain the public welfare, a contemptuous attitude toward authority also figures largely in the relations between government officers and public. Here is one more of the basic ambivalences underlying Australian values—a passive dependence on authority combined with a contemptuous and even aggressive attitude toward it.

A psychological analysis of the Australian's attitude toward authority would be especially interesting; so far, to our knowledge, no such analysis has been made in any systematic form. (Why, for example, is the only traditional hero of Australia a small-time gangster outlaw—Ned Kelly?) Such an analysis might consider, for instance, the tendency to rely on regulation rather than self-control to provide the foundation for public morality. This seems to be a manifestation of "other-direction" as opposed to "inner-direction."[25] For a democracy, there is probably an unusual amount of legislation imposing restrictions on gambling, drinking, obscenity, and profiteering. In view of the ambivalent attitude toward authority just described, it is not surprising that flouting these laws is common.

There is further evidence that the predominant social character in Australia is other-directional, for example, in the belief that its national characteristics are the result of the way people are brought up rather than congenital. In the UNESCO survey,[26] Australians—together with Americans—were far more likely to agree with this environmental explanation of their own characteristics than were the residents of the other countries. (In Australia 74 per cent agreed, compared with 29 per cent in western Germany.) Such results would be expected from a people who believe that it is possible to engineer progress by public policy. When it comes to the people in other countries, however, Australia's insularity seems to lead to a much more pessimistic attitude. In the same UNESCO survey Australians were more pessimistic than the average that human nature can be changed, or that world peace is possible.

Another characteristic value in Australia concerns social relations, and is summed up by the term "mateship." The term dates back to the nineteenth century when itinerant agricultural workers usually traveled in pairs. The essence of mateship[27] is the uncritical acceptance of reciprocal obligations to provide companionship and material or ego support as required. Such comradeship is, of course, not confined to Australia, but it appears to have colored social relations there in many ways. The feeling for comradeship has produced one important effect in its tendency to inhibit the adoption of a "success" mentality, since achievement in a competitive society is often obtainable only at the expense of one's comrades. Strikebreakers have always been hard to find in Australia. "Success-ship" versus "mateship" are two conflicting approaches to life about which there is considerable ambivalence, especially in the middle class. Accompanying this conflict is a gross suspicion, if not antagonism, toward the person who lifts himself above the average in any way, and there is little respect for leaders or experts and little appreciation of local talent. The philosophy of "success-ship," however, seems to be gradually gaining ascendancy over mateship under the influence of a growing industrialization that makes it necessary to acquire complex technical and social skills.

A quite different aspect of behavior that also could well emanate from mateship is the *attitude toward the status of women.* There is a tendency for recreation to be sought in a sex-segregated way. Thus only men drink in public bars, and in social gatherings men and women usually form independent groups, even when together in one small room. Despite early political equality (votes for women were first granted in 1894 in South Australia), or perhaps because of it, Australian women have always suffered from an economic and social discrimination that is inconsistent with the democratic ideals of the country and, perhaps, partly owing to the tradition of mateship, a purely masculine concept in its origin.

One last value that should be mentioned is that of *leisure*. Presumably most humans value leisure, but perhaps no people in an industrially advanced country would attribute as much value to leisure as to material comforts. Almost all workers are on a five-day, forty-hour week, with at least ten days paid annual leave plus eight regular public holidays. The main Labor Day holiday commemorates the achievement of the eight-hour day one hundred years ago, in Victoria, by building workers. The strong eight-hour-day movement by labor extended this standard workday to all workers, and pressure to reduce hours and extend holidays has been maintained ever since.

What Australians prefer to do with their much-valued leisure time will be discussed later under "Cultural and Leisure Activities."

BASIC AMBIVALENCES IN THE BELIEF-VALUE SYSTEMS

We have already suggested several conflicting values concerning which Australians are ambivalent, and these are summarized below. Much of the ambivalence arises from trends toward new values, and the probable direction of these trends is indicated by the second side of the dualisms.

Elimination of class differences *versus* class consciousness and class conflict.

Mateship *versus* success-ship.

Respect for rural way of life *versus* urban industrial outlook.

Irreverence toward and rejection of authorities *versus* reliance on government initiative and welfare.

Belief in rights of the individual *versus* reliance on government initiative and welfare.

Idealism *versus* pragmatism and materialism.

Sense of national destiny *versus* fatalism and cynicism.

Isolationism *versus* dependence on and respect for overseas cultures.

Willingness to take risks *versus* concern about security.

Conservatism regarding innovations *versus* enterprise and desire for progress.

NATIONAL TRAITS

It may be expected that there are certain outstanding traits associated with the key national values, but there is very little objective evidence on the basis of which the characteristics of Australians can be compared with those of other nationals. There is, however, a great deal of subjective opinion, and we must rely on the most unanimous of these opinions as our least unreliable source of data, at the same time being mindful that they may be only logical inferences drawn from the national values and mores. In one study of stereotypes conducted by Australian-born students and high-school teachers,[28] the subjects were asked to select from a list the traits most appropriate to the nationals of seventeen varied countries, including Australia. The following represent, in descending order, the traits about which there was most agreement that they apply to Australians in contrast with the other nationals: sportsmanlike, happy-go-lucky, generous, pleasure-loving, heavy-drinking, tolerant, argumentative, boastful, jovial, warm, straightforward, lazy, practical, materialistic, individualistic, and gregarious. Almost all these traits have been attributed to Australians in the last hundred years by observers, but whether this long-standing consistency validates the stereotypes, or whether it merely points to their origin, we cannot say. Other traits which observers have mentioned are cynical (or disillusioned), crude, superficial, uncultured, casual, informal, fair-minded, friendly, and hospitable; but the uniqueness of such traits to Australians is not always implied. Public opinion polls[29] suggest that the Australian public sees itself as more easygoing, practical, and generous, and less progressive and hard-working than do other people in advanced industrial countries. Most significant of all, perhaps, is the finding[30] that Australians describe themselves as "very happy" more often than do people of other countries.

If we are to accept the above descriptions as correct, Australians may be summarized as unsophisticated, materialistic, and pleasure-loving extroverts. To some extent this is consistent with the other-directed character but without the sophistication usually associated with it. The Australian personality, despite "capitalism, industrialism, and urbanization," seems to bear more resemblance to the American personality of the nineteenth century (de Tocqueville's time) than to that of today. On the evidence available we cannot say to what degree the difference is due simply to the fact that industry is less developed in Australia, and to what degree it is due to historical factors.[31]

Economic Institutions

A MIXED ECONOMY

While Australia must be classed among the capitalist countries of the world, it is essentially a mixed economy, in which public enterprise co-exists with private enterprise, economic activity is subject to much government control, and all sections of the community constantly resort to political action to achieve economic objectives. On a hypothetical scale running from the unregulated market economy at one extreme to the completely planned economy at the other, Australia stands rather nearer the planned economy than do many capitalist democracies.

Government enterprise has always been an important sector of the Australian economy. In a sparsely populated extensive country colonized mainly by government action, governments had to take over railways from private enterprise, and this laid a foundation on which governments have built up other large public utilities such as those supplying power, water, banking, telephone, telegraph, broadcasting, and airline services. Although some public enterprises are not without substantial competition (particularly in transport, banking, and radio), they are much larger than private enterprises and account for most of the total government employment.

In general, Australians believe their public enterprises to be less efficient than private business, although this opinion is probably unduly influenced by the published accounts which often show government enterprises to be running at a loss, without showing the contribution of these enterprises to the economy as a whole. The economic value of Australian government railways, for example, cannot be assessed without taking account of their role in earning Australia's export income and their contribution to the general development of rural areas.

In addition to government enterprises trading commercially, the government sector of the economy includes the provision of community facilities and services such as defense, roads, education, health services, unemployment relief, and pensions. Also to be included are the civil servants who administer government policy. Together with employees in government enterprises, they constituted 26 per cent of the work force in 1952.

The relative size of the government sector of the economy is only one aspect of the role of the state in Australian economic life. The second notable feature is the degree of government control of private economic activity. Such controls may be divided broadly into those aimed at maintaining general prosperity and those aimed at regulating certain particular economic activities regarded as inimical to the general interest.

In common with other democratic countries, Australia found it necessary to institute comprehensive economic controls to meet the demands of modern war, although the nature of her participation in World War I required a far less extensive economic mobilization than that experienced by

European countries. When the world depression of 1929–34 hit Australia hard, governments were led to try to achieve greater control over the general level of economic activity, and their efforts laid a foundation of economic policy for the thorough economic mobilization forced on the country during World War II. When the war ended, there was a strong public reaction against detailed regulation of economic life, but nevertheless Australia continued her wartime controls longer than almost any of the victors except Britain. In the postwar discussions of full employment as an over-all goal of economic policy, Australia adopted a more literal interpretation of full employment than most democratic countries, and campaigned consistently in international economic councils for concerted international action to maintain high employment.

The principal instruments of economic policy available to Australian governments in their attempts to control the general level of prosperity are the budget, with its corollary instruments of taxation and loan policy, the tariff and associated measures controlling imports and exports, the foreign exchange rate, and the central bank. In the last twenty-five years each of these instruments has been increased in power and scope, and a stage has now been reached in which a federal government has a fairly complete grasp—within the limits of political feasibility—of the factors determining the prosperity of the country. As in other democracies which do not attempt directly to control prices and production, the principal gap in the government's armory of general economic controls is the lack of a wage policy. The extensive government machinery for settling industrial disputes does not involve the government in direct legislation on wages, although Australian governments generally submit their views to the wage-fixing tribunals in key cases, and in this way probably exert more direct influence on money wages than do most democratic governments.

Government regulation of particular forms of economic activity has not proceeded so far as the control of general prosperity. Although some state governments have legislated against monopolies, nothing of practical significance has been achieved, and the regulation of working conditions and trade practices has followed the British pattern, somewhat hesitantly. The most important areas of government intervention have been in the marketing of primary products, where controls have become increasingly comprehensive.

The third aspect of the role of the state in Australian economic life is the extent to which all sections of the community resort constantly to politi-

151

cal action in order to gain economic objectives. Although it is true that pressure groups operate in all countries, Australians appear to invoke government intervention more readily than other peoples. The dominance of economic interests in Australian politics has often been remarked by observers from other countries. This point will be referred to again.

STRUCTURE OF THE AUSTRALIAN ECONOMY

After a brief period of subsistence farming, the Australian economy rapidly became dependent on its export trade. By the 1830s, a pastoral society was developing, with wool as the staple export. In the second half of the nineteenth century, although wool (and to a lesser extent, wheat) remained the basis of the export trade, mining (especially gold) assumed major importance, stimulating immigration and a long wave of prosperity that collapsed in a sharp depression in the 1890s. In the twentieth century, particularly since the 1920s, manufacturing has become an important sector of the economy, but Australia's prosperity is still influenced to a great extent by export prices.

These changes in the structure of the Australian economy, together with the mechanization of agriculture, have led to a decline in the proportion of the work force engaged in rural industries. In the decade 1911–20 the work force in these industries for the first time fell below the numbers in manufacturing and construction, and Table 2 shows the dramatic changes that have occurred through industrialization of the economy in the last eighty years, a process that has proceeded at approximately the same speed as in Sweden and the United States. The proportion of the population engaged in agriculture has fallen strikingly, and the table shows a

Table 2. Distribution of the Work Force in Australia, by Industries, 1871–1954

Type of Industry	1871	1901	1933*	1947	1954
Primary†	44.1	32.9	26.7	17.6	14.9
Manufacturing and construction	26.5	26.9	27.1	37.1	38.6
Transport and communication	3.6	7.2	8.8	10.1	9.1
Commerce	8.2	13.2	17.8	16.2	18.3
Personal and professional services and other occupations	17.6	19.8	19.6	19.0	19.1
Total	100.0	100.0	100.0	100.0	100.0

Source: Colin Clark, *The Conditions of Economic Progress* (London, Macmillan, 1940), p. 194, and Commonwealth Bureau of Census and Statistics, *Census Bulletins*, 1947 and 1954.
*Excluding unemployed.
†Including fishing, trapping, agriculture, forestry, mining, and quarrying.

growth of manufacturing and of service occupations characteristic of the industrialization of technically advanced countries. (The only important exception to the general trend is personal and domestic service, where the numbers have fallen.) Manufacturing has grown with remarkable rapidity since World War II. The proportion of the Australian occupied population engaged in manufacturing and construction industries is now exceeded by only about half a dozen nations, of which the most important are Britain, Germany, and Sweden; in the United States and Canada the proportion is slightly below the Australian figure. The proportion employed in commerce, transport, and communication is also very high, being exceeded only by a few countries.

PRODUCTIVITY AND INDUSTRIAL ORGANIZATION

Industrialization has been accompanied by rising productivity. Productivity per man in agriculture rose by 100 per cent in the twenty-five years ending in 1940–41, the rise being 60–70 per cent for all primary industries. In industry as a whole, the rise in productivity per man-hour has been estimated at 56 per cent between 1901 and 1947, compared with 183 per cent in the United States, 97 per cent in Britain, and 74 per cent in Canada in the same period.[32]

Changes in occupational status have occurred in the process of industrialization. The proportion of employers and self-employed in the work force has fallen steadily while the proportion of employees has risen, being 80 per cent in 1947. This is a higher proportion than in almost any other country except Britain, although it is only a little higher than a number of other industrialized countries.

Compared with more populous countries, the typical Australian business enterprise is relatively small, an enterprise employing 500 persons being considered a large business. While average factory size has not grown beyond 20 employees since 1909, the larger factories have become relatively more important. In 1909 factories employing 100 persons or more constituted 3.3 per cent of the total number of factories, but employed 37 per cent of the total factory workers, whereas in 1952–53 the corresponding figures were 3.0 and 48 per cent.

No adequate data exist on the degree of monopoly and industrial concentration in Australia, but it appears to be rather higher than in the United States. The high proportion of employees, taken in conjunction with the high proportion of small factories, lends support to this view.

Geographical factors encouraged large-scale operations in rural and mining industries, and low population density has fostered monopoly in transport and manufacturing. Integration has been both vertical and horizontal, and some of the larger industrial and commercial empires bear international comparison, e.g., steel, coal and shipping; retailing; sugar; newspapers.

THE LABOR FORCE

The proportion of the population in the work force (about two fifths) has not changed significantly for the last sixty years, and is about the same as in the United States and Britain.

Women workers now constitute nearly one quarter of the labor force, compared with 15 per cent in 1871. (The proportion remained constant between 1901 and 1921, but has risen since.) In 1947 about 20 per cent of Australian women were in paid employment, a proportion that is at about the middle of the world range.[33] Many women workers have moved from personal and domestic service to other occupations. This transfer and the general expansion of women's employment parallel the experience of other young countries — the United States, Canada, and New Zealand — and contrast with older countries.

Compared with the United States, Australia has a much higher proportion of young people at work, no doubt because of the lower age of leaving school. The proportion of young men at work is the same in Australia as in most industrialized countries, but the proportion of young women at work is among the highest in the world.

In Australia the proportion of men over sixty-five years old still at work (one third) is at about the middle of the world range, but fewer elderly women work than in most countries. The proportion of elderly men at work has fallen markedly in this century, as it has in other industrialized countries.

REGULATION OF INDUSTRIAL RELATIONS

One of the most interesting Australian economic institutions is the governmental machinery for compulsory arbitration of industrial disputes established by the governments of all states and the Commonwealth at the turn of the century. Aimed at instituting "a new province for law and order," most systems envisaged the settlement of industrial disputes by arbitrators drawn from the judiciary and from the legal profession. Although there have been various attempts to introduce "practical" men, with no legal training, as conciliators and arbitrators, most systems remain legalistic in form, and to a large extent in procedure, imposing fines and other penalties on unions and employers who engage in illegal strikes or lockouts, or who break the arbitrators' rulings. These industrial tribunals have developed a complex system of industrial-relations law, as well as exercising important functions in adjusting wages in the light of economic conditions. Over 90 per cent of Australian employees work under arbitration awards.

Evaluation of the effectiveness of this complex institution is very difficult. International comparisons tend to be invalidated by social and economic differences, and it is practically impossible to disentangle the influence of compulsory arbitration from other factors active in the historical development of Australia. Nevertheless, it is clear that the noble vision of an enforced industrial peace has not been fulfilled, for the working time lost through industrial disputes in Australia is among the highest in the world.[34] Stoppages have become increasingly concentrated in certain industries, however, and in some industries compulsory arbitration has proved an essential factor in promoting peace, although in others it has been disruptive. In general, the system seems to have attempted too much and to have been insufficiently flexible in operation, particularly in meeting the varying problems of different industries. Many relatively minor changes have been made in the system since it was established, but there has been little serious inclination to abolish it. At first, employers opposed the system because it enforced collective bargaining and the recognition of unions, but gradually this attitude changed to one of support. Unions have generally favored arbitration but have not been willing to forgo the right to strike.

Australian trade unionism had grown strong by the end of the nineteenth century, and as an objective of compulsory arbitration was to encourage organization among employers and workers, it has grown further in strength in the last fifty years. By 1921 half the employees in the country were union members, and in 1952 the proportion was 60 per cent, while the largest state, New South Wales, had made membership in a union compulsory for employees covered by the arbitration tribunal's awards. Australian unionism has advanced much further in rural and white-collar occupations than in most countries. Employers' associations developed rapidly in the 1920s, and are now strong in practically all industries.

TAXATION

The expansion of government activities during this century has meant a great rise in taxation. In 1901–2, the total tax paid per head in Australia was £3. 0. 6., about 1.5 weeks' wages for the lowest paid worker. In 1951–52, the total tax per head was £116. 14. 10., about eleven weeks' wages for the lowest paid worker. About half of this taxation was income tax in 1951–52 (as late as 1939 the proportion was only one third), a quarter was customs and excise, and one tenth was sales (purchase) tax. Indirect taxation has grown in relative importance, being used as an instrument of economic policy as much as a means of raising revenue.

Comparisons of the weight of taxation in various countries are extremely difficult, but the available information indicates that Australia's postwar level of approximately 25 per cent of the national income is about as high as Canada and the United States, a little below New Zealand, and well below Britain, where the proportion was 35 per cent in 1950.[35] The proportion of direct taxation to total taxation is comparable with all these countries except Canada, which has a much lower proportion of direct taxation.

Australian income tax has tended to be rather more steeply progressive in the middle incomes than in the United States, especially under Labor governments, but has not approached the steepness of the British income tax since World War II. In 1951–52 the average worker on the lowest adult wage rate paid about 6 per cent of his income in tax. The average taxpayer earning twice as much paid about 10 per cent.

CURRENT ECONOMIC PROBLEMS AND POLICIES

Since World War II Australia has entered upon a vast program of development of the country's resources, stimulated and aided by her ambitious immigration plans, and assisted by overseas capital. Overfull employment with imminent inflation are persistent problems in this situation, aggravated by the world boom in the prices of wool and other exports at the time of the Korean War. At the same time the economy has been developing unevenly, with rapidly expanding consumer-goods industries draining resources from the basic industries and services. With personal incomes high, and continuously stimulated by heavy investment expenditures, the Australian economy has recently developed a serious balance-of-payments problem through very free spending on imports.

Australia's fundamental economic problem has always been her dependence on overseas prosperity, both for her export income and for her supply of capital. Despite a considerable advance in general understanding of the economic mechanisms involved, much remains to be done both in economic research and in resolving the administrative and political issues. A central issue is the division of powers between federal and state governments, for since 1943 the federal government has been almost entirely responsible for raising revenue and loan funds for the governments of all six states as well as the Commonwealth, but has very little effective control over the spending of these funds by state governments. At a time when the country's resources are overcommitted by the many aspects of rapid development, this divided control raises many problems which are aggravated by political differences between the various governments.

The persistent economic problems of a rapidly developing country create the acute issue of how far governments should go in controlling economic activities. The working of the Australian federal Constitution also affects this issue, for the federal government's limited powers in peacetime force it to rely entirely on fiscal measures and import controls. Non-Labor governments, officially committed to protecting free enterprise, have been slower than Labor governments to apply the controls within their powers, but the differences in their actions have not been as great as might have been expected from their political platform. This suggests that the long-run solution of Australia's economic problems will turn more on advances in economics and public administration than upon political programs.

Political Institutions

THE BRITISH INFLUENCE

Government in Australia follows the same general pattern of democratic constitutional monarchy as in Britain, with differences of structure and outlook that reflect local conditions and problems. At first the governors put in charge of the colonies by the British government exercised absolute power within the scope of their commissions; but under pressure from local sheep farmers, legislative councils were established. These were made increasingly representative and responsible until, by the 1860s, all the colonies except Western Australia had gained responsible government.

The office of governor (and, since federation in 1901, that of governor-general) has been retained under responsible government. Its constitutional functions are much the same as those of the monarchy in the United Kingdom, giving the people effective control of their own government.

Although in the last hundred years Australia—in common with other former dominions of the British Empire—has achieved effective political independence of the mother country, her ties with Britain have remained close. In this connection, it is difficult to overestimate the role of the crown, which acts as a symbol of ethnic and social unity. Queen Elizabeth II is Queen of Australia as well as of the United Kingdom, and in Australia she refers to herself as "Queen of Australia." The lives and activities of the royal family are regarded with interest and affection throughout the country.

In general, Australians are happy to remain members of the Commonwealth of Nations, regarding it as a family of which the queen is the titular head, and the members of which consult freely as equals on matters of common concern. Jealous of their independence in their own affairs, Australians are nevertheless glad to contribute to the common fortunes of the Commonwealth. Actually, Australia is not committed by any British declaration of war, and she can withhold approval of changes in accession to the throne. For many years Australian foreign policy largely reflected Britain's, but recently it has struck a more independent note, particularly when Labor has been in power.

THE PATTERN OF GOVERNMENT

Australian parliamentary institutions derive from those of Britain, each Parliament having originated from a British act, and subsequent changes have mostly been procedural. All the Parliaments except that of Queensland are bicameral, the upper house generally being elected on a restricted franchise or by some other procedure which ensures that its power to block legislation passed by the lower house will be used for conservative ends. Sporadic efforts to abolish the upper houses have failed except in Queensland. Elections are held triennially, and voting is compulsory; state and federal elections are therefore fairly regular events in the life of the Australian citizen. Preferential voting is used, and proportional representation has recently been adopted in the federal upper house.

Likewise, the general administration of government follows the British model. The legislative, executive, and judicial functions of government are strictly separated. The judiciary are appointed from the legal profession by the government, and are protected from political control. The Cabinet is composed of members of Parliament drawn from the majority party, or a majority coalition. Each minister of state is responsible to Parliament for the actions of his particular department of government. Since the end of the nineteenth century, the civil service has become firmly established as a bureaucracy free from political interference in recruitment and promotion, and enjoying permanent tenure. Juries are widely used in the legal system.

Although the extent of political corruption is difficult to estimate, the Australian record would appear to be reasonably good compared with that of the United States and the Latin American republics, but considerably poorer than that of Britain.

It is significant that although Australian parliamentary institutions are cast in the British mold, the tide of political democracy met with less resistance in the fluid social structure of the new country, with the result that Australia was ahead of Britain in reforms such as manhood suffrage, the secret ballot, and votes for women.

Another important difference from Britain is the relative weakness of Australian local government and the high degree of centralization in the federal government. Various factors have been responsible for this. Local government was costly for a widely scattered population; it was therefore natural for the colonial government, which had carried so much responsibility for founding and peopling the colony, also to carry the main burden of developing the remote areas. The aboriginal population was not a sufficient danger to enforce the development of independent fortified centers as in America, and the economic geography of the continent has not been conducive to closer settlement. In the cities, the central government having got in first, residents preferred to accept this situation and keep property rates to a minimum.

LOCAL, STATE, AND FEDERAL GOVERNMENTS

Local feeling is not absent in Australia, but politically it is associated with states rather than with local government areas. The federal Constitution of 1901 followed the United States pattern of giving the federal government specific powers, leaving the rest to the state governments. However, the structure of the upper house of the federal Parliament is designed to give some additional weight to state interests. The relation of state and federal powers is complicated. Some powers are exclusive to the states, and some are exclusive to the federal government, for example, posts and telegraphs, customs and excise. However, some federal powers are shared with the states, whose legislation on these matters remains lawful until federal legislation covers them, whereupon the federal law is paramount. The legal issues involved are interpreted by the High Court, which functions rather like the United States Supreme Court in this respect, and also acts as a general court of appeal from the state supreme courts. Further appeal may be carried to the Privy Council in the United Kingdom.

Discussion of the relations of federal and state governments would take us far into technical, constitutional, and political issues. Our purpose here will be served by noting that events have strengthened the relative power of the federal government, despite the almost complete failure of twenty-four referendums to change the Constitution. The economic mobilization involved in two modern world wars gave the defense power of the federal government far more social significance than it had possessed in 1901, and its financial and banking powers have been used to extend its control over economic policy; but the states retain important functions concerning public works and social services. There has been a tendency for social security payments to be expanded by federal rather than state action.

The relations of federal and state governments complicate the political situation by providing scope for political parties to play off one against another. Federal legislation is assumed to be valid unless challenged and ruled unconstitutional by the High Court, with the result that many federal activities, which would almost certainly be declared invalid if challenged, are allowed to continue because they run counter to no powerful interest. A powerful group, or a state government which challenges a federal law, can usually be assured that all states will not pass similar legislation, because of divergences of political color or economic interests. The outstanding exception has been price control, which the states re-established by interstate agreement when its federal form was challenged successfully by business interests. In general, however, federalism in Australia has put a brake on rapid social change, whether to the left or to the right. Recent examples were Labor's attempt to nationalize the banking system and the Liberal and Country parties' attempt to proscribe the Communist party. Both measures were blocked by constitutional limitations, the Labor government losing an appeal to the Privy Council on the bank nationalization plan.

ATTITUDES TOWARD GOVERNMENT

The reluctance of the Australian citizen to grant more inclusive power to the federal government has probably been a reaction to the wider assertion of government power in an age in which this power has grown remarkably. Australian attitudes toward government are a mixture of demands for government action in the interests of special groups and resentment at the use of authority over the individual. Referendums have been viewed as a formal request to hand more power to those in authority, and their rejection has been motivated more by hostility to authority than by deliberately formulated views on constitutional issues.

This dislike of authority comes out in the Australians' generally unfavorable attitude toward politicians, who are regarded as particularly obnoxious if they show any signs of intellectual or social superiority. (Australian politicians are drawn largely from the working and middle classes.) This attitude is also reflected in the organization and staffing of the civil services, which until very recently opposed direct recruitment of university graduates for fear of encouraging an administrative elite based on social position or superior education.

Australians' mixed feelings toward authority are no doubt linked with the class structure and attitudes toward class distinctions. The historical basis for these feelings of suspicion and dependency is clear, for from the start Australia has had many citizens who either suffered at the hands of authority or were opposed to it on religious or political grounds, but the pressure of economic forces has nevertheless forced them to rely heavily upon government activity.

POLITICAL PARTIES AND THE VOTERS

The familiar observation that Australians are not interested in politics is correct only to the extent that Australian politics focus on clashes of economic interest groups rather than issues of doctrine. Broadly speaking, while prosperity is maintained and community development keeps pace with the needs of the people, Australians are not much interested in politics. However, despite the political apathy of the average citizen, since 1946 proceedings of the federal Parliament have been regularly broadcast by one of the federal government radio stations. According to Gallup Polls at various times, from 50 to 75 per cent of the population favor this practice, although only 17 per cent listen to a parliamentary broadcast in an average week.

A fairly wide range of settled policies exists to which the three major parties are committed, thus removing certain basic areas of dissension from the political arena. The more important of these settled policies are "white Australia," compulsory arbitration of industrial disputes, protective tariffs, regulated marketing of most primary products, social services, full employment, and general community development. The political parties differ in the emphasis placed on these policies and on the speed and means by which they are put into effect, but the general direction of policy is clear.

Within such settled policies, each of the major political parties represents the interests of a section of the population. The Labor party represents the wage earner, the Country party the farm owners, and the Liberal party a less clearly identified group which includes manufacturing and business interests, and the professional and middle classes. The Liberal and Country parties are usually in coalition against Labor, and the composition of the community is such that in order to stay in power, both Labor and its opponents have to attract the support of swinging voters. Compulsory voting relieves the parties of the need to get their own regular supporters to the polls, leaving them free to concentrate on winning temporary adherents from the undecided. Each of the major parties has been in power over considerable periods, and is accustomed to office. The Australian Communist party has never gained any real political strength; only one Communist member has ever been elected and the Communist vote is negligible. Other small political parties are formed from time to time but none has achieved importance.

As a result, the policies of Australian governments, whatever their political complexion, do not usually vary much from those of preceding or succeeding governments; evolution rather than revolution marks the trend in social change. This situation encourages political apathy in the electorate, except in a group whose interests are directly affected by a particular government policy. In these circumstances the political power of the middle classes could be decisive, but they have remained unorganized and diffuse in orientation, acting as a buffer rather than an independent political force. Splinter parties separating from the major parties have failed entirely to capture the allegiance of the unorganized middle classes. The actual course of politics at any time is thus a process of accommodation among the powerful interest groups that happen to be concerned with the matters in question, and it is determined much more by pragmatic compromises and deals than by doctrines.

The Family

STRUCTURE

Almost 90 per cent of Australians marry, the legal framework of Australian marriage being broadly similar to that of other countries of Western culture. Thus marriage in Australia is more than an ordinary civil contract; it bestows legal status as well. For example, the tests of capacity to make marriage contracts differ from those applied to other contracts; mutual agreement is not a legal ground for dissolution of a marriage, as it is for other contracts. And although the courts have been forced—in actions for "restitution of conjugal rights"—to make operational definitions of the obligations of marriage, these are much wider and vaguer than the obligations assumed under a typical civil contract.

In conformity with Western norms, Australian marriage is monogamous, bigamy being illegal and severely punished. There are no important restrictions on the choice of spouse except the prohibition of marriage of close blood relatives and males under the age of 14 years and females under the age of 12 (in one state the minimum ages are 18 and 16 years). The consent of parents is required for the marriage of persons under the age of 21, but in most states the courts can override unreasonable refusal of consent. The modal age at first marriage is 22–23 years for men and 21 for women; the corresponding medians are 25 and 21. These ages have remained relatively stable throughout this century except for a tendency for the age of marriage to rise during economic depressions and to fall during prosperity and in wartime. However, there are proportionately more bridegrooms and brides under 21 years of age today than there were fifty years ago. Marriages may be performed by ministers of religion registered for the purpose, and about 90 per cent of all marriages are accompanied by a religious ceremony. The proportion of civil marriages has remained unchanged since the beginning of the century.

Grounds for annulment or divorce vary among the Australian states. Failure to consummate the marriage and unnatural offenses are grounds in all states, and adultery and desertion are also generally recognized as grounds although the laws vary importantly in detail. Habitual drunkenness, violent assault, and criminality are grounds for divorce in most states, and incurable insanity is generally admissible except in the important state of New South Wales. These interstate differences, together with difficulties in establishing legal domicile, have led public opinion to favor a uniform federal divorce law, although the majority do not want a general relaxation of the divorce laws.[36] In fact, however, divorce laws have been altered to make divorce much easier to obtain now than in the nineteenth century, and divorce rates have risen greatly. In the last eighty years the annual divorce rate has risen from 1 per 10,000 marriages to 35. Such a rise is characteristic of all countries of Western culture. International comparisons show Australian divorce rates to be in the middle of the range of such countries, England and Wales having the lowest rate and the United States the highest.[37] As in other industrialized countries, divorce is more frequent among childless couples and those with one child, those married less than seven years, and those living in the cities.

Australian marriages are arranged by the parties themselves after a courtship during which neither sex is severely controlled by the parents. The rarity of coeducation for adolescents probably contributes to a rather later commencement of courtship than in the United States. No reliable information exists on the extent of premarital sexual intercourse, but it is widely agreed that it has greatly increased in the middle and upper classes in this century. About 12 per cent of brides are pregnant when they marry, and about one sixth of first births are conceived before marriage or occur out of wedlock. Births not followed by marriage account for about 4 per cent of the total number of births, the rate having fallen from 6 per cent in 1901–10. Romantic love is generally regarded as the basis for marriage, although other factors enter into many marriages. Husbands and wives, for example, tend to come from the same social classes.

Upon marriage, a wife usually takes her husband's name, but otherwise retains most of her former legal rights. She may own and bequeath property, earn a separate income, and vote.

The effective family unit in Australia is the conjugal family, comprising man, wife, and children. To an increasing extent this unit is independent of the wider group of blood relatives on both sides. Influence by "in-laws" is generally regarded as an illegitimate interference. Legally, marriage is patrilocal, but this rule does not imply any greater importance for the male line, and is not invariably followed. Neither of the two family groups linked by the marriage has any priority of influence, except through force of circumstance or personality factors, and descent is multilineal. In this respect Australian norms are nearer American than English or European.

As noted above, the size of the typical conjugal family has shrunk a great deal in the last two generations. In 1954 the average private dwelling had 3.2 persons living in it whereas in 1933 the figure was 4.1, and in 1901 it was 4.5. This reduction results partly from fewer children, but partly also from increasing reluctance to have unmarried or elderly relatives living in the house, where their presence might interfere with the autonomy of the conjugal family.

SOCIAL FUNCTIONS

As Australia has become more urban and industrialized, and as families have grown smaller, the social functions of the family have diminished in much the same way as in other countries that have undergone similar social changes. The process has been carried further in metropolitan areas than in the country, but is extending there as the rural areas are brought into closer contact with city ways of living.

The contrast between urban and country families is perhaps most marked in *economic function*. Unlike the city family, the country family largely retains its original function as a productive unit. The trend away from a "family economy" has a long history but is still continuing, and the last fifty years have seen many productive activities pass from the home which were once exclusively carried on there. The preparation of canned goods and other foods, and both the manufacturing and the cleaning of clothing, are striking examples. Except in family businesses, the productive activities of the various members of the city family are unlikely to bear any organic relationship to each other; their economic interdependence is limited to income and consumption, and no longer includes production, except for home gardening, and similar minor activities.

An important aspect of the economic functioning of the Australian family, which has a considerable impact on the performance of its other functions and on the relations between its members, is the virtual disappearance of domestic servants in the last thirty years. This applies not only to full-time servants living in the home but also to part-time help. Increased availability of labor-saving devices in the home has not compensated fully for the added claims this change has made on the middle-class housewife's time and energy. The trend toward smaller families has reduced the amount of housework and child care to be done, but the smaller household of today also has fewer hands to help with these tasks.

The *protective functions* of the family have been greatly attenuated by advances in public health and social services. Practically all children are now born in hospitals, and through old-age and invalid pensions the state is assuming increased responsibility for the care of the elderly and the incapacitated. Health services have been extended, although not so far as in Britain.

Educative functions of the family will always remain important so long as children spend a large part of their early life in the home, but the community has steadily expanded its provision for the formal education of children, and the drift of population to the cities has brought more people into contact with educational institutions other than the home. The consolidation of small rural schools, which has been extended recently by the provision of bus transport over long distances, may reduce the time a country child spends at home by up to two hours daily, illustrating the exchange of family influence for a higher quality of formal education.

Religious functions of the family have not been transferred to another social institution, but have suffered a decline parallel with the general decline of religious observance. About one Australian family in three claims to say grace before meals.[38]

Recreation for young people has moved out of the home to a considerable extent, but apart from sport the preferred leisure activities of Australians, especially those who are married, include many activities that can be done at home or shared with the family.

No comprehensive data have been collected on the extent to which Australian families participate in social relations with neighbors; the one available study of urban families found very little participation of this type.[39]

Procreative functions might be thought to have diminished with the trend toward smaller families, but modern Australian parents would probably claim that their children are just as important in their marriage as their grandparents' children were to them. The desire to make a better provision for each child is no doubt a factor in restricting the size of the family. But the increasing proportion of childless marriages (one in six at the beginning of the century, now one in five) suggests that fewer couples regard children as an essential part of marriage.

The attenuated functions of the family as a social institution leave the *personality functions* of marriage to bear a greater strain, which is no doubt partly responsible for the increased instability of marriage in the last two generations in Australia and other countries where similar factors have operated.

The changes in the family's social functions are relevant also to the general position of women in Australia. As mentioned earlier, Australia was among the first countries of the world to give women the vote. Educational emancipation has been complete for over a generation. Economic emancipation has been slower, although speeded up by wartime emergencies in which women proved their ability in occupations previously regarded as male preserves. Women now practice all professions in Australia, although prejudice raises barriers against their appointment to the highest positions. In industry and government women are usually paid less than men on the ground that they have fewer dependents and similar responsibilities, and women in government positions must resign on marriage. The first woman member of parliament was elected in 1922, but there have been very few others. In general, emancipation has proceeded a long way, but not so far as in the United Kingdom or the United States.

PATTERNS OF FAMILY RELATIONSHIPS

In Oeser's community studies in Australia,[40] detailed surveys of family life in both a city (Melbourne) and a rural community distinguished several types of family pattern. The *autocratic* pattern has either the husband or wife dominant, whereas in the *autonomic* pattern the partners have their own areas of activity in which they are free to decide and act. In the *syncratic* pattern, the partners make decisions jointly and act in concert. In general, syncratic and autonomic patterns were found to predominate. Dissension between husband and wife was found to be greatest in autonomic families, and although no systematic data exist for earlier generations, it may be surmised that the trend has been away from the autocratic pattern in which the husband was dominant. This view is supported by the fact that in the rural community, where the impact of social change on the family has been less, the husband is the ultimate source of authority; whereas in the urban families the wife is generally the major source of authority. Furthermore, the particularly high tension in many urban families when the husband is dominant suggests that the trend away from the husband-autocratic pattern will continue.

Analysis of the control and performance of various activities of the members of the family revealed characteristic stages whereby the Australian husband has come to participate more in activities traditionally regarded as appropriate for the wife. The principal activities of the spouses may be classified in the order of increasing participation by the husband and decreasing participation by the wife. In what may be described as primarily the wife's household area, she performs such tasks as ironing, dusting, washing, and cooking the evening meal. In the common house-

167

hold area, husband and wife may divide the tasks of setting the table, buying groceries, and washing dishes. The husband increasingly participates in the care and control of the children, in the social activities of the family, and continues to assume economic responsibilities. Finally, in the husband's household area, he performs the duties of making repairs around the house, chopping wood, and mowing the lawn.

In the urban families one fifth of the husbands participated in all activities, but only 9 per cent of the wives did so, although the wife's participation appears to be extending into the family's economic activities. The wife's basic role consists of her household duties and child control, and the husband's of his job. In considering such patterns, however, it should be noted that they appear to be established early in marriage and to persist throughout its duration. The trend away from the autocratic pattern and toward wider participation by the husband is therefore not discernible in the history of particular families, but only in the relative proportions of the various family patterns in successive generations.

Class differences in family patterns have not been comprehensively studied, but there are clear indications that employers and the self-employed have autonomic family patterns while a large proportion of skilled workers have syncratic patterns. Autocratic families are found mainly in the semiskilled groups. These differences may be explained partly by differences in sociopolitical ideology, partly by lower education and cultural lag in the less skilled, and partly by the higher job-satisfaction of husbands in the middle and upper classes, providing an alternative to power in the home.

These family patterns are relevant to child-rearing practices. In the first place, the roles of sons tend to follow the participation of fathers and the roles of daughters the participation of mothers. Secondly, differences in child-rearing practices are obviously involved in the various patterns, with consequent differences among social classes. In the predominantly autocratic families of the semiskilled group, the child is expected to be more independent in social relations and adult behavior is demanded earlier than in other social classes. Emphasis is laid by these parents on the child "not being a trouble." Boys in these families are less controlled than children in any other group, but girls are restricted fairly closely to activities in the home. In general, parents of these families are concerned with dealing with the daily demands of child-rearing rather than with the child's advancement to a higher class. The syncratic families of the skilled group stress "independence" and "intelligence" as desirable qualities in children, and the father participates more in family life. Disciplinary methods are less punitive and less corporal than in other classes, but parental control is greater. In the white-collar class, a variety of family patterns is found, the homogeneity of the group resting primarily on educational level and occupation. Parents desire their children to be "good" and "well-mannered," and sharply differentiate the roles of boys and girls. They hold high aspirations for the boys' advancement and control their children's activities strictly, especially the boys'. Employers and the self-employed alike have high aspirations for children but do not control their children very directly or strictly.

In farming families the children appear to be more family-oriented than in urban families, where more stress is laid on relations with peers. In farming families children participate more in the work of the household and are under fairly strict control in this area of activity.

In general, Australian parents tend to control their children rather more than American parents but probably less than English parents. Girls are subject to more control than boys, although the treatment of boys and girls probably does not differ so much today as in former generations. Parents stress moral training more with girls than with boys. Parents are primarily concerned with the child's behavior in the home rather than in the community as a whole. Children are not as a rule expected to contribute to the family income.

In summary, the family in Australia reflects the uncertainty of a social institution in transition under the pressures of the rapid social changes experienced in the last two generations by most countries of Western culture.

Education
PRIMARY AND SECONDARY EDUCATION

Schooling in Australia was first provided entirely by denominational schools subsidized by the states. State government schools were founded in 1830, and when the subsidies to nongovernment schools were withdrawn by the various states in the 1880s and 1890s, free and compulsory education was introduced up to the ages of fourteen to sixteen. The first school of this type was established in Western Australia in 1871. Even in convict times, in the early nineteenth century, approximately one half of the children in the colony were receiving some schooling, and in the latter half of the century the demand for universal and free education was one of the central features of the political "platform" of the worker's leaders. Subsequently, however, much disillusionment set in concerning the power of education to raise the worker's lot, and the extension of general educational facilities has long since ceased to be a vital public issue. The majority of children still leave school soon after completing the obligatory eight to ten years of schooling, and little more than one quarter of school-leavers successfully complete the examination which is given at the end of the tenth grade (Intermediate Certificate). Many school-leavers proceed to part-time vocational training for several years after finishing full-time school, but only an extremely small percentage of young persons (12 per cent of those aged fifteen through nineteen years in 1947) are full-time students. The emphasis is on vocational skill rather than general education.

Preschool kindergartens, for children of two and one half to five and one half years, do not exist in sufficient numbers, and probably less than 5 per cent of the children in that age group attend them. The kindergartens are supported by small government subsidies, but are mainly dependent on fees and charitable collections for their revenue. In general, they are not considered to be important in a child's education, but their popularity is increasing.

At the time of writing (1956) there appears to be occurring a radical upswing in the popular evaluation of education, manifested particularly in a tendency for children to remain at school beyond the legal minimum age much more frequently than in the past. The reasons for this development are manifold, but perhaps the most important ones are the prosperity of the community and the increasing industrialization which entails a greater demand for more educated personnel.

Primary and secondary education in Australia is carried out by three different school systems: schools controlled by the education departments of the state governments, Roman Catholic schools, and other "private" schools, covering approximately 75 per cent, 20 per cent, and 5 per cent of all school children respectively. There are no local education authorities, and the state schools are under the control of a permanent director of education in each state who is invariably appointed by the state government on his professional rather than political merits. Popular and political control of education is kept at a minimum, and the only local committees— the "Parents and Citizens" committees—are school auxiliaries rather than controlling boards. This centralized system leads to uniformity and a good deal of inflexibility in educational techniques compared with the local control systems used in other countries, but it also tends to preserve a fairly high average standard and to avoid the excesses of neglect that would otherwise occur in country districts. This is most important in a country where the sparseness of population requires three quarters of the state primary schools to be one-teacher schools and where 17,000 children can be reached only by correspondence and radio-broadcasting methods. An elaborate system for the government inspection of schools preserves standards and at the same time unintentionally inhibits the willingness of teachers and principals to make innovations. Teachers are comparatively well paid, and promotions are obtainable on grounds of merit and qualifications as well as seniority. A small minority of primary school teachers and the majority of secondary school teachers have university degrees. There are as many male as female teachers (unlike the United States), and few married women are employed. Due to a shortage of teachers and buildings, classes of over fifty pupils are not uncommon. With classes of that size, it is not surprising that collective activities are the rule and discipline is rather strictly enforced.

State secondary schools include technical high schools, which have more pupils than the other high schools. Unlike Britain, the choice between three types of secondary school—technical, academic, and general—is almost completely at the option of any pupil who has completed the sixth grade, except in a few academic high schools. Highly developed under governmental auspices, vocational-guidance facilities assist pupils to make their choice of school.

The Roman Catholic schools duplicate the state school system in many respects; approximately 70 per cent of the Catholic children of school age attend them. The other private schools are also largely denominational, but they are more independent in determining their policies.

Most of these private schools accept a number of boarding pupils, but the majority attending are day pupils. Fees for the latter range up to $150 per annum,[41] although a number of scholarships are granted. These schools are theoretically more flexible in their programs than state schools, but denominational school boards and the influence of alumni tend to keep them conservatively in the tradition of the English "public" schools. Most of the private and Roman Catholic schools are also subject to a minor degree of inspection by state authorities, but interference is minimal. The educational emphasis in the private schools is predominantly academic rather than vocational, and they provide the majority of the students who matriculate in universities.

The main distinguishing features of Australian child education, viewed as a whole, are the uniformity and conservatism of both the curriculum and the teaching methods in primary schools; the pragmatic (rather than humanistic) orientation adopted in secondary and tertiary education, manifested by a marked tendency for vocational training to commence early; the constant use of competitive examinations in secondary school as a device for barring promotion to pupils who have not met standards; and, finally, domination of the school system by the state universities through control of curriculums and examinations. Coeducation in secondary schools is the exception rather than the rule, even in state high schools, and the schools do not usually regard the development of social poise as one of their educational functions. Mathematics and the physical sciences are stressed at the expense of social science in the secondary schools, and the standards in these subjects are high.

HIGHER EDUCATION

Australia has eight state universities, including one university of technology, and a postgraduate research university sponsored and well endowed by the federal government. There has been a great postwar expansion, and by 1955 there were approximately 30,000 students at these nine institutions. Unlike the secondary schools, all universities are government sponsored but administered independently by nonprofessional boards representing different community interests. Political interference in matters of academic freedom is minimal, perhaps because of the inherited British university traditions, but Australian universities are obviously vulnerable should political pressures be exerted, especially since over half of their total income comes from government grants. Annual tuition fees for students vary from approximately $20 to $250 (medical course), but scholarships and living allowances are freely available to the more able students, and many of the students, perhaps one third, pay their way by taking their courses part time. Most of the universities are located in the large cities and most of the students are nonresidential. A minority of the students, however, are in residence at "colleges" which are endowed and administered by the various religious denominations, and which endeavor to supply the traditional university atmosphere of the Oxford and Cambridge colleges. On the whole the organization of the universities is derived from the Scottish system and—like other Australian educational bodies—they tend to be pragmatic in outlook, encouraging early specialization. The proportion of graduates who receive a degree in arts is only one fifth. Professional courses are all commenced in the first or second year after leaving secondary school, and there are very few postgraduate research students. As in secondary schools, highly competitive examinations provide barriers to the student's advancement in each year of his course; consequently, the academic standards are high. The universities are coeducational, but there are five male graduates to every female (compared with two to one in the United States).

Nonuniversity training in teaching and in various technologies is provided by special colleges which are administered by the state education departments. A majority of the students attend only evening classes at these colleges, and the total enrollment represents over 80 per cent of the 200,000 students at the tertiary level in Australia.

The place of tertiary education in the Australian community could perhaps best be summarized by the statement that its total annual cost, including university research grants, is less than four dollars per head of population. If the general public shows any positive interest in the universities at all, it is to demand "practical" research projects, professional training, and advisory services; the expression "long-haired professors" is a favorite byword among journalists and politicians.

Religion

Australia is nominally a Christian community, but—like the United States—it has avoided an established state church and has long extended complete legal equality to all its residents irrespective of religious affiliation. Religious freedom is guaranteed by the federal Constitution. Australia has never known any lengthy period in which its church officials and leaders have been politically privileged persons, and this probably accounts for a virtual absence of anticlericalism, splinter sects, and militant atheism. In their first few years, the convict settlements employed Anglicans (Episcopalians) officially as chaplains, but Roman Catholic and nonconformist settlers (mainly Presbyterian) demanded their own clergy. These non-Anglican groups successfully kept up pressure for equal privileges with Anglicans, and today government bodies, e.g., the Broadcasting Commission and the Registrar of Marriages, scrupulously avoid giving preferential treatment to any denomination.

The history of government subsidies to schools provides a record of the changing attitudes toward established religion. Up to the 1830s, Anglican schools were the only church schools subsidized; eventually subsidies were extended to all denominational schools, but with the advance of state schools in the 1880s all subsidies were abolished. There is occasional agitation today by Roman Catholics for the restoration of these subsidies, but the matter is not a central political issue. More recently there have been signs of the restoration—without public protest—of some minor subsidies to church schools, although more non-Catholics are against this than for it.[42] By and large, the churches and all their related institutions are financed by the voluntary contributions of their adherents, supplemented by the proceeds of their various fund-raising projects.

The religious affiliations of the population in 1954 (expressed as percentages of the total population) were:

Anglicans 37.9
Roman Catholic 22.9
Methodist 10.9
Presbyterian 9.7
Other Christian 8.0
Non-Christian (mainly Hebrew) 6
No religion 2
No reply or indefinite 9.8

Although many of the smaller Christian sects have adherents in Australia —even the Father Divine movement—it is notable that 92 per cent of the people associating themselves with a specified denomination choose one of the "Big Four." The weakness of the small denominations and sects probably reflects the comparative apathy of Australians concerning doctrinal matters. Most of the smaller denominations are still diminishing in proportion to the larger ones, but a few are gaining from the arrival of certain immigrant groups—Lutherans, for example. The proportion of the population who describe themselves as Anglican is also declining.

The only denomination whose relative increase in the past twenty years has been substantial is the Roman Catholic, which has increased from 22.2 per cent of those *declaring* their adherence to a particular religion in 1933 to 25.4 per cent in 1954. Apart from a possibly disproportionate number of immigrants who are Roman Catholics, this increase is also attributable to a higher birth rate of the members of this Church. Undoubtedly the success of the Roman Catholic Church in maintaining its adherents in the face of strong secularizing pressures is also partly a tribute to

174

its well-organized and all-embracing system of primary and secondary schools, which it has achieved through a great effort in self-help and sacrifice. The strength of this Church in Australia arises from the constancy of its members rather than their numerical total, and on any Sunday it is probable that more than half of those attending church will be Roman Catholics.

There are some socioeconomic differences between the denominations. Higher level occupations tend to be pursued by Presbyterians, Hebrews, and Congregationalists, followed by Methodists, Baptists, and Lutherans. Roman Catholics, members of the Salvation Army, and those not disclosing any denomination tend to follow lower level occupations, while Anglicans are evenly dispersed on both levels. But the lines are not clearly drawn, and ethnic origins appear to play a far more important role than economic status in differentiating the denominations.

Most Presbyterians are of Scottish ancestry, most Catholics of Irish, and most Lutherans of German. There is no native denomination of any consequence, and most of the religious groups retain fairly close ties with their counterparts overseas. Although obvious adaptations have been made by the religions to local conditions—for example, in education—the churches in Australia have in many instances rigidly retained practices and attitudes which are not altogether appropriate.[43] A disproportionate number of the church leaders are born and trained overseas, especially the senior personnel, and no university in Australia has a chair of divinity. Preparation for the clerical profession is usually provided by special seminaries, many of which do not require university matriculation standards.

Official relations among all denominations are cordial but the pooling of resources is rare, even in those areas where one might most expect it—in training clergy, for example, or in serving sparsely populated areas. Despite the maintenance of correct relations between Protestant and Catholic leaders, there is considerable mutual sniping by lay members and there are frequent cases of prejudice in employment and social relations, somewhat reminiscent of the "gentlemen's agreement" type of ethnic discrimination.

ATTITUDES TOWARD RELIGION

Australians, with their pragmatic rather than abstract values, show little concern for evangelism or theological sectarianism. Fundamentalism is almost extinct. There is little suggestion of a religious revival, although

175

there have recently been a few stirrings, for example, the Moral Rearmament movement and the Methodist "Mission to the Nation." With some notable exceptions, the overworked and poorly paid ministers of religion also have little time to concern themselves with social and moral questions outside the limits of their own congregations. The ministers who constitute the exceptions in this regard tend to be attached to nonconformist denominations. On the whole, the public shows little desire for pontifical exhortations by the clergy outside of the pulpit, and is inclined to resent any intrusion by the churches into politics.

Australian church bodies are particularly active in the missionary field among the aborigines and neighboring non-European communities, but—apart from the Methodist Mission, which concerns itself largely with social questions—evangelical activities are restricted to a minor role among European Australians themselves; such activities are not particularly welcomed. Care is usually taken to keep separate the renderings unto God and Caesar, but there is a definite Christian bias in public expression vis à vis non-Christian or atheistic ideologies. Lay leaders in public life usually take pains to conform outwardly to the requirements of conservative Christianity.

Regular weekly church attenders constitute only 23 per cent of all adult Australians, and only 6 per cent of those calling themselves Anglicans. Fifty-three per cent "rarely or never" go to church.[44] These attendances are well below corresponding figures for the United States and, if allowance is made for the proportion of Roman Catholics, below those of Britain. On the whole, Australian women are considerably more religious than the men by any criterion, but the majority of women are not churchgoers.

On the other hand, respect for religion is shown by the fact that over half the respondents agreed that a religious revival is needed in Australia.[45] Furthermore, half the respondents opposed the showing of movies on Sunday. In fact, Sunday public entertainment is banned in several Australian states,[46] and Sunday observance is strongly maintained in certain districts where Sunday newspapers and even the use of public sports grounds are forbidden by local regulations. When asked why people stay away from church,[47] the respondents were inclined to blame the people rather than the church. There is no lack of belief in God or in an afterlife, compared with people in other countries.[48] Nevertheless, the typical Australian attitude toward religion signifies apathy rather than opposition. Generally speaking, Australians are not churchgoers but they are by no means in revolt against the church or its institutions. The general public shows tolerant patience toward the sometimes successful activities of certain church leaders who attempt to reduce its drinking, gambling, and Sunday recreational activities.

Cultural and Leisure Activities

Educated European immigrants in Australia frequently bemoan the absence of "cultural facilities" and the alleged inability of Australians to appreciate cultural and artistic values. We suspect that these judgments are partly class biased, but it may be true that popular support of the arts is less marked in Australia than in Europe, class for class. Popular support for the arts in Australia probably compares closely with that in the United States, but in the absence of any "index of culturedness" it is very difficult to compare relative levels accurately. Each state in Australia has a permanent orchestra, and there are national opera and ballet companies and a National Theatre Trust. These developments are recent, whereas art galleries, libraries, and adult education (nonvocational) facilities were already established on a comparatively grand scale in the middle of the nineteenth century, paralleling the enthusiastic development of child educational facilities at the time. The plateau in cultural development from 1890 to 1940 also paralleled that in the popular support of educational activities. Since World War II there has been a noticeable upswing in cultural pursuits, and today there is much popular enthusiasm for a number of artistic endeavors, particularly music.

Perhaps the most characteristic feature of Australian cultural life to date has been, ironically, the lack of characteristic features. There have been few indigenous developments of note in music, the graphic arts, and architecture, although outstanding executants have been produced, including singers and political cartoonists. Some use has been made recently of aboriginal themes in art and music, but no influence from neighboring Asia has gained entry. The tendency has been to take over uncritically the styles of expression current in Europe and America, frequently introduced by immigrants. Talented local artists are seldom appreciated unless they have first established a reputation abroad. As with other public activities, government bodies are looked to for the support of artistic endeavors, but this has seldom been forthcoming except through the Australian Broadcasting Commission, a government agency, which has done a great deal to stimulate music and intellectual discussion. Private patronage of the

177

arts is almost nonexistent, and—probably as a consequence—experimentation and innovation are very rare. Australia's class attitudes, which are antagonistic to the esoteric artistic pursuit of an elite, undoubtedly also have much to do with musical, artistic, and architectural conservatism.

Literature in Australia has shown a more indigenous influence than other aspects of culture. The nineteenth century produced a body of notable literature that was firmly rooted in the "aggressive democracy" of the era. This literature, which dealt almost entirely with rural themes, was concerned largely with the struggles of the "common man," but also expressed the lusty nationalism of this period. Modern writers are still inclined to adopt themes concerned with the social and environmental struggles of the people rather than with introverted soul-searching; accordingly, character studies are rare. Considering the urban emphasis in Australian life, the emphasis in literature is still markedly rural and provincial. A high proportion of the better works are historical or period novels, although a trend toward the novel of social criticism, based on urban life, is noticeable. Contributions by Australian authors have included many short stories and sketches, but few plays. Until recently, poetry has been predominantly ballad in form.

A great drawback to literary creativity is the virtual impossibility for a writer to make his art a livelihood or self-sustaining profession. Although by world standards, Australians read many books—they are still ante-television—they do not read Australian works. A Gallup Poll in 1953 found that two thirds of Australian adults state that they read books, claiming an average of twenty-eight a year. Adolescents also read books at a similar rate, not counting the paper-covered American "comic" books that are also popular.[49] The average reader concentrates almost entirely on "popular" novels, while the educated reader shows a preference for works that have already been acclaimed overseas. Commonwealth government fellowships are now available to assist writers, but no significant influence has yet been felt from this source.

Each state has active adult-education organizations, usually associated with the universities, and these provide lectures and short courses in arts and crafts, politics, practical psychology, and philosophy. They also provide libraries of books and music. There are usually no educational prerequisites for their courses; fees are nominal, and no diplomas are given. Attendance is fairly large in some of the courses, especially in those offering topics of seeming pragmatic interest—for example, "practical parenthood."

Newspapers are also relevant to culture; there are only fifty-five daily papers, of which the fourteen published in the five large cities account for 90 per cent of the total circulation. The combined circulation amounts to 410 issues to every 1,000 persons, compared with 624 in Britain and 350 in the United States.[50] The bulk of the newspapers are controlled by a few nationwide syndicates, and there is an absence of both a "quality" paper and a mass-circulation yellow press. There are several popular-type weekly and monthly papers and magazines with a large circulation, many of them being produced by the large newspaper corporations. The "highbrow" periodicals are constantly menaced by bankruptcy and they come and go with considerable rapidity, leaving few survivals.

Listening to the radio is by far the most popular way to spend an evening,[51] followed by reading a book and attending movies. Among the population as a whole, visiting friends in their homes and playing cards are each more popular than attending a dance. We have no comparable data on the leisure habits and preferences of adolescents and young adults, but undoubtedly movies, dancing, and parties figure more prominently than among older adults. The first preferences of adults are mainly for activities in the home, while for adolescents activities outside the home are comparatively more popular.

Almost every home has at least one radio, and most listeners have the choice of two government and up to six commercial stations. Short-wave stations relay the government and commercial programs to outlying listeners. The government stations are financed by license fees amounting to four dollars per household, and the programs offered range from the proceedings of Parliament and educational broadcasts to popular serials and "hit parades." Television is scheduled to start in 1956, with parallel government and commercial channels following the present pattern of radio broadcasting.

Movie attendance, while lower than in Britain and the United States before television, is comparatively high, averaging sixteen times a year for the total population and more than twice that figure for older adolescents. There are some very large and comparatively luxurious cinema houses, and the films are predominantly American. Attendance at "live" shows in the cities is small except when overseas celebrities are performing; "runs" of over twelve months in one location are unknown. The average adult

Australian attends three concerts or plays a year. Amateur acting is also popular; many small provincial towns maintain their own thriving repertory companies.

Attending or participating in sports is a popular way to spend a Saturday afternoon. Spectators at one football game or a special horse race sometimes account for a tenth of the total population in metropolitan areas. Sporting skill is highly valued, but training is inclined to be rather casual in most amateur sports. Swimming and—to a lesser extent—tennis are by far the most popular participation sports; most Australians can swim, and in some states swimming is a compulsory subject at school. Other common weekend activities include gardening and going for drives, while a great many Australian men gain satisfaction from making household appurtenances for themselves. We might add that the moderate climate of both summer and winter favors outdoor activities during the day. The joy of sheer physical expression is highly valued by both young men and women, and sport and physical development have been given official support through the government-subsidized National Fitness Councils. These councils stimulate the provision and use of recreational facilities and sponsor youth-leader training and youth camps.

Gambling is highly institutionalized; there are government-supported lotteries in five of the six states, and legalized off-course betting shops for horse races in two. A Gallup Poll indicates that 87 per cent of the adult population buy lottery tickets and 53 per cent gamble on horses. It has been estimated that the average Australian over nineteen invests about $100 on race horses each year. (This estimate is derived from the amounts paid in the form of betting taxes.)

Australians regard themselves as heavy drinkers even though closing time for almost all bars and liquor shops ranges from 6 P.M. to 10 P.M., and most of them are closed all day Sunday. With increased prosperity the consumption of alcohol per person has doubled since 1939, but the rate is probably not much greater than that of the United States or Britain. Perhaps because of daylight drinking hours it is not uncommon to see drunks on the street; yet, despite considerable public tolerance of excessive drinking, arrests for drunkenness are high (twenty times the number in Britain). Seventy per cent of adults in a Gallup Poll claimed that they drank at least a little, but there are no reliable statistics available on the extent of alcoholism. Workers' strikes and union boycotts have occurred several times in disputes over the price of beer. This interest in beer has become a tradition in Australia as a result of many factors, among which are probably heat, reckless attitudes, short working hours, British tradition and the semiprohibition involved in limiting the hours during which liquor may be sold.

Paid annual holidays have been the custom for white-collar workers for fifty years; for factory workers, only thirty. Today these are granted to over 80 per cent of all employees,[52] and half of the population goes away for about a fortnight's holiday each summer, preferably to a seaside resort. Workers and employers do not differ in this respect. Most families take their holidays together, frequently in the form of camping under primitive conditions. Although short-term (one or two weeks) youth camps are often organized by service organizations (for example, the Scouts), longer camps for children and adolescents sponsored by either institutional or commercial interests are virtually nonexistent.

In summary, Australians take their right to leisure seriously and tend to spend it in varied ways. On the one hand, sport, drinking, and gambling possibly play a larger role than in other comparable countries. Cultural activities and voluntary organizations, on the other hand, possibly play a smaller role, although interest in these is increasing.

Social Movements and Ideological Organizations

As indicated in previous sections, Australia has not proved to be a fertile soil for the growth of ideologies, despite the fact that the immigrants of the nineteenth century included many radical and dissident elements, some of whom were deported from the British Isles for this reason. The ideological drive of these dissidents seems to have been dissipated by the success they had in getting their ideas accepted in their new country, where they were supported by the mass of the population and where there was less opposition to the tide of social reform than in the more traditional and tighter social structure of Britain.

Trade unionism flourished and achieved social power much earlier than in America, favored not only by the political temper of the population but by an economic climate which was inhospitable to the independent small businessman. In a contest of power over union recognition in the pastoral industry, then the center of the economy, the unions suffered a temporary setback in the depression years of the 1890s, only to recover their strength soon after, when they founded the Labor party in order to use political pressure for their protection. The Labor party rapidly became an important political force, achieving office as early as 1899 (in Queensland). Labor gained general recognition of unions in the systems of compulsory arbitration established around the turn of the century. Both these victories, however, were won on terms that introduced certain stabilizing elements into the situation, and these have slowed down further progress toward Labor's objectives. Labor could only stay in power politically if it moderated its radicalism toward the conservatism of the swinging middle-class voters, and unions which were grateful to compulsory arbitration for guaranteeing them recognition and the right to bargain collectively found that they were expected to forgo direct action in return for these gains.

These and further successes of the labor movement blunted the edge of its various ideologies, none of which has ever achieved a dominating grip on the movement, which has been essentially pragmatic and pluralist, carrying its doctrines lightly. The earliest major ideological influence was Chartism. In the middle of the nineteenth century this movement appealed strongly to the large section of the population owning no property but its own labor, which saw its main hope in full political democracy. Then the doctrines of Henry George enjoyed a vogue when the problem of land distribution became acute as the decline of alluvial mining drove the miners onto the land. Both these ideologies received some expression relatively early in Labor's political career.

The Australian Labor party also became much more nationalistic than the other political parties. The pressure for democracy was mingled with resentment against the controlling economic and political interests in Britain, and the drive for higher labor standards in industry was associated with the attempt to exclude colored labor. The earliest official objective of the Labor party, issued in 1905, included as its first item "The cultivation of an Australian sentiment, based upon the maintenance of an enlightened and self-reliant community." White Australia was the immediate expression of this aim, and in its emphasis on Australia's independent role within the British Commonwealth, the Labor party has continued to show this nationalist strain throughout its history. However, in this sphere, as in others, progress toward the goal of independence has been sufficiently rapid to remove the basis for any emotive nationalist movement.

Socialist doctrines have been current in Australia since the 1880s, and in various forms have been influential on the ideological fringe of the labor movement, without diverting it from immediate practical politics. The social, economic, and political environment in Australia was receptive to the basic ideas of socialism, which—in the form of government enterprise and state intervention in economic life—received practical expression quite early.

Nonrevolutionary socialism was influential in the foundation of the Labor party. It envisaged a gradual constitutional transformation of the social order through the good sense and good will of men, once the vision of the new society had been brought before them by education and propaganda. This utopianism fused with the Australian nationalism of the 1890s; freed from the shackles of the Old World, Australians were to build a new social order.

Revolutionary socialism, first of the syndicalist orientations favored by the Industrial Workers of the World and later of the communist variety, has had much more influence on the organization and conduct of the Australian labor movement than on its doctrines. Although revolutionary influence was strong enough to establish the socialization of "all principal industries" as an aim of the Australian Labor party in 1921, this goal was to be achieved by constitutional methods, and six years later the socialization aim was limited to a few key industries. Nevertheless, Communists have wielded considerable power in the trade unions, particularly in coal mining, transport, and the metal industries. Their success in the unions contrasts sharply with their failure at the polls and can be attributed to their efficient organization and militant policies rather than their political views. Their influence reached a peak soon after World War II, but in the struggle for control that has taken place in the last few years, they have lost ground. One of the main active sources of opposition to communism is Roman Catholicism, which has always been strong in the Australian labor movement.

The conflict in the labor movement came to a head in 1955 over the role played by its leader, Dr. H. V. Evatt, in the Royal Commission on Espionage (the "Petrov Commission") that led to a split in the parliamentary Labor party. The split, like an earlier one in the 1930s, was complicated by personalities and sectarianism, and although the breakaway group has been practically annihilated in subsequent federal and state elections, the rift was too deep to be easily healed and the labor movement remains confused, uncertain in policy and program.

In historical perspective the Australian labor movement appears as a stream diverted from the main flow of social reform in Britain, the accumulated pressure behind it carrying it rapidly forward over the unresisting terrain of the new society. The large dissident element among the settlers of Australia and the absence of a substantial group of small property holders favored the growth of a strong labor movement. The same factors also made the movement one of an amorphous mass of people who, although favoring government intervention to further their own interests, have not been sufficiently underprivileged to embrace ideologies envisaging the peaceful transformation of society, let alone by force.

Perhaps the absence of doctrinaire revolutionary ideologies partly explains the fact that right-wing totalitarian movements have had even less success than those of the left. Minor fascist organizations have developed from time to time without becoming a major social influence.

Indeed, apart from the labor movement, no social movement has wielded great influence in Australia. The non-Labor political parties have no positive social philosophy guiding their advocacy for the sections of the population that they represent, and are mainly parties of resistance to Labor. Various movements—like those for social credit, protectionism, and the single tax—have achieved a brief vogue, but none has won the allegiance of a substantial part of the population. Religious and ethical movements, such as Moral Rearmament, Catholic Action, and Freemasonry, have made determined bids for influence through inconspicuous organizing. Others, such as the Methodist Mission to the Nation, the Christian Social Order movement, and The Call (an interdenominational appeal for a higher standard of public morality) have worked more openly and with relatively superficial impact. Political parties other than the Labor party have had their junior branches, such as the Young Nationalists of the Liberal party and the Eureka League of the Communist party, but none has kindled the imagination of the younger generation, which remains more concerned with vocational aims and leisure pursuits, especially sport.

Voluntary Associations and Community Organizations

Many of the types of association found in the United States are also found in Australia: for example, sporting clubs, fraternal lodges, veterans' organizations, church fraternals, and social clubs. In view of their prevailing urban culture and typically extroverted personality, we should expect most Australians to belong to voluntary associations. Although actual statistical data are lacking, we surmise that this is, in fact, the case. Unlike Americans, however, Australians do not have the reputation of being "joiners." Most of their memberships are superficial affiliations with large organizations in which the member is merely a passive dues-payer—if that. More than half the members of voluntary organizations *never* attend functions.[53] Informal social pressures to join organizations are sometimes so strong that the membership is barely voluntary: for example, in the cases of occupational associations and veterans' organizations.

"Social-influence" types of organizations[54] usually fail to attract the participation of more than a few persons. As in France,[55] the dependence on centralized rather than local government breeds apathy toward local matters. Municipal and shire rate-payers' meetings on seemingly important matters are poorly attended, and local projects—kindergartens, school parents' committees, and community center movements—are left in the hands of a diligent few. For this reason, perhaps, retail cooperatives have never succeeded, except in small one-industry towns where the trade unions have organized them. In provincial centers in the country there is usually a greater degree of participation in local organizations and more enthusiasm about local social improvements than in the cities. But different localities vary greatly in this regard, owing largely to local traditions, personalities, economic structure, and ethnic composition.

Australians are fairly ready to cooperate in worthy public causes, provided someone else takes the organizing initiative; thus the same leaders often fill executive positions in several organizations. Such leadership in social-influence organizations is often the road to successful candidature for political office, so that such organizations—not only trade unions—can serve to bestow political power on persons who otherwise could not obtain it. Except in trade unions, however, the leaders are seldom of lower-class origin.

Undoubtedly some associations are used by the members to confirm or to gain social status, but we doubt whether the class identifications of these associations in Australia are as clear-cut as they apparently are in the United States.[56] As mentioned previously, Australians are probably less socially mobile than Americans, but there are some exclusive social clubs, at the upper-upper level, aimed at excluding middle-class "upstarts." There are also exclusive workers' clubs, open only to members of the working class. Membership in war-veterans' organizations also has some prestige value, derived from the voluntary nature of active war service. Ethnic origin makes some contribution to the formal associational structure in the cities, but practically none in country districts. The membership of ethnic clubs and associations is almost exclusively first-generation, and these clubs probably enhance the acculturation of their members to Australia almost as much as they retard it.

There are many charitable and social-improvement organizations, and public subscription appeals are fairly successful. Such appeals frequently take the form of street collections, in which individual contributions tend to be nominal only. Few communities have general charity funds, and appeals for funds are usually for very specific, emergency purposes. In general, the public looks to the government to provide for charities and social welfare; consequently, political lobbying often is an important element in the role of the leaders in social-improvement organizations.

Although men greatly outnumber women in total voluntary memberships, women probably predominate in social-improvement organizations. Most of the purely social associations for adults are unisexual and predominantly male. Australian men make a frankly admitted virtue out of seeking fellowship with other men under conditions that exclude women. On the other hand, women seldom join women's social organizations in order to have fellowship with members of their own sex only.

Child and youth organizations mostly include both sexes, and embrace a comparatively high percentage of young people. They are mainly devoted to social, recreational or educational purposes; only in exceptional cases do they concern themselves, even incidentally, with charity or social reform. The youth clubs associated with churches, which are often well attended, also tend to emphasize their social and sporting sides. Secret societies and exclusive clubs for young people, comparable with American fraternities, are very rare.

Most of the internationally known organizations that exist in Britain and the United States have their counterparts in Australia; for example, the Y.M.C.A. and the Y.W.C.A., the Rotary International, Freemasonry, the Boy Scouts, the Red Cross, and Catholic Action. There are also, however, many thriving nationwide organizations whose origins and scope are purely Australian, for example, the Australian Natives' Association, the Young Australia League, the Country Women's Association, and the Legacy Clubs, which are service organizations for deceased soldiers' families.

The development of voluntary associations has been enhanced greatly by the traditional role which Friendly Societies and lodges have played— and still play—in disbursing medical and other social welfare benefits. The legal limits on drinking hours also stimulate the existence of various clubs, mostly for men, which enable after-hours drinking to be conducted within the law.

Interrelationships of Institutions

Our treatment of the relationship between the Australian social institutions will deal with three aspects: the relative dominance of certain institutions, the degree of integration of the society, and present trends.[57]

It is difficult to determine which institutions are the dominant ones; that is, which institutions influence other institutions more than they are influenced by others. In this respect economic and family institutions appear to be the dominant ones in Australia at present. Most sociologists regard economic institutions as the dominant ones in industrial societies, if not in all societies, but we are not prepared to decide on the evidence whether or not the Australian economic institutions actually do dominate such aspects of family life as marriage and kinship patterns, child-rearing practices, and ascribed social status. On the other hand, certain aspects of the political institutions, the party system for example, are clearly dominated by the economic institutions. The religious, ideological, cultural, and educational institutions seem to us to be subordinate to both the economic and political. The recreational institutions, while also playing a subordinate role in Australian society, perhaps are more important there than in many other advanced cultures. To some degree, underlying recreational values—leisure, horse-racing, beer-drinking—are allowed to prevail against the values operating in the other institutions, such as the family, religion, and economic materialism. Voluntary organizations, outside of those connected with the other institutions already mentioned, play a very minor role in the society, but those connected with the economic structure, especially trade unions, are very important.

Despite the interrelationships among the institutions referred to above, the society is highly differentiated, and the various institutions have achieved a certain degree of autonomy. Let us consider the integration of Australian society from two viewpoints: among institutions and within institutions. Conflicting values *among* the institutions do not appear to be a paramount problem in Australia, although they have appeared prominently from time to time. For example, there was an attempt in recent years to associate trade-union activities more closely with religion as embodied in the Roman Catholic Church, but after some fairly intense public conflict, the Church appears to have withdrawn at least temporarily from this comparatively unsuccessful attempt.

Individual participants in the various institutions are largely protected from the possible harmful personality effects of conflicting role requirements by a fairly general acceptance, by the society, of pluralism together with compartmentalization among institutions. As crude indices of the degree of integration or disintegration, as reflected in individual behavior, we might point out that the rates of divorce, violent crime, mental disease, and suicide in Australia are low to average for industrialized countries. (The suicide rate in Australia averaged 1 per 10,000 persons in the last twenty years.) Also, as we have seen, a comparatively high number of Australians describe themselves as "happy." Either the role conflicts associated with social differentiation are not great in Australia or the social values ameliorate the effect of these conflicts on the individual.

Lack of integration *within* institutions would reveal itself openly in social strife rather than in personality disintegration. Undoubtedly there are many conflicting interest groups associated with the various institutions, for example, Labor and Liberal in politics, Catholic and Protestant in religion, parents and adolescent children in family life, country and urban interests, and employer and employee organizations in the economic system. The latter conflict is the only one of these which has led to any open strife in the last hundred years. By the standards of other countries, Australia has been remarkably free from bloodshed and riots; there have been a few minor incidents of this type associated with employer-employee conflicts, but these conflicts are much more often manifested in strikes that are accompanied by very little heat.

The basic economic conflict spills over into other institutions, especially into political and social movements and voluntary organizations, and it tends to dominate the other group conflicts. Even in wartime, employer-employee conflicts have been quite marked and overt. They have rarely been associated, however, with totalitarianism of either the right or the left; that is, neither side aims at eliminating the other by force.

One type of social conflict that is not closely associated with any one of the above institutions is ethnic conflict. While Australians have always been somewhat prejudiced against immigrants, there have never been any serious social disturbances associated with these prejudices. However, on a number of occasions in the past, there have been local riots—against Chinese gold-diggers in the nineteenth century and against Italian workers during the 1930s. These riots occurred mainly under conditions of extreme economic insecurity. Hostile acts against aborigines, however, have more often been caused by social prejudice than by economic factors.

To sum up the integration of Australian society, there are few signs of disintegration; on the other hand, it is not a highly integrated society. There is some tendency for economic institutions to dominate the others, but not to an all-pervading degree. There are a number of conflicting interest groups within the community, but these do not threaten to split it into militant partisan groups.

Looking ahead a couple of generations, it seems reasonable to predict that, with further industrialization, Australia will move in the direction of a "managed" society, in which the community, in various ways, intervenes to guide the activities of its citizens. Economic institutions are likely to move basically in the direction of more community intervention in market processes through the action of both the government and private enterprise. Social services will become more comprehensive and take more initiative in providing for the individual. The influence of state educational organs on the socialization process will increase, and social relations will be increasingly stimulated and guided by trained recreational leaders. The individual will become still more independent of family ties, although family life will continue to be very important. We predict that the Australian social character will approximate "other-direction" more and more.

Finally, one may ask to what extent the present institutional structure of Australian society may be expected to change, as a result of the stresses between and within institutions. So far, since at least the last decades of the nineteenth century, the development of the various institutions and their relationships have evolved in a comparatively smooth and continuous way. The industrialization of the country has proceeded without any notable social disorganization or change in direction, even under the severe stress of depressions and wars. We suggest that this was the result of the early urbanization of Australia and the urban origin of a large proportion of the immigrants, which spared the society the trauma of transforming large masses of peasants into an urban proletariat.

The present social institutions provide a solid, relatively integrated foundation upon which the future may be built, and, barring some unforeseen catastrophe, we do not anticipate any notable increase in either personal or social disorganization.

Notes

[1] Net value of production without deduction of depreciation or maintenance costs. Unless otherwise indicated all statistics are derived from figures published or supplied by the *Australian Commonwealth Statistician* and various *State Statisticians*. The last census was conducted in 1954 and figures are derived from this wherever they are available.

[2] Colin Clark, *The Conditions of Economic Progress* (London: Macmillan, 1940). W. S. and E. S. Woytinsky, *World Population and Production* (New York: Twentieth Century Fund, 1953).

[3] C. H. Northcott, *Australian Social Development* (New York: Columbia University Press, 1918), p. 41.

[4] W. D. Borrie, "Australia's New Population Pattern," in H. E. Holt *et al.*, *Australia and the Migrant* (Sydney: Angus & Robertson, 1953), p. 53.

[5] The term "British" is usually employed in Australian sociological writings to include Irish as well as English, Welsh, and Scottish.

[6] A. P. Elkin, "Native Peoples," in Grattan C. Hartley (ed.), *Australia* (Berkeley: University of California Press, 1947).

[7] Gallup Poll, December 1954. The polls held by the Australian Public Opinion Polls will, for convenience, be referred to in the text of this chapter as Gallup Polls.

[8] Gallup Poll, September–October 1952.

[9] See, for a discussion of the possible frame of reference, R. Taft, "The Shared Frame of Reference Concept Applied to the Assimilation of Immigrants," *Human Relations*, 6 (1953), 45–55.

[10] *Ibid.*

[11] O. A. Oeser and S. B. Hammond, *Social Structure and Personality in a City* (London: Routledge, 1954). A. Richardson, "British Immigrants in Western Australia: A Study of the Immigration Process," unpublished honors thesis (University of Western Australia, 1953).

[12] As described, for example, in R. Centers, *The Psychology of Social Classes* (Princeton: Princeton University Press, 1949). R. M. Williams, *American Society: A Sociological Interpretation* (New York: Knopf, 1952).

[13] W. Buchanan and H. Cantril, *How Nations See Each Other: A Study in Public Opinion* (Urbana: University of Illinois Press, 1953).

[14] R. Taft, "The Social Grading of Occupations in Australia," *British Journal of Sociology*, 4 (1953), 181–188.

[15] Buchanan and Cantril, *op. cit.*; Oeser and Hammond, *op. cit.*; O. A. Oeser and F. E. Emery, *Social Structure and Personality in a Rural Community* (London: Routledge, 1954).

[16] See Oeser and Emery, *op. cit.* as compared with Centers, *op. cit.*

[17] Buchanan and Cantril, *op. cit.*

[18] *Ibid.*, and Oeser and Hammond, *op. cit.*

[19] *Op. cit.*, Chapter 22.

[20] Oeser and Hammond, *op. cit.*

[21] Oeser's data, the only relevant material available, are subject to a number of limitations for our purpose. Most important is the fact that the proprietor and white-collar groups cover a wide range of statuses, with considerable overlap between the proprietor, white-collar, and skilled-worker groups. Further, Oeser's data cover mobility during a period occupied largely by the depression and the war, and it is possible that the postwar prosperity period has changed the picture. His sample of upper-middle-class families is also probably biased through the exclusion of families whose children attend private schools.

190

[22] S. N. Lipset and Natalie Rogoff, "Class and Opportunity in Europe and the U.S.A.," *Commentary*, 18 (1954), 562–568.

[23] R. M. Crawford, *Australia* (London: Hutchinson's University Library, 1952), p. 191.

[24] Buchanan and Cantril, *op cit.*

[25] D. Riesman, N. Glazer, and R. Denney, *The Lonely Crowd* (New Haven: Yale University Press, 1950).

[26] Buchanan and Cantril, *op. cit.*

[27] "Now this is the creed of the Book of the Bush,
Should be simple and plain to a dunce:
If a man's in a hole you must pass round the hat
Were he jail-bird or gentleman once."
Henry Lawson
From Will Lawson (ed.), *Australian Bush Songs and Ballads* (Sydney: Frank Johnson, 1944).

[28] K. Morris, "A Study on Racial Stereotypes," unpublished undergraduate investigation (University of Western Australia, 1954).

[29] Buchanan and Cantril, *op. cit.*, and Gallup Poll, June–July 1953.

[30] Gallup Poll, October 1948.

[31] See Riesman's discussion in Riesman *et al., op. cit.*, p. 35.

[32] *Review of Economic Progress* (Queensland Bureau of Industry, August 1949).

[33] Woytinsky and Woytinsky, *op. cit.*, p. 351.

[34] K. F. Walker, *Industrial Relations in Australia* (Cambridge, Mass.: Harvard University Press, 1956).

[35] R. C. Gates, "The Weight of Taxation in Five Countries, 1938 to 1950," *Economic Record*, 27 (1952) 222–237.

[36] Gallup Polls, July 1951 and September 1952.

[37] Woytinsky and Woytinsky, *op. cit.*

[38] Gallup Poll, July 1951.

[39] Oeser and Hammond, *op. cit.*

[40] *Ibid.*, and Oeser and Emery, *op. cit.*

[41] Figures expressed in dollars are converted from Australian pounds at the exchange rate of approximately £A1 = $2.25. Actually, in terms of purchasing power, the Australian pound is probably worth three to four dollars at present.

[42] Gallup Poll, June–July 1955.

[43] E. H. Burgmann, "Religion," in Hartley, *op. cit.*

[44] Gallup Poll, September–October 1950.

[45] Gallup Poll, November–December 1953.

[46] Gallup Poll, November 1952.

[47] Gallup Poll, November–December 1949.

[48] Oeser and Hammond, *op. cit.*, p. 20.

[49] Material in this section concerning adolescents is derived from an unpublished report of a study conducted in Sydney by W. F. Connell and others.

[50] The British and United States figures are quoted from G. A. Lundberg, C. C. Schrag, and O. N. Larsen, *Sociology* (New York: Harpers, 1954), pp. 449–457.

[51] Gallup Poll, September–October 1952.

[52] Gallup Poll, November–December 1949.

[53] Oeser and Hammond, *op. cit.*

[54] A. M. Rose, *Theory and Method in the Social Sciences* (Minneapolis: University of Minnesota Press, 1954).

[55] *Ibid.*

[56] *Ibid.*

[57] This treatment owes a great deal to Williams, *op. cit.*, for its orientation.

Supplementary References

Australian Quarterly (various issues). Sidney: Australian Institute of Political Science.

Caiger, G. (ed.), *The Australian Way of Life* (London: Heinemann, 1953).

Commonwealth Bureau of Census and Statistics (Canberra); A.C.T. and various state statisticians; yearbooks and other publications.

Economic Record (various issues). Melbourne University Press.

Garnett, A. C., *Freedom and Planning in Australia* (Madison: University of Wisconsin Press, 1949).

Hancock, W. K., *Australia* (London: Ernest Benn, 1930).

*

Heikki Waris

FINLAND

*

THE main fact which has deeply influenced all social institutions in Finland and which has shaped its history is its geographical location. Finland is a *borderland*. Finland's location and its historical function have made it a bridge and a meeting ground between Russia in the East and Scandinavia in the West. Thus, the flora and fauna of Finland show a mixture of both Western and Eastern elements and, likewise, from earliest prehistoric times up to the twentieth century Western as well as Eastern cultural influences are discernible in Finland. There are already Western and Eastern patterns in the ornaments of pottery from the stone age in Finland. And in the twelfth century religious influences emanating from the two centers of the Christian world, Rome and Byzantium, met among Finnish people and produced the westernmost monasteries of the Greek Orthodox church (at Valamo and Petsamo) and the easternmost fortresses of the medieval Roman Catholic countries (at Viipuri and Savonlinna). And through seven centuries fierce battles have been fought on Finnish soil again and again. The Karelian Isthmus—north of present Leningrad—is one of those historic regions in Europe where fighting armies have met through several hundred years. In this region the Finnish and Soviet armies met again during the early phase of World War II.

Finland is a borderland. Yet, from the point of view of its social institutions Finland always was and is today a Western country. In many respects it resembles Sweden, with which Finland was politically united for more than six centuries.

During more than a hundred years (1809–1917) these Western peoples lived under the supremacy of the Russian czar, but this period scarcely changed the basic nature of social institutions in Finland. Finnish institutions remained, on the whole, intact. Finland's Western heritage of institutions, cultural patterns, and social values has only been strengthened in the years of independence. Although Finland's position as a borderland has been challenged, its response has been to stand in defense of its Western institutions.

Finland's geographical location and its historical development have produced the second basic fact. Finland belongs to the *northern countries* of Europe, which, for many non-Europeans, are identical with the *Scandinavian countries*. The long common history with Sweden, and more remotely with Denmark and Norway, has brought the most significant social institutions of Finland under the influence of the same factors that have affected institutions in these other countries. Inter-Nordic cooperation today, which covers practically all fields of economic, social, and cultural life, is based on the similarity or parallel development of social institutions in the northern countries.

One significant aspect of this affinity with the Scandinavian countries is the high degree of *homogeneity* in the Finnish society. *Racial homogeneity* particularly characterizes the Finnish people, who have practically no racial minorities (fewer than three thousand Lapps in the northernmost arctic communities make up the largest racial minority group). Consequently, racial prejudice and discrimination are nonexistent. A second important aspect is the very high degree of *religious homogeneity*—which is common to all Scandinavian countries with their established Lutheran Church—with more than 90 per cent of Finland's population retaining formal membership in the Church. Finland's location in the northernmost corner of the European continent has contributed to the fact that the country has never become a passageway for migrations nor a target for immigration. As a result, the number of persons of foreign extraction in the population is very small. A *national homogeneity* is apparent in all northern countries, including Finland, despite its linguistic minority of Swedish-speaking peoples (9 per cent in 1950).

When dealing with social institutions in Finland a fourth aspect of Finnish homogeneity has to be kept in mind. *Finland is one of the small countries of Europe.* Compared with the other countries of Europe included in this volume, Finland is the smallest in size. Greece has a population nearly twice as large as that of Finland, Yugoslavia four times, France nearly ten times, the United Kingdom more than twelve times, and Germany more than sixteen times. Finland is small when compared with these countries, although there are other countries in Europe with a long history of their own and social institutions clearly differing from those of their larger neighbors. Finland has a population of approximately 4.2 million, which puts it in the same category with Norway (3.4), Denmark (4.4), and Switzerland (4.8).

There is in these smaller countries of Europe, perhaps, a comparatively high degree of self-assertion and pride in *national traditions*. In this respect Finland resembles some of the older small countries of Europe where an ideological nationalism of the Romantic period—as well as a political nationalism, based in Finland on Hegelian philosophy—molded the minds of some leaders during the nineteenth century. Lacking political independence, however, the Finns expressed their national sentiments primarily in the nonpolitical field, in the collection of folklore, in philosophy, literature, and music. And so, Elias Lönnrot, the collector of folk poetry, Johan Ludvig Runeberg, the national poet, Johan Vilhelm Snellman, the philosopher and statesman, Aleksis Kivi, the novelist, and later Jean Sibelius, the composer, became the national heroes to whom the Finns erected their first statues. Such were the ideals that challenged the minds of Finnish young people in the early years of the twentieth century, when Finland sought to gain her political independence.

Since medieval times, the Swiss waged their wars of defense against their feudal lords and neighbors, and the Danes defended their country against the expansion of their southern neighbors in Germany. In Finland, which gained its political independence at an entirely different stage of European history, the active nationalistic attitude, characteristic of all smaller nations in Europe, is of a later date. It was strongly accentuated by the passive resistance of the Finns to Russian oppression during the later period of the last czar's regime (1899–1917), by the war of liberation (1918), and by the more recent wars of defense (1939–40, 1941–44) against the overwhelming numbers and military power of the Soviet Union. Nationalism, ideological and political, pervades the culture of this small people in contemporary Europe. Their social institutions cannot be fully understood without taking these basic nationalistic attitudes into account.

The discussion of these four aspects of Finnish homogeneity has stressed certain similarities between Finland and a number of other European countries. There are, however, also certain striking dissimilarities that should not be overlooked and some peculiarities of Finnish institutions that have to be borne in mind.

It is true that Finland is one of the smaller countries of Europe. Of the numerous young states separated and liberated from the old pre–World War I Russian, German, and Austrian empires, only Finland and Yugoslavia have retained their independence and real sovereignty without succumbing to their neighbors during or after the turbulent years of World War II. Dismembered and torn by wars, Finland still maintains its political independence. Its recent entrance into the United Nations is only an external sign of its special role in the family of nations.

One fundamental difference between the Finns and their neighbors is linguistic. The Finns speak Finnish, a language which with its fourteen or more cases is unlike any Indo-European tongue and is not related to any of the great European language groups. Finnish belongs to the Finno-Ugric group of languages, and is thus related to Estonian and, more distantly, to Hungarian. This linguistic affinity, however, has had no influence on the development of Finnish institutions. More recent and prolonged contacts with Indo-European peoples, notably Scandinavians, are today dominant in Finnish culture. There is the possibility that this difference in language may have emphasized a sense of isolation among the Finnish and strengthened irrational sentiments of prejudice and dislike against former members of an upper class that in earlier times was not able or willing to speak Finnish. Today all educated Finns, in their cultural contacts with other peoples, resort mainly to Swedish, German, or English.

In many respects the Finns resemble other northern peoples in Europe. Under the surface of a great many similarities, however, present-day Finland stands apart, in striking contrast with the Scandinavian countries, in possessing a deeper *attitudinal climate*. Among Finnish labor, a sense of hostility toward the existing social order was clearly discernible during the first decade of this century and occasionally burst out, external conditions permitting, into violent demonstrations and bloody revolts. The pressure of the czarist regime in the early years of this century brought about in 1905 a general strike in Finland, "Red guards" and mass demonstrations following the pattern of revolts in Russia after its defeat in the Russo-Japanese war. The Marxist doctrine of irreconcilable class interests and inevitable class struggle found ardent adherents in Finland, not only among urban industrial workers but also among the rural proletariat. And so, in 1917, the year of great revolutions in Russia, the accumulated bitterness of Finnish labor broke loose in waves of violent strikes and resulted in a cruel civil war in the early months of 1918 between "Reds" and

196

"Whites," with atrocities on both sides. The mere fact of civil war threw its long and gloomy shadow over all internal social relations during the two first decades of Finland's independence. The split of the labor movement in the 1920s between Communists and Social-Democrats; the deep-rooted distrust between managers and labor, particularly during the 1920s; the emergence of a violent reaction at the trough of the economic depression in 1930–31 among the defenders of the cause of the "Whites"—all this reflected, in part at least, the lingering effects of the civil war. These aspects of internal hostility and distrust were unlike the more peaceful atmosphere in the Scandinavian countries, with their more even and gradual development. There was a difference in the attitudinal climate.

However, this is not the whole story. There is in Finland a counterbalance to feelings of hostility against the social order. When the external pressure reaches a certain strength it calls forth a dormant sense of *national solidarity*. This was clearly visible in the joint passive resistance and the successful campaign of nonobedience to the czar's suppression of the rights of the Finnish people. This latent sense of national solidarity became still more obvious in the early days of Finland's Winter War. It was demonstrated by the unanimity of all classes, including Finnish labor, during the long period of wars against the Soviet Union from 1939 to 1944.

It is not necessary—nor possible—to dwell here at length on the motivation for the awakening of this sense of solidarity at the crucial moment in 1939. It may suffice to quote one American authority on Finnish history:

It is an interesting fact that the literature of freedom and liberty in the abstract does not loom large in Finnish culture. This does not mean that the concepts or practices of freedom have been ignored. What it means is that freedom, liberty and government under law have been taken for granted. National freedom and the liberty of the Finnish citizen and Finnish cultural independence—these have been accented more than the general idea of human liberty. Man's search for freedom has not been the important concern; the Finns' own desire to be free, to escape foreign domination, to be masters in their own house, has been the inspiration.[1]

Economic Institutions

Industrialization began in the northern countries of Europe during the 1860s, rather late in comparison with the major industrial nations. In Finland it did not begin until the 1870s, and moved slowly during its first decades. Since World War II the expansion of industry has become more

Table 1. Occupational Structure of the Population in
Finland, 1900–50

Occupational Group	1900	1920	1940	1950
Agriculture and forestry	68%	65%	51%	44%
Industry.....................	11	15	21	30
Commerce	2	3	5	6
Transport and communication ..	3	3	5	7
Other	16	14	18	13

rapid and has changed the *occupational structure* of the Finnish people, as shown in Table 1.

Compared with other northern countries of Europe, Finland lags behind in the expansion of industry, i.e., manufacturing, mining, and handicrafts. Yet, Finland represents a society which is now moving rapidly toward the dominance of industrial production. In this respect it is interesting to compare the southern and southwestern counties where 32–39 per cent of the population is engaged in industry with the eastern and northern counties where the corresponding figure is only 18–22. In those sparsely populated regions, partly beyond the polar circle, modern industrial production entered very late. Here old forms of social organization and rural folkways were preserved until recent years, when the construction of power plants and increasing electrification brought about rapid changes. In these forest-clad regions the majority of men work part of the year—summer and fall—in agriculture on small farms of their own and, in addition, from a few weeks to several months in winter and spring in forests, felling and hauling and floating wood (as has been demonstrated by an intensive study of the rural labor force and its annual round of activity).[2] These men are thus producing the raw material needed by Finland's timber, pulp, paper and other woodworking industries. In this way industrial production enters the lives of men still living, widely scattered, in rural surroundings. These northern farmer-lumbermen defy the standardized classifications of occupations appropriate to countries with another kind of industrial structure. And at the same time this group also seems to defy the regulations and patterns imposed by a society with a higher degree of stability, as is shown by a study of the drinking patterns in Lapland.[3]

Finland, like the other northern countries of Europe, has escaped the concentration of industry in large and sooty urban agglomerations like those found in older industrial countries. To be sure, a number of industrial plants are located in the capital and other major cities but, on the whole, manufacturing in Finland as well as in the Scandinavian countries is characterized by a high degree of decentralization. This applies especially to the woodworking industries, which produce most of the goods used for exports.

The economically active population (as of 1950) is distributed among the principal industries as shown in Table 2.

Although eclipsed by the rapid and recent expansion of manufacturing, *agriculture* remains the major industry in Finland as well as in other northern countries. Owing to climatic and geological conditions the agricultural land is relatively meager, amounting to only 8 per cent of the total land area, as compared with 69 per cent for forest. Compared with forestry and industry, the productivity of agriculture remains low.

Farming in Finland is that of a borderland. There is first the physical border of settlement. "In most countries of western Europe, land clearance belongs to history. In Finland, it is of the past; but also very much of the present. Here, the farm story not merely begins with land clearance; but continues with land clearance as an accompaniment. Finland is engaged more energetically in land clearance than any European country west of the Russian border. Such reclamation gives to its farming a pioneer character." This is the view of a British geographer, an expert on Finland, who adds the following observation to his analysis: "As in many other farming countries, that which is traditional is still too persistent in the place of that which is economically profitable and desirable."[4] This traditional aspect of all farming seems to exert a strong conservative influence on the

Table 2. Distribution of the Economically Active Population
in Finland among Principal Industries in 1950

Industry	Number Employed	Total
Agriculture and fishing	795,000	
Forestry	117,000	912,000
Mining	6,000	
Manufacturing and handicraft	421,000	
Construction	123,000	550,000
Commerce	160,000	
Transport and communication	107,000	267,000
Services	227,000	227,000
Other	28,000	28,000
Grand total		1,984,000

development of agriculture in a country so close to the physical border of human settlement. But the proximity of the political border has also had a direct impact on Finnish farming, illustrated by the postwar resettlement of displaced farmers.

Finland's territorial losses in World War II have meant a turn of the screw for Finnish farming. Land was lost—more than 10 per cent of Finnish territory—but there was no corresponding decline in population and animal stocks. The change of political boundaries was forcibly complemented by a change in property boundaries inside the state. The Land Acquisition Act, passed by the Finnish Parliament in May 1945, prescribed expropriation of land to meet the needs of farmers displaced from the ceded territories in Karelia and also of war veterans with families. Within less than five years this operation was completed.

Unlike other European countries facing similar problems, Finland gave the displaced farmer an opportunity to continue as a farmer. And the Karelian has responded to this challenge. A recent sociological investigation by the author into the social adjustment of these displaced persons has proved that the migration of rural people to towns was no greater among the displaced Karelians than the national average. These farmers, with their traditions from the earliest settlements along the shores of Lake Laatokka and the Karelian Isthmus, have at least tried to continue their traditional way of life. They have worked on the new farms on land they themselves cleared, constructed houses, and freely associated themselves in cooperatives and other local groups with their new neighbors. Their participation in municipal and church activities, in farmers' associations and educational pursuits, and a relatively high proportion of intermarriage, seem to reflect their good adjustment. They continue their traditional way of life in new surroundings but still within the boundaries of their old native country.[5]

This is the sociological aspect of resettlement. It has, however, an economic aspect, too. The dismemberment of existing agricultural units added greatly to the number of small farms. In 1950 the resettlement was nearly completed; the resulting distribution of arable land among farms is shown in Table 3.

The small size of the farms is characteristic of Finnish agriculture. When all units are taken into account the average arable land area is only 5 hectares (12 acres) per farm. Nearly 80 per cent of the Finnish farms today have less than 10 hectares or 25 acres of arable land. The

FINLAND

Table 3. Distribution of Arable Land in Finland
after Resettlement in 1950

Hectares per Farm	Number of Farms	Percentage of Farms
0.25–2	95,306	26.6
2–10	187,834	52.6
10–25	62,479	17.5
25–50	9,931	2.8
50–100	1,284	0.4
Over 100	223	0.1
Total	356,787	100.0

postwar resettlement has been severely criticized from an economic point of view but, as the British geographer concludes: "Whatever criticism may be leveled against the form of the resettlement programme, its necessity has been unavoidable. Only the passage of time will permit the new pattern of ownership to be seen in its true perspective. Meanwhile Finland has demonstrated in the international field that at least one country has made constructive and practical efforts to solve its problem of displaced people. By 1951, all farm families had been resettled. Finland's solution for a major domestic problem is part and parcel of the settlement of a wider European issue. . . . The revolution in landholding of the postwar resettlement has not been economic for Finland; but the social integrity of the country demanded it."[6]

One further aspect of Finnish agriculture is the farmers' cooperative movement. Cooperation plays a significant role in the total picture of Finnish society, as in all Scandinavian countries, but is particularly dominant in the daily life of the Finnish farmer. He sells his milk through the cooperative dairy, his cattle and hogs through the cooperative slaughterhouse, his grain and eggs through the cooperative store, where he also does most of his purchasing of machinery and fertilizers as well as consumer goods, and the cooperative credit society is his local bank for deposits and loans. As in most Scandinavian countries the cooperative movement is highly specialized, with separate cooperative societies for special functions so that a vast net of cooperatives has spread all over the country. The combined membership in all cooperative associations has grown very rapidly—particularly in the postwar years—and, consequently, now far exceeds the number of farmers. It seems justifiable to speak of a bureaucracy within the cooperative movement, although the individual farmer-member has retained all his formal rights and the local committees and auditors exercise their important controls—yet the most important decisions are made on upper levels of the organization. Relatively speaking, the cooperative dairies have assumed the most dominant position in the life of the Finnish farmer. It was estimated in 1954 that 76 per cent of the milk and dairy products brought to market are delivered to cooperative dairies. Milk deliveries are the main source of income for the farmer in an agricultural economy based mainly on dairy farming. The marketing of different agricultural products varies. Another estimation shows that 79 per cent of all farm products are marketed through cooperatives—if the consumers' cooperatives are taken into account.

The farmers' cooperatives are only a part of the total cooperative movement that started around the turn of the century, at a time of rapidly changing economic and social conditions for the Finnish farmer. This change was brought about by industrialization on the one hand, and by agricultural competition from foreign countries on the other. The establishment of cooperative societies would hardly have achieved the dimensions it did, if, under the threat from czarist oppression, this movement had not awakened national enthusiasm. The cooperative movement has become one sector of the national front, and enjoys the high prestige of a patriotic movement.

Again, in this respect, Finland, with its numerous cooperative societies, their significant role, and their high prestige, is typical of all northern countries. In Scandinavia the farmers' cooperatives are among the most important and functionally highly specialized social institutions. The network of local, district, and national cooperative organizations covers all phases of a farmer's life. The cooperative is not merely an economic institution, but has assumed a more comprehensive social function.

Among industries in Finland, the *forest industry* occupies a place of primary importance. Within recent decades the industrial utilization of forest products has made enormous strides. Sawed timber, for domestic construction as well as for export, remains an important product, but emphasis has shifted increasingly toward the manufacturing of more highly processed goods. Today paper and pulp play a decisive role in the forest industry. And as a result of continuous research new products are being discovered, the production of artificial textile fibers, wallboard, and plastics being but a few examples of the rapidly expanding branches of the industry. Forest products in various forms account today for 80 to

90 per cent of the total exports. Most of the factories in these branches represent the highest stage of development, with the newest technological innovations, and employ highly skilled craftsmen along with a comparatively high proportion of women laborers. As a rule, these factories are located in the smaller industrial communities in a rural environment. In these communities the workers have easy access to the surrounding forests and lakes.

Another branch is the *metal industry* with its 83,000 workers (1953). There is only one copper mine of importance in Finland and very few smelting furnaces, but the most significant sector of this branch is formed by the engineering works and shipyards. They were formerly, as a rule, modest in size but had to be expanded at once to meet the demands of war reparations. Out of the total of reparation goods demanded from Finland nearly two thirds or 66.3 per cent were products of the metal industry, or various kinds of ships. As a result of this, the capacity of Finland's metal industry had to be increased overnight. In 1938 the metal industry of Finland employed 45,000 workers, but in 1948 their number had risen to 84,000 and the output had doubled. Large investments were necessary in these industrial plants, whose capacity had thus grown much greater than would have been necessary to meet the demands of the home market. After the compulsory reparations had been paid off—in full and on time—in 1952, the total capacity could be employed to meet additional Russian orders based on a five-year trade agreement. So the threat of impending unemployment in the metal industry was removed—at least for the time being. Dependent on imported raw materials and facing keen competition from older industrial nations, the Finnish metal industry has to rely for its exports almost exclusively on the large and expanding Russian market.

The war indemnities imposed on Finland necessitated a very rapid expansion of the industrial capacity of the country and brought about full employment which, in turn, made the absorption of displaced workers easier and greatly facilitated the adjustment of industrial workers into the postwar economy.

The *textile industry*, too, relies mainly on imported raw materials, and is able to supply practically the entire domestic demand. It employs nearly 40,000 workers, more than 80 per cent of them women. Because of the rising standard of living, particularly in the postwar years, the textile industry is assured of a relatively stable demand. Expanding social services for married women in industry seem to encourage the inclination of Finnish women to remain in factory work after marriage.

In *other branches of industry,* individual plants in different parts of the country are expanding their capacity and their labor force. In particular, the food and tobacco industries are having to meet a greater demand for their products, owing to the rising standard of living, changing habits, and the loss of old family functions. In Finland, as in other industrialized countries, industry performs more and more of the functions that used to belong to the family. In this respect, rural areas, too, resort more and more to factory-made goods, a trend noticeable in all branches of the production of food and beverages. The consumers' cooperatives have established some of the most prosperous factories in this particular industry.

Finnish industrial plants are, as a rule, comparatively small. Only 23 per cent of all industrial workers are in plants employing more than five hundred workers in contrast to 26 per cent in plants requiring a work force not exceeding fifty. In smaller plants the industrial organization is rather simple; in many of the rural industrial plants the management has been able to retain a personal and paternalistic attitude toward workers. With the growth of plants, however, the attitudes change. As in other countries during and after World War II, demands for industrial democracy were effectively expressed. In Finland a law was passed in 1946 according to which all industrial plants employing more than fifty workers had to establish a joint production committee, consisting of representatives of management, of white-collar employees, and of workers. These committees, limited to a consultative function only, were intended to further internal communication within the plant and thereby increase productivity. Certain pilot studies point out, however, that these committees have not been able to establish themselves as an important new institution in the Finnish plant community. The committees have not won the allegiance and confidence of either the management or the workers. In this respect the Finnish reaction parallels the experience with similar institutions in the Scandinavian countries. In all these northern countries the shop steward, as an elected representative of the trade-union local, has become the most important channel for internal communication. Although there is no grievance procedure in the American sense of the word, the shop steward has assumed a central position in the plant. In Finland, with its strong and active Communist element, the shop steward's influential position and his prestige in both the plant and the community have provoked much bitterness and dissension among different elements in the work force.

The expansion of Finnish industry since the war has increased the demand for power. In a country which has so many sources of water power, the obvious answer is to increase the production of hydroelectricity. This would have been necessary in any case merely to recover lost ground, since about a quarter of the hydroelectric capacity installed before the war was in territory ceded to Russia by the armistice of 1944. An ambitious program of building new power plants was undertaken and is now nearly completed, mainly in the far north where the great Kemijoki and Oulujoki rivers have been harnessed by power stations. Most of the new large hydroelectric power stations are state-owned and operated. Thus the very large investments required by this construction program have increased direct state control in economic life.

The greater part of Finnish industry is in the hands of private joint-stock companies. There are, however, a number of important industrial corporations which have retained their legal status as private companies, and are administered as such, but where the majority of shares is in the hands of the state. So the largest corporation in the woodworking industry, the largest mine companies, and a number of other industrial enterprises are state-owned. The percentage of state-controlled companies in the total production varies in different branches of industry; in mining it is 94, in power plants 38, in foundries and other metal-working factories 42, in chemical industry 33, in engineering industry 18, in woodworking industries16, and so on. Direct state control is not confined to industry only. The corresponding percentage for commercial airlines is 90, and for broadcasting 100. The state liquor monopoly is based on special legislation, and has an exclusive monopoly on the production and distribution of all wines and liquors. Its annual profit plays a significant role in the national budget.

Public ownership and control of the economic life of the country has gradually increased during nearly forty years of Finland's independence. The same is true of the collective ownership of the producers' and consumers' cooperatives. In this respect, Finland probably has traveled somewhat farther than other countries in western Europe. Certainly there is strong criticism of "creeping socialism," especially by certain bourgeois groups in Parliament and by certain economic organizations. On the other hand, shortage of private capital is at least partly a cause of this development. Moreover, this widespread public control seems to be accepted more or less as an accomplished fact, and all political groups share in the administration of state-owned companies. In this connection it is, perhaps, necessary to mention that state ownership of railways is taken for granted in Finland as in other countries on the European continent. The same holds true for municipal public transport and other public utilities. Private enterprise is often excluded from these services, which at times are run with a deficit paid directly from municipal taxes. There are no scientific studies available on this point, but it seems that the nature of ownership in an industrial enterprise has only little influence, if any, on relations between management and workers.

The *trade-union movement* is one of the most powerful social institutions in Finnish society today. In 1957 the Central Federation of Trade Unions in Finland (Suomen Ammattiyhdistysten Keskusliitto, known usually as S.A.K.) will celebrate the fiftieth anniversary of the establishment of its predecessor, the first central federation of trade unions, in 1907. Its membership was small, and it was composed mainly of craft unions. In contrast with the other northern countries where the trade-union movement has achieved a relatively even growth, the Finnish unions have passed through periods of external crisis, such as the civil war in 1918, and internal dissension between Communists and Social-Democrats, particularly in the 1920s. These struggles culminated in 1930 in the dissolution through court action of the federation of trade unions, which had been infiltrated by Communists. A new central federation (S.A.K.) with Social-Democratic leadership was formed. Its membership grew only slowly during the 1930s, but immediately after the war it experienced an influx of newly established national unions and tens of thousands of new members. The total membership soared from 106,000 in 1944 to 300,000 the next year and 340,000 in 1947. Now it included not only manual laborers but considerable groups of salaried people and lower civil servants. Inner dissension and constant fights with Communists led to the expulsion of certain national unions from the central federation. As a consequence, membership in the S.A.K. tended to fall in spite of the steady growth of the national labor force during a period of full employment in the early 1950s.

The S.A.K. proclaimed a general strike in March 1956, which led to the almost complete acceptance—after twenty days—of the demands of the S.A.K. This successful action has strengthened the position and added to the prestige of its present Social-Democratic leadership in the working class at large. On the other hand, it has alienated some white-collar groups in the unions and many people outside who contend that the trade-union movement has expanded beyond its legitimate sphere of influence and has encroached upon the prerogatives of Parliament.

This is the issue of today. Whatever answers may eventually be discovered to resolve the issue, the modern trade-union movement—with all its ramifications—is at present an indisputably central social institution in Finnish society as well as in all the Scandinavian countries. Whatever the "legitimate" boundaries of unionism may be, it is self-evident that the sphere of trade-union influence has greatly widened in postwar years and is by no means confined to wages and benefits for labor only. Alongside other voluntary special-interest organizations, such as the agricultural producers' and the employers' federations, the farmers' and the consumers' cooperatives, and the trade associations, trade unions of all shades of opinion exert influence and pressure on public opinion, especially on the Parliament as the supreme legislative body.

A feature common to all northern countries is that the majority of salaried employees have their separate unions, which as a rule do not belong to the central federation. These unions—representing intellectual workers, civil servants, foremen, and other white-collar people—have attained sizable dimensions. They have a central federation of their own, which today has a membership totaling 67,000. The progress made in the organization of nonmanual workers within the last decade must obviously be viewed against the continuous expansion, found in all Western industrialized countries, of administrative personnel in private business and in the government sector. This trend, coupled with reduced chances of promotion for the individual, has clearly provided a powerful stimulus for the development of organizations in this field. Results obtained by the older trade unions have been another contributing factor.

When all trade unions are taken into consideration, including those outside the two central federations, all organized laborers and salaried employees account for about 40–45 per cent of all workers in Finland, which is roughly equivalent to the corresponding percentages for Norway (45) and the United Kingdom (45) but lower than Denmark (50) and Sweden (60). The great number of workers attached to agriculture and forestry, and the relatively high proportion of female labor, partly explain the somewhat lower figures for organized workers in Finland.

Trade unions are open, in principle, to all persons employed in the trade or industry covered by the union. Freedom of association also includes the right to refrain from joining a union, although in practice any refractory worker encounters informal pressure from other workers in an industrial plant (but scarcely in an office or in agriculture). The ideological dissensions and internal struggles between Communists and Social-Democrats seem to strengthen democratic discussion and debate in locals as well as throughout the whole movement. Furthermore, the relatively small size of federations, the largest not exceeding 40,000 members, emphasizes this aspect. Consequently, the passivity or apathy typical of huge bureaucratic organizations does not seem an imminent danger in the Finnish trade unions. Yet, the executive boards of the federation or the national unions have the actual power of decision. There is a clear trend toward concentration of power and coordination of action, but the structure of organization has remained democratic.

The trade-union movement, represented by large federations, is matched by powerful *employers' organizations*. The unions were established to fortify the weak bargaining position of the wage earner as against the employer, and correspondingly the employers' organizations have had as their main purpose strengthening the hand of the individual employer in dealing with the union. In Finland, as in other northern countries, there have been no industrial giants potentially strong enough to meet the trade union single-handed as is the case in the United States. The structure of Finnish industry, with its many small and medium-size enterprises standing face to face with large trade unions, tended to promote the delegation of decisive powers to a central employers' association. In addition, the same industrial firms have established a network of special trade organizations to defend the rights and interests of industry in problems of tariff, taxation, regulation, licensing, and price control. This is one aspect of functional specialization in social institutions. The relative weakness and inner dissension in the trade unions in past times have not made the concentration of power on the employers' side as imperative as in other northern countries. Negotiation and bargaining in Finland, however, tends to become inclusive for a whole branch of industry, with more variations in the nonindustrial field. The Finnish Employers' Confederation (founded in 1907, reorganized in 1918) sets the pattern for all wage negotiations with unions.

The dominant attitude on the employers' side during the twenties and thirties found expression in a general sentiment of distrust toward trade unions, whether Communistic or Social-Democratic in leadership. It was not until the external pressure had risen to its highest pitch during Finland's Winter War that the main exponents of both parties, the Employers' Confederation and the Central Federation of Trade Unions, were prepared for negotiations and willing in January 1940 to sign an agreement of recognition. It was based, at least in part, on older patterns of similar basic agreements in Denmark (1899) and Sweden (1938) where national federations of employers and trade unions laid down certain principles of mutual acknowledgment and collaboration. The Finnish "January Agreement" was then amended in 1944 and 1946. This basic agreement between the central federations has been included in all subsequent collective agreements between unions and employers' associations. Much later than the Scandinavian countries Finland has now reached a stage of nationwide and industry-wide collective agreements.

The concentration of actual power in the hands of the central organizations, nearly all located in Helsinki, diminishes the independence of decision at plant level on wages and benefits. Simultaneously, this concentration of the bargaining accentuates a very marked long-term tendency toward the concentration of all economic, social, and cultural forces in the capital of the country.

In our age of rapid industrialization with its strong influx of population from rural communities to towns, from the periphery toward the centers, this concentration of administration, public as well as private, in the capitals or principal cities can be observed in many countries. Such a concentration has, perhaps, more influence on a balanced development of resources in a country like Finland, with its relatively large size and its sparse population.

Political Institutions

Finland is one of the young countries of Europe. It has been a politically independent country only since December 1917, when—having been a grand duchy under the Russian czar—it issued a declaration of independence. Yet Finland's political institutions are of older origin. In particular, the Finnish Parliament and system of government have old traditions. An appreciation of these traditions is widespread among Finnish as well as Scandinavian people.

According to the present Constitution, which dates from 1919, sovereign power is vested in the Finnish people, represented by their delegates in Parliament which holds legislative power in conjunction with the president of the Republic. The president also has supreme executive powers and the government is carried jointly by the president and a council of ministers, the Cabinet.

The Parliament consists of a single chamber and is composed of two hundred members who are elected on the basis of universal suffrage and proportional representation for a period of four years. The voting age was reduced in 1944 from 24 to 21. Laws enacted by the Parliament must be signed by the president. If Parliament, after general elections with a qualified majority, re-enacts the same law, it becomes effective without the president's signature.

The president is elected for a six-year term by a college of three hundred electors, chosen each time for this purpose by popular vote. Owing to the multiparty system there are, as a rule, more than two presidential candidates and, consequently, the electoral college has to make the final choice among several candidates. Twice already (1931 and 1956) it has happened that the final votes in the electoral college were 151 to 149. Thus the electoral college is not only a formality—as in the United States—but performs a highly significant function in the actual election. The president enjoys relatively wide powers. These powers of the president are more extensive than the prerogatives of any of the remaining constitutional monarchs in Europe. And what is significant is that they have not remained merely a dead letter. The first president (1919–25), K. J. Ståhlberg, in particular, made actual use of these powers and did not hesitate to dissolve the Parliament. Likewise, the president has more recently made full use of his wide constitutional powers in critical situations.

The Finnish Cabinet consists of a prime minister and up to eighteen other ministers. According to the parliamentary system the members of the Cabinet must enjoy the confidence of the Parliament. A minister of the interior, belonging to the Communist party, was dismissed in 1948 because he refused to resign after a vote of censure had shown that he had lost the confidence of the Parliament. Most of the Cabinets have been relatively short-lived. During thirty-eight years of Finland's independence since 1917 there have been forty Cabinets in power, only a single one staying more than three years. However, the change of Cabinet has in many cases meant only a change of a few members since the same coalition of parties remained in power.

This apparent instability of the Cabinet has an important counterbalance in the office of the president. By dividing the power between a stable authority, the president, and a temporary authority, the Cabinet, the Finnish Constitution has considerably lessened, if not eliminated, the apparent instability which is the great weakness of the parliamentary system in multiparty countries. The Finnish system, in spite of its many shortcomings, has assured a certain continuity of policy. The significance of this aspect becomes evident when compared with the instability of the executive power and the political regime in certain other countries of Europe which have a multiparty, parliamentary system.

Many political problems in postwar Finland arise from the nature of Parliament, which in turn reflects the different shades of opinion among the Finnish people at large. The results of the last parliamentary elections, in 1954, are shown in Table 4.

Table 4. Results of the Parliamentary Elections in Finland, in 1954

Party	Number of Votes	Total Deputies	Women Deputies
Social-Democrats	527,000	54	12
Agrarians	484,000	53	5
Communists	434,000	43	7
Conservatives	257,000	24	4
Liberals	158,000	13	2
Swedish Peoples Party	140,000	13	..
Others	8,000	...	..
Total	2,008,000	200	30

There are six parties represented in the Parliament. Some of the party names have changed and some realignment has taken place, particularly among the Liberals. The front organization of the Communists is called "The Democratic League of the People of Finland," established in 1944. It is fully under the strict control of the Communist party and has today only a small remnant of left-wing Socialists, not formal members of the Communist party. The other party names and organizations date from the early years of this century, when modern political parties sprang up: the Social-Democratic party in 1899 (with its present name since 1903), the Agrarian League in 1906, the Conservative, or the National Coalition party in 1918, and the Swedish People's party in 1906.

This is the political setup of parties today. It is unnecessary here to enter into an analysis of their ideologies and programs. Some general observations of the political institutions must suffice.

The Parliament is the most important political institution in the country. The Finnish Parliament is rightfully proud of its long history and its old traditions. Its earliest predecessors were the assemblies of nobles and clergy to which representatives of the burghers from towns and peasants from the rural countryside were invited in the early part of the fifteenth century; 1435 is usually given as the date for the birth of the four-estate Parliament in Sweden-Finland. Here the Finnish people had their representatives as did the provinces of Sweden. Finnish peasants and townspeople developed in this way a tradition of having representatives of their own to take some part in legislation and to give their consent to internal revenue taxes. In this respect Finland, Sweden, and Switzerland are the only European countries where the peasants never were serfs under feudal lords.

This Diet of four estates from the Swedish period of Finnish history was preserved through the nineteenth century under the Russian domination. When, under the influence of liberal ideas, the Finnish Diet was revived in the 1860s, it became a focus of public attention and brought about a lively discussion of public affairs in the country. This Diet initiated legislation to meet some of the demands of a modern dynamic society and reflected liberal, new ideas. Most important of all was the modernization of the Diet itself, long overdue, when the four-estate Diet was superseded in 1906 by a single-chamber Diet based on universal suffrage extended to all adult citizens, men and women alike.

The *scope* of the Parliament has greatly expanded. The establishment of Finland's independence in 1917 led in itself to an expansion of functions and an increase of power of the central legislative body; the Diet of an autonomous grand duchy became the Parliament of an independent republic. And since that time the scope of legislation, expansion of the state budget, increase of taxation, establishment of new services, not to speak of the exceptional nature of wartime controls—all have added to the power and enlarged the scope of the Parliament. In Finland, the expansion of the state sector in economic life means additional power for the Parliament.

Finland like all continental countries of western Europe has a *multiparty system* which compels different parties to seek collaboration and compromise. No single party seems to find sufficient backing to be able to assume the responsibility of government alone. It has to align itself with some other party with a different program. But what are the actual possibilities of coalition?

Theoretically there could be a coalition of the two labor parties. In Finland the Social-Democrats and the Communists won 99 seats out of 200 in the first elections after the war, in 1945; but in subsequent elections they lost a few seats. Yet, since the break between them in 1948, the dividing line between these two parties is sharp and definite. The Social-Democrats have aligned themselves to the bourgeois parties of the political center. In all Cabinets since 1948, with one exception, the two largest parties of the Parliament, the Social-Democrats and the Agrarians have joined with additional members from the Liberals or the Swedish. The Communists, on the left, and the Conservatives, on the right, remain to fulfill the important function of a parliamentary opposition and critic of the Cabinet. The pattern of Finnish postwar democracy is domination of the center kept in balance by criticism from both extremes. Yet, Social-Democrats represent mainly the interests of wage earners and consumers, and Agrarians are the chief exponents of farmer and producer interests. The clashing interests of their constituents perhaps more than their divergent ideologies give rise at times to discord. In presidential elections and on certain issues in the Parliament the partners in this political marriage may be found opposing each other.

The Finnish voters have, as a rule, kept faithful to their *party allegiance.* A certain conservatism seems to be typical of the political behavior of the Finnish people irrespective of their party. Real landslides have not occurred on the political terrain of Finland with the exception of the first elections after the defeat of Finland in 1944, when the Communists reappeared on the political scene. Consequently, Parliament has changed little from one election to another. Only certain long-term trends in changes of the political climate can be observed. A similar faithfulness and consistency in voting behavior can also be demonstrated regionally. Although there are only a few scientific studies on electoral geography in Finland and in Scandinavia, the influence of strong regional factors affecting the voting behavior can be demonstrated. In his illuminating work, *Atlas of Finnish History* (1949), and in an article based on it, Jutikkala observes that the social system of a past time seems to live in the political climate of today.[7]

Thus, the Social-Democrats captured 40 per cent of all votes in the first elections for the single-chamber Diet in 1907, which was more than this party gained in any European country in the pre–World War I period. The Social-Democrats attracted adherents not from urban labor primarily but from rural regions where the system of tenantry had been widespread. The landowner-tenant relationship was instrumental in producing the political climate where socialism—and later communism—seemed to thrive. A recent ecological study of Finnish communism in two provinces[8] seems to corroborate, in part at least, some findings of an investigation made in Sweden.[9] There is no single explanation for the adherence to communism. In particular, there is a tendency to overestimate the role of economic factors as if the rise of the standard of living in itself would counteract the spread of communism. The Communists in Finland as well as in Sweden— where they play a very minor role nationally—derive a substantial part of their support from distant backwoods and isolated agricultural areas where emotional experiences of past injustices seem to live in the memory of these people. Here the communist ideology has only little relevance, if any, to its adherents. "If we wish to locate communism in the human body it would be rather in the stomach and the heart than in the head." The political climate of a region as well as of a country has been shaped by its past, by the social relations and experiences of a previous generation.

An interesting instance of this tradition-bound political behavior is given by the displaced persons from the ceded territories in Karelia. In spite of a fundamental change in their conditions, in spite of the loss of their homes and home province, in spite of the entirely new issues faced in postwar years, the Karelians seem to remain faithful to their traditions in voting behavior. In many other respects they have been willing and able to adjust themselves to their new environment in western Finland, but in parliamentary elections they remained faithful to their old political ideals and did not vote for the Communists.[10]

The *active interest* of the Finnish people in their political institutions has varied considerably. There is, however, a long-term trend toward more active interest, as measured by frequency of voting at all elections. When the first elections for the Diet based on universal suffrage took place, in 1907, 70 per cent of all those entitled to vote turned up at the polls. Active participation soon decreased, however, during the Russian period when no positive achievements by the Diet were visible and reached a minimum of 51 per cent in 1913. It was not until the first elections after World War II that the percentage from the first elections was surpassed, with 75 per cent voting in the parliamentary elections. In 1954 this percentage had risen to 80. This rise was not caused by lowering the voting age from 24 to 21, as the frequency of voting in this youngest age group remained low—

214

in the capital as low as that among people over 70. A recent sociological study of voting behavior seems to indicate that voting frequency was highest in homogeneous communities where one party seemed to dominate and where the voters were not subjected to the pressure of conflicting norms. This study seems to support the so-called cross-pressure hypothesis.[11]

Frequency of voting has been substantially lower in municipal elections and in presidential elections, which seems to indicate that these local elections do not arouse the same degree of public interest.

It is typical for the Finn to turn up at the polls and cast his vote and then leave the elected member of Parliament—or of the municipal council —a free hand to use his mandate with only infrequent, if any, efforts by the voter to try to influence his delegate. Sending telegrams and letters to his member of Parliament is not a part of the political behavior of the Finn. Nor does the delegate often report back or open a discussion with his constituency. Nor do local party organizations as a rule control or exert pressure on the delegates. More pressure comes from outside institutions, from the highly developed special-interest organizations of trade unions, of private business, of landowners, of recipients of resettlement farms, of tenants, of war-disabled citizens or other invalids—all trying to influence members of Parliament in favor of their special interests. Furthermore, local or provincial interests, strongly advocated by powerful organizations, unite delegates belonging to different political parties to fight for privileges for their home town or province. A railway line, a new road, or a new hospital have a high priority in the mind of every delegate from the region.

Let us now consider the role of *women* in political institutions. In 1906, earlier than in any other European country, the women of Finland received full political equality with men. What has been the attitude of Finnish women toward their political privileges during half a century? Evidence from Finland seems to confirm the experience of other countries that women's interest in all political institutions is weaker than that of men. Their participation in elections is, as a rule, not so active as men's. This applies apparently to all age groups. But what is more important is that the great majority of women elect men to the Parliament, to municipal councils, and to the electoral college for presidential elections. Out of the 200 members of Parliament there were less than 20 women through the twenties and thirties, and only in postwar years has the number of women in Parliament begun to rise, reaching 30 in the last elections. Nearly two thirds of these women are labor delegates. In general, the political activity of women in elections as well as in party organizations is considerably livelier among labor groups than in other circles. It was the Social-Democratic party which introduced the first woman member into the Cabinet in 1927. Since 1945 all Cabinets have had one or two women members.

The early women's movement of the nineteenth century started in Finland and the Scandinavian countries, inspired by the feminist movement in the Anglo-Saxon countries. It was confined to the educated people, and fought vigorously for the principle of equality of women, for equal opportunities in education, in professions, and in political life. These early feminists fought against special protective legislation for women in industry, but they in turn were strongly opposed by women from the labor movement who had had personal experience in industrial work. Thus the feminist movement soon branched out into many idealistic associations and separate women's sections in political parties. Class consciousness and political ideals have been stronger than special women's issues. In the meantime, the women in Finland—as well as in the Scandinavian countries—have gained equal rights with men not only regarding suffrage but in the civil service and in other professions. With the rapid spread of university education for women, they have in great numbers entered such professions as dentistry, where 75 per cent today are women. More important from a national point of view is the relatively high proportion of women in industrial occupations. The percentage of women in the industrial labor force increased gradually with the growth of modern industry, reaching 40 per cent of the total labor force in 1935. It has receded from 50 per cent, reached under the exceptional circumstances of the war, but still remains at 38 to 39 per cent, which is approximately double the corresponding figure for Sweden.[12]

With all these relatively early and easy victories in Finland, feminism has lost a great deal of its enthusiasm and challenge. The younger generation of Finnish women are not belligerent feminists. They take their suffrage for granted, but seem to prefer men as their delegates in Parliament and municipal councils.

There is in Finland a unique political institution, the autonomous province of Aaland, the *self-government* of which was endorsed by the League of Nations. The Aaland Islands at the entrance to the Gulf of Bothnia have an enormous strategic importance in the Baltic. Their inhabitants asked in 1918–19 to be united with Sweden but the matter was referred to the decision of the League of Nations. The decision left the islands under

Finnish sovereignty but required that extensive guarantees be given to the 21,000 islanders, all Swedish-speaking. The settlement of this problem was probably the only successful solution of international tensions through peaceful mediation by the League of Nations. With so many discouraging examples of failure this was often cited as a promising opening for a new era in international relations. Bitterness between Finland and Sweden and a disappointment among the Aalanders themselves had gradually subsided when the challenge of an external threat called forth an inherent sense of solidarity. The autonomy granted has not destroyed the sense of joint responsibility. Here, probably, lies the significance of the self-government of Aaland.

Aaland is the only province enjoying self-government. All other provinces—or counties—are only districts for state administration under a governor appointed by the president. This limitation in the Finnish administrative system has been compensated, partly at least, by federations between groups of neighboring communes to erect and maintain common social institutions, such as mental hospitals, tuberculosis sanatoriums, trade schools, and child guidance clinics. Units of self-government are local municipalities. Towns as well as rural communes have since very early times enjoyed extensive rights in taxation and in administration of their local affairs. In spite of the trend toward expansion of state functions, local municipalities have retained a significant role in public administration. Municipal councils, elected by all residents over the age of twenty-one, exercise—mainly through their specialized committees—extensive rights regarding taxation, town planning, housing, schools, adult education, social welfare, public health, and hospitals. Administration of these and many other services are regarded as a function of municipalities. They are in turn subsidized from state funds, partly according to a differential and progressive scale so as to give relatively more state aid to communes in the poorer eastern and northern parts of the country.

Most of the municipal functions, including many exceptional wartime controls, were administered by laymen in municipal councils and committees, which have thus served as a practical training ground for the assumption of wider responsibilities in the democratic system of the country. Members of Parliament have often had their initial political training in municipal councils. With rapid expansion of the range of social welfare and other municipal services in recent times, trained social workers and other professional employees — in increasing numbers — have been en-

217

trusted wtih the actual administration of these services. Their adequate professional training in universities and specialized schools has become one of the essential tasks of towns and rural communes trying to preserve the high standard and prestige of local self-government.

The Family as a Social Institution

Finland lives at present in a period of transition. Although agriculture remains the major industry with the largest number of people attached to it, its domination belongs to the past; and modern industry and communications are spreading all over the country. Compared with central Europe and also with the Scandinavian countries, urbanization in Finland is fairly recent. At least, Finland has had—up until recent years—"backwoods areas" in the sparsely populated northern forest area and isolated rural villages in the wide lake district, where all social institutions, including the family, were dominated by the old traditions of a self-supporting economy. This self-sufficiency combined with old family attitudes and patterns is now rapidly changing. This trend is accentuated by two recent developments.

First, the expulsion of Karelians from the easternmost provinces, in particular those distant forest regions inhabited by Greek Orthodox people, has shattered the closed village communities with their venerable traditions and institutions, including the large-family system with three generations under the same roof. Their displacement meant, as a rule, abrupt transition to a small-family system.

Second, the very rapid expansion of electrification and of modern transport in postwar years has more or less destroyed the self-sufficiency of the farmers' families in many rural areas. The pattern of family life has come under urban influences. Consequently, family patterns all over the country have become more uniform.

There is, however, a strong trend in postwar Finnish society that retards the transition toward this urban family pattern. The establishment of resettlement farms for displaced persons and war veterans has greatly added to the number of very small agricultural units. More than 280,000 farms with fewer than 25 acres of arable land are all family-size farming units. As no hired labor can be used on such small farms, it is the family, in particular the farmer's wife and children, that makes up its main labor force. In most cases the farmer himself has to find outside employment during several months of the year. In countless cases the small-holder's family still performs significant productive functions which have been lost by the urban family. But, as in older times, most of his children must leave the family, the farm, or the village community as soon as they approach the age of twenty.

Changing family patterns are clearly reflected in birth and fertility rates. There is a high correlation between these rates on the one hand and rates of industrialization on the other. The more industrialized and urbanized southern counties have low birth rates and low fertility rates, and the northern counties comparatively high rates. In 1950–51 Lapland, the northernmost county, had a crude birthrate 77 per cent higher than that for the southernmost county, Uusimaa, including the capital, Helsinki. The difference is one between rural and urban areas, it is true, and emphasizes the contrast between family life bound by traditions in a relatively undeveloped forest region and the more individualized patterns of family life in towns and urbanized countryside.

These more urbanized family patterns have spread gradually during this century. A penetrating study of marriage and sex in Finland[13] has shown that Finnish radicalism in matters of sex and marriage received its main inspiration from liberal and Marxist ideas and sought to emancipate minds from more traditional and strict religious conceptions. This radicalism had already reached its culmination before 1910. A fight between an absolute and a relative sexual morality resulted in a defeat of relativism. The radical ideas of marriage and sex never reached more than a narrow segment of urban people and had already receded when the new phase of rapid industrialization set in during the 1920s. Advocacy of "free love" remained merely an episode. The notions of a decline in the significance of the family proved to be exaggerated. Many functions of the family have been partly transferred to other institutions in the industrialized society, and this trend has in many respects fortified the potentialities of a relative morality. Likewise, risks attending free sexual relations have become less dangerous. Nevertheless, the development of urbanized family patterns also seems to have strengthened the institution of monogamy. Particularly, the general spread of marriage for love and the growth in importance of mental compatibility between man and wife have constituted a notable aspect of the modern family. The institution of the family has emerged as victor from the attacks directed against it.

The falling birth rate reached its low ebb during the economic depression in the early thirties (18.4 for Finland in 1933 and 13.7 for Sweden in 1934). As an immediate reaction to this alarming trend there arose in the minds of certain social scientists, simultaneously in Finland (Modeen) [14] and in Sweden (Alva and Gunnar Myrdal), [15] a concern for the future of their small nations. Population forecasts and recommendations for an active population policy had a deep influence on public opinion in the post-depression years. If the population trend was to be reversed, the whole attitude of the community toward the institution of the family had to be radically changed. Means had to be found to enable couples to have children without suffering undue setbacks in their standard of living. Governmental population commissions were appointed in Finland, Sweden, and Denmark to study the matter and to submit recommendations for action. These commissions called for the formulation of a policy in harmony with the basic views of a democratic society, a policy that would counteract depopulation while simultaneously constituting a progressive step in social development toward better, healthier, and more secure living conditions for the people as a whole. Efforts to arrest the decrease in birth rates should serve also as a contribution toward a better adjustment of community and family life to the changed conditions of modern times.

This is the characteristic double ambition of a family-welfare policy in all northern countries. Although declining birth rates provided the stimulus for the inauguration of this policy, its demographic ambition has been modest. Coupled with this quantitative preoccupation is a natural concern for improving the quality of the population, and with passing years increasing emphasis has been placed on this latter aspect. The population approach of the thirties has developed into the family-welfare approach of the forties and fifties. Separate population measures have developed into an inclusive social policy aiming at redistribution of national wealth and income in favor of children. This seemed to be well in harmony with the general feeling of social justice in the democratic countries of northern Europe. By now these family-welfare programs extend—directly or indirectly—to all essential aspects of family life: health, housing, nutrition, education, and leisure.

The development in all northern countries has been parallel. In Finland the first sign of an awakened interest in population problems was a revision of state taxation in 1935 which imposed an additional tax, 20 per cent of the tax assessed on income and property, to be levied on all persons over twenty-four who had no responsibility for maintenance. In 1940 this "bachelor's tax" was increased to 40 per cent. In 1937 the first maternity-allowance act was passed. This was the first step in legislation aimed at equalizing the standard of living of families with many children and that of families with few or no children. After the Winter War, interest in population problems was prompted by the bitter experience that "we were too few."

A special Population League was established in 1941 by over twenty national organizations, and has since become a strong pressure organization for family interests and a driving force for the new family-welfare policy. A great number of measures have been introduced: interest-free marriage loans for persons under thirty, extension of maternity allowances to all expectant mothers irrespective of their economic standing, school meals free of charge to all children, rebates on housing rents to large families—all referring to specific items in the family budget. In addition, other allowances are aimed at the leveling of family costs. Family allowances are paid to families of small means with a minimum of four children. More important from a national point of view are the child allowances which are paid to all mothers for every child under sixteen. This scheme is financed mainly by a special tax of 4 per cent of the total wage bill, paid by all employers. This child allowance amounts now to 14,400 marks annually, which in a family with three children equals approximately two months' wages for an unskilled laborer. The total sum paid in child allowances in 1954 was 20 billion marks, which is as much as the total state expenditure for all education. This amount indicates clearly the dominant role of family welfare in Finnish society. The whole body of social policy has thus been pervaded to an increasing extent by family-welfare considerations. Needs of the family have come to be accepted as the central issue, with priority over all others. It is significant that the major family-welfare programs have been introduced only during and after the war, when demographic development—due to increase in birth rates—no longer caused the same anxiety as in the thirties. The family has been acknowledged as a central social institution. It ranks high in the scale of social values. Mother's Day—originally an American invention—has developed from a family affair into an important national festivity at which mothers of large families from distant parts of the country, in the presence of the president of the Republic, are honored and decorated with medals.

The renaissance of the family and the high prestige it enjoys are partly reflected by the fact that the proportion of unmarried in the total population has continued to decline even since 1950. In Finland as in other countries there was a marriage boom in the postwar years (1945–48) which has since receded, but still remains higher than in prewar times if due consideration is given to the changing age structure. In particular, it is interesting to observe that the marriage rate has continued to increase in the youngest, i.e., 15–25, age classes. Another aspect of the same trend is the lowering of the mean age at first marriage. In 1949 it was 29.0 for men and 26.0 for women; five years later it was 27.6 and 25.2; and ten years later 26.4 and 24.3, respectively.[16]

There is another side of the picture. Simultaneously with the marriage rate the divorce rate has risen, too. The annual total of divorces (in 1936–40, approximately 1,500) began to rise steeply in the war years, attained a peak of 5,600 in 1945, and declined to nearly 3,500 in the period 1950–54—equal to just over one tenth of the annual number of marriages. It can be shown that marriages contracted during and even after the war have ended in divorce relatively more often than was the case earlier. An intensive study of the ecology of divorces in Finland[17] demonstrates clearly the close correlation of divorces with the stage of urbanization and also with norms prevalent in towns, particularly in Helsinki, the capital, which has by far the highest divorce rate. Mobility of population, diversified occupations, and urbanized ideas seem to determine the degree of permanency of marriage and the family as social institutions. The capital is leading in the number of divorces, yet the great majority of Finnish families live in smaller towns or in the countryside where marriage rates and fertility rates are high. Therefore, rural attitudes still dominate the family scene in this northern country.

Educational Institutions

Literacy is a usual measure in comparisons of educational standards in different countries. By 1930 there were already fewer than 1 per cent (0.9) illiterates among all persons above 15 years of age in Finland. Since that time their number has dropped rapidly and they are no longer counted in the census. In this respect the Finns stand alongside the other highly advanced and educated peoples.

In its zeal to lay the foundations of a political democracy, the new single-chamber Diet of Finland in 1910 approved as one of its earliest proposals a bill for compulsory education. This bill—like many others pertaining to social legislation—was not, however, signed by the czar and had to wait for the political independence of the Finnish people (1917). Now, after more than one generation, the system of compulsory public schools, free of charge to all children between seven and fifteen, has spread to the remotest regions of the country. It is built on the solid foundation laid by the Lutheran Church, beginning in the seventeenth century. As an independent school system it has developed since the 1860s. The compulsory primary school has today seven grades with an additional two years of optional continuation grades. The school population has continued to increase throughout the country, and today the public schools, with the great numbers of postwar children now of school age, are faced with the double problem of too few and too small school buildings, on the one hand, and the training of a sufficient number of competent teachers, on the other.

The Finnish secondary schools take their students not after the completion of primary school but from the fourth grade. On an average, four out of five children in the compulsory-school-age category spends seven years in the primary school, and the remaining one in five is in a secondary school. There is a very high correlation between the proportion of children in secondary schools in an area and the density of that area's population.[18]

The secondary school lasts, as a rule, eight years. These eight plus the four years of primary school total twelve years until the student takes a matriculation examination, which, if passed, admits him—usually at the age of eighteen or nineteen—to the university. This is the double-track system of most European countries. This heritage of the old Latin school has been strongly criticized in Finland and in other countries as an undemocratic system, because it compels a division of the children at the early age of ten or eleven into a lower and a higher category based not exclusively on the child's abilities but, at least in part, on the parents' ability to afford the expenses of further education. This debate has lately calmed down. The main issues in today's lively discussion are deeper problems concerning the role and aims of secondary education in a rapidly industrialized society as well as the more pedagogical problems of proper balance in the curriculums of the school.

Partly on the basis of their experience with experimental secondary schools where six years of study have followed six years in a primary school, practically all educators today give preference to an eight-year secondary school designed to prepare its students for university studies. In particular, the teaching of foreign languages, a necessity in small nations, requires a longer, continuous learning process. Today Finnish children in most secondary schools have eight years of Swedish—the second internal language and the bridge with Scandinavia—seven years of English and three years of German or, optionally, Latin, French, or Russian. The Swedish schools in Finland, equally state-supported, have eight years of Finnish.

There is another favorable aspect of the present system. In spite of the double-track principle, criticized as undemocratic, the Finnish secondary schools have promoted rapid social mobility, carrying increasing numbers of students from humble origins to their destinations in universities and professional careers. Social mobility through secondary schools has fundamentally changed the stratification of the Finnish society.

A recent sociological investigation[19] into the social mobility of farmers' children has given convincing proof that great structural changes in Finnish society — particularly changes in agriculture — have led sons and daughters from farmers' homes to the secondary school, especially since World War II. The decreased average size of the farm and the mechanization of farming offer a livelihood on the farm to a smaller number of children. Farmers are eager to open new opportunities to their children, boys and girls alike, through schools that lead them to nonagricultural occupations.

Earlier investigations into the social origins of university students seem to corroborate these more recent studies of secondary-school students.[20] Three fourths of the university students come from homes where the father has had no university training. With the expansion of secondary schools to distant rural communities more children come today within the reach of a secondary school, which, it is hoped, will help them to enter other occupations and ascend to a higher social stratum. Trade schools, agricultural as well as industrial, which are urgently needed during the phase of rapid industrialization of the whole economy, lag far behind the secondary schools. This disproportion is seriously retarding the necessary adjustment to the industrialization process.

Sending one's sons—and, more recently, daughters—to a "learned" school has developed into a cultural pattern. It was originally a response of educated people, as well as enlightened farmers, to the challenge of the Russian period in Finnish history when no political avenues and too few business paths seemed open for young Finnish men, and when intellectual investments seemed more profitable. This cultural pattern has persisted. In spite of all the destruction during the war and the heavy indemnities to be paid afterwards, the secondary-school population in Finland is relatively greater than in Scandinavian countries. The same is true of universities: the total number of university students (14,000) is relatively greater than in Sweden, Denmark, or Norway. In the old state university, the University of Helsinki, founded in 1640, the present student body of 9,500 is in striking disproportion to the teaching staff and appropriations. (Traditionally, no fees are collected from the students in the universities of the northern countries.) This disproportion at the University of Helsinki will increase, further complicating the problem, when the great tide of postwar children, born in 1945–49, reaches university age in the middle 1960s.

Different forms of adult education have played an important role since the 1880s among educational institutions. They have shaped the attitudes and opinions of farmers and workers. Libraries, folk high schools, workers' institutes, social settlements, study clubs, amateur theaters, choirs, young peoples' associations, and similar activities have all been instrumental in awakening democratic ideals, clarifying cultural aims, and strengthening national solidarity. Thus adult education has greatly encouraged the rapid social mobility that has been channeled through the formal school system.

Social Movements and Religious Institutions

In contemporary Finnish society voluntary bodies based on freedom of association play a central role. Owing to Finland's history under the political pressure of the Russian regime, freedom of association, one of the cornerstones of liberalism, was strictly limited and under rigid control by the authorities. The early history of trade unions, of athletic associations, of educational societies, and similar organizations tells of all kinds of petty regulations and annoying obstacles, in particular since 1899, when the first period of systematic Russification set in. Here again is the same retarding of the unobstructed evolution of free institutions that has occurred in other small countries living in the gloomy shadow of a large empire. The same oppressive conditions prevailed even more strongly in many subjugated provinces and among national or religious minorities in the control of Russia, Austria, or Germany before World War I. In this respect the past of Finnish organizations is typical of many European nationalities and small countries.

On the other hand, however, Finland stands today as a mature member in the family of northern countries where freedom of association is taken for granted and where democratic organizations founded by free citizens enjoy high prestige. In this respect present Finnish organizations are typical of free Scandinavian countries.

It is unnecessary here to enumerate all categories of voluntary associations. It may suffice to analyze four types of organizations that have a highly significant function in Finnish society today.

Labor market organizations, trade unions, and employers' associations have already been discussed among economic institutions. Two important aspects ought to be stressed once more. The membership of trade unions and employers' associations has grown rapidly in recent years. At the same time the scope of their influence has greatly expanded.

One group among *cooperative societies* has already been dealt with, that is, the farmers' cooperatives. There are, however, also the consumers' cooperative stores, which have at least an equally significant role in Finnish society.

The principles of the Rochdale weavers were accepted by the pioneers of the cooperative movement between 1901 and 1910 in Finland as in all northern countries. They subscribed to the principles of open membership, democratic government, limited interest on capital, and distribution of the annual surplus to members as dividends or as a refund proportional to their trade with the cooperative. Even today these principles are strictly adhered to. The local consumers' society remains the key unit in the system. Each local society is democratically governed by its individual members. The principle has been "one member, one vote" ever since the first cooperatives made their appearance.

An important phase in the development of cooperatives began when local societies initiated joint purchases. As long as each society operated alone the movement's range of action was restricted to competition with private retailers. The founding of the first wholesale society, called the S.O.K., took place in 1904, but in 1916 the organization already had split in two. The urban branch of consumers' cooperatives, dominated by organized labor, left the central organization and established a wholesale society and central organization of its own, called the K.K.

This split into two competing factions of consumers' cooperatives two years before the civil war reflects the deep political and emotional controversies in Finnish society which have no equivalent in other northern countries. The first branch (S.O.K.) is closely associated with the producers' cooperatives and is farmer-dominated. The other (K.K.) is dominated by industrial labor. In fact, it is regarded by many of its members as an integral part of the labor movement. For them the principle of cooperation stands out as a compensation for the free-enterprise system. The two central organizations compete commercially, not only with private business but also with each other, establishing their stores—often on opposite corners—in towns and rural villages. Likewise, they compete with each other for new members and their purchases. This competition in a sparsely populated country means, of course, uneconomical and wasteful investments of capital as well as unnecessary strife and controversy. On the other hand, this internal competition seems to safeguard, to some extent at least, the movement against the danger of bureaucratization into a huge mass organization. The two organizations are today about equally strong. During and after the war the two competing systems developed a number of joint projects. In addition, both central organizations have founded a great number of factories, and thus the consumers' cooperatives themselves have entered industrial production.

Membership in all consumers' cooperatives has grown strongly, especially since the war. In 1945 the combined membership in both branches was 767,000. In 1954 this figure had risen to 1,023,000. With this high figure Finland, with its 4,200,000 inhabitants, leads the northern countries —and probably the world—in percentage of membership in consumers' cooperatives compared with the total population: Finland 24, Sweden 14, Denmark 11, and Norway 8 per cent. Since each member usually represents a family, these percentages should be multiplied by three or four in order to arrive at the actual extent to which the population is directly or indirectly affiliated with consumers' cooperatives. The two central organizations of cooperatives are estimated to account for no less than a third of the total retail trade, and thus in many branches they hold a dominating position in the economy of the country. The increase of trade brings in new members, and these new members add cumulatively to trade figures.

The rapid growth of membership has deeply affected the nature of the movement. Many local cooperatives are too large to allow direct control by the members. With the growth of membership, the societies have had to develop an indirect democracy with a hierarchy of elected delegates to a council, which in turn elects the board of trustees and appoints the executive committee composed of salaried managers. Yet local cooperative societies elect their representatives to regional and national conventions of their central organizations. These big parliaments of cooperators have retained their democratic forms; however, as in any mass organization, they are actually led by relatively small groups of key persons. As social institutions, large cooperative organizations face the same problems as all large private corporations or any other secondary group.

During fifty years (1905–55) one of the consumers' cooperatives in the capital has become the largest of all: it has 490 stores and a great number of factories, with a total of 5,200 employees. Its membership is 101,000 out of a total population of 520,000 in the metropolitan region of Helsinki. Such a huge dominating organization requires exceptional measures to maintain sufficient communication between different groups and strata. Accordingly, the large consumers' cooperatives—as do all national organizations—publish monthly or weekly papers which are distributed free of charge to all members, and all together these publications have one of the widest circulations among all papers in Finland. It is the important function of these papers, as well as of festivities and exhibitions, to keep the spirit of cooperation alive in a mass organization.

To counteract the trend of bureaucratization, the large cooperatives have established local consultative councils for each store and formed special womens' committees to attract housewives to the movement and to help them participate in the ideological and educational programs of the society. All cooperative organizations are not content to develop their business services only, but stress continually the message and ideology of cooperation. Their educational work is an effort to cultivate the grass roots of a mass movement.

A third group among social institutions are *sports organizations*. They too belong to the "popular movements" or "folk movements" typical of the northern countries. They too are based on the principle of voluntary association, and their internal structure resembles other mass organizations in many respects.

Like the consumers' cooperatives, sports life in Finland is divided between two major national organizations. There are workingmens' sport associations, called T.U.L., and non-Labor—often called bourgeois—associations, belonging to the S.V.U.L.

Interest in modern competitive athletics arose during the first years of the present century. The splendid successes of Finnish athletes in the Olympic games in Stockholm in 1912 brought about the first wave of enthusiasm for athletics in the younger generation. Athletic associations sprang up all over the country. Then came the civil war in 1918, with young sportsmen fighting on both sides. This led to a split, mainly on political grounds. During more than thirty years, all efforts to reunite the organizations or to establish an entirely new top organization, which would cover all of them and make participation in international events easier, have been in vain. Growth in size on both sides and the traditions, prestige, and symbols of both organizations seem to stand in the way of an amalgamation. There have been similar rifts in certain other countries, as in Norway, but nowhere else has such a division lasted. The two major national organizations share many common projects, however, involving joint committees and joint participation in international sport events, but the pattern of class dichotomy that separates them persists.

A high degree of specialization and differentiation is characteristic of athletic organizations. Most branches of sport, such as skiing, skating, ice hockey, boxing, fencing, tennis, basketball, and track, as a rule have separate local associations, and these in turn belong to national federations in their special fields. These are finally members in either of the two national organizations, or—as in many cases—remain independent. In addition, both national organizations have their districts, 16 and 14 respectively, with committees, competitons, and championships of their own on the district level. Thus, the wide net of associations in the field of sports is very unevenly meshed.

All sport associations have had a continually and rapidly increasing membership. The total number of members, as a rule seventeen years old or more, in all sport associations was 366,000 in 1945. In 1954 this figure had risen to 792,000, which means a rise of 117 per cent in ten years. There is a great deal of overlapping in these figures, it is true, as individuals often are members of several associations. The very rapid increase in figures cannot, however, be explained merely by this multiple membership. These growing figures are an indication of the increasing interest in sports and sport associations. The civil guards, a citizens' voluntary military organization, which had been strong and powerful in prewar years, was prohibited by the armistice with the Soviet Union in 1944. The war veterans' large organization had to be disbanded. Much of the voluntary interest and energy has since been diverted to sport associations. It is significant that these sport associations have a stronger appeal for boys and girls; on the whole, their membership represents a younger generation than that of many other voluntary organizations. It is on the "pesäpallo" (Finnish version of an American baseball) field that a farmer boy comes into contact with the social institutions of a large organization, and it is in the gymnastic exercises that a teen-age town girl experiences for the first time the atmosphere of democratic and voluntary associations.

In Finland there is a strong interest in competitive sports and an appreciation of sport stars, particularly of track athletes; yet the organizations put much emphasis on sport performances of great masses, arranging large-scale gymnastic exhibitions and competitions in skiing, swimming, and other athletics.

One further point about sport associations: More than in any other field, members of these associations have direct international contacts. They travel abroad as members of their teams and meet foreigners who come to athletic events in their home towns. Groups and teams of sporting people make full use of modern facilities for international travel. Inter-Nordic athletic events offer ample proof of this.

The trade unions, consumers' cooperatives, and sport associations, which have been described here to represent the social institutions of voluntary organizations, have certain common features.

First, they all have shown a marked growth in membership during and since the war. Voluntary organizations seem to satisfy certain basic needs of modern men. Hundreds of thousands of persons belong to these institutions, which have become huge mass organizations.

Second, they are all voluntary associations based on the principle of democratic government and control by their individual members; with the growing size of these institutions, the distance has grown between the bottom and the top—between the individual member in a local association and the leadership of a grand national organization; the hierarchical and bureaucratic features of mass organizations are thus emphasized, and the role of the individual member is more subordinated to the collective goals of the institution.

Third, with the growth of voluntary organizations the demand for professional officers has rapidly increased. Secretaries and presidents of trade unions; storekeepers, employees, and officers in cooperatives; professional trainers and coaches in sport associations; all have entered voluntary organizations as salaried managers who perform the most important functions within their organization.

Fourth, all these voluntary organizations have developed a rich system of symbols, visible and audible—such as badges, pins, flags, and songs—all symbolizing the common aims of their movement and enhancing the solidarity of its members. Conventions, performances, and parades, where these symbols are exhibited before great crowds, all serve the purpose of strengthening an emotional attachment and a sense of solidarity in individual members marching in the parade, joining the common song, reverently saluting the flag. Often these emblematic devices resemble national or international symbols, and thus reach beyond one's own organization to larger collectivities. The individual member identifies himself, and his expectations and ideals, with his own organization.

Some sociological research is under way in this expanding field of voluntary associations, but no final results can as yet be quoted. However, a few pilot studies seem to indicate that education is an important variable in the increase of membership in organizations. Consequently, we may expect that with the trend toward industrialization and a rising standard of education these voluntary organizations will continue to grow and attract more new members. This trend then would imply that we are moving more and more away from a nineteenth-century conception of liberalism and individualism.

Last but not least come the *religious institutions*, which represent the oldest cultural influences in this distant and northern corner of Europe.

Foremost among religious institutions is the Lutheran Church, which in Finland—as in the Lutheran countries of Scandinavia—enjoys the privileges of an established church. There is a close bond between the state and the Lutheran Church, symbolized by a Lutheran service at the opening and closing ceremonies of a parliamentary session and by the appointment of the bishops by the president of the Republic. But it is not only this formal position of the Church that is important from a sociological point of view. More important is the fact that the Finnish people have largely retained their membership in the Church, although there has been full religious liberty since 1922. Traditions are strong. In 1950 as many as 95.2 per cent of all Finns belonged to the Lutheran Church, and only 2.8 per cent had withdrawn and were included in a secular register. This small percentage amounted to 120,000 people, including children, but is nonetheless an impressive figure, considering that at the same time the Communists as well as the great majority of Finns prefer to remain members of the traditional Church and even to pay taxes to support it. Most children are baptized and entered in the church register. Most boys and girls at the age of fifteen go to a church confirmation school, although all have had religious instruction in primary and secondary schools. Most marriages are solemnized by the Church; only one marriage in twenty is performed by a secular officer. Consequently, formal membership in the Lutheran Church is upheld by strong traditions and folkways. The Church plays at least a formal role in the private lives of people who may be personally quite indifferent to religion.

An estrangement from personal religion has taken place in remarkably large segments of the urban population, and may be attributed to the same influences operating in so many other Protestant countries of Europe. But this is not true for the country as a whole. On the contrary, there is in the Finnish countryside a strong and active tradition of religious life. In spite of secularization and religious indifference there is within the Church of Finland a great deal of genuine religious vitality. Popular revival movements, which have their historical roots in eighteenth-century pietism, have not died out.

There are four separate currents in this religious stream. They all started from the mountains of inspiration erected by an especially great leader and religious personality (Paavo Ruotsalainen) more than a hundred years ago, and have since kept faithful to his particular emphasis. They differ from each other in their dogmatic views on problems of the individual religious life, but all have kept within the main stream of the Church. A great number of Lutheran clergymen have come from one of these sects with which they openly identify themselves. These religious sects develop strong in-group sentiments that are strengthened in small house-meetings during the week and in large annual conventions gathering twenty to thirty thousand people together. The character of these popular religious movements is definitely rural, and they have won comparatively fewer adherents and less influence among people in towns.

Yet, in spite of its strength there remains for the Christian Church in Finland the challenge brought about by industrialization. In this respect Finland faces the same problems as all Western countries with advanced cultures.

Notes

[1] John H. Wuorinen (ed.), *Finland and World War II, 1939–1944* (New York: The Ronald Press, 1948), p. 10.

[2] Lauri Heikinheimo, *Maaseudun Miestyövoiman arkiajan käyttö. Maaseudun työvoiman tutkimuksia II.* Summary in English: *Use of Rural Manpower in Finland,* Finnish Rural Labour Force Studies II (Helsinki: Acta Forestalis Fennica 63, 1955).

[3] Sakari Sariola, *Drinking Patterns in Lapland* (Helsinki: Väkijuomakysymyksen Tutkimussäätiö, 1956).

[4] W. R. Mead, *Farming in Finland* (London: The Athlone Press, 1953), p. 43.

FINLAND

[5] Heikki Waris, Vieno Jyrkilä, Kyllikki, Reutosuo, and Jouko Süpi, *Siirtoräen sopeutuminen* (Social Adjustment of Displaced Persons) (Helsinki: Otava, 1952).

[6] Mead, *op. cit.*, p. 204.

[7] Eino Jutikkala, *Suomen historian kartasto* (Atlas of Finnish History), with texts in Finnish and English (Porvoo-Helsinki: 1949).

[8] Jaakko Nousiainen, *Kommunismi Kuopoin läänissä* (Communism in the County of Kuopia) (Joensuu, 1956).

[9] Sven Rydenfelt, *Kommunismen i Sverige* (Communism in Sweden) (Lund: Gleerups, 1954).

[10] Waris, *op. cit.*

[11] Erik Allardt, *Social Structur och politisk aktivitet* (Social Structure and Political Activity) (Helsingfors, 1956).

[12] Elisabeth Elfvengren, *Finland arbetskraft. Struktur ock utvecklingstendenser.* Summary in English: *The Finnish Labour Force. Its Present Structure and Tendencies of Development* (Helsinki: Taloudellinen tutkimuskeskus, 1955).

[13] Armas Nieminen, *Taistelu sukupuolimoraalista I.* Summary in English: *The Battle over Sexual Morality. Problems of Marriage and Sex in Finland from Approximately 1860 to 1920,* Part I (Helsinki: Väestöpoliittinen tutkimuslaitos, Publications A:6, 1951).

[14] Gunnar Modeen, *Suomen väkiluvun tuleva kehitys ja sen taloudelliset seuraukset* (The Future Development of Finland's Population and Its Economic Consequences) (Kansantaloudellinen Aikakauskirja, 1934).

[15] Alva and Gunnar Myrdal, *Kris i befolkningsfrågan* (Crisis in the Population Problem) (Stockholm: Albert Bonnier, 1935).

[16] Aarno Strömmer, *Recent Demographic Development and Population Policies in Finland* (Princeton: Population Index, January 1956).

[17] Erik Allardt, *Mijöketingade differenser i skilsmässofrekvensen* (Environmental Differences in the Frequency of Divorce) (Helsingfors: Bidrag till kännedom af Finlands Natur och folk. Utgivna af Finska Vetenskaps–societeten. H. 96, No. 1, 1953).

[18] Kosti Huuhka, *Talonpoikaisnuorison koulutie. Tutkimus talonpoikaisnuorison koulunkäynnistä ja siihen vaikuttaneista tekijöissosiaalisista tekijöistä Suomessa 1910–1950.* Summary in English: *A Study of the School Attendance of Young People of the Farming Population in Finland, 1910–1950* (Helsinki: Suomen Historiallinen Seura, 1955), pp. 94–98.

[19] Huuhka, *op. cit.*, pp. 208–220.

[20] Heikki Waris, *Suomalaisen yhteiskunnan rakenne* (The Structure of Finnish Society) (Helsinki: Otava, 1948), pp. 321–331, and "Yliopisto sosiaalisen kohoamisen väylänä" (The University as a Channel of Social Mobility), *Historiallinen Arkisto,* Vol. 47 (Helsinki, 1940). Sven-Erik Aström, "Literature on Social Mobility and Social Stratification in Finland, Some Bibliographical Notes," *Transactions of the Westermarck Society,* Vol. II (Copenhagen, 1952).

Supplementary References

Aaltonen, Esko, *Consumer Co-operation in Finland* (Helsinki: Kulutusosuuskuntien Keskusliitto, 1954).

Economic Survey of Finland, published annually by the Economic Department of the Ministry of Finance.

Hall, Wendy, *Green Gold and Granite: A Background to Finland* (London: Max Parrish, 1953).

Harmaja, Leo, *Effects of the War on Economic and Social Life in Finland* (New Haven: Yale University Press, 1933).

Jaantila, Kirsti, *Political, Economic and Social Writings in Postwar Finland: A*

233

THE INSTITUTIONS OF ADVANCED SOCIETIES

Bibliographical Survey (Washington, D.C.: Library of Congress, European Affairs Division, 1952).

Kallio, Niilo, *The School System of Finland* (Helsinki, 1956).

Kannisto, Väinö, *Kuolemansyyt väestöllisinä tekijöinä Suomessa.* Summary in English: *The Causes of Death as Demographic Factors in Finland* (Helsinki, 1947).

Koli, Paavo, *Ennakkoluuloista teollisessa organisaatiossa.* Summary in English: *On Prejudice in Industrial Organization* (Porvoo-Helsinki: Werner Söderström, 1955).

Labor-Management Relations in Scandinavia, Bulletin No. 1038 (Washington, D.C.: U.S. Department of Labor, 1952).

Lento, Reino, *Maassamuutto ja siihen vaikuttaneet tekijät Suomessa vuosina 1878–1939.* Summary in English: *Internal Migration and Factors Affecting it in Finland in 1878–1939* (Turku, 1951).

Mazour, Anatole G., *Finland between East and West* (Princeton, N.J.: Van Nostrand Co., 1956).

Nelson, George R., (ed.), *Freedom and Welfare: Social Patterns in the Northern Countries of Europe* (Copenhagen, 1953).

Pihkala, K. U., "The Position of the Karelian Agricultural Displaced Population before and after the War," *Integration,* Bulletin International No. 1, 1955.

Platt, Ray R., (ed.), *Finland and its Geography: An American Geographical Society Handbook* (Boston: Little, 1955).

Sariola, Sakari, "Defining Social Class in Two Finnish Communities," *Transactions of the Westermarck Society,* Vol. II (Copenhagen, 1953).

Siipi, Jouko, *Palkkatyöväen viihtyvyys.* Summary in English: *Workers Satisfaction with their Place of Residence* (Porvoo-Helsinki: Werner Söderström, 1954).

Social Legislation and Work in Finland (Helsinki: Ministry of Social Affairs, 1953).

Statistical Yearbook of Finland (New Series, 51st Year, 1955; Helsinki, 1956).

Suviranta, Br., "Finland's War Indemnity," *Integration,* Bulletin International No. 1, 1955.

The Scandinavian States and Finland, A Political and Economic Survey (London: Royal Institute of International Affairs, 1951).

Toivola, Urho, (ed.), *The Finland Yearbook 1947* (Helsinki, 1947).

Tuominen, Arvo (Poika), "The North European Communist Parties: Saint Anthonu's Papers on Soviet Affairs III," *Occidente,* Vol. XI, No. 3 (Torino, 1955).

Wahlbeck, Lars, *Om inkomstnivans geografi i Finland ar 1951,* I–II. Summary in English: *The Geography of the Income Level in Finland in 1950,* I–II (Helsingfors: Söderströms, 1955).

Waris, Heikki, "Finland's Solution of Its Displaced Persons Problem," *Integration,* Bulletin International No. 1, 1955.

————, and Procopé, Victor, "The Problem of Compensating Property Losses: Experiences Gained from the Compensation Policy for Displaced Persons in Finland," *Economia Internazionale,* Vol. VI, No. 3 (Geneva, 1953).

————, and Siipi, Jouko, *Resettlement of Displaced Persons in Finnish Society* (Helsinki: Unitas, 1951).

Westermarck, Nils, *Finnish Agriculture* (Helsinki: Pellervo Society, 1954).

Wright, J. H., "Economic and Commercial Conditions in Finland," *Overseas Economic Surveys* (London: H.M. Stationery Office, 1953).

Wuorinen, J. H., *Nationalism in Modern Finland* (New York: Columbia University Press, 1931).

*

Jan Szczepanski

POLAND

*

Basic Sociological Characteristics of the Culture

IN SPITE of many differences in definitions and theories sociologists have always regarded institutions as a stabilizing factor of societies and cultures. Therefore, if one wants to describe the culture of one's own people to the outsider, one must give, first of all, a picture of its institutions. But difficulty begins with the definition of *institution*. There are many definitions formulated in textbooks, special papers, and systematic studies on this subject, but I believe that the view which the authors have in common may be presented as follows: institutions are purposive groups or sets of patterns, created by societies by means of legislation or tradition and customs, or both together, having a definite organizational form and being able by the use of symbols and other means to influence human behavior.

This is not a precise definition, only a device serving to limit the field of my description. I shall distinguish between the formal institutions having clearly formulated statutes or laws and informal institutions functioning by virtue of traditions, customs, and habits. In every institution, of course, formal and informal elements are discernible. The most formal institutions create in time their own informal customs and habits. The proposed definition deliberately does not differentiate among associations, institutions, ways of life, and folkways, for reasons which are important for the description of characteristic processes going on in the Polish culture of today. In all societies which are in a state of planned and radical

AUTHOR'S NOTE: The author is obliged to Mrs. Stefania Dziecielska-Zaleska, an assistant at the University of Łódź, for gathering materials and for valuable help in writing this paper. She bears, of course, no responsibility for its content.

EDITOR'S NOTE: The reader should note that this paper was completed after the October 1956 Revolution in Poland but before the January 1957 election.

rebuilding of their economic and political structures there are to be seen two coexisting processes: the radical changes in formal institutions almost always go hand in hand with the intensified conservative functioning of traditional and informal institutions; and the radical changes in macro-structures (e.g., class structures) parallel conservative tendencies in micro-structures. As a result changes in the society as a whole develop at different speeds on different levels and not always in the planned direction, and the picture of the social life as a whole changes rather slowly.

Such phenomena may be observed today in Poland. The basic economic and political institutions, and the class structure of Polish society, have been changed in a revolutionary manner. All formal institutions and groups controlled by the state work according to the new aims and tendencies. But to give a picture of the whole social life the formalized institutions not wholly depending on the state must also be described, like the family and religious institutions, and informal institutions which in all societies are regarded as factors of stability and continuity of social life.

In Western countries the following questions have often been posed: What are the causes of the Polish acceptance of Stalinism? What is the mechanism in Poland for a gradual transformation into a Stalinist society? How deep are the changes? What is the social significance of the "Polish October Revolution"? What is the nature of recent Polish transformations and what are their sources? These are very interesting questions for sociologists, but to answer them is not an easy task, and a wholly satisfactory answer could be given only as a result of vast investigations—which up to now have not been carried out. So my attempt to explain some Polish institutions and processes of change must be considered a very superficial one.

If we are even to begin to understand the culture of Polish society, we must first consider the specific historical conditions under which that culture was formed.

To these conditions belong, first of all, the partitions of Poland among Russia, Prussia, and Austria and the consequent lack of political independence in the years 1795–1918. During this time the Polish people lost their own political institutions, including political parties, and could not engage in what may be called normal political life. I do not mean by this that political life in Poland died out. On the contrary, the striving for political independence was one of the strongest national characteristics during the whole of the nineteenth century, and all spheres of Polish culture and life were saturated with it. Almost all Polish institutions, associations, and groups thought it a "national service" to seek out the ways that would prepare the country for recovery of its political independence. Literature, science, arts, the family, education, the Church, economic activity —all were under the strong influence of this ideology of independence and political freedom.

The situation of the people was not the same under the three foreign dominations: the limits of freedom, the forms of repression, the policy of the three governments toward the Poles differed according to states and historical periods. But, independently of the degree of repression and oppression, their policies had some sociological effects in common. For instance, in all English-speaking countries people create special committees, societies, or associations even for trifling purposes, but in Poland all three governments severely limited the possibility of founding new Polish associations or societies. Therefore all the existing institutions and associations took on the functions of those which could not be created: the scientific periodicals undertook the functions of scientific societies, scientific research institutions, and even universities. The parishes not only performed their religious duties, but also sponsored social and educational activities. Families substituted for nonexistent national schools. Philanthropic societies conducted political and educational business. This was a struggle for the maintenance of the national cultural values, as the basis for recovery of political independence. It must be stressed that this tradition, revived during the war, is still alive in Poland.

In order to understand the development of Poland, we must remember that the Polish state that was conquered at the end of the eighteenth century was a feudal republic controlled by the landed gentry, and that the nobility remained the leading social class during the first half of the nineteenth century. Its prestige and ideals had a profound influence on the formation of social ideas and social relations throughout the century. The struggle of the gentry for the preservation of their position and the struggle of other classes against them have strongly influenced Polish political ideas and—most important of all—the development of the Polish idea of democracy. Since the people did not have their own state and lacked proper political experience, they became greatly interested in other nations' political ideas and state organizations, above all those of western Europe. This interest was the source of an admiration for Western social models called

Occidentalism. It was also the source of a certain inferiority complex and at the same time of a mighty stimulus to Polish national pride.

Democratic public institutions in Poland have little tradition. It is necessary to remember this in analyzing the present Polish institutions and their actions. During the partition period, lasting until 1918, the Polish people had no practical acquaintance with liberal democracy. Immediately after the liberation in 1918 Poland involved herself in the war with Soviet Russia and was ruled by a military government. The short period of democratic government between 1920 and 1926 ended with the dictatorship of a colonels' group, led by Pilsudski, which lasted until 1939. Nevertheless the ideal of a liberal democracy always had a large number of followers, and not only among the intelligentsia. The working and peasant classes also formed a strong opposition to the Pilsudski dictatorship.

During the period of partition, governments were those of the enemy and conquerors, and therefore it was a patriotic duty to fight against them. There were, of course, certain loyalist tendencies, but they never dominated the attitudes of all the nation. As a consequence there is in the Polish people a deeply rooted attitude of distrust of every government. It is not easy to govern in Poland. And the vast opposition against the government of Pilsudski revived and maintained these attitudes. Then in 1939 came the war with Germany, and military occupation accompanied by the extermination program. The only answer was the resistance of the whole people in all spheres of life and work and in all possible forms.

These conditions caused the basic political attitude of the Poles to be rather anarchic, characterized by distrust and lack of esteem for government, by a lack of respect for the law, and by an "individualism" in interpreting the governmental political line. The Poles have had little experience with a modern government chosen in a legal election and sufficiently competent and efficient in action.

But in spite of these individualistic political attitudes, the Poles have a deeply inculcated sense of patriotic duty. One may say, rather sadly, that the Polish nation has preserved its political and cultural existence because, during the last 150 years, every generation has been ready to fight and to die for freedom. This is exemplified by the wars and uprisings in 1792, 1794, the Napoleonic wars, 1830–31, 1846, 1848, 1863–64, 1905, 1914–20, 1939–45; the October days of 1956 have confirmed this readiness of the whole nation once more.

Besides this readiness to fight, the Polish people, their institutions, and culture developed during their stormy history many features enabling them to adapt to changing conditions. Above all it was necessary to preserve the culture and national characteristics, to maintain the cultural values and the national traditions, to maintain Polish literature, arts, and science, to educate every generation in the national spirit in order to have a basis for recovery of political independence at a favorable moment. This required a conserving action for 150 years, but it was done. It required also a great capacity for adaptation. Since these processes of preserving and renewing the Polish culture have been as yet little investigated by historians and sociologists, it is rather difficult to tell exactly which institutions have historically played the decisive part. But we must stress the great social role of the Roman Catholic Church. It was the most powerful institution integrating national life during the partition. The clergy managed to maintain in the masses the belief that Polish customs and Polish nationality were identical with Catholicism. It was among the peasants that the attachment to the Church was the strongest, though they did not have a very deep religious culture. This identification of national feelings with religious faith, connected with religious fanaticism, became a powerful influence in the struggle for national independence.

Although the role of the Roman Catholic Church in the formation of Polish national character has not been yet fully studied, clearly its influence on Polish culture and life has always been great. Today, the Church is the most powerful organization whose internal affairs stand beyond the state's political control. This fact gives the Church a special position in Polish social life. I shall have some more to say about this later.

In the urban working class nationalist feelings were attached to socialist revolutionary ideas and tendencies. The leftist group led by Rosa Luxemburg never had a great influence on the masses because it neglected the question of national independence, regarding it as unimportant. The same patriotic tendencies were also powerful in the peasants' political movement.

What was the social and economic background of this formative process of Polish institutions and culture? Everybody who wants to understand present Polish institutions must remember that Poland has always been a backward agricultural country. As in all eastern Europe, capitalism made slow progress here; the elements of the feudal order persisted longer than in Western countries. Only after 1945 did the question of industrialization receive full attention. A process often called the "construction of the foundation of socialism" in reality was the realization of the delayed first Industrial Revolution. The low standard of life among the peasants and workers, largely the result of the almost colonial labor conditions in industry before World War I (the situation was of course different in the three separate occupied zones), though they changed between the two world wars, remained low when compared with western Europe. World War II caused great new devastations. About 295,400 urban buildings were destroyed or damaged, and about 466,900 farm buildings. And so the nation, which never had known prosperity, which after the ruin of the Great War undertook the reconstruction of its social and economic setup, had again to pay heavily at the cost of its standard of living.

I have already indicated the central role of the landed gentry in the formation of Polish culture. It would be very interesting to determine to what extent elements of the typical attitudes of the landed gentry found their expression in the draft of the Six Year Plan formulated to build the foundations of socialism in Poland. The gentry culture was first of all a romantic culture, and its dominating patterns were an imposing gesture, individualism, chivalry, and dash. The contrary virtues characteristic of the Western liberal bourgeoisie—like economy, foresight, and devotion to a good prospering business—were never held in esteem in Poland. There are some exceptions to this in western Poland, which had belonged to Germany and where the *petit bourgeois* attitudes had a deep influence on behavior patterns. But the migration of millions of Poles from eastern Poland to the western territories, after 1944, caused a mixing of population from all parts of the country.

The class structure also had a deep influence on the development of Polish national culture, because of the strongly marked barriers and great differences in living standards. In the nineteenth century and the beginning of the twentieth century there were the rich classes of big proprietors, both capitalist and landowners, and the masses of peasants and workers living in misery. Under a thin layer of intellectuals fully participating in the international "European" culture, there were masses of illiterate people living in a traditional folk culture. Illiteracy as a mass phenomenon disappeared only in the years after 1947.

Therefore in Polish cultural life there is always to be found a strong current of folk culture, and Polish musicians, painters, and writers have drawn from it the motifs for their works. The process of creating a unified national culture, combining the values of the cultural life of the intellectual classes and those of the folk masses, is still going on. The acceleration of this process is now one of the goals of the state cultural policy.

National pride and national megalomania in Poland are not, perhaps, greater than in other nations. Like all other peoples the Poles have the feeling that in some way they are better than others. They are proud of their history, their gallantry and great deeds, their heroes and their martyrs. They are also prone to forget their misfortunes of the past which were due to their own incapacity in handling economic and political affairs. An illustration will help to clarify this point. In the nineteenth century there existed in Poland a relatively strong ideological current called Polish Messianism, affirming that the Polish nation was a Messiah sacrificed for the sins of all peoples, and that the sufferings caused by the rapacious conquerors of Poland had a salutary influence on the fate of mankind. That was of course a very flattering historiography. But there was also a Cracow school of historians who asserted that Poland's fall was not due to the messianic virtues of the Polish people, but that it had been caused by an amazing concentration of all sorts of social sins, with political unreason at the head.

The history of the past twelve years (1945–56) presents a series of interesting questions. But there are also many difficulties in describing contemporary Polish society and explaining properly the processes that are going on in it. It is a society in transition. But this transition is peculiar in many aspects. Poland was liberated from German occupation by the Red Army, and political power was transferred from this army to the workers' party. The nationalization of industry and land reform began the period of construction of a socialist society. The first state plan of economic reconstruction in the years 1947–49 aimed at rehabilitation, the second plan (the Six Year Plan) sought to lay the foundations of socialism. Economic rehabilitation went hand in hand with a reconstruction of all political, social, educational, and cultural institutions. Especially after the defeat of the tendencies represented by Gomulka in 1948 and after the victory of the Stalinist tendency in the Polish United Workers' party, all spheres of public and social life were developed in conformity with the Soviet model. It seemed in 1951 that the victory of Stalinism was complete. But in 1954–55 there came the revolt of the intellectuals and under its pressure came the "thaw," and then the retreat from Stalinism ended with the full victory of Gomulka and the "Polish way to socialism."

All these processes were not systematically recorded and investigated by sociologists for obvious reasons. They are too complicated to be explained in this essay. But it seems to me that in order to understand these processes we must take into account the following facts.

After the war out of about 33 million making up Poland's prewar population, about 6 million had been killed and several million were returnees from concentration and hard-labor camps and from P.O.W. camps. Several hundred thousand remained abroad or emigrated. There was a general striving for peace, for the rehabilitation of normal life, for a reconstruction and revival. The new political and social system presented a vision of a new life in a society of welfare and social justice. It must be said that many Poles, mostly those who returned from the Soviet Union with bitter memories of their experience, were skeptical about this ideology. But the Polish Communist leaders stressed the essential differences between the Soviet Union and the proclaimed Polish way to socialism, and the belief that the Western countries would help in the fight for independence from the Soviet Union was broken. The events of the year 1939 and the Yalta Conference of 1945 also shook Polish faith in the good will of Western democracies. The fear of a third world war was great, too. Therefore, together with the rehabilitation of the country in the years 1945–47 and with the rise in the standard of living, a positive attitude toward the new system grew. It must be stressed that the land reform gave the peasants much desired land, that the workers in this period really felt they were the owners of industry. There was no unemployment. Schools were open for the youth of all social classes. The government created a network of reading rooms and other cultural establishments throughout the country. Books and newspapers appeared in great numbers and were very cheap. It seemed that all able and industrious people had an open road to social advancement.

It was a period of great vertical mobility. Not only were many schools for adults and many vocational schools opened, not only were many new courses and different forms of education offered, but also there was a great increase in the number of academic schools. All these were factors affecting the general acceptance of the new social regime. It must be said also that there were some groups which resisted it in various ways, even with arms, but after three years they were broken by force or they capitulated as a result of an amnesty.

The attractive features of the new order helped establish it, but it was also strongly backed by a system of political administration, political police apparatus, and the psychological pressure of propaganda. It was not a liberal democracy but a "People's Democracy"—a form of dictatorship of the proletariat. And all dictatorships, without regard for their names, must obey the same sociological laws. After the victory of the Stalinist tendency in the party, the system of political police control and intimidation was strongly built up. Political life was beyond the control of the masses. Decisions were made among small groups without regard to public opinion. Even the first election in 1947 brought deep disappointment. While the spread of the new form of political control influenced the development of institutions, it also concomitantly increased the consciousness of resistance. But the resistance found its expression in rather a passive attitude called "internal emigration," which meant abstention from participation in pro-regime activity.

And now let us put the question as to how this development influenced the institutions.

Immediately after the German troops left Polish territory, the people returning to their prewar institutions and workshops started their rehabilitation—limited of course by the wartime destruction and the shortage of labor due to German killing and deportation. For instance, it was impossible to rehabilitate institutions in Warsaw immediately, because there was no city at all. But in a few months even this ghostly town of ruins awakened to a new life. In the years 1944–46 most of the prewar social, cultural, educational, religious, and even economic institutions were restored on the old plan. Of course there appeared also, first of all in politics and the economy, new forms and institutions providing a basis for the process called the "introduction of socialism." In practice this meant the reforming of existing institutions and the creation of new ones. But this was only the beginning.

More radical changes began with the victory of Stalinist tendencies in the party. All institutions and associations were put under state control, and associations concerned with social problems were disbanded. This was a consequence of a vulgarization of the Marxist theory, a pretense that social problems are a simple consequence of class conflict and capitalistic conditions. The doing away with capitalism and class differences was held to cause also the disappearance of social problems. It was naively believed that, with the building of socialism, social and economic relations would influence people in such a way that new and better men would be reared almost automatically. Later I shall try to show what the elements of Stalinism in the institutions were and what its specific patterns of social life were.

An adequate description, not to say explanation, of all these processes would be a difficult task for many reasons. We in Poland have witnessed a total reconstruction of economic and political institutions. We have witnessed the disappearance of great social classes, the nationalization of industry and commerce, the partial collectivization of agriculture, the submission of almost all spheres of national life to political state control, the introduction of planning not only in the economy but in all branches of culture. This radically changed the face of the nation. But under this surface the traditional patterns, the ways of life and values, the informal circles and institutions, the latent opposition, were working. Thus, when Gomulka returned to power in 1956, proclaiming the Polish way to socialism, we witnessed again the sudden emergence of many institutions and associations disbanded in the previous period. Events are still in flux and it is impossible to say what shape our institutions will take in the future. In October 1956, we had a real revolution, carried on with enthusiasm and also with anxiety caused by the tragedy of Hungary.

So the complexity of the subject is one source of difficulties for me. But there are many others. I had no studies available, and only few data concerning different institutions. I had neither case studies nor comprehensive studies, for there were very few sociological investigations made in the Stalinist period. There was, of course, the official literature, but it did not distinguish between *soll* and *sein*,*and treated *soll* rather as *sein*. Statistical data were secret for many years, and between 1948 and 1955 no *Statistical Yearbook of Poland* appeared.

Bearing all this in mind, the reader can understand why the author is sometimes vague in his descriptions and analysis and will excuse him.

Political Institutions

GENERAL CHARACTERISTICS OF POLITICAL ORGANIZATION

The official name of Poland's political organization is the People's Democracy. Its principles, elaborated by the Polish Communist organizations, were published for the first time during the war and were made known to all the people by the Polish Committee for National Liberation

---

*EDITOR'S NOTE: Did not distinguish between *what should be* (what was theoretically expected) and *what actually existed*.

in Lublin in July 1944; they were then accepted by the new Polish government. The People's Democracy was to be a form of dictatorship of the working class acting in alliance with peasants and having the support of the intelligentsia. The aim of this political organization is to build the foundations of a socialist society. It follows, then, that the People's Democracy is only a transitional political organization, realizing all the aims of the proletarian revolution but without violence and civil war. This could be done because the political party of the working class, leading in this process of transition, had the help of the already established socialist power of the Soviet Union and could profit by its experiences.

The general conception of the theory and practice of the People's Democracy changed over time. Three main periods in its development may be distinguished, the first from 1944 till 1948, the second from 1948 till October 1956, and the third after the October Revolution in 1956.

In his speech delivered at the First Congress of the Polish Workers' party on December 6, 1945, Wladyslaw Gomulka described the People's Democracy in the following manner. As a result of the war and of the fascist regime there awakened in the masses of workers and peasants a strong striving for freedom and democracy. The defeat of fascism liberated these political forces and enabled these people to participate in political power. Then he formulated the following definition: "In the situation in which, at the helm of the country and the state, democratic forces consisting of the elements of the liberal and of the popular democracies are to be found, in which the monopolistic financial capital has been destroyed, and in which all the basic means of production and transport as well as the banks have been nationalized—the state assumes the character of a popular state, its social constitution is a popular constitution in which financial capital does not hold a dominating position in economy and politics, and this democracy is a People's Democracy."*

Gomulka thought that the People's Democracy in Poland could make its own way and organize the socialist order in such a manner as to take into account the specific historic and economic conditions in Poland, which were different from those of the Soviet Union. But a fear that Poland might become too independent strengthened the Stalinist elements and they proclaimed Gomulka's program a "nationalist right-wing deviation." So a Stalinist conception of the People's Democracy as a form of dictator-

---

Ku nowej Polsce (Toward a New Poland), Katowice: Wydawnictwo Literatura Polska, 1945, pp. 78–79.

245

ship of the proletariat, based on a centralized bureaucracy, secret-police terror, centralized planning of the economy and social life, and rigid socio-techniques for keeping the people in the "right line" of thinking and activity came into being. The People's Democracy became a transitional stage toward a socialist society based upon the Soviet model. The Stalinist wing in the Polish United Workers' party (P.U.W.P.) molded not only the party life, but all spheres of political, social, economic, and artistic activity according to patterns established in the Soviet Union.

But when, at the eighth plenary meeting of the Central Committee of the P.U.W.P., Gomulka returned to power, the conception of the People's Democracy changed once more, making necessary the total reconstruction of all institutions established in the second period (1948–56). We are, then, at the beginning of an era in which the hopes for freedom and welfare are taking real shape. As Gomulka put it in his speech in October 1956, there is in socialism one unchangeable element and that is the abolition of the exploitation of man by man, but the forms and ways leading to that may be, and often are, different.

And now, let us have a look at the political institutions that express the People's Democracy.

THE FORMAL STRUCTURE OF POLITICAL AUTHORITY: ADMINISTRATION

According to the Constitution adopted in 1952 (which, however, is going to be changed by the new Seym elected in January 1957) the supreme political institution is the one-chambered Parliament (Seym), elected by all citizens over eighteen years of age. The Parliament controls all the organs of state authority and administration. It is the only organ with the power to enact legislation. It votes the state's budget. It decides about war and peace. It appoints and revokes the government's executive and controls its activity. It is the only body that may change the Constitution.

The Seym elects the State Council, an institution which is something like a collective president. The latter is subject to the Seym and is responsible before it. The State Council organizes the general election, may propose bills, and is the interpreter of the statute laws. In the intervals between Seym sessions, the State Council may pass bills in the form of decrees, which afterwards are confirmed or rejected by the Parliament, and it may perform other functions of the Seym. It controls all the local people's councils, nominates the high state officials, confers distinctions, may pardon criminals, represents the Republic before other states, ratifies international agreements, can introduce martial law and decide on mobilization. The State Council consists of a chairman, four vice-chairmen, and nine other members. Their decisions are made by majority vote.

The highest organ of state administration is the Cabinet Council, which consists of the prime minister, the deputy prime ministers, ministers, and chairmen of commissions which have the functions of a ministry (e.g., State Commission for Economic Planning). The functions of the Cabinet Council are—I believe—in the main the same as in all other countries. However, it must be stressed that it also directs all the presidiums of all people's councils—that is, the provincial (*województwo*), county (*powiat*), and town organs of the state authorities.

The councils ought to be the real organs of people's authority. Article 35 of the Constitution states with rather pathetic bravado that the councils express the will of the laboring people and develop their creative initiative and activity in order to increase the strength, welfare, and culture of the nation. There are village, town, county, and provincial people's councils, subject to the State Council. The members of the local councils are elected in general, equal, direct, and secret elections. The last election to the people's councils took place on December 5, 1954. Among the 204,399 councilors elected, 46.8 per cent were workers, 41.2 per cent peasants, 7.9 per cent members of the collective farms, and 4.1 per cent others. The councils deal with all the affairs of the territory subject to their administration. They elect their presidiums, which are the actual bureaus of the state administration subject to the respective ministries. Besides the bureaus of the presidiums, the councils have their committees consisting of the councilors who control the respective bureaus of the presidium. For instance, the Education Department, which is responsible for school administration and all educational matters, and is subject to the Ministry of Education, is controlled also by the council's Committee for Education. This committee seeks to implement local interests in the educational policies of the department.

The formal structure of the political authority and administration is as shown in the accompanying diagram.*

This formal structure, created in the second period of the development of the People's Democracy, did not function according to the letter of the

*From Nasza Konstytucja, *Our Constitution* (Warsaw, 1956), p. 157.

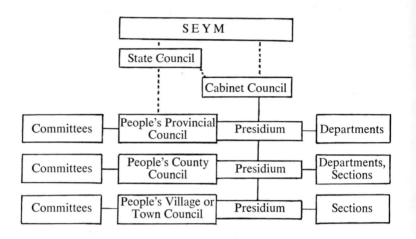

Constitution. The structure presented here was the *soll*, but the *sein* was different, because there was another powerful political force which concentrated the real authority in its hands—the Polish United Workers' party.

THE POLITICAL PARTIES

Today in Poland there are three political parties: the Polish United Workers' party, the Peasants' United party, and the Democratic party. They are political representations of the main social categories: workers, peasants, intelligentsia, and artisans.

The leading role is played by the P.U.W.P. as the real political force directing the building of socialism. It is not easy to describe a political party like this. It is a party of the Leninist type, a type treated at length in an immense literature in political science, but—I believe—there are many things still unrecorded about it. Especially in the years of "the cult of personality" when myths were treated as reality, and social reality was "transformed" by the decrees of the party which was regarded as an incarnation of historic reason and of historical necessity—there was established a model of party organization and activity connected with the Stalinist theory of socialism. It is true that the basic party principle of internal organization, namely the principle of democratic centralism, greatly facilitated the development of Stalinism. This principle requires that all party decisions be discussed by all party members, but when adopted by the majority, they must be implicitly obeyed by all the members. Since the party authorities are the executors of these decisions taken collectively, in practice this means obedience to the people standing at the top. It is difficult to keep harmony between democracy and centralism; there are always shifts toward centralism. Therefore the processes which are now going on in the Polish United Workers' party are watched with very great interest, because Gomulka wants to organize a new model of a democratic Communist party. In the period of Stalin's dictatorship, the party was transformed into a strictly centralized organism, where an iron discipline united all the members into a body which was highly efficient in all actions.

The Polish United Workers' party was created in 1948 when the Polish Workers' party merged with the Polish Socialist party. The first was a continuation of the Polish Communist party, disbanded by the Comintern in 1938 under false accusation (and rehabilitated in 1956.) The second was a Democratic-Socialist party of the Western type. Both parties merged on the ideological basis of Marxism-Leninism. The party of the Leninist type is a revolutionary party, leading the workers to socialism through the dictatorship of the proletariat. The party is the executor of this dictatorship. In order to attain its goals, the party must direct all spheres of social life through its members. It must also steadily educate its members, give them necessary instruction, and thereby influence the entire nation. So the party has built up a mighty propaganda machine always working on the centralistic party line. At the same time the party keeps its members in discipline through the Commission of Party Control and a system of sanctions applied to members who do not respect the party line.

In the system of the People's Democracy, the working class is expected to play the principal role, but it is supposed to work in alliance with the peasants, the artisans, and the intelligentsia. In other words, in that system, according to its basic conception, there is no place for a single-party rule. But in fact (and this was reflected in the attitude of the P.U.W.P. toward other parties and in its attitude toward the Parliament, the government, all social organizations, and all citizens) the principle of party leadership really meant a monopoly of rule.

Although nominally the P.U.W.P. is a workers' party, it is composed not only of workers but also of peasants and intelligentsia. The problem of party composition has been widely discussed, and the disadvantage of including too great a number of intelligentsia debated. The party has been characterized by an influx of members striving for different goals. There were the convinced communists, believing that the party really transformed society according to the Marxist vision. But there were also a number of upstarts and opportunists, who joined the party because, in spite of formal declarations to the contrary, membership was also connected with some privileges.

In order to realize its principal aim—political leadership in building a socialist society—the party must draw its members from all occupations, social strata, and organizations. The party's political leadership is the essence of the Communist social system. It must direct all activities of all the people toward the same aim: socialism. It must control all spheres of social life in order to mobilize the right effort and to prevent or suppress the activity of the enemy. The party does not directly govern and administer, but in all governmental and administrative institutions and offices are to be found party organizations, consisting of the people who work there. These organizations play a leading role, acting as watchdog for the party line of policy.

But carrying out party aims, while avoiding direct management and administration is a very difficult task, and in the Stalinist period, it was actually the party committees that had the real power in their hands and dictated the decisions and activities of all the administration. It could hardly be otherwise. The principle of political leadership without management is, maybe, a beautiful thing, but in practice there has always been a tendency to direct management. The Central Committee of the party is therefore the highest political institution in the country, directing and deciding all political, economic, and social affairs.

The basic principle of political guidance of the P.U.W.P. influenced also its relations with other parties. As was stated several times after the eighth plenary meeting of the Central Committee in October 1956, these relations in the Stalinist period were also warped. Briefly stated, the other parties were totally subject to the Workers' party, their programs consisted solely of support for the political line of the Workers' party. But now both the other parties are in feverish action, trying to attain their own political aims.

The United Peasants' party is supposed to represent the interests of the rural population. Its members are not only peasants but also the intellectuals of peasant origin. The tradition of the peasants' political movement in Poland is older than that of the workers' movement. In the system of the People's Democracy, the United Peasants' party (U.P.P.), which came into being after the fusion of the radical and the right wing in the peasants' political movement, should be an autonomous political party, acting in alliance with the working class and ensuring the influence of the peasants in the people's government. But in the Stalinist period the role of the U.P.P. was reduced to assisting the P.U.W.P. in the process of building socialism, especially in the rural areas. Its old leader retired. But after October 1956, new life came into the Polish villages. In the process of disbanding the collective farms, economically weak and created by force, the old rural social and cultural institutions have returned to life. The peasant masses can again express their will, and the U.P.P. regained a large measure of autonomy following an agreement with the P.U.W.P. As Gomulka has put it: "The Polish way to socialism differs from that in other countries in that in the building of socialism it admits the collaboration of non-Marxist parties supporting socialism." On this principle the U.P.P. seeks now to work out its own program of political and social activity in order to organize the peasants, defend their economic and cultural interests, and promote their development.

We must say the same about the Democratic party. It is expected to group in its ranks the members of the intelligentsia and the artisans. The Polish intelligentsia has always had rich revolutionary and progressive tendencies. In the Stalinist period the Democratic party, like the United Peasants' party, was only an echo of the Workers' party and its political activity consisted in supporting that party's political line. Now it looks for its own political program. This may be a very interesting task in view of the special role played by the intelligentsia in a society like Poland's, but rather a difficult one. The Democratic party faces the same difficulties as the U.P.P. in keeping harmony between centralism and democracy, between leadership and administration, and between its autonomous policy and a recognition of the leading political role of the P.U.W.P.

Both the Peasants' and the Democratic parties in recent years had only a relatively small number of members. But after October 1956, with the revival of political life, both parties became more important in the process of democratization. We must stress, above all, the strong activity of the peasants who have returned to their traditional belief in their own political movement, adapted to the new situation.

THE PARTICIPATION OF CITIZENS IN POLITICAL POWER

According to the Constitution all organs of state authority and administration are obliged to work in close contact with all citizens, give account of their activity to the people, carefully look into all motions, complaints, and desires of all citizens, and explain to the masses the essential aims of all political activity. All councils and all the members of Parliament are directly responsible to the electors. Every citizen may express his opinion about the activity of any state or political institution or employee, whether the latter is a minister or a simple usher. Such is the letter of the Constitution. Moreover the press is obliged to accept letters of complaint from all citizens and intervene in all cases of abuse, of neglect of duties, and so on. About the press we shall speak later. But it must be said now that, in the Stalinist period, all the means of popular participation in political power and all the means of popular control over the government were theoretical only. The Stalinist system was a dictatorship of a mighty centralistic bureaucracy. And one of the main problems of Gomulka's reform is to find ways to ensure democratic participation of the masses in government, at the same time preserving the leading role of the party. This means a reconstruction of the party's internal structure and new relations between the party and the citizens. The electoral campaign which began in December 1956 was the first decisive step in this direction. For the first time under the People's Democracy, the Poles have the right not only to vote but to elect. The new Polish model of democratic socialism will bring the provisions of the Constitution to life.

A few words must also be said about the "National Front," called now "The Front of National Unity." It was an organization totally subject to the party leadership, proclaiming national unity in the struggle for socialism and peace, and working for nationwide support for the people's authority. Its aims were to unify all people in political actions like elections or the peace campaign. We may say that its weakness consisted in proclaiming that *soll* is already *sein*. But we must observe that there was in the Polish nation a deep feeling of unity on all questions of vital importance for national existence. The influence of state and party ended in the formal institutions and groups. But the other current of political life ran in the informal circles, in families, in all such microforms of social life. And in the October days all the Poles stood behind Gomulka ready for sacrifice in the struggle for independence. It was a true manifestation of a real "Front of National Unity."

Now, in order to complete the picture of the political life, we must describe the role of the press. In a Stalinist society the principal aim of the newspapers had been to explain and glorify the people's government, to mold the desired attitudes, to fight against the remnants of capitalist mentality, and to educate the people in the spirit of socialism. The press had the right to criticize but this had to be done only from the correct position; that is, the press had to criticize all that was a deviation from the right line, or was harmful for socialism. But this changed with the "thaw." The Poles have too acute a sense of comedy to be for long good dogmatists. Newspapers and periodicals became the organs of nationwide criticism, showed the economic weakness of the system, the bureaucratic abuse of citizens' rights, the incompetence of many officials, the unsolved social problems proclaimed to be nonexistent, and so on. We can say that the Polish newspapers and periodicals truly played a leading role in the process of democratization and de-Stalinization.

There is one more question: What about the opposition? There is no political system without opposition. But we must distinguish opposition as a psychological phenomenon, as a social process, and as a political party. There were, in Poland, feelings of opposition against many aspects of the People's Democracy system. They found their social manifestation in many forms of activity—ranging from sabotage to "internal emigration" (the abstention from all pro-regime social and political activity) and an attitude (called the "positive tendency") reflecting the intention to safeguard national values in quiet work without any external manifestation of political opposition. But in a People's Democracy there is no place for an opposition party, because in principle this political system works to realize the vital interests of all laboring people, who form the immense majority of the nation. As a kind of dictatorship, it excludes the possibility of giving freedom of activity to the enemy. The system of self-criticism is expected to play in some way the role of opposition and preserve the political system from deterioration and degeneration. It did not. So the aroused general feeling of opposition against abuses and distortions found its general expression in October 1956.

Economic Institutions

As we have already seen, the political institutions of the People's Democracy are based on a system of economic organization. The only possibility of maintaining and developing this system toward the final goal of a socialist society consists in building up an economic organization which gives economic power to the political authority. The most important traits of this economic organization are a certain form of property relations and a planned organization of production, distribution, and investment. All other characteristics of Polish economic institutions are derived from these.

PROPERTY RELATIONS

Today in Poland there are the following different—coexisting—economic systems: (1) the socialist system, (2) the small producer system, and (3) the capitalist system. The socialist system is the dominant one. All these economic systems have their foundations in different types of property relations.

The socialist system is based on the socialization (or nationalization) of property. There are two kinds of socialized property: state property and cooperative property. The state or national property came into being through the nationalization of all industrial enterprises, banks, communication systems, and some estates which were not parceled out among the peasants. This national property consists of mineral resources, waters, forests, mines, all kinds of transport, means of communication, national industrial enterprises, state farms, state machine centers, national trade enterprises, and communal enterprises. The administration of this national property is vested in the government, and it is the main basis for a planned economy. The second kind of socialized property, cooperative property, arises as a result of the voluntary union of individual proprietors who pool their means of production for their common use and begin to work collectively. This property is not national property, but the common property of the cooperative members. In this way different kinds of cooperatives have been created: collective farms, artisans' cooperatives, trade cooperatives, consumers' cooperatives, and so on.

There are essential differences between state and cooperative property. In the state enterprises *all* means of production have been socialized; in the cooperatives only the *basic* ones have been socialized, and the rest remain as the individual property of the cooperative members. Workers in the state enterprises receive wages; members of the cooperatives share the income. The production and activity of state enterprises are centrally planned and directed by state organs, of the cooperatives only indirectly so. But they have this in common: in principle both kinds of property exclude the exploitation of workers, and therefore both are called socialist property.

The small producer system comprises all farms and artisans' workshops which do not employ wage earners. This system is dominant in agriculture where the process of collectivization made rather slow progress. After the Eighth Plenum in October 1956, many collective farms were disbanded, and the peasants returned to individual farming. During the second period of the People's Democracy the policy toward the small enterprises consisted in the development of their productivity and, at the same time, in directing them into the cooperatives, which two goals proved to be rather difficult to reconcile in practice. I shall say more about this when speaking about agriculture. But I must stress that even before the Eighth Plenum there was a tendency to strengthen private enterprises because of the failure of cooperatives. Gomulka's program is to stop the process of creating cooperatives by administrative pressure and to maintain private economic initiative, within limits, in order to revive all economic forces. But at the same time he has stressed that the collective economic forms are better.

The capitalistic system within the Polish economy comprises larger peasant farms, private trade enterprises, and small industrial enterprises. In the years 1948–56 the policy toward this system was that of isolation and limitation, in order to prevent a revival of capitalism. This policy has also been changed since Gomulka's return to power, in the direction of using this system to raise the standard of living.

The main aim of nationalization was to direct the profit which all enterprises create from private hands to the use of all the nation, and, primarily, to the laboring people. But the plans were not fulfilled to the extent that had been hoped for. A great part of this income was directed into new investment and the greatly expanded administration consumed too much. Also, the centralistic system of planning and administration of industry hampered the development of productivity.

I must also mention something about personal property, which consists of all things for personal use, including houses and gardens. Article 13 of the Constitution states that the government guarantees the private holding of this property and the right to inherit it.

THE PLANNED ECONOMY

The main points of the Marxist theory of the socialist society are these: the abolition of private enterprise which makes possible the exploitation of the workers by the proprietors, the nationalization of all means of production, and the planned organization of the economy in order to stimulate a rise in the standard of living of all laboring people. The principle of planning, which replaces freedom of enterprise, is of basic importance for the socialist economy. Having in its hands all forms of social property, the state is expected to organize the collaboration of all kinds of industry, trade, and transport; to divide the income and plan investments; and to provide goods in order to satisfy all the needs of the society. So the socialist economy is expected to have a mighty and efficient organization for planning.

It is rather difficult to present an adequate description of the Polish model of planned economy, because at present the system developed in the years 1948–56 is being radically changed—changed because it failed.

Planning began as early as 1945 but it consisted only in making plans concerning some limited spheres of economic activity. The application of the first nationwide plan began in 1947. It was the so-called Three Year Plan of Economic Rehabilitation which had as its purpose the reconstruction of what the war had destroyed. Its goals were realized in 1949, after the victory of the Stalinist element in the party. In the next year, a new Six Year Plan of Economic Development and Construction of the Foundations of Socialism came into operation. It was in this period of 1950–56 that the now-changed model of planned organization and planned economy was elaborated. In this model the supreme institution for the economy was the State Commission for Economic Planning. Then all the ministries and the presidiums of the provincial, county, and town councils had also their departments of planning, subject to the control of this State Commission. These departments elaborated the essentials of the plan for their respective territories, and the State Commission provided a detailed national plan. There were plans for long periods, as, for example, the Six Year Plan, and short-time plans for one year each. The various enterprises had their yearly, monthly, weekly, and daily plans. The over-all plan established the manner of production, the productivity expected of labor and investment, and the employment policy.

In the State Commission there were departments for all branches of the national economy, and during the application of the Six Year Plan that commission was transformed into a sort of economic government which not only originated, but also directed the application of the plan. The national economy became a highly centralized but less efficient machinery, with an immense administrative apparatus. Even trifling affairs in factories needed the consent of the central economic authorities. The initiative of the local management was fettered with many rules. The "plan" became an idol, and since wages and salaries were tied to its success (workers and employees could increase substantially their low basic salary if they met the demands of the plan), very often its goals were realized at an unnecessary waste of time, effort, and raw materials.

In such a system of planned economy the Six Year Plan, though it produced many new factories and investments, did not bring about the rise of the standard of living in the desired measure. It must be said that armaments and the war industry absorbed many products originally destined for consumers. But the growing discontent of the working population, expressing itself first in the strike and riots in Poznań, was directed not against the effort and sacrifice asked of them but against the centralized, bureaucratic administration, which became a machinery existing for itself and not for the service of all citizens.

After the Eighth Plenum, the Seym abolished the State Commission for Economic Planning. In its place a Planning Commission was created in the Cabinet Council, composed of economists and other experts. Its aim is to provide general direction for economic activity. The basic principles in the reorganization of all planning institutions, now in full progress, are to remove the rigid rules of planning in order to mobilize all economic forces and to decentralize decisions and provide for the participation of workers in factory management. The ideal of democratization in economic life is that the workers should decide the affairs of their factory, the peasants should determine their respective affairs, and in all spheres of economic activity the people directly affected should replace the central administration. (I must add that the word "bureaucracy" in Poland today has an offensive as well as pejorative meaning. A "bureaucrat" is a man without imagination, without initiative or a feeling of responsibility, without human understanding, acting only according to rules, seeing no wider implications of his activity.)

In the course of democratization workers' councils have been created in the factories. They are expected to provide an opportunity for the workers to manage the factory and to direct all their own economic and social affairs. This is being organized under the influence of the Yugoslavian example, but has different forms and aims. The workers' councils are expected to deal first of all with such problems as a yearly plan for the factory's production, the internal structure of the enterprise, a plan for technical development and investments, the division of the income from the enterprise, and the establishing of the norm system. As I am writing these lines, the workers' councils are still in the stage of experimentation.

THE TRADE UNIONS

The Stalinist theory of trade unions followed from the general theory of the socialist society. In such a society, where the exploitation of workers is abolished and the factory becomes national property, there is no antagonism between management and workers and no contradictory interests. The management and the workers strive toward the same goal: increasing productivity and bettering the welfare of the whole people. Therefore the aims of the trade unions consist in the organization of devices for increasing the output and productivity of labor, such as encouraging competition for greater output, providing for the political education of the workers, and establishing reading rooms and leisure-time activities. These trade unions were to be the means of "transmission from the party to the masses."

Actually, to state the matter briefly, the trade unions were an overly developed centralized, parasitical, bureaucratic, administrative apparatus. The Stalinist theory of socialist society proved false. There was no exploiting class but there was an administration which did not care about the vital interests of the working class. The strike in Poznań showed that the discontent among the masses was too great to be ignored or suppressed by police force. In August 1956, at the plenary session of the Central Council of the Trade Unions, as a result of wide discussion in the press and at meetings, the proper tasks of the trade unions were reformulated: to protect the vital interests of the laboring people, to work for better wages, housing, and living conditions, to seek real participation by the workers in the management of the factory and in the political government in the country, to organize the workers' cultural life, and so on.

This movement deepened and expanded after October 1956. It can be said that the Polish trade unions are passing through a crisis, that they are looking for new organizational forms, new methods, and new aims. There are many questions to be settled: the relation of trade unions to the workers' councils, the relation to the state administration, the extent of participation in economic planning, and, above all, how to raise the standard of living.

The Stalinist conception of trade unions has been rejected; the new one has not yet crystallized. But in the conception of the Polish way to socialism the trade unions will play an important role.

THE ECONOMIC ORGANIZATION OF AGRICULTURE

As indicated above, agriculture in Poland is organized in three sections: state farms, collective farms, and individual farms. Before October 1956 the state farms owned 12 per cent, the collective farms 13 per cent, and the individual farms 75 per cent of the agricultural land. But the production picture was different: the state farms contributed about 15 per cent, collective farms 5 per cent, and individual farms 80 per cent of agricultural production.

The state farms are national property administered by the Ministry of State Farms.* Their area varies from 10 to 2,000 hectares. They were created after the land reform from the estates not parceled out among the peasants. The individual state farm as a productive unit is directed by a manager and his staff. Several such productive units create a set of state farms which in turn becomes an administrative unit. Every province *(voivodship)* has its director of state farms.

There are three categories of workers on a state farm: permanent workers, who dwell there with their families; semipermanent workers, who are small peasants and their families living in neighboring villages; and seasonal laborers working only occasionally in spring, summer, or autumn. Since the wages are relatively low, the state farms often have scanty manpower. The organization of labor—as one critic has put it—is neither capitalist nor socialist, just bad. State farms are expected to be model farms and the centers of progress in agriculture, but they assume this role only very slowly.

The collective farms are of four kinds. The first is called an Association for Land Cultivation and is the simplest type of collective farm. The members unite only their arable fields for common cultivation, leaving some area for individual use. The houses, farm buildings, and all equipment belong to the members, who are obliged to provide all the tools needed for the common use. The second type is an Agricultural Cooperative Association where all the fields, meadows, and pasturage grounds are united for common use, but the members are still proprietors of their fields. Each member retains some land, his house, and equipment (horses, cows, machines, etc.), but he must provide what is necessary for the common use. The third kind of collective farm is called an Agricultural Production Collective Farm. Here, the members give for common use not only their fields but also all their equipment. Every member has the right to own a small individual farm, two cows, and as many small animals and poultry as he likes. Every member must work at least 100 days in the common fields. The fourth type differs from the third only in the method of dividing income among the members. Whereas in the third type the income is shared

---

*Now under the administration of the Ministry of Agriculture, the Ministry of State Farms having been disbanded.

by members according to their investment in land and tools, in the fourth type the share is calculated only according to the labor contributed.

The process of collectivization made slow progress and then only under administrative pressure. Thus when Gomulka declared that "The peasants have the free choice of the way of farming" a great number of collective farms decided to disband. The forced collectivization had caused a drop in agricultural production; the collective farms created by various kinds of pressure were economically weak, needed state assistance and credit, and consumed large sums while producing poor results. But it must also be stressed that there are hundreds of collective farms that are economically sound and highly productive.

Individual farming has always been the main form of agricultural organization in Poland. This term is perhaps not wholly accurate, since in spite of recent developments the peasant farm in Poland is still more a family undertaking than an individual economic institution. In any case, the peasant farm is undergoing a crisis both in its economic and in its social aspect. Industrialization and the development of education have attracted great numbers of young people away from the villages. The state and collective farms are not the only ones hampered by insufficient manpower; the peasant farms have the same problem. The economic organization of the peasant farm was connected with the family organization, and now, as the family changes, the farm economy must also undergo a change. With these factors went hand in hand the pressure toward collectivization, which took the form of imposing higher taxes on individual farms and higher

Table 1. Distribution of Farm Land in Poland, by Size of
Peasant Farms in 1954

Size of Farms (in hectares)	Percentage of All Farm Land	Percentage of All Farms
0.5–1	1.1	8.0
1–2	4.4	15.4
2–3	6.6	13.7
3–4	8.1	12.0
4–5	8.8	10.1
5–7	18.5	16.1
7–10	23.8	14.6
10–12	9.6	4.5
12–14	5.6	2.2
14–20	7.7	2.4
More than 20	5.8	1.0
Total	100.0	100.0

compulsory quotas for corn, potatoes, milk, and livestock. It is easy to understand how such a policy led to a drop in production.

The distribution of farm land in 1954, according to size of peasant farms, is shown in Table 1.*

THE PEASANT SELF-HELP ORGANIZATION

The Peasant Self-Help Organization was to be something like a peasants' trade union. Its aims were to increase agricultural production; to organize professional assistance and instruction; to raise the cultural standard of the peasants through the provision of reading rooms and courses in agriculture and the publication of books and periodicals; and to prepare for collectivization. These aims were being realized in a way similar to that of the aims of the trade unions. Beside this political organization there are the peasants' cooperatives of Peasant Self-Help, which supply the villages with all sorts of goods and buy agricultural products from the peasants. The cooperatives also run their own enterprises—bakeries, mills, and inns.

The economy of the People's Democracy is closely connected with its political aims. The party leadership also has control of the economic life. Thus the first trait of economic institutions is that they are subject to political aims. The second trait of the economic system is rigid regulation by a great number of laws, rules, orders, and the like. The third is the replacement of personal initiative by centralized administrative activities. The recent changes are characterized by a tendency toward decentralization of decisions, by giving more autonomy to enterprises, by democratization, and by stimulation of economic forces.

The Family

There are some questions concerning the family and its basic social functions common to all societies. In every society the family is an institution securing that society's biological and cultural continuity. This basic social function gives the family a special importance among all institutions. Since the existence and the future of the society depend upon the family, the interest in the family on the part of the state, the church, and many other groups and associations is easy to understand. But the family satisfies also the needs which every man considers most intimate: sexual

*All tables and statistical data quoted in this paper are taken from the *Statistical Year Book of Poland, 1956* (Warsaw, 1956).

needs, love relations, the rearing of children. As a result of these two divergent tendencies the family has two different sides of existence. On the one hand, it is an institution controlled by the society and regulated by laws, religious commandments, mores, and customs; while on the other hand, it is an institution of great internal strength which can deeply influence the whole life of the society.

These two sides of the family can be better observed in a period of quick and violent changes in the structure of the society. Every revolution, each of which changes the system of values, must of necessity fight against the resistance of the family, which hands down to the next generation the traditional values recognized as the most important. It is therefore the task of a revolutionary government, in the service of the revolution, to remove the youth from the influence of the traditional values, social patterns, and customs of the family. We have witnessed such a process in all revolutionary societies. Then when the families were transformed into institutions of a new type, in conformity with the spirit of the revolution, the states drew them once again to their educational tasks. But the struggle between the traditional tendencies of the family and the revolutionary tendencies of some states is always a source of disorganization.

Many social problems concerning the family in postwar Poland arise only partly from this conflict. Their roots are to be found in the political, social, and economic situation of the last seventeen years. The war beginning in 1939 and the partition of Poland between Nazi Germany and the Soviet Union have had a disastrous effect on hundreds of thousands of families. Soldiers in P.O.W. camps, emigrants to the neighboring and Western countries, refugees separated by the new German-Soviet frontier —all this meant the breaking up and separation of families. And then there were the concentration camps and the deportations which destroyed additional hundreds of thousands of families. For several reasons we shall never know the exact numbers, but we do know that millions of Poles spent the war years as forced emigrants or in different kinds of prison, concentration, or labor camps; many were deported to Germany or to the eastern part of the Soviet Union, and only after Gomulka's visit to Moscow in November 1956 were they allowed to return home.

The German occupation and extermination program evoked a great resistance movement. The conspiratorial activity, in which almost all people in Poland took part, also had a disastrous effect on family life. We have as yet no history of the Polish resistance movement, and we have no sociological analysis of its social and moral effects; like many other subjects, it has been politically taboo. But generally speaking, the conspiracy and the underground activity, the participation in the underground armies (these were the Home Army and the People's Army), the participation in the merciless struggles, the cruel repression by the German police forces—all had a profound and disorganizing influence, weakening all social and moral ties. Families were forced to adapt to the new conditions by rejecting most of the previously accepted and established norms because of the hardships of everyday life, the uncertainty of the future, the difficulty of living in an honest way—in brief, because of the regime of slavery, the "times of contempt."

Thus, when the war was over and the time of reconstruction came, there were a great many broken, separated, disorganized families in Poland. There were also great numbers of people accustomed to violence, contemptuous of the laws and moral rules, demoralized by the war, the underground struggle, and the monstrosities of the concentration camps. But there was also a longing for peace and for a revival of quiet, normal life.

Let us examine how general social conditions influenced family life. As the reader has already seen from the previous description, the revolution, which came after the war and the German occupation, changed the class structure of the Polish nation, began the reconstruction of the economy, and aimed at the creation of new moral and cultural values. But, in a rather vague manner, families strove to reconstruct their lives on the basis of prewar norms and values. The revolution proclaimed the new, revolutionary, and socialist morals, condemning at the same time the bourgeois or petit bourgeois morals. For example, the revolution condemned religion as the "opiate of the people" and as a tool in the hands of the exploiting classes. But this was not the only conflict of values that influenced the families.

The revolution also created new labor relations, accelerated industrialization, drew thousands and thousands of peasants to the towns and women to the plants and other places of work, and gave the youth access to an extensive school system. Moreover, the revolution proclaimed that youth was the great force in building the future society and therefore it had special rights and duties. It is easy to imagine how all this evoked tension and conflict in families. In order to provide the conditions for a new organization of family life, to restore harmony between the family and the society, and to provide a system of protection for women and children, the state began the codification of existing family laws and the creation of new laws. Family laws in Poland were very complex. As a result of Poland's former partition, there were five different series of laws operating in as many parts of Poland during the period 1918–39, and three of them recognized marriage as a religious institution. In the years 1945–46 some decrees began the unification of family legislation. In 1950 a new family code appeared with the following basic principles: the family was to be considered a secular institution, there were to be equal rights for women, and provisions were to be made for the stability of the family settlement following divorce and for the protection of children.

What are the main problems faced by Polish families recently? Let us begin with some figures, as shown in Table 2. As we see from this table, after the war there was a considerable increase in the marriage and birth rates. Table 3 shows that people were getting married at a somewhat younger age. There was also a considerable increase in the employment of women: in 1938 there were 23.5 women per hundred of the employed; in 1953, 31.0; in 1954, 32.0. The distribution of men and women employed in socialist enterprises in 1954 is shown in Table 4. Briefly summarized, the figures tell us that there is an increase in marriages, that there are more young marriages, that there is an increase in women's employment, and that the average age of employed women is lower than that of men (probably because older women are less often employed outside the home).

Today Poland is a country of hard-working people. "Real" wages and salaries are low. It is difficult to maintain a family on the salary from only one job, and many hold down two jobs. The result is that family members seldom even see each other. Often children of working parents see their parents only late in the evening. There are also great difficulties in housing. All this does not strengthen the internal ties of families.

Another problem arises from the process called "social advancement." It may be described as an intensive upward mobility, the rise of a new social and political elite. Many workers, peasants, and humble clerks can and do attend various schools and advance themselves, or through political activity attain better (sometimes even high) posts in industry or state administration. It has been a mass process which has caused many tensions and conflicts in families, especially when the husband has advanced and the wife has remained on the family's former cultural level. But there are not many divorces in Poland: in 1950 there were 0.43 divorces per thou-

Table 2. Marriage, Birth, and Death Rates in Poland (per thousand population)

Year	Marriage Rate	Birth Rate	Death Rate	Rate of Natural Increase
1936–38	8.2	29.8	15.3	14.5
1950	10.8	30.7	11.6	19.1
1951	10.7	31.0	12.4	18.6
1953	10.0	29.7	10.2	19.5
1955	9.5	29.0	9.6	19.4

Table 3. Marriage Rates by Age Group in Poland
(per thousand of each sex and age group)

Age Group	Men		Women	
	1931–32	1954	1931–32	1954
To 19	6.9	11.1	34.8	51.9
20–24	58.1	88.0	70.2	100.4
25–29	70.6	79.3	37.7	38.4
30–34	26.8	27.5	16.6	16.8
35–39	13.3	14.8	8.9	9.4
40–49	7.5	8.1	3.9	4.7
50 and over	3.7	4.4	1.1	1.2
Average age for marriage (in years)	26.3	25.5	23.4	22.6

Table 4. Percentage of Men and Women, by Age Group,
Employed in Socialist Enterprises in 1954

Age Group	Men	Women	Percentage of Total Employed
To 18	4.4	7.1	5.3
19–30	35.3	48.7	39.7
31–40	21.5	18.0	20.4
41–55	29.1	21.2	26.5
56 and over	9.7	5.0	8.1

sand population; in 1951, 0.44; in 1952, 0.49; in 1953, 0.49; in 1954, 0.46; in 1955, 0.49.

There are other causes of loosening marital and familial ties. For instance, the planned distribution of manpower, sending workers to different parts of the country in the new enterprises built up during the Six Year Plan, separated thousands of families for a shorter or a longer period. We must also mention the not always reasonable number of meetings and other near-compulsory social activities, which consume time normally spent in the family.

The next set of problems to be considered concerns parent-child relations, family and school relations, family and youth organizations and movements — that is, generally speaking, educational problems. It was stated previously that youth supported the revolution with enthusiasm, that the pathos of building a new society of justice and welfare appealed to young minds and hearts with an irresistible force. But the life of the revolutionary youth has been a hard one, especially when the revolution was directed by such an elite as the Stalinist group. There were many tensions and conflicts between the older skeptical generation and youth; there were the conflicts between the family values and the new values and educational goals represented by the party-controlled school system; and later there were many and deep psychological tragedies among the young people after Khrushchev's report on Stalin. There were also other phenomena like the self-defense of youth against the ideological pressure of the school and the party propaganda, which some young people understood to be false and hypocritical. From this struggle arose the attitude of revolt against the *dretwa mowa* (numb speech) of the official propaganda and against the deceitful customs of the privileged elite. There arose the search for humanistic socialism. That is why youth has given Gomulka their full support.

In spite of all these difficult conditions, I believe I can state that the strength of the Polish family is, as it always has been, great. During the partition period and then during the war and occupation the family was the unquenchable source of the strength of the whole nation. And this is also true today.

Educational Institutions

One of the basic socialist principles is the faith in the power of education. To build up a new socialist society means economic and political reconstruction, but more than that, an education of the whole society. Therefore Polish educational institutions of all kinds embrace with their activity almost all the people in the country. I mean not only the school system, but all existing organizations from political parties and trade unions down to youth organizations and other associations. All these carry on educational work. The trade unions organize the so-called ideological education, as also do the peasant organizations. The Society for the

Popularization of Science (in existence since 1950) has organized yearly more than 100,000 lectures on different themes in all kinds of communities. There has also been built up a vast system of vocational training of all kinds and degrees from short courses to the evening engineering schools. This process of re-educating the whole nation raises many sociological problems. It is not only an education of a new generation. Many times the roles are reversed, and young people become the educators of their parents. It is not my task here to present the details of these processes, but only to give a short review of the formal structure of the Polish school system. As is true of all institutions, this system changed several times in the past twelve years, and after October 1956 it will undoubtedly change once more.

The first educational institution is the nursery school, which receives children between three and seven years of age. In 1955 there were in Poland 8,460 nurseries with 377,804 children; that is, of every 1,000 children aged three to seven, 142 were placed in the nursery schools. In 1949 the corresponding number was 170. The nursery schools were expected to free women from their household tasks and let them work in industry.

At the age of seven children go to the basic school, where they study for seven years. Attendance at the basic school is compulsory for all children (there are special schools for defective children). In the school year 1955–56, out of 3,325,600 children aged seven to thirteen, there were 3,256,500 in the basic schools—97.9 per cent. Besides the ordinary basic schools there are artistic primary schools for particularly capable children who are preparing for the secondary artistic schools.

The system of secondary schools is more complex. In 1955–56, 43.8 per cent of all youth aged fourteen to seventeen were entered in some type of secondary school. The lyceums provide a secondary general education for four years. They issue a certificate of completed secondary education (*matura*), which enables a young person to enter a university or other higher academic schools. In 1955–56 there were 201,421 pupils in the lyceums. There are also secondary general education schools for adults (with 53,843 students in 1955–56).

Then there is a wide system of secondary vocational schools, of the following kinds: basic vocational schools, secondary technical schools (the *technicum*), vocational lyceums, secondary medical schools and lyceums, secondary artistic schools. The basic vocational schools train skilled workers in two or three years. In 1955–56 they had 129,659 pupils. The secondary technical schools are of several different kinds: agricultural, commercial, technical (to train technicians for industry), and those providing education in physical culture. Then there are lyceums for nursery school teachers, for teachers of the basic schools, and for cultural workers like librarians and reading-room heads. Furthermore, there are the three-year secondary schools for nurses and secondary schools for pharmacists. There are also medical lyceums for midwives, dental technicians, pharmacists, and assistant surgeons, but the entrance here is restricted to those who have previously finished two years of secondary general education. These secondary vocational schools may be for young people or for adults. The former trained 270,240 pupils in 1955–56, the latter 54,409 pupils. The secondary artistic schools had 8,065 pupils in 1955–56.

The higher academic schools are administered by the following ministries: the Ministry of Higher Education, which controls the universities, higher economic schools, higher agricultural colleges, and the polytechnic and higher engineering schools; the Ministry of Education, which runs the pedagogical higher schools; the Ministry of Health, which operates the medical academies; the Ministry of Culture and Arts, which organizes the higher schools of arts, drama, and music; and the Committee for Physical Culture, which administers the physical training colleges. In 1955–56 there were 78 schools of all these types with 134,554 students.

As we may infer from the figures cited, the sums and effort spent for education are immense.

Besides the schools there are many other educational institutions: reading rooms for children and young people, children's clubs and children's homes, youth houses of culture, and other special educational establishments for juvenile delinquents, orphans, and the like. There also are a number of short courses for both general and vocational education. The popular and workers' universities must also be mentioned, and the Sunday universities organized by the Society for the Popularization of Science and other organizations.

We may or may not be satisfied with the result of the educational institutions—personally, I am not wholly satisfied—but one thing must be said in conclusion to this short review: never before has the Polish nation undertaken such an effort to overcome ignorance and to give all the people their proper education. We may be unsatisfied with the methods of education applied, particularly in the Stalinist period when often the methods were those of propaganda instead of education, with the failure to master all the educational problems, with the fact that there have been so many delinquent children and young people, with the number of hooligans who have become a grave problem—but in spite of all this we must also acknowledge that the Polish nation can look forward with hope. Polish teachers and educators have proud traditions and now after the abolition of distortion and a return to proper educational methods we may expect better results.

Recreational and Artistic Institutions

The Polish Constitution guarantees all citizens the right to rest. In order to implement this right the government created a Workers' Leisure Fund administered by the Central Council of the Trade Unions. The fund is used for maintaining workers' leisure houses in all kinds of holiday resorts throughout the country. Every employee may spend a fortnight a year in one of these houses for a price relative to his earnings or free of charge. In these houses he finds not only the conditions necessary for a good rest, but also opportunities for playing games and practicing sports or artistic activities, and a reading room.

There are several different kinds of government-sponsored leisure: the above-mentioned fortnight of leisure in the houses of rest; a "tourist leisure," that is, an excursion through a particularly beautiful part of the country during two weeks; a vacation for mothers with small children; a family vacation for whole families; a vacation in Warsaw for country people; a medical-treatment vacation of three weeks for those threatened with illness; a vacation abroad in other People's Democracy countries.

The directing of people to these forms of leisure lies in the hands of the trade union organizations. In 1955 there were altogether 1,344 rest houses with 35,600 places in which 454,900 working people found relaxation.

The most numerous institutions connecting recreation with artistic activities are the houses of culture, clubs, and reading rooms. In these institutions different forms of activity take place. The houses of culture are organized in villages, in county towns, and in provincial cities. They are directed by central institutions from Warsaw, and it is the duty of a house of culture in a provincial city to take care of the other houses throughout the province. The services and activities of the houses of culture include various courses and lectures popularizing the sciences; libraries; amateur theaters, cinemas, orchestral and dancing groups, and choirs; and laboratories for amateurs (e.g., photographic laboratories). The houses have rooms for amusement and play. Of course not all the houses offer all these opportunities for artistic expression and not all of them are well equipped and directed.

The same kinds of activity may be found in the reading rooms, but on a modest scale. In 1955 there were 254 houses of culture, 289 clubs, and 16,988 reading rooms in Poland. The statistics show that 357,200 members were active in artistic groups and 349,900 in library and scientific groups, but I think we must be careful in drawing optimistic conclusions from these numbers. Some of the groups operate on a very high level, but others do not.

In speaking about artistic and recreational institutions we must mention the Song and Dance State Ensembles, some of them widely renowned (like Mazowsze or Slask). They have been the model for many other regional groups, and this movement to rediscover and revive regional folk music, songs, and dances is one of the more important evidences of cultural revival in postwar Poland.

In 1955 there were 106 professional theaters in Poland (including 28 traveling theaters) which gave 30,314 performances seen by 11,458,000 spectators. There were 2,672 cinemas (including 285 traveling cinemas) which gave 999,000 showings seen by 183 million spectators. In the same year there were in Poland 3 million wireless sets registered, 155 museums with 6,249,000 visitors, 7,199 books and pamphlets printed in a total of 95,684,000 copies. There were 51 copies of newspapers and 14 copies of periodicals per person that year.

One thing must be said in conclusion to this section: Everybody must agree that, as in education, a great effort has been made to raise the standard of the whole nation in artistic and cultural life. If the results have not been all that might be hoped for, still they are significant enough to be felt in the future.

Religious Institutions

The separation of the Church from the state in Poland is a consequence of the Marxist theories on religion and revolution. The Church is the only powerful organization not integrated politically in the socialist system of institutions and organizations building socialism. Religion is considered a private affair of an individual. For a long time even such a statement would have been regarded as indicating a right-wing socialist position on this question—as an apparent neutralism, which, in fact, is objectively hostile to true socialism. But the Polish people are religious and their religion has been deeply rooted in national tradition and customs. The government, not wishing to jar these religious feelings, made its policy elastic. The Constitution guarantees to all citizens, professing all possible religions or none at all, full freedom of conscience and worship. But religion was eliminated from public life, including educational institutions. The October Revolution of 1956 has changed this attitude. Religious instruction returned to the schools as a noncompulsory subject. An agreement between the government and the Church has regulated the controversial questions.

There are in Poland today more than twenty-five churches and denominational organizations. No official statistics are available concerning the number of their members, but the Roman Catholic Church is by far the largest. According to the census of 1931 the percentage of membership in the different denominations in Poland was Roman Catholic, 75.2; Protestant, 2.6; Orthodox, 11.8; other Christian, 0.5; Jewish, 9.8; other, 0.1. Following the almost total extermination of the Jews, the removal of Germans (mostly Protestant), and the transfer of the eastern territories with their Orthodox population to the Soviet Union, the Roman Catholic Church must now have a still more dominating position.

I have already said that the Poles, mainly the folk masses, have been a religious people, and it must further be observed that the war and the occupation and their horrors deepened this religious spirit. Hence since the war there has been an intensification of religious life. Under these conditions the attempt to educate the whole nation in the spirit of scientific materialism has proved to be a hard and thankless task.

The victory of the Stalinist group in the party strengthened anticlerical tendencies in the political, educational, and cultural activities; however, it must be pointed out that liberty of worship was absolute, that there were never any attempts to interfere with the priests' worship activities. The government reacted only against the interference of the clergy in political matters. Still, as every sociologist knows, politics and religion always meet. When a political party tends to integrate all social, artistic, educational, and moral life according to its own patterns and values, and when a church like the Roman Catholic Church gives the faithful a philosophy of life with similarly integrating tendencies, it requires a great diplomatic ability and much cultivation of good will to avoid conflicts. Therefore, besides the practical aspects of great importance for Poland's future, the development of friendlier relations between the government and the Church after

Gomulka's return to power is an interesting sociological experiment: a peaceful cooperation of two systems that are incompatible in principle.

The history of religious life in the Poland of the People's Democracy has not been written yet. The activity of different groups, organizations, and tendencies among Polish Catholics deserves the attention of sociologists, but there has been practically no research done until now. The basic social unit of all churches is the parish. The churches understand this well, and know that the foundation of their power lies here, and they have assigned a great importance to parish work. Eliminated from public life, religion sought its support in the sphere of private life, in the nonformalized social circles, in families, in morals and faith. But that does not mean that the Catholic Church gave up its social aims.

Conclusion

It is possible that the above description of Polish institutions will be inadequate when it comes into the hands of the reader. This essay was finished in December 1956, when the revolution against Stalinism was still going on. We have witnessed the emergence of many new tendencies in Poland. For instance, the Polish Youth Association ceased to exist and new associations are emerging from the ferment. There are discussions and searches for new ways. It is difficult to say what tendencies will win, and which will disappear. The social forces now in action are numerous: the party and the working class, the peasant masses, the intelligentsia, the Catholic Church, the youth. There is also a large stratum of administration bureaucracy—the managers of all sorts—struggling for position. There are in the country diverging political tendencies, and different conceptions of democratization. In January 1957, a new Seym will be elected. There is a strong pressure among workers for the raising of wages. There is also a critical economic situation. There is a struggle against Stalinist ideas in literature, the arts, education, and other cultural activities. There is a crisis concerning the government police technique because of the elimination of the powerful Security Office. The young Communist generation is very severe in its criticism of the party leaders. And there is a tense international situation.

What are the prospects for creating a stable set of institutions? What are the integrating forces and institutions? I believe that a return to liberal democracy, free enterprise, and capitalist property and production relations is simply impossible, and nobody, except for relatively small groups, wants it. The integrating forces are the strong national traditions, the idea of democratic socialism, and a growing sense of political realism. In the Stalinist conception of socialism, the party was the integrating institution taking under its guidance and control all spheres of national life. It seems that the issue facing the new form of democratic socialism is the problem of integration without administrative pressure and control. Is it possible that in a socialist society we shall see voluntary associations integrating the whole national life on the basis of common values, that we shall see the socialist society preserving all the essential achievements of liberalism in the sphere of human rights but without capitalist property relations? Is it possible that in the present international situation Poland will be able to carry on her experiment?

These are really vital questions not easy to answer. The cruel experience of the last war and occupation are still alive in the memory of the Polish people. They passed through a hard school to attain political realism. Let us hope that by linking their traditional valor with this new political realism the Polish people will solve their problems, regarded by many as insoluble. I believe that many other people in the world warmly wish them that solution.

*

Oleg Mandich

YUGOSLAVIA

*

Geography and Population

THE Federative People's Republic of Yugoslavia was proclaimed on November 29, 1945, as a community of six People's Republics: Serbia, Croatia, Slovenia, Bosnia and Herzegovina, Macedonia, and Montenegro. It has a land surface of 255,804 square kilometers, including Serbia proper with 55,897, the Autonomous Province of Vojvodina with 21,774, and the Autonomous Region of Kosovo and Metohija with 10,690. The People's Republic of Croatia comprises an area of 56,553 square kilometers, Slovenia 20,226, Bosnia and Herzegovina 51,139, Macedonia 25,713, and Montenegro 13,812.

Yugoslavia is bordered by Italy, Austria, Hungary, Rumania, Bulgaria, Greece, and Albania and has land boundaries 2,969 kilometers long. The Adriatic coast of Yugoslavia is 1,993 kilometers long. It has a large number of islands and 408 square kilometers of peninsulas, bays, channels, and the like. About three quarters of Yugoslavia is mountainous while the rest consists of valleys and plains. The land abounds in rivers that belong to three systems. Most important is the Black Sea system, the largest river being the Danube and its most important tributaries the Sava, the Drava, the Morava, and the Tisza; while the mountainous rivers of the Adriatic system are short, with many waterfalls such as the Krka and the Cetina. To the Aegean system belong the Vardar and the Strumica.

Yugoslavia is one of the richest European countries in minerals and other natural resources. Oil, bituminous shale, and natural gas are found in Serbia, Croatia, Slovenia, and Macedonia; anthracite coal is found in Serbia and Croatia, but in small quantities. Much larger are the brown coal and lignite reserves in Serbia, Bosnia and Herzegovina, Croatia, and Slovenia. The Yugoslav subsoil is also rich in iron ore, especially in Bosnia and Herzegovina, Serbia, and Macedonia. Outstanding are its resources in colored ores: chromium, in which Yugoslavia is the richest country in Europe, copper, manganese, molybdenum, nickel, cobalt, bauxite, tungsten, antimony, lead, zinc, mercury, pyrite, arsenic, gold, silver, and vanadium. There are also large quantities of nonmetallic ores: salt, magnesium, barite, plumbago, and marl.

About one third of the land surface is forest (7,895,000 hectares), forming another source of Yugoslavia's natural riches. A large amount of the remaining area is arable land—14,600,000 hectares.

According to the census of March 31, 1953, the population of Yugoslavia amounted to 16,927,275. The density then, is 66.5 inhabitants per square kilometer. In 1954 after the annexation of the districts of Buje and Kopar, which were formerly in the Free Territory of Trieste, the total number of inhabitants rose to 16,990,000. They live in 3,984,000 households with an average of four persons per household.

The population of Yugoslavia is divided among the federated republics as follows: Serbia, 6,983,544 (Serbia proper, 4,460,405; the Autonomous Province of Vojvodina, 1,713,905; and the Autonomous Region of Kosovo and Metohija, 809,234), density of population, 73.9; Croatia, 3,437,000 (density, 66.8); Slovenia, 1,502,000 (density, 71.1); Bosnia and Herzegovina, 2,843,486 (density, 50.4); Macedonia, 1,303,906 (density, 44.8); and Montenegro, 419,625 (density, 27.3).

According to the national census there are in Yugoslavia 7,064,000 Serbians, 3,970,000 Croatians, 1,492,000 Slovenes, 897,000 Macedonians, 476,000 Montenegrines, and 992,000 who did not indicate their nationality. Among the national minorities are 752,000 Shqiptars (Albanians); 507,000 Hungarians; 254,000 Turks; 83,000 Slovaks; 80,000 Gypsies; 62,000 Rumanians and just as many Germans; 57,000 Bulgarians; 37,000 Walachians; 34,000 Czechs; 33,000 Italians; and 65,000 persons of other nationalities.[1]

The 1954 data show that the number of males is lower than the number of females—8,191,000 to 8,737,000. Consequently there are in Yugoslavia 566,000 more women than men: 1,061 women to every 1,000 men. Among 11,752,000 persons older than fifteen years, 1,718,000 men and 1,502,000 women are unmarried; 3,549,000 men and 3,615,000 women are married. Furthermore, there are 229,000 widowers and 996,000 widows as well as 42,000 men and 78,000 women who are divorced.[2]

Yugoslavia's Past

BASIC SOCIOLOGICAL CHARACTERISTICS

There is one very important consideration to be taken into account when studying the evolution of Yugoslav society. It is possible to speak of a Yugoslav society beginning only with 1918 when the former Hapsburg possessions, Slovenia, Croatia, Slavonia, Dalmatia, Bosnia, Herzegovina, and Vojvodina, parts of the decayed Austro-Hungarian Empire, formed a common state—the Realm of Serbs, Croats, and Slovenes—with the kingdoms of Serbia and Montenegro.

Before that date every one of the above-mentioned lands had a separate history: Slovenia and Dalmatia were the Austrian crown lands; Croatia and Slovenia formed a common realm, which was in union with Hungary; Vojvodina was part of the Hungarian territory; while Bosnia and Herzegovina, until 1878 Turkish territories, were occupied and in 1908 annexed to Austria-Hungary. Therefore, the Yugoslav peoples—Serbians, Croatians, Slovenes, Macedonians, and Montenegrines—have not had a common history and each had its particular evolution over many centuries, although segments of these peoples—Croatians and Serbians, for example—lived in the same territory, as in Bosnia and Herzegovina, and thus had a common destiny.

The southern Slav peoples[3] in Yugoslavia are derived from the Slav invaders who occupied vast regions of the Balkan peninsula in the seventh century. They settled down in more or less compact social groups and even penetrated the Peloponnesian peninsula.

There are very few documents which establish the essential events in the evolution of the southern Slav social groups before the formation of their states. Nevertheless it is possible to demonstrate that already in this early period the southern Slavs had fallen under the influence of the two strongest powers in the Europe of that time—the Frankish Kingdom and the Byzantine Empire. The influences of these powers clashed just on the territories where the southern Slavs settled down, so that one part of them—the western group, composed of Croats and Slovenes—came under the economic, political, and cultural institutions of the Byzantine social organization, while the rest remained under the Franks. These contrasting social forces originated differences among the various Slavic ethnic groups which found their solution for the first time in the Yugoslavia of the People's Revolution, 1941–45.

The first great political organizations of the southern Slavs were the tribal alliances that developed into national states. The Slovenes had already formed their state by the seventh century. After a period of Frankish domination, the Croatians formed their state in the ninth century, and the Serbian state grew up during the same period. The Macedonian state originated later, in the tenth century.

During the tenth century the southern Slavs were Christianized. The Slovenes and Croats were Christianized by the Franks, who used this tactic to consolidate their dominion. However, the new religion spread also from the cities on the Dalmatian coast, which were under Byzantine government. Among the Serbians and the Macedonians the new faith in the beginning spread from the Byzantine cities on the Adriatic and Aegean coast. The Christian faith came from the West with divine services celebrated in Latin, which was for the Slavs a foreign language. In the second half of the ninth century two brothers, Cyril and Methodius, translated the Bible into the Slav language. Thus a rapid popularization of the Christian faith among the Slav populations was made possible. Among the Macedonians the work of Clement and Naum, disciples of Cyril and Methodius, was very important because they checked the Byzantine political influence, which was extended under the cover of religious propaganda.

Macedonia was the cradle of the Bogomil or Pataren faith, one of the Manichaean offshoots. It spread with the resistance of the lower strata of the population to the process of feudalization, which was being imposed by the landowner nobility and the clergy. Afterwards Bogomilism as an ideology not only moved to Bosnia, Serbia, and Bulgaria, but also sprang up in western Europe (northern Italy and France). The use of the Slav language in the church permitted the formation of national ecclesiastic organizations, which gave a strong support to the Slav states against foreign influences. Among the Slovenes and Croatians, however, the foreign organization of the Roman Church remained one of the strongest factors influencing their internal affairs. This situation has lasted until the present, with the religious cover hiding the political aims of the Roman Church.

The early feudal epoch of the southern Slav states was closed in different ways. The Slovenes and Macedonians lost their independence; the Croatian regime formed a personal union with the Hungarian Kingdom (1102) under Koloman who assumed the title of King of Croatia and promised to maintain its independence. From this date all Hungarian kings had the title of King of Croatia.

277

In the thirteenth century Serbia was already a feudal state with definitely formed feudal classes: landowners—high nobility (*vlastela*), lower nobility (*vlastelichichi*), and high clergy—on the one side, and dependent peasants (*sebri*) on the other. The peasants were of different conditions; the most numerous were the *meropses,* who had set obligations to the landowner. The *meropses* were the most important direct producers of material goods in the Serbian Empire. Moreover, they were obliged to work on the feudal estates and to furnish the labor force for the building of fortifications, castles and bridges, road-making, and so on. The other direct producers were *vlachs,* the tenders of cattle, which were the property of the feudal lords.

The *meropses* and *vlachs* lived in great family organizations (*zadrugas*), which comprised all descendents of one living or dead ancestor and their families. By uniting the labor force of all its members, a *zadruga* produced all that was necessary for its own maintenance. As a particular form of producers' group in the Yugoslav territory, such associations existed until the People's Revolution. The last group of the exploited in medieval Serbia were the slaves (*otroci*), personal property of their owners, who employed them either as house servants or as agricultural workers. The urban populations had to fulfill economic obligations to the lords, on whose territory the city was situated. Social relations in Croatia and Bosnia were generally the same as in Serbia.

The Turkish invasion of regions inhabited by the Yugoslav peoples in the fourteenth century was the decisive event that determined their ultimate evolution. First they were split among different states. The Croatians were divided among Austria, which governed Croatia proper; Turkey, which occupied Slavonia; and Venice, which ruled in Dalmatia. Turkish rule in the occupied lands and the incessant peril of Turkish invasions in the nonoccupied countries determined a particular way of development. The life of the Slovene peasant, who worked on the lands of his lords in Gorizia, was quite different from that of the Croatian peasant in the region of Turopolje, between Zagreb and Sisak. The first had a more peaceful life than the second in Turopolje, where the incursions of the Turkish irregular militia were continuous. The most important social function of the population in Croatia was to constitute a barrier against the Turks and to defend Europe from their further infiltration.

Naturally, a territory subject to military discipline is not favorable to the development of manufacture and commerce. It was not possible to exploit natural resources, to develop manufactures, and to organize comercial relations within the boundaries of the state and with the neighborng lands. Moreover, the government had to spend large sums for the permanent maintenance of armed forces, for the construction of strongholds all along the frontier, for the building of fortresses as at Karlovac (1579), and for other military expenses instead of investing these sums in productive undertakings. All this was a first cause of economic regression among the population in Croatia and Slovenia. The Croatians were in the worst situation because of their immediate contact with the enemy. All the weight fell on the dependent peasants, whose unbearable economic situation frequently caused uprisings—the largest the rebellion of Croatian and Slovenian peasants under the leadership of Matija Gubec in 1573.

The frontier dividing the Croatian people into two parts was, at the same time, the frontier between West and East. It was not an impervious barrier, but like a diaphragm permitting circulation between separated fluids it allowed migrations of populations from one side to the other. The most numerous migrations consisted of the flight of Christian populations from the invading Turks. But later, when the boundaries were more or less stabilized, there was a continuous passage of people from the Turkish side of the frontier to the Christian and from the Christian to the Turkish in search of a better settlement and a more peaceful way of life. As a consequence of these migrations, in some parts of Croatian territory there appeared a more or less compact Serbian population composed of refugees who had fled Turkish domination.

The refugees generally settled down in the frontier zone. There was a specific reason for this: On both sides of the border there was feudal exploitation of the peasants, who had obligations to their landlords. Near the frontier line, however, the peasants were free of every form of economic dependence. They lived in *zadrugas* and, therefore, earned their living by means of their common work. All served in the armed forces by turns, so that in every *zadruga* there were some men left for field work. Since the social position and living conditions of these bordermen were better than those of the dependent peasants or serfs, the zone attracted dependent peasants from other regions. This belt on both sides of the frontier was under military government, and so there came into being a new territorial institution—*vojna krajina*, the Military Border—which was exempt from civil government. This border constituted a new social system which influenced in a particular way the evolution of its population.

Turkish rule in Serbia arrested the development of the Serbian people. There was incessant guerilla warfare during the whole period of Turkish domination. Those who were not able to support Turkish misdeeds or acted against Turkish orders took refuge in the forests where they formed bands of insurgents—*hajduks*—who regularly attacked the Turks.

The situation in Bosnia was more favorable for the Turkish government because many of the peasants were Islamized and there was not so much religious and political antagonism between the higher and the lower strata as there was in Serbia. Nevertheless, in Bosnia too there were uprisings and riots.

When the crisis in the Turkish empire grew graver, the ruling class of tribal chieftains began a liberation movement under the leadership of the high clergymen from the Petrovich phratry. During these struggles the Montenegrine territory became an independent state. It resisted Turkish attempts at annihilation and remained in existence until 1918 when it was united with other Yugoslav lands in the Kingdom of Serbians, Croatians, and Slovenes.

The nineteenth century brought emphasis on the aims proclaimed by the French Revolution. The ideas of liberty, equality, and fraternity made popular the capitalist organization of the economy, which was at the beginning of the century an accomplished fact in Great Britain, the United States, Holland, and France. The economic organization in the Austrian and Hungarian crown lands was still retarded, but the feudal foundations of the state were gravely shaken. At the end of the Napoleonic wars Austria reincorporated Slovenia and annexed Dalmatia, which, after the fall of Venice, together with Slovenia and parts of the Military Border had formed the French Empire's Illyric Provinces. The progressive French administration in these regions was remembered by their populations, and it represented an example to follow.

The structure of capitalism began taking shape in the Austrian lands of the Hapsburg monarchy, which, from the economic standpoint, were the most highly developed. Expansion into the neighboring territories of the Hungarian crown met the resistance of the Hungarian ruling class, which considered the Croatian lands an object of its economic expansion. The Hungarian nobility and bourgeoisie did not regard Croatia as a *regnum sociurn*—that is, an associate kingdom—but attempted to make it dependent on Hungary as an annexed land—*pars adnexa*. The Croatians stood firm against these attempts. The period of relative peace that the civil part of Croatia profited by in the eighteenth century had allowed the revival of agriculture, manufacturing, and commerce. This economic activity caused the formation of a bourgeois class in Croatia, which defended its economic interests against the expansionistic attempts of the Hungarian ruling classes—nobility, clergy, and bourgeoisie.

This resistance took shape in the formation of a Croatian national sentiment, the first manifestation of which was the literary-cultural movement of the Illyrismus under the leadership of Louis Gaj (1809–72). Gaj's ideas grew out of the narrow frame of Croatian nationalism. Putting aside the Kajkavski dialect spoken in Croatia, Gaj began to publish the *Narodne Ilirske Novine* (People's Illyric Journal) in the Shtokavski dialect of the Serbo-Croatian language, which dialect the Serbian linguist Vuk Karadzhich declared to be the Serbian literary idiom. Since a large part of the Croatian nobility participated in this movement, there was a compact front resisting Hungarian expansion. The Illyric movement also influenced the neighboring Slovenes, among whom nationalism began to grow after the revolutionary events of the year 1848.

The 1848 revolutions in the Austrian and Hungarian parts of the Hapsburg monarchy were attempts by the bourgeois to shake off the feudal forms of government that slowed down the rapid growth of capitalist economy. But the revolutionary leaders did not intend to liberate the Slav peoples from the monarchy since they regarded these peoples as possible objects for exploitation. The revolutions did not bring any important changes in the position of the Slav peoples in their relations with the Austrian or Hungarian ruling classes. Under the pressure of events, however, the government did set the peasants free from their obligation to the landlords. This fundamental modification of productive relations signified official recognition of the end of the feudal period.

The second half of the nineteenth century was characterized in Serbia, Croatia, and Slovenia by a rapid growth of bourgeois and workers' classes. In each land the source from which the members of these classes came was the peasantry.

The passage from the autarchical type of production characteristic of the feudal period to free trade and competition led to the disorganization of social relations. The *zadrugas* suffered first because their production system could not withstand the attraction of the towns where industry needed much labor. The sons of richer families had a greater opportunity to get an education which, with the help of their families' capital, enabled them to climb the social scale. Those who did not have such favorable conditions were employed as workers and constituted the industrial proletariat.

The emigration to the towns led to the dismemberment of the archaic producing and consuming collectives. In the overpopulated regions hereditary laws contributed to the disorganization by allowing the fractioning of land among a large number of heirs, everyone receiving a small portion which was not sufficient to assure the maintenance of himself and his family. The laws also permitted the dissolution of the *zadrugas* if their members wished it. All these factors led to the breaking up of *zadrugas* in the fertile regions and the appearance of small peasant property, which is one of the social characteristics of Yugoslavia. *Zadrugas* remained in isolated mountainous regions where the majority of the population were backward cattle breeders. Such were Herzegovina and Macedonia, where the *zadrugas* existed until World War II.

The bourgeois class was the bearer of nationalistic sentiments that constituted the most effective weapon in the struggle against the economic expansion of Hungarian capitalists on Croatian soil. In defending the national independence of Croatians and Serbians the bourgeois class contributed to the raising of the people's cultural level. This process began with establishing elementary schools and augmenting the number of secondary schools. The University in Zagreb was founded in 1874 and the Yugoslav Academy of Sciences and Arts in 1866. Much credit for the raising of national culture and education goes to Joseph Georg Shtrosmajer, Bishop of Diakovo (1815–95), who gave large funds for scientific and educational activity and for the promotion of the arts. Shtrosmajer was a sponsor of the Yugoslav Idea, which aspired to the union of all southern Slavs in one state. He opposed the Hungaro-Croatian Agreement of 1868 and greatly influenced the political life in Croatia.

In order to prevent a possible alliance among the southern Slavs, the Austrian and Hungarian governments began to foment discord among the Serbians and Croatians in Austria-Hungary, trying to divert their national resentment from the Austrians and Hungarians and to direct it against each other, creating an artificial enmity between these peoples. This was one of the frequent applications of the Austrian government's tactics, *Divide et impera*. The fomenting of such national antagonism was easiest to accomplish in the regions with mixed population, as in the former Military Border and in occupied Bosnia and Herzegovina, where there were both Croatians and Serbs.

The economic rise of the small bourgeoisie in villages and little towns provided a material foundation for these conflicts, and economic competition between Serbian and Croatian artisans, small manufacturers, and dealers took on a nationalistic coloring. In the rural regions such nationalistic antagonisms were sometimes fomented by clergymen, Catholic and Orthodox, but with very little success. The majority of intellectuals did not accept this policy and encouraged intimate reciprocal collaboration among these peoples.

In artificially creating these national antagonisms the aim of the Austrian and Hungarian government was to consolidate the internal situation in the pluri-national Hapsburg monarchy and to prevent the collaboration of Croatians and Serbians for the realization of their independence in a Yugoslav state. Before this time, from their arrival on the Balkan peninsula there had not been a single case of conflict, armed or ideological, between the Serbians and the Croatians. The best proof of this is the amity of the Serbian and Croatian populations in the Military Border, where Serbian and Croatian immigrants from Turkish territory settled down in neighboring villages or in the same village. Consequently, the Austro-Hungarian policy created the first source of conflict between the Croatians and Serbians. In World War II these conflicts degenerated into the Ustasha and Chetnik movements, which led to reciprocal massacres of innocent Serbian and Croatian populations in the regions where they lived together.

At the end of the eighteenth century, after the Austrian-Turkish war of 1788–91, Serbia (that is, the Belgrade *pashalik*) received partial autonomy. The Turks did not bother much about the interior life of the peasant villages or about their administration. The villages were autonomous and their population elected officials—*knez* and *seoski kmet*, as they were called—who were confirmed in their charges by the Turkish authorities, but not appointed or paid for their functions. The interests of these people's officials were identical with those of the population they represented, and they directed their energies against exploitation by Turkish landlords in the uprisings of 1804–13 under the leadership of Karadjordje and in 1815 under that of Milosh Obrenovich. The second uprising succeeded in increasing autonomy, reducing taxes, and partially liberating Serbia from occupation by military forces, imposed after the first uprising of 1804–13.

Further, a central government was formed under the leadership of

Milosh Obrenovich, who became the first hereditary prince of Serbia (1830). The government's policy had as its main purpose the securing of complete independence from the Turkish Empire, and the promotion of the country's economy by putting a stop to the export of natural riches. The Serbian state consolidated its structure under the protectorate of the Russian Empire and the later guaranty of the European Powers (1856). The occupation of Serbia ended in 1867 and complete independence was gained in the Russian-Turkish war of 1877–78.

The economic and political situation in Serbia was less complicated than that in Croatia. There the growth of the bourgeoisie and the working class had taken about the same course. There were struggles, too, but between different parts of the capitalist class. Two principal factions emerged, each of whom supported one of the two dynasties—Karadjordjevich and Obrenovich—that fought for the Serbian throne. The government's structure was a centralized, well-developed bureaucracy. As a matter of fact the Serbian kingdom was a police state and this was also the chief characteristic of the later Kingdom of the Serbians, Croatians, and Slovenes. In the meantime a new political movement arose. Svetozar Markovich in 1869 began spreading socialist ideas and organizing a workers' political movement. He was the initiator of socialist political organizations among the southern Slavs.

An organized socialist movement began in Croatia in 1892, and in 1894 the Social-Democratic party was founded. In Slovenia such a party originated in 1896, and in Serbia the Serbian Social-Democratic party was organized by D. Tucovich in 1903.

The Macedonians remained under Turkish rule until the defeat of the Turkish Empire in the Balkan war of 1912–13 and lived as their ancestors had done in the past centuries.

THE TWENTIETH CENTURY

The main economic characteristics of the Yugoslav peoples on the eve of the twentieth century remained the same: The rural population constituted the greatest part of the inhabitants in all southern Slav lands. The industrial towns were more numerous in Croatia than in Serbia, but this circumstance did not influence much the evolution of the lower strata of the Croatian population. A large majority of the factories belonged to foreigners so that their profits were not spent in Croatia, but were exported. In Serbia although industry was weak, this was compensated for by the fact that its profits were reinvested in the country.

Among the Slovenes, who were still divided among the Austrian crown lands of Kranjska, Korushka, Stajerska, Gorizia, and Istria, national sentiment demanded the union of all Slovenes into one territory. This aim was a necessary consequence of the fact that, after the liberation of the serfs, Slovenia became an economic unit with relatively well-developed agriculture, cattle breeding, and handicrafts. The living standard had risen thanks to the activity of the peasants' cooperatives, which were founded and administered with the particular feeling that the Slovenes have for organization, a feeling which developed out of the struggle against German national oppression. The successful end of this struggle was a consequence of the activity of liberal cultural societies and also of the Slovenian clergy. On this basis the political movement in Slovenia fell under two contrary influences—liberal and clerical—which slowed up the political evolution of the people.

The occupation of Bosnia and Herzegovina was intended to furnish Austria-Hungary with a colony possessing immense natural riches. Therefore the administration in Bosnia and Herzegovina was Austrian, the official language German, so that none of the population had any influence on public affairs. The necessity of raising the intellectual level of the lower social classes in order to increase their capacity for handling machines led to the introduction of elementary schools.

The beginning of the twentieth century was characterized by revolutionary movements in Serbia and Croatia. A military *Putsch* in Belgrade, led by a group of officers who decided to get rid of the bureaucratic clique headed by King Alexander Obrenovich, succeeded in overthrowing the government. On that occasion the king was killed and the People's Legislature elected as king Peter Karadjordjevich.

At the same time in Croatia the revolutionary riots began, headed by *Hrvatska napredna omladina*—the Croatian Progressive Youth. All forces agreed in requesting that Croatia should be independent in financial matters because it gave to the Hungarian exchequer far more than it received, and received far less than promised by the "agreement" of 1868.

When the Hungarian government rejected these just requests, demonstrations were launched; the peasants demolished the railways; there were armed clashes with the government's forces. The Vienna court, impressed by the Belgrade *Putsch* and the violent death of King Alexander, moderated the methods of government in Croatia but did not change them in essence.

285

Influenced by these revolutionary attempts the progressive Croatian and Serbian bourgeois politicians in Croatia and Dalmatia proclaimed in the Resolutions of Rijeka and Zadar (1905) their common political aims and formed the Serbo-Croatian Coalition under the leadership of Franjo Supilo, the most farsighted and influential Croatian politician.

Meanwhile the Croatian peasants began to enter into political life under the slogan People Must Help Themselves. The brothers Ante and Stjepan Radich were the founders of the new Popular Peasant party, which became important in educating the Croatian peasant masses and in raising their cultural level.

At the same time a bourgeois party arose. This was the party of extreme nationalists, headed by Dr. Joseph Frank. It attempted to realize its political aims with the help of the Austrian ruling classes. Its policy was declaredly anti-Serbian. The clerical party, sponsored by the heir to the Austrian crown, Archduke Franz Ferdinand, had the same aims and anti-Serbian tendencies. These were the two parties that joined together to try to form a Great Croatia at the expense of the Serbians, giving rise later to the bloody Ustasha movement.

During the Balkan war (1912–13) Serbia, Bulgaria, and Greece succeeded in liberating Macedonia, which they divided among them.

After World War I all Yugoslav peoples were united in one state. The idea of the union was sponsored by the Allies under the program of national self-determination enunciated by Woodrow Wilson. The Serbian government, headed by Nikola Pashich, preferred to unify all lands inhabited by orthodox Serbians in a Great Serbia and to secure an outlet to the sea. However, the activity of the Yugoslav Committee, whose members were emigrated Croatian, Serbian, and Slovenian politicians, many of whom belonged to the Serbo-Croatian coalition, upset such plans. The Yugoslav Committee succeeded in awakening the interest of the Allied governments, excepting Italy, in the unification of the Yugoslav peoples. Italian politicians with their imperialistic aims, which were later continued by the fascists, were not happy about facing a united state on the opposite shore of the Adriatic Sea. The Russian government's declaration of March 24, 1917 recognized the formation of Yugoslavia as one of the war aims to be realized, and gave a push to the ultimate development of events. In July 1917 the Yugoslav Committee and the Serbian government agreed to set up a new state, the Kingdom of the Serbians, Croatians and Slovenes in which all the peoples would enjoy equal rights and each would have an autonomous government. At the end of October 1918 the Croatian People's Council proclaimed the separation of Croatia and Dalmatia from the Hapsburg monarchy and their union with other Yugoslav peoples. A similar declaration was issued in Slovenia. On December 1 the new Kingdom of Serbians, Croatians, and Slovenes was proclaimed, which was recognized by the Allied powers.

The peace treaties did not realize the union of all Yugoslavs in the new state. A large number of Croatians and Slovenes in Istria, about 550,000, had to be left under Italian rule, and a smaller part of the Slovenes fell under Austria. The fascist government in Italy, during more than twenty years, tried with every means at its command to denationalize the Slav population in Istria. But these coercive measures had no success, because the population conserved its national feeling and joined the *Partizan* movement in World War II that led to its liberation.

The Constitution of the new state set up a single, centralized government, contrary to the Corfu pact and the desires of the Yugoslav peoples. They wanted a decentralized and autonomous form of government, which would guarantee their independent development within the framework of a common state. The supporters of the centralizing tendencies were the Serbian bourgeoisie, headed by King Alexander and his military and bureaucratic clique, which considered the whole Yugoslav territory as an object for its economic expansion and exploitation. Such tendencies met fierce opposition on the part of the Croatian bourgeoisie, which was joined by the Croatian Peasant party headed by some representatives of the Croatian little bourgeoisie like Stjepan Radich. A new and important political factor were the Communists, who founded the Socialist Workers party in Belgrade (1919), which at the Vukovar Congress (1920) changed its name to the Communist party of Yugoslavia. The main points of the party's program were the following: transfer from private to national ownership such means of production as permit the labor force's exploitation; liquidation of class rule; workers' control of enterprises; equality of all citizens without discrimination on the basis of sex or nationality; civic freedom; a republican form of government with autonomy where possible and desirable; elected judges and government officials; protection of national minorities; separation of church and state. The realization of such a program was subordinated to the achievement of power. Fearing the Communist party's influence among the broad masses of the population, the government prohibited it. From this moment the Communist party worked illegally, persecuted by the police and tribunals. But persecution could not hinder it from spreading its influence and preparing the exploited masses of the population for the socialist revolution.

The government instituted a hegemony of Serbia over all other nationalities. The nature of this hegemony is revealed in the declaration of the Slovenian deputy Koroshets, who in 1926 said in a parliamentary debate: "The government in its very majority is Serbian, Serbian are all the generals without exception, the central administration is Serbian, too, in the measure of 98 per cent."[4]

Such a crushing majority of Serbian elements in the government permitted them to favor the Serbian bourgeoisie at the expense of other nationalities. This policy led to national conflicts with the bourgeois classes in other parts of the country. These were substantially economic conflicts, which originated in the wish to secure all sources of exploitation on behalf of the Serbian bourgeoisie and which oppressed the peasantry. The objective of the bourgeoisie was to keep prices for agricultural products low and taxes high.

The position of workers was also very grave: their small wages did not permit an adequate living standard. A great majority of the population were more or less indifferent spectators of the battle between the Serbian and the Croatian bourgeoisie, whose object was economic domination of the state.

The government tried to impose the will of the Serbian ruling class on the rest of the population, using constitutional forms. The opposition was strong, and the result was that from the origin of the Yugoslav state till the end of 1928 — that is, within a period of ten years — there were twenty-nine ministerial crises.

Radich's Peasant party and the Democratic party had constituted the "Peasant-Democratic Coalition," which represented the kernel around which the opposition parties concentrated. This coalition sought a solution within the framework of the Yugoslav state, and a large part of the Croatian bourgeoisie adhered to it. A small minority followed the program of the Frankovci Party which wished to dismember the Yugoslav state so that Croatia, Dalmatia, and Bosnia with Herzegovina would constitute a Catholic state, from which the Serbs would be banned. The Frankovci intended to realize their aims by the use of arms for they had secured the help of the Italian fascist state and of the Hungarian kingdom. They created abroad a terroristic organization, *Ustashki pokret* (Insurgent Movement), consisting of emigrants, which was financed by the Italian and Hungarian governments.

On the eastern frontier Bulgaria looked with suspicion on her larger neighbor and hoped to annex Macedonia. Such a plan was prompted by the bad policy of the Yugoslav government in this part of the country. It did not recognize the national personality of the Macedonians, considering them as south Serbians and maintaining them in a backward way of life not much different from their standard under Turkish rule.

The attempts of the government to give a constitutional appearance to the virtual dictatorship of the king and the Serbian bourgeoisie could not withstand the pressure of events when some Croatian parliamentarians were slain and Stjepan Radich was mortally wounded during a parliamentary debate in 1928. The king began in 1929 the dictatorship that lasted until his murder in Marseille in 1934.

The international situation became worse every day. The union of Italian Fascism and German Nazism signified a great peril for the little states which had not yet been absorbed by these powers. After the Ustashas murdered King Alexander, the Regency took over the functions of the sovereign, because his son was under age. The annexation of Austria by Germany in 1938 and Czechoslovakia's dismemberment in 1939 under the pressure of the Nazi armies made it clear to the members of the Serbian ruling class that there was no time to waste if they wanted to maintain, at least in part, their economic and political positions in the country. Therefore, in August 1939, the representatives of the Serbian and Croatian bourgeois parties signed the "Agreement Svetkovich-Machek" after the family names of the government's minister-president and the head of the Croatian Peasant party. The Croatian Peasant party was peasant in name only; it really defended the interests of the Croatian bourgeoisie. The newly reconstituted Croatia became an autonomous territory, composed of Croatia proper, Dalmatia, and parts of Bosnia and Herzegovina, which was reserved for the rule of and the exploitation by the Croatian bourgeoisie.

After the beginning of World War II, Yugoslavia, like other small countries, had no choice but to bend its head before Germany's superior forces or to rebel against them. In this dilemma the bourgeoisie and the rest of the population divided. In 1941 the government sent its representatives to Vienna, who agreed to the German request for a treaty of alliance. This was an attempt to avoid a conflict with the Germans and to assure to the Yugoslav bourgeoisie a continued enjoyment of their position. But two days later, on March 27, 1941, a popular insurrection in Belgrade supported by part of the military overthrew the government and the Regency, thus demonstrating the anti-German feeling of the population. This insurrection found a favorable reception among the masses, which were united in their will to resist the Germans.

The German, Italian, Hungarian, and Bulgarian attack, which began on April 6, 1941—with the bombardment of Belgrade but without a declaration of war—led to the occupation of Yugoslavia. But the shifting of the German armies due to the Yugoslav campaign caused the Germans a loss of several weeks in their preparations for invading the Soviet Union from which it was not possible to recover. The insurrection of March 27 was a grain of sand hampering the gears of the German war machine, which was not able to win a decisive battle before the advance of the winter season of 1941–42.

King Peter II and his government fled into exile, and the army capitulated after giving little resistance to the invaders. Yugoslavia was dismembered. Slovenia was divided between Germany and Italy; half of Dalmatia was annexed by Italy; Croatia, the other half of Dalmatia, and Bosnia and Herzegovina were united in a puppet Ustasha state; parts of Croatia and Vojvodina were occupied by the Hungarians; Macedonia fell to Bulgaria; Montenegro was proclaimed a state under Italian protection; parts of Serbia and Macedonia were annexed to Albania; and the rest of Serbia constituted a provisory state, whose fate the Germans intended to decide after the war.

The Ustasha state of Croatia was headed by Ante Pavelich. He installed a regime of terror. Not only progressive-minded persons, but all who were suspected of being opposed to the Ustasha government were sent to concentration camps (the most ill-famed of which was Jasenovac) where they were mercilessly slain. The Jews and the Serbs were exterminated without pity because they were considered enemies by reason of their racial and ethnic membership.

The illegal Communist party began organizing insurrections among the masses of the population over the whole territory occupied by the enemy or by quisling forces. In July 1941 armed insurrection began in Serbia, Croatia, Slovenia, Bosnia, Montenegro, and Macedonia, with the aim of liberating the country and realizing the Communist program—social and national equality, nationalization of the industrial means of production, agrarian reform, and abolition of class rule.

The armed forces consisted at first of loose formations and individual groups of volunteers whose most important task was to seize arms and munitions from the enemy. At the end of the war the fighting strength of the National Liberation Army amounted to fifty divisions. After the Soviet Union, the United States, and Great Britain, Yugoslavia's armed forces were, at that time, the largest allied army in Europe. The contribution of the National Liberation Army to the Allied cause consisted in killing more than 450,000 enemy soldiers; in capturing 4,530 cannon, about 7,200 mine throwers, 14,000 machine guns, 500,000 rifles, 309 airplanes, 928 tanks, and about 20,000 motor trucks; and in destroying large quantities of war material.

Civil administration grew with the army. As soon as a part of the land was liberated elections were held to form the territorial government organs. In 1942 the People's Anti-Fascist Council of the Liberation of Yugoslavia was constituted as the highest authority on liberated territory, and in the beginning of the next year such anti-fascist councils were formed for Croatia, Slovenia, Serbia, Macedonia, Montenegro, and Bosnia with Herzegovina, each of which was the highest legislative and administrative authority of these lands. On November 29, 1943, in Jajce (Bosnia) a session of the Anti-Fascist Council of Yugoslavia was held which definitely fixed the structure of the Federated State of Yugoslavia. The council elected its first government under the presidency of Josip Broz-Tito, the head of the Liberation movement, on whom the council conferred the title of Marshal of Yugoslavia.

The enemy army, aided by the quisling formations of Ustashas and Chetniks, launched seven offensives against the Liberation movement, all of which failed to destroy it. On every occasion the occupier's forces proceeded with utmost brutality, pillaging and murdering the civil population. A very large number of villages were razed to the ground and their inhabitants slain or driven into concentration camps.

At first the Yugoslavs struggled alone. Help did not begin to arrive until 1944 when it came both from the Western Allies and from the Soviet Union. The Partisans had to seize from the enemy the arms and war supplies they needed. In this uneven struggle, lacking heavy armament, they suffered heavy losses. But the breaches left by the fallen were filled with fresh volunteers coming from the people.

A crisis broke out in 1942 when some officers belonging to the former Yugoslav army organized an armed movement, sponsored by the government in exile. This Chetnik movement, as it was called, at the beginning appeared to be directed against the occupying forces. Therefore, the Liberation movement's command invited a collaboration directed against the occupation, but this was not accepted. Some days later the Chetniks attacked the Partisan forces and from this moment sided with the Germans and the Italians, becoming—with the Ustasha—their most obedient helpers. As had the Ustasha, the Chetnik forces, too, proceeded with utmost brutality, slaughtering prisoners and the sympathizers with the Liberation movement and burning down their dwellings.

In the summer of 1944, an agreement was reached between the Liberation movement's government and the king's government in exile. A Council of Regency was formed to head the state until the Yugoslav people at the end of the war could declare themselves in favor of a republican or a monarchic form of government. A common Minister's Council was also formed.

The consequences of the war were tragic. As casualties numbered more than 1,700,000 dead, every ninth inhabitant of Yugoslavia lost his life during the war. Among them, 305,000 soldiers were killed in battle, a figure that corresponds to 2 per cent of the total population, the highest rate in World War II. At least 90,000 skilled workers and 50,000 intellectuals, besides more than one million peasants, constituted a heavy loss for the national economy and Yugoslav society in general. War damages were estimated at approximately $46 thousand million on the basis of 1938 prices—the cost of destroyed material goods and of damages caused to buildings, factories, means of communications, agriculture, and the like. Industry was destroyed or suffered damage amounting to 36.5 per cent of its value, and 822,237 buildings were destroyed or heavily damaged.

After the war elections were held to elect the members of the Constituent Assembly, which proclaimed the Federative People's Republic of Yugoslavia on November 29, 1945. The Constitution was adopted on January 31, 1946, giving sanction to all the achievements of the revolution.

The new republic has had three principal tasks to fulfill on her territory: to eliminate war damages; to foster the brotherhood and unity of the Yugoslav peoples, definitively molded during the military operations against the occupiers and their helpers; and to conclude the revolution begun during the war. Under the guidance of the Communist party, the population worked to realize these tasks. A Five Year Plan of Socialist Development was launched in 1947 with the purpose of eliminating the backwardness of the country, strengthening its productive forces, and developing the socialist sector of the national economy.

Great difficulties had to be overcome. The Western powers' misunderstanding of Yugoslavia's aims at the beginning blocked the help that the new republic badly wanted. Second, many more difficulties were created by the Soviet Union and the neighbors of Yugoslavia: Albania, Bulgaria, Rumania, and Hungary. The Soviet Union's attempt to put Yugoslavia under its domination encountered obstinate resistance in 1948. The Yugoslav people, misunderstood by the West and attacked from the East, had to rely only on their own resources to defend their independence. Many productive plans were put aside or postponed in order to create a war industry able to assure sufficient armaments and munitions for the Yugoslav People's Army, which was at that moment the only guarantee of Yugoslav independence. The events in South Korea confirmed the wisdom of such a policy. A turning point in the development of Yugoslav society was the introduction in 1950 of the workers' management of industry. All enterprises and higher economic associations that belonged to the state came under the management of their workers. This was the beginning of deep changes in Yugoslav society that led to further decentralization of the government. In 1953 the new constitutional law which embodied these changes was passed.

Yugoslavia's foreign policy, directed to assure independence and to unite all peaceful forces within the United Nations, has led to success. Today Yugoslavia is held in esteem by many peoples of the world because it is a small country that stood firm in defending its peoples' equality, freedom, and independence and in struggling for universal peace.

Yugoslavia's Present

THE NATIONAL ECONOMY

According to the *Statistical Annual, 1955*, based on the 1953 census results, Yugoslavia had, in 1953, an economically active population of 7,838,000—5,145,000 men and 2,693,000 women. The active population is distributed as follows: Serbia, 3,381,000; Croatia, 1,872,000; Slovenia, 705,000; Bosnia and Herzegovina, 1,199,000; Macedonia, 528,000; and Montenegro, 153,000.

This active population is occupied as follows: industry, 715,000 persons; agriculture, 5,179,000; building enterprises, 199,000; communications, 162,000; commerce, banking, the hotel industry, 240,000; handicrafts, 412,000; public administration and the liberal professions, 466,000; without a specified occupation, 427,000.

According to the functions they perform in various occupational branches, the active inhabitants are classified in this way: 5,327,000 agriculture and forestry workers, fishers, and hunters; 1,150,000 industry and handicraft workers; 471,000 unskilled workers; 362,000 central and local government officials, deputies, and those employed in state economic enterprises; 225,000 scientists, specialists, artists, and liberal professionals; 102,000 workers in communications; 96,000 commercial employees, sellers, and the like.

Such an enumeration permits a look at the numerical relations among different occupational groups in Yugoslavia. It is clear that the most numerous occupational group is the workers in agriculture—farmers, cattle-breeders, and so on. This is a consequence of the economic backwardness of many parts of the country. The government's main effort is now directed toward the development of industry in order to assure the economic independence of the country with regard to the basic needs of its population. The attention paid to industry and handicraft is evident from the number of industrial, craft, and unskilled workers.

But this outline is not sufficient to permit a final judgment on the relations among the different occupational groups. The statistical data do not mention a large number of persons who are at the same time farmers and industrial workers. Of the 5,327,000 agriculture and forestry workers, fishers, and hunters there were 5,131,000 persons who, during the census, stated that they earned their living by agricultural work alone or combined it with forestry work, hunting, or fishing. Persons declaring themselves to be solely agriculturists numbered 173,000. The rest had in addition another occupation: 8,000 worked in mines and industry; 2,000 in building enterprises; 2,000 in commerce; the same number were artisans; and 6,000 were occupied in the central and local administrations. Such a duality of occupations is a phenomenon characteristic of the transitional period of Yugoslav society.

In Yugoslavia several types of property exist—social, cooperative, social organizational, and private. Of the 7,838,000 persons in the active population, 2,004,000 work in the sector of social property, as for instance, the factories; 697,000 in the cooperative sector, as workers in agricultural cooperatives; 41,000 work for social organizations, as in the Alliance of Working People of Yugoslavia, or for cultural societies; and 5,015,000 work on means of production, private property possessed by farmers or artisans.[5] This coexistence of social and private property is also a characteristic sign of the transitional period of the Yugoslav economy.

The foundations for a socialist development of the Yugoslav economy were first laid down in the Constitution, which abolished the exploitation of direct producers by the possessors of the means of production. The nationalization of industrial enterprises, commerce, and banking houses and agrarian reform were measures in that direction. The Five Year Plan (1947–52) tried to reinforce the Yugoslav economy and make it independent of importations in some industrial branches.

As the concentration of large numbers of industrial enterprises under state control led to a growth of bureaucracy and to state capitalism, this way of organizing the economy, modeled on the Soviet example, was abandoned. The Law on the Administration of State Economic Enterprises by Working Collectives (1950) brought a revolutionary charge in the management of industrial enterprises and the higher economic associations, putting into effect the socialist axiom that the factories belong to the workers. The administration of the factories is composed of a Workers' Council and a Managing Committee. All workers and employees of the enterprise have the right to vote in the election of the Workers' Council, which is elected by general, direct, and secret ballot. The Workers' Council determines a general production policy, approves the plan of production, sets up the regulations, gives its approval to annual accounts, decides about the distribution of the funds at the disposal of the enterprise, and appoints and recalls the members of the Managing Committee.

The Managing Committee is the executive organ of the council. It carries out the council's general directives, hires and dismisses workers and employees, makes decisions about their salaries, plans annual vacations — in other words, performs all acts necessary for the regular functioning of the enterprise. Three fourths of the Managing Committee must be workmen engaged in various departments of the plant. The enterprise's director is also a member. Formerly the director had very extensive functions, which are now greatly reduced. He is now an employee of the enterprise and works under the control of the Managing Committee.

The most important achievement of the workers' management is that the workers and employees of an enterprise are alone responsible for the distribution of the sums earned by the enterprise. After the subtraction of funds fixed as a contribution to the state, amortization, new investments, and the like, the workers and employees determine the distribution of remaining sums as extra wages.

Such is the general outline of the organization of the economy of Yugoslavia in industry, commerce, and communications. The same principles of social self-government are in force in other branches of social activity.

Industry. The economic backwardness of prewar Yugoslavia was a direct consequence of its undeveloped industry. The huge natural resources could not be exploited in the country and were exported as raw material. For instance, from 1937 to 1939 Yugoslavia exported 86 per cent of its zinc and lead ores and 94 per cent of its bauxite, and at the same time had to import the final products of these materials in order to satisfy the economic and other social needs of the population. The Yugoslav government directed its economic policy to build up those industries which would produce finished and semi-finished products from the raw materials found in the country. Thus, in 1947, the Five Year Plan was adopted with the purpose of laying the foundations for the industrialization and electrification of the country. Some of the items in the plan had to be changed because of the conflict with the Soviet Union. As a result the accomplishment of the plan was delayed for another year.

A general outline of Yugoslav industry can be sketched as follows. Yugoslavia occupies today an important place in the world market with its nonferrous metallic ores: copper, chromium, lead, zinc, aluminum, mercury, antimony, manganese, and molybdenum. Its subsoil is also rich in iron ores, coal and lignite, petroleum, and nonmetallic minerals such as marl, magnesite, asbestos, graphite, and salt. Therefore all industries which extract or transform the above-mentioned minerals are important. One should also enumerate the lumber and food manufacturing industries, the glass and chemical industries, and the textile, leather, and tobacco industries as important branches of Yugoslavia's national economy.

At the end of 1954 Yugoslavia had 2,482 enterprises. The largest was the food production sector with 546 enterprises; then the plants producing building materials, 358; the lumber industry with 279 factories; the metal industry, 246 enterprises. There were also 142 electrical plants, 92 coal mines, 55 tobacco factories, 30 paper plants, and 22 dockyards.

In 1954 Yugoslav industry gave employment to 85,200 office employees and 600,600 workers. Of 2,482 enterprises, 114 had more than 11,000 workers and 276 not more than fifteen. The most numerous group is constituted by 536 factories which gave employment to a number of workers ranging from 61 to 125 each.

Industries which give employment to more than 20,000 workers are the following: metals, 101,101; wood, 94,550; textiles, 84,969; coal mining, 74,831; food manufacturing, 41,365; black and colored metallurgy with 30,789 and 31,974 workers respectively; and nonmetallic ores, 26,205 workers. On the lowest steps of this scale are the film industry with 438 and the rubber enterprises with 2,114 workers.

Among industrial workers is a group who have not broken away entirely from their original rural environment. These are the peasant industrial workers. According to data collected by C. Kostich, of the 516,000 industrial workers in 1952 one half belonged to this category. They live in the villages in the neighborhood of the towns or great factories, and have two sources of income. On the one hand they receive wages for their work in industry, and on the other they enjoy the income from their land, which they cultivate in their spare time. The statistical data show that the area of ground possessed by a peasant industrial worker is in inverse proportion to his attachment to industry. A large area—more than a half hectare of arable land—lowers the peasant's interest in the obligations deriving from industrial employment. For instance these workers do not try to acquire the new skills necessary to improve their position in the production process and often leave their working place for agricultural labor. The efficiency of their production is lower because they come to work in the plant already tired from cultivating their land. They consider agriculture as the main basis of their existence, while their wages serve to round out the family budget. At the same time the peasant industrial workers slow up modernization of agricultural production. This occupational group is a natural phenomenon in a largely rural society undergoing the pains of rapid industrialization.

The extent of industrialization can be seen by comparing the present achievements of Yugoslav industrialization with the situation in 1939. In the metal industry the production of pig iron rose from 101,000 tons in 1939 to 356,000 in 1954; steel from 235,000 to 616,000 tons; refined lead from 10,700 tons in 1939 to 66,700 in 1954. The coal mining industry increased its production from 7,032,000 tons in 1939 to 13,663,000 tons in 1954. The petroleum industry, which was completely neglected before the war, in 1954 produced 216,300 tons compared with 1,100 tons in 1939. The electrical energy production rose from 1,173 million kilowatt-hours in 1939 to 3,440 million kilowatt-hours in 1954 thanks to newly constructed plants. The development of Yugoslav industry in the postwar period is shown in Table 1.

Industrial progress in the various republics ranged from an index of 190 for Serbia in 1954 through 202 for Croatia, 217 for Slovenia, 226 for Bosnia and Herzegovina, 351 for Macedonia to 443 for Montenegro, as compared with an index of 100 for the year 1939.[6] It can be seen that the most underdeveloped republics have progressed faster in proportion

Table 1. Development of Yugoslav Industry from 1939 to 1954

Year	Extractive Industry	Manufacturing
1939	100	100
1947	110	125
1948	126	159
1949	145	176
1950	152	179
1951	148	170
1952	153	165
1953	158	189
1954	184	214

Source: *Statistical Annual, 1955*, p. 157.

to the more developed. Industrial development in Yugoslavia suffered in 1951 and 1952 because of the conflict with the Soviet Union. Afterwards the help received from the Western powers contributed to its rise.

Industrialization has had other consequences, too. The development of industry stimulated many peasants to change their occupation and to abandon agriculture, wholly or partly, as the principal source of their income. In 1952, 497,500 workers were employed in industry and mining; in 1953 there were 517,000, and in 1954, 600,600—in two years an increase of more than 100,000. The same phenomenon occurred in the building enterprises, in commerce, and in the cooperative handicrafts, so that it is not an exaggeration to conclude that in 1952 and 1953 about 200,000 abandoned agriculture, thus reducing the labor force in that economic sector.

Agriculture. Up to the present agriculture has been the economic sector in which the largest percentage of the active population has been occupied: 5,179,000 out of 7,838,000, or 66 per cent. Yugoslavia produces cereals such as wheat and oats; Indian corn, vegetables, fruits; industrial plants like hemp, flax, sunflowers, sugar beets, castor-oil plants, tobacco, and cotton; wine, oil, fodder, and medicinal herbs. An important industry on the rivers, lakes, and seas is fishing.

In prewar Yugoslavia there was a disproportion between the large estates, owned by lay landowners and the churches, on the one hand, and the property of small farmers, on the other. One of the first measures undertaken by the government after the war was intended to reduce this disparity. The Agrarian Reform Law (1945) rendered possible the formation of an Agrarian Fund of 1,566,000 hectares, which was distributed as shown in Table 2.

In 1953 the Federal People's Assembly passed a law limiting the size of individual ground property. The permitted maximum is 10 hectares, but there are exceptions for collectives composed of two or more families or for properties in regions where the land is of poor quality. In any case, however, the size of a farm can never exceed 15 hectares.

Table 2. Distribution of Agrarian Fund Lands among
Various Landholding Groups in Yugoslavia

Group	Thousands of Hectares	Percentage
Individual peasant proprietors	797	51.0
State agricultural estates	288	18.3
State industrial enterprises	40	2.5
Peasant cooperatives	41	2.6
Health institutions	20	1.3
Forests, land to afforest, etc.	380	24.3
Total	1,566	100.0

Source: *Statistical Annual, 1955*, p. 109.

Table 3. Size of Private Farms and Number of
Farmers in Yugoslavia

Size (in hectares)	No. of Farmers
Without land property	55,000
Not more than 0.5 ha.	170,000
0.5–1 ha.	307,000
1–2 ha.	399,000
2–3 ha.	336,000
3–5 ha.	422,000
5–8 ha.	282,000
8–10 ha.	93,000
Over 10 ha.	153,000
Unknown	30,000

Source: *Statistical Annual, 1955*, p. 62.

Yugoslavia's agricultural area, amounting to 14,600,000 hectares, is divided as follows: arable land, 7,419,000; orchards, 384,000; vineyards, 274,000; meadows, 1,905,000; pastures, 4,551,000; moors, 68,000. By type of property, this area is classified as follows: social property, 2,799,000 hectares; cooperative property, 501,000; and private property, 11,300,000 hectares.

Notwithstanding the large amount of private property, the individual land estates are small. Table 3 shows the area of 2,245,000 farmers' households.

Thus, there are 1,634,000 households with 5 hectares of land or less and only 528,000 households with more. These figures indicate that Yugoslavia is an overpopulated country from the agricultural point of view. The small farms slow up development of agricultural production. As we have seen, industry in Yugoslavia has developed more rapidly than has agriculture. Although Yugoslavia was predominantly an agrarian producer before the war, in 1954 agriculture contributed to the national income only 30.2 per cent while the share of industry was 42 per cent.

There are several reasons for the decrease of agricultural production. At first it is difficult to apply modern agro-technical methods to small-farm production because of their higher costs, which the single owner cannot afford. The low standard of living of the peasants leads them to take advantage of every occasion that permits them to find an auxiliary source of income or to change their occupation. In this manner they are completely or partially lost to agriculture, and this decrease of the agricultural labor force causes a decrease in production.

The small-farm system does not permit large-scale specialization of those crops best suited to the climate. For personal use the peasants sow wheat or other cereals or Indian corn which often does not ripen, instead of planting such crops as would yield a maximum production for the particular climatic conditions of the region. Lowered production has also been attributed to natural phenomena—floods and droughts which several times befell the most fertile regions, specially in 1950, 1952, and 1954. Compared to 2,876,000 tons of wheat produced in 1939, 2,284,000 tons were grown in 1951, 1,684,000 in 1952, 2,513,000 in 1953, and 1,381,000 in 1954. The fluctuations in the production of Indian corn have been approximately the same: in 1939, 4,046,000 tons; in 1951, 4,040,000 tons; in 1952, 1,474,000; in 1953, 3,840,000; and in 1954, 3,004,000 tons. The production of cereals, required as raw material for industry, has increased.

For instance, in 1939, 27,287 tons of sunflower seeds were produced and in 1954, 125,223 tons. The same is true of sugar beets: 922,000 tons in 1939 and 1,249,000 in 1954.

To develop agriculture the present defects must be remedied. First it is necessary to eliminate the large number of small farms which hinder the application of modern agricultural techniques. Only the combination of a large number of individual farms can enable them to acquire the agricultural machines and equipment necessary for raising the average yield. The use of machines in agriculture neutralizes the labor loss caused by migration from the country to the factories and also produces better crops. In present-day Yugoslav society, there is only one solution: the forming of cooperatives, thus creating large estates able to accumulate machinery and the necessary labor force. Such collectives, if they wish, can sell their products directly to the consumer, organizing retail outlets in the cities.

Cooperatives are of two types: general agricultural and peasant-producers. In the general agricultural cooperatives the members cultivate their own farms, which generally remain their private property, and unite only in order to organize the selling of the product and to distribute the income from its sale. Such a concentration of funds enables the members of the cooperative to acquire, collectively, agricultural machinery and equipment, which is of use to all of them. In 1953, 7,114 general agriculture cooperatives had 3,100,000 members, and possessed 4,177 agricultural machines, 11,361 shops, 4,727 restaurants and inns, and 5,865 craft shops and workshops.

In the peasant-producers cooperatives, the members contribute their land property and agricultural inventory to the cooperative, but each household retains its dwelling with a piece of land nearby which its members cultivate for themselves. The cooperative's work is done by organizing the activities of its members so that they fulfill their individual tasks in the whole community's interest. Generally the wages correspond to the quantity of work done, but in some cooperatives of this type the former owners of land and inventory receive rents proportional to the amount of their contribution. In 1953, 1,165 peasant-producers cooperatives had 194,000 members and 4,351 machines with a land property of 328,900 hectares. Further they possessed 118 shops, 93 restaurants and inns, and 2,246 craft shops and workshops.

The first type of cooperative fulfills principally the task of satisfying the consumers' food needs. In 1953 they sold directly to consumers goods to the amount of 67,243 million dinars, while the second type of cooperative received from the same source only 636 million dinars. But on the other hand 7,144 agriculture cooperatives produced in their workshops goods worth 6,579 million dinars while the 1,165 producers' cooperatives produced 12,440 million, or about 47 per cent more.

The creating of cooperatives goes on more rapidly in those regions where the *zadruga* traditions of collective life still exist—that is, in the more backward parts of the country.

Handicraft. The handicraft organization of production constitutes today an important factor of the Yugoslav economy—and is a sign of its underdevelopment. In 1954, 463,942 persons were occupied in this branch of the national economy: 200,862 declared they were the owners of the enterprises; 191,261 were workers; and 71,824 were apprentices.

The total number of handicraft enterprises in 1954 amounted to 217,352, of which 198,644 were private property and 18,708 were cooperatives. They encompass various activities: preparing food supplies; carrying out electro-techniques; working in chemistry; construction; processing metal, wood, minerals, paper, textiles, and leather; personal and communal services such as barber and cosmetic shops and laundries. The number of workers is as follows: 162,746 enterprises are without workers; 48,572 have from 1 to 5 workers; 2,253 from 6 to 10 workers; and the rest employ more than 11 workers each. Consequently 75 per cent of the craft shops are individual enterprises, while only 25 per cent have workers. And this second category is mostly composed of handicraft cooperatives.

These cooperatives are organized as collectives of workers, who unite their activities in order to improve their personal position and that of the enterprise. The managing committee of each cooperative carries on the routines of administration, but accounts for its work to the members of the collective, whose decisions are final in all matters related to the activity of the cooperative.

Commerce and Transport. As a direct consequence of the postwar difficulties domestic trade was characterized by administrative measures regulating the production and distribution of goods. Ration cards were issued, assigning to every person a limited quantity of food and other consumer goods. The peasants who produced these goods were obliged to deliver fixed quantities of their agricultural produce to the state. This system was abandoned in 1951 when the economic situation improved. The limitations were removed little by little until the law of supply and demand again operated. The peasant quotas were discontinued. The price system is now free from state interference, which encourages competition among enterprises and the production of higher quality goods.

In 1954 commerce gave employment to 157,677 persons. The organization of commercial enterprises has the same structure as factories with workers' councils and management committees. There are also commercial undertakings which depend on cooperatives and social organizations. In 1954, there were 35,228 shops: 20,171 were managed by their employees; 12,215 belonged to cooperatives; 1,977 to social organizations; and 865 were private property. The circulation of goods in 1954 was estimated at 459,055 million dinars. In wholesale trade there were 1,485 enterprises, of which 535 dealt in food products, 378 in other consumer goods, and 572 in other kinds of products.

Yugoslavia's foreign trade balance has a deficit. Although the quantity of goods exported is larger than that of imported goods—3,443,000 tons to 1,704,000 tons in 1954—their value stands in reversed proportion—72,113 million dinars to 74,743 million—with a deficit of 2,603 million.[7] Yugoslavia exports agricultural products of various kinds, but less now than in 1952 and before that year. This diminution is caused by a decline in cereal production, the result of floods and droughts,[8] and by the increased needs of a population attempting to raise its standard of living. Other exported goods are minerals, metals, and finished metal goods. Then follow lumber, cattle, and meat products. The principal characteristic of Yugoslav foreign trade is that most of the exported products are still nonprocessed goods or products of simple manufacture, which amount to 59.4 per cent of the total export value. In 1954 Yugoslavia exported its products as follows: in first place to Western Germany, 19.7 per cent; then to Italy, 14.7 per cent; Turkey, 10 per cent; the United States, 9.5 per cent; Great Britain, 9.5 per cent; Austria, 8.2 per cent; and the remainder to other countries.

The principal items of import are machine tools and other manufactured products amounting to 43.8 per cent of the total import value. Then follow food products, 24.3 per cent; raw materials, 15.5 per cent; petroleum and its derivatives, 8.8 per cent. In 1954 the United States was the largest exporter of goods to Yugoslavia, accounting for 27.9 per cent, followed by Western Germany, 16.9 per cent; Great Britain, 7 per cent; Italy, 7 per cent; Austria, 6.4 per cent; France, 5.6 per cent; Turkey, 5.3 per cent, followed by other countries.

Table 4. Railway Equipment and Services in Yugoslavia from 1939 to 1954

Years	1939	1946	1950	1951	1952	1953	1954
Length of lines (in kilometers)	9,647	9,900	11,541	11,581	11,548	11,619	11,622
Number of locomotives.................	2,295	2,079	2,397	2,378	2,368	2,367	2,346
Number of passenger cars	5,189	3,610	5,430	5,553	5,704	5,332	5,572
Number of freight cars	53,524	42,723	63,112	63,041	64,664	66,332	....*
Travelers transported (in thousands)	58,316	78,443	179,022	169,544	104,277	130,978	147,388
Goods transported (in thousand tons)	21,133	19,518	46,072	41,917	37,939	39,335	43,669

Source: *Statistical Annual, 1955*, pp. 187, 189, 190.
*No data are available for 1954.

304

Transportation, an essential factor for the development of commerce, has improved in comparison with the situation before the war. The railways are the most important means of transportation. Table 4 gives various data on railways in Yugoslavia.

The large increase in railway lines and in travelers and goods shows that the efforts made to open new regions for economic development and to improve the organization of transportation have had good results. The number of locomotives and cars, however, is not sufficient to satisfy the needs of the far larger number of travelers and of a much increased traffic in goods. While the length of lines rose by 20 per cent, the number of travelers by 152 per cent, and traffic in goods by 106 per cent, the number of locomotives increased by only 2 per cent, passenger cars by 7 per cent, and freight cars by 24 per cent.[9] The actual increase over the prewar figures is low because of the heavy losses suffered during the war that had to be replaced with new material.

Yugoslavia's Adriatic coast has an air-line length of more than 600 kilometers (from Koper to the estuary of Boyana) while the real length of the coast is 1,993 kilometers and that of its islands is 3,000 kilometers. This circumstance is convenient for the development of shipping between ports and for trade with foreign maritime countries. But the war damages were so heavy that the renewal of maritime transport took much time. (See Table 5.)

The administration of single transport enterprises is in the hands of their workers who elect the administration in the same manner as in all other socialized enterprises. There are 102,000 workers employed in transport.

Other Occupations. The preceding survey covered the most important

Table 5. Increase in Number of Vessels and BRT in Yugoslavia
from 1939 to 1954

Year	No. of Vessels*	No. of BRT
1939	185	400,944
1946	86	141,165
1950	124	222,539
1951	134	246,109
1952	147	248,252
1953	176	255,631
1954	206	291,539

Source: *Statistical Annual, 1955*, p. 191.
*Ships and motor sailers of 100 BRT (British Registry tons) and more.

occupations of Yugoslavia's population. Several other occupational groups should be mentioned. There are 212,712 persons who are employees of the state, the republics, and the local people's councils—135,115 men and 77,657 women. After the decentralization of many state functions, which passed to local authorities, the number of state officials decreased. In 1954 the state employed 7,916 persons, and the rest of the 204,856 were distributed among the federal republics and local authorities. Another occupational group consists of 225,000 scientists, specialists who work in the institutes and other scientific and nonscientific institutions, creative artists, and those in the liberal professions. The professional activity of counselors and attorneys (the two functions are considered as one) is independent of every official influence. In 1954 Yugoslavia had 2,022 counselors—1,987 men and 35, women. Physicians have the right to engage in private practice, but they must also work part of the day as employees of community health institutions. This measure was instituted because of the very low number of physicians in proportion to the entire population. In this manner, the physicians are obliged to work as sanitary employees in the interests of the community before devoting themselves to their own patients. Architects are in a similar position although they are not obliged by law to be so employed; they are employed mainly on public works but a large number of them also work in private studios in their free time.

Labor Unions and Social Insurance. The labor unions of Yugoslavia in 1954 had 1,556,721 members. Every occupational branch has its own union, for instance the labor union of textile workers, of state workers, of metallurgical workers, of commerce workers, of sanitary workers, and the like. The associations of teachers, professors, and educators who work in elementary and secondary schools, as well as the unions of journalists, of creative artists, of museum associations, and of librarians and the associations of superior schools teaching staff are united with the above-mentioned labor unions in a common Union of Labor Unions of Yugoslavia.

The functions of labor unions in Yugoslavia differ from those of similar organizations in capitalistic countries, where union activity is one-sided in that its main concern is protecting the workers' interests from the abuses of exploitation. In Yugoslavia the workers alone administer their factories and other enterprises, and make decisions about all matters concerning their individual position in relation to the enterprise. Naturally, it may happen that a workers' council does not function in a satisfactory manner.

In this case, it is a duty of the relevant labor union to call attention to abuses and to take action to revoke the council and elect a new one. The labor unions have the very important task of training their members in the managing of the enterprises where they work and of helping them in all situations in which they encounter difficulties. They also exercise social control in the interest of the whole community, pointing out management's weaknesses and failures and giving hints for their elimination. Therefore, the functions of labor unions in Yugoslavia are twofold: they prevent unjust practices against individual workers, and they prevent abuses which cause loss to the enterprise, thus slowing up the economic development of the socialist community.

Another kind of workers' organization in each republic is the Establishment for Social Insurance, which assures health, old-age, and social protection to all workers, clerical employees, officials, and war invalids, including their family members, as well as to certain orphans, to the unemployed, to students, to pregnant women. The establishments pay all costs of health service, physicians, medicines, and clinical treatment, so that all members and their families enjoy these services free of charge. Pensioners, after retiring on pension, enjoy health protection until their death. Old-age protection makes it possible for workers and clerical employees to retire on pension after reaching an age determined by law—55 years for men and 50 years for women. Workers, employees, and officials with children receive 3,000 dinars monthly for the first child, 2,500 for the second, and so on.

The funds for such broad social assistance are provided by a 45 per cent tax on all wages and salaries which every employer—state, cooperative, association, or private—is obliged to pay in addition to wages or salary issued directly to its workers or clerical employees. These funds are managed by representatives of the workers, clerical employees, and officials, who are elected by free and secret ballot. In 1954, social insurance establishments in Yugoslavia included 2,239,946 persons, without counting their family members. The income of these establishments and of dependent institutions amounted to 118,726 million dinars, and the expenses to 103,319 million. The expenses were distributed as follows: health service, 30,174 million dinars; pensions, 27,061 million dinars; family help, 43,032 million dinars; unemployed, 374 million dinars; miscellaneous, 2,678 million dinars.

National Income. The national income is composed of the value of new

Table 6. National Income of Yugoslavia for 1952 and 1953
(in millions of dinars)

Item	1952*	1953
Social income	948,817	1,134,490
Depreciation	94,987	111,814
National income	853,830	1,022,596

Source: *Statistical Annual, 1955*, p. 103.

*In the preceding years national income was not calculated on the basis of free market prices and, therefore, cannot be compared with the 1952 and 1953 data. The 1954 national income had not yet been calculated when the *Annual* was published in July 1955.

Table 7. Distribution of National Income in Yugoslavia, by Republic
(Average National Income = 100)

Republic	1952		1953	
	Millions of Dinars	Relation to Average National Income	Millions of Dinars	Relation to Average National Income
Serbia	42,647	83.6	53,056	88.2
Croatia	56,070	109.9	66,382	110.3
Slovenia	102,274	200.4	110,777	184.1
Bosnia and Herzegovina	39,858	78.1	47,068	78.2
Macedonia	33,660	65.9	41,782	69.4
Montenegro	28,609	56.1	35,713	59.3

Source: *Statistical Annual, 1955*, p. 105.

Table 8. Contribution Made by Various Industries to the National Income
of Yugoslavia (in millions of dinars)

Type of Industry	1952		1953	
	Amount	%	Amount	%
Industry and mining	402,581	47.0	430,302	42.0
Agriculture...........................	217,024	25.2	310,031	30.2
Lumber	3,780	0.4	11,966	1.2
Building	63,529	7.5	74,345	7.3
Transport	42,654	5.1	47,068	4.6
Commerce	56,325	6.6	76,761	7.6
Handicraft	41,160*	4.9	48,691†	4.8

Source: *Statistical Annual, 1955*, p. 103.
*Unspecified: 26,777 million or 3.3 per cent.
†Unspecified: 23,432 million or 2.3 per cent.

Table 9. Expenditure of National Income in Yugoslavia
(in millions of dinars)

Item	Amount	%
Personal expenditures	598,100	49.8
Capital investment	362,600	30.2
Social and government	214,400	17.9
Miscellaneous	25,500	2.1
Total	1,022,600	100.0

Source: *Statistical Annual, 1955*, p. 105.

products created throughout the war after subtracting the depreciation of the productive plant. The income for 1952 and 1953 is shown in Table 6. Average national income in 1952 was 51,039 million dinars and in 1953, 60,185 million dinars. Yugoslavia's national income is distributed among the six republics as shown in Table 7. Table 8 shows the contribution made by the various industries to the national income. Table 9 indicates how the national income was spent.

POLITICAL STRUCTURE

Basic Principles. In Yugoslavia the political structure of the state has been devised to encourage economic democracy and socialist collaboration. The relations between persons and things and among persons have been shaped to eliminate the different forms of exploitation of man by man and to encourage mutual aid in executing social functions. One of the most important functions in every society is its government. Government officials organize the economic and other relations among various social groups and single persons and thereby strive to realize the aims which the ruling strata set up.

The most efficacious form of government is that in which government officials are best acquainted with the needs of the population and with the local situation. In other words the best government can be found where the citizens administer their own affairs either directly or by means of their elected representatives. This is a basic principle of the structure of the government in Yugoslavia. Another basic principle is the responsibility of representatives to their electors. Every deputy—federal, republican, or local, without exception—must give an account of his activity to his electorate, which has the right to approve or to censure it and to recall him if it considers his activity harmful to the common interest. Consequently, the people are not only the formal holders of the sovereign power, but are also executors of it in fact. The third basic principle is that of the unity of power: the legislature, the administration, and the judiciary are only various special forms in which this authority shows itself.

The Structure of Government. The foundation of the social order of the Federative People's Republic of Yugoslavia is expressed in the Federal Constitution of January 31, 1946, with the modifications brought about by the Constitutional Law of January 13, 1953.

Yugoslavia's citizens are all equal by law regardless of sex, race, nationality, or social origin. Marriage, the family, and children are under the protection of the state. The right to vote and to be elected to office belongs to all citizens over eighteen years of age. Citizens enjoy freedom of thought, conscience, speech, assembly, press, and worship, and have the right to hold meetings and demonstrations. Nobody can be held under arrest for longer than three days without appearing before the proper legal authorities and cannot be sentenced if not legally ordered to appear before the court. Moreover, freedom of the home, secrecy of correspondence, the sanctity of private property, and the right to inheritance within limits fixed by law are guaranteed.

The highest legislative body and the representative of the sovereign power of the Yugoslav people is the Federal People's Assembly which is made up of two houses—the Federal Council and the Council of Producers, the latter a new institution springing from the particular conditions of Yugoslav social development. The national assembly directs the whole activity of the state. It has the power to change the Constitution; it approves the Federal Social Plan and the State Budget; it gives directives for foreign policy; it makes decisions about war and peace; it elects and recalls its executives—the president of the republic and the members of the Federal Executive Council—as well as the members of the Federal Supreme Court.

The Federal Council is composed of 352 deputies, selected by two methods. The majority are elected by general, direct, and secret ballot; the rest of the council consists of seventy deputies, ten from each of the six republics, six from the Autonomous Province of Vojvodina, and four from the Autonomous Region of Kosovo and Metohija. These deputies are appointed by the legislatures of their republics and regions. There is a reason for the two methods. The general ballot favors the republics which have a large population, hence a larger number of deputies. This could create some inequities when questions of vital interest to single republics are discussed. Therefore, when it is necessary to debate changes in the Constitution or the social plan of the whole federation, the small group of appointed deputies constitutes itself a separate house—the Nationalities Council—which makes its decisions independently of the Federal Council and the Council of Producers. In all other matters before the Federal Council these deputies remain part of the Federal Council. The deputies of the Federal Council cannot be, at the same time, government officials. They receive fixed pay, being permanently at work as members of various commissions and committees.

The Council of Producers is composed of deputies elected by the three principal productive groups of the country—industry, agriculture, and handicraft. The number of deputies is in proportion to the respective participation of the productive group in creating the total social production, and they are elected by the workers and clerical employees in their branches of production. Their number in the present legislature amounts to 202. Since the deputies' participation in the productive process is a necessary condition of their parliamentary functions they do not receive fixed salaries, but only compensation for wages lost during the parliamentary session. The competence of this council as well as that of the similar republican and local councils includes all matters pertaining to the economy —problems of work and social insurance—and the election of the highest state officials. All remaining functions of the Federal Assembly are exercised by the Federal Council alone.

Such a limited competence shows the particular character of the Council of Producers. It is concerned with economic problems, in which its members are highly skilled because they participate directly in production and have a clear perception of problems in their branch of production. Deputies of the Council of Producers may not be elected as members of the Federal Executive Council. This prevents the possibility of removing the best workers from their employment, which would damage their enterprises.

If the houses of the Federal People's Assembly should fail to agree on an issue, a joint commission would seek a solution. If such an attempt failed, the assembly would be dissolved and new elections fixed.

The Federal People's Assembly elects the president of the republic, who is the head of the state, and the Federal Executive Council, which is a body of thirty Federal Council deputies controlling the state administration and making its general policy directives. This council is an executive organ which carries out the decisions of the Federal People's Assembly. Its principal task consists of assuring the supremacy of democratic political forms over bureaucracy.

The chief governing organs are the five state secretariats: for Foreign Affairs, for National Defense, for Home Affairs, for National Economy, and for General Administration Affairs and Budget. They depend upon the Federal Executive Council, which appoints and recalls the state secretaries. Other autonomous bureaus—such as the Government of Foreign Trade, Government of Maritime and River Transports, Government of Civil Airlines, or the Federal Establishment of Social Health, Federal Establishment of Economic Planning—are also appointed by the Federal Executive Council.

The relations between the federal government organs on the one side and those of the republics and localities on the other are based on the principle that all affairs are governed by the republics and local organs because on their respective territories federal authorities do not exist. In addition to this the republican and local organs are not under the control of the federal authorities even in matters of federal jurisdiction. The same principle is applied to the relations between the republican government organs and the local administrations. There is only one exception—the Yugoslav National Army, which is organized on hierarchical principles.

The structure of the government of the republics is, in general, the same as the federal one and is founded on the constitution of each republic. There is the republican people's assembly composed of two houses—the republican council and the council of producers, with deputies elected in the same way as for the Federal Assembly. The republican assembly elects the republican executive council which has a jurisdiction similar to the federal one in controlling the activity of government organs and in giving them directives for acting. The number of republican state secretariats, determined by republican constitutions, consists everywhere of the important secretariats for home affairs, for national economy, and for general administration affairs and budget.[10]

The republican structure of government contains a particular type of council, which is needed in the transitional period of passage from state government to social government. These councils are composed of persons selected by the republican executive councils and of others designated by the social associations concerned. So, for instance, a republican council of education, science, and culture is formed by the executive council's appointees and the delegates of the Association of Superior Schools Teachers Staff, Association of Teachers and Professors, Association of Museum Workers, and other important scientific cultural and educational associations. There are also councils for health, for social protection, and so on.

The Autonomous Province of Vojvodina and the Autonomous Region of Kosovo and Metohija, which are parts of the people's republic of Serbia, have their own republican forms of government because of the large number of national minorities — Hungarians in Vojvodina and Albanians in Kosovo and Metohija. The autonomy granted to these territories where the different nationalities are intermixed is the best way to guarantee them a peaceful development.

Since 1955, the lowest self-governing unit of local government has been the commune. In some cases communes form a county. The formation of these territorial units was carried out by applying the principle that every communal territory with its population must constitute an economic productive unit able to develop in the best possible manner its means of production and its natural resources under the self-government of its population. The task of the counties consists in uniting nearby communes in order to coordinate and control their activity. These communes and counties, formed in 1955, have only their names in common with the earlier territorial units which were regularly much smaller. So it was not a rare event that during the reorganization an earlier county became a commune and the former commune was abolished. This territorial reform was made on an economic basis and was intended to concentrate the means of production of a territory under its own guidance in order to raise productivity.

The basic organ of local self-government is the people's committee which is a legislative and executive organ for a defined territory, acting within the frames fixed by the federal and republican laws and other regulations. The committee is divided into two houses. One is the county's council, elected by general, direct, and secret ballot of all inhabitants of the territory. The other house is the county's council of producers which is elected by the same categories of producers as the federal and republican producers' councils.

For governing some important public activities such as the sanitary service, building activity, culture, science, and education, the people's committee forms special councils and appoints as their members such citizens as take active part in these particular branches of social activity. The appointed citizens, together with the delegates of interested associations, compose a council of culture, science, and education, or a council of health service.

These councils represent one form of direct intervention by citizens in the regulation of governmental matters.

Another such form is the electors' meeting. The electors composing an election district meet together when some of them agree on the necessity of discussing important matters of common interest. The deputy, whom they have elected, is often invited to attend the meeting. After discussion of the items on the agenda of the day, conclusions are drawn up and the deputy is obliged to execute them. At electors' meetings the deputies are, on occasion, also called to account about their activity in representing the electors. They can be censured and even recalled if a qualified majority of electors maintains that the deputy's activity was insufficient or prejudicial to the interests of the electors.

All judges in Yugoslavia from the lowest to the highest are elected. The federal and republican assemblies elect and recall the judges of the federal and republican supreme courts, while the people's committees do the same with the judges of the lower courts. The single republics have state secretariats for justice, supervising the judiciary organization on their territory but not interfering with the administration of justice, for the courts are quite independent in their deliberations.

The courts appointed to try cases consist of professional judges and lay judges who are selected by the people's committees and have equal rights with the professionals. The public prosecutor is elected in the same manner as the judges, but his position before the court is equal to that of the defendant, to whom is granted the right of defense. If the defendant has not appointed his own counselor, the court does it for him.

The courts deal with civil, penal, and administrative cases. Every citizen has the right to bring a formal charge against acts committed by all government organs without exception, and may carry his case to the higher courts. For instance, a complaint against the decision of a school council is brought to the commune's council of education. If the complainant is not satisfied with the new decision, he may sue the school council in the republican supreme court. Against the decision of the republican supreme court in administrative matters, the contending parties may appeal to the Federal Supreme Court.

All the present achievements of the Yugoslav social order are the result of incessant governmental action directed toward creating the conditions of a socialist way of life. There is still much to do, but the foundations already stand firm and make possible still greater improvement in the general conditions of life in Yugoslavia.

In 1945, after the end of the war, centralization of state authority was made necessary by the social conditions in Yugoslavia. The government's structure inclined to centralism; the lower organs, although elected, depended hierarchically in one way or another upon the higher government. Also, there were many functions denied the republican and local governments and reserved to the authority of federal organs, as for instance, the departments of home affairs, justice, industry, transports, and commerce. The execution of a large rehabilitation and reconstruction program; the putting into operation of new collective forms of state organs; the installation of a large number of newcomers in government, who lacked administrative experience; the development of the national economy; the elimination of the vestiges of the past—all these tasks required a sure guide rising from a center and making possible the distribution of available means to the critical points.

Such a centralistic system of government arose from the necessity of that particular historical moment. But after fulfilling its tasks, the government began to degenerate, making it possible for the officials in economic and other administrative branches to exploit government bureaus and industrial enterprises in order to create special privileges for themselves, and to influence the development of social life in the manner most useful for themselves. Such tendencies revealed the peril of bureaucratization and menaced the working population.

A radical change in the organization of the governments began with the Fundamental Law on Workers' Administration. This constitutional law abolished the principle that only the state organs could administer national economic enterprises and placed all such enterprises under the management of their respective workers and other employees. This principle was followed in other branches of administration and has led to a complete democratization of government, which was definitely fixed in the Constitutional Law of January 13, 1953, abolishing outdated portions of the 1946 Constitution.

The development of the whole economic, political, and cultural life of Yugoslavia represents a broad social movement of the large majority of the population. In one way or another, all social classes—workers, farmers, and employees of all sorts—are uniting their efforts to accomplish the transformation of Yugoslav society into a socialist collective. There are many obstacles standing in the way: economic underdevelopment, an insufficient number of specialists of all sorts, backward and inadequate educational systems, self-centered behavior characteristic of bygone times, outdated traditions, old-fashioned usages and customs, and so on. But the achievements attained in the past eleven years by the efforts of the population and with foreign help prove that a long and coordinated endeavor can lead to a successful end.

Political Organizations. After the end of the war, the force behind government activity came from political organizations—the Socialist Alliance of the Working People of Yugoslavia and the League of Communists of Yugoslavia.

The Socialist Alliance is the largest organization in the land, consisting of 7,744,880 persons. It grew up during the war as a political body offering a common platform to all progressive social forces in the country. The Alliance had great success throughout the entire war, assuring the political mobilization of the people and the supplying of the Partisan armed forces. The Alliance had the same function after the war, that is, to unite its members for the reconstruction of the country and to consolidate the Yugoslav peoples. The Alliance is today a popular political organization composed of individuals and associations of different political, idealogical, and religious views, all of whom are united in their intention to work for the construction of a socialist society and for the protection of Yugoslavia's independence.

After Josip Broz-Tito became the secretary general of the illegal Communist party in 1937, it began a vast organizing activity to increase the number of its adherents, who later constituted the Partisan Movement. From the beginning the party led the war operations and the People's Revolution. The war's end signified for the party the beginning of an intensive political activity within the Socialist Alliance in order to promote the reconstruction of the country. It had very important tasks to fulfill in organizing resistance to the pressures of the Soviet Union after the Cominform Resolution of 1948. The further development of democracy after 1950 changed the tasks of the Communist party. It transferred its political and organizational functions to the broad masses of the people united in the Socialist Alliance, which now alone makes decisions concerning economic, political, cultural, and other manifestations of social life and takes measures appropriate to realizing its aims. The social role of the Communists is now confined to the political and ideological education of the population for the new conditions of economic democracy, training the citizens for their political functions and striving to eliminate backwardness in all sectors of social life. Having renounced its role as a political organization, the Communist party in 1952 changed its name to the League of Communists of Yugoslavia. It had, in 1954, 700,030 members.

THE FAMILY

The family in Yugoslavia, as well as children without a family, are under the protection of the state. The composition of the family is the same as in all civilized countries: it is a legal community of man and woman which involves duties between them and toward their children.

There are some ways in which the Yugoslav family differs from families in other countries. Husband and wife have a completely equal position. Both husband and wife are obliged to contribute to the household within the limits of their ability. If the wife is not employed, the domestic work she does is considered her contribution to the household.

They are not legally obliged, however, to form a common household. In this case they agree about the contribution for their common maintenance. Husband and wife maintain separate ownership of things they possessed before marriage, but all that they acquire during their married life becomes their common property. Moreover, they are not limited in their rights, while married, to make contracts as is the case in some other countries.

In prewar Yugoslavia only religious marriage was recognized as legal, with the exception of the territories which formerly belonged to Hungary, where civil marriage existed. Since the war only civil marriage is legal. If a couple wish to have their marriage blessed in a church, that is a private matter. In 1954, there were 171,313 marriages, or 9.9 per thousand inhabitants.

Divorce is permitted under circumstances fixed by law — incompatibilty, adultery, unjustified adandonment of the household, and so on. In 1954, 15,730 divorces were granted by the judicial authorities, 0.9 per thousand inhabitants.

Rights over the maintenance and education of children belong to husband and wife equally, so that the father and mother collectively exercise such rights. The law abolished the old-fashioned patriarchal principle which made the father alone the authority in the family circle. The law recognizes the position of children born both in and outside of marriage. It is possible to sue for the determination of paternity in order to force the father to recognize his children.

In 1954, 492,025 children were born—28.4 per thousand inhabitants. In the same period there were 187,042 deaths or 10.8 per thousand. The rate of natural increase was, therefore, 17.6 per thousand inhabitants.

The peasant family still maintains its patriarchal traditions and has a tendency to educate children as their ancestors did. Eight years of compulsory schooling and service in the Yugoslav People's Army counterbalance this influence of past times and outdated traditions. Service in the army is a very important period in the life of a young peasant, because the officers take much care with his education, particularly that which will enable him to conclude his formal schooling, discard old usages, and become a productive member of the community. Young peasants are often unable to attend school regularly. Peasant parents often consider the child more useful if he is doing some work rather than going to school. One must not forget that 24.4 per cent of the whole population were illiterate in 1953,[11] and that the army alone is in a favorable position to eliminate this defect among enlisted men.

Families in the towns and cities educate the younger generation in a manner more appropriate to the social necessities. The elementary and secondary schools give to a child living in a city a far better education than he would receive in rural areas. But there are also negative factors. In the towns, and far more in cities, both parents are often working in factories or are employed elsewhere. If there are no grandparents or other relatives living with the family, the half-grown children are many times left to themselves, and they frequently fall under the bad influence of the streets. Parents leave small children in special institutions that take care of them during working hours. But school children are left unsupervised when the parents are absent and often, too, when they are at home occupied with domestic or other work. Although the situation is now improved when compared with the conditions of some years ago, nevertheless this looseness in family life causes a diminution of the family's influence on the education of some children. The bad effects of this are partly neutralized by the educative action of the People's Youth of Yugoslavia. But this organization receives as members only boys and girls from fourteen years upwards, and the problem remains acute for the children below that age.

Children who attend secondary schools outside their parents' place of residence can find accommodation in special homes operated by the establishments of social insurance. In 1954, 1,172 different institutions and homes of the social insurance establishments helped children and youth. Three hundred and twenty-three were concerned with small children up to seven years of age and had 18,226 inmates; 122 were for children of elementary school age with 8,530; 632 were for secondary school children with 59,248; 28 university students' homes with 10,774; and 67 homes and institutes were for blind, dumb, invalid, and mentally retarded children with 4,446 inmates. The total number of inmates amounted to 101,224.

CULTURE

Languages. The population of Yugoslavia speaks three languages—Serbo-Croatian, Slovenian, and Macedonian. With the Bulgarian language they compose the South Slavic linguistic group. The Serbo-Croatian tongue is spoken by the populations in Serbia, Croatia, Bosnia and Herzegovina, and Montenegro—12,390,000 in all; Slovenian is spoken by 1,483,000 inhabitants of Slovenia; and Macedonian is spoken by the people in Macedonia (931,000 persons). All these languages are equal before the law.

The national minorities use their own languages: Hungarian is spoken by one part of the population in Vojvodina, 506,000 persons; Albanian is spoken in Kosovo, in Metohija, and in West Macedonia by 780,000 persons; the Walachian language is spoken by 197,000 persons in Serbia and Vojvodina; Turkish is spoken by 173,000 inhabitants of Macedonia; Rumanian, Italian, and other minority languages are used to a lesser degree.

The Serbo-Croatian, Slovenian, and Macedonian languages are closely related so that people from different regions of the country can understand each other. Intellectuals are more or less acquainted with all three languages. To the young workers and peasants from Slovenia and Macedonia the People's Army provides the opportunity to learn Serbo-Croatian, because generally they serve in units located among Serbo-Croatian-speaking populations.

The Serbo-Croatian language is divided into three dialects—Shtokavski, Kajkavski, and Chakavski, so named after the form they give to the interrogative pronoun *what?* (shto? kaj? cha?). The Shtokavski dialect was accepted as the literary language by the Serbians and Croatians in the first half of the century. The Slovenian language, which is related to the Kajkavski dialect of the Serbo-Croatian tongue, developed without foreign interference because Slovenia's territory was not affected by migrations during the Turkish domination. The Macedonian language has a remarkable likeness to the Serbo-Croatian and the Bulgarian tongues. It obtained recognition as a language from the Partisan Movement because in prewar Yugoslavia, Macedonia was considered a Serbian region and the tongue of its population a Serbian dialect.

There are two alphabets in use in Yugoslavia—the Latin and the Cyrillic. From the legal standpoint, they are equal. The peoples and regions which, in their historical and social development, were under the influence of the West use Latin, and those influenced by the East use the Cyrillic alphabet. Therefore, the Croatians and Slovenes employ the Latin letters and the Serbians, Macedonians, and Montenegrines, the Cyrillic. In Bosnia and Herzegovina both alphabets are in use by the population.

Education and Science. The basic principle of education in Yugoslavia is to give at least a minimum of instruction to the broad masses of the population. Therefore, the state requires every child to attend school for eight years (not for only four years as in prewar Yugoslavia), that is, from the seventh to the fifteenth year of age. Not only during this compulsory period of schooling, but also later in the higher grades, education is free and accessible to all young people without discrimination by sex, nationality, social origin, or religion. The way to the universities is open to all scholars who have completed studies in a secondary school of general or vocational education.

In elementary and secondary schools, the teaching is done in the language spoken in the region, that is, in the pupils' mother tongue. The national minorities, therefore, have their own schools, maintained by the government, where the pupils are educated in their own language.

The eight years of compulsory schooling takes place in the elementary schools. Where eight-grade schools do not yet exist, the pupil attends four years at a secondary school after four years of elementary school. The number of elementary schools, of their teaching staff, and of their pupils is shown in Table 10.

The number of teachers diminished from 1938 to 1950 because the elementary school teachers were part of the progressive movement. Always in the first lines, they suffered heavy losses during the war, and afterward many of them became officials of the state and local governments.

Illiteracy is a grave problem. Of 13,366,000 inhabitants over ten years old, 3,339,000 read only a little without being able to write, or cannot either read or write; 881,000 of them are men and 2,458,000 women. The illiterates are distributed as shown in Table 11. These proportions show that the largest number of illiterates are found in regions that were under Turkish rule in the nineteenth century and that the women predominate among them.

The secondary schools offer a general education, including study of the mother tongue; two foreign languages with a choice among English, Russian, French, German, and Italian; social sciences, such as history and philosophy; natural sciences; mathematics; moral education; drawing; and physical culture. There are also a small number of grammar schools where Latin and Greek are taught. At the end of his studies in a secondary school, the pupil must pass a final examination which enables him to enter a university or any other superior school.

There are also lower vocational schools for working youth which educate qualified workers for different branches of industry, handicraft, and agriculture. In addition, there are secondary vocational schools: economic,

Table 10. Growth of the Elementary School System in Yugoslavia from 1938 to 1954

Year	No. of Schools	No. of Teachers	No. of Pupils
1938–39	8,956	32,144	1,428,223
1950–51	13,466	26,873	1,527,387
1951–52	13,574	29,892	1,427,267
1952–53	13,872	32,576	1,387,523
1953–54	14,044	36,040	1,401,608

Source: *Statistical Annual, 1955*, pp. 305–307.

Table 11. Number of Illiterate Persons in the Population of Yugoslavia (in thousands)

Item	Serbia	Croatia	Slovenia	Bosnia and Herzegovina	Macedonia	Montenegro
Population older than 10 years	5,584	3,201	1,190	2,116	957	318
Illiterate men	384	128	12	229	106	20
Illiterate women	1,148	379	15	628	222	73
Total	1,532	503	27	857	328	93
Percentage of illiteracy in relation to the population older than 10 years	27.4%	15.7%	2.2%	40.4%	34.2%	26.7%
Percentage of illiterates in each republic in relation to the total of illiterates	45.9%	15.0%	0.8%	25.7%	9.8%	2.8%

Source: *Statistical Annual, 1955*, p. 54.

321

technical, agricultural, and medical. All graduates from secondary vocational schools can continue their studies, that is, a graduate of a specialized economic school or of a sanitary school can continue his studies in the faculty of economy or faculty of medicine, respectively.

In Yugoslavia, there are two elementary and secondary art schools, secondary schools for training teachers, and specialized schools for defective youth. There are also schools for adults who wish to complete their education. Table 12 provides figures on the various types of schools.

As did other branches of social activity, education increased after the war: from 1938–39 to 1953–54 there was an increase of 379 per cent in the number of schools of general education, 165 per cent in their teaching staff, and 212 per cent in the number of pupils. This progress is a consequence of the efforts made to assure an adequate education to the largest possible number of youth. But there are still some inadequacies. The increase of the teaching staff is not proportional to the increase in the number of schools and pupils. While in 1938–39 there were 18.5 teachers in every general educational school and 20.6 pupils per teacher, today's proportions are changed: the average is 10.3 teachers for every school and

Table 12. Increase in Number and Size of Various Types of Schools
in Yugoslavia from 1938 to 1954

Type of School	1938–39	1950–51	1951–52	1952–53	1953–54
Schools of general education ..	439	1,706	1,875	1,918	2,106
Teaching staff	8,126	14,294	15,940	19,549	21,749
Pupils	167,848	587,379	455,886	493,307	523,076
Lower vocational schools	770	1,129	926	871	892
Teaching staff	6,197	12,235	9,420	7,933	8,352
Pupils	69,872	120,648	111,318	101,632	103,944
Secondary vocational schools..	53	245	217	201	182
Teaching staff	879	5,361	4,403	4,285	3,650
Pupils	10,689	66,067	44,982	43,046	35,831
Teachers' training schools	37	81	79	80	79
Teaching staff	555	1,313	1,372	1,589	1,499
Pupils	4,268	28,002	24,716	23,059	20,762
Art schools	21	143	150	151	159
Teaching staff	277	1,789	1,789	1,848	1,954
Pupils	3,173	18,506	15,414	16,249	17,007
Specialized schools	21	34	54	60	58
Teaching staff	232	274	428	430	489
Pupils	3,175	3,958	4,894	4,725	5,171
Adult schools	29	188	187	248	229
Teaching staff	311	2,039	2,969	1,954	1,798
Pupils	4,008	14,313	10,281	11,869	13,005

Source: *Statistical Annual, 1955*, pp. 305–307.

24.1 pupils per teacher. It is also necessary to keep in mind that the pupils are not equally distributed among the schools; the number of pupils is far greater in the cities than in small towns. Practically every teacher in the cities deals with a far larger number of pupils than the average given above. In addition, every teacher specialized in some field has classes with far larger numbers of pupils than the average class. Efforts are being made to increase the number of teachers.

The smaller number of pupils in the lower and secondary vocational schools from 1950–51 on is due to an increase in the number of pupils attending general education schools. This is a consequence of the tendency of a large number of youths to choose a general education rather than a specialized one, because it permits greater choice of studies in the superior schools. But at the same time, such a tendency leads to a decrease in the number of specialized workers and technicians in the coming generation.

In Slovenia, superior schools date from the end of the sixteenth century; in Croatia, they began in the seventeenth century, and in Serbia in the nineteenth century. The first university was inaugurated in Croatia at Zagreb (1874), while in Serbia a university was founded at Belgrade in 1905, in Slovenia at Ljubljana in 1919, and in Macedonia at Skopje in 1920. In Bosnia and Herzegovina, the first faculty was established at Sarajevo, and the university was inaugurated in 1949. In 1955, three faculties were founded in Vojvodina at Novi Sad, as a kernel of a new university.

The universities consist generally of the faculties of law, economics, philosophy, natural science and mathematics, engineering, medicine and stomatology, pharmacy, veterinary medicine, agronomy, and forestry. Until the school year 1952–53 the faculties of theology were integral parts of the universities and afterward became separated from them. The increase in university faculties is shown in Table 13.

There are also in Yugoslavia three academies of fine arts; two academies of applied arts; three academies of music; and three academies for the theater arts. The increase in the number of faculties, teaching staff, and students is a consequence of the need for top specialists in all branches of activity to help in the development of the country.

In 1954 the social government of the universities came into being. Direct interference by the republican government consists only in approving the university and faculty statutes, while the administration is done independently by bureaus of the state and people's committees. The main governing bodies are the councils of universities and of faculties com-

Table 13. Growth of the Universities in Yugoslavia from 1938 to 1954

Item	1938–39	1950–51	1951–52	1952–53	1953–54
Number of faculties	23	53	53	55	55
Teaching staff	1,129	4,528	4,037	3,778	4,226
Students	17,247	52,487	46,885	47,876	51,752

Source: *Statistical Annual, 1955*, p. 320.

Table 14. Number of People's and Workers' Universities in Yugoslavia,
Number of Lectures, and Attendance

Type	Number	Lectures	Attendance (in thousands)
People's universities	1,873	24,776	3,158
Workers' universities	32	2,169	232

Source: *Statistical Annual, 1955*, p. 328.

posed of professors elected by their faculties, of practicing specialists in specific branches of social activity, and of eminent representatives of cultural life, appointed by the republican government. A very important role belongs to the people's and workers' universities which organize lectures and courses serving to complete the education of adults. (See Table 14.)

For the increase of general culture, great credit goes to the libraries— scientific, public, and scholarly. In 1954 there were 583 scientific libraries, 4,183 public libraries, 11,053 scholarly libraries for pupils, and 10,224 for teachers.

Scientific work is done in the universities, academies of science, and state establishments and institutes. In 1842 the Society of Serbian Science was founded, which in 1886 became the Serbian Academy of Arts and Science. In Croatia the Yugoslav Academy of Science and Art was established in 1866. The Slovene Academy of Science and Art began as a scientific society in 1921.

The state also contributes directly to the development of science by founding autonomous establishments and institutes with determined spheres of action. There are, for instance, federal and republican establishments for compiling statistics; for geological and mineralogical research; for physical research; and economic institutes.

Arts. Literature in Yugoslavia has had a popular tradition from the Middle Ages. In epic and lyric poems the customs and beliefs of the population in various regions were sung. Historical events were often the occasion for poetry in which popular fantasy expressed the people's feelings, wants, and desires. In such manner came into being the popular poems of the Kosovo cycle, which commemorated the Battle of Kosovo fought against the Turks, praising the people's struggle against an overpowering enemy; or the Kraljevich (Prince) Marko cycle, which in the idealized person of Marko, the son of King Vukashin, glorified the resistance of the people against Turkish rule and its misdeeds. The leading idea is the same in the *hajduk* (insurgent) cycle, where the resistance and the love of freedom of the *hajduks* was an object of praise.

In the free merchant city of Dubrovnik, under the influence of humanism and the Renaissance, poetry, drama, and comedy developed. Somewhat later literary activity began in other parts of Croatia and in Slovenia.

Very important in the nineteenth century for the development of Yugoslav culture was the lifework of Vuk Stefanovich-Karadzhich, who fixed the basis of the literary language while collecting the popular poetry of the people. The Croatians accepted his linguistic formulations as their literary language, abandoning the Kajkavski dialect they formerly had used for this purpose. The epic poems *The Death of Smail-aga* of Ivan Mazhuranich in Croatia and *The Mountain Wreath* of Petar Petrovich Njegoch in Montenegro, in which the authors treated the resistance of the people against the Turks, are outstanding creations.

Among the outstanding contemporary writers, Miroslav Krlezha in his novels, stories, and plays describes the antagonisms in the decaying Croatian bourgeois society of the first quarter of the twentieth century, and novelist Ivo Andrich depicts past and present relations among the population of some parts of Bosnia.

Among noteworthy literary creations of recent years are *The Kurlans* of Mirko Bozhich in Croatia, treating of the hard life of a peasant family in the mountainous region of Dalmatia before the war, and Oskar Davicho's *The Song,* in which the author describes the struggle of Belgrade's progressive youth against the German occupiers and their helpers.

In the domain of modern fine arts, the foundations were laid by the epochal work of Ivan Meshtrovich in sculpture and by impressionist painters like Nadezha Petrovich, Miroslav Kraljevich, and Rihard Jakopich. There are two tendencies reflected in the work of Yugoslav artists: the realistic and the abstract. The first seeks to give realistic form to man's impulses and actions and to social events in their environment and in the history of the Yugoslav peoples. Typical of this group are painters Krsto Hegudushich, Marijan Detoni, and Djordje Andrejevich-Kun, and sculptors Vanja Radaish, Antun Augostinchich, and Boris Kalin. Abstract and nonrepresentational techniques, significant of the second tendency, are employed by painters Edo Murtich and Zlatko Prica and sculptors Kosta Andjeli Radovani and Vojin Bakich.

In Yugoslavia, theater activity makes an important contribution to the raising of the cultural level of the population. (See Table 15.) The repertoire of opera, drama, and comedy includes all international standard works, as well as domestic productions based on works projecting problems of contemporary life. The Yugoslav people have a well-developed sense of music that takes shape in an unlimited number of popular songs and melodies. Therefore, the best works of Yugoslav composers are those based on popular music, like the compositions of Stevan Mokranjac, Josip Gotovac, Petar Konjovich.

Religion. The Constitution of 1946 proclaimed the separation of state and church and assured freedom of conscience and worship to all religions in the territory of Yugoslavia: Orthodox, Roman Catholic, Islamic, Protestant, and so on. Table 16 presents data (based on the census of 1953) on the religious composition of the population.

According to the Law on the Legal Position of Religious Communities the members of a religious community are completely free in their religious

Table 15. Number of Theaters, Capacity, Attendance, and Number of Performances, in Yugoslavia

Item	1938–39	1951–52	1952–53	1953–54
Number of theaters	24	73	72	73
Number of seats	19,628	36,978	36,944	37,204
Number of performances	4,233	10,821	13,374	12,285
Attendance in thousands	1,421	3,821	5,154	4,772

Source: *Statistical Annual, 1955,* p. 329.

Table 16. Religious Composition of the Population in Yugoslavia, According to the Census of 1953 (in thousands)

Group	Number	Group	Number
Orthodox	7,011	Islamic	2,083
Roman Catholic	5,383	Jewish	2
Protestants	148	Non-Christians	1
Other Christians	71	No answer	126
Believers not belonging to a religious community	11	Unknown	5
Atheists	2,085	Total	16,926

Source: *Statistical Annual, 1955,* p. 58.

activity. The penal law sets up sanctions against hindering or frustrating the exercise of religious functions.

Religious organizations showed varying attitudes toward the new social order. The Orthodox, Moslem, and Protestant clergy soon accepted the new situation, but the Catholic clergy stood in opposition to the government. In recent years a large part of the lower Catholic clergy have taken a more conciliatory position and have followed the example of other churches, the clergy of which united in associations. These associations were formed to assure to their members the rights which appertain to other citizens because of their occupation. By making contracts with the establishments of social insurances, the clergy class associations obtained for their members the same rights as all working citizens—the right to be assisted in case of illness or disability, the right to receive the invalid, old-age, and family pensions, and so on.

The state supports the religious communities when they require it, according them allowances which they manage alone. A formal exception had to be made for the Catholic Church, which did not settle its relations with the state; nevertheless, on several occasions the republican governments have made grants to Catholic communities.

The Orthodox Church has a faculty of theology at Belgrade, and some secondary schools. The Roman Catholic Church has two faculties of theology at Zagreb and Ljubljana besides twenty-five secondary schools in Croatia and Slovenia, while the Moslem community conducts three schools for priests.

The religious communities may publish freely. The Roman Catholic Church publishes eight periodicals, the most important of which is *Gore srca* (Hearts on High), the Orthodox Church publishes two, and the Moslem community, one. All communities occasionally publish books, almanacs, pamphlets, and leaflets.

Recreational Institutions and Other Associations. Spread all over the country are a large number of cultural and educational societies, often connected with the labor unions, which organize the recreational activity of their members with such projects as amateur theatrical performances, concerts, chess tournaments, excursions, travel, and dancing.

Sports are important in Yugoslavia. There are 6,449 sports organizations (with 900,094 members) [12] of which the largest number are shooting associations, followed by soccer football clubs. Other associations practice gymnastics, swimming, skiing, mountaineering, handball, basketball, volley ball, tennis, and the like.

Interest in sports is continually increasing, particularly among the youth. The local organizations of the People's Youth of Yugoslavia often mobilize their members for the voluntary construction of sports places. The People's Youth of Yugoslavia had, in 1954, 1,142,856 members —workers, peasants, scholars, students, and employees from fourteen to twenty-five years of age. The organization was formed during the war, but its members distinguished themselves in the reconstruction period also. The People's Youth of Yugoslavia participate voluntarily in the building of railways, factories, electric power plants, and students' cities. During the Five Year Plan, the contribution of its members was more than 60,000,000 voluntary working days.

Other organizations are the Union of the Veterans of the National Liberation War, the Union of the War Invalids, and the Yugoslav Red Cross. The first two are engaged in a vast program of assistance for their members. The activity of the Red Cross is especially important for raising the level of sanitation in the villages.

Notes

[1] 12,000 persons have not declared their nationality. All statistical data are derived from *Statistichki godishnjak, FNRJ (Statistical Annual of the Federated People's Republic of Yugoslavia)* (Beograd: Savezni zavod za statistiku, 1955).

[2] 21,000 persons did not specify their status.

[3] The concept of southern Slavs is broader than that of Yugoslavs. The Bulgarians are southern Slavs, too, but they do not belong to the Yugoslavian people because they have their own state.

[4] Gilbert in Der Maur, *Die Jugoslawen einst und jetzt* (Leipzig and Wien: J. Günther, 1936), III, p. 217.

[5] 81,000 did not specify the property sector in which they work.

[6] *Statistichki godishnjak, op. cit.,* p. 156.

[7] Foreign economic aid, which in 1954 consisted of 1,390,000 tons of goods valued at 27,076 million dinars, is not included.

[8] In 1952 Yugoslavia exported 481,000 tons of cereals and in the next year only 57,000 tons, while in 1954 exported cereals amounted to 128,000 tons *(Statistischki godishnjak, op. cit.,* p. 210).

[9] This is the relation between the situations in 1939 and 1953.

[10] Foreign affairs and national defense are under the exclusive jurisdiction of the federal government.

[11] Vladimir Bonach, "Illiteracy as a Social Factor," manuscript presented before the Third World Congress of the International Sociological Association, Amsterdam, 1956, p. 3.

[12] These are the official numbers of registered associations and sportsmen. But a far greater number practice various sports in associations not recorded by the sports federations.

YUGOSLAVIA

Supplementary References

Broz-Tito, Josip, *Borba za oslobodjenje Jugoslavije* (The Struggle for Liberation of New Yugoslavia) (Beograd, 1945).

Chermelj, Lavo, *La Minorité Slave en Italie* (Union Yugoslave des Associations pour la Société des Nations, Association de Ljubljana, 1938).

Chubrilovich, Vaso, *Politichka proshlost Hrvata* (The Political Past of Yugoslavia) (Beograd: Politika, 1939).

Djordjevich, Jovan, *Ustavno pravo FNRJ* (Constitutional Law of the Federative People's Republic of Yugoslavia) (Beograd: Nauchna knjiga, 1953).

Eisner, Bertold, *Porodichno pravo* (Family Law) (Zagreb: Shkolska knjiga, 1950).

Guzina, Ruzhica, *Knezhina i postanak srpske burzhoaske drzhave* (Kneshina and the Origins of the Serbian Bourgeois State) (Beograd: Kultura, 1955).

Historija naroda Jugoslavije (A History of the Yugoslav People), edited by Grafenauer Bogo, Perovich Dushan and Shidak Jaroslav (Zagreb: Shkolska knjiga, 1953).

Horvat, Josip, *Politichka povijest Hrvatske* (A Political History of Croatia), I–II (Zagreb, 1937).

————, *Stranke kod Hrvata i njihova ideologija* (Croatian Political Parties and Their Ideology) (Beograd: Politika, 1939).

Humo, Avdo, "Socijalne promjene i industrijalizacika u Bosnia-Herzegovina" (Social Changes and Industrialization in Bosnia and Herzegovina), *Nasha Stvarnost* (Beograd, 1953), No. 5, pp. 12–24.

In Der Maur, Gilbert, *Der Weg Zur Nation* (The Way to Nationhood) (Berlin-Wien-Zürich: Payer, 1938).

Jirechek, Konstantin, *Istorija Srba* (History of the Serbians), I–II (Beograd: Nauchna knjiga, 1952).

Kardelj, Edvard, *Povodom novog uredjenja Srezova i opchina* (About the New Organization of Counties and Communes) (Beograd: Politichka biblioteka, 1955).

————, *Problemi nashe socijalistichke izgradnje* (Problems of Our Socialist Construction), I–III (Beograd, 1954).

Kos Milko, *Zgodovina Slovencev* (History of the Slovenes) (Ljubljana: Slovenska Matica, 1955).

Kostich, Cvetko, *Seljaci Industriski radnici* (Peasant Industrial Workers) (Beograd, 1955).

Mandich, Oleg, "Il Consiglio dei Produttori nell' Ordinamento Constitutionale Jugoslavo" "The Council of Producers in the Yugoslav Constitutional Order), *Rivista di Studi Politici Internazionali* (Firenze, 1953), No. 3, pp. 411–421.

Mitrovich, Zhivam, *Srpske politichke stranke* (Serbian Political Parties) (Beograd: Politika, 1939).

Paulova, Mylada, *Jugoslavenski odbor* (Yugoslav Committees) (Zagreb: Prvjetna Nakladna Zadruga, 1925).

Pbvichevich, Branko, *Stvaranje crnogorske drzhave* (The Making of the Montenegrin State) (Beograd: Rad, 1955).

Prokop, Ana, *Komentar Osnovnom zakoju o braku* (Commentary on the Fundamental Law on Marriage) (Zagreb: Shkolska knjiga, 1953).

Stojanovich, Nikola, *Srbija i jugoslavensko ujedinjenje* (Serbia and Yugoslavia) (Beograd, Politika, 1939).

Shishich, Ferdo, *Povijest Hrvata u vrijeme narodnih vladara* (A History of Croatians in the Time of the National Sovereigns) (Zagreb, Naklada shkolskih knjiga, 1925).

Vukosavljevich, Sreten, *Istorija seljachkog drushtva* (A History of Peasant Society) (Beograd, Srpska Akademija Nauka, 1953).

*

John Koty

GREECE

*

National Traits and Basic Sociological Characteristics of the Culture

"IN THE complexity of its contour and variety of its natural features, Greece surpasses every country in Europe . . ." wrote one of the authorities on Greece some years ago.[1] Indeed, the historian and the geographer who visit this country are always impressed by the variety and the contrasts of its landscape.

Greek society, no less than Greek nature, often presents irreconcilable aspects. The urban and the rural communities seem to belong to two different worlds. Life in the capital, or in some other big towns, is not very different, at least outwardly, from that in any other part of the Western world, but the social conditions of most remote and isolated villages remind one of the semibarbarous medieval communities. Mountain regions shelter a population of nomadic shepherds that bears little resemblance to the open-minded, alert, and quick-witted islanders. The conservative inhabitants of the fertile valleys have acquired a different attitude toward life from the people of the coastal regions.

No systematic and thorough studies of the Greek national character have, as yet, been published.[2] This is, of course, not surprising, for the problem of "national character," in spite of its great sociological importance, has only recently become the object of scientific investigation. There are still many unsolved methodological problems and unanswered details regarding the essence and the formation of national character.[3] Bearing these reservations in mind, I shall venture a description, even though tentative, of some striking features of the Greek "national character."

Generally speaking, the Greek national character is the product of three major, essentially antagonistic, historical forces: the classic antiquity,

330

which is alive in the language and folkways; the Christianized Byzantine Empire with its theocratic conservatism, centralism,[4] and spirit of bureaucracy; and the Turkish domination, which isolated Greece from the West and strengthened the Asiatic influences that had been penetrating the country even before the conquest. The invasions of different groups (Visigoths, Ostrogoths, Vandals, Huns, and Avars), as well as the transitory rule of the Franks, Venetians, and the Genoese, had only a slight influence on Greek life. The periodic immigrations of the Albanians and the Slavs, however, in spite of the great power of Greece to assimilate foreign groups, did not fail to leave some traces in the social patterns of the native people—a fact not readily admitted by some scholars. As the power of the Sultan gradually waned, influences from western Europe began to trickle into the country and after the Liberation (1829) they became prevalent, especially in the urban centers.

Considering the variety of determining influences, one need not wonder that the Greek national character presents many contradictions. The student of modern Greek society will certainly be impressed by the spirit of democracy, as well as by stubborn conservatism; by expressions of extreme individualism and even selfishness, which are peculiarly combined with cooperativeness and touching hospitality; he will come across examples of patience and stoic endurance, side by side with excitability and an inveterate tendency to grumbling and discontent. Skepticism, and not seldom a morbid inclination to criticism, are paired with religious credulity and superstition; inquisitiveness and the passion for learning are often marred by intolerance and distrust of free inquiry; haughtiness is often coupled with servile subordination. One observes on the one hand warm patriotism which makes any sacrifice seem easy, and on the other, flagrant disobedience of the laws of the country. Trickiness and thirst for profit are often relieved by boundless generosity; cordiality, kindness, and expressions of sympathy for others may go together with total disregard of human rights—especially of social inferiors—verging at times on unpardonable indifference. Outbursts of enthusiasm, which may lead to daring exploits, are followed by spells of gloom, dejection, and despair; great sensitiveness to abstract justice on the one hand, and an incurable dependance on favoritism, on the other; meticulous cleanliness, and complete indifference to the most elementary principles of hygiene.

The traits enumerated above do not, by any means, exhaust the list of virtues and defects, for the psychology of nations, perhaps more so than that of individuals, is an intricate maze of conscious and subconscious elements, the detailed analysis of which lies beyond the scope of this paper.

Significant for the formation of the social structure and the character of the Greek people was not only its history, but also the configuration of the country and its peculiar geographic situation. Unilateral explanations of social phenomena, frequently resorted to because of their convenient simplification of reality, should be carefully avoided. "Determinism" has no place in the interpretation of social reality. Life with its various aspects offers to human groups, as Toynbee rightly pointed out, only a "challenge," but does not determine the nature of "response." The manner in which human groups will respond to this challenge is seldom, if ever, predictable. Bearing these remarks in mind, perhaps it would not be an idle task to look at the natural habitat of ancient and modern Greeks for clues to an additional explanation of their mental attitudes and emotional reactions.

Greece has for centuries served—except during the period of the Turkish domination—as a bridge joining three continents. Because of this privileged geographic position, it became the converging point of influences from West and East. Perhaps this fact also can account, at least in part, for the complexity of the inner life of the Greek people and for the striking contrasts in its character. The ubiquitousness of the sea on the Greek scene, the indented coast offering splendid shelter to the ships, the host of islands situated at convenient distance from the mainland and from one another, the mountainous character of the country, the absence of good roads, and the relative poverty of the soil—all induced the Greeks, when no other factors counteracted these inducements, to accept the challenge and become adventurous mariners, roving tradesmen, enterprising colonizers, or reckless pirates.

It is not improbable—so little is known of the biologic determinants of character—that the restlessness, the passion for adventure in every field, the deeply rooted curiosity—traits which modern Greeks share with their ancestors—are the result of the maritime and trading pursuits and of the stimulating contacts with the neighboring peoples, some of whom were in ancient times bearers of advanced civilization.

The mountain ranges which broke the country into many isolated valleys, making contacts difficult, gave rise to the creation of small autonomous communities, which, in spite of similarity of race, of language, and of cultural traditions, were independent of, and frequently antagonistic to, one another. It is not unlikely that this geographic factor has contributed, at least in part, to the development of local patriotism and the spirit of individualism. These two traits, which worked for good and for evil, are traceable all through the long history of the Greek people, as there never operated in the past a force strong enough to check, or even to moderate, their expression, and it is only in the last decades of the nineteenth century that the new social conditions facilitated the emergence of different tendencies. In ancient times, even in the face of deadly danger, the Hellenic city-states acted as separate units and not infrequently followed their own interest to the detriment of the group endeavor. Two thousand years later, when all the Greeks rose in arms against the Turkish overlord, we again meet the same spirit of narrow localism and individualism in the attitude of the local groups and the different war chiefs, who very often showed unwillingness to cooperate, and in pursuit of their private aims did not hesitate to thwart the common cause. Quite different, however, was the spirit of the nation in 1940, when it rose as one man to confront the Italian invader. It was probably the first time that the Greeks acted as one undivided nation, without hesitation and with supreme loyalty to the common cause. This glorious historic event marks a new stage in the development of the Greek spirit, and it is indeed an eloquent refutation of the theory that national character does not change.

The Greeks have always been noted for their mental alertness and ambition to learn and to progress. And yet, Greece, the heir of classic antiquity and a member of the west European family of nations, if gauged by the standards of Western civilization will have to be classed as a rather "retarded" country. Even in larger towns the Western cultural atmosphere is limited to a relatively thin layer of the population. On many an occasion a careful observer will be able to detect under the superficial veneer of modern civilization signs betraying former stages of culture. It is for this reason that the stranger will sometimes be surprised to hear sharp expressions in quarters where such language is least expected.

Some scholars, like Falmerayer, tried to explain the decline of the Greek society by the "biologic" deterioration of the human material. They asserted that the many wars, the natural catastrophes, and epidemics decimated the old Hellenic stock, while the immigration of semibarbarous and barbarous ethnic groups "diluted" the "noble" blood of the Greek population that survived. The problem of interrelationship between the biologic structure and the character of peoples is still unsolved, but no scientist would probably dare nowadays to support the "pure race" theory, or attribute "magical" properties to blood.

It is not, after all, "pure blood" or the biologic continuity which some good patriots are so eager to defend, but the cultural continuity that counts. The folklorist will find no difficulty in detecting in the language,[5] in social patterns, in beliefs and superstitions, and, in general, in the details of everyday life of modern Greece, countless traces reminiscent of classic antiquity.[6]

The relative backwardness of the Greek society is, undoubtedly, due to other than biologic causes. It must not be left out of sight that Greek society has been greatly handicapped by the Turkish domination, which, especially in the first two centuries, not only retarded, but almost altogether interrupted its normal evolution. Greece has not had her period of Renaissance, for, just as the first signs of the new spirit began to appear, all ties with the Western world were abruptly broken by the relentless Asiatic master. Greece won her freedom four centuries later, but with all the cultural heritage of the past (classic antiquity and Byzantine Empire) it was not easy for the Greek people to pass from a semibarbarous stage to the cultural atmosphere of the West. Civilization, that is, the technological achievements and the outward forms of social life, can be readily borrowed and imitated; the acquisition of culture is a slow organic process. P. Kanellopoulos, the former minister of war, probably had this truth in mind when he wrote in his lucid study on modern society that Greece had many excellent "specialists" in practically every province of science, but a relatively small number of really "cultured" people.[7]

The cultural development of Greece has also been retarded by the poverty of the state, by the imperfectly functioning social selection, and by the frequently inefficient management of public affairs. There are, however, many hopeful signs that may make us look confidently into the future. After the two world wars, the cultural contacts with the West became more frequent and permanent. The exchange of professors and students is being organized on an ever larger scale. The interest of the United States and of the United Nations in the retarded and economically weaker countries is becoming more active and systematic. The most cheerful sign is that in the country itself the voice of honest and progressive people who clearly realize the needs of the masses becomes louder and louder. All these factors of social dynamics will not fail to produce an intellectual and social fermentation that will help raise the country to a higher cultural level.

GREECE

Economic Institutions

The foreign visitor who has become acquainted only with the central section of Athens will certainly form a very inadequate picture of the economic situation in Greece. He may have the illusion that he has visited the capital of a prosperous country. And yet, the central part of Athens is not typical of the rest of the city, and the city itself, inhabited by almost a million and a half people (Greater Athens) does not represent Greece as a whole. Athens is a misleading façade of the country: our visitor would not suspect the existence of many villages which have been almost entirely neglected by most governments, liberal as well as conservative, and where most people live in dire necessity, deprived of most of the basic requirements that make human life tolerably comfortable and respectable. Greece, like many underdeveloped countries, is a land of striking contrasts: a relatively small group of very wealthy people on the one hand, and a great mass of underfed or poorly nourished population, on the other.

The United Nations' Food and Agriculture Organization mission reports that in Greece, even before World War II, the food available for consumption provided only 2500 calories per capita, as compared with the average consumption levels of 3000 to 3200 calories in more privileged countries. The per person consumption of protein—65 grams per day—was considerably smaller than in most other countries of Europe. Moreover, the composition of the Greek diet was poor: only one fifth of the protein came from animal sources, as compared to one third to one half in western Europe. This deficiency in diet is, however, balanced by the rather high consumption of fresh fruits and vegetables.[8]

Various factors combined in the past to bring the country to its present plight: the relative poverty of the soil, which was, moreover, overused or badly used; the wasteful economy *(Raubwirtschaft)* of foreigners and of natives; the ignorance of the people; and the unwise or irrational management of many governments (there were outstanding exceptions) of free Greece.

Before the Liberation War (beginning in 1821) Greece was almost entirely an agricultural country, but even now, in spite of recent economic developments and the fact that only one fourth of the total area is arable land, about 57 per cent of the population still depend on land for their living. (This compares with an agrarian minority of 15 per cent in the United States and 35 per cent in France.)

Thanks to the land reforms, the first of which was inaugurated in 1917,

335

most of the very large estates were broken up and distributed among the landless peasants. This fact explains why Greece has an insignificant number of land proletariat. According to the recent statistics, there are only twenty-two "giant" estates (2500 hectares or upwards) and these represent less than 0.01 per cent of all landholdings, while the very large, large, and medium farms (2500–500 hectares, 500–50 hectares, 50–20 hectares) comprise only 0.63 per cent. The greatest number of landholdings (about 99.37 per cent) in this country are the "dwarf" farms and small holdings (0.1–20 hectares),[9] but as the peasants are the owners of the plots they cultivate, it is not surprising that the agrarian population, even though politically weak, has been relatively unreceptive to the communistic ideology. The average farmer is, indeed, far from being prosperous, not only because the acreage available per farmer is much smaller than that in Europe, but also because the soil in most parts of Greece is poor in both nitrogen and phosphorus. Consequently, the average grain yield per acre is low, only one half to one third of the average yield in most countries in Europe and the United States and only slightly higher than the average yield in India.

One may get a clearer idea of the situation in Greece by examining Table 1.

Since the Greek is traditionally a great bread eater, much of the arable land is cultivated in cereals (wheat, corn, barley, and rye). In spite of the

Table 1. Land Available to Greek Farmers and Grain Yield
Compared with Eight Other Countries

Country	Acres per Farmer	Bushels per Acre
Greece	1.31*	13.5
Italy	1.68	24.4
Rumania	2.45	14.3
France	3.34	21.7
Germany	3.51	29.8
United Kingdom	5.36	31.0
Denmark	6.12	39.3
United States	17.03	18.6
India	1.28	12.0

Source: Food and Agriculture Organization of the United Nations, p. 155. *Report of the FAO Mission for Greece.* Washington, D.C.: U.S. Government Printing Office, March 1947.

*If orchards and vineyards are included, the figure may come up to 1.57 acres per head of farm population. F. Smothers, W. McNeil, and E. McNeil, *Report on the Greeks* (New York: Twentieth Century Fund, 1948), p. 51.

fact, however, that 74 per cent of the arable land is devoted to grain, Greece has to import 30 per cent of the grain needed for food.

Besides cereals, Greece produces tobacco, cotton, currants and raisins, olives (and olive oil), wines, grapes and figs, citrus fruits, and the like, the so-called commercial crops that are of great importance to the country because they secure a high financial return. From the economic standpoint, some of these products are very profitable, for, their yield per acre being considerably higher than that for grains, they require less land while at the same time they give employment to more people: 25 man-days per hectare are needed for grains, 120 man-days for cotton, and 328 for raising and processing tobacco.[10]

Unfortunately, many of the products (namely tobacco, raisins and currants, olives and olive oil, and fresh fruit) on which Greece largely depends for the creation of export trade in order to buy from abroad the necessary commodities not made in the country (in the prewar period, approximately one fourth of all products consumed in the country were obtained from abroad) belong to the semiluxury or luxury category of goods and, therefore, are likely to be demanded only when the other nations are prosperous.

Only a relatively small part of the rural population is engaged in purely pastoral pursuits. Being a Mediterranean country, Greece does not have natural pasturage all year round, and therefore not many cattle are found here (904,000 head in 1953). But Greece is rich in smaller animals, sheep (8,254,000) and goats (4,510,000), which are of great economic value—while requiring no special care since they can graze on the mountain slopes when the valleys get dry in summer, they provide the people in addition to their wool with meat, milk, and cheese, and relieve somewhat the monotony of their diet.[11]

This is a very brief survey of the Greek agricultural situation, but before we take up some of the other aspects of the economic life, let us give a rapid glance at the causes that make the peasant's life so hard and unhappy.

One of the most serious problems agriculture in Greece has to face is *water*—either its insufficiency or its harmful abundance. The country as a whole gets plenty of rainfall during the year, but it is unevenly distributed. The summers in most parts of the country are very dry, while during the other seasons torrential rains frequently occur, which wash away from the mountain slopes valuable soil, or cover with stones and gravel good land in the valleys. (The destructive effect of rains has been further intensified by the wanton deforestation that has been carried on for centuries.) Until recent times little was done to harness this powerful element of nature and make it subservient to human will. The tragic consequences of the two world wars and the constructive advice of friendly foreign agencies (Near East Foundation, UNRRA, and ECA) served as strong incentives to a more systematic study of the economic situation of Greece as a whole. The conviction is growing that there is considerable room for improvement, if persons in leading positions would give a more full-hearted attention to the problems of the peasant world.

The proposed measures aiming at radical improvements are reclamation of land by draining marshy areas, control of floods and erosion by constructing embankments and through planned afforestation, better and more abundant utilization of fertilizers, substitution of antiquated methods by more modern technical means, expert guidance, professional education of the growing peasant generation, redistribution of land so as to avoid unnecessary waste of human energy caused by the strip system, better medical care, more efficient means of fighting parasites destroying plants or animals,[12] improved seeds, greater credit facilities offered to peasants, and, finally, the extension of village cooperatives. With foreign technical and financial assistance, the progressive local agencies have been able to realize many of these goals: between the wars, the total area sown to six main crops increased from 1,048,500 hectares (1925–29) to 1,523,000 hectares (1935–38), and the yield from 753,000 tons to 1,393,000 tons for the same years.[13] In the postwar period, the use of chemical fertilizers was considerably increased (21 per cent), while the cultivated area has been enlarged by 8 per cent and the irrigated surface—it is calculated—by 20 per cent.[14] The production figures for 1953 were wheat, 183 per cent; cotton, 214 per cent; and rice 2000 per cent of prewar rates.[15] Some of the suggested long-range projects (e.g., electrification of most sections of the country, irrigation improvements, flood control) are also well under way. By the expenditure of American aid funds and of money obtained from German and Italian reparations (in all $117,388,000), 175,000 kilowatts have been added to the existing electric power, which has more than doubled the production of such power. For the first time in the history of the country, electricity is available in most sections of the land.[16]

In visualizing the future of Greece the FAO report draws a very optimistic and attractive picture of the rural communities,[17] and undoubtedly much in the way of lightening the labor of the peasants, of improving their living conditions, and of offering them greater cultural opportunities is feasible and well within the range of possibility. But careful observers are becoming more and more convinced that even if all the improvements suggested are achieved, the land will still be too overcrowded.

The comparison of Greece with her neighbors regarding the density of population in relation to the area of cultivated land tends to justify this view, as the accompanying tabulation shows.[18] The Greeks, especially the

	No. of Persons per Sq. Km. of Cultivated Land
Greece	336
Bulgaria	140
Yugoslavia	181
Rumania	128

peasants, are still rather prolific. Since no agency has undertaken to organize a systematic popularization of modern birth-control methods, such practices are ignored by the peasants; nor does the official church favor the artificial limitation of the population. Besides, the steadily improving public health service in the country as a whole has considerably reduced child mortality (from 133.55 per thousand children under one year in 1931, to 43.61 per thousand in 1953).[19] On the other hand emigration and urbanization have not so far brought about any considerable decrease of the agrarian population. It is not unlikely, therefore, that in the course of years the agrarian problem may be seriously aggravated. In view of this fact, foreign and Greek experts suggest that occupational openings be created capable of absorbing the surplus agrarian population. By offering suitable opportunities in industry and other occupations, the FAO mission believes that "over a considerable term of years, the proportion of the workers in Greece dependent upon agriculture might be reduced from the present level of about 60% to 40% or even lower."[20] The shifting of the population to other occupational channels would, certainly, not appear as a revolutionary governmental measure, for this trend has already begun in the past. The responsible authorities will only have to encourage and systematize this movement.

Because of natural and social conditions, industry in Greece is of recent development. The scarcity of fuel, of skilled working hands, and of capital did not encourage the establishment of factories. Nor was the opinion of political and economic circles wholly undivided with regard to the industrialization of the country. It was only after the serious agricultural crisis of 1893 that greater impetus was given to industrial development, and in 1917, when the first industrial census was taken, some 282 large industrial establishments and 2,000 smaller workshops were already functioning, giving employment to 35,000 workers. The territorial expansion following the Balkan Wars and World War I, but more especially the arrival of some 1,500,000 refugees from Asia Minor and other districts, gave a great push to the growth of industry. See Table 2.

During the German occupation, industrial activity was considerably hampered by the shortage of material and fuel, and the restrictions imposed by the foreign authorities. Not a little damage was caused to industrial installations and stock by air raids and by sabotage. According to semi-official estimates, the losses sustained in buildings and machines amounted to $40,000,000, while the damage caused to stocks and raw material totaled $470,000,000.[21] Thanks to foreign assistance (UNRRA and Marshall Plan) and to the vitality and enterprising spirit of the Greek people, postwar industrial production has been able to approach prewar levels, and in many cases even surpass them. In 1945 it reached 33 per cent of prewar production; 53 per cent in 1946; 88 per cent in 1949; 123 per cent in 1951.[22]

It must, however, be noted that, judged by Western standards, even the largest industrial enterprises (most of which are located around Athens, Piraeus, and Salonika[23]) cannot be compared with similar establishments of Western countries. Very few factories are equipped with modern machinery and employ a great number of workers. Many of the "industrial establishments" are not infrequently family concerns, use very little power and simple—if not primitive—machines, and employ only one to five men.[24]

Remarkable results have been achieved in manufactures such as ciga-

Table 2. Industrial Development in Greece

Year	No. of Factories	No. of Workmen
1920	2,905	60,000
1929–30	4,000	110,000
1938	4,515	140,000*
1951	88,674†	318,686‡

*N. Svoronos, *Histoire de la Grèce* (Paris: Presses Universitaires, 1953), p. 106.
† This number includes also handicraft establishments.
‡ National Statistical Service of Greece, *Statistical Summary of Greece* (Athens, 1954), p. 53.

rettes, paper, and tools, in building materials and furniture manufacturing, and in tanneries, but the most noted progress has been in textile, chemical, and food industries. The great significance of this development lies in the fact that these industries use raw materials mostly extracted or produced in the country, and thus reduce the dependence of Greek industry on material imported from abroad.

As mentioned above, Greece has been handicapped by the absence of coal and any other natural fuel. There are, indeed, substantial deposits of lignite, but it is of no great value to industry, because it contains much moisture and little carbon.

Greece has considerable mineral wealth (bauxite, manganese, emery, chrome, iron pyrite, nickel, zinc, copper, and sulphur), but the exploitation of these minerals has been in most cases inadequate. Few serious attempts have been made until recent years to use these minerals in local manufactures and many of them were exported as raw material and reimported as fabricated goods.

We have already referred to the recommendations of FAO and of some Greek authorities regarding the diversion of the surplus agrarian population to other occupational fields, but a rapid survey of economical journals and daily papers convinces one that it is still a much-disputed question among experts (the people at large are rather indifferent to these issues) whether Greece should retain her mainly agricultural character, or whether, because of the nature of her agriculture produce intended for export, the main emphasis should be shifted to the industrialization of the country. Some economists maintain that Greece should remain a primarily agricultural country since she does not possess resources in fuel. Others (for example, Varvaressos) categorically discourage the establishment of heavy industry, because the necessities for successful development in this direction are lacking. Still others, while acknowledging the necessity and feasibility of encouraging small industry, insist that—since to date no careful surveys of the mineral resources of the country have been made nor any exhaustive investigations into the general economic and demographic conditions attempted—competent authorities should abstain from any hasty and drastic resolution. Even if one does not share the sanguine expectations of some enthusiasts, postwar achievements in the utilization of the hydroelectric potentialities of Greece certainly warrant a profitable extension of light industry, which would considerably increase the production of articles (heretofore imported from abroad) mainly intended for home consumption. Most of these developments (for example, in Macedonia, Peloponnesus, Epirus, and Euboea) are long-range projects which are carried out primarily for the interest of the country as a whole and not for the benefit of small interest groups.

The foreign missions that made a thorough study of the economic situation of Greece are of the opinion that commercial pursuits should be so organized as to create new openings for the surplus population. Trade, for which the Greeks have great aptitude, has always played an important role in their economy. In the census of 1928 some 200,000 were recorded as employed in commercial business (banking, merchants, and shopkeepers).[25]

Greece has needed to export her mostly semiluxury or luxury goods, in order to procure staple foods (wheat, sugar, meat, and the like), which the country was unable to produce in sufficient quantities to feed her population. In order to establish an equilibrium in her payments, Greece has been making an effort to increase the volume of exports (especially of goods not classed as luxury items, like ores, textiles, rice, and cotton). By a more rationalized organization of agricultural and industrial production, it is hoped that the value of imported goods may be reduced to indispensable limits,[26] while the volume of exports is considerably increased so as to secure a better balance in visible trade. For the present, however, it is not possible to foresee whether Greece will ever succeed in establishing a favorable balance between exports and imports. See Table 3. Fortunately, Greece has had in the last decades three important sources of foreign exchange: emigrants' remittances, revenue from shipping, and tourism.

Shipping has been in the past a prominent feature in Greek economic

Table 3. Greece's Imports and Exports from 1922 to 1952
(in millions of dollars)

Year	Imports	Exports
1922–30*	$236.8	$122.5
1931–38*	118.1	70.9
1946	383.0	40.3†
1948	553.0	94.0
1950	428.2	90.4
1952	346.3	119.9

Source: Royal Institute of International Affairs, *Greece, A Political and Economical Survey, 1939–1953* (London, 1954), p. 184.

*Annual average.

†The drop is caused by diminished manufactural and agricultural activity due to civil war.

life. During the struggle for independence, the merchant marine of Greece was greatly reduced, but since then it has been making a steady and noteworthy comeback, so that, before World War II, Greece (with her 1,837,315 tonnage) occupied the third place in the Mediterranean and the ninth in the world.[27] After the war, thanks to the purchase of a hundred United States Liberty ships and tankers on extremely favorable terms, Greece succeeded in recovering her prewar position, and in spite of the heavy losses suffered during World War II—78 per cent of her vessels and 72 per cent of the tonnage—she now holds the eleventh rank in international shipping, with 1,270,221 tons (1955).[28] It must be noted, also, that many native shipowners register their ships under foreign flags in order to evade the heavy taxation levied on Greek shipping companies. According to recent figures (1955), there were 7,653,341 tons of Greek-owned shipping registered under foreign flags.[29] The Rally government, by offering favorable terms, succeeded in convincing some of the Greek shipowners residing abroad to register their ships under the Greek flag.

Before the war, the earnings of the merchant marine contributed nearly $12,000,000 to the balance of payments, and shipping offered employment to about 30,000 seamen (with their families they numbered from 150,000 to 200,000 people).[30] If, in addition, all those employed in occupations directly connected with shipping are included, one may easily realize the great importance of this branch of Greek economy.

Greece is usually referred to as a very poor country. The issue of great sociological interest is not that the vast majority of people have lived in squalid poverty and that the national income is very low ($192 per capita, as compared with $1,800 in the United States),[31] but whether, as some inveterate pessimists claim, Greece is doomed to be forever a poor country. It is true, Greece is not particularly favored by nature to become a rich agricultural country. But not all countries depend for their prosperity entirely on fertile soil. Switzerland, like Greece, is mountainous, but this does not prevent her from being one of the economically soundest nations of Europe. Before the final verdict about the future of Greece is passed, one must examine the important question whether this country has exhausted all its potentialities, so that there remains no room for further improvement.

The Greek state has enjoyed 130 years of free life, but the more or less careful investigations of the economic problem as a whole, and of the economic potentialities of the country, are of but recent date. The conviction one is bound to form after studying the data supplied by foreign missions and by Greek specialists is that Greece has been, as a rule, an unwisely managed country and that many of her resources have not yet been efficiently exploited. Most of the important branches of economic activity, like agriculture, dairying, fishing, and forestry, have to be placed on an altogether new footing, if a considerable improvement in the living conditions of the economically weaker classes is to be effected. Serious efforts have to be made to eliminate waste and to spread knowledge of up-to-date methods.

Fishing, for instance, which could have supplied the people with cheap, abundant, and wholesome food, has been carried on most inefficiently and altogether wastefully.[32] Thus, although Greece is surrounded by sea, much foreign exchange had to be used for the importation of 20,000 tons of fish every year.[33] Greece has considerable forest wealth, and it could be of outstanding importance to her economy. And yet, the country has not been able to draw much profit from this valuable source because of wanton destruction and inadequate forest policies, while great sums of foreign exchange have to be used for imported wood and wood pulp. Another much neglected and unexploited natural resource is the great variety of flowers and pharmaceutical and scented plants and herbs. The FAO mission and native scientists stress the importance of these resources, which could help build up useful and profitable industries capable of providing occupational opportunities to a considerable number of people.[34] Greece, above all, has unusual advantages that would enable her to become a first-class attraction for tourists. The land is rich in historic traditions and monuments; the natural scenery presents an infinite variety and great beauty; many springs with excellent curative properties are to be found everywhere; and yet, while other states like Switzerland, Italy, and France have for many years in the past been drawing huge profits from tourism, Greece only recently began to give a serious attention to this industry.

This brief survey, it is hoped, will suffice to show that Greece, in spite of certain disadvantages, has sufficient natural possibilities, which, if wisely and efficiently used, may secure a more comfortable and decent living for its people.

No survey, however, would be complete if mention were not made of the organizations of the factors of production. Although the constitution of 1836 made a provision for the voluntary organizations of merchants and industrialists, it was only in 1869 that the first associations of this class were founded at Patras. The main object was the promotion of professional interests, but the nature and structure of these associations was originally quite different from the form they assumed at a later date. In some respects they resembled the medieval guilds, for they consisted of employers and employed, and besides purely professional objectives, they pursued philanthropic and social aims. It was only in 1914 that the Venizelos government (in Law 281) prohibited the existence of mixed associations. Since that period, various employers' associations (for example, the Chamber of Agriculture in 1914, the Shipowners Union in 1936) have sprung up.

These professional associations are classed in two categories: the voluntary and the state-founded ("Chambers"); participation in the latter is obligatory for all persons concerned. Both types of associations play an important role in the economic life of the country.

Since there was in Greece no real industry, the emergence of trade unions was considerably retarded. The first labor union was formed in Syra in 1879 when the carpenters of the shipyards combined to improve their conditions. This movement was gradually extended to many other professional branches, but in spite of the many strikes that periodically occurred in the principal industrial centers (Patras, Volos, Athens, and Piraeus), the trade unions did not become "class-conscious" until the end of the first decade of our century. There were many attempts to unite all the workers into one great body, but it was only in 1918 that the formation of the confederation GSEE was achieved. Since that time, the labor movement has made considerable progress, for, while in 1919 there were 385 unions comprising 84,926 members, in 1949 (according to the report of the International Labor Organization) the number of unions rose to 1,850 with a total membership of 200,000–220,000.[35]

After World War I, the socialist movement began to grow in strength, and, especially after the influx of a great number of refugees from abroad, its influence among the working classes was by no means negligible. Strikes not infrequently assumed a political character. Before August 4, 1936, when the dictatorship of General Ioannis Metaxas was established, the trade unions were split into two political wings: the right ("Reformist") and the left, led by the communist leaders. The foreign-directed leftist party has repeatedly attempted to bring the labor movement under its sway and use the trade unions as an instrument of its subversive policy. The state interfered, however, and the communist danger was eliminated, but the problem of how to establish a confederation free of all political influence has found as yet no satisfactory solution.

Some observers believe that the failure of the labor unions to improve their living and working conditions is due, first, to the individualistic spirit of the Greek, which frequently hampers concerted action, and, second, to their political orientation. According to the report of the British Parliament delegation in 1946, "politics are the dominating motive in trade union activities, to the detriment of the proper business of such bodies, namely the improvement of the condition of the workers in the various industries."[36]

With all the drawbacks the Greek trade unions are becoming an important weapon in the hands of the working people. They are no longer isolated but are connected with foreign, especially American, labor organizations and send delegates to the International Labor Organization conferences. In spite of occasional intervention on the part of the government (for instance, the Decrees of October 24, 1938, and October 31, 1942), the trade unions are run on a democratic basis, and select their leaders, who are usually past middle age, from their own class. Strikes, intended to manifest the workmen's discontent, are rather frequent but invariably of short duration.

The relations between employers and laborers are on the whole by no means cordial. Since not all laborers have as yet acquired a "work conscience," they not infrequently try to "cheat" their employer by not doing their tasks conscientiously; on the other hand, the employers do not always approach their employees with friendly feelings. Mention must be made, however, of some employers, as for instance Papastratos, Matsagos (tobacco manufacturers), who on their own initiative have offered to their workmen advantages (economic, sanitary, cultural) which go far beyond the ordinary measures prescribed by law. These are exceptional cases, but one may hope that, in view of the menacing communist danger, or, if for no other more noble motive, at least out of pure "enlightened selfishness," the labor situation in Greece may be given in the future far more earnest attention.

Political Institutions

No country's politics exist in a vacuum. International forces in combination with natural factors and the social structure determine the policies of any nation, regardless of its size and power. But the political development of smaller and weaker countries, even though the semblance of "sovereignty" is preserved, is occasionally interfered with by stronger powers, now invisibly and now with cynical frankness.

Greece was drawn into the limelight of international politics, not because of her natural resources, but because of her geographic position. It must be emphasized again, lest the above statement be misinterpreted, that geographic factors may acquire special significance only in consequence of the operation of political and social forces.

It was only when the Russia of Peter the Great launched upon expansionist adventures that the Balkan peninsula, inhabited mostly by the Christian subjects of the Sultan, began to draw the attention of some European powers. In order to weaken and ultimately destroy the Ottoman Empire—the only serious obstacle to Russia's southward drive—Catherine II tried to arouse the national aspirations of the Greeks. Great Britain followed Russia's machinations with an anxious eye, for she well knew that the realization of the plans of the Northern Empire might seriously endanger the freedom of communications between London and the colonies. Thus Greece, studded with islands—a good number of which offered strategic advantages—became the battleground of conflicting interests of the Great Powers. Three important parties were formed which, instigated and supported by the diplomatic representatives of the three Great Powers (England, France, and Russia), engaged in stubborn conflict and acted as disruptive forces in a country that had just emerged from the Liberation war and needed internal peace and cooperation.

The discovery of oil in the Middle East area, at a later date, added a new dimension to the geographic importance of Greece; she could be conveniently used as a steppingstone to that rich oil region or she could serve as a vital link in the defense chain protecting it. The full significance of the December civil strife (1944), and the destructive activity of the Greek guerrillas (1946–49), may be understood only in the light of the conflict between Russia, which in pursuit of her political aims skillfully exploited the misery of the masses, and the Western democracies, which endeavored to prevent her from setting foot on the eastern Mediterranean shore. Thus, because of her geographic position, as well as because of her traditional orientations, Greece was involved in the conflict between the East and the West, and became the outpost of the democratic block. If one realizes that a small country like Greece, just emerging from so many successive catastrophes, has to spend almost half of her budget in order to be a worthy link in the Western defense line, one may understand what heavy obligations—

and the economic, political, and social effects resulting from them—this role imposes on her.

Another powerful factor in the evolution of the political and social life of Greece was the "Megali Idea," whose full significance we shall analyze later. Here it is only necessary to indicate that the pursuit of this *fata morgana,* in spite of some undoubtedly beneficial social influence, considerably retarded the normal evolution of the country, and what is worse, frequently became a dangerous weapon used by unscrupulous demagogues either to overthrow political opponents or to launch the people upon doubtful military adventures. The preparations necessary for the realization of the "Idea" absorbed a large portion of the nation's budget and tended to divert the attention of capable statesmen from the solution of vital economic problems.

When Greece won her independence, there were a host of political, administrative, economic, and social problems that demanded immediate solution. Practically every sector of social life was dislocated; and it seemed, indeed, a Herculean task to create order out of this chaotic condition. Nevertheless, on this retarded society an attempt was made to impose a parliamentary system of the Western pattern.

Democracy is a growing principle and its normal functioning presupposes a long political experience; but in Greece even the basic prerequisites for such an institution were lacking. In appraising the political evolution of modern Greece, it must never be overlooked that, during the long Turkish domination, the people had not been given a chance to experience the benefits of a liberal and efficient state machinery. It is true that under the Turkish rule a rudimentary form of "self-government" was practiced in Christian communities, but one would look in vain for any evidence of a just, efficient, and respectable state. These communities were retained by the conqueror as convenient means of farming out the various taxes, and the management of local affairs was entrusted to the prosperous landowners (*Kotchabashi*) —many of whom were as rapacious as the Turkish high functionaries. The Turkish administration showed no interest whatever in the welfare of the Christian subjects; it limited itself to the task of keeping them subservient and of collecting many onerous taxes, the worst of which was the notorious "child tribute." (Christian-born children of six or seven years of age were snatched from their parents, Moslemized, and enlisted in the Janissary troops.) As the process of decay penetrated deeper and deeper into the social and political body of the Turkish Empire, injustice, favoritism, arbitrary use of power, bribery, and deceit became the usual methods the higher officials, Moslems and Christians, employed in order to attain their selfish ends. In this atmosphere of dissoluteness the Greek people and its leaders received their first lesson in the "disciplined and democratic" way of living. The rights of the economically and politically weaker classes were disregarded since these latter were unable to organize and defend themselves against the encroachments of the "mighty." The official political agencies were disinclined to undertake a wholehearted protection of the masses or curtail the unjust rights of the privileged groups. Is it surprising that, even today, the general attitude of the citizens toward the state is that of distrust and unfriendliness,[37] since, even after the liberation, not all Greek governments lived up to the ideals of the modern welfare state?

Ioannis Capodistria, the first president of free Greece, realizing the tremendous difficulties he had to face, and understanding full well that a wholly democratic government, imposed on a country completely unprepared for this kind of regime, would at best be a parody of genuine democracy, tried to introduce a kind of "hierarchically centralized" administration, namely, a mild form of authoritarian rule. He was often severely criticized for his political views, but no careful and unprejudiced observer of social reality will fail to admit that certain stages in the evolution of politically immature nations justify just and "humane" dictatorial methods. The Greek people were by tradition undisciplined and atomistic. It must not be forgotten that a large proportion of people, during the Turkish rule, led a brigand-like life in the mountains, free of any state control and supervision. These were the legendary outlaws, the *armatoli* and the *klefts*, who, like so many Robin Hoods, defied the state and the orderly social life, and were living by plundering the Turks and occasionally wealthy Greek landowners.[38]

Some foreign observers have remarked that Greece has had statesmen, but no "state."[39] This observation is a gross exaggeration and it might be applied with some justification only to the period which preceded Capodistria's arrival in Greece and to the confusion that ensued after his assassination. No state, however primitive, can in the long run exist without a minimum of administrative functions, and Greece, even in her darkest days of the earlier period, had some rudimentary forms of political organization. It must, nevertheless, be admitted that the above statement about the "nonexistence" of a state in Greece might be considered correct if it means that the welfare of all citizens, regardless of their social status, has not always been the primary concern of the government, and that many statesmen have been unable to subordinate their party or group interests as well as their personal ambitions to the general weal. The Greek people could not always say that they were governed by a benevolent "service state," by a political organization that was "run by the majority for the interests of the totality" and not for the benefit of a few privileged groups.

Formally, of course, Greece has had a parliamentary system, but the development of the genuine democratic spirit and traditions was greatly impeded by the unfortunate tendencies bequeathed by the long period of unfree life. The common people, most of whom were illiterate peasants, were unable to take an intelligent and active part in the political life of the country. Thus, the management of public affairs fell into the hands of the influential military chiefs or to their families and to the *Phanariots** who were capable and highly educated, but who, because of their training in the corrupt political and social atmosphere of the Turkish capital could not always exercise a wholesome influence in the newly formed Greek state. These leading families (*tzakia*, from *tzaki*, meaning hearth, hence old and influential family) jealously kept for themselves the higher positions in every field of social life and the "new blood" had few chances, if any, of climbing the social ladder.[40] The fact that so many flagrant social evils (illiteracy, absence of sanitary organization in villages, etc.) have been tolerated for such a long time may perhaps find its partial explanation in undemocratic social selection. The leader of the newly formed National Radical Union, Mr. Karamanlis, who won in the last elections (February 19, 1956) and became prime minister, is an outstanding exception to the general rule, since he does not come from the privileged groups.

Greek political life is not devoid of paradoxes. One may witness, on the one hand, extremely democratic patterns, unknown even in countries with long parliamentary tradition, as for example, easy access to ministers of the state: every citizen, no matter how humble his social standing, has the right to present his case personally to the responsible minister. However, few important cases would be given favorable consideration on their own merit solely and without consideration of strong social or political

---

*From *Phanar*, the quarter around the premises of the Patriarchate at Constantinople, hence the Christian aristocratic residents of this quarter, who filled high posts in the Turkish administration.

influence. Until recently, centralistic and bureaucratic tendencies—vestiges from Byzantine times—hopelessly retarding the solution of urgent problems, were quite evident in the country. But, at the same time, centrifugal forces, the strong spirit of localism and private initiative, were by no means lacking. One would be puzzled at times by the disheartening indifference governments used to show to vital problems; at other times one would be struck, especially in exceptionally critical periods, by the able leaderships and organization, in the case, for example, of the rapid and efficient settlement of the thousands of refugees from Asia Minor.

Students of Greece have repeatedly pointed out that one of the characteristics of its social life has been the presence of many political parties and, with few exceptions, the fluidity of their guiding principles. Indeed, with the exception of the old Conservative (royalist) and Liberal (E. Venizelos) groups, the recently dissolved Rally of Papagos, and the Communist party (before it was outlawed) with its iron discipline and its consistent foreign-directed policy, most parties have been founded less on a clear-cut "ideology" than on the adherence to a political leader. This fact accounts for the frequent reshufflings of party memberships. In the last elections (February 19, 1956), this "fluidity" was amply proved by the readiness with which the conservative and the moderate parties, in order to face the new, dynamic opponent, Mr. Karamanlis, allied themselves with the extreme left. The principal parties in recent years have been the following:

National Radical Union (ERE) (moderate right). The strongest party of today. Leader, Mr. Karamanlis. The main bulk of its membership consists of the dissolved Rally party, but it is also joined by members of other groups.

Populist (conservative and royalist). Leader, Mr. Tsaldaris. Now no longer of any significance on the political scene.

Liberal. Leader, Mr. Papandreou. Formerly the Social Democratic party.

Liberal Democratic Union (FDE). Leader, Mr. S. Venizelos. The remnant of the once powerful liberal party led by his father, E. Venizelos.

Progressive. Leader, Mr. Markezini, who was once, as minister of coordination, one of the most dynamic members of the Rally party.

National Progressive Union of the Center (EPEK) (moderate center). Leader, Mr. Papapolitis. Party created in 1949 by the fusion of the followers of General Plastiras and Mr. Tsouderos (former liberal) who in 1951 joined the Rally and in 1956 the ERE.

Agrarian Labor party (moderate leftist). Leader, Mr. Mylonas, who was formerly an adherent of the Liberal party of E. Venizelos.

Democratic Party of Working People (Socialistic). Leaders, Mr. Kartalis and Mr. Svolos. Formed in 1953 by the merging of the Socialist ELD with a group of EPEK.

United Democratic party (EDA) (extreme left wing). Leader, Mr. Passalidis.

Communist party of Greece (KKE) now outlawed, but exerts its influence through EDA.

No one familiar with Greece will fail to observe that the absence of continuity, of consistent policies, of efficient "housekeeping," as well as the inability to conceive and to carry out long-term projects, have often been the unfortunate features of her political life. Although the statement about the paucity of prominent political leaders in modern Greece may to some extent be warranted by historic facts, it would be quite unfair to overlook the splendid efforts made by such outstanding statesmen as I. Capodistria (1776–1831), first president of Greece, "enlightened" conservative; C. Trikoupi (1832–85), liberal; E. Venizelos (1859–1936), liberal; I. Metaxas (1871–1940), royalist dictator who with his historic "No" (October 28, 1940) rejected Mussolini's outrageous demands; and Alexandros Papagos (1883–1955), leader of the Rally party. No impartial historian can deny the ability of these men and their sincere aspiration to better the lot of their countrymen. If their work did not always come to its full fruition, it was primarily due to successive wars, to adverse political constellations, to cultural lag, as well as to unforeseen natural catastrophes (like the two destructive earthquakes which ruined prosperous towns and villages within the three years of General Papagos' government).

In concluding this section, one must consider briefly what steps were taken by the Greek governments to improve the general living conditions of the population. Even though, because of unfavorable political and economical circumstances, as well as of other less important handicaps, constructive policies have not always been pursued consistently and systematically, considerable progress has been made in this direction since World War I, and especially after World War II. It may be mentioned in this connection that malaria fever, which formerly ravaged the country (and every year in rural districts alone meant the loss of 30–60 million wage-days) has now almost entirely disappeared.[41]

The governments were greatly assisted in the economic and welfare field by foreign agencies (Near East Relief, UNRRA, AMAG, ECA), by local communities, and by some powerful philanthropic organizations.

The Ministry of Welfare is, of course, mainly concerned with the welfare of the society in general, but the other ministries (National Economy, Labor, Public Health, Education) are responsible for the implementation of social welfare programs that come under their jurisdiction. Since industry in Greece began to develop only in the latter part of the nineteenth century, labor legislation is of recent date. Since 1909, when labor legislation was inaugurated, many beneficial laws have followed in rapid succession. As a member of the International Labor Organization, Greece, through the Ministry of Work (founded in 1935), follows the decisions of this institution on the maximum hours of labor, Sunday rest and holidays, minimum wages, hygienic conditions of work, employment of women and children.[42]

A semipublic agency, Ergatiki Estia (Workmen's Club) is responsible for furthering the welfare of laborers, by encouraging their cultural development, by organizing recreational opportunities, and by offering them other different facilities. In larger towns (Athens, Piraeus, Salonika, Volo, Cavalla) twenty-five placement offices for the unemployed function.

The rights of the working classes are further protected by the laws of 1935 and 1936. In case of disagreement in a certain occupational branch between the employers and the employed, the latter have the right to manifest their dissatisfaction by going on a "demonstration" strike. If, however, the issues of collective bargaining concern the working classes as a whole (for example, the determination of the minimum wage), resort to the arbitration committee is compulsory, and in this case its decisions are binding for both parties.

Social insurance in Greece, as in some other countries, had its origin in the efforts of private organizations (the first being founded in 1861) to secure, in case of accident, invalidism, or death, better protection for their members and those dependent on them. In 1934, by Law 6298, a special organization, IKA (Idryma Koinonikon Asfaliseon, i.e., Institute of Social Insurance), was instituted which made social security obligatory for all employed people who did not belong to any private insurance organization. IKA, although a semipublic agency, is placed under the auspices of the Ministry of Labor and now covers about 450,000 employed persons. There also exist, in addition, about 150 private funds which cover some 350,000 persons, as well as 800,000 members of families of insured persons. These private funds are permitted to function as separate units, but no new organization may be established (Law 6298). The state made repeated efforts to absorb all independent security funds in one great national institution, but so far opposition on the part of the private organizations, which secured for their members by far greater benefits, is so strong that nothing short of dictatorial measures can achieve this end. There are, unfortunately, some 2,300,000 people who are not yet protected by any security fund. To this class belong the persons employed in agriculture,[43] domestic work, and a few other occupations.

To protect family life, the state has worked out an extensive program for aid to dependent children (namely, children of men serving in the army, children of disabled breadwinners, and orphans) in their own homes or in the homes of relatives. The amount of assistance varies according to the category to which the children belong. In November 1950, over 37,900 such children were given assistance.[44]

There are 64 orphanages functioning in Greece, 30 of which are public and 34 state subsidized. There are 10 homes for foundlings, which care for some 1,200 children. Two of these institutions are state supported, while most of the others are run by municipalities.

Free breakfast (550 calories per day) is provided for school children between the ages of six and twelve years. In spite of the law providing for regular medical inspection, the health of school children, especially in the villages, is not sufficiently taken care of, because there is only one school doctor for every 10,000 school children.

There are 50 health centers, one in each region (*nomos*). In 1950 there were some 161 hospitals in the country, with a total bed capacity of 21,108. Of these, 93 were state hospitals and 68, although not public, were almost entirely under state control. Free hospitalization is provided to indigent persons in all state hospitals. A short time ago a new up-to-date lying-in hospital, the Alexandra—one of the best on the Continent—was established, which will accommodate some 300 patients. The poor are given free treatment.

These are splendid achievements, but the criticism on the part of some observers, that equal attention has not been given by the state to the health needs of the rural population, is not groundless.

The Family

As one passes from the primitive Greek villages with their medieval and oriental character to the cosmopolitan atmosphere of the larger towns, one will certainly not fail to notice the difference in the attitude of the members of the family toward one another, and the diversity of views regarding the position of women, the problems of marriage and divorce, and the relation of the sexes in general.

It would, indeed, be surprising if, considering the rapid transformation the country is undergoing,[45] it did not present a variety of social patterns and notions regarding such vital human problems. And yet, regardless of the cultural level of the community, a considerable uniformity, at least outward, is secured on matters immediately connected with legal and religious regulations (legal marriage age; degrees of relationships, natural or conventional; illegitimacy; and divorce).

Although the modern Greek family is patterned after the form prevalent in Western civilization, in rural communities and not infrequently in urban centers—particularly among the middle classes—one may still observe vestiges of patriarchal mores. For example, even grownup children approach parents or elders with great respect. Sons, on marrying, not infrequently bring their wives to the paternal home. The widow usually takes her husband's place in the household, and her daughters, especially the unmarried, her sons, and their wives show her due attention and respect and consult her on all important matters. The solidarity that binds close relatives, a typical patriarchal trait, is still the ruling principle in primitive Greek villages, although cases of family quarrels arising from property differences are not unknown, notably in villages which have already been affected by the individualistic tendencies of modern society. The dowry is still an important factor in contracting marriages, and the provident father quite early—sometimes right after the birth of a female child—begins to put aside a part of his earnings in order to secure a good marriage portion for his daughter. Although usually all the male members of the family cooperate in bringing about a successful match for each girl, the main burden of this obligation formerly fell upon the oldest brother, who assisted his father in case the latter was not well-to-do. When the head of the family died, the oldest son was expected to remain single until all the female members of the family were married. The inconveniences arising from such social patterns are quite evident, and perhaps the postponement of the marriage of the male members has been a cause of the sexual irregularities observed in some villages.

In recent years, owing to the gradual infiltration of Western ideas and to the occupational opportunities offered to women outside the home,[46] elder brothers are no longer required by the mores to delay their own marriage, nor are they willing to make a serious material contribution to their sisters at the expense of their own happiness and prosperity.

It would be wrong, however, to assume that because of the radical changes in Greek society the dowry ceased to be an important factor in matrimonial arrangements. Although there are already many young men who, in selecting a mate, stress other than financial considerations, the dowry still plays an important role, and a girl who has none to offer, in spite of an attractive appearance and intelligence, may not always be sure of finding a suitable mate easily.

Another survival from patriarchal times is the so-called "honor of the brother," a custom which imposes on him, or, if necessary, on another male member of the family, the obligation to murder his sister's lover, especially when the latter refuses to redress the wrong by marriage. Murders of this kind, it is true, are becoming rarer and rarer, and in upper and middle classes are now practically unknown; nevertheless, such drastic solutions are still occasionally reported in the daily papers. Although public sentiment, mostly in urban communities, is increasingly against such procedures, one is often surprised at the leniency with which the jury examines these cases.

In the villages, where girls are given very little freedom and have no opportunity to make important decisions, the arrangement of marriages lies in the hands of the parents. When the right young man is found—in these matters they usually use the services of professional matchmakers (*proxenitis* or *proxenitria*)—the parents of the prospective couple proceed to the settlement of the economic side of the match, which occasionally assumes the unedifying form of commercial bargaining, the final settlement of which is officially confirmed at the notary's.

In spite of the fact that in the villages the young girls are very closely watched by the older folk, love marriages do occur. Such marriages are, of course, of frequent occurrence in bigger towns, where—especially since World War II—young people find many opportunities to meet one another and to take the responsibility of their action almost entirely upon themselves.

In no country of Western civilization, no matter how advanced, has the problem of the relation of the sexes found a wholly satisfactory solution. In societies like that in Greece, in which the institution of the family has not been completely readjusted to modern conditions of life, these problems often assume a tragic aspect. Modern Greek youth in urban communities are given greater freedom, but no guidance. Boys and girls are exposed to all kinds of temptations, but are very inadequately equipped to face reality. Confusion regarding sex problems is prevalent: patriarchal notions about sex and women versus up-to-date ideas about sex expression; frank admission of the Freudian libido theory versus persistence of the double standard of sex morality. Parents very seldom are in a position to show real understanding of the problems of youth. The two generations are frequently separated by an unbridged gap. Most parents would still frown upon an open and intelligent discussion of sex and kindred problems. The young people have few chances of obtaining wholesome information. In spite of the seriousness of the situation, the sociologist would look in vain for definite data regarding sex problems. Greek society is still playing the ostrich game in these matters. There are no exact statistics to be found regarding divorces, sex aberrations, and illegitimacy.

One of the peculiar features of modern Greek society is the fact that, while greater occupational, educational, and social opportunities are offered to women, oriental attitudes regarding the female sex and antiquated ideas about its inherent—biologic and mental—inferiority still persists. In villages, of course, women hold, as a rule, inferior positions in all departments of social life. The mother is highly respected, the sister protected, but otherwise, women are excluded from any participation in village public affairs. Women do not appear in the village coffeehouse alone, and in some more conservative rural homes women serve the meals, but do not sit at table when male strangers are entertained. At family celebrations (marriage, baptism, and the like), however, and on great holidays, separation of the sexes is not very strictly observed, and the young people may dance in the public square under the approving supervision of the older folk.

The double standard is still prevalent in both rural and urban communities. Society winks at the premarital and even postmarital freedom of the male. But public opinion is very severe—although less so in great urban centers—toward the moral misconduct of a woman. One frequently reads in the papers of an aberrant wife being killed by the wronged husband, or by some other male member of either family; for, not only the husband's family but also that of the wife feels "dishonored" by the woman's misconduct.

The growing number of illegitimate children—even in the rural districts, in spite of the rigid social patterns—and of divorces now being granted on the ground of the infidelity of the wife are unmistakable indications that

Greek society is undergoing a radical transformation. In some circles, fortunately very limited, where the models of certain French novels are readily adopted and the Freudian theory is highly welcome, infidelity in marriage, on the part of man or woman, is considered a mark of progressive mentality. However, an increasingly greater number of the younger generation has been able to outgrow some of the older as well as the "ultramodern" notions, and has come to consider the relation of the sexes as a wholesome and sincere comradeship.

The two world wars, the influx of a million and a half Greek refugees from Asia Minor, Caucasus, and South Russia effected great changes in the status of women. One hears less and less frequently the statement that the only fitting career for a woman is marriage, although the opinion that the unmarried woman is a "social failure," worthy of pity, has not yet altogether disappeared, even in urban communities. Society offers now many occupational opportunities to women. According to recent statistical reports (1955), in addition to the 1,085,000 women who were engaged in agricultural pursuits, some 170,000 are now employed in different industrial establishments, 31,000 in public services, 45,000 in commercial enterprises, and 69,000 are occupied in other branches.[47] The old-fashioned prejudice that education beyond the acquisition of socially approved skills —sewing, embroidery, weaving, cooking, and (in towns) the mastering of one or two foreign languages, or learning how to play the piano—is superfluous for girls has become a thing of the past.

Since 1890, when the first woman had the courage, in spite of severe criticism and general ridicule, to register at the University of Athens, all higher educational institutions have been admitting an increasingly greater number of girls. Women in Greece have been slowly but steadily acquiring greater and greater social, economic, and political rights, until finally a law passed in the National Assembly on May 28, 1955, extended to them political equality. There still are certain deeply rooted prejudices to overcome, but when the legal foundations are laid, progress is inevitable and rapid.

Religion

In discussing the religious situation of culturally retarded peoples, one must be prepared to find not one "religion," but many "religions." In the same religious community one may discern several different levels of belief. It has already been pointed out in a previous section that the cultural difference between the classes is very great. Should it then be surprising if the content of religious ideas and the quality and intensity of religious emotions presented a considerable variety?

In Greek society one may distinguish the official religious institution—the Greek Orthodox Church—whose dogma, the product of a long evolution, is based on interpretation of the Scriptures and tradition. Religious views of the uneducated masses, however, present a peculiar mixture of Christian teaching and superstitions. The beliefs of these simple folk consist, to no small extent, of a blind observance of customs and rites, some of which date from classical antiquity, while others have probably been borrowed from the neighboring peoples. The religious attitude of the great bulk of the townspeople, on the other hand, is considerably different, since the spiritual content of the Scriptures is accessible to them;* while they also observe, more or less faithfully, the outward forms imposed on them by the Orthodox Church (e.g., fasting on certain days of the year) and perform symbolic practices (e.g., making the sign of the cross, kissing the holy images, lighting candles in churches), they are, nevertheless, free of the magical conceptions which constitute such a prominent feature of the peasant's spiritual world. Finally, one may distinguish the religious notions of the "intelligentsia," a class to which belong quite a number of scholars, thinkers, men of letters, students of higher educational institutions, and people who think it fashionable to play the intellectual. Here are mingled all the shadings from "pure," abstract deism to agnosticism, skepticism, or even outright denial; communist ideas about religion being the "opiate of the people" are no less common here than mystical tendencies and pantheistic leanings.

The Greek Orthodox Church, whose doctrine is formulated in the Nicaean creed (first stated in 325 A.D. and reaffirmed by the first Council of Constantinople), recognizes, as does the Roman Catholic Church, seven sacraments (Baptism, Confirmation, Holy Eucharist, Penance, Holy Orders, Matrimony, and Extreme Unction). Celibacy is required only of the higher clergy, but a widowed priest cannot marry a second time.

Since the decisions of the ecumenical councils are considered to be divinely inspired, they are unalterable in their essence; therefore, no radical changes may be introduced until another ecumenical council is convoked. This explains why the religious situation today is pretty much the same as

* The Scriptures are written in an ancient dialect which only the educated people fully understand.

it was in the eighth century (the last ecumenical council took place in 787 A.D.). Every attempt, consequently, on the part of progressive religious heads to introduce certain reforms or innovations (for example, translation of the Bible, introduction of organ music,[48] simplification of priestly garments) has been consistently discouraged. One may still meet people, both clergymen and laymen, who refuse to accept the "new" style of reckoning and stubbornly cling to the old (Julian) calendar.

The political and social events of the last decades did not pass without leaving profound traces in the minds of the people. The trying experiences of two world wars; the acquaintance with the manners and ways of thinking of foreigners, friends and foes, who came to Greece; the increasing number of Greek youth who had the privilege of studying abroad—all tended to broaden the mental horizon of the thinking Greek public. The articles on the religious situation of modern Greece that fill the columns of the more serious dailies of all political shadings indicate clearly that public feeling is becoming ripe for thoroughgoing church reforms.

The Greek Orthodox Church has always occupied a peculiar position in the minds of the people. When the Byzantine Empire ceased to exist as an independent political unit (1453), the astute conquerer Mohamed II, seeking to avoid political complications with the West, granted to his Christian subjects considerable religious freedom and raised the Patriarch to almost royal dignity. Thus the Patriarch was not only the supreme head of the Church, but also the political representative of the Christian subjects and the leader of the Greek nation (*Ethnarch*). It was owing to this arrangement that the Greek nation was able to survive. It is no wonder that Church and nation came to represent in the minds of the people one undivided entity, and even now, when in the face of outside danger people take up arms and fight, they give their lives for "fatherland and faith" (*yper pisteos kai patridos*).

After the formation of the Greek kingdom, the religious and political authorities felt that it was desirable, if not necessary, that the Church within the new borders should become independent of the Patriarch of Constantinople. This decision was well justified, for many inconveniences and political frictions were likely to arise, owing to the fact that the Patriarch resided on Turkish soil, and was considered as a functionary of the Ottoman Empire. Accordingly, in 1833 the Church of Greece was declared "autocephalous" and was henceforth to be governed by a Holy Synod, consisting of five ecclesiastics and a royal commissioner representing the king, who was declared supreme head of the Church. The constitution of 1844 confirmed this decision, but it recognized that an "inseparable dogmatic union" existed between the Church of Greece and "the Great Church in Constantinople."[49] The official relations between the two churches began in 1850 when the Patriarch issued a "Synodal Tome" recognizing the Holy Synod of the Greek Kingdom with the Metropolitan of Athens (now styled Archbishop of Athens and of all Greece) as its president. The sacred oil for anointing is still provided by the Great Church in Constantinople.

During the Turkish domination the Church concentrated in its hands many political and civil functions. It not only administered to the religious needs of the people, but also, insofar as circumstances permitted, cared for their education and for their welfare in general, since no other state agencies existed that could relieve the suffering of the sick, protect the debtor, the widow, and the orphan. In spite of all shortcomings and failures, the Church was the only bright point in the lives of people who were under a heavy yoke, full of misery and uncertainty. But perhaps the greatest service that the Church rendered to the Greek nation was that it helped the people retain the faith of their fathers and thus keep their nationality. Above all, it kept alive their hope in the regeneration of the nation sometime in the future. The records of history are filled with the names of bishops and parish priests who defended the faith of the people and sacrificed their lives for national independence. During the War of Liberation, the priests not only held the cross with which they encouraged the fighters, but also the gun which they handled no less skillfully than the experienced warriors.

When the nation won its freedom, the Church began to concentrate its attention once more on primarily religious and welfare duties. Although most of the estates owned by the Church were expropriated by the law of 1930, it still possesses considerable wealth, acquired mainly from generous donations of religious and philanthropic people. These funds are used for welfare purposes (maintenance of orphanages, asylums for the aged, support of widows and the poor), as well as for promoting religious education of the youth and of the public in general (the Sunday school system, religious organizations and publications).

The education of the Greek clergy has been one of the serious ecclesiastical problems since the foundation of the free state. As mentioned above, during the enslavement the cultural level of the people was so low that even the intellectual regeneration of the eighteenth century was unable to effect marked improvements. The monasteries, once seats of learning, were now mostly peopled by ignorant and superstitious monks. Maurer, the viceroy of the Othonian dynasty, stated that among 1,000 priests only 10 were able to write their names.[50] Capodistria, realizing the important role the clergy played in Greek society, established the first ecclesiastical seminary at the monastery of Poros in 1830. This marked the beginning of the many subsequent efforts to raise the educational level of the lower clergy. Higher religious instruction is now given at the theological school in Athens, founded in 1837. In addition, since 1843 many theological seminaries have been established in the larger towns, the most important being the Rhizareios School of Athens, so called from its founders, the wealthy Epirote patriots. A number of minor seminaries give elementary theological training to the graduates of the primary schools who intend to become village priests.

It is also generally felt that, besides education, greater attention must be given to the economic problems of the lower clergy, if it is to be raised to a more dignified position in Greek society. The salaries, paid from a special Ecclesiastical Fund, are very low. The salary of the lowest ecclesiastical rank is 700 dr. a month ($23.30), and of the highest 1,420 dr. ($47.30). In richer towns the priests get extra fees for performing religious ceremonies and rites (marriages, baptisms, funerals, extreme unction, and the like). In the villages, however, where the parishioners are so poor that the priests have few chances of getting these extra fees, they are obliged to work in the fields, do some carpentry, or perform any other work, except commerce, in order to be able to support themselves and their families. The improvement of the economic status of the clergy will certainly contribute to the elimination of certain evils, which little accord with the religious spirit, and will raise this class to the dignified position it deserves.

Just a few words must be said about monastic life, which is gradually disappearing. In Byzantine times and during the Turkish domination the monasteries were important religious, cultural, and welfare centers, but after the beginning of the nineteenth century their influence and importance began to decline, so that it is not surprising that the government of the new state suppressed in 1821 more than 300 small monasteries and secularized their revenues. In 1833 there still were 563 monasteries with 3,000 monks and 18 nunneries with 277 nuns. The number of the monasteries does not now exceed 170 with 1,600 inmates, and 4 nunneries with 250 nuns. In 1926 the Holy Synod decided that the monastic system should be discouraged and that no new monasteries should be established. There are few people who are willing today to retire into the monastery, and this change in the people's thinking accounts for the rapid depopulation of these religious institutions and for the small interest the public in general shows in them. It is true, however, that some important monasteries like Megaspeleon, Lavra (where the standard of the Revolution of 1821 was unfurled), Meteora, and Mt. Athos still attract a few genuine hermits who are determined to withdraw from worldly affairs, as well as scholars, archaeologists, and artists, who visit these places for their incalculable historic treasures, their historic associations, and their exceptional natural location.

Education

It is an irony of history that a people which had produced one of the greatest cultures should gradually sink into "the darkest night of ignorance" (sixteenth and seventeenth centuries). The Greeks have always been noted for their zeal for learning. Professor William Miller, an authority on the Near East, writes: "There is probably no people so keen about learning as the Greeks, letters are for them a sign of distinction, an unlettered man is a term of contempt." And yet in spite of the keen intelligence of the average Greek, in spite of his inquisitive spirit and "great love for book learning," the percentage of illiteracy in this country is still very high. According to the unpublished official census of 1951, there were 2,450,714 illiterate people—some 32.1 per cent of the entire population that could neither write nor read.

Several causes contributed to the gradual decline of the nation; but one of the chief ones, undoubtedly, was the long servitude under a conqueror who had no inclination for cultural achievements because his interests were absorbed by military pursuits. The cultural decline was accelerated by the murder of many scholars and learned men who fell into the hands of invading troops, as well as by the flight of many representatives of Greek culture to the West before and after the fall of Constantinople. In the course of time the masses were plunged into "intellectual slumber"[51] and the knowledge of letters became the privilege of some clergymen and wealthy functionaries who were serving the Turkish master.

During the eighteenth century and especially after the beginning of the nineteenth century, there was an intellectual awakening. Earnest efforts were made by wealthy and patriotic Greeks residing abroad to establish schools in order to combat widespread ignorance. No great improvement could be expected, since these endeavors were private, uncoordinated, and unsystematic. The provisional governments of the Liberation War (1821–29) tried to introduce compulsory primary education, but the social conditions were so chaotic that these measures remained paper decrees.

The chief concern of King Otto and his Bavarian advisers, who were invited to rule the young nation, was to organize the educational system. Unfortunately, they had but vague knowledge of local conditions, and in working out their ambitious projects they followed foreign models that were little suited to Greek reality. The law of 1834 requiring all children who had completed their sixth year of age to attend free primary schools for seven years, and charging the community administration (*demoi*) to maintain the schools and appoint the teachers, was not a success. Such a law, certainly, could not function easily since all the necessary prerequisites were lacking. The land was devastated, few villages could offer a school building, the treasuries of many communes were empty, while the administration of local affairs lay mostly in the hands of conservative, ignorant, and inexperienced committees. Even in subsequent periods compulsory primary education has never been consistently and generally enforced, in spite of a long series of reforms (1899, 1912, 1929, etc.). This is true not only in remote and isolated villages, but even in larger urban centers.

Secondary education did not fare much better. In 1837 a law was published regulating the middle schools, which were supposed to serve a double purpose: to impart general knowledge and to prepare for superior schools those who intended to continue their education. The curriculum of the secondary schools, which was imposed by the Ministry of Education, was not well balanced. Too much emphasis was laid on formal instruction of the classics (a method of teaching still common) while much less attention was paid to practical information.

The University of Athens was founded in 1837, but following the medieval tradition it had only four schools: theology, philosophy, law, and medicine. Later, however (in 1901), certain branches separated from the old schools and functioned independently. Sometime after the annexation of Macedonia and Thrace, the responsible authorities thought it expedient to establish another university in the capital of Macedonia, Salonika (1925).

Industry and commerce, which had made steady progress since the latter part of the nineteenth century, created a great need for practical education, and in 1887 the Superior Technical School was founded in Athens, one of the few superior educational institutions in this country; it ranks high, even if judged by western European academic standards. In order to satisfy the growing demand for well-trained specialists in different fields of social life, a number of superior schools sprang up in rapid succession. The Superior School of Commercial and Economic Studies (1920); the Superior School of Agriculture (1920), later transferred from Athens to Salonika, the main center of an important agricultural region; the School of Advanced Industrial Studies (1938); and finally, the Superior School of Political Studies (1938), chiefly attended by public officials who wish to acquire a thorough knowledge of civil administration and of politics.

Since the public schools did not respond adequately to the growing demand for good education, many private establishments of preschool, primary, and secondary level began to appear in the larger towns. The number of these private institutions appreciably increased, especially after 1860. Professional schools, night schools, and foreign (American, French, English, and before World War II, German and Italian) lyceums or academies were founded at different times in the more important urban centers and attracted a great many young men and women. All private and foreign schools, of course, were subject to the Ministry of Education and had to follow the general regulations. Nevertheless, the quality of instruction they offered was, as a rule, much better than that in the public schools, for these establishments—possessing greater economic means—could buy more adequate equipment, engage better paid teachers, and apply more up-to-date methods. Those foreign schools that offer specialized instruction beyond the high-school level enjoy greater academic autonomy in the subjects taught and in the choice of the teaching staff. In certain parts of the country there are special schools for the national minorities (Armenian, Jewish, and Moslem), which are granted by the state certain privileges and may give a part of the instruction in their respective vernaculars.

Although one of the most serious problems that Greece had to face before and after the liberation was the absence of qualified teachers, no measures were taken before 1880 to remedy the situation. Both primary and secondary school teachers were appointed without their having had even elementary pedagogical training, and it was only after 1910 that some teachers' seminaries were founded and a permanent chair of pedagogy was established at the University of Athens. In spite of this improvement, there still were in 1928 some 5,000 primary school teachers out of 12,000 who had not attended the teachers' seminary.[52] Since 1929—the year inaugurating thoroughgoing reforms in education—drastic measures have been taken to improve the quality of the teaching staff. Women teachers intended for the "kindergartens," after the completion of their primary education, have to go through a special four-year pedagogical course. Academies for primary school teachers were founded in 1934. There are now fourteen such academies in the principal towns of the country and they provide training for 3,000 students.[53] The teachers intended for the secondary schools are required to complete the four-year university course.

One must acknowledge the efforts made by different ministers to raise the educational system to a higher level, and recognize the improvements already achieved. Of course, no one would dare ignore the problems that still await solution. Serious periodicals and daily papers abound with articles criticizing the evils that have not yet been removed. The roots of some defects and abuses may be sought in the vestiges of long servitude—as was mentioned above—in wars, civil conflicts, economic crises, and natural catastrophes; but also bad "social selection" must be considered one of the serious causes that retarded educational development. People of ability, people who were broad-minded enough to grasp the significance of the educational problems, were not always entrusted with the responsible positions. Besides, the Ministry of Education was not regarded as of "primary" importance; few capable statesmen "condescended" to accept this post.

As late as 1896, the tenure of the teacher was not permanent; political influence and favoritism, not ability, experience, and academic qualifications, determined appointments and dismissals. Any change in the government and the consequent shift of the power of the parties resulted in considerable disorder in the composition of school personnel.

Another serious drawback has been the shortage of teachers. Bulgaria, Greece's Balkan neighbor, whose population in 1929 amounted to 5,000,000, had 17,000 primary school teachers. In that year Greece with a population of 6,200,000 could boast only 12,000 elementary teachers. Although no marked changes in the population of these two countries were noted, Bulgaria had in 1936 some 27,000 primary school teachers, while the official figures for Greece were 19,000 teachers for this school level. A high functionary of the Ministry of Education stated that in order to secure satisfactory results in the primary educational system, Greece actually needed at least 25,000 teachers.[54]

The teachers of both primary and secondary schools have not been fairly treated by the postwar governments. They were very poorly paid and in spite of the importance of their profession, they were placed in the low rank of the social hierarchy. The services of many other occupational branches are much better rewarded. This irregularity is probably due to the fact that the teachers' unions are politically weaker than those of other professions. No due consideration has been given to the unfavorable circumstances under which teachers, especially of primary schools, have to work. The classes in most public schools are very large. Many villages are cut off from regular contact with the rest of the country, so that the teachers serving in these isolated districts are deprived of every cultural advantage (daily paper, radio, library, legitimate amusement) which their more fortunate colleagues in towns enjoy. In order to combat illiteracy the government required (by the law of January 1955) all village primary school teachers to give, in addition to their regular daily routine, special evening courses (from 6 to 9 P.M.) to boys and girls who had not attended school. The teachers are not paid for this extra task. These village teachers are, indeed, the anonymous heroes of the nation, for, although underpaid, they go on laying the foundations of a better society in the future. And to the teacher as well as to the priest do the poor villagers, who have been neglected by the "official" state, turn for the solution of their problems.

The shortage of good school buildings is another acute problem in Greece. In recent years a number of up-to-date schools have been constructed, but there have always been fewer buildings than needed to accommodate the growing number of students. Many buildings are entirely neglected and are quite dilapidated.[55] This deplorable state should not be attributed in every case to the negligence of responsible authorities, for in times of stress these buildings had to be requisitioned, now to house thousands of refugees, now to billet the troops of friend and foe, and now to hospitalize the victims of wars and civil conflicts. The shortage of school buildings has inevitably resulted in overcrowded classes (120–160 pupils), lack of playgrounds, and what is worse, illiteracy.

The country needs 10,000 kindergartens to give adequate training to preschool-age children, but actually only some 881 have been able to function normally. According to official data, in 1954 the number of state-owned elementary schools was 9,026 with 90,000 pupils. Of these schools 5,000 had only one teacher for all six grades, that is, the instructor divided his working day into three parts and met the children in three groups (first and second class together, then third and fourth grade, and finally fifth and sixth) for two hours each. The quality of education resulting from such a system needs no comment. Only a relatively small percentage (according to some calculations, 5 per cent) of schools could afford the luxury of having six teachers, one for each class separately. It is maintained that there still are some 2,800 communities, comprising 200,000 people, with no schools at all. According to official data, in 1954 there were also 420 private elementary schools with 37,000 pupils.

The secondary schools are called by the traditional name "gymnasia." In 1954 there were 280 gymnasia subsidized by the Greek state with 184,000 students, and 153 private gymnasia with an enrollment of 23,000 students. For the benefit of students who had to work, there were 15 public and 18 private night secondary education establishments.[56]

Few schools, primary or secondary, are adequately equipped. If the reports are valid, only 106 gymnasia own a library, and only 52 offer laboratory facilities to their students. This condition, tragic as it is in itself, is further aggravated by two important factors: the language and the curriculum. The students are obliged to concentrate their attention on three varieties of Greek: the ancient (with its different dialects), the "purist" (i.e., the official), and the popular, the modern everyday language. Even a cursory examination of the entrance examination papers of the candidates for the superior schools convinces one of the confusion which results from the peculiar language situation.[57]

The curriculum of all school levels is mostly antiquated, and needs considerable revision. Enormous emphasis is laid on the formal aspects of the language (grammar and syntax) at the expense of content, so that the students have little chance to appreciate the beauty and the cultural wealth of Greek classic literature. Neither do practical aspects of modern life receive due consideration.[58] History and—even more so—geography are taught very inadequately. Civics forms a part of the curriculum in very few schools. Vocational training is only now beginning to occupy the attention of competent authorities. The textbooks leave much to be desired. They are as a rule unattractive and treat the subject matter in a dry and uninteresting manner, and, what is worse, they are not always free of errors or of out-dated information. The school authorities have no freedom in selecting their textbooks, for all schools have to use the same textbooks selected by a special committee and approved by the Ministry of Education.

GREECE

A country like Greece, which abounds in vestiges of classical and Byzantine culture, should have been a source of inspiration and emulation to the younger generations; unfortunately, however, owing to many untoward circumstances, it has not been possible to create the proper cultural atmosphere for the masses of people. There are few libraries accessible to the general public that have been systematically kept up to date and enriched.[59] No scholar who specializes in sciences like economics, anthropology, biology, psychology, or sociology can do serious research work or make a valuable contribution to science if he has to depend on local libraries.

This disheartening situation is to some extent relieved by the efforts of private or semipublic agencies to encourage learning. The Academy of Athens encourages research in different fields by awarding generous prizes. Wealthy people (for example, Marazli) or associations have undertaken the publications of popular and scientific works. Another bright spot in Greek cultural life is the various learned societies (the Archaeological Association, the Medical Association of Athens, the Historic and Ethnologic Association, the Byzantine Society, the Medical and Surgical Association, the Society of Psychic Research, and many others), some of which have a long tradition and are a convincing proof that the longing of the Greek for intellectual achievements has been kept alive all through the centuries, in spite of enormous difficulties and drawbacks.

The Arts

There have been two great incentives to artistic creation in Greece: the models of classic art and Greek nature. It would, indeed, be surprising if the people, in spite of widespread poverty, did not feel an imperative urge to produce objects of beauty with these models all around them.

The long servitude interrupted the normal evolution of artistic expression. Byzantine religious art (mostly fresco and mosaic) and the traditions of church architecture, which reached its peak achievement in the cathedral of St. Sophia of Constantinople, were cut short when the new masters not only prohibited the construction of new churches but also the repair of old ones. From this period no glorious monuments, no magnificent churches or palaces could be erected. But the artistic spirit of the Greek people did not die; it only became less conspicuous and continued its activity "underground." It manifested itself in iconography, which, following faithfully the Byzantine patterns, was diligently carried on in the monasteries until the latter part of the sixteenth century, mostly by anonymous monks. It manifested itself also in popular art, which reproduced in endless variations classic and Byzantine motifs on garments and objects of everyday use; in folk poetry, some roots of which may be traced to the Homeric period; and, finally, in popular songs, which glorified the exploits of the prerevolutionary mountain rebels *(Kleftica)* or expressed the aspirations of the nation and the hopes in the future revival of the Greek state.

Modern painting first made its appearance in the Ionian islands, and since they were a Venetian possession until the end of the eighteenth century, many young Greeks studied art in Italy. Although these artists were influenced by Italian traditions and techniques, they did not forget their country and usually depicted different aspects of Greek everyday life. Great impetus was given to artistic development when King Otto and his Bavarian advisers established the School of Art at Athens (1836). The most promising graduates of this academy completed their art training in the then flourishing artistic center of Munich. To this generation belong some names of European renown — Nikif, Lytras, Ghyzis, Jakobidis, Volonakis. As contact with western Europe became more regular, different artistic tendencies (impressionism, symbolism, realism, expressionism, and futurism) exercised considerable influence on Greek painting. One may in general say that in the earlier period of Greek art the main interest lay in historic scenes, in portraits, and in "genre"; in our day, on the contrary, this type of artistic creation occupies a minor place, while the interest in landscape painting is predominant. Bold attempts to open new horizons to artistic expression may be observed in the works of some artists (Parthenis, Gounaropoulos, Hadjikyriakos-Ghikas, Bouzanis), but it must be said — to the honor of modern Greek painting and sculpture — that extravagant modernism and pathological artistic aberrations have so far found little appeal in the land of classic traditions.

In architecture, with only few notable exceptions, achievements have been less remarkable. In the Ionian islands one can easily distinguish the influence of the baroque; in the capital many public buildings and mansions of wealthy people betray the traces of neoclassicism or pseudoclassicism, while most of the new churches are imitations — frequently quite "unorthodox" — of Byzantine models. After World War I, huge apartment houses sprang up in great number in the larger towns. These huge structures, mostly influenced by nondescript Western styles, satisfy more the practical demands of life than the artistic taste of the descendants of

Phidias. It is only in the islands of the Aegean that one may enjoy the sight of original specimens of modern Greek architecture, the so-called island architecture, in the low, flat-roofed, invariably whitewashed private houses, or in the vaulted churches or chapels with their detached bulky belfries.

In music Greece has not yet found her Bach. Since our knowledge of classic and Byzantine music is still imperfect, scholars are uncertain as to how much popular songs and church psalms reflect the genuine classic or Byzantine tradition, and how much has been adulterated by Turkish and Oriental influences. Many of the earlier Greek composers and musicians assimilated Italian operatic traditions; the later generations have been considerably influenced by the French schools, so that much of modern Greek music is really west European in character. Dimitri Mitropoulos, who has now become prominent in American musical circles, has composed "classic" music to accompany the performance of ancient Greek dramas. This composer as well as some other musicians (Kalomiris, Petrides, Scalkotas) has made notable efforts to write "Greek" music, but it seems (unless the future generations have different criteria of appreciation) that Greece has not yet been able to produce music of permanent value.

The Ionian poets and writers were the pioneers of modern Greek literature until 1888, when the Athenian school of literature emerged and formed the second stage in the rebirth of Greek letters. The Ionian Islands produced a whole pleiad of prose writers as well as of satiric, lyric, and epic poets. The most famous poet of this group was Solomos (1798–1857), whose *Hymn to Liberty* (put to music by the Corfiot composer Mantzaros) became the national anthem of Greece. Since then literary production has been rich and varied. It is, of course, impossible to do justice to this significant achievement of the Greek spirit, but even a brief account should not fail to mention some outstanding poets and writers, like Palamas, Kavafis, Sykellianos, and Kazatzakis, whose names have become familiar in literary circles beyond the narrow limits of their native country, for their works were translated into more than one European language.

Recreation

In spite of great poverty and frequent frustrations, the Greeks, no less than other peoples, like to relax and amuse themselves. Recreational opportunities differ greatly. The capital, with its cosmopolitan character, offers almost everything that one could expect to find in any big city of western Europe and America. All tastes may find gratification; for, during the winter season especially, there are concerts of local and foreign artists, lectures, art exhibits, sports, athletic shows, horse races, cabarets, and so on. Summer and winter the theaters present a varied repertory from classic, foreign, and modern Greek literature. The light satirical reviews are well attended, but the fact that well-staged serious dramas attract numerous audiences shows that the capital has acquired a select and cultivated public capable of appreciating good art. Unfortunately, no other town in Greece, not even Salonika, the capital of a wealthy district, has a permanent theater. It is only when Athenian troupes go on tours that the inhabitants of the provincial towns have the opportunity to enjoy a good play. Corfu and Zante once formed an exception. Before World War I, these island towns possessed their own opera houses, where, following the musical traditions of their former masters, the Venetians, they could entertain their inhabitants by offering them Italian operas. The wealthier families owned their boxes or hired them for the winter season.

The cinema, of course, is a common feature in every Greek town and it is practically the only organized entertainment. The picture halls, where one may see American wild west movies as well as the best productions of the sixth art, are always overcrowded. Both in the provincial towns and in the capital, American films of the light revue type, with an abundance of dancing and singing of modern airs, are exceedingly popular with the younger generation.

Another common feature is the pastry shop, which is something like the American cafeteria, with the difference that the people who frequent it, mostly in the afternoons and evenings, stay for hours and gossip or engage in more serious conversation over a cake or a cup of coffee. Such establishments serve also as a trysting place for young couples, at least in larger towns.

In very small villages where there is only one coffeehouse it is patronized by the male members of the village, regardless of age, although usually the younger people out of respect do not mingle with older men. In more sizable villages which boast two or more such establishments, often different age groups frequent different shops. In towns, especially the larger ones, the class and occupational differentiations are more clearly reflected in the clientele of the cafes, the most fashionable of which serve also as pastry shops. Some are more exclusive and attract people of the well-to-do classes. Others are less pretentious and consequently more democratic, and are frequented by the representatives of the middle and lower classes. A number of such establishments also serve as the "traditional" meeting places of some groups—for example, public officials, pensioners, veterans, or artisans.

The coffeehouse is an important institution in Greek social life, for it serves many purposes. It satisfies man's craving for fellowship. There may be found a welcome shelter when one wants to escape from the monotony of home; one may discuss important business projects, sign a contract, scrutinize a prospective employer or workman; one may spend a whole afternoon or evening reading all the daily papers kept at the coffeehouse and satisfy one's political instincts. The coffeehouse is a kind of unofficial parliament where the Greek highly interested in politics may air his political views, criticize governmental measures, offer his opinions on international politics, or even suggest panaceas that would save the world from misery and suffering. Some customers prefer to play cards, chess, or tric-trac. These people usually play purely for pleasure, or for a cup of coffee, or a glass of *ouzo* (an alcoholic drink). The Greek, however, is a gambler rather than a drinker. One sees very few pubs and very seldom drunken people. It is a tradition in this country not to take alcoholic drinks without some *meze* (sour cucumber, cheese, salami, etc.). Card playing has become very fashionable, and wealthy ladies organize afternoon bridge parties from which some depart with lighter purses.

The Greek is fond of music, although neither his voice nor his musical talent may equal the accomplishments of his Italian neighbor. Since the radio is accessible to the average townsman, use of this feature of modern life has become widespread. Many coffeehouses, restaurants, and other establishments entertain their customers by switching on programs from local and foreign stations. Not infrequently a passer-by may hear popular airs emerging from the radio of a kiosk or of a parked taxicab. Television is still quite unknown.

The only entertainment which the villagers indulge in is singing and dancing—on special occasions. No engagement, marriage, or baptism is celebrated without due tribute paid to the muses of music and of dance, and, to a lesser extent, to Bacchus.

In the last decades a wholesome interest in sports, athletic pursuits, and outings has been observed. Greek climate greatly encourages open-air life and, fortunately, the taste for vigorous exercise and long excursions, which are now very efficiently organized by many associations, is becoming quite general. Traveling abroad is also becoming fashionable, and, thanks to the good service of many tourist offices, not only the well-to-do people may enjoy a two- or three-week visit to a foreign country. One may only hope that greater facilities will be offered to the peasant folk, so that they may also acquire an interest in things beyond the narrow bounds of their village world.

Social Movements and Ideological Organizations

Many threads connect every phase of modern Greek society with the culture of the past, but the awareness of these connections and of their significance has been but slowly becoming common. The cultural trends coming from the West usually failed to take deep roots, as the masses, but a few decades ago awakened from "intellectual slumber," remained on the whole unaffected by cultural "subtleties," while the intelligentsia, constituting a thin social layer, had no real influence on the average citizen. The interests that could stir the general public and lead to mass movements were elemental, emotionally tinged, and centered around such idea-complexes as "nation," "national language," "national religion," or "social justice."

The "Megali Idea" was one of the most powerful influences that activated Greek society until after the end of World War I. It had both a political and a religious background and it contained realistic as well as utopian elements; as a typical expression of nineteenth-century Irredentism, it strove to free the "enslaved" brethren; as a romantic ambition, it aspired to revive the Byzantine Empire and to replace the crescent by the cross on the dome of St. Sophia, the symbol of eastern Christianity. The magic appeal of this Idea was general: it was the slogan of all classes and political parties; it kindled the imagination of the older generations and of youth; it filled with enthusiasm the erudite scholar, and the poet no less than the simple peasant.

The origin of the Megali Idea goes back to the fall of Constantinople (1453). Immediately after this national catastrophe many legends began to circulate among the subject people, promising a miraculous rebirth of the nation. These mythically founded prophecies of national regeneration acquired flesh and blood after the restoration of the Greek state.

The Great Idea became a great social force and (although in the hands of unscrupulous demagogues and chauvinistic organizations it exercised a baneful influence) it offered to the young people an ideal to work for, and moved some of the ablest statesmen (Trikoupis, Venizelos) to introduce far-reaching social reforms.

The social significance of the Megali Idea may be more adequately appraised if one compares it with postwar developments. The new political climate deprived the Great Idea of its fundamental reality and left a great void in Greek society, because the democratic world proved unable to present to the young people an appealing aim; unfortunately, not many leaders of the "democratic" world, liberals as well as conservatives, made a sincere and consistent effort to apply the fundamental principles of democracy, i.e., social justice, equality before the law, equality of opportunity. The growing generations could not be persuaded of the supreme worth of the democratic ideal by the mere professions of its official bearers, who repeatedly failed to exemplify it in their lives and political activity. It should not be surprising, therefore, that many of the younger generation lost the deeper meaning of social life and narrowed their activity to merely materialistic pursuits, while the more earnest and restless gradually gravitated toward leftist ideologies.

The Megali Idea was the ideal of the entire Greek people; it was not an official group organization, but an atmosphere within which moved the whole nation. The leftist ideologies had fewer adherents, but they were well organized and well disciplined. Socialistic ideas did not penetrate the country until the end of the last century, and the repeated attempts to form groups on a strictly ideological basis, because of the peculiar structure of the Greek society, proved abortive. The peasants, who constitute a great proportion of the population, are small proprietors, and by tradition very individualistic. This being the case, it is very natural that the radical ideologies could have very little appeal to them. The social and political developments immediately before and after the world conflagration of 1914 made certain of the Greek people (the workers and some intellectuals) more receptive to the radical ideologies.[60]

The KKE (Kommounistikon Komma Ellados) was founded in 1919, and because of its iron discipline, abundant funds, and underground foreign support, rapidly became the most dynamic and disruptive organization of Greece. This group drew its membership primarily from economically weaker classes—factory laborers, lower government officials, employees of private enterprises—from frustrated refugees and intelligentsia, and from well-to-do classes who "embraced" this ideology less from conviction than out of snobbism or ambition.

During the German occupation (1941–44), the Communist party under the guise of the "national" resistance movement (EAM) and of a youth organization (EPON) skillfully camouflaging its real Marxistic airs, attracted a great number of people—some of whom were decidedly nationalistic—and ultimately organized them into the notorious guerrilla bands, the National People's Liberation Army (ELAS). The stubborn effort of the Communists to gain control over the state led to the tragic December civil strife and the guerrilla war (1946–49). The KKE, as a member of the Third International and late of the Cominform, gave ample proof of its intention or obligation to further Soviet policies rather than to promote national causes or inner social reform. In view of this antinational activity the party was finally outlawed in 1947.

The conflict that was waged with so much fanaticism and vehemence about the so-called language question did not resemble the social movements so far referred to, for it was limited to the university circles and to the intelligentsia and never assumed (except in the matter of the proposed translation of the Bible, considered by many as a sacrilegious act) the dimensions of a mass agitation.

After the liberation the leaders of the new state, finding the spoken language too "vulgar" and inappropriate for higher literary expression, created on the basis of ancient grammatical forms an artificial "official" written language. This had catastrophic effects on the intellectual development of the country and as we have seen, it obliged school children to devote, at the expense of more practical knowledge, much of their precious time to the mastering of three language forms, the ancient (Homeric and Attic idioms), the "purist" (the official), and the spoken (the demotic). A struggle to establish the spoken forms as the sole vehicle of thought ensued.

The language question itself was only a surface problem; in its essence it was the clash between two mentalities, the conservative, which was looking backwards to the glories of the past and proved incapable of adjusting itself to the exigencies of modern life, and the progressive, which hopefully turned its attention to the future, endeavoring to break the nation away from the clutches of the deadening old traditions. On the one hand is seen the negation of the creative genius of the people; on the other, the determination to cast overboard all unnecessary ballast of antiquated standards and to set free the "life-asserting" values. It is for this reason that all progressive-minded people, royalists no less than leftists, fought under the same banner for the supremacy of the modern language and of the new life outlook. General Metaxas wanted to solve this problem once and for all, but the war and his untimely death put an end to his worthy efforts. The question is still pending and perhaps it is one of those Gordian knots that in retarded countries only "benevolent" dictatorships dare cut.

Private Voluntary Organizations

People everywhere combine with their fellow men outside their ordinary occupation and their routine life in order, on the one hand, to satisfy their craving for companionship, and on the other, to find an outlet for their various propensities, altruistic or individualistic. It was natural for the Greek, who since his enslavement had lost his confidence in the state — a situation not entirely remedied even in our own day — to depend for the solution of problems primarily on his own resources and initiative, acting either alone or, often, in voluntary association with others.

Following the convenient classification used by Professor Arnold Rose in one of his articles, one may distinguish two principal categories of private organizations: the "expressive" groups tending to "satisfy the interests of their members in relation to themselves" (scientific societies, sporting, athletic, recreational or hobby clubs, etc.), and the "social influence" groups, which "wish to achieve some condition or change in some limited segment of the society as a whole."[61]

The limited scope of this paper precludes even the mere mention of the numerous "expressive" groups in Greece, but the second category, because of its greater sociological significance, should arrest our attention at least briefly. It is, indeed a psychological paradox that the Greek, robust individualist that he is, is also moved by ardent patriotism, a fact amply demonstrated by the many associations privately organized for the promotion of worthy causes (national, philanthropic, and cultural), which the state, either because of poverty or inefficiency, has proved unable to support.

Some of these private agencies have centered their interest on the economically weaker classes, trying to improve their living conditions in various ways; others have undertaken the protection of children; and still others have accomplished outstanding achievements in their efforts to raise the cultural level of the people. The Philekpaidevtiki Etairia, probably the oldest institution of this kind (functioning uninterruptedly since

1836), at the beginning directed its attention primarily to the education of indigent girls and women, but later it widened its scope to include the instruction of girls of well-to-do families. The Parnassos and the Society of the Friends of the People, founded in 1865, and the Society for the Propagation of Greek Letters, established four years later, also pursued cultural aims. The first of these associations organized free public lectures, concerts, and exhibits, but its noteworthy activity undoubtedly was the maintenance of night schools for needy children who had to earn their living during the day. The imposing number (some 100,000) of young people who have graduated from these schools since their foundation is an eloquent proof of the contribution of Parnassos to the Greek nation. No less important service to Greece was rendered by the Lyceum of Greek Women, established in 1911 by Caliroe Parren. Inspired by its founder's ideal, this society did remarkable work for the emancipation of Greek women and for their education within the framework of the noblest national traditions. Following Parren's example, her followers also did praiseworthy pioneering work in encouraging and promoting peasant handicrafts. Very important work was also done by the Society for the Propagation of Useful Books, founded in 1899, which used its funds to publish cheap books imparting encyclopedic knowledge, in a language accessible to the average person.

Two women's organizations have recently been doing a splendid reform work: the Queen's Fund, which, under the auspices of the queen, was very active in rehabilitating the guerrilla-stricken population, and in founding in the northern provinces "children's homes," intended to serve as centers of recreation, vocational training, and enlightenment for the rural population.

Numerous religious organizations also function, the most notable of which is Zoe (Life), which has thousands of members, possesses great funds, and is able to maintain Sunday schools, organize lectures, publish periodicals and books, and contribute to the cultivation of the religious and moral nature of man.

Interrelations among the Institutions

Although the influence of the Church has always been very strong in Greek society, and nothing fundamental has usually been undertaken without the participation of the clergy, the state has always been supreme. Greece, while neither socialistic nor fascistic, has been characterized—and not without good reason—as the most centralized of the Marshall-Plan nations. Indeed, the spirit of centralism and bureaucracy, a prominent feature in the Byzantine Empire, regardless of discontent and criticism on the part of the people, is still alive in every phase of everyday life.

All branches of economic life are controlled very closely by the state. Every little detail has to be settled by the competent officials of the different ministries. One reason why some of the big enterprises tended in the past to concentrate near large cities was their desire to be in closer touch with the organs of the central government, thus enabling them to settle their questions with the least delay. It is significant that the Agricultural Bank, which did a great deal to relieve the hardships of the rural population, was established in 1929 by the order of the official state. It must, however, be admitted that some of the organized interest groups (e.g., industrialists, wholesale merchants) cooperate with the state and occasionally exercise a considerable influence on its economic and even political policies. The professional organizations (voluntary and state founded) render great service to the government by studying the different economic problems, either on their own initiative or on the recommendation of the state, by keeping statistical records, investigating the possibilities of future developments, offering their opinion on the feasibility and usefulness of new bills, and finally by organizing periodic fairs. The activity of these associations has been valuable, for, in addition to the effort they make to safeguard and promote their occupational interests as stated in the Constitution "within the limits of general welfare," they also contribute greatly to the economic progress of the country.

There is no strict separation of the Church from the state, and the king, not unlike the Byzantine emperor, is the head not only of the state but also of the Church. In spite of the relative autonomy which the latter enjoys in strictly ecclesiastical matters, many of its affairs are administered at the Ministry of Education; nor is the Church wholly free from *occasional* state pressure.

The clergy are considered as civil servants, but they are excluded from any "official" participation in political life. On the other hand, however, the Church has never limited itself to strictly religious duties; it continues to perform functions that in other countries fall within the jurisdiction of civil authorities. Since Greek law has no provision for civil marriage, this institution acquires validity only after it has been sanctioned and recorded by the Church. Although considering marriage a sacrament, the Greek

Orthodox Church does not share the notions of the Roman Catholics regarding the indissolubility of the matrimonial tie. The Greek law grants divorces for certain serious reasons, but the civil courts may not begin any legal procedure unless the efforts of the Church have failed to bring about a reconciliation of the two parties, nor do court decisions acquire validity until they have been approved and registered by the clergy. Funerals are also an entirely religious matter. The civil authorities only interfere in case no medical statement regarding the death of a person has been properly secured. Being considered an integral part of the state, the Church has rendered to it great service by performing certain political functions. It nerved the patriotism of the Greek people and has repeatedly promoted national causes by having its most capable ministers preach on important political issues or even participate in political conferences.[62]

Education, primary and secondary, is entirely in the hands of the central government. The appointments of teachers, the choice of textbooks, curriculum problems, and the construction of school buildings are decided by the competent authorities at the Ministry of Public Instruction. The superior educational institutions, most of whom have their own funds, are granted considerable self-government, but that their connections with the government are by no means very loose is amply proved by the not infrequent tension that arises concerning problems of common interest.

The local units, the communities (*demoi*), following old traditions, are supposed to be autonomous, but in reality their finances and their functions have never been, in the free Greek state, altogether independent of government control.

Much of the voluntary enterprise, no matter what its nature may be (economic, scientific, literary, or recreational) is more or less controlled by the state. No private organization may be founded unless it is granted special license by the court of first instance. The trade unions which are also voluntary workers associations are often subject to state interference.

Some of the above observations may be of interest to the sociologist, for they show how potent the influence of the past can be, and how obstinately traditions persist in spite of changed conditions. Legislation has of course, been gradually removing some of the cultural lag, but certain attitudes and practices continue to exist until they lose altogether their validity and meaning, or are finally discontinued by a forceful act of a bold reformer.

GREECE

Notes

[1] James D. Bourchier, "Greece," *Encyclopædia Britannica,* Vol. 12 (13th ed., 1926), p. 426.

[2] The author has been collecting material on "Greek character" from ancient, medieval, and modern sources, but the study has not yet been published.

[3] A. Inkeles and D. Lewinson, "National Character," in G. Lindzey, ed., *Handbook of Social Psychology* (Cambridge, Mass.: Addison-Wesley, 1954), Vol. 2, Ch. 26.

[4] The Byzantine Empire, the historic product of many conquests, consisted of vast provinces whose governors not infrequently manifested separatist tendencies. In order to eliminate the danger of these centrifugal movements, the emperors tried to concentrate all the administrative power in the capital. The modern Greek state followed the same centralistic tradition, but in view of the many inconveniences involved in this system, the tendency toward decentralization has increasingly been gaining ground.

[5] C. Whitman, *The Vitality of the Greek Language and Its Importance Today* (New York: Office of Greek Education Bureau, 1954).

[6] J. Lawson, *Modern Greek Folklore and Ancient Greek Religion* (Cambridge University Press, 1910). L. Garnett, *Greece of the Hellenes* (London: I. Pitman and Sons, 1914), Ch. 14.

[7] P. Kanellopoulos, "Modern Greek Society," *Great Greek Encyclopædia (Pyrsos),* Vol. 10 (Athens, 1934), p. 861.

[8] Food and Agricultural Organization of the United Nations, *Report of FAO Mission for Greece* (Washington, D.C.: U.S. Government Printing Office, 1947), p. 159. See also *New York Herald Tribune,* Special Supplement (Paris, May 1955), p. 16.

[9] National Statistical Service of Greece, *Statistical Summary of Greece* (Athens, 1954), p. 31.

[10] L. Stavrianos, "Greece," *Encyclopedia Americana,* Vol. 13 (1954), p. 371.

[11] A. Gomme, *Greece* (London: Oxford University Press, 1946), p. 102. *Statistical Summary of Greece, op. cit.,* p. 42.

[12] Since there was no efficient veterinary service, the losses from animal diseases were rather heavy; they were estimated at 10 per cent annually of the value of all livestock. Smothers, *et al., op. cit.,* p. 59.

[13] B. Sweet-Escott, *Greece, a Political and Economic Survey, 1939–1953* (London: Royal Institute of International Affairs, 1954), p. 119.

[14] C. Evelpides, *I chronia georgiki krisis is tin Ellada* (Athens: Argyris Papazisis, 1953), pp. 7, 8, 9.

[15] H. Stroup, "Social Changes in Greece," *Sociology and Social Research,* 39 (1955), 388.

[16] *Ibid.*

[17] *Report of FAO Mission, op. cit.,* pp. 22–23.

[18] Gomme, *op. cit.,* p. 103.

[19] *Statistical Summary of Greece, op. cit.,* p. 19.

[20] *Report of FAO Mission, op. cit.,* p. 21.

[21] Stavrianos, *op. cit.,* p. 372.

[22] S. Sineossoglou, "Survey of Industry," *Continental Daily Mail* (Supplement, March 14, 1950), p. 10.

[23] The electrification of the country (achieved with the money obtained from German and Italian reparations as well as the American aid funds) will make the establishment of factories possible in strategic parts of the country other than the above-mentioned centers (Athens, Piræus, Salonika). Stroup, *op. cit.,* p. 388.

[24] Sweet-Escott, *op. cit.,* p. 127.

[25] Gomme, *op. cit.,* p. 98. The *Statistical Summary of Greece (op. cit.,* p. 120) gives approximately the same number for the year 1951.

[26] There has been some improvement in this direction. In 1948–49 the imports primarily for human consumption amounted to $167 million, while the exports of agricultural origin were only $83.7 million. By 1953–54 the situation was reversed, with the imports for human consumption dropping to $40.2 million, and the agricultural exports reaching $111 million (Stroup, *op. cit.*, p. 388).

[27] *Statistical Summary of Greece, op. cit.*, p. 107. E. Baron, *La vie économique du globe* (Paris: Editions Magnard, 1947), p. 101.

[28] *Navtika Chronika*, No. 494, 253 (1956) 61, 67.

[29] *Ibid.*, p. 67. See also *New York Herald Tribune, op. cit.*, p. 18.

[30] W. Chadbourne, "Greece and Her Ships," in G. H. Chase, *Greece of Tomorrow* (New York: American Friends of Greece, 1943), p. 70. Eidikos (Expert), "O Ellinikos emporikos stolos," *Nea Oikonomia* (January 1947), p. 132.

[31] G. Diamantikos, "To oikonomiko mas provlima," *Kathimerini*, 12 (January 1956), 4.

[32] *New York Herald Tribune, op. cit.*, p. 3.

[33] *Report of FAO Mission, op. cit.*, p. 147.

[34] *Ibid.*, p. 45. S. Papadakis, *Importance de la culture des plantes médicinales et aromatiques* (Athens, 1954), pp. 9 ff.

[35] Rapport de la Mission du Bureau International du Travail, *Les Problèmes du Travail en Grèce* (Genève, 1949), p. 258.

[36] Sweet-Escott, *op. cit.*, p. 138.

[37] K. Varvaressos, *Ekthesis epi tou oikonomikou provlimatos tis Ellados* (Athens, 1952), pp. 48–49.

[38] J. Marriott, *The Eastern Question* (London: Oxford University Press, 1947), p. 199.

[39] C. Woodhouse, *Apple of Discord* (London: Hutchinson, 1951), p. 10.

[40] Smothers, *et al., op. cit.*, p. 12.

[41] Evelpides, *op. cit.*, p. 7.

[42] United Nations, *Greece: Biennial Report on Community, Family and Child Welfare for 1949 and 1950* (1953), p. 11.

[43] The premier, Mr. Karamanlis, declared that a new law which would include the agrarian population was being prepared.

[44] *Greece: Biennial Report, op. cit.*, p. 4.

[45] P. Bardis, "The Changing Family in Modern Greece," *Sociology and Social Research*, 40 (1955), 19 ff.

[46] In 1950 33 per cent of the gainfully employed people were women (Bardis, *op. cit.*, p. 21).

[47] L. Dertilis, "I Poreia tis ellinikis oikonomias," *Archeion Oikonomikon kai koinonikon Epistimon*, 35 (1955), 5, 98.

[48] One church in Corfu forms an exception since its chorus is accompanied by an organ.

[49] W. Miller, *Greece* (London: Renn, Ltd., 1928), p. 200.

[50] Chryssostomos, Archbishop of Athens, "Ekklesia tis Ellados," *Great Greek Encyclopædia* (Pyrsos), Vol. 10 (Athens, 1934), p. 681.

[51] G. Finlay, *History of Greece under Othman and Venetian Domination* (Edinburgh: Blackwood, 1856), pp. 193–94.

[52] T. Haralambides, *Die Schulpolitik Griechenlands* (Berlin: Neue Deutsche Forschungen, 1935), p. 115.

[53] *Greece: Biennial Report, op. cit.*, p. 9.

[54] K. Georgoulis, "Ellinik Ekpaideusis," *Encyclopædia Helios*, Vol. 5 (Athens), p. 1557.

[55] Smothers, *et al., op. cit.*, p. 118.

[56] Address delivered by his excellency, the minister of education, Mr. Gerokostopoulos to the American Fulbright grantees to Greece, September 1954. See also

GREECE

Greece: Biennial Report, op. cit., p. 9. I. Ekpaideusis, Elefteria (Greek daily), March 3, 1954, p. 1.

[57] I. Ekpaideusis, Elefteria (Greek daily), February 23, 1954, p. 1 and March 3, 1954.

[58] Smothers, et al., op. cit., p. 118.

[59] A notable exception is the Greco-American Marazleion Library that is very efficiently kept up to date. Unfortunately it contains mainly books on Greek and Near East history and archæology.

[60] W. McNeil, The Greek Dilemma (London: Fanfare Press, 1947), p. 27.

[61] Arnold M. Rose, Theory and Method in the Social Sciences (Minneapolis: University of Minnesota Press, 1954), Ch. 3, p. 52.

[62] One may clearly see the political role of the Church in the activity of the Bishop of Cyprus, Makarios.

Supplementary References

Battle for Survival (Weekly Bulletin), Athens: Ministry of Coordination, No. 2 (July 12, 1950).

Forster, E., A Short History of Modern Greece, 1821–1945 (London: Methuen, 1946).

LeFeuvre-Méaule, M., La Grèce économique et financière (Paris: Libraire Félix Alcan, 1916).

Mears, E. G., Greece of Today (Stanford: Stanford University Press, 1929).

Mirabel, A., La Littérature Grècque Moderne (Paris: Presses Universitaires de France, 1953).

Sanders, I., Village Social Organization in Greece, reprinted from Rural Sociology, 18 (December 1953).

Svoronos, N., Histoire de la Grèce moderne (Paris: Presses Universitaires de France, 1953).

Zarra, F., "Epagelmatikai Organosis," Great Greek Encyclopædia (Pyrsos), Vol. 10 (Athens, 1934).

*

S. N. Eisenstadt

ISRAEL

*

THE analysis presented in the following essay will attempt to provide both
a historical and an analytical description, placed within a wider, comparative setting, of the institutional framework of Israeli society. While
it is not the purpose of this essay to analyze the institutions of other
societies, I shall attempt to point out some of the basic frameworks to
which the Israeli social structure may be related. It seems to me that there
are three such foci or frameworks of comparison.

The development of Israeli society may be compared to other colonizing movements which have attempted to transplant Western social institutions into a new setting. As compared with such other trends the Israeli
has some distinct features. First, this attempt at colonization was not
effected in an entirely new, culturally vacant place (as was Australia),
but in a country which was part of the traditional setting of the Middle
East, with all the major characteristics of what are now called underdeveloped countries. Thus the Jewish colonists and pioneers had to face
problems of adaptation and adjustment which perhaps did not present
themselves with such acuteness in other colonizing movements. Second,
this colonizing movement was prompted and motivated not only by economic needs, but also by a national and social renaissance.

This is closely related to the second framework: the fact that while we
witness here a process of transplantation of Western institutions to a non-
Western region, this process is strongly connected with attempts to effect
some basic changes in these institutions—especially to limit by various
social means the effect of purely formal "mass"-relations, and the free
play of economic forces. Hence the numerous attempts at establishing new
types of social life—the communal settlements being the best known ex-

ample of this type. Hence the development of the institutional structure of the Yishuv (as the Jewish Community in Palestine was called) and of Israel should also be considered from the point of view of its attempts at social transformation.

Finally, I shall analyze the social structure of Israel from the point of view of absorption of immigrants. The Yishuv and the State of Israel were built up by waves of immigrants, which absorbed each other continuously. This process may be compared to a similar one in other immigrant countries. I shall later analyze this process in greater detail; here it may perhaps suffice to point out that the traits which distinguish it from other modern waves of migration are closely connected with the afore-mentioned strong national and social emphasis of this movement.

Even from the brief foregoing remarks it can be inferred that, for a number of reasons, a full understanding of the Israeli social structure necessitates a broad historical perspective—perhaps more than for other modern societies. It is important to remember that this social structure has evolved very recently, in no more than fifty to sixty years, and most intensively during the last forty years or so.

Historical Background

Before proceeding with an analysis of the main problems of immigration to Israel I should first briefly outline some of the historical periods in its development and provide some basic demographic data. It is customary to denote six waves of immigration (Aliyah) to the country since 1882 (as shown below), the waves varying in the number of immigrants and in the character of their composition.

	Period	*No. of Immigrants*
First Aliyah	1882–1903	20,000–30,000
Second Aliyah	1904–1914	35,000–40,000
Third Aliyah	1919–1923	35,000
Fourth Aliyah	1924–1931	82,000
Fifth Aliyah	1932–1944	265,000
Mass immigration to State of Israel	1948–1956	900,000

The first Aliyah was inaugurated in Russia and Rumania by the first Zionist movement, Hovevei Zion, with the wave of pogroms which flooded South Russia in 1881 as its main driving power. These immigrants regarded settlement on the land as a primary condition for the rejuvenation of the Jewish people. During this period the first Jewish agricultural settlements in Palestine, such as Petah Tiqva, Rishon Le-Zion, Rosh Pina, Zikhron Yaacov, and Hedera were established, and the foundations of the new Yishuv were laid.

The second Aliyah was mainly one of working elements. Its pioneers were members of various Zionist labor groups in Russia who had become disappointed with the social reform movement there, in which they had taken an active part, and with the October revolution of 1905, which ended in pogroms against the Jews. During this period, too, the world Zionist organization started work in Israel (1908), and the first mixed farming villages were established. This period also witnessed the beginning of urban development, with the foundation being laid in 1909 for the Jewish town of Tel Aviv, and here and there could be found even a rudimentary beginning of industry.

The third Aliyah received its impetus while World War I was still raging. This was after the Balfour Declaration, which the Jewish world understood as meaning the creation of a Jewish state. In this Aliyah, the pioneering element predominated, that is to say, young people who had been trained through the Halutz organization before their departure for Palestine and on their arrival were ready and willing to do any work that the country might require of them, however difficult.

The fourth Aliyah, beginning in 1924, was mainly actuated by improved economic conditions in Palestine that made possible the absorption of further immigrants, and by the economic position of the Jewish community in Poland, hard hit by the Polish government's policy of eliminating Jews from many trades. The main element in this immigration was the middle class, persons with some small means, most of whom settled in the towns and entered commerce or industry, or became artisans.

Although the fifth Aliyah actually began in 1929, it was only in 1932 that a large column of immigration was resumed, one resulting in great economic prosperity. Up to 1935 about 150,000 Jews, many of them from Germany, brought into the country a good deal of capital and developed industry, trade, and agriculture on a large scale. From 1936 to 1940, a period of severe troubles in the country, immigration was limited by the government, and only about 100,000 Jews, including a sizable number of "illegal" immigrants, entered.

The last stage, the sixth of the immigration waves, came with the establishment of the State of Israel in 1948 when a flood of mass immigration was loosed which brought about 900,000 immigrants into the country up to 1956.

Patterns of Absorption of Immigrants[1]

The basic motivation for migration among the immigrants who gradually established the Yishuv was rooted in the crisis engendered by the decomposition of traditional Jewish society as it was reduced to the status of a secondary group in modern, universalistic societies. Certain youth and young adults rebelled against this decomposing process and developed a strong aspiration for an entirely new kind of Jewish society to be established in Palestine. Thus their aims in migration were not purely adaptive and instrumental—as was the case with most of the Jewish immigrants to overseas countries—but mostly solidary and cultural, looking to the establishment of a totally new type of communal life. The economic motives were subordinated to the solidary and cultural ones—as can be seen in the "upside-down" occupational trend.[2] In all spheres of social life the immigrants showed a relatively high predisposition to change, not adhering to the specific cultural and social traditions of their countries of origin.

The immigration process itself usually took place in new social groups— usually primary groups—composed of relatively young people and formed with the direct purpose of preparing for migration to Israel. Even when migration took place in small family groups, these groups usually transformed their values and roles before and during the process of immigration. For the most part they cut themselves off from the institutionalized ties that bound them to their countries of origin, and oriented their levels of aspiration to the new country.

The absorbing society was itself gradually built up through the activities of the various groups of immigrants, but it developed, in time, a structure of its own which was of great importance for the processes of absorption. Its ideology was based on an over-all social and cultural identification with incoming immigrants and on ideas of social justice and welfare that assured complete social and economic equality to new immigrants. From the institutional point of view, it was greatly dependent on new immigrants for, first, the development of its economic manpower and resources in order to stabilize its economic and occupational structure, and, second, the maintenance of semipolitical activities which could not be legally required and regulated because of the lack of state power. These structural necessities enhanced the basic assumption of equality among the immigrants.

It was through the interaction between the immigrants' motivations and the institutional demands of the absorbing society that the processes of absorption and of institutionalization of immigrant behavior developed within the Yishuv. Their main characteristics were the following: (1) Strong neutralization of the immigrants' cultural and social background. (2) Almost complete dispersal of successive waves of immigrants among the various strata of the institutional structure. (3) Lack of any particularist identification on the part of any immigrant group. (4) Total transformation of the leadership of immigrant groups according to the institutional demands of the new country. (5) Utilization not only of formal institutions but also of primary groups closely interwoven with the formal institutions. (6) A relatively rapid transformation of the immigrant groups as well as participation by them in the institutions of the absorbing society, and a relatively high degree of social activity and orientation to the society's central values.

The new country which developed through the mingling of these many immigrant groups was relatively highly integrated in comparison with other immigrant countries. Within its main strata but few of the deviant tendencies characteristic of immigrant countries could be seen. It was most closely integrated, however, within the solidary and expressive spheres, and only to a smaller extent within the instrumental one. There it was part of a wider—the Palestinian Mandatory—framework, and the extent of its internal integration and of its adherence to common norms and rules was much smaller. Because of the intensive transformation of immigrant groups, cultural and educational background was of relatively little importance in determining a given group's position in the new society.

There were, however, some cases of unsatisfactory integration of immigrant groups. But these groups were of a distinct type and were distinguished by a different motivation for immigration from that of the majority of immigrants in the Yishuv. Some were made up of various refugees who came to Palestine with mainly adaptive and instrumental orientation, and with but little predisposition to change in the solidary and, especially, in the expressive fields. The main disintegrative tendencies to be found among them were a disinclination to enter into active social participation and to identify closely with the collective values of the community, and a proneness to develop particularistic groups and identifications. Most of the particularistic tendencies lessened in the second generation, without giving rise to any strong inter-generation conflicts.

The rate of immigration during the first four or five years of the state's existence was such that the population was doubled by the end of that period. Under the Yishuv, immigration had never taken place on such a scale. This meant that the proportion of old inhabitants to those who had to be absorbed became small. The composition of the immigrants as distinguished by country of origin greatly changed. More and more came from Eastern and Oriental countries, and the proportion from Central European countries significantly decreased. This, however, was not merely a change in "ethnic" composition. It was connected with a change in the basic social and demographic characteristics of the immigration, both from Eastern and from European countries. The lowest age groups (0–4) increased, while those in the middle range decreased. From our point of view this means that immigration was no longer a matter of selected groups detaching themselves from their former communities and backgrounds, but was becoming something more like a displacement of population. It took place in existing social groups, families, groups of families, local areas, sometimes (as in the case of the Yemenite Jews and those from Bulgaria and Yugoslavia) almost complete communities. The proportion of those groups who had no vested interests, emotional and social, in their previous cultural and social patterns considerably decreased. This tendency finds its counterpart in the considerably larger proportion, among the immigrants, of people with no fixed, productive occupation. Side by side with the increasing rate of immigration and the changing composition of immigrant groups, an entirely different and changing pattern of absorption evolved.

First, there was a decrease in the importance of those types of settlements where absorption was effected through incorporation into existing primary groups, as for instance, the Kibbutzim. The relatively large proportion of small holders' settlements indicates mostly not absorption into already existing settlements, but the creation of new Moshavim by the immigrants. Second, the immigrants tended to settle in special, segregated areas, where they usually maintained a high degree of social homogeneity, especially apart from the older inhabitants. Not only did many of them settle in entirely new places—such as abandoned Arab villages and towns—but even those who settled in existing towns or villages usually did so in new neighborhoods where they were more or less concentrated and, from the ecological point of view, relatively segregated. This segregation was very pronounced when the mass immigration began, and although it has since been somewhat lessened because housing projects have thrown old and new inhabitants together, it still persists as the main institutional feature of the new immigration. As immigration increased, new types of special transitional settlements for immigrants were created—the immigrant camp and the Ma'abara—many of which were built all over the country. If those who made their homes in abandoned settlements did not always have worse housing conditions than some, at least, of the old population, those who settled in Ma'abaroth usually did, since most of the Ma'abaroth were composed of tin and wooden huts, and the contrast between old and new inhabitants became quite striking. The ecological segregation also implied, of course, that even those formal institutions in which the immigrants had to participate (such as the school system or the local government organization) often provided separate services for them, and were not necessarily common meeting points for old and new inhabitants.

Changes in the Patterns of Absorption

The new pattern of initial absorption was closely connected with some changing characteristics of the absorbing society and with the new social pattern and basic motivations of the immigrants themselves.

The main motivation for migration was different. The commonest motive was the attainment of economic and social security and basic solidarity within the existing Jewish community, and not the creation of new kinds of community and culture. Predisposition to change varied greatly among the different groups of immigrants, ranging from a totally negative attitude among those with a "ritual" status image, through a purely instrumental attitude, to a more general predisposition (i.e., one including to some extent the social and cultural spheres); but even among those with more positive attitudes there was a disposition to adapt to a given situation and not to create an entirely new one. This could be most clearly seen in the more traditional communities (for example, Yemen, North Africa), but was evident also among the European communities. Group-clusters of families, neighborhoods that emigrated intact, and bands of emigrants from local areas rarely changed their original values and orientation through the process of migration—except for some general solidary orientation toward the new country.

Nowhere among the later immigrant groups was there so great a predisposition to change or so complete a fusion of expressive, solidary, and instrumental orientation (with the first supreme) as in the first Aliyah. In the pioneer stage of the Yishuv, occupational change and "normalization" was an important element in the new national identification and aspirations of the early immigrants, and hence there was a great emphasis on agriculture and industry as "basic" occupations. Occupational standing was valued mainly in terms of its contribution to the economic structure of the Yishuv. From the material at our disposal, however, it would seem that among the later immigrants occupational aspirations were not directly connected with national identification. Their valuation of occupational possibilities was usually made in terms of various status aspirations, as well as in terms of social and economic security.

This change in the pattern of occupational motivation could be clearly seen among those of the new immigrants who chose to join agricultural settlements of various kinds. During the period of the Yishuv, settlers on the land usually had a strong collectivist feeling and an appreciation of the high value of agriculture in relation to national rebirth. Among the new immigrants, on the other hand, the change to agriculture usually resulted from their conception of it as providing economic stability and conferring relatively high prestige within the Yishuv.

A similar change could be seen in the patterns of absorption evolved by the absorbing society. Most initial absorption was accomplished through bureaucratic activities, under the aegis of formal, bureaucratic agencies. From their first steps in Israel, most of the immigrants were met by various officials—of the Jewish Agency, the government, the Histadruth—whose function it was to deal with them, to direct them to their various places of settlement, to distribute to them various facilities (housing, furniture, food rations, medical help), and to assist them generally. Both the state and the Jewish Agency set up special administrations to perform these various functions for the immigrants. The formal, bureaucratic relation was the first which the immigrants experienced in their new country, and for a long time it remained—and in some instances still remains—the main one for many of them. Even their introduction to the basic, universal roles incumbent on them as citizens was usually effected through bureaucratic channels—whether in education, the military service, or in securing economic rights. In later stages of absorption (though not all immigrants passed beyond the initial stage) the main contacts with the representatives of the absorbing country were also with various secondary bureaucratic agencies—those of the various political parties and organizations—all of which began to compete for the potential political value of the immigrants as voters. Quite often there was also an outspoken party bias in the functioning of the first absorbing agencies. Beyond that there existed only minimum contact with the primary groups and informal circles of the old Yishuv. Except for those who had relatives, old acquaintances, or friends in Israel, few new immigrants could enter such informal settings at the first stage of absorption, for the old Yishuv groups were often reluctant to open their ranks to newcomers. It was only toward certain select cases, such as immigrants of a high professional and economic level from Anglo-Saxon and Western countries, that the attitude of the older settlers was somewhat different. But these formed only a small community within the new immigrant population as a whole.

The strong emphasis on the allocation of political and economic power and the policy of social welfare which developed within the Yishuv tended initially both to segregate the immigrants and, on the other hand, to assure them some minimum of social and economic rights. Special new fields of economic activity were developed for them, such as public works of various kinds (afforestation, repair of abandoned property, and so on), and in general, at the beginning, the new immigrants occupied lower economic positions than the old inhabitants. The incidence of seasonal unemployment was—and in certain types of immigrant settlements, such as the Ma'abaroth, still is—fairly high; and, perhaps even more important, many of the occupations had only a temporary character, without any permanent or future prospects. These immigrants, however, were allotted certain basic facilities, such as housing (even if of an inferior type), some furniture, initial financial help, and continuous social security allowances, as well as basic rations, all of which contributed to their economic security. In time, some degree of occupational mobility and integration came about, but this initial situation persisted as the basic set of conditions under which absorption took place.

This initial situation was, then, a rather paradoxical one. On the one hand, the immigrants were given some primary rights and privileges on the basis of a more or less universal criterion ascribed to them as citizens or Jews. But, on the other hand, their place in the social structure was a relatively low one, and they were initially but passive objects of the bureaucratic agencies of absorption. It is this paradoxical connection between these two aspects of absorption that prevented this initial situation from becoming static. The basic equality and universal civil rights granted to the immigrants were fully legitimized within the social structure, while the initial, relative segregation had no basis in either the law or the ideology of the state, which emphasized the complete equality of all citizens and their dedication to the task of the "Ingathering of the Exiles."

In addition to this ideology, and strongly connected with it, were other factors that tended to mitigate the initial conditions of absorption. First among these was the extension of various universal agencies, such as the schools and the army, which made important demands on the immigrants and directed them in the performance of new, universal roles. Second, the economic structure of the state developed throughout these years, and new enterprises were launched, all of which demanded additional manpower at various levels of specialization. The old Yishuv could not provide sufficient manpower, and as no legal discrimination existed, many of the immigrants were drawn within the various economic strata in the Yishuv. While there have been, and will be, periods of economic retrogression and unemployment to which immigrants are more susceptible than older inhabitants, a general tendency toward economic advancement and development has become evident.

Third, with the stabilization of immigration, many of the bureaucratic agencies dealing with absorption limited their personnel, and many positions in local activities and the like were opened to the immigrants. Fourth, and most important, was the fact that the immigrants were granted basic political rights, and this necessarily enhanced their political value to the competing social groups and parties within the Yishuv and the state. All these groups developed activities among the immigrants, extended their organization toward them, and thus necessarily drew many people within their orbits.

It was the impact of all these factors that gradually broke down the initial segregation of the immigrants, and gave rise to processes of group-transformation and institutionalization among them.

Thus a close connection exists between the internal changes in the structure of the Yishuv and the problem of absorption. The Yishuv provided the basic framework into which the immigrants were absorbed, while the process of absorption and the immigrants' own social and cultural predispositions tended to reinforce changes in the Yishuv's system of values and stratification. Truly enough, the tempo of absorption of new immigrants is even now much quicker than in most other modern immigrant communities. However, the present pattern of absorption—the basic solidary, even if formal, identification and acceptance—greatly differs from that which prevailed in the Yishuv. According to a current Israelite saying, two "nations" now exist in Israel. But although there is a grain of truth in this saying, it does not accurately describe or analyze the situation. The fact is that in spite of segregation there is but one society in Israel today—a society built up of many sub-units in different degrees of segregation from one another. This fact has its repercussion on the system of stratification of the society and on the nature of its integration. First of all, most of the common meeting points between the new immigrants and the old ones in the economic sphere and the army enhance the importance of economic and instrumental criteria in the system of stratification and the importance of the formalized, bureaucratic apparatus as the main bearer of the collective solidarity. The most important channels of mobility open to new immigrants are the economic one and the bureaucratic political one, and the mobility which takes place in these channels tends either to remove individual immigrants from their group of origin or to limit the contacts between old and new immigrants to the more formal spheres. In turn, this tendency is connected with the growing segregation of solidary relations in "private" spheres. Thus most of the immigrants still live, from the social and cultural point of view, in relatively segregated spheres, and have few primary contacts with other groups.

The Family Structure in Israel

Of all the different institutional spheres the family was given the least emphasis in the socialist ideology of the Zionist colonizing movements. With the sole exception of the Kibbutzim, which consciously limited the scope of the family, and the Moshavim, which consciously enlarged it, there was no conscious attempt at planning in this social field. Here the trend of development was mostly the outcome of other institutional pressures and trends. A differentiated family structure, rather akin to that of most modern societies, developed. In most of the strata of the Yishuv, the scope of the family unit became much more limited than in the traditional Jewish society from which the majority of the immigrants originated, as a result of both the general trend toward economic differentiation and specialization in urban settings and the exigencies of adaptation to a new country. Although in this respect not many data exist it seems that the main patterns of urban families in the Yishuv were rather similar to those in other modern small urban settings. The only significant exception was provided by the Oriental Jews.

A recent survey of family types in Israel has postulated the existence of the following main types: [3]

A. The "non-familistic" family predominates among immigrants from Europe. It is most prevalent in various strata of the bureaucratized middle class, among members of the professions and among organized and skilled workers. The family in these sectors does not function as an independent economic, political, or cultural unit. Different members of the family participate in different organizations and associations and perform many roles which are independent of their familial roles. Authority patterns tend to be equalitarian. Husband and wife are basically equal. The authoritarian element in parent-children relationships is not strong, although parents insist on their right to supervise their children and try to determine their choice of future occupation. Marriage is beyond the control of the parents. Economic contributions of both families of orientation, or only that of the wife, help in the establishment of new households, but each family unit tends to be economically independent of its predecessors. The nuclear family is small and partly isolated. It should be stressed, however, that it is not completely atomized. The basic family lives as a rule in a separate household, but it has many rights and obligations which bind it to other kin. The wider kinship category is amorphous and ill-defined but there exist within it some economic continuity, financial assistance and mutual aid. Families maintain close relations through frequent visits. In spite of the disruption of kinship ties brought about by immigration, it seems that the processes of isolation of the basic family unit are not as intense here as in large-scale modern industrial societies. This is probably due to small-ness of scale and to the persistence of strong, wider family ties which are characteristic of the typical Jewish family.[4] . . .

The "non-familistic" family is most prevalent in European urban sectors, although it is by no means confined to them. Due to frequent changes of occupation typical of any immigrant community and due to the Zionist policy of "return to the land" and to manual labor, a considerable number of immigrants changed their occupation when immigrating to Israel. Many families now living in villages or employed in lower urban occupations were formerly middle-class town dwellers. The breakdown of the statistical data according to urban-rural place of residence and present occupation is, therefore, not as significant as in other countries. Estimates of mean age at marriage until 1940[5] suggest that farm wives married at about the same age or even later than women in urban areas. Farmers had about the same fertility as those in higher urban occupations, except the small group of Oriental farmers who married at a considerably lower age and had a higher fertility. Wives of men in higher urban occupations married later and had fewer children than wives in lower urban occupations. But, with the exception of Orientals, differences were very slight. . . .

B. The traditional family in some Oriental groups comes nearest to the "familistic" type.[6] There is very little specialization in these groups and they tend to follow their traditional occupations, mostly simple crafts and small-scale petty trade. In Israel, many of them had to shift to unskilled labor and agriculture. The patrilineal, patriarchal and sometimes even polygamous household unit is comprised of three or four generations. Parents control their children and determine their choice of spouses. The exchange in connection with marriage prevalent in these groups is the payment of bride price. There is no unilineal, clearly defined kinship unit although extensive and stable relations exist between kin. The community is in fact an aggregate of families and within it families of kinsmen tend to cluster and to form united power groups.

Although most of the Oriental communities are familistic it should be stressed that they are not undifferentiated in their family type. Families from Turkey, from Iraq, and from the urban sectors of North Africa are appreciably less familistic. Differentiation according to occupation is considerable, too. . . .

The "familistic" patterns have persisted in Israel but are undergoing a process of change. The traditional unspecialized economy on which this type of family is based is incompatible with the more specialized and more varied economy of Israel. The impact of the new system results either in a shift to unskilled manual labor or in frequent fluctuations and instability.

Apparently, then, most of the urban and rural types of family structure (with the partial exception of family units in the Kibbutzim) conformed generally to those found in similar settings elsewhere.[7] Although the scope of family life greatly diminished, in accordance with the general modern pattern, family and kinship relations still retained great importance—especially in the well-established social strata. Only on the margin of society, in areas of delinquency and destitution, did the family pattern become entirely disorganized. Significantly enough these tendencies were much more prevalent among those sectors (like part of the Oriental Jews) that retained the traditional family pattern. But here also the picture was not uniform. Only among those Oriental families that did not adapt themselves to the modern social setting of the Yishuv and did not find an accepted place within it—even as an accepted subculture—were these processes of disorganization strong and evident. Many Oriental families succeeded in finding for themselves an accepted place, and among them no manifestations of disorganization appeared. They usually succeeded in maintaining a more extensive family pattern than that found in other urban strata, but this pattern became an established and accepted subculture in the Yishuv.

Insofar as this was the case, these families succeeded, like the major parts of the rural and urban strata of the Yishuv, in retaining the main social functions of the family: they socialized the children and placed them in the social structure. Perhaps the most significant fact about the Israeli family was that, despite the exigencies of immigration and adaptation to the new surroundings, most families maintained, in the new setup almost from the very beginning, their basic function as the main channels of socialization and transmission of status.

As in most other spheres, the institutional pattern has greatly changed with the establishment of the state and the mass influx of immigrants, especially Oriental ones. Although few data are available on the changes of family patterns among these immigrants, some general characteristics may be pointed out. First, a much greater number of families evinced a more traditional pattern of extended family organization and of traditional relations in other institutional spheres—for example, in the economic and political fields. Thus, for instance, in many new-immigrant agricultural settlements both the economic and the political structure is based to a large extent on the extended family. But it is very difficult as yet to predict to what extent the mutual adaptation of this family pattern and of the more modern institutional structures in the political and economic spheres will be peaceful and stable and to what extent it will become a focus of social disintegration. This problem is obviously connected with another—the extent to which the new immigrants will become fully integrated within the status system of the total society, or, conversely, will continue to remain isolated in their own sectors. It is possible that the relative strength of the old family pattern in the settlements and urban quarters of the new immigrants is mainly due to their relative isolation, and so far as this isolation becomes weakened, not only will this pattern of family life greatly change, but it will also become a focus of social disorganization. However, all these trends belong to the future and at this stage it is difficult to predict their results.

INTER-GENERATIONAL RELATIONS IN ISRAEL

These tendencies became much more articulated in the sphere of intergenerational relations—a sphere of great importance in any new country with a largely immigrant population, as a focus of either social continuity or disorganization. The most important aspect of this problem was usually the development of special youth groups, peer groups, and the like, and their relation to their own families on the one hand, and to the absorbing society on the other.

Within the Jewish community in Palestine and in Israel, diverse types of youth groups and youth movements developed,[8] distinguished according to the following main classifications: organized, legitimate youth movements, some of them linked with pioneering movements; others of a more recreational type; relatively unorganized or loosely organized cliques; delinquent groups.

While these various youth groups provide some common psychological function for the adolescent, they differ greatly in many other respects that are of crucial importance to our analysis. First, they differ in the extent to which they are fully organized and legitimated in the social structure, or conversely the extent to which they are only informal groups or even outright deviant groups. Second, they differ in the type of their internal organization and structure. Of the greatest importance to our central problem is the first difference—the way in which inter-generational relations are solved and social continuity is maintained in immigrant communities. Our problem here is to see under what social conditions these different types of youth groups arise. Before answering this specific question, it would be worth while to survey in a general way the extent to which some sort of specific youth culture developed in different social sectors of the Yishuv, and the conditions of its development.

Various researches have already indicated that the most important factor in the development of youth culture is the extent to which the general conditions of family transformation and of the establishment of a social division of labor, not based on the family, take place.

A cursory examination shows that a specific youth culture is most highly developed among the professional, bureaucratic, middle-class, and upper working-class sections of the urban population, in the communal settlements (Kibbutzim), and among those Oriental Jews who are going through rapid processes of "culture-contact" and culture change. It is lowest among those Oriental families which retain their traditional setting, in the cooperative settlements (Moshav Ovdim, which is a cooperative village consisting of family farms), in the Moshavoth, and among some of the lower urban classes.[9]

The different sectors of the Jewish community in Palestine have solved in their own ways the problems of inter-generational tensions and relations. Some sectors have succeeded in overcoming almost entirely any strong tensions by giving full legitimation to organized youth groups and youth movements. Others have attained the legitimation by developing more informal types; in other cases, these groups may have become foci of tension; while in still others delinquent youth groups have been developed. The solution of the inter-generational problem is, however, connected not only with the relative importance of the family and the social structure, but also with its place in the socioeconomic and stratification system of the country.

Classification according to socioeconomic status does not, however, fully explain the problem. Even this classification does not follow the usual pattern, because a unique element entered into the social stratification of the Jewish community in Palestine—namely, the element of "pioneering." Within some of the most important sections of the community the social status of the individual depends to a great extent not so much on his economic position as on his participation in the "pioneering" activities and groups. It is among those sections of the population most imbued with the "pioneering" values that the youth movements—especially those with pioneering ideology—take root.[10]

This orientation toward identification with the values of pioneering and social change finds its full institutional expression in the youth movements. This was achieved mainly in the following ways: (a) by placing strong emphasis on the ultimate common values of the society; (b) by continuous participation in social activities with future citizens and the perception of the place of one's own activities within a wider range; and (c) by mutual identification with these age-mates and with the common values upheld in these activities.

In this way youth culture became organized within the institutional structure, legitimized, and closely connected to the ultimate common values. The possibility that the youth culture will take on disruptive characteristics and oppose the values of the adult world is in this way overcome. Although many psychological tensions between children and their parents may arise, the degree of *structural* incompatibility between the family, the total social structure, and the youth movement is minimized. This may be clearly seen in the ideologies of the youth movements in which opposition to the family and the social structure is minimized while the articulation of common values is emphasized.

The avowed aim of most of the pioneering youth movements is to bring about social change through transferring urban (mainly middle-class) youth to the working life of rural communal settlements, which are supposed to form the basis of a utopian socialistic community. They are intended to mean for the youth a break with the life of their families. However, the results of numerous researches indicate that the choice of movement itself is to a large extent influenced by the status or status security of the family. Similarly, the child's role in the movement seems to be, to a large extent, a reflection of status factors. This is the case not only in such near-bourgeois movements as the Scouts (even this movement has a socialistically tinted ideology), but also in such almost expressly "revolutionary" movements as the Hamahnoth Haolim. Many middle-class parents seem to direct their children to this movement, or at least tacitly to agree to their participation in it. They regard it as a suitable agency of education for social life and the inculcation of the idealistic values of socialist Zionism. The continued harmonious contact between parents and children does not, therefore, point to a complete break in social continuity, and indeed a very small proportion of members joins a communal settlement—the path definitely prescribed by the movement and strongly identified with by almost all members as long as their membership lasts. The actual meaning of membership is therefore not education for social change, but the inculcation of some of the basic and collective values, which have acquired a place in the central value and symbol system of the society, and to which lip service is paid even by broad strata of the middle classes. From this point of view the function of the movement is complementary to that of the family.

In those sectors of the social structure where the orientation toward the common values is weak, youth culture loses its organized character and the distinctiveness of its goals. It takes on more and more the shape of loose cliques—with mainly recreational goals and activities—whose aim is not any longer to change the social orientation of their members. As in the "pioneering" families, there does not exist here any marked structural opposition between the different generations, but the degree of discontinuity and tension between the generations may be greater—especially if the children want to join the more organized movements.[11]

From the above analysis the peculiar position and features of the "working-youth" movement may be understood. Among the common "pioneering" values, those of social justice and security are the most basic. The opposition between these values and those of "individualistic" advancement may be most acute among the lower economic strata where the demands of competition are severe. The purpose of the working-youth movement then becomes not so much to change immediately the status and economic welfare of its members as to effect their mobility toward those sectors where the common values—especially those of social security—prevail, and in this way to improve the economic standard and to widen the scope of social participation. It should be then expected that the degree of incompatibility between the generations would be higher among some sections of this movement, but at the same time, considering the society as a whole, the movement may and will provide an important channel of stabilization and social control.

The "deviant" types of youth culture are—according to our analysis—connected with those situations where there exists an incompatibility between the social orientations and values of the family and their realizability within the social structure. Although this tendency may exist—in a mild form—in many individualistic families, it is intensified only in specific situations, occurring mainly in two typical instances. First, as in many Western societies, there are families in the interstices of the economic system lacking economic stability who cannot enable their children to realize their goals. Second, and to a larger extent, these disrupting tendencies become greatly enhanced in situations of immigration and culture-contact. In those situations the parents' effective symbolization of the social structure is minimized and the discontinuity in the transference of identification becomes more acute. It is then quite understandable why the degree of juvenile delinquency is highest among some sections of the Oriental Jews, where the processes of culture-contact are most acute.

Some sectors of the Oriental Jews—all of whom account for about 20–25 per cent of the population of the Yishuv—are, as is well known, the less integrated sectors from the point of view of adaptation of immigrants. They evince various forms of social disorganization—lack of stability of family life and relations, occupational and educational retardation, and other manifestations[12]—all of which seem to be closely related to the high incidence of juvenile delinquency among them.

The most important difference among the various categories of youth can be found in the fact that only a very insignificant part of the new immigrant youth tended to join any of the youth movements existing and still developing within the established Yishuv.

Before the immigrant youth there opened up various possibilities of social mobility toward the absorbing society of the Yishuv and the state. Among these channels the most important were the para-military and military organizations that made available various means of acquiring technical knowledge and offered special vocational courses. But it seems that only a small percentage of the immigrant youth availed themselves of these opportunities,[13] although this picture has been changing continuously since then. Thus in several surveys undertaken in various immigrant settlements in 1953–54 it was found that the average percentage of youth availing itself of the various existing training services was about 15 per cent, while those participating in various youth movements accounted for about 8–10 per cent. Among all kinds of immigrant youth there developed manifold types of informal peer groups, youth groups, and the like, which became the main form of youth culture among them and which were quite often homogeneous—at least from the point of view of the distinction between "old" and "new" groups.

Most of these groups of new immigrant youth evince certain distinct social characteristics. First, as has already been indicated, they are usually relatively unorganized and but little connected with the more formal organization of the society. Significantly enough their relations with the school system are very meager. Second, they have relatively weaker orientation to the common values of the society, and their social orbit and perspective are rather limited to their own immediate surroundings and social setting, with a strong emphasis on attainment of a limited social status and instrumental goals within that field. Third, as their groups are not as yet fully integrated in the total social structure of the state, and as they are in a process of constant change and occasionally clash with the absorbing society, we observe within these youth groups a relatively strong tendency toward social disorganization and juvenile delinquency. Obviously enough, the strength of these different tendencies varies greatly among different groups of immigrants. However, it is beyond the province of this essay to analyze these differences.[14] Suffice it to say here that the over-all picture, as compared with that of the Yishuv, evinces these characteristics. This picture is obviously closely related to the different patterns of family life found here, to the new patterns of absorption of immigrants, and to the different degrees of integration of different groups in the total society.

Economic Institutions

The main interest of an analysis of the economic institutions of Israel does not necessarily lie in the enumeration of some of the basic statistical data. From my point of view Israel can be described as a small-scale, modern economic system, which is based on modern agriculture, on small and medium-size non-heavy industries, and on an overdevelopment of some of the tertiary occupations, and is as yet greatly dependent on outside resources for the maintenance of its standard of living and the absorption of the doubled population.[15] This economic system has developed certain social directives and limitations on economic activities, which to some extent are unique. To a certain degree, the system evinces some of the most important characteristics of a welfare state, but these characteristics are also closely connected with a very strong colonizing drive and expansion. The relation between economic activities and incentives on the one hand, and social values and incentives on the other, are patterned here in a manner different both from modern Western economic systems and from those of underdeveloped and colonial societies. Some of the basic socioeconomic orientations of many underdeveloped societies, such as emphasis on welfare, some planning, and the encouragement of co-operative ventures, do, however, already exist in Israel as a basic part of the institutional structure of the absorbing society.

THE HISTORICAL AND SOCIAL BACKGROUND OF ECONOMIC DEVELOPMENT IN THE YISHUV

The set of values, social orientations, and ideologies which existed at the outset of the pioneering immigration to Palestine placed their main emphasis on the establishment of a new national community. They stressed diffuse relations and ideals and aspects of social life, such as "belonging to the Jewish people." Although these ideals could only be achieved in practice through specific activities of a new kind, their ultimate goal was the establishment of a new over-all pattern of collective life. From this, some general characteristics and problems of the economic institutions have developed.[16]

1. The Yishuv was largely created on the basis of an ideology which

stressed occupational discontinuity, which wanted to turn its back on the "traditional" Jewish occupations in the Diaspora and to emphasize primary occupations such as agriculture and industry.

2. Accordingly, the scale of prestige of occupations was, in this ideology, greatly different from that obtaining in most modern countries.[17] At the same time, however, this very ideology emphasized the importance of creating a viable *modern* economy, with most of its features of specialization and differentiation. In this way some basic contradiction—or at least a problem—existed within this ideology.

3. This problem was accentuated by the prevailing socialist egalitarian ideology which greatly influenced the internal wage and economic policy in the Yishuv.

4. At the same time there took place in the Yishuv a continuous expansion of the economic structure, with stronger development of secondary and tertiary occupations, which necessarily gave rise to various functional problems common to all such modern structures, and which gradually opened up more and more positions in these various tertiary spheres—in management, in the professions, in civil service and other public bureaucracies.

In the economic field, specialization and achievement were tempered by a sense of general collective obligations, by a concern with the welfare of the community as a whole, and by the realization of the collective ideals, as can be seen in several interconnected ways—first of all, in the importance attached to agricultural settlements and the emphasis within them on fundamental human equality and on identification with the community. Although most of these settlements aspired to the highest standard of technical achievement, it was everywhere assumed that any personal specialization in this direction should be concerned only with the communal welfare, and should not entail any marked variation in rewards. This was most evident in the communal settlement (the Kibbutz), but in the Moshav, the smallholders' settlements, limits were also established in order to reduce possible differences in standards of living. The strong community spirit of these settlements overrode—at any rate, during the first period of their development—the various structural demands of differential reward for specialization.[18]

Second, the same principle was realized in the urban setting through the wide schemes of social security. The continuously rising standard of living meant that workers were usually assured a relatively high minimal standard. Many of the socioeconomic organizations, both middle-class and Histadruth, undertook numerous activities for their members' benefit that were beyond the usual scope of activity of a trade union or labor organization, such as the provision of housing and educational facilities. The social security schemes became particularly important at the outset of World War II, when the cost-of-living index was introduced, thus gradually reducing somewhat the real differences among various salaried groups.

A third indication of this development was the strong encouragement given to various cooperative enterprises in the cities, especially the transport cooperatives, and the extended chains of consumers' cooperatives.

A fourth indication was the strong emphasis, within cooperative and noncooperative sectors alike, initially placed not only on the provisions of various facilities and securities, but on the "pioneer" tasks of various branches of the economy. A very marked ideology of the "conquest of labor" and of various other sectors of the economy prevailed. This ideology was strongly rooted in reality, and usually entailed even for the capitalist sectors an orientation toward those branches of the economy that were most necessary to the developing social structure, relinquishing the possibility of using cheap Arab labor in the interest of building up a self-sufficient economy rather than a colonial society.[19]

This sense of national dedication and collective social emphasis within the various branches of the economy was most clearly shown in the development of organizations of professional workers—such as teachers, physicians, and to a somewhat smaller extent, lawyers. These professional associations did not begin with the sole purpose of ensuring rights, salaries and remuneration, or setting up standards of membership. Their initial purpose was to create new professions that would serve the new community—to create, as it were, "Hebrew" professions—and to organize pioneer work within various sectors of the population and create a new culture. In the beginning strong emphasis was laid on these ideals, and problems of direct professional interest took a secondary place. It was only with the growing development of the Yishuv and the gradual normalization of its social and economic structure that purely professional and economic interests prevailed and the various associations—both labor and professional—became centers of vested interests and holders of important power positions as well.[20]

Finally, these various developments had their repercussions on the distribution of both economic facilities and power. The differences among the standards of living of various strata of the Jewish population signified a double trend. On the one hand, these differences grew with the development of the Yishuv; on the other, however, even at the close of the Mandatory period, they were not very great compared to those in other countries.

The differences between various income-levels and occupations were not very great, particularly if the strong concentration of the "middle-income" groups is taken into account. It should also be mentioned that the differences were still smaller within the non-Oriental majority, and that it was the Oriental Jews who gave special weight to some of the lower income classes.[21] An interesting feature is the relatively high income of the transport branch—mostly in cooperative hands—which is one of the indications that such differentiation as existed was not always parallel to that in other industrialized countries.

From this point of view it is interesting to note that in the National Institutions (the Jewish Agency, the Vaad Leumi—the National Council of Jews in Palestine), and within the Histadruth, a special system of remuneration was arranged. In the Histadruth the peculiar system of basic family salary prevailed; that is, the basic salary was roughly equal for all workers and employees, with very small additions for specialization, education, and so on, and varied mainly according to family status, number of children, and seniority of employment.[22] In the National Institutions such an extreme system did not exist, but still there were only six or seven grades of remuneration, based not only on specialization but also on seniority, with large family allowances. It quite often happened that a janitor of an institution, with his six children and seniority, earned more than its director with only two children. While this system of remuneration was not universal and did not obtain in the free market, it is significant that it existed within those organizations which, in a way, bore the maximum of social prestige, and to some extent also of power. It was the most important manifestation of the ideology of "service"—national or social—in accordance with which all were basically equal even if performing different functions.

Even in the second generation the ideal of "service" continued to be of some importance. Several partial inquiries into the vocational interests of urban youth[23] indicate that this consideration prevailed among them to some extent in their choice of vocation. During a later period (the thirties and forties), it was seen in the large number of volunteers for fully mobilized formations of Haganah and, during World War II, among the volunteers for the British Army, especially the Jewish Brigade. About 25,000 men and women joined the British Army.

The same inquiries show, however, that with the normalization of the Yishuv's social structure more purely economic motives gradually developed, and that the relatively strong—though not general—occupational continuity in the basic productive branches of the economy in the second generation was due not only to ideals of social service, but also to the economic amenities existing in these branches and to the general scheme of social security.

A rather similar trend can be traced in the distribution of economic power. There was a tendency to concentrate at least some of this power not only in the hands of private individuals or concerns with capital of their own, devoted to making maximum profits, but also, to some extent, in the hands of public corporations and the like, with the manifest aim of developing the country, promoting social security, and caring for the consumer and his standard of living. One of the most important examples of this is the inflow of national capital into the various kinds of agricultural settlements. But the extent of concentration of economic power in the various concerns belonging to the Histadruth is of the greatest importance in this connection.

With the rising standard of living and developing economic opportunities there was a stronger tendency to distribute rewards in accord with individual achievement and investment of time; and a growing restiveness appeared against the pure ideology of service, which denied, as it were, some of the simple rewards to the most faithful. It became obvious that one could attain greater success in life by not devoting oneself to purely collective goals alone.[24] Many of those who did devote themselves to such goals found, after a time, that the more lucrative positions were held by those who followed a different path. The several partial investigations into the vocational interests of youth, mentioned above, show that side by side with the collective tendencies there also developed a very strong trend towards economically secure trades. As the need for technical experts in various fields grew, it sometimes became necessary to give them special emoluments disproportionate to the general principles of national wage policy.

The tension between collectivism and individual security tended to resolve itself in two different ways. The first and more pronounced way was by a growing emphasis on achievement patterns in certain sectors of the life of the Yishuv, and a growth in "conspicuous consumption." This meant generally both a growth of individualist emphasis and a certain apathy toward the Yishuv's central values, with an accompanying lessening of social participation. Only with the growing differentiation in the Yishuv did there develop also, within all sectors, a strong connection between emphasis on private, individualistic, or subgroup interests and some degree of apathy toward the central values. This became especially pronounced as new and more purely "refugee" types of immigrant waves increased the relative weight of the more passive elements.

The second way of resolving this tension did not pass beyond an embryonic stage during the period of the Yishuv; but it was nevertheless of great importance both as a social phenomenon and as a forerunner of certain future trends. Its essence was a combination of differential allocation of rewards and of political power and social prestige to those groups which were connected with the collective ideology of the Yishuv, and which wielded the various collective economic interests. Many of the social security schemes, cooperative institutions, and the like, led to the development of vested interests which were furthered by their representatives in the political sphere; these were justified on the basis of the collective ideology and of the national service they performed in the development of the country, and they secured collectively for their members various rewards and benefits. These vested interests gradually came to be accepted as having basic rights because of participation in the collective enterprises and their devotion to these ideals. An outstanding example which began to show itself even during the Mandatory period was the growth in property and remuneration of the various transport cooperatives, which developed into one of the principal vested interests. But many parallel instances could be observed in other fields.

Thus the collective values gradually became more and more emphasized not only in ideology but also in the allocation of economic rewards. As already indicated, these developments were not of great importance during the period of the Yishuv. This was mainly because of its basic power-structure. The necessity of maintaining a common loyalty, which could not be founded on coercive-political power, and of directing various activities of a political nature (defense, colonization, and so on), precluded any excessive development of a ruling, privileged class clearly marked off from the rest of the population. Characteristically, this tendency inclined to show itself mainly in the somewhat lower strata of the collective-minded sectors, and not among the upper elite elements, during the Mandatory period.

PATTERNS OF ENTREPRENEURSHIP AND ADMINISTRATION
IN THE YISHUV

All these developments and problems were manifested in the types of entrepreneurial activities first developed in the Yishuv. The strong emphasis on *social* values within the realm of purely economic activities may have hindered the development of economic entrepreneurship and stifled economic development. This problem could be especially acute because of the fact that most of the colonizing expansion was financed by outside sources (by money raised through the different national organizations), that there was but little direct economic risk involved, and that the internal market was developed and expanded only gradually and was geared to and dependent on the colonizing activities. Only in the late thirties did the internal market develop a more autonomous structure. What happened, however, was not the nondevelopment of entrepreneurship but rather the development of some very specific entrepreneurial types.

Perhaps the most important single type of the new entrepreneur is what may be called the "institutional," entrepreneur colonizer. He is a man who holds a key position in a settlement, in a cooperative enterprise, or in one of the public or semipublic economic enterprises (such as the Histadruth-owned factories and the public water companies). His main concern has been to maximize the scope of economic activities, the assets and the profits of his own group and organization through the best manipulation of both the market possibilities and the sources of capital and credit—especially from the colonizing agencies. He does not view his role, however, as a purely economic one. He sees himself as furthering the general social values of the society, as helping the colonizing movement through the enlargement and development of his own organization—an assumption with some elements of reality in it. While very adept at economic calculations, he regards them as subsidiary to these social goals, expecting other people to see his activities in the same light. He is not generally a bureaucrat of the usual type—although gradually more and more purely bureaucratic managers have developed. He sees himself rather as an elected representative of his group or organization, its emissary, and, in general, as an economic pioneer.

In these types of entrepreneurship there could be found a very strong economic motivation—geared to and strengthened by noneconomic but not traditional values. A similar pattern could be found in the development of another aspect of institutional life in Israel—that of bureaucracies and administrative organizations.

At the same time there developed in the Yishuv two types of capitalist entrepreneurs. One was the large-scale entrepreneur who was able—through appropriate use of his own financial resources, of some of the liquid capital in the country, and of some of the credit facilities extended by the colonizing agencies—to exploit some strategic possibilities of the developing internal market and the export outlets, and to establish some relatively big industrial enterprises in key areas. Good examples of this are the Ata Textile Industries and some of the industries that process different kinds of agricultural produce.

What characterizes the large-scale entrepreneur is that he also had to take into account many of the social values found in the semipublic enterprises. First, most of these entrepreneurs subscribed to the basic tenets of social security, collective bargaining, family and cost-of-living allowances. Second, they sometimes found it beneficial to their interests to go into partnership—usually on a limited basis and in subsidiary companies—with public or semipublic enterprises. This tendency has especially increased since the establishment of the State of Israel. Third, most of these enterprises availed themselves of the various facilities (especially financial credit) of the colonizing agencies and, later, of the state, and shared in some of the "pioneering" and colonizing ideology. This showed itself in their relative concentration in industries of strategic importance for economic development.

The second and more general type of capitalistic entrepreneur that developed in the Yishuv was the small industrialist, merchant, or businessman, whose activities were mostly oriented toward the growing internal market. His range of activities was not very wide, and on the whole he was rather conservative in his approach. He was not usually in close contact with the colonizing agencies, although quite often he would enter into some competition with the public cooperatives.

It is evident, then, that the special set of social forces and values impinging on economic development in the Yishuv resulted in a special type of entrepreneurship that utilized the combination of these values and colonizing activities and was able, so long as there was a continuous flow of both capital and manpower, to maintain a high rate of expansion. To be sure, some of the basic administrative functions were performed by the Mandatory government, especially communications, posts, and routine police functions. But in health, education, and colonization, as well as in many spheres of local government, the Yishuv developed its own administrative framework and skills. Whatever the level of performance, the carrying out of these basic functions provided both the Yishuv and, later, the State of Israel, with parts of an administrative framework necessary for economic development, although they gave rise, of course, to problems of their own. At the same time there was a continual increase of technically skilled people within the economic organizations. For many the development of administrative skills and activities was more a matter of "pioneering" and social service than of professional careers.

ECONOMIC DEVELOPMENTS IN THE STATE OF ISRAEL

All these developments were given a great impetus by the establishment of the State of Israel, with the concomitant mass immigration.[25] These constituted major developments of the economic and social structure. As a result of the establishment of the state a new occupational sphere was created—the civil service. It was within this sphere together with the appropriate higher echelons of political activity that a great part of the power of the society became concentrated, and the men in these positions began to enjoy great prestige—much greater than was given to employees of the national institutions in the Mandatory period. In the civil service itself, new systems of gradation came into existence, within which a much greater differentiation existed than in the former national institutions. During this period there came about also in the Histadruth a change from the gradation based on such qualifications as size of family and seniority to one based upon professions and occupations. While the difference between the lowest and highest grades in the civil service is still one of the least evident in the world, yet the system of gradation constituted a major development within the state, forming a compromise between the socialist-egalitarian ideology and the pressure of occupational and economic developments. It was, and continues to be, a rather uneasy compromise, as the various strikes or threats to strike among the upper echelon and professional strata of the civil service bear witness.

The recent manpower survey conducted by the General Bureau of Statistics has indicated that services, professions, and commerce constitute 20.4 per cent, 10.3 per cent, and 12.8 per cent respectively among the Jewish population. This heavy percentage in the various services is among the highest in the world, and appears to go somewhat contrary to the original Zionist goal of normalizing the occupational structure.

The first period after the establishment of the state—until 1952—was also a period of inflation during which many unstable sectors of the economy thrived; during which it became relatively easy to earn money; during which the standard of living of many strata of the Yishuv rose, and together with it, the evaluation of pecuniary success.

All these developments and problems have had their repercussions on the patterns of economic absorption of the new immigrants. While no full statistical data are as yet available, some general indications can be offered. The main problem here concerns the extent to which specific institutional characteristics of Israeli economy are impeding or facilitating this absorption.[26]

The absorbing structure itself, for example, has tended to impede the economic development and adaptation of the Oriental immigrants. The first, most general impeding effect is due to the ascriptive allocation of various services, rights, and possibilities of consumption without basic relations to productivity. While this could, at a certain stage, provide a minimal security and other prerequisites for the acquisition of new skills—such as certain standards of health and education—beyond this level it could easily impair productivity if no steps were taken to avoid it.

Closely connected with this is the problem of dependency on various bureaucratic agencies of absorption, which give rise to passivity and lack of interest in advancement coupled with strong aggressive demands on the agencies, on the part of the immigrants.[27] All of these problems could become especially acute if the capital available to the absorbing agencies should not be sufficient to effect a rapid integration of the immigrants in productive work and have to be spent on maintaining a given level of consumption. Obviously, all this could easily develop into a vicious circle.

A second major impediment is connected with some inherent tendencies of a bureaucratic administration. In these agencies power and authority are concentrated in the hands of the absorbing sector, while the immigrants have only the more passive functions and are thus extremely dependent on the former. This state of affairs has been particularly conspicuous in the immigrants' reception camps, and it persists today, to a considerable extent, in transitional work settlements and other places. Such a formal bureaucratic and authoritarian relationship usually constitutes one of the decisive factors in the creation of social and vocational apathy and in the development of various other negative phenomena, such as peremptory demands, aggressiveness, and unwillingness to persist in any job seemingly "imposed" from above.

The last, most important impediment is connected with problems deriving from the types of entrepreneurship that are most strongly favored by the absorbing structure. Quite obviously there are many formal and informal pressures on the immigrants to produce types similar to those that existed in the Yishuv—especially the more specific "institutional" type.

Although no reliable statistical materials are as yet available, some general impressions can be given. Of the three main types of entrepreneurs that have been found in the Yishuv, only the first (the "institutional") and the third (the "petty capitalist") seem to be prevalent to any great extent among the immigrants. The second type, that of the "large-scale capitalist," is very rare—mostly owing to the very small number of new immigrants with adequate capital resources of their own. Those few having such resources have not greatly affected the over-all structure of the immigrants' economic activities. Moreover, some of them have tended to use their capital in various speculative ventures instead of in productive investments.

Many immigrants have continued, to some extent, their old pattern of activities, becoming small-scale entrepreneurs of the third type. Some have continued to be artisans of the traditional type, while many others have been drawn into the less productive sections of the economy, which expanded during the inflation and the rapid growth of the population.

The most original development among the immigrants is the "institutional" type of entrepreneur—the secretary of a cooperative settlement, the small-scale agricultural organizer, the director of a cooperative plant, the foreman or official of one of the larger agricultural or industrial enterprises, an official of one of the public or semipublic enterprises. This type developed under the impact of the specific new conditions, although obviously the other ones were also able to develop owing to various facilitating factors in the absorbing setting. Few of these new entrepreneurs have attained top economic positions, but their very development is significant.

It is also significant that, in a way, this type is being given greater chances for productive activity than the other types, although quite often a more mixed type of entrepreneurship may arise and develop. But within this framework many problems and difficulties have arisen.

The basic problem here is the hidden, but nevertheless very real competition existing between the channels of political mobility and those of clear vocational mobility. Many immigrant settlements present the following phenomenon: Because of the pressure exerted by the various absorptive frameworks—local government institutions, political parties, and the like—many of the most active immigrants choose "public activity" as the "trade" affording greatest security, and do not tend to learn any primary vocation or to persevere in one. The influence of this attitude penetrates also beyond the active stratum, into the wider circles of immigrants, who regard office work in the public sector and political activity as the most important sources of income. Moreover, the over-all sociopolitical structure of Israel, with its pressure and power groups, often influences adversely the very devotion to professional functions and the motives for maintaining a high productivity. Not infrequently the immigrants learn that it is more important to belong to a certain political trade organization than to keep up a definite standard of output and production in the plant they work in; they readily perceive that their membership in such a body will cover for low productivity. The effect of this attitude on the level of productivity and the economy is obvious.

But these impeding factors could be set off by more favorable, facilitating ones. Some of these are, in a sense, merely the other side of the impediments. Others are developments of other possibilities inherent in the absorbing structure.

One important facilitating factor is the basic social security given by the absorbing institutions. This security perhaps strengthens some of the internal forces among the immigrants, making for greater predisposition to change, greater willingness to acquire new skills and develop new attitudes toward work and economic activities. Very important in this context is the fact that these services—if properly administered—could very quickly raise the general standard of health and physical prowess. But this basic security is only the first step—and one which has dangers of its own. It is only insofar as additional reinforcing factors have been developed that the potentialities of this basic security can be maximized.

The second basic facilitating factor is the ability of the absorbing structure to sometimes provide *new social settings* in which new skills, activities, and attitudes may be learned. The best examples of this are the agricultural settlements, various urban cooperative enterprises, as well as some of the more general social and political organizations touching on economic and labor relations, such as local trade-union councils, local workers' committees, and the like. In all these cases the immigrants have not been entirely thrown into the "open" market with its impersonal relations and possibilities of disorganization, but have been enabled to participate in new, relatively stable, social groups that incorporate many of the new types of economic activities and motivations within a framework of new social values and incentives. In this way the immigrants could be spared some of the "anomic" experience of the total loss of social meaning and regulation of economic activities that often accompanies processes of detribalization and urbanization.

It has already been pointed out that inflexible, authoritarian, bureaucratic attitudes, which tended to disorganize the existing groups, usually had totally disruptive results. Insofar as family and inter-generational relations were not purposefully disrupted, insofar as the agents of the absorbing society worked, at least to some extent, with the traditional elites and groups, and tried to maintain the status of these elites in some parts of the social structure—as in the traditional spheres of religious activities or in dealing with certain daily problems—to this extent the general process of adaptation and learning and the development of new types of elites and entrepreneurs in the economic and political spheres proceeded successfully. The interesting fact, from the point of view of this analysis, is that such a flexible approach was one of the possibilities inherent in the structure of the absorbing society and its institutions with their emphasis on social values, on "ascriptive" rights of different groups, and with their need to incorporate the immigrant groups speedily both in the political and the economic spheres.

Obviously enough this means—perhaps somewhat paradoxically—that the best adaptation is made not when the traditional groups are completely disorganized and their traditional values disrupted, but when they are to some extent transformed and incorporated as legitimate subgroups (or subcultures) in the new settings. This, however, poses an important problem that has been often mentioned in the discussion of these topics,[28] namely, whether the more traditional groups, with their somewhat larger emphasis on family and other particularistic relations, can behave successfully in a modern economic setting. The answer to this in our setting is two-fold. The first lies in the nature of the specific type of entrepreneurship which has developed in the Yishuv and which contained some such orientations. Secondly, this very type of entrepreneurship could develop then, and even more now, among some of the immigrant groups, because of certain basic economic and absorption policies of the state—the effect of most of which is to minimize to some extent the risks to be directly borne by the enterprising unit.

The government itself has afforded some basic economic security within which the immigrants' development can take place. Within this framework the immigrants can much more easily find a place for some of their traditional social structures than if they were entirely thrown on their own resources in an open market. The government has also minimized some of the graver risks of the immigrants by tying their investment to the broader policy of the various settlement agencies. This has also enabled the maintenance of "wider" economic relations within the family, so that the small family unit need not be entirely dependent upon its own resources and the open market.

The government (or other public bodies) may also provide the immigrants—through its various enterprises—with guidance and help in their transition to new types of economic activities and time orientations. As most of the long-time measures and problems of economic development are closely connected with various state activities and policies, the adaptation of the immigrants to new organizational skills and the new time perspective may be greatly facilitated and made gradual.

Both the impediments and the facilitating factors of the immigrants' adaptation to modern economic activities are closely connected with problems of capital formation and productivity. The facilitating factors can be greatly reinforced through the existence of adequate capital for long-term industrialization. Their effects on the industrialization and full occupational absorption of the immigrants, and on the level of productivity of the economy as a whole, will be fully discernible only in relatively long-range terms. In the future they may raise many problems and difficulties because of the outlay of capital they demand. The impeding factors use up, in the short run, less capital—but this is spent entirely on consumption. They may also seem to facilitate the occupational absorption of the immigrants —but mostly in the less productive secondary and tertiary occupations.

ISRAEL

Political Institutions

The preceding sections analyzing economic patterns and inter-generational relations have already touched on the value and status system in the Yishuv. In proceeding to a more detailed analysis of these institutional problems it seems best to analyze the political sphere on the one hand, and that of social stratification and value-orientation on the other. In the organization of these spheres the ways in which the society was integrated can be discerned. Moreover, it will be mainly in these fields that the major changes which took place after the establishment of the state can be fully discovered and their implications most clearly seen.

THE SCOPE OF THE YISHUV'S POLITICAL ACTIVITY

What may be called the "realm of power" of the Yishuv and its national institutions, the scope and framework of the political activities of these institutions, and their sources of power are of particular importance. The various national institutions of the Yishuv and the Zionist movement (the Vaad Leumi, the Jewish Agency, etc.) dealt mostly with the following matters: (1) development of Jewish colonization, both rural and urban, in Palestine; (2) arrangements for immigration into Palestine from various countries of the Diaspora; (3) maintenance and development of Jewish military defense—the illegal Haganah, various semilegal and legal police groups (and during World War II, mobilization in the British Army); (4) development of an active "foreign" policy—oriented mainly toward the Mandatory government and League of Nations—the main aim of which was to increase the scope of immigration and colonization, to maintain the political autonomy of the Yishuv and ultimately to create the Jewish State; (5) maintenace of an autonomous system of education; (6) maintenance of an autonomous religious organization; (7) maintenance of some social services, especially of a wide network of health services which had in themselves a colonizing and pioneering aspect. Significantly enough, the first four tasks were primarily in the hands of the Zionist organization and the Jewish Agency, while the others were mostly in the hands of the Vaad Leumi (National Council). In this way the fact was emphasized that the actual Yishuv at any time was only one stage in the constant development of the Zionist enterprise.

The various routine tasks of administering the country—communication services, police, legal system, and, to some extent, local government also—were mostly in the hands of the Mandatory government. Many tensions existed between the government and the national institutions both in major issues of policy (immigration, etc.) and in those spheres where their activities encroached on each other. But the interesting fact is that the Jewish institutions dealt mostly with what may be broadly called "colonizing" tasks which had a marked future-orientation. Thus Jewish institutions did not have to deal to any great extent with the allocation of purely economic facilities, nor with the maintenance of instrumental relations and order within the society. The only major exception was the allocation of the various funds for colonization and for "constructive" works. However, in this respect most of these facilities were constantly allocated to *new* groups of pioneers and immigrants and not necessarily to the existing population. Many of these new groups were strongly connected with existing groups— they belonged to the same party or movement and had common political interests.

The main sources of power of the Jewish institutions were the various voluntary contributions gathered among Jews all over the world and in Palestine. Their main moral and social basis was the preparedness of most of the social groups in Palestine to accept their discipline in political matters and to volunteer for various tasks—participation in the defense force (Haganah), in colonization work, and in various types of "passive resistance" toward the Mandatory power. In addition, the national institutions could rely on the Zionist movement abroad and on Gentile and Jewish public opinion as a potential source of influence, if not direct power.

THE PARADOX OF INTENSIVE POLITICAL ACTIVITY
IN A STATELESS COMMUNITY

Those are, however, only the more formal—although important—aspects of the power resources of the Jewish national institutions. They pose a more crucial problem. All the various political and semipolitical functions that were performed by the national institutions, as well as the sources of their power, were not based on coercive political authority and state power. They were all recruited and performed on the basis of voluntary sacrifice and work. How then was this paradox—the performance of political functions without state power—performed? It is not enough to point out that the Yishuv was in part created by revolutionary pioneers who consecrated themselves to these colonizing tasks. Although true in itself, this does not provide a full explanation. These pioneer groups were not monastic sects shutting themselves off from participation in wider social and political life. Through their work and through the work of the movement from which they came they continuously created a powerful social and economic reality, with many positions of power and many consequent problems. They performed, as noted above, political functions, and although many of these were oriented towards the future, yet through them new frameworks of power were constantly created.

It is also important to remember that there did not exist only one pioneer group. There were many of them, of different political parties and ideologies, and the continuous creation of power and wealth only intensified the problem of how to keep them united in one common framework and maintain their common allegiance to the national institutions, which had no coercive power. Again, it is not sufficient to give a formal answer only, i.e., to point out that the governing bodies of these institutions were democratically elected and were usually formed by a coalition of the main groups and parties. It is important to analyze how the actual social and political processes were organized within these institutions and how this organization enabled them to solve this paradox of performing intensive political functions by a stateless community. It is, however, worth while to indicate here that during the greater part of their history the Yishuv and the Zionist organization were governed by a coalition of the main parties — from left to right, with but few extremes. This is very significant as it indicated clearly that these institutions could be maintained *only* through the widest possible popular support.[29]

THE DISTRIBUTION OF POWER IN THE YISHUV

The most important fact concerning the distribution of power in the Yishuv was a relatively wide dispersal of political power and prestige. This was due not only to the fact that political institutions lacked coercive power, but also to the fact that some, at any rate, of the sources of political and economic power were not in themselves concentrated. They were based, as we have already seen, on the voluntary discipline of the Zionist groups abroad; consequently there were always many different points of pressure and possibilities of influence, none of which could easily be concentrated or controlled. As a result, this wide dispersal of power developed. Many and diverse social and political groups and organizations existed. Many such associations, parties, and groups were constantly created and claimed scope for their activity. They were primarily semi-autonomous groups which did not derive their power and prestige from the national institutions even if they acknowledged their supremacy. There did not exist within the Yishuv any central "fountain of honor" with complete monopolization of prestige and power. Most of these associations and groups also served as channels of prestige and emphasized the centripetal tendency in the distribution of power.

THE COMPOSITION AND ACTIVITIES OF THE ELITES

The factor of wide dispersal of power and prestige can be clearly discerned also in the composition of the elites and in the pattern of their values and activities. The political elite of the Yishuv can be identified with the leaders of the various national institutions, their main parties and movements, their main officials, civic leaders, the heads of the main Jewish municipalities. All the bodies, headed by the elites, were more or less democratically elected by most of the adults in the Yishuv, in a given municipality.

The focus of their values and ideology was the idea of national service and also, although to a somewhat lesser extent, social service. It was maintained that those most active and most powerful in the realization of the main values and aspirations of Zionism should be the political leaders. On this point there were not many substantial differences between the left, center, and right-wing groups of the Yishuv and the Zionist movement, the main difference being in the interpretation of what constituted the "best" way of serving the Yishuv. It was only gradually that a second full-fledged ideology developed according to which economic power and wealth were *in themselves* justification for political power. Until the end of the Mandatory period, this ideology and value orientation were but secondary in the Yishuv's social structure. Thus it came to pass that a disproportionately large part of the officeholders and influential people in the Yishuv's political organization consisted of members of collective settlements, former workers in the agricultural colonies, intellectual leaders of the various movements (there was very definite overlapping between the last two categories), leaders of youth movements, and the like. At the outset there were not many holders of private economic power or pure political or trade-union "bosses" among the first rank of leadership. Only gradually did the last type develop among the second and third strata of leadership.

The basic ethos of the elite and the whole Yishuv gave rise to a minimal differentiation in the standard of living of the elite members as distinct from that of other groups, and the predominant attitude was that economic gain was not appropriate as remuneration for elites. As we have already seen above, the wage policy of the national institutions and of the Histadruth usually did not give rise to any great distinction in the standard of living of the entire elite as compared to other strata of the population. The pioneering ethos was very pronounced from this point of view, and satisfaction with proper performance of service and the personal esteem derived from it had to be adequate compensation for political and social activity. Social status and prestige were largely dependent on these criteria, and although various strata with a more individualistic achievement orientation developed, the basic ethos of the volunteer and pioneer persisted and manifested itself in style of dress, of dwelling, and the like. The leadership of the Yishuv and the strata with highest social prestige (insofar as a unitary criterion existed) did not belong to high income brackets, and emphasized their simple way of life as part of the legitimization of their power.

This tendency was even more pronounced from the point of view of the exercise of political power, of what Lasswell calls "accountability" and the concomitant distribution of power within the Yishuv. The first was exercise of authority through largely informal relations. This was rooted in the necessity to use persuasive—and only to a very limited extent coercive—power in order to assure political obedience and identification. Hence there were always many informal, direct relations among the various strata of leaders and between them and the general public. This is in line with the general importance of the multiple primary group relations outlined above. To these various parties, groups, and associations described earlier, the elite were largely accountable and they usually participated actively in them.

The main social characteristics of the elite were also in line with the activities of these groups. Thus we have already mentioned that most of the upper ranks of the elites were "pioneer leaders," many of them members of the various agricultural settlements, and many of them engaged in various cultural and social activities. Many of them had an intellectual background, and many of the intellectuals and literati of the Yishuv participated in the various groups and associations.

This pattern of elite activities signifies the great importance which ideology—the Zionist and socialist ideology—had in the political life of the Yishuv. There was a very strong interest in ideology and adherence to it, especially among the elite, and the various tenets of the ideology served as important criteria for evaluation of daily political activities. While with the growth of the Yishuv and the development of various economic power structures the importance of ideology began to wane somewhat, yet until the end of the Mandatory period and the War of Independence, it held an important place in the political life of the community.

POLITICAL ACTIVITY IN THE YISHUV: THE

RESOLUTION OF THE PARADOX

In general it may be said that a very great part of the political activity of the Yishuv was maintained within primary, nonformalized groups, and that the various formal bodies and frameworks (the formal organizations of the national institutions, the various political parties, etc.) developed mostly from such informal groups and maintained their activities through these groups, although more and more formal power organization developed. This was even true, to a very large extent, of the Haganah, the illegal army of the Yishuv. It is worth while to mention that, unlike many other immigrant countries, the new immigrants in the Yishuv were very quickly absorbed not only within the framework of the formal political institutions, but also within the various primary groups. This explains the relatively weak development of specific "ethnic" associations and political parties in the Yishuv.[30]

It seems that these various characteristics of political activity in the Yishuv can explain how the basic paradox of intensive political activity in a stateless society was solved. This paradox was solved in a twofold way. On the one hand, most of the political activity and power relations did not deal to a great extent with internal instrumental activities. It was mostly oriented either toward "external politics" or toward increasing efforts in colonization and defense. It may perhaps be said that one way in which the strong solidarity of the Yishuv was maintained was through the segregation of day-to-day regulation from future-oriented politics. The colonizing activities enabled the various political groups to find ample scope for their activities without impinging to excess on other groups and without the necessity of excessively intensifying various internal conflicts. Thus it was significant that the formation of any strong political consensus in the Yishuv did not involve much of an adherence to formal rules of procedure in allocation of various facilities, in settlement of disputes, and

422

the like.[31] Only at the end of the Mandatory period—in the forties—did such problems become more and more acute, but even they were overshadowed by the intense political struggle with the Mandatory power. In this way the adherence of most groups and parties—with the exception of the "dissident-terrorist"[32] organizations—to the national institutions was maintained.

But the future-oriented colonizing and political activities demanded much self-sacrifice, discipline, and volunteering for various tasks. These were attained and maintained through the strong internal identification of the various political and social groups of the Yishuv, and through the small differentiation between elites and non-elites on the one hand and close relations between them on the other hand. In this way a very strong internal solidarity of the various strata of the Yishuv was achieved and their preparedness to fulfill the various political duties was intensified.

THE CHANGE IN THE FRAMEWORK OF POWER

The basic framework of power of the Yishuv was entirely changed with the establishment of the State of Israel. While from the formal point of view the main changes were in the establishment of an independent, democratic government, with a parliament and a judiciary, the internal changes in the social process of political life were no less significant. The major change brought about by the creation of the state was the development of new power frameworks and positions. First of all, the new state took over all the various parts of the Mandatory administration. Second, a new national army was created. Third, owing to the various plans of development, many new administrative frameworks and posts had to be created and maintained. Fourth, the influx of so many immigrants and the necessity of absorbing them and of allocating facilities also necessitated the expansion of such frameworks and organizations. All these developments gave rise to a whole gamut of new political power positions which had not existed before. The basic social and economic policy of the new government—a policy of social service, of strong socialist traditions and of a welfare state—only increased the scope of the new society's potential political power.

The most important change was not in the mere increase of power but in the change in its nature, organization, and scope. All these changes in power took place without great changes in the social structure of the political institutions. The major change was, of course, that an independent

423

system of government had been established with its own parliamentary institutions, but to a great extent there was a continuation of the political arrangements that had existed in the national institutions. This was especially true of the composition of successive governments. All of them were coalition governments, with the moderate labor party (M.A.P.A.I.), some moderate religious parties, and the "progressives" almost always participating. During some periods more rightist groups of the "general Zionists," the more orthodox religious groups, and the more leftist groups of MAPAM and "Unity of Labor" have participated. Only the two extremist groups, the Communists on the left and the "HERUT" (Liberty) party on the right have never participated.[33]

New principles and ways of allocation of power and facilities developed within the state. It should be emphasized that what is meant here are the actual processes of allocation within the framework of a democratic state, based on free elections and parliamentary responsibility of the government.[34] The basic democratic principles were also actually upheld through the constant competition for power, which was maintained within legitimate limits and based on freedom of speech and opposition. However, the nature of such competition and of the basic principles of allocation of power and of the actual norms regulating the competition for it changed tremendously from those that existed during the period of the Yishuv. The four main changes were the following: (a) a growing centralization of the basic framework of power within the hands of the government and its administrative appendices; (b) a rise in the social evaluation of power and power relations; (c) a shift in the type of political activities; and (d) a concomitant growth in the differentiation between various strata in general, and between elite and non-elite in particular, with respect to the allocation of facilities in various social and economic fields.

The trend toward centralization could be seen in the attempts of the government to concentrate in its hands the control of various power possibilities within the state. This was done both through the government's undertaking certain enterprises directly (with the incident possibilities of allocation of power positions), or through the exercise of control with the help of regulations in the economic sphere—in allocation of import and export licenses, regulation of prices, and the like. While all this did not, of course, do away with other centers of power—economic and political— vested in various nongovernmental groups, it did necessitate the orientation of these groups to the framework set up by the government. Thus the government and its various agencies became the focal point of distribution of power and allocation of facilities, even if they did not have an over-all monopoly of them. In addition, the government made several attempts— not always entirely successful—to concentrate all the external resources of power, such as foreign loans and moneys from the United Jewish Appeal, in its own hands (or those of the Jewish Agency) and to minimize the direct approach by various groups within the state to these external sources of power.

Side by side with this there developed also an increase in the value of power and power positions; and the holding of such a position gradually became a value in its own right. This probably was the result of several interconnected reasons. The state was seen as—or at least declared to be by the elite—the embodiment, even if a partial one, of Zionist values and aspirations, which now were given the first opportunity to be realized in an unhampered way. The power of the state could thus easily be seen as the fullest expression of these ideals. Furthermore, the very achievement of independent power by people and elites long deprived of it, tended to make them put a great value on it and see in it a recompense for all past sacrifices. In addition, the dependence of the population on the bearers of political power in many other fields served also as a contributing factor.

But in order to understand fully this change in the evaluation of power, it is important to remember and to analyze the shift in the type and direction of political activity. The strong emphasis on colonizing activities, on "foreign policy" as contrasted with the regulation of internal power and instrumental relations, the strong future-orientation as opposed to emphasis on the present have rapidly changed. Truly enough, many new colonizing activities were undertaken and masses of new immigrants, which doubled the population, were taken in. But these activities were now maintained not as a means toward future goals, but as a part of the existing machinery of the state. Even though the society of the state was constantly changing and developing, this change was effected within an existing political framework. Hence most of these processes became more and more concerned with the internal processes of allocation of power and not only with development of future-orientation and political solidarity.

THE ORGANIZATION OF POLITICAL ACTIVITIES

The main change in the organization of political activities can be described as follows: growing formalization, bureaucratization, and loss of the cohesiveness of the various primary groups and of their direct relation to the central values of the society. The process of formalization and bureaucratization may be summarized briefly as follows:

First, it could be discerned in the growing number of various bureaucratic organizations — those of the government, the Jewish Agency, the Histadruth, and the various political parties. It was estimated that about 30 per cent of those gainfully employed were in the "service" class. One small party with only eight members in the Knesseth (Parliament) had about five hundred officials on its payroll. This bureaucratization proved to be a heavy burden on the state's economy and became somewhat of a problem as it tended to give undue weight to the so-called "tertiary" occupations in the economic structure of the society.

The rising value of power as such was necessarily connected with a parallel growth of differential distribution of rewards in other, mainly economic, fields—particularly in the field of consumption. Although the growing differentiation in the standard of living was not very great as compared to other countries, it was real enough, especially with regard to rare commodities, such as housing, transportation facilities (cars), various utensils for domestic use, trips abroad, and the like. Thus competition for power positions was strongly connected with an orientation toward the attainment of facilities in other fields, namely, in the economic field.

Second, the growth of bureaucratization was evinced in the fact that the various bureaucratic frameworks, whether political or economic (the two were usually closely interwoven), became the most important channels of distribution of the various scarce facilities (housing, food, trips abroad, etc.). This was probably truer of the various bureaucratic hierarchies than in the case of the top elite. This does not necessarily mean that there was a very unequal distribution of those facilities among different strata of the population. Obviously no exact data are available, but it seems that such inequality, although it did exist, was not overwhelming (i.e., among the old inhabitants). The most important fact was that most of the distribution was directed through bureaucratic channels, and those who were far from them could become underprivileged in this respect.

Third, and even more significant, bureaucratization could be seen in the tendency to resolve most social and economic problems by bureaucratic regulations and laws rather than by voluntary civil action. A rapid abatement developed in the variety of voluntary civic associations and groups that existed within the Yishuv. Some of them, like the Haganah, became naturally transformed into formal, compulsory units. But others, whose fields of activity were not necessarily so regulated, either disappeared or lost their significance. The enormous concentration of power and competition for it gave rise to the attitude that most social problems could be solved by legislation and administrative regulations, and many attempts at voluntary civic activity died out because of lack of proper encouragement.

Accordingly, the importance of formal, bureaucratic bodies became great not only within the general framework of the state, but also within the sphere of civic life and associations. Within them there was little scope for nonbureaucratic, nonparty associations and activities. Parallel changes could also be discerned in the internal organization of the parties. Everywhere there was growing formalization and bureaucratization and growing dissociation between the formal institutions and frameworks and the primary groups of members. Within the various parties themselves there was also strong competition for allocation of facilities and power. The formerly strong solidarity became weakened, and more and more utilitarian orientations prevailed in the attitudes of the members to their parties.[35]

All this did not give rise to a pure Weberian type of neutral bureaucracy. The nonbureaucratic elements existed not only on the top, directive levels —as in all bureaucratic systems—but became strongly interwoven also at other levels. Thus, for instance, many ministries were staffed, at least beyond the purely technical levels (and sometimes even on these levels) by members of the party or group to which the minister belonged. Most of the main positions were already filled before attempts at establishing a purely nonpartisan policy of appointment were made. This does not necessarily mean that these positions were filled without regard to professional qualifications, but only that there usually were additional considerations not of a neutral character. In addition, the mere fact that various bureaucratic machines were competing for the allocation of various facilities and that numerous interrelations existed between the various machines necessarily diminished the possibility of a "neutral" state bureaucracy.

CHANGES IN THE STRUCTURE AND ACTIVITIES OF THE ELITE

As could be foreseen, this gave rise to a marked change in the composition of the elite, in their relations to various public groups and their accountability to these groups, and in the general nature and organization of political activity.

Owing to the growth of power positions, the number of the elite has increased considerably. The process of internal differentiation within the elite has also developed intensively. There was the "natural" differentiation between various layers of the elite, and a very rapid growth within the middle and lower layers (small party "bosses" and secretaries, various underlings of big bosses, and party bureaucrats).

In a parallel fashion there began to develop, on the one hand, more professional elites—in the bureaucracy, in the army, in the judiciary—while on the other hand there developed also the more "professional" politicians and bosses. Significantly enough, many tensions and divergencies arose between these two groups. The relative homogeneity of the elite of the Yishuv—a homogeneity both of social origins and of patterns of activities —gave place to a marked differentiation. This differentiation was also closely connected with the rising value of power. This led to a greater concentration on purely political activities, to a lessening of the cultural activities of the elite, and to a relatively strong dissociation from the intellectual and cultural elite of the country. Thus the internal homogeneity and cohesion of the elite became weakened to some extent.[36]

All this had, of course, repercussions on the relations between the elite and non-elite. The strong permeation of the elite by various primary groups and the direct "accounting" by the elites to these groups and their emotional dependence on them were weakened to a great extent. The elite members somehow detached themselves and formed groups of their own—although, it seems, with but little internal primary cohesion—and their pattern of life and association began to be distinguished from that of the non-elite and dissociated from them.

The increasing formality of relations and social differentiation also necessarily changed the internal relations between elite and non-elite groups in the sphere of political activity. Instead of more or less common action, with only differentiation of roles in the realization of common tasks, there developed relations based on the allocation of patronage and different facilities at the disposal of the central political agencies. As there was a parallel increase in the scope of affairs managed by the political agencies, owing to growing bureaucratization and the development of a welfare-state policy, the scope of such allocation became enlarged. The various social and civil groups which existed within the Yishuv quickly transformed themselves into pressure groups for the achievement of maximum allocation from the "common pool." Relations between them and the elites were focused on the maximal exploitation of their mutual connections. There developed a continuous "trade" over the distribution of the various allocations within the scope of the elites. Most of the internal political activity within the state—including to some extent the distribution of portfolios, of nomination for administrative positions—became directed into these channels. The same applies also to the various economic and professional groups. The strong cohesion and interrelation of social and political groups, which was to a great extent maintained by the performance of common tasks and a common way of life with but little differentiation, tended to disintegrate.

An additional important aspect of the changes in the political activities in the Yishuv was the growing dissociation between ideology (Zionist, socialist, etc.) and the realities of social and political life and activities. While the official ideology was strongly adhered to, particularly by the elite, and even new aspects—e.g., "the ingathering of exiles"—were added or strongly emphasized, yet apathy increased toward it within the wider public. "Talking Zionism" became a cynical, derogatory term. It was only in strongly oppositional circles—mostly left-wing parties—that ideology still played an important part. Otherwise the importance of ideology, and adherence to it, became weakened because of all the processes described above—the weakening of collective values, the increasing emphasis on power, and the dissociation between elite and non-elite. Wider and wider social spheres became dissociated from ideology and more and more instrumentally oriented. Ideology increasingly began to serve as a cloak for various interests of this kind. The most significant fact in this respect was the already mentioned dissociation of the political elite from the intellectual and literary groups.

A new important factor in the political structure of the strata was presented by the recent immigrants, who acquired the right to vote usually after a very short period of residence (about half a year to a year), and thus became of great significance to the several competing parties. But their participation in the political process differed greatly from the pattern of political participation that existed in the Yishuv. They were at first mostly passive objects of the political activity of the different parties. They were promised various rewards for voting for this or that party, and the allocation of different services to them was often used as a means of political pressure. The extent of their own active and conscious participation in political life was at the beginning very small, but it has since increased; in the last (1955) elections they showed some independence of the government parties. The great majority of them also developed a purely instrumental attitude toward political activities and organizations. Only a very small number of people from among the new immigrants became really interested and active in political life—and even here the greatest proportion were motivated to do so as a means for attaining better economic positions. Conscious political activity and interest developed only in certain places, as in some of the settlements which became well established. But during the first steps of absorption, manifestations of interest in political affairs were exceptional. Despite, or because of, the great concentration of power in the hands of the political elite and the bureaucratic organizations, and efforts to capitalize on the political value (because of their great number) of the new immigrants, the latter evinced a growing apathy toward political activity, interest, and ideology. They felt their dependence on various agencies, but were either confident of being able to wrest from them the rewards they were interested in, and/or they despaired of gaining any possible influence over them. At the same time, however, the gradual development and increased stability of some institutions took place, reflecting the trend toward the concentration of power and indicating a degree of public interest in political affairs. The growing prestige and popularity of the presidency (although largely a nonpolitical office) is one manifestation of this. But the most important one is perhaps the growing prestige of the Supreme Court and the whole judiciary, which seems to be a very significant development; but as yet it is difficult to estimate fully the significance of all these changes.

Aspects of Cultural Life

The two main starting points toward attaining a better understanding of certain aspects of cultural life in Israel are (a) the fact that one of the basic goals of the Zionist movement was the renaissance of Hebrew culture—a renaissance which would include both modernization and "going back" to its original sources; and (b) the fact that most of the population of the Yishuv had a relatively high degree of literacy and a wide range of cultural interests, partly brought over from the countries of origin and partly developed in Israel, which made these people important consumers of cultural goods. Thus two trends developed, one of cultural creativity, the second of cultural consumption, which sometimes reinforced and sometimes opposed each other.

In the field of cultural creativity and renovation a number of great feats were accomplished. The most important was the total regeneration of the Hebrew language, which became the official and the paramount language of the Yishuv and was rapidly adapted to the needs of a modern society. Hebrew theaters developed and flourished, a wide net of newspapers was established, the whole educational system—from the kindergarten to the university—was conducted in Hebrew. Hebrew literature also developed vigorously; many modern works have been and are being published by writers of high literary achievement. But it was not only the quantitative development of the Hebrew language and literature that was here important. Of no small significance was the strong identification of many groups in Israel wtih cultural creativity in general. Most significant were the numerous attempts to create festivals or to give new meanings to old ones, to develop folk dances and folk art. These attempts were especially strong in the agricultural settlements and in youth movements, but spread also to wider strata of the population, and today many of them have become a part of daily and festival routine. Most of these attempts were rather secularly oriented, although they sought to revive, in part, ancient, especially biblical, traditions.[37] But these attempts at cultural creativity could not satisfy all the cultural needs of the population; great areas of cultural consumption in the fields of literature, motion pictures, and plays were based either on Hebrew translations of foreign plays or on direct reading in foreign languages. (While at the beginning the various languages of the countries of origin predominated, the English language gradually became the main foreign language taught in schools in Palestine.) In this way the cultural contacts with European tradition and culture were maintained, although quite often tensions developed between the emphasis on original cultural creativity and this "foreign" consumption. But these tensions became less acute with the years, for two reasons. One was that with the total victory of Hebrew it became easier to avail oneself of foreign languages, and the second was that the general level of cultural interest and sensitivity seemed to decline a little with time, especially among the second generation. The latter grew up in a new cultural setting, and many of the acute cultural problems of the former generation were not so important for them. This gave rise on the one hand to a lesser *general* interest, among the population, in many of the "higher" aspects of culture while at the same time it enabled smaller groups to develop creative and professional interests in literature and the arts.

But this stabilization of cultural patterns did not mean that a more or less homogeneous and unified pattern should develop. The whole situation is as yet in a state of constant flux, the end product of which it is difficult to envisage. While the general pattern was secular, religious and traditional values still had a hold in daily life on many of the non-Orthodox. The secular renaissance was so strongly interwoven with the revival of tradition that it was difficult—even if people really were interested—to distinguish between religious and secular values. Within the field of the renaissance itself, there were many selective processes, each of which emphasized different aspects or periods of the tradition. Biblical or Second Temple times; Palestinian versus general Jewish values; agricultural versus urban; and so on. With the destruction of east-European Jewry under the Nazis, great parts of their tradition—against which many of the original settlers rebelled—were also rediscovered and incorporated in literary works and in other cultural activities. With the influx of the new Oriental immigrants who had a rich folklore tradition, a new element came in. All these trends are still developing, each claiming the allegiance of different groups which often overlap one another.

It is perhaps possible to indicate one point on which the change in cultural orientation was full and which enabled, in a way, the coexistence and constant development of these different trends. In contrast with traditional Jewish society, the new cultural activity was dominated by a strong historical awareness focused on the continuity of the Jewish nation and its relations with Palestine. This was no longer a ritual-mythological relation. The common value orientation which encompassed all cultural activity was historically oriented. Even among most of the religious people this transformation took place. And it was this strong historical emphasis and orientation, the over-all attempt to re-create the continuity between the past and the future, that became the common denominator of most of the cultural activity and cultural consciousness in the Yishuv, and which at the same time enabled the flexibility and coexistence of many different trends and patterns of development.

Value Systems and Stratification

Many significant changes took place in the systems of stratification and main value orientations of the Yishuv after the establishment of the State of Israel, and it is possible to indicate some of the probable future trends of development. This analysis will not deal, however, with these institutional spheres alone. As these institutions constitute the integrative foci of the whole social system, I shall deal here, even if only by implication, with the interrelations among institutions, and with the nature of social consensus and integration.

The main changes in the value systems can be described as the relative weakening of the old pioneering, social-national values; the growing importance and autonomy of instrumental, economic criteria and orientations; the weakening of the strong future orientations; and the growing importance of political power. It is this growing importance of political power that maintained the continuity of the collective orientations in the social system but at the same time created many social tensions and foci of malintegration. This was so because the high evaluation of political power did not "neutralize" the importance of purely economic factors and criteria, as was the case with the former pioneering social values, but recognized their importance while at the same time it tried to subjugate them to considerations of power and political expediency. This was, in its turn, strongly connected with the weakening of the former future orientation and the shift in every-day life to considerations of allocation of rewards.

A strong trend toward conspicuous consumption, well above the standard of other strata of the population, was confined mainly to the top economic elite, to some parts of the political and bureaucratic elite, and to the professional elite. The existence of many channels of mobility made this pattern a focus of emulation and envy, with concomitant tensions, among the other strata. There also developed a growing proximity between the purely economic elite and the political and bureaucratic elite, while a dissociation developed between these and the intellectual and cultural elite. The points of social and cultural contact between different strata diminished and became more and more formalized. But at the same time, possibilities of economic advancement for many groups continued to exist, owing to the constant emphasis on economic development. The general impression, however, is that these possibilities of mobility have not yet caught up with the process of differentiation and dissociation among different groups and strata. Moreover, it seems that the process of mobility does not give rise to growing primary contacts among different groups and strata, but rather to the development of somewhat segregated clusters of different economic and professional groups. In most of these groups there seems also to develop a style of life which greatly emphasizes different types and levels of conspicuous consumption and rather mass types of entertainment and cultural consumption, with great emphasis on mass media. All this is in line both with the growth of segregated, private spheres of life and the increased formalization of over-all social relations. These changes were perhaps most manifest in the field of general, social, associational activity—in the structure of the so-called voluntary associations.[38]

In the Yishuv there were a large number of voluntary associations and groups of various kinds. Their apparent aims were manifold, relating to culture, literature, recreation, maintenance of various social services, and so on. There are no exact statistics in regard to these associations, but that their number was large is well known. Despite their great variety, these associations had some basic characteristics which were shared by most but not by all of them. The most important characteristics of these groups were the following: (a) Most of them were closely related to, and quite often a part of, general social movements, organizations (the Labor movement, the Zionist organizations), and political parties. (b) Most of them performed certain functions of vital importance within the community, such as guard duty and defense (as was the case with the Haganah, the semilegal defense organization, which also consisted mostly of voluntary groups), medical aid (the Red Shield Society), social welfare, propagation of the Hebrew language, helping the communal and cooperative settlements, advertising local products, and developing various professional and cultural activities. (c) Because they performed these functions, most of the groups were closely connected with the central social and political activities of the community and its centers of power and influence. (d) Most of the groups conceived of themselves as realizing, in one way or another, the Zionist ideal of national rebirth. In the majority of cases, just as in the dominant value system of the Yishuv, there was usually little differentiation between social, political, and cultural aspects and ideals, although one or another of these would obviously receive stronger emphasis in certain groups.

The structural pattern of the associations described above was largely absent in those sectors of the Yishuv which did not share in the dominant pioneering value system.[39] This was true both of the sectors usually called "private," in which to some extent a purely economic scale of values prevailed, and of the groups, usually concentrated in those sections of the lower and middle economic strata, which were entirely apathetic to the common values of the society or only partly interested in them. Within these sectors the connection between the purely "social" side and active participation in the central spheres of the society was either entirely absent or very weak. In the higher levels of the purely economically oriented strata, there existed certain forms of social, philanthropic, and cultural activities (e.g., lodges and clubs), which symbolized to some extent their wider interests and cultural orientation, without, however, always being directly related to the central values of the society or to the performance of central tasks in it. In the lower, more apathetic strata the main types of social life outside the family and place of work could be found in informal social groups and gatherings, in which the main preoccupations were eating, playing cards, dancing, and similar pastimes. These people lacked special cultural activities of any specific symbolic value, and their activities did not extend beyond the maintenance of internal, solidary relations.

The whole pattern of associational activity in the main sectors of the Yishuv changed considerably after the establishment of the State of Israel. While here, also, adequate statistical data are lacking, it is possible to establish the general trends on the basis of documentary material. Moreover, a survey of various research findings found in other studies, comprising about 1500 individuals (even though these are not an adequate sample of the whole population), also indicates these general trends. On the basis of all these data, it can be postulated that the most important changes were the following: (a) multiplication of the purely social type of association, which had existed in the more passive sectors of the Yishuv, and its diffusion among many social groups and sectors; (b) a strong decline in the semivoluntary activities and associations which had performed various civic activities in the community, with a relative increase in purely philanthropic associations; (c) the transformation of many of the former groups and associations into pure pressure groups aimed at exerting pressure on governmental bodies for the purpose of receiving various facilities; and (d) the development of several new types of associations and groups.

Among the new associations the following were found to be rather prevalent: (a) variations of the purely social type, whose activities usually combined leisure-time activities with talks and discussions of a topical or intellectual nature; (b) purely or mainly ideological clubs or groups, the purpose of which was either to discuss topical issues or to develop a generally intellectual orientation in contemporary society, and which dealt with various problems of Zionism, problems of the state, government, education, and the like (in contrast to the former type, the purely social side was not strongly emphasized, as reflected in the fact that married couples rarely participated together); (c) formal clubs which combined ideological discussions with more or less explicit political orientation, and which aimed at attaining some degree of influence in the political life of the state, cutting across various parties; and (d) the Volunteers' group (Shurat Hamitnadvim), which aimed at giving new impetus to voluntary work in Israel, improving relations with the new immigrants, and combating various manifestations of corruption, official bureaucracy, and general apathy in public life. This group also conducted certain activities which were oriented toward active social participation and influence in public life.

These new associations differed from the older ones in several important structural characteristics, among which the following were the most important: (a) Within most of them the close association between the purely social, solidary side and accepted and legitimized participation in the central political and cultural spheres of the society did not exist. (b) As has already been mentioned, most of the accepted and fully recognized civic duties were not undertaken or successfully performed by them, and their interest in such activities dwindled to a very great extent. (c) Most of these associations (with the partial exception of some of the ideological groups) were not related to any existing social movements, organizations, parties, and the like, and usually emphasized their dissociation from such groups. Even those with a strong activistic tendency (like the Volunteers' group) emphasized either their nonpolitical bent, or at least their tendency to draw adherents from various political parties, and in this way to cut across them. (d) Most of these groups had no direct or strong contact with the upper elite of the country.

A parallel pattern—closely connected with the former one—can be discerned also in the sphere of cultural activity and participation. While the general trend of cultural and intellectual activity has continued, and the number of theaters, literary magazines, and institutions of higher education has increased considerably, all these activities have become more and more segregated in special organizations and the participation of the general public has greatly, if not totally, decreased. Here also we have a reversal of the former pattern of relatively active participation and interest in cultural creativeness. Private "consumption" of different types of cultural creation has greatly increased. Moreover, interest has become much more heterogeneous, even from the point of view of the language (the number of non-Hebrew magazines, newspapers, and dramatic performances has been greatly increased). Together with this there developed a trend toward somewhat greater emphasis on religious traditions. Here the situation was somewhat complicated and even paradoxical. The gulf between the ultra-Orthodox and other strata of the Yishuv became perhaps greater, sometimes even giving rise to outright tension and small-scale collisions. But at the same time, the nonreligious majority of the population evinced a greater tendency toward the observance of some aspects of religious life without becoming religious in other ways.

The government itself, from considerations of coalition and party politics, enacted a law through which only religious marriages are legal and binding. Although many objections were raised against this law, more people began to participate in synagogue services on the Sabbath and holidays, and the number of children's religious confirmations (Bar Mitzvah) increased. At the same time, the intensive secular rituals of the youth movements and of various labor groups seem to have abated except in the collective and cooperative rural settlements. An additional factor, apparently augmenting the religious trend, is, of course, the relative strength of religious traditions among the new immigrants. But, significantly enough, among them and especially among their younger generation, a process of rapid secularization under the impact of the absorbing society has taken place. Insofar as they maintain their religious traditions, this is mostly done in their own segregated spheres, and has at most but an indirect impact on the general society. Insofar as they participate in recreational and ritual activities with the older inhabitants, this is done mostly through anonymous mass contacts—as in walking through the main streets of the town, participating in public celebrations (as on Independence Day), or in frequenting cinemas.

Another phenomenon, indicative of the whole process of change described here, is the changing place of the collective and cooperative agricultural settlements in the social structure of the Yishuv and the state. During the period of the Yishuv these settlements—and especially the collective ones—were viewed as the apex of the whole process of Zionist and socialist realization (Hagshamah). The Kibbutzim claimed to be the purest fulfillment of the ultimate values of the society, and this claim was accepted by many, if not all, sectors of the society. Many of the political leaders and elite of the Yishuv came from Kibbutzim and Moshavim settlements, and membership in them conferred a certain prestige. The simple style of life of these settlements—manifested in dress and housing—was accepted as a model for emulation by large parts of the Yishuv, especially by the bread strata of the workers. The official ideology of most of the youth movements encouraged membership in these settlements as the ultimate goal of all educational activity. Great numbers of boys and girls spent some time of their life at these settlements doing various forms of "national service," not the least important among them being "service" in the Haganah, which had many of its training bases in these settlements. Furthermore, these settlements were often looked upon as centers of the Jewish cultural renaissance. It is significant, too, that the prestige of the Kibbutzim was higher than that of the Moshavim. This was because the Kibbutzim were often regarded as more "socialistic" than the Moshavim, in which the property and land were allocated to family units; by their very social structure, the Kibbutzim were better able to free their members for "outside" political and cultural activity.

This whole picture changed immensely after the establishment of the state. There was a rather widespread reluctance among several groups of the new immigrants to go into agriculture, and an even greater reluctance to experiment with various forms of cooperative and communal life. While many new Moshavim were established by new immigrants, there were even more immigrants who preferred to be employed as agricultural workers in different types of bureaucratically managed farms. But among the different types of settlements the Moshavim fared much better from the point of view of the intake of new immigrants than did the Kibbutzim. The strong ideological emphasis in the several Kibbutzim, their relatively more rigid social structure, and their sectarian outlook on life—manifest in their strong social and political identification—did not greatly attract the new immigrants, who lacked the strong ideological background of the early settlers. The Moshavim, on the other hand, with a much more flexible social structure, a less rigid ideology, and a stronger emphasis on economic stability and status, drew much greater numbers of immigrants.

This fact alone exerted an influence on the relative prestige of the two types of settlements. But there were several additional factors. First, the very establishment of the state, with its claims to high prestige, weakened the claims of these settlements to symbolize the main values of the society, since many national tasks formerly performed by them were now undertaken by the central, bureaucratic offices of the state. Moreover, some of the new political elite, who had been closely identified with the Kibbutzim in the past, and feeling the contradiction between their present attitudes and that past, began to underrate and even, perhaps unconsciously, to undermine them, especially by using them as pawns in the political game.

This was made relatively easy by the inherent rigidity of the Kibbutzim, by their strong sectarian character which made it difficult for them to adapt to changing circumstances. This may perhaps explain, in part, the splitting up of existing settlements according to party lines. The split has greatly weakened their influence, as can be witnessed both in the smaller number of elites recruited from them and by the smaller number of new members they attract. While in the last year or two this decline has been somewhat checked, and a new period of relative stabilization can be discerned, the general downward trend is quite clear.

Conclusions

The foregoing analysis of the main features of the institutional structure of Israel has placed special stress on its development from loosely coordinated, primary groups of pioneers to a full-fledged autonomous state and society. The gradual changes which developed in every institutional sphere throughout the period of the Yishuv, and the far-reaching and, to some extent, sudden changes which developed after the establishment of the State of Israel, have been noted. In the last sections an attempt was made to show how these changes have transformed the whole structure of consensus and integration of the society.

These changes were mostly in the direction toward a more formalized and differentiated social structure, in itself a "normal" development which has gradually made Israeli society more like other Western societies. But the picture is not so simple and straightforward, and these changes have given rise to many problems and internal tensions. While some of these problems are but natural outcomes of this transition, others are perhaps more acute and may greatly affect the extent to which this society will develop and achieve stability. Having undergone these various changes, Israeli society has nevertheless retained many of the specific characteristics which distinguished it from other Western societies and which were rooted in the historical background of the Zionist movement. Even now the strength and partial primacy of nontraditional collective values is much stronger than in many other modern societies, and the extent of social and economic differentiation and stratification much smaller.

Compared with other modern countries which have increased their population by the intake of immigrants, the tempo of integration in Israel has been much faster, the whole process much smoother, and the extent of tensions much smaller. A policy of social welfare is more or less the official policy of the state and of most of the parties, and is evident not only in vast schemes of social security but also in the relatively high standard of wages, in the power of the trade unions (from which the new immigrants also benefit), in the great part which public, semipublic, and cooperative organizations play in the economic development of the country, and in the relatively wide distribution of wealth—even though social differentiation became much greater after the establishment of the state. Of great importance here are the cooperative settlements of new immigrants, whose relative success points to some continuation of the social values in economic enterprises.[40]

It is therefore clearly evident that the strong emphasis on solidary integration is still an important, if not the predominant, aspect of Israeli society, and leaves its imprint on institutional patterns in general and on that of absorption of immigrants in particular. But this continued emphasis on solidary and collective values gives rise to several problems, the solution of which will largely determine the future development of Israeli society. Most of these problems are derived from the fact that among the various collective values, the power values assumed great importance and gave impetus to the process of bureaucratization. This affected the very nature of internal cohesion and participation, gave rise to growing competition for power and its rewards, and stimulated attempts to create ever larger concentrations of power and vested interests. But curiously enough, this very fact has impeded the development of a highly democratic tradition of government opposition. Since economic rewards can be derived from participation in the government, the main struggle among the different parties centers on their securing a share in the government coalition and the concomitant opportunity to benefit their adherents. This has produced interesting effects on the structure of Israeli society as a democracy. While on the one hand citizens enjoy freedom of speech and assembly, and the private sphere of an individual is relatively wide, the simple citizen has but few direct contacts with—and receives few benefits from—the state which are not mediated by one of the parties or pressure groups. Associations that cut across party lines have become relatively weak and ineffectual, and independent public opinion has exerted little influence, although a slight reversal of this trend seems to have taken place in the last two years. But the probability of any significant changes in the parties composing the government remains small.

The main problem here is not so much the actual situation today, but the ways in which the new immigrants will be taken into the political orbit of the society—whether they will be entirely swallowed up by the bureaucratic and party machines, either as active members or as passive objects, or whether they will be absorbed into nonpolitical groups and organizations.

The second important aspect of Israeli society which is strongly influenced by the growing power-orientation and bureaucratization is that of economic development and industrialization—the gradual attainment of relative, economic self-sufficiency. While to some extent the strong collective orientation fosters economic development, beyond a certain point it hinders and may even endanger it.

Israeli society stands today, then, at the crossroads of social and economic development, one road leading to a more authoritarian-bureaucratic structure and the other to a more democratic society. Thus Israel shares many of the problems of underdeveloped countries. Within the various institutions a silent battle is going on between these tendencies, and in the growing public interest in this struggle rests the main hope for its outcome.

Notes

[1] A full analysis of the process of absorption of immigrants can be found in S. N. Eisenstadt, *The Absorption of Immigrants* (London: Routledge and Kegan Paul, 1954; Glencoe, Ill.: The Free Press, 1955).

[2] See the section on economic institutions, pp. 403–416.

[3] Quoted from Mrs. Yonina Talmon-Garber, "The Family in Israel," *Marriage and Family Living*, 16 (November 1954), 343–345.

[4] P. Young, "The Reorganization of the Jewish Family Life in America," *Social Forces*, 6 (December 1928).

[5] R. Bachi, "La Population Juive de l'Etat d'Israel," *Population*, 7 (1952) 405–452.

[6] S. N. Eisenstadt, "The Oriental Jews in Palestine," *Jewish Social Studies*, 12 (July 1950) 199–222 and *The Absorption of Immigrants, op. cit.*

[7] For lack of space I shall not deal here with the somewhat special type of family life which developed in the Communal Settlements (Kibbutzim). It is mainly characterized by these features: "The basic features of the Collective Settlements (Kibbutz) are common ownership of all property, except for a few personal belongings, communal organization of production, consumption, and the care of children. The community is run as one economic unit and as one household. (a) The family has ceased to be an autonomous group from the point of view of the division of labor. (b) Husband and wife have independent jobs. Roles are allotted to individual members by a central committee elected yearly by the general assembly. Main meals are taken in the communal dining hall and are served from a common kitchen. Members' needs are provided for by communal institutions. Families look after their own rooms but have few other household responsibilities. (c) In most of the collectives, children live apart from their parents and are attended mainly by members assigned to this task. From their birth on, they sleep, eat, and study in special houses. Each age group leads its own life and has its autonomous arrangements. Children meet their parents and their siblings every day in off hours. They spend the afternoons and early eve-

nings with them. Parents put their young children to sleep. On Saturdays and on holidays children are with their parents most of the time except for short intervals when they take their separate meals. There are thus frequent and intensive relations between parents and children, but the main socializing agencies are the peer age groups and specialized nurses, instructors, and teachers. The age group is a solidary unit and it substitutes the sibling unit. It duplicates the structural lines of the community and inculcates communal norms. Basically the children belong to the community as a whole." (Quoted from Talmon-Garber, "The Family in Israel," *op. cit.*). See also S. N. Eisenstadt, *Age Group and Social Structure, A Comparative Analysis of Socialization in Cooperative and Communal Settlements in Israel* (Jerusalem, 1950). Despite its general theoretical interest, this type of family does not play a large part in the picture of the whole society.

[8] For fuller details, see S. N. Eisenstadt, "Youth Culture and Social Structure in Israel," *British Journal of Sociology,* 2 (July 1951).

[9] *Ibid.*

[10] The following are the main types of youth movements: 1. Scouts. 2. Hamahnoth Haolim (left-wing socialists). 3. Tnuah Meuhedeth (right-wing socialists). 4. Hashomer Hatzair (extreme left). 5. Betar (extreme right). 6. Hanoar Haoved (a movement influenced mainly by the left wing of Israel labor, which tried to recruit its membership from among young workers).

[11] For a fuller description of these groups, see Eisenstadt, *The Absorption of Immigrants, op. cit.* and Y. Ben-David, "The Research on Youth Movements," *Proceedings of the 2nd International Congress of Sociology* (London, 1955), Vol. I. See also S. N. Eisenstadt, with the cooperation of Y. Ben-David, "Intergenerational Tensions in Israel," *International Social Science Bulletin* (April 1956).

[12] See Eisenstadt, "The Oriental Jews in Palestine," *op. cit.*

[13] See, for a fuller report, A. Brodersen, ed., "The Report on Intergenerational Tensions in Israel," to be published in the *International Social Science Bulletin* (April 1956).

[14] For fuller details, see Eisenstadt, *The Absorption of Immigrants, op. cit.* See also D. Bobell and H. Weill, *Immigrant Youth* (Jerusalem: The Department of Sociology, Hebrew University, 1955), in Hebrew.

[15] For full details, see D. Horwitz, "The Economy of Israel," *Yearbook 1949–1955* (Tel-Aviv: Government of Israel, 1955), in Hebrew.

[16] For a fuller analysis, see Eisenstadt, *The Absorption of Immigrants in Israel, op. cit.,* pp. 74 ff.

[17] For a general exposition of this problem, see S. N. Eisenstadt, "The Sociological Structure of the Jewish Community in Palestine," *Jewish Social Studies,* 10 (January 1948) 3–18.

[18] See the paper on this problem by Yonina Talmon-Garber, "Social Differentiation in Cooperative Communities," *British Journal of Sociology,* 3 (December 1952), 339–357.

[19] There were many disputes about the employment of Arab labor, and in several economic branches it was used seasonally; but the general ethos was against it, as leading to the establishment of a colonial economy with the Arabs as "natives."

[20] I am indebted to my colleague, Mr. Y. Ben-David of the Department of Sociology of the Hebrew University, for suggestions on the analysis of professions in Israel.

[21] See C. Cyderowitz and S. Bavly, *Inquiry into the Living Standard and Nutrition among the Jewish Urban Population of Palestine* (Jerusalem, 1947).

[22] See G. Muenzer, *Jewish Labour Economy* (London, 1946), p. 217.

[23] See B. Malinowsky, *The Vocational Interests of Urban Youth* (Jerusalem, 1945), in Hebrew, and H. Ormian, *The Vocational Interests of Pupils* (Tel-Aviv, 1952), in Hebrew.

[24] See Eisenstadt, "The Sociological Structure of the Jewish Community in Palestine," *op. cit.*

[25] For fuller details, see Eisenstadt, *The Absorption of Immigrants, op. cit.*

[26] For a fuller analysis, see A. Bonne, "Economic Absorption of Immigrants," *International Social Science Bulletin* (April 1956) and S. N. Eisenstadt, "The Interrelation of Traditional and Modern Social Values in Their Impact on Economic Development: A Case Study of Israel," *Annals of the American Academy of Political and Social Science,* 304 (May 1956).

[27] For fuller analysis of these problems, see S. N. Eisenstadt, "The Process of Institutionalization of Immigrant Behavior," *Human Relations,* 5 (August 1952), and *The Absorption of Immigrants, op. cit.*

[28] See, for instance, M. Levy, *The Rise of the Modern Chinese Business Class* (New York: International Secretariat, Institute of Pacific Relations, 1949).

[29] For an account of these various parties, see B. Akzin, "The Role of Parties in Israeli Democracy," *Journal of Politics,* 17 (November 1955).

[30] For further information, see Eisenstadt, *The Absorption of Immigrants, op. cit.* It is important to stress that there were some exceptional cases, from this point of view, within the Yishuv, particularly the Oriental Jews and, to a small extent, also some of the German immigrants. They constituted also exceptional cases from the point of view of the political organization of the Yishuv, and most of the analysis presented here does not apply to them. Inasmuch as they did not change the over-all pattern of the Yishuv, I shall not dwell on them here in any detail. It is worthy of mention, however, that the ethnic groups participated to a disproportionately large extent in the various dissident "terrorist" groups, such as the Irgun Zvie Leumi. I shall not deal here in any great detail with these groups because, despite their historical importance and interest, they did not change very much the main characteristics of political activity in the Yishuv. They perhaps only intensified some of these characteristics. For a detailed discussion, see Chapter 4 of the above mentioned book, and Eisenstadt, "The Oriental Jews in Palestine," *op. cit.*

[31] It is interesting to notice that the Jewish institutions did not develop—despite several abortive attempts—any autonomous system of law and legal regulations which could bind their various groups in the Yishuv. This was done entirely by the Mandatory government or by the religious courts (in personal matters).

[32] But even their dissidence was caused mostly by the intensification of the national-political identification and, to a smaller extent, by disagreement on allocations of internal facilities.

[33] For fuller details, see Akzin, *op. cit.,* pp. 507–596.

[34] For the details of the formal political structure of Israel, see, for instance, N. Bentwich, *Israel* (New York: McGraw-Hill, 1952). See also O. Kraines, "Israel," *Western Political Quarterly,* 6 (1953), 518–542, 707–727.

[35] This came out clearly in numerous researches on absorption of immigrants undertaken by the Department of Sociology of the Hebrew University. See, for instance, S. N. Eisenstadt, "The Absorption of Immigrants in Israel," *Human Relations* (November 1952).

[36] It is interesting to note that the number of members of the elite among members of agricultural settlements has diminished, as has the general prestige of the settlements which were divided by intensive political strife.

[37] The great popular interest in local archæology is one of the manifestations of this tendency.

[38] For a fuller discussion, see S. N. Eisenstadt, "Voluntary Associations," *Studies in Social Sciences,* 3 (Jerusalem, 1955), 100–125.

[39] See *ibid.* and Eisenstadt, "The Oriental Jews in Palestine," *op. cit.*

[40] For a more detailed discussion, see Eisenstadt, "The Interrelation of Traditional and Modern Social Values in Their Impact on Economic Development: A Case Study of Israel," *op. cit.*

François Bourricaud
Translated from the French by Caroline B. Rose

FRANCE

Introduction

THIS interpretation of France, confined to such a few pages, is limited by the paucity of adequate studies. I shall try to point out how certain hypotheses could be verified, but I would not pretend that more than a few have been so.

In order to characterize present-day French society, it is necessary first of all to choose a point of view. No society is entirely homogeneous; none of its activities ever express the whole of the society. Yet there is nothing in its past or present which does not in some manner bear witness to the nature of the society. In describing a society, therefore, one must be arbitrarily selective.

It is the political aspect of present-day French society with which I shall begin, an arbitrary decision on my part, but one which is not surprising because politics is of so much importance in French society. By politics is understood the activity which aims, either deliberately or implicitly, to maintain or to change the distribution of power and authority among the various social groups. But it seems most difficult to distinguish between that which is political and that which is nonpolitical.

There seems to be no social activity which is not able, at one time or another, to produce political consequences. But in the place of this meaning, almost unmanageable by reason of being so comprehensive, it is possible to substitute a second meaning, narrower but more precise. We shall regard as political all activity able to maintain or to change the relation of forces among individuals or groups that exert public constraint on others.

To study the functioning of a society in its political aspect means to

444

ask how it formulates the alternatives imposed on it, how and if they are resolved, and if the proper decisions are applied. In brief, politics can be defined as the science of community deliberation, decision, and execution. Now, one opinion widely held about the French, both among our compatriots and among foreigners, is that we do not know how to discuss our affairs, that we are never able to decide, much less execute, our decisions. Briefly, this country does not know what it wants and never attains what it considers wanted. France today presents, in the processes of deliberation, of decision, and of execution, some peculiarities by which political analysis can distinguish it without difficulty from other occidental countries.

The French Political Regime

The French Constitution, if read literally, is not notable, still less original: a president without responsibilities, a cabinet, an attenuated bicameralism—nothing at all to attract attention. The most interesting statutes in French constitutional law concern the French Union. They betray the obstacles met by the 1946 constitutional convention in seeking to mitigate the customary tendency to centralize, with a pronounced leaning toward liberal and humanitarian language. The October 1946 text is a compromise: a first draft had been rejected in June of the same year by a popular referendum, even though the two parties of the left, Communist and Socialist, had made a common campaign in favor of this draft.

During the summer an agreement to restore some luster to the presidential function had been made by the three large parties of this period— the Communists, the Socialists, and the MRP. The appointment of the president of the Council (the premier) was restored to the head of the state (the president), who, in the text of June 1946, was limited to transmitting to the president of the Assembly (the speaker) the list of people declaring themselves as candidates for the head of the Cabinet. The second Assembly, baptized, curiously, "Council of the Republic," in order to avoid even the name of the former senate, had its power of suspension of legislation increased. But the fundamental shape of the first draft was hardly altered. Basically it consisted of a chamber (Chamber of Deputies) exercising complete legislative power without presidential or senatorial counterweight. Thus the practice of the Third Republic on the first point, regarding the president, was modified, and on the second point, regarding the Assembly, a tendency was reversed that between the two wars had continually increased the powers of the upper branch of the Assembly, elected by a limited suffrage. But, following the intentions of its authors, the text of October 1946 did not entrust all power to the discretion of a single Chamber of Deputies. Without doubt the "counterweights" (senate and president) set up by the constitutional deputies of 1875 had been dropped. Still, to balance the Chamber, the text of 1946 organized, or at least pretended to organize, a cabinet directed by a president of the Council (the premier) whose title was not even mentioned in the constitution of 1875. It is not very difficult to imagine the intentions of the constitutional deputies of 1946. On the one hand, they disliked the idea of a presidential system framed after the American model, mainly because of the fear of General de Gaulle; neither did they want a strong senate, a "fortress of reaction." Instead of the old theory of the division of powers there is substituted the idea of a division of tasks and of agencies. All power proceeds from the same source, but it is not held in the same hands. The Assembly (Chamber plus Council) is not able to govern and even less able to administer; the Cabinet is to be its arm. These different functions demand specialized aptitudes.

The experts debate whether such a system can still be considered "parliamentary." Certainly it is not parliamentary in the nineteenth-century sense, as when the Cabinet was an intermediary between the elected Assembly and the monarch. This conception is evidently without value in the eyes of the constitutional deputies of 1946, since they deprived the head of the state of all purely political functions; they had, in the language of M. Cot, reduced him to a "thinker" or, in an even more elevated style, turned him into a "moral magistrate."

The form of government of 1946 can, however, be called parliamentary in that it attempts to organize a functional separation of the Assembly and the Cabinet. This presupposes two conditions: it is necessary that the Assembly not be subservient to the Cabinet and that the Cabinet not be subservient to the Assembly. Add that the two conditions should be realized simultaneously, and the difficulties begin to be evident. This problem also explains the embarrassment of the constitutional deputies when they treat of the right of dissolution. To permit the possible dissolution of the Assembly is to risk making it dependent on some agency (Cabinet or president) to which is confided the exercise of this right. To make it constitutionally impossible to dissolve the Assembly is to deliver the Cabinet to the discretion of the Assembly. The deputies of 1946 have resolved this difficulty by a somewhat hypocritical compromise. In principle the

Assembly can be dissolved; but the application of the principle is suspended by clauses so numerous and so complex that, practically speaking, dissolution remains very improbable.

This point of constitutional technique, important though it is, ought not to mask a more serious difficulty. In order for the Cabinet and Assembly to cooperate, that is, to reserve to each of them special tasks in pursuit of a common goal, it is necessary that they proceed from the same source and that they develop the same aims. If a "real" majority exists in the Assembly, the Cabinet becomes spontaneously the agent of this majority. This is the most usual situation in Great Britain. But, if a majority does not exist in the elected chamber—which has been the case since 1946 in France—conflicts are carried from the Assembly into the Cabinet, which is not only constantly menaced from inside but becomes besides the target of the diverse parliamentary factions.

The text of 1946 supposes an Assembly capable of achieving a clear and coherent majority. This postulate is clearly formulated by the publicists of the era. M. Vincent Auriol, in *Hier...Demain,*[1] hopes that the restored republic will have a system of large organized parties. The MRP also, in its constitutional proposal, presents some analogous considerations and solutions. But the accusation of "monolithism" was soon raised against the three parties that governed France after the departure of General de Gaulle (January 1946) up to the exclusion of the Communist ministers (March 1947). Perhaps this reproach was aimed at first at the Communists, but the Radical party and M. Herriot made their return into politics by denigrating all the "monolithic parties" and by exalting the old republican individualism. This individualism existed under the Third Republic because of the two rounds of balloting in the *arrondissement,* which made the candidates familiar to the electors, and because of the absence in Parliament of party discipline, which permitted the deputy to refuse the orders of irresponsible committees and to vote "according to his conscience."

The gravest charge that one can make against the deputies of 1946 is not the mediocrity of a prolix and banal text; it is the fragility of the postulate on which the regime they have elaborated reposes. The functional separation of Assembly and Cabinet requires, in effect, large organized parties and the desire to cooperate. But never in its parliamentary history has France known the large organized party, with the exception of the Communist party, and, perhaps, the Socialist party.[2] In default of two large parties, does France have a small number of political blocs—three or four—able to coalesce into two rival squads? Not any more.

It should be recognized that French parliamentary maneuvering develops an incoherence and complication rarely if ever equaled, and that this situation has existed throughout French political history. Since the Revolution, all through the nineteenth century up to the establishment of the Third Republic, France has retained two traits, among others. It is notorious for constitutional instability: two parliamentary monarchies, two empires by plebiscite, three republics—all in less than seventy-five years. Now that the chances of a restoration of a monarchy are close to nothing, the instability of cabinets replaces that of charters. Where should we seek the cause? Certainly there are some permanent causes for our extraordinary consumption of political regimes in the nineteenth century. There are some accidents, but there are also some basic causes. The folly, perhaps exaggerated, of Charles X and the ambition of Louis Philippe are, upon the whole, accidents. What is most curious is that they have exercised such an influence on our history. The harsh struggle between legitimists and Orléanists, which killed the constitutional monarchy, poisoned our conservative parties. This rivalry between the partisans of the younger dynasty (Orléanist) and those faithful to the older (Bourbon-Legitimist) symbolizes in miniature the observable conflicts among our conservatives today. The legitimists could conceive only of a throne that firmly supported the Church. They dreamed of a France that abandoned its revolutionary past to return to the religious and monarchical tradition. They rejected the tricolor, holding fast to the *fleur de lys*, and the Count of Chambord destroyed with his own hand the last chance of restoration by refusing all compromise on the symbol of the flag. We note this rigidity so characteristic of the French conservative—defiance of the regard of the modern world, refusal to engage in any compromises for fear that should he begin thus, he will end by abandoning all his values. "It is this weakness which has destroyed my brother" (Louis XVI), said Charles X, the last legitimate king, whose beautiful manners and very poor intelligence illustrate well this type of conservative. From the same prince, we quote again: "I would prefer to saw wood than to reign in the manner of the English king." The Orléanists, on the other hand, regarded themselves as liberals, even though they were basically more pessimistic about the virtues of democracy. They liked to invoke the memory of the great Revolution; Louis Philippe was a veteran of the battle of Jemmapes; his father, the

Duke of Orléans, was a cousin of Louis XVI but as a "Montagnard" deputy to the Convention he voted for the death of the king. The Orléanists flirted with liberalism, a game which Louis Philippe played with a great deal of adroitness. He likewise invoked the military glories of the Empire. For the legitimists, Napoleon was the tyrant, "the Buonaparte usurper," as they affected to write his name. Louis Philippe chose his ministers and his especially docile and decorative presidents of the Council from among the marshals of the Empire: Soult, Bassano, Mortier. On the pediment of Versailles he wrote: "To all the glories of France." And in this country where, according to Renan, "history itself is a kind of civil war," this wish for conciliation and for reconciliation is worthy of being retained. The Orléanists were distinguished again by their distrust of the Catholic clergy. Louis Philippe finished by marrying his heir to a Protestant princess. He distrusted the "church party" and the traditional nobility. At the beginning of his reign, Louis Philippe was baptized the citizen-king. It is rather as the bourgeois-king that he had wanted to speak.

Orléanism is not dead. It illustrates the best aspect of French political tradition, still alive today: the somewhat visionary idea of the "golden mean." The Third Republic, in its beginnings, is not very far from the Orléanist model; and it is Thiers, one of the great ministers of Louis Philippe, who consecrated and shaped it. The famous words, "The Republic will be conservative, or it will not be," express marvelously the Orléanist wish for a regime politically liberal and socially conservative; or again, a regime which accepts necessary social changes to the extent that they do not disturb the peaceable and ordained habits of a hard-working and economizing bourgeoisie. Another saying of Thiers about the Republic, "the regime which divides us the least," underlines the concern for equilibrium and compromise.

One sees without difficulty that the two versions of conservatism are rivals and incompatible. The mistrustful, prudent spirit of Orléanism is regarded as egotistic and flat by the conservatives, who uphold the splendor of the true monarch against the pot-boiling of the citizen's monarchy. Chateaubriand expresses this point of view in some admirable pages of his memoirs. And the Orléanist himself mocks the Carlist dreams and opposes the Count of Chambord, who refuses a crown rather than renounce the *fleur de lys*.

In the present French conservative tradition one rediscovers traces of this schism; on the one side a conservatism ready to accommodate itself to the world as it is, but always fearing the worst and disposed to any political compromise in order to save the essential, that is, that wise management of material interests; in brief, those conservatives who call themselves the moderates. On the other side, a confined conservatism which sees treason and shameful capitulation in all accommodation; in brief, those conservatives whom all the others call reactionaries and who occasionally recognize themselves with pleasure in this name.

Among the second group anything other than a "strong" regime is suspect; in default of an impossible restoration of the monarchy, Vichy satisfied them, certainly in preserving nostalgia. They desired a government that would not be elected but whose members would be selected from among the "notables" and the "most competent"—that is, from among themselves and their friends—a government that would defend the traditional order. "Family, Work, Country"—this is their hope. Without the occurrence of exceptional circumstances, they are—and they know it—incapable of realizing their project. Such is the drama of the reactionaries. They also attack universal suffrage because the majority of the voters remain insensible to their preaching. This variety of conservatism sours in its feeling of impotence and has, without doubt, sterilized the party of the right, which morosely delights in prophesying the worst catastrophies and, infatuated with origins, exalts the glories of the French past. "I told you so" is the watchword of the reactionaries. In the first part of the twentieth century, a man with a mind as narrow as it is vigorous, Charles Maurras, revised and codified the doctrine and furnished to his followers a set of responses very efficiently adjusted to their disappointments and desires. With the monarchy, according to Maurras, the Gothic accouterments that enchained the romanticism of Chateaubriand had disappeared. One no longer needs the Church or the Scriptures. Maurras pretends to deduce the excellence of royalty out of reason and experience; traditionalism loses its esthetic and religious veneer. M. Maurras has defined it as a "positive" doctrine. That democracy is in itself bad, that it is so particularly in France, is what M. Maurras holds demonstrable in the most rigorous sense of the term. This rational method gives to the reactionary rightist unshaken assurance and at the same time isolates him in a savage opposition.

This hard conservatism, much accused, attracted no more than a handful of followers. Before the war, the paper *Action Française* did not have more than 40,000 subscribers. But now and then it diffuses widely and reaches distant strata of opinion. M. Maurras did not convince many of the

French of the necessity of restoring their royal house. But he contributed to maintaining alive among them a certain image of the traditional order, of hatred for the Revolution, of contempt for the republican regime held culpable of feebleness toward the foreigner and the "new French." Thus was support of the regime, on the part of conservative groups, retarded and troubled, even among those who proclaimed themselves republicans; these often escaped into dreams of the traditional order or sought consolation in a hoped-for but unexpected Caesar.

The temptation of Bonapartism is recurrent throughout the nineteenth and twentieth centuries. To this current may be attributed not only our two emperors but also some abortive movements like Boulangism, the leagues of the Dreyfus affair or of the 1930s, and, most recently, the RPF. These diverse attempts have some common traits. They present themselves as "syntheses" but register as "reaction." Bonaparte considered himself the founder of the fourth French dynasty. In general they pretend to continue the Revolution rather than to abrogate it. Even with a man of conservative education like General de Gaulle, references to the 1793 Committee of Public Safety are constant and favorable. With Bonaparte, with Boulanger, with Colonel de la Roque, or with General de Gaulle, one discovers the same distrust of "lawyers," of parliamentarians, and more generally, distrust of "the system." They advocate returning power to the people, betrayed by their representatives; then they would appoint a tribune, a consul, an emperor. But if Bonapartism is a permanent temptation it could not be more than a provisionary expedient. Its rebuff does not lie only in military history. Waterloo and Sedan concluded the two empires, but in the case of the last Bonaparte his Caesarean attributes had already been crushed. Recourse to the strong man is a spontaneous response among French conservatives. But it is a response as short as it is intense and frequent. The conservatives have not attained the building of the correct regime of which they dream vainly and constantly, nor can they take seriously a restoration of the order anterior to the Revolution, nor are they willing to trust their interests in the hands of the masses of the people. This accounts perhaps for their inconstancy. They deeply want to support the republican regime, and as soon as things seem peaceful and favorable they do not fail to support it: a Méline, a Poincaré, appeases them. It sufficed in 1948 that the administration of M. Queille and M. Petsche resulted in a certain price stability, for a great conservative newspaper like *Le Figaro* to support the regime, to wage a subtle but very efficient campaign against General de Gaulle and the RPF, and to recognize the merits of parliamentary democracy. But if popular agitation develops, the same conservatives dream of the saber, which will return the *canaille* to reason.

Fear is probably one of the strongest motivations among French conservatives. It is the revolutionary inclination of the masses that frightens the bourgeois. When the masses act in a revolutionary manner, neither the republic nor the monarchy—nor the junior or senior dynasty—matters; the bourgeois is concerned only with saving private property and protecting the family, both menaced by the "sharers."

In the revolution of 1848 this great fear had two effects. First it united the various conservative groups. Next it revived in them the feelings of death and aggression that Flaubert shows unchained, when the Sparticist revolt had been broken by the troops of Cavaignac. His description of the captive insurgents imprisoned in the Tuileries strikes a note of sickening horror: "There were nine hundred men packed pell-mell together in filth, black with dust and clotted blood, shaking with fever, crying with rage. Sometimes at the sudden noise of an explosion, they believed that all were about to be shot; they threw themselves against the walls, then fell back into their places. Because of the fear of epidemics, a Commission was named. At the entrance, the President recoiled sharply, overcome by the odor of excrement and cadavers." And lest we should attempt to impute these ignominies to any cause other than the gratuitous wickedness of men, Flaubert adds: "When the prisoners approached the air-hole, the national guards—who were serving as sentries to keep them from shaking the bars—thrust their bayonets into the mass of men." The novelist also underlines the absurd and foolish cruelty of the repression. "They, the national guards, were in general pitiless. Those who were unbeaten wished to demonstrate the fact; it was an outburst of fear; they were avenging themselves."[3]

But this fear and this cruelty are not the delirious products of *petit-bourgeois* imagination. For De Tocqueville himself there was no doubt that the triumph of the insurgents of June had been the return of barbarism. From the "mixture of greedy desire and of false theories," which according to him were the motives of the insurrectionists, nothing but evil could result.

In brief, it is fear that unites the conservatives. As soon as they are reassured, they scatter and divide. Traditionalists, reactionaries, moderate

Orléanists, Bonapartists, and plebiscitists then accuse each other endlessly, in acid and obscure recriminations. Let us not imagine that the "left" is very much more united. Clemenceau declared once that the Revolution is a bloc. This is a correct formula if one understands that images or stereotypes hold the revolutionaries together and sometimes even bring together groups of the left so diverse that they are the only cement in the union; it is an affirmation evidently fallacious if it makes us neglect the heterogeneity of the groups that claim the label of "left"—Constitutionalists, Feuillists, Girondists, Montagnards, Dantonists, Robespierrists, which prey upon each other to the point of total extinction.

The instability of coalitions of the left, so notable in the accords made between radicals and socialists in 1924 and 1932, more accentuated still in the case of the popular front of 1936, appears since the beginnings of our republican history. It can be explained in large measure by personal rivalries and incompatability of temperaments. But it has another source. In addition to a "radical" left in France, there is a socialist left. And to this first antithesis is added a second. By the side of a liberal left, distrustful of power, is set an authoritarian left, centralist and Jacobin. The radical left gives priority to political reforms. Under the July Monarchy they insisted on universal suffrage. After 1880 the Radical party, then in all the flame of its young vigor, battled for the suppression of the second chamber and the abolition of the presidency of the republic. For Ledru-Rollin in 1848, as for Clemenceau in 1880, these political reforms were preliminary to all social change. The left socialists, on the contrary, believe that this insistence on political reform is but a maneuver to maintain the *status quo* in social matters. The people expelled Charles X in 1830; but according to an expression of the era, it was the bourgeoisie who "confiscated" the Revolution. This misadventure was repeated in 1848, and again in the 1870s when, for the second time, attempts to install *La République Sociale* were strongly repressed. From then on there is for the left socialists a certain temptation to abandon the radical bourgeois whenever they face Caesar.

In the twentieth century the "radical" left and the left socialists met again more easily, and if in the 1930s "fascism did not succeed," it is evidently because the union between the two groups of the left in the popular front was made sufficiently viable. A very unstable, very tempestuous union it was; indeed, the Radical party feared unceasingly that it would be debauched and kept checking the initiative of its Socialist and

Communist allies. A second difficulty, very apparent in our time, occurs when the Communist party achieves a preponderance in the French left, imposing its views in marked contrast with the views held by the liberals and Jacobins. The main goal of the radicals is to check, to arrest, to hinder; their ideal is "the citizen against power." The philosopher Alain has developed these views, eminently critical, with a great deal of spirit. In terms close to those of Lord Acton ("Power corrupts; absolute power corrupts absolutely"), he has insisted on the evil character of political power, denouncing the "important ones," a category in which he includes the rich, the military, the clergy, certain professors who defend the *status quo,* in brief, all the people he does not like. For him the task of the left, its vocation, is the constant harassment of these people. This mission, let us note, is not temporary. Alain considered illusory the hypothesis that power was a means exercised directly by citizens for their common good. It is in the nature of things, he thought, that the citizen should be annoyed, hampered, exploited by the coalition of the "important ones" whose membership changes but which endlessly reconstitutes itself. The citizens would do well to keep their eyes open always if they would pretend to defend themselves against these encroachments. This philosophy of the *petit bourgeois,* as it has been disdainfully called, seems strongly differentiated from the Communist perspective in which the state takes charge of the affairs of all and imposes on recalcitrants respect for the "general will." But the vision of a violent catastrophe, by which the despoilers are forced to disgorge, remains one of the most vivid in the imagery of the left; from time to time, it warms up even the sober *petit bourgeois.* This image of the Revolution still remains in the idea of the "general strike," "the great evening before the revolution." It vibrates across the formula—so equivocal, so seductive —of Léon Blum, announcing "the vacation of legality." The terror and the dictatorship of the proletariat fascinate the imagination and obsess the will, because they express in a most startling manner the forbidden charms of violence.

The left, then, is no more fixed than the right in its desires and its objectives. It wants the full flowering of individual liberties. But it does not recoil before the test of terror. It distrusts the state and affirms that it attaches itself to its "withering away." But in the period of "transition" it reinforces the state in the name of "public safety." Without doubt the point in question is that it is no longer the same "state." And this is why the reduction of liberties, when it is decided upon by a revolutionary government, is considered as an increase of liberty. In this metamorphosis, the Revolution, as image, holds an essential place; of all the symbols of the left it is the most efficacious and the most irreplaceable, particularly in reconciling the contradictions between individualism and collectivism, between violence and liberation. Without it the tensions analyzed here would reinforce themselves to the point of breaking the unity of the left. The Revolution abolishes privilege and throws the "important ones" into confusion, thus realizing the desires of the liberal and radical left for equality of all before the law. But it assures, at the same time, to each, the legitimate satisfaction of his "needs"; this pleases the equalitarian dreams of the left socialists. The Revolution thus reconciles the otherwise incompatible desires of various groups of the left; better still, it promises the simultaneous realization of these desires. Thus the left, without ceasing to seek an impossible unity, succeeds in rallying its scattered members in some rare and brief moments preceded by laborious approaches and followed by sharp deceptions. The "three moments of glory" in 1830, the days which followed the exile of Louis Philippe in June 1836, and the first days of the revolution of 1848 are the most memorable of these rallies.

It does not take long for this euphoria[4] to disappear and for the various groups of the left to separate according to a process that Marx has admirably analyzed in the *18 Brumaire de Louis Bonaparte*. There are the liberals who are scared away at the very first; they soon become uneasy in the face of violence and confusion. In their turn, the *petits bourgeois* who regard themselves as Jacobins begin to desert when the Revolution becomes socialist. The road is then open for reaction or for a return to normalcy.

These remarks on the French political cycle are very brief, let us admit. The crises of 1948, of 1871, and of 1936, not to mention the months that followed the liberation of 1944, were quite different from each other. The rise of a Communist party after 1920 again poisoned the relations among the different components of the left. To the traditional divisions, already described here, was added another: the "nationalist aliens," that is, the Communists, according to the term by which Léon Blum described them, excited a very active distrust among their allies. As long as France was the source of the socialist movement (until 1870) the conciliation between patriotism and internationalism was made without pain. Things began to be spoiled by the time of the Second International. Between 1900 and 1914 the French left followed Jaurès toward a reformism influenced by the German model—in certain respects not too different from the then rising British trade unionism. The authoritarian and Jacobin tendencies were almost rooted out. The appearance of the Third International interrupted this movement. Between the two wars "the man with a knife between his teeth" haunted the bourgeois imagination. Again the left returned to its exaltations, causing the recurrence of great fear among the conservatives.

It can be said that in France conservatives and revolutionaries are not conscious of themselves except in time of crisis. Then the diverse factions rally in order to fight their opponents jointly, *en bloc*. Fear joins the conservatives together; a lyrical exaltation fills the left with a kind of euphoria, with the feeling that everything has suddenly become easy. But more often, when there is no crisis, the coalitions tend to break up and political maneuvers are characterized by an extreme fluidity and at the same time by secrecy. Political groups swap roles and positions readily. It is this parliamentary intrigue that holds the attention rather than mass movements and popular ferment. Ministerial instability[5] is a trait of French political life. It has become highly apparent in the present time. But the July Monarchy suffered from it at least as much as the Fourth Republic. The imbroglios of 1950 (after the fall of the Bidault ministry) or of 1953 (between the fall of M. Mayer and the investiture of M. Laniel) have some analogues in the great crisis of 1836 when Louis Philippe, after having cleverly opposed Thiers, Guizot, and Molé, in the hope of beating each in coming to the aid of the other two, set up a "provisional" cabinet. The great parliamentarians of the July Monarchy during the entire regime never stopped their harsh struggle, one against the other. The same unyielding opposition between ideologically similar politicians was characteristic of Caillaux, Briand, and Clemenceau between 1906 and 1914; of Herriot, Briand, and Poincaré between 1920 and 1930; again, of Laval, Flandin, and Reynaud on the eve of World War II, not to mention the recent duel between Edgar Faure and Mendès-France. These battles are all the more violent when they occur between men whose opinions and attitudes are very close on basic problems. Thiers and Guizot united, painting Molé as "the man of the chateau," that is, "the man of the king." But Guizot, in his turn, was not at all unwilling to be made the mouthpiece of the monarch. Between 1840 and 1848 Thiers himself did not attack his rival with much force, because he hoped to ingratiate himself with the king. Nevertheless, Thiers, Guizot, and Molé, whose disputes fill the chronicles of the regime of July, were in accord on the essentials: to maintain in the political and social order the compromise of July, although their inexcusable battles helped shake it to ruin.

Up to this point I have specified some traits of the French political complex that I have not yet explained, but merely grouped and ordered. First a contrast should be established between parliamentary maneuvers and public opinion. The antithesis between the "legal"[6] country and the "true" country has been abused: Extremists, reactionaries, and revolutionaries have pretended to be interpreters of the "true" country (the people, as against the elites) and view the majorities—for the most part feeble and incoherent—who designate and sustain the heads of the "legal" country, as malleable elements, subtly betrayed. The accusation of usurpation of power and of occupation by force or by ruse, directed against the legal country, was common during the nineteenth century. In the eyes of the liberals, the restored monarchy of 1815 returned on the ammunition wagons of foreigners. The two Bonapartes were regarded as usurpers by both the royalists and the republicans. The Orléanist solution was generally described as fraudulent. Louis Philippe duped the liberals who dreamed of a republic, and betrayed his cousin, Charles X, who had confided to him "the crown of a child." The Third Republic was installed only after difficult negotiations. Moreover, it was arrived at accidentally, one could almost say negatively, by only one vote. No French regime of the nineteenth century was held to be absolutely legitimate by all sectors of opinion. However, not enough firmness was generated to rally the opposition. The Third Republic lasted seventy years. This exceptional longevity permitted it to discourage the more impatient of its adversaries. But support for it was never complete. In the eyes of the least blind of the reactionaries, it ended by imposing itself as the regime of fact. This acceptance, resigned at first, became more positive after World War I. The Third Republic obtained Alsace and Lorraine; it brought back victory; the regime had become entirely national.[7] But when the "divine surprise" of the defeat of 1940 occurred, the old dreams of a restoration of the traditional order multiplied and bloomed once again. The first months of the Vichy regime are curious in that some dreamed of re-establishing the governors in the traditional provinces.[8] A psychoanalyst would see in this a kind of liberation, an acting out of desires held back and repressed for a long time.

But it does not suffice to observe merely that these French regimes are weakened because their legitimacy appears always suspect to one sector of opinion or another. It is not only the reactionary who cannot be relied upon or, at least, who is never won over frankly and totally. The attitude of the revolutionary left is no less ambiguous. By definition it is not able to recognize as legitimate any existing political regime. But its hostility, or rather its distrust, has some gradations. Evidently the republic of Méline or of Pinay is not that of the popular front. The Third Republic had one advantage over all the regimes that preceded it; it was able to create a "union with the left" in case of need. It is doubtful that Louis Philippe, when an attempt like that of the Duchess of Berry made difficulties for him, would have been able to count on the liberals. After the *coup de force* of Louis Napoleon, the bourgeois majority in the Assembly tried, on December 2, 1851, to rally the faubourgs (workers' districts); but the workers would not budge. The later liquidation of Boulangism at the time of the Dreyfus affair (about 1900), the victory over the National Leagues, and between 1934 and 1936 the blocking of the fascist movements, were greatly facilitated by the temporary reunification of the left. The reflex "defend the Republic" has several times saved the regime from reactionary enterprises. Thus the Third Republic somehow acquired legitimacy. Even though support from the right was confused and uncertain, the Third Republic was able to pass for a national regime, of which the symbol was the great man, Clemenceau, "patriot and Jacobin." In the eyes of the left, it was able to pass as the most "progressive" of the bourgeois regimes. This precarious legitimacy affects more than the regime. It also influences the parties and, generally, all groups interested in politics.

French lack of confidence in political chiefs is far from being uniform. It is probably more marked among the conservatives than among the revolutionaries. At any rate it would seem so, according to a 1952 public opinion poll: "Together with the moderate electors, the Radicals are less numerous in having total confidence in their party."[9] "The Socialist voter has little confidence in the leaders of his party."[10] There are at the present time two groups of voters attached to their chiefs and having confidence in them: The Communists and the RPF. But in the second case this confidence is directed to one man and in the first it is directed to the program.[11]

These feelings are explained without difficulty as resulting from the conditions of political maneuvering. "A Jacobin minister is not always a minister for Jacobins," Mirabeau once said. The deception of their constituents by the conservatives can be compared to that of the revolutionaries by their "renegade" chiefs or by those who simply become "bourgeois." The second phenomenon is less often noted than the first, but it seems considerable because it underlines the regime's ability to absorb and assimilate. The Chamber elected in the euphoria of the victory of 1918, but also in resentment against the prewar politicians, did not delay in turning for leadership to Briand, whose past, whose personage, whose proclaimed intentions, expressed to perfection all that against which the Chamber had been elected. The adventure of General de Gaulle with the RPF deputies after the elections of 1951 confirmed this tendency of elected conservatives —even though they had been elected on an antiparliamentary program— to rally around the moderates on a program to administer material interests or, if one is severe, to "expedite current affairs." The rightist voters also glide from one party to another, successively deceived and seduced by the diverse formulas that are generously offered to them. Thus French opinion does not have a taste for the extremes, and French government oscillates by feeble displacements about the center. Political opinion is both stereotyped and confused. The French have a tendency to think by summary opposites—between resistance and movement, revolution and tradition. But this spontaneous dualism is tenable only on the plane of opinion, that is to say, on the verbal plane. In practice it is modified and corrupted, and makes of both the left and right blocs each a loose coalition, which does not regain its unity of behavior except in rare circumstances. Also, political action in France takes place on two levels. On the one hand, there is action with principles first, and on the other, the practical "administration of things." This observation is not at all original but it seems characteristic of France that the conditions of the ideological struggle most of the time force the administration of affairs into the hands of the "moderates." The battle to death between a left revolutionary and a right reactionary is not observed only in France; nowhere else, however, has it such toughness and rigidity. But the most startling result of this antagonism is that left and right each prevents the other from attaining power. Power rests in the hands of the "center," which forms either a coalition of the left (the radicals in the popular front) or a coalition of the right (the same radicals in a cabinet of national union), for example, in the Poincaré cabinet of 1926 or in the Doumergue cabinet of 1934. Thus the center, to a certain point, is able to control and to check right and left successively wherever it takes the initiative and assumes the responsibilities (a situation similar to the opportunistic combination of the year 1880 or, recently, the governments of the third force between 1947 and 1951).

In normal times such a government is deeply divided: the center is not much less "social" than the left, nor much less "national" than the right; that which constitutes a government as "center" is fidelity to the regime with which it is identified. Whenever such a government is simultaneously attacked by the reactionaries and the revolutionaries, the center must unite. Then the opposition — between clerical and ainticlerical, between MRP on one side and socialists and radicals on the other, between authoritarians and liberals, between socialists and MRP on one side, radicals on the other — disappears or is, at least, attenuated.

Even when the groups of the center do not exercise control on the parliamentary plane, the influence of the moderates remains, probably, more than proportional to their strength. This is because the majority of the *conseillers d'état* (top civil servants), of the *inspecteurs des finances* (tax inspectors) or of the magistrates of the *cour des comptes* are resolute defenders of the traditional, or even of the bourgeois, order. Yet a good number hold socialist opinions, and these they hear the parties of the extreme right denounce viciously. But, by their profession, by the nature of their work, they are ready to check certain projects of the left if they appear useless or arbitrary.

The top civil service does not intervene only in important circumstances. The more feeble political power is, the more the "administration" gains in prestige. The growth, irregular but continuous, all during the Third Republic, of the large agencies like the *Conseil d'État* and the *Inspection des Finances* is an example of this. Daniel Halevy tells how the *Conseil d'État*, a Napoleonic institution which had ceased to exist from September 1870 to June 1872, was surreptitiously re-established and how its recruitment was made independent in the constitutional laws of 1875. "By the subterfuge of an Article introduced at the last instant, these same constitutional laws which organized parliamentary power in France, rendered it (the *Conseil d'État*) independent at the beginning of our administrative bodies."[12] It is its total independence from political power that the top administration seeks constantly to protect. The *conseillers d'état* are recruited for the most part by competitive examination, but the board of examiners is made up of senior members of the "corps," which works discreetly but firmly to reduce the percentage of auditors, of *maîtres des requêtes,* or of councilors in ordinary service whose designation is left to the government.[13] The same process of bureaucratization[14] is observed in diplomatic and prefectoral careers. The top functionaries tend to become irremovable.

Yet without doubt they are not independent of political and parliamentary fluctuations. On entering into such or such a ministry, a man is enabled to move to the top without stopping and win, while still very young, a brilliant reputation by attaching himself to a specific minister. Conversely, when the "patron" falls, his protegé risks disgrace. Although change of status depends on favor, promotion and demotion are tempered by strict and well-defined rules. A minister of foreign affairs can exile the principal collaborator of his predecessor by naming him minister of France to Amman. He can also remove a civil servant, but unless extremely grave professional faults are evident, he is not able to dismiss him. Thus is constituted a bureaucracy much affected by political maneuvers but protected against their worst abuses, thereby assuring continuity and stability to the administration despite parliamentary turbulence.

Perhaps one can describe the French regime as immobility in convulsions. The word "immobility," launched in the spring of 1949 by M. Pleven against M. Queille, is appropriate to describe one tradition of "moderate politics." *Quieta non movere*—when things are quiet, the government takes no action—would be the first rule. But more fundamental is the fact that whenever things cease to be calm, it is necessary to intervene with a hand trembling with fear lest the remedy be worse than the disease. Distrust of the "new" characterizes the moderate, who sees the menace of deterioration in all changes. Guizot in the 1840s illustrates wonderfully the opinionated defense of a charter built on dogma, the obstinate refusal of all revision or concession, out of fear that the least breach in the edifice will shake it down entirely. In this refusal to negotiate there is without doubt a confused feeling of insecurity, perhaps even of bad conscience, but especially the fear of being outmaneuvered. "As soon as one begins to discuss, it is impossible to put a stop to the quarrel." The regime of Grévy and of his opportunist allies in the 1880s followed this same tradition with a little more suppleness. At that time the question was to defend the constitutional laws of 1875 against the enterprises of the radicals and, on the right, against the attempts at restoration of the monarchy. Then the Boulangist storm calmed; the Panama fever fell; and the administration of Méline fell into immobility; "Neither Reaction: do not re-open the dynastic quarrels—Nor Revolution: do not repeat June, '48 or the Commune." But these episodes are often no more than pauses, a time of recuperation after paroxysm.

Guizot installed himself after the crisis of 1840 when the throne had been gravely shaken by a passionate rise of French opinion and by the menace of a Europe newly united against France. It was the repulsing of an abortive revolt which permitted the opportunist to develop the politics of compromise. Méline came to power only after the passions and excitement brought about by Boulangism and Panama had been appeased. In brief, the solutions of compromise are never actively sought for themselves or highly praised. They are imposed for lack of a better solution; do they also lack, if not artfulness and cleverness, at least force and appeal?

At bottom Grévy, Méline, even the Poincaré who stabilized the franc in 1926, are no more than second best. One supports them, one even renders homage to their administration, at the same time deploring the need for their services. "France is a country which tires." The famous *mot* of Lamartine in his polemic against Guizot accords with all the pauses which characterize each episode of moderate government. "The great halt," as the count said *apropos* of the July Monarchy, weighs on the French. The revolutions, the Days, the mass movements reawaken them, fill them with fear or enthusiasm. This cycle where excitement and depression alternate, separated by a plateau, can be used as a symbol of the vanity of our political life.

But we should not pass judgment without appeal or without reserve on the French regime. Let us recognize first that all exercise of this kind is for the most part rhetoric. How do we decide that one regime is preferable to another for a given country? We are free to imagine what France would be today if, on January 21, 1793, the head of the king had not been cut off; or if the monarchy restored after 1815 had been consolidated or . . . . Let us observe, however, that when the Third Republic began, it had to face three kinds of problems that, by the time of World War I, it had almost resolved correctly. It was necessary to prevent the constitutional quarrels from being continually reopened, as had been the case during the nineteenth century. In brief it was necessary that the regime win for itself at least a quasi-legitimacy. This was almost accomplished by 1910. The republic had above all to assure the security of the nation, beaten in 1870, against the enterprises of its redoubtable conquerer. In 1918 the victorious French army had become the strongest in Europe which, at that time, signified the strongest in the world.[15]

Finally, we can judge the Third Republic on another criterion: the administration of material affairs. The economic expansion of France by

1914 was not very rapid, but it followed a continuous rhythm, placing France among the great exporters of capital, and made the franc one of the solidest and most sought after currencies. In brief, the republic on the eve of World War I cut a good figure, and it is not unreasonable to think that of all the regimes since 1789, the Third Republic alone had succeeded as well as could be expected in resolving a number of difficult problems that would have faced any regime during this epoch in France. It is not even certain that the years 1920–1930, taking into account the blood-letting of World War I and the difficulties of the reconstruction, should be inscribed to the debit of the regime. During these years industrial production mounted in France, less than in Germany but significantly more than in England or Belgium. The worst mistakes were made between 1932 and 1940: the monetary and financial policies, directed at any cost to retain the gold standard, prolonged the economic crisis far beyond all need; the "social" politics of the popular front (rigid application of the forty-hour work week in particular) ruined the effects of the devaluation of 1936; timid and outmoded military politics threw the French soldiers almost unarmed, or at least badly equipped, into the atrocious rout of June 1940.

The regime restored in 1945, more and more impotent and more and more convulsed, is still not without merit nor totally inefficacious. It has been confronted by grave difficulties that have almost dragged it down; good observers, since the beginning, have predicted its almost inescapable collapse. Caught between the Communist agitation and the Gaullist movement, the chances for parliamentary democracy in France seemed, toward 1947, very slim indeed. The pressures were gradually eased; the regime made its way through. The inflationary pressure has been reined little by little; the worst has been averted, in part by the Marshall Plan, in part by the skill of the technicians of the Bank of France and of the Minister of Finance, in part by the physical and human resources of the country. The heaviest deficit is in the overseas account. More generally it can be said that the Fourth Republic has shown itself almost incapable of defining a political line in any domain, particularly in those domains where this definition would have demanded perseverance and lucidity. The regime has employed all the energy it has in preserving itself and assuring its survival [16] and in this spontaneous and almost unconscious art, it has exhibited some admirable abilities.

463

Political Parties and Social Structure

Fluidity of parliamentary maneuvers, rigidity and unreality of ideological stereotypes, such are some traits of our regime. In bringing these things together, it appears that France may be condemned to moderate governments more than it dreams—or does not want to dream—rather than to revolution or to a restoration of the traditional order. The instability of our governments is a symptom; probably there is no specific remedy.[17] It bears witness only to certain peculiarities in our social system. Let me add that the sketch I am about to draw here is evidently much simplified. It concerns only those groups who are professionally interested in political life, the "elites."[18] It is false to try to apply such explanations to the motivations or to the conduct of workers, of peasants, or of members of the liberal professions. Thus, the analysis of political behavior demands sociological explanation. Can it not be that these opinions and attitudes that I have discussed are themselves conditions of, or causes of, certain broader characteristics of French society?

It is not a great discovery to observe that the workers vote for the left and that their employers vote for the right. It is somewhat more curious to note that opinions manifest a certain stability in their geographic distribution. M. Labrousse[19] has shown that a map of the elections of 1848—the first which took place in France under universal suffrage—if superimposed on one showing the results of the referendum of May 1946, is in large part the same. The superimposition is particularly startling in regard to Montagne, where the strengths and weaknesses of the various political groups remained in 1946 as they were a century before.

A recent article on "The Social Democrats in the Elections of 1849"[20] confirms these results. The author writes that in 1849 two regions showed a marked orientation toward the extreme left. The departments of the Southeast—in particular Provence, where the democrats without having a majority have carried a large number of votes—are notable: unfavorable to the imperial regime, they constituted, as a consequence, one of the solidest bastions of the advanced parties. The political pattern of the Massif Central is also shown to be stable. Berry, Bourbonnais, Marche, and especially Limousin leaned toward radicalism, later showing Marxist tendencies. But the Auvergne and the Cévenol country,[21] where the democratic influence was restrained in 1849, remained turned toward the right. The West,[22] the Parisian Basin, and the Northeast, with some exceptional places, have remained hostile to the extreme left. While Socialist in 1919,

Alsace is oriented toward the parties of the center and of the right. The Southwest also is still wavering, now as in 1849. By contrast two new regions, the Parisian suburbs and the North, have notably accentuated their movement toward the extreme left in connection with both industrialization and the development of a proletariat, still nonexistent or dispersed in 1849. In the North, an opposition is manifested between rural and industrial *arrondisements*.[23]

The value of these studies, both historical and geographic, is to find in the structure of a region the social conditions and the psychological motivations on the basis of which the pattern of elections becomes comprehensible. In his celebrated work on western France, André Siegfried has discovered some essential variables of the conservative vote. Western France is characterized first as a rural region with a dispersed population in which the family is a strong institution. Next, in this region of large property, the land often remained in the hands of nobles; they continued to reside here, exercising thus a direct and continuous influence on local affairs. Finally, it is a region (and is this last trait perhaps more significant than the others?) where the nobles do not wage war against each other, but support each other and become stronger. In France, "the country of divided elites" according to M. Raymond Aron, an alliance among the lords of the castle and the priests, imposing thus their pre-eminence on other social groups, is unusual. With this background a certain type of conservative emerges, identified by rural spirit, respect for the upper classes, and fidelity to the Church. This exact and finished description, if one limits it strictly to the model that M. Siegfried wishes to paint (western France at the beginning of the century) would give a wrong impression if one generalizes from it the "ideal type" of the French conservative. The relations between his conservatism and the Catholic Church, for example, are more complex.

A most instructive, even troubling, paradox arises from a reading of these regional studies. They underline the stability of the electorate, the fidelity to the same great tendencies of opinion, even though the French parliamentary game is characterized in the opposite way by its extreme fluidity. These studies help to explain the existence and the functioning of a great conservative party playing together with a great progressive party. Yet, it is perhaps the most startling trait of French parliamentary history that such a couplet has never been able to effectively constitute itself.

Another method of study consists of comparing voting behavior with occupational structure. In this manner, an inquiry of the French Institute of Public Opinion (one section devoted to each of the different political parties then active, the Socialists, Communists, Radicals, MRP, RPF, Moderates) mentions the percentages of the social origins of the votes. The most obvious conclusion is that no party could pretend to represent alone one or another social class, still less any of the numerous social groups (workers, peasants, and civil servants, for example). The most interesting example in this respect is the Communist party. "The Communist Party claims to be 'the advance guard of the working class in the struggle against capitalism.' "[24] But the inquiry reveals that "of 100 Communist voters, 38 are workers (the percentage of workers in the total population is 19 per cent), 8 per cent are white-collar workers, and 5 per cent are civil servants. Moreover, 82 per cent of these voters are not property-owners; 89 per cent do not own an automobile and 97 per cent do not have domestic servants. The Communist party influences the largest mass of workers and the voters having the lowest standard of living."

The relation between the Communist party and the working class is important. The party attracts to it the largest percentage of votes no matter whom it competes with; 38 per cent of the workers' votes go to the Communists against only 21 per cent to the Socialists, 19 per cent to the MRP and 15 per cent to the RPF.[25] If one adds the 38 per cent of the industrial workers to the 8 per cent of the agricultural workers who vote Communist, one is able to write with MM. Reynaud and Touraine: "The working class has only one political expression which properly belongs to it: this is the Communist Party. But does the working class give the majority of its votes to the Communist Party?"[26] "Expression" is without doubt a little strong. All that one can find out, at least on the level of votes and of public opinion polls, is that the Communist party carries off a plurality of the workers' votes.

But this remark raises two questions: first, how do the 50 per cent of the workers who do not vote for the Communist candidates vote? Nearly half of the rest (21 per cent of the total) support the Socialists (S.F.I.O.). Accordingly, two thirds of the workers' votes are attracted to the parties of the extreme left (Socialist and Communist). Concerning this, M. Maurice Duverger writes, "In France and in England, the same proportion of wage earners votes for the Socialist and/or Communist Parties."[27] But a substantial group of workers' votes also goes to the MRP (the Catholic social liberals) and to the RPF (the Gaullists); the center parties (the radicals and the moderates) being among all French parties those that attract the smallest number of workers.

In brief, the social heterogeneity in the recruitment of the French parties (as much among their voters as among their militants) now seems well established. "The Socialist Party appears," writes the anonymous author of a special number of *Sondages*,[28] "as the opposite of a class party. It is above all the party of the civil servant, active or retired. But its composition is such that the most diverse influences are manifested in its electoral clientele." This heterogeneity has an important consequence on the functioning of the political regime. Each party lies in wait for the clientele of all the others; no interest is foreign to them. The Communists make advances to the peasants and to the middle classes. M. Jacques Duclos, addressing himself to M. Pinay, declared himself ready on April 1, 1952 "to amnesty the small and middle-sized taxpayers, victims of your fiscal and one-sided injustices."[29] "One can note recently," writes M. Lavau from another point of view, "the eagerness shown by two Communist deputies, MM. Thamier (elected from Lot, the home of the movement of Saint-Ceré) and Tourtaud (Creuse) to support, during the budgetary discussions, the claims of the movement of M. Pierre Poujade [the U.D.C.A.]. One can infer that in these departments, the Communist clientele is composed in part of the clientele of the U.D.C.A."[30] Does the author, perhaps, go a little too far here? What appears probable is that there are some contacts and some exchanges established between the two groups, and that certain individuals pass from one to the other. In brief, the heterogeneity in the recruitment of parties causes their instability, which in its turn probably contributes to producing among them a form of competition by challenge and outbidding that one could risk describing as demagogic.

Thus the working class, of all social groups probably the most articulate, is far from being expressed by a unique political presentation. And if MM. Reynaud and Touraine make of the Communist party "the only authentic expression of the workers' world," it is to be decided whether they consider only the choice of interests or also other more complex criteria like the relation between the classes that support the party and the origin of its leaders.[31]

The case of the peasants is even more instructive. We have a tendency to represent our peasants as conservatives. There is nothing more false than this stereotype. Let me underline the extreme diversity of demographic, technological, political, and juridical conditions. The small peasant proprietor in the southwest of France, particularly in the valley of the Garonne, is in juxtaposition with the large proprietors in the West, for example, or the owner renting his lands to farmers or sharecroppers. But the area of large holdings is itself far from being uniform. The vast domains of the Parisian region (or the wheat lands of Beauce or of Brie) are worked by the large farmers in lots that attain and sometimes exceed 100 hectares—a picture which contrasts with the West, where the farms or the sharecroppers' lands are generally of much smaller dimensions and even the rich proprietor includes in his patrimony some isolated lands of mediocre quality. Let us add that sometimes—and this is the case in the West—the large proprietor resides on his land still keeping control over local affairs, and sometimes he resides in town, living off his farm rents and content to return to his lands for summer vacations or for hunting (in Bourbonnais, for example). These differences in the manner of working and in the nature of the property are not the only things that distinguish French agrarian systems. Variations in the techniques and economics of production induce some deviations that individualize the regions profoundly. The production of more than 45 *quintaux* of wheat per hectare is not exceptional in the department of the North or in the Parisian Basin. But 15 *quintaux* does not appear exceptionally low to the farmer of Aveyron. Such a discrepancy between productive techniques is probably matched by a discrepancy between incomes. These contrasts can be observed not only in regions very different or very far apart, but within the same homogeneous zone, the returns and the profits show a very significant discrepancy[32] which can be explained by the varying degrees of skill among the workers, the more or less favorable topography and climate, and the quantity, the quality, and the age of the implements.

French agriculture is not then correctly understood if one insists upon its archaism (especially observable in the Center and some arid regions of the Southwest) or if one exalts its efficiency (the North and the Parisian Basin). Furthermore, the methods of production technically the most efficient (wheat in the good lands, beets, some grapes) are not economically the most efficient, for they accumulate unsaleable surpluses (wheat, wine, alcohol), the purchase of which (at a loss) is incumbent on the Treasury.

From the demographic point of view, the differences are no less notable. A certain conservative tradition has taught the French to see in the peasantry the "demographic reserves of the nation." The remark is true if applied to the West, the East, the North, or the Parisian Basin but entirely false concerning the Center, the Southwest, or the Mediterranean region. The valley of the middle Garonne is depopulated, not simply by the exodus of its inhabitants but by the deliberate sterility of the small proprietors who protect their fields from partition by reducing the number of their heirs.[33] And the rate of reproduction is not rising significantly in these regions beyond the rate observable in the urban areas.[34]

Our rural world is no more homogeneous in regard to religious practice. For more than thirty years, a very learned historian of canon law, M. Gabriel Le Bras, has undertaken to measure religious practice (Catholic) according to certain criteria such as attendance at Sunday mass, confession, Easter communion, and recourse to the Church and its rites in the principal episodes of the individual's life: birth, marriage, and burial. These rich observations show that "the faithful" occupy the wooded areas of the West, the East, and certain regions of the Massif Central. But the country of the Center (Creuse), Bourgogne, the heart of the Parisian Basin (Yonne and Aube) are as profoundly dechristianized as the urban parishes most impervious to Catholic penetration.

It is not surprising that a group as scattered and diversified as the peasants are never able to find, or at least never for long, a coherent and efficacious political expression. "Forty-seven per cent of the French live in communities of less than 2,000 inhabitants. . . . The active agricultural population amounts to 35 per cent of the active population. Moreover, the peasant world has no unity toward politics."[35] The departments where the rural population is the strongest are Creuse (85.8 per cent of the population, 39.9 per cent of whom voted Communist in 1951); the North (81.5 per cent, of whom 37.7 per cent voted for the MRP and the RGR); Gers (80.9 per cent, of whom 46.5 per cent voted for the S.F.I.O. and the RGR; Vendee (80.4 per cent, of whom 43.8 per cent voted RPF) and Haute Savoie (80.4 per cent, of whom 35.7 per cent voted MRP). Thus the five most rural departments show diametrically opposed political behavior.[36] Another expert, M. François Goguel, writes even more trenchantly: "There does not exist *any correspondence* at all between the number of the population actively working in agriculture and the political orientation of the department."[37]

There probably does not exist a solid correlation between any of the sociological data generally advanced: type of production; property law; manner of exploitation of the land; demographic rates; religious practice

—and the political orientation of the peasants. "The France of wheat," says M. Fauvet, "is not necessarily to the right; the vine-growing departments of the Midi (Hérault-Gard, Aude Pyrénées, Orientales) vote left (Radical or Socialist, with a strong Communist percentage). But the Gironde—another wine region—votes Moderate or Radical, and the Côte d'Or (Bourgogne) votes Independent and Peasant. The only correlation, and that vague, that one is able to find between political orientation and production concerns, is that of meat and especially that of milk and butter." But this correlation does not appear so clear to us as to M. Fauvet; a cattle-rearing region like the Haute Vienne votes Socialist and Communist, while the Charolais (Saône and Loire) votes Radical.

There is no greater correlation between the vote and the property laws. The farmers and sharecroppers of the West vote for the conservative candidates whom the large proprietors and the Catholic clergy designate. But some other farmers and some other sharecroppers in the Bourbonnais (department of Allier) vote Socialist and Communist, that is to say, against their employers. The small winegrowers, (Girondins) vote Moderate. But the small individual proprietor is not always associated with a vote for the right; indeed, often the contrary holds. Corrèze, Lot, and Garonne, all departments of small holdings, have a percentage of Communist votes much higher than the national average. In 1951, Corrèze was, according to M. Fauvet,[38] "the reddest department in France; the canton of Brive attained a Communist vote of 41 per cent." In 1932 the same title belonged to another entirely rural district: Lot and Garonne. Religious practice or demographic vitality are not sufficient to sway the political vote of winegrowers; Girondists and Malthusians are politically moderate; the peasants of Aube, one of our most dechristianized departments, vote for the right. Even in the territory of the "faithful people" in Bretagne, a vote for the left is not incompatible with fidelity to the Catholic Church.[39]

This example is too favorable to my thesis of the heterogeneity of the recruitment of French parties for me to insist on it further, but a few points should be emphasized. First there is the impotence of the peasant world to give itself political expression, owing to its divergent interests and regional differences. But it is also necessary to point out an unforeseen consequence. This is the extremely efficacious protection of the interests of the peasant world by virtue of their extreme dispersion. The vinegrower, the cattle-breeder, the wheat producer, even though they have only a few common interests, have also few contradictory interests. A subsidy for meat does not disturb the vinegrower. It may even encourage him to seek a subsidy for his own product. This variety, this dispersion, produces another consequence. In each party, or each parliamentary group, the rural world has some representatives. "The committees for studying"[40] the vine, the tobacco, and the beet, and the representatives of the distillers are not recruited only from the "independent" or "peasant" deputies. The Socialists do not disdain to take an interest. And under cover of defending the "small" cultivators, the Communist party cooperates with this protection of rural interests.

Between belonging to a social group and allegiance to a party no clear liaison can be observed. This thesis evidently demands clarifications, qualifications, and temperate consideration. Between membership in the working class (industrial and agricultural wage earners) and voting Communist or Socialist there is a correlation in two thirds of the cases. The working class, more than any other group, is able to set up a somewhat constant and definite political expression of its own because, in contrast to the other political formations, the parties for which the workers vote manifest a most pronounced "class" character.

This point is well illustrated by a public opinion poll of the I.F.O.P. appearing in the magazine *Réalités* in May 1952. Examining "why five million of the French still vote Communist," the authors affirm that "It is because they seek a legitimate and energetic defender who will aid them in ameliorating their material conditions that five million French choose the Communist Party."[41] Above all other considerations, economic reasons motivate the Communist voter. To the question "What are the points on which you would particularly like the party to insist?" 50 per cent said: the amelioration of the lot of the working class, stopping the price rise, improving social security; 25 per cent of the others spoke of "peace." The ideas of "class struggle," "struggle against capitalism," "struggle against the profiteers," and "the emancipation of the working class" appeared in only 10 per cent of the cases. Ideas about foreign politics, "the struggle against American guardianship," or "stopping the Indo-Chinese war"[42] appeared in only 20 per cent[43] of the cases. And the authors add: "We have asked our respondents if they thought that the standard of living generally conditioned the vote and if they thought this was the case for them personally; 76 per cent of the Communist voters responded that that was true in general and 58 per cent among them answered that they thought this was true for them (against 52 per cent of the S.F.I.O., 28 per cent of the MRP, 34 per cent of the moderates). By this response the Communist voters acknowledged that they voted Communist because their living conditions were difficult, because they thought themselves to be the victims in the division of wealth, and because they thought that the party of their choice would be their defender and advocate."[44] On themes more closely political, the Communist voter cannot be neatly distinguished from others. "We have asked our respondents if they believed that their situation could be ameliorated by reforms or only by a revolution. Among those voting Communist, although 41 per cent responded "by revolution only" or "by a revolution if necessary," *the majority declared themselves reformists.*[45] Thus the Communist party appears to these voters as the most efficacious instrument by which the "disinherited" can defend their interests. It is this basis on a kind of community feeling that gives the party its strength. The Communist party, then, exemplifies a party whose membership is motivated by its origins and its class affiliation.

However, two difficulties should be considered here. To speak of the "disinherited," of those "unfavored by fortune," is to underline the protesting character of the Communist vote. But is this only a *workers'* protest? Evidently not, even though the strongest contingent of Communist voters comes from the ranks of the workers. Are the mechanisms of frustration and protest that move these voters to the extreme left the same even when they concern a rural school teacher, a metal-worker from Renault, or a student from the West "whose parents have some property, an automobile, and domestics," whose answers are reported in the public opinion poll of I.F.O.P.?[46] There is a second and more serious difficulty. I have described the majority of Communists as "malcontents" who wish to ameliorate their standard of living, as reformists rather than revolutionaries, attached to parliamentary institutions and well decided[47] "in case of war between the U.S.S.R. and the United States to do everything to see that France remains completely neutral."[48] Let us admit the exactitude and fidelity of this image, but if it is true of the Communist *voter,* is it true of the *leaders* of the party? Presumably, the answer is negative. We touch here upon a proposition both banal and very important. That there is or is not a connection between the vote of the electors for a party and their class does not prove that that party expresses or does not express the points of view, defends or does not defend the interests, of this class. Even if *all* the workers voted Communist, before it would be safe to say that the Communist party "constitutes the political expression of the workers," we should have to take account of the "effect of domination" that the leaders of the party exercise or, at least, are susceptible of exercising over their electors. In the same way, from the social heterogeneity of "Peasant," "Independent," or "Radical" party voters, one cannot conclude that these parties are free vis-à-vis the large economic interests. The nature of a party is knowable not only from the social condition of its voters, or even of those it elects, but also by the effect that the electors and their representatives are able to exert.

One cannot hope to find the key to French politics in a sociological summary which makes various parties correspond to well-defined classes or groups, and which would see in our political regime the epiphenomenon of the conflicts and struggles of opposing classes and groups, one against another. I do not say, of course, that politics have no relation to the social structure but only that it is vain to seek to reduce the first set of facts to the second. There are some analogies between our social and political structures; both are remarkably complex. Our agriculture is disproportionately important compared with that in other occidental societies; 25 per cent of our active population devote themselves to it. French agriculture, as I have pointed out, is heterogeneous in practically all respects: technique, economics, and legal status. There are other differentiations in our society: the commercial interests, among which very small units proliferate, are very sensitive to the threats that press upon them; but, never resigned to change, they remain convinced—if one believes their chosen spokesmen—that they constitute the seat of national grandeur. Let us point out another heterogeneous group that holds a place apart: the liberal professions, both the ancient ones (of an independent type, like lawyers and doctors) and the new ones (like the salaried groups in industry). Each of the professions has a hyperbolic awareness of its originality and a tendency to regard its interests as separate from those of others. Is the incessantly repeated sentiment that one's self is—and is alone—indispensable so intense and so widespread among us that we can regard it as a specifically French trait? I should not like to risk affirming it. But with this caution it seems advisable to determine whether these mechanisms of differentiation between social groups are of a pathological intensity among us. This extreme differentiation evidently complicates politics. There are, at the least, more interests than there are groups, but it is necessary to add that these interests change, and that there are practically none (apart from the religious denominations) to which all parties would not successively or simultaneously appeal to attract voters.

So far, this explanation of the inconstancy of the French political party is not completely satisfying. Interests in America are no less numerous or less voracious. But are they perhaps less capricious, and are the groups concerned more flexible? American interest groups are not so ready to put forward their claims in absolute terms. Perhaps they are less disdainful of compromise and delay. French peasants occasionally threaten to bar the roads if their demands are not satisfied. French civil servants chronically threaten to strike if prompt satisfaction is not accorded them. It is not that American farmers are less demanding or that French civil servants have lost their sense of responsibility. Without doubt, this method of discussion is more familiar to the French, seeming more efficacious and more in accord with French "national character."

The complexity of our social structure does not explain the inconsistency of French politics—or at least it does not explain the frequent incoherence of the French political scene. American society and English society are, one might say, less complicated. It is true that American society is not embarrassed with pre-industrial survivals. It is true that in America a society largely dependent on technology exerts great pressure toward uniformity. However, the regional, ethnic, social, and religious differences are considerable, and the extreme diversity renders impossible complete synthesis and unanimous compromise. But American society does not leave the observer with this feeling of unbalanced heterogeneity which strikes one in the case of France. The English example confirms our analysis; that which appears simple and relatively unified at a certain level —in the political perspective, for example—appears diverse from another view. Let us agree that in England politics and parliament are simpler than in France; but it is doubtful if England is more homogeneous socially and less complex than France.

In brief it is not correct to seek the explanation of the French political regime in the social structure alone. It is true that our society is remarkably complex. Interests are expressed in a plurality of groups. These negotiate with political parties equally numerous and feebly integrated, producing forced coalitions. There is nothing in this picture that is specific to France; why these coalitions are so inefficacious, so much more gloomy, so much more violent than in other countries needs to be explained, but it can scarcely be understood by viewing the complexity of French social structure alone.

Some Tensions and Conflicts in French Society

Since World War II, France has often given foreign observers the impression of a sick country, skeptical, and profoundly unsure. But what struck these observers especially was the discontent and the protests of the workers. To reduce the conflicts and tensions of French society to a struggle between employers and workers would miss the main points.

These divisions are multiple and of variable intensity, but always very apparent; they follow the nature and the process of stratification observable in French society. "There is something that one has never seen under the sun," writes La Bruyère, "and that according to all appearances one will never see . . . a small town which is not divided into any parties, where the families are united . . . , where a marriage does not engender civil war, where the quarrel between ranks does not sound at all moments during the offering, during communions, during the processions and during the obsequies, where one sees the bailiff and the president speaking together, or the representatives and the assessors, where the dean lives well with his canons, where the canons do not snub the chaplains or where the latter suffer the choristers." [49] In this context it is necessary to underline the "quarrel among ranks." Saint-Simon has unforgettably described this extreme sensibility to social precedence. [50] It is evidently a characteristic trait of noble society, where the name, the antiquity, "the alliances," the "illustriousness," that is to say pure "vanities" according to the words of the bourgeois, conserve all prestige. But the French bourgeois seems never entirely cured of these chimeras, which he has, however, so strongly criticized among the nobility. The contrast between the pretensions of the lord and his often mediocre fortune amuses the merchant or the good bourgeois. However, when his fortune is solidly established he dreams only of titles for himself or for his children. The bourgeois' interest in moving out of his class of origin has been noted many times by French writers. It is M. Jourdain, Molière's character, who insists that his wife cease to receive their former acquaintances. It is M. Poirier himself, so aware of being bourgeois, who, in the story of Émile Augier, cannot resist the seduction of the peerage and ends by abandoning himself to a delicious dream of becoming a baron. But nowhere is this more pathetically illustrated than in *Le Père Goriot,* the story of the old vermicelli maker who amasses a fortune and despoils himself of it for his daughters. The paternal passion which inspires this sacrifice in him becomes aggravated by the humility with which the old bourgeois devalues himself and the extent to which he plunders himself. His daughters become ladies (one marries a marquis, the other a baron) and do not receive their worthy father. Goriot dies abandoned and ruined in a room of the sordid pension Vauquer, looked after by Rastignac alone, whose youthful cynicism has no need of this hard lesson.

The French bourgeoisie has spent part of its time in envying the nobility and a good part of the rest in mimicking them. One sees this emulation in the hunger for ennoblement which drives the rich bourgeois—up to the end of the nineteenth century, that is—to the moment when titles, being no longer controlled, are often false; one sees it in the relative ease with which the sons of family, even nonentities, marry the rich heiress ("fertilizers," they are called). How much jealousy and resentment on the part of even the rich bourgeoisie are manifested in obscure struggles for which the stake is, perhaps, a chair in the Academy or the control over the "good works" of M. le Curé!

Jules Vallés, in the first volume of his admirable trilogy, *Jacques Vingtas, L'Enfant,* describes how he and his mother (an elementary teacher at the Lycée du Puy) behave toward three passengers in the third-class train, one a commercial traveler, the second a woman hawker, and the third a "little old man." "A pleasantry of which I understood nothing was spoken by the salesman to the woman, pulling apart his lips and drawing from hers a loud laugh. From this moment they did nothing but enjoy themselves and he even gave her a few playful slaps to the great scandal of my mother . . ." Here are the commentaries which this spectacle inspires in a son of the "petits bourgeois": "How much gayer she is than my mother. What am I saying? . . . My mother is a pious woman who does not laugh, who does not love flowers, who has to keep up her position, to guard her honor."[51] Distrust and envy by the "superior" class of their neighbors below (and of those above) appears to be a notable trait of French society. This rivalry is probably more apparent because French society is relatively homogeneous; there are no ethnic groups who maintain their autonomy; there is the predominance of a rural population[52] or at least of small villages "where everybody knows everybody else."

Furthermore, French society lacks a precise and unilinear criterion of stratification. Even the bourgeoisie has never frankly admitted the indisputable pre-eminence of money. The "nouveau riche" is a suspect person-age, both ridiculous and odious. Rapid enrichment resulting from specula-tion or from the war has been judged not only as scandalous and shocking but as vulgar. "No origin is noble," Bossuet once said, and still less "noble" the origin of fortunes. It is necessary to ennoble one's wealth by some increment of prestige: to buy some land; to raise one's children at great expense, to acquire some high pretensions for them; to furnish one's house with antiques. The vulgar behavior of a salesman, a farmer, or a doctor, is thoroughly avoided by his children or grandchildren, raised in a grand style and with well-bred manners. But the recently enriched family who continues its habits of thrift, excites mixed reactions. "He who is not a gentleman has to put on a good front," one says of the peasant recently become a millionaire who walks as in the past, in wooden shoes and a beret. The antiquity of a family counts as much as its richness. Also im-portant is the occupation of the head of the family. "At Bordeaux," says M. François Mauriac, "wine ennobles." One even speaks of a "nobility of the cork." Banking, maritime commerce, the judiciary, and medicine are also honorable occupations. But production in lumber has less prestige than that in wine, even though one would not perhaps dispute the quality of a "shipowner." The pharmacist or the dentist enjoys a prestige well below that of the doctor. The prestige of the professions is not independent of their remuneration. But it is probable that remuneration is not the only thing that counts. The income of a pharmacist or a dentist is often as large, sometimes even larger, than that of a doctor. But a bourgeois family, happy to marry its daughter to a surgeon, would perhaps show less ur-gency if the suitor were a pharmacist or a dentist.

Money it appears, holds a large place in the system of French stratifi-cation. Thrifty habits are profoundly rooted among the majority of social groups. The peasant who heaps up bank note upon bank note to give himself some reserves or to round out his field is a familiar image. A good number of workers, despite low incomes have some savings: more than three months wages for 19 per cent of them; two or three months for 24 per cent of them; less than a month's for 24 per cent.[53] If there are a few years of relative monetary stability, individual savings accounts begin to be built up.[54] Without doubt one can see in this the mechanical fact of the lowering of "the propensity to consume." But in the case of the French there are a number of specific motivations for saving. Money, in this perspective, appears essentially as security, as an assurance. "To put by a flask against thirst," "to have some hay in the trusses," these peasant expressions have their equivalent in the mentality of the French entrepreneur who has a tendency to accumulate surplus in the balance sheets of his corporation and to be unwilling to distribute the profits.[55]

Between the "bourgeois" money criterion and more aristocratic criteria —antiquity of family and connections—the bourgeois hesitates. This ambiguity explains in part, perhaps, why his relations with the workers have been so difficult. A recent investigation of I.F.O.P., published in the February 1956 number of the magazine *Réalités*,[56] showed a level of satisfaction among workers higher than was generally supposed. To the question "Do you like what you are doing at this time?" 36 per cent answered "very much"; 50 per cent answered "well enough." One cannot put too much faith in vague questions, and this impressive 86 per cent who declare themselves satisfied with their work no doubt hides some significant regional and professional differences. A community study by Pierre Clément and Nelly Xydias in Vienne sur le Rhône[57] modifies some of these findings. These two researchers asked their subjects not only about their satisfaction with their employment but also about their wages or income; 72 per cent of the men declared themselves not satisfied as over against 20 per cent satisfied. In answer to the question "Would you like to change your work?" (a question comparable to the I.F.O.P.'s "Do you like what you are doing at this moment?"), 75 per cent of the population studied by Clément and Xydias responded negatively. On a second point, the inquiry of the I.F.O.P. showed some results worthy of interest: To the question "From the point of view of the quality of the products fabricated or of the quality of work, would you say that the firm for which you work rates very well, pretty well, not so good, or poor?" 90 per cent considered that things went very well or pretty well. Concerning the engineers and staff, 32 per cent of the workers questioned judged them very competent and 50 per cent pretty competent. And finally two rather explosive questions were put. To the first—"In the relations between the employer and his employees, is there more confidence or more distrust?" —53 per cent responded "more confidence," 27 per cent responded "more distrust." To the second—"Do you think that the employer himself is too arrogant, just about enough, or insufficiently?"—42 per cent responded "too haughty," 41 per cent answered "just about enough."

The over-all results of the I.F.O.P. investigation seem confirmed by the findings of the Clément-Xydias monograph. "Are you satisfied with your bosses or your superiors?" was asked of the workers in Vienne sur le Rhône; 75 per cent of the men and 72 per cent of the women responded "yes." Let us add that to the question "Are you satisfied with your subordinates?" 80 per cent of the male working staff and 77 per cent of the female staff responded "yes."[58] The results of the I.F.O.P. study have been commented upon with some sarcasm in a brilliant article in the radical weekly *France-Observateur* of March 1956. Both the title — "The Little Model Workers of *Réalités*"—and the drawings which accompany the text speak of the distrust of the author and his irritation at seeing the workers painted under "reformist" colors. First the feeling of workers' insecurity is said to be juggled away by the inquiry of the I.F.O.P. "Generally the French workers experience little unemployment," writes *Réalités*. "It would have been instructive to test this extremely broad sentiment in an always possible economic crisis," writes the editor of *France-Observateur*. "The workers' standard of living is overestimated by *Réalités*," adds our critic. "The inquiry speaks only of a total monthly budget of a family where the wages and the family allocations are arbitrarily mingled . . . 40,000 francs per month does not represent the same standard of living for a bachelor or a family of five or six persons. . . . Another point on which the inquiry of *Réalités* seems optimistic concerns workers' savings. The expansion of credit sales, the existence of systems of savings credit such as the 'bons de la Semeuse,' make us think that the proportion indicated as saved is somewhat low." Finally, while the standard of living is presented in the most favorable fashion, by contrast the desires of the wage earners are rather reduced. "One learns that 21 per cent of the workers 'do not desire' a bathroom; that 33 per cent do not want washing machines and that 41 per cent do not desire refrigerators, which is at the least curious." It is perhaps the relation between the level of aspiration and the actual level of income which constitutes the best index for understanding workers' satisfactions. That 41 per cent of the workers "do not want" refrigerators evidently does not mean that if Santa Claus put them in their stockings, they would return them to the sender. For these 41 per cent, the purchase of a refrigerator does not appear possible on their incomes or in their family situation. Even if the expense were not absolutely impossible for these families, a refrigerator is not regarded by them as a primary necessity. This is a motivation similar to that of the bourgeois who could afford to spend two weeks at Cannes, but prefers to pass a month "in a little place not so dear."

It remains to ask if the lack of a refrigerator is regarded as a cruel frustration or as an annoying but temporary lack. Interesting in this respect is the list of objects that workers lack but regard as worth having: 21 per cent, for example, would like a house of their own; 22 per cent would like an automobile; 59 per cent a bathroom; 34 per cent a washing machine; and 40 per cent hot water. Going on from there, two questions pose themselves, "What percentage increase of income would make these desired goods accessible without a price increase?"[59] Between 5 per cent and 30 per cent is the estimate of 61 per cent of the workers questioned. To this subjective question it is necessary to add an objective one. Is the French economy able to satisfy such needs? And under what conditions? At least the inquiry of *Réalités* suggests the potentially reformist tendency of the workers. To the question "Are you interested in politics?" only 11 per cent responded "very much," 39 per cent answered "not at all," and 50 per cent said "a little." But it must be noted that 72 per cent answered that they always voted in the general elections and only 10 per cent said they never voted. It is necessary to point out also that the inquiry was conducted during a period of political inactivity, and that in a period of effervescence the workers furnish their contingent of militants. If 19 per cent believe that the situation would be improved by a revolution, 30 per cent prefer slow change and 42 per cent answer that they do not know.

In order to draw a picture shaded to include all cases, two facts should be underlined. First, 52 per cent of workers estimate that their standard of living has not been improved for five years, even though the official statistics show an increase of real income, per capita, of about 20 per cent. Is the pessimism of the workers more marked than that of other social categories? Taking account of everything, one cannot be sure. The majority of farmers and shopkeepers also refuse to admit that the economic situation has improved. Next, 34 per cent of workers estimate that if French prosperity increases, their standard of living will increase even though 31 per cent estimate that they would have nothing to gain from the general prosperity. There are 35 per cent who do not know.

On the basis of this short analysis it is difficult to give an idea of "what the workers want," but the data permit the elimination of two current stereotypes. The French working class is not united in a wild revolutionary drive, and the myth of the "grand soir" (that is, outbreak of revolution) is probably more of the kind that will "mobilize the masses." The worker resembles but little the allegorical "proletariat" of M. Sartre who, in having been freed himself, would "reconcile at one blow man with himself, with nature and with other men." Perhaps, he would be well advised not to count on himself to make history and to incarnate liberty. But it would not be more reasonable to imagine the average worker as a patient reformist who hopes for a slow improvement of his condition. What is probably most characteristic of the French workers is their instability, their oscillation between attitudes in apparent contradiction. We have underlined above the constancy of the worker's vote in favor of the Socialist and Communist parties; how may we now speak of indetermination and indecision? The two observations, far from being contradictory, call forth, we believe, the same explanation, as we shall now see with a discussion of the alternate swelling and reduction in the numbers of active unionists.

Before the schism of Tours, (between Communists and others, mainly Socialists) the C.G.T. (the main federation of trade unions) had in 1919 about three million members. At the time, two rival organizations were formed which paralleled the division between Socialists and Communists: the C.G.T.U. (of Communist inclination) and the former C.G.T. (more allied to the Socialist Party); the membership of the two organizations combined was not over a million and a half. In 1935, at the time of the popular front, the two trade union federations decided to reunite. At the end of 1937 the membership of the combined C.G.T. was more than five million. But in 1939, on the eve of the war, it had fallen again to less than two million. After the war, the same alternation took place: an increase from 1945 to 1947, followed by a decrease after the new schism which opposed the Socialist F.O. (Force Ouvrière) to the Communist C.G.T.[60] Today a third of the workers are unionized. The instability of the workers' world is well attested to by this index. But this instability, this indecision, does not mean that the worker indulges naively in the grossest exaltations, or abandon himself to despair. The workers' attitudes vis-à-vis their union representatives, vis-à-vis the parties (the Communist party in particular since it pretends to represent them) indicates that their wishes are badly known and have not yet been systematically studied. All that one can presume is that they are more complex and more ambiguous than the current stereotypes would lead us to believe. The total and perfect identification of the working class and "its Communist party" is very probably merely a legend. The workers who vote Communist remain freer vis-à-vis the "party" than many intellectuals who do not vote for it. They manifest a reasonable and critical attitude toward their leaders, or toward the

481

"party line." It is useless to try to prove that the conservative stereotype according to which "the good workers are duped by bad leaders" is entirely laughable. The C.G.T. was resisted at the schism of 1947. Without doubt its active membership has decreased, but its working-class membership has not deserted it. Rather, workers renounced provisionally all union activity. Only one very weak faction has been seduced by the appeal of the F.O. The great mass of the working population remains, in general, faithful to the unions and to the parties which pretend to represent them, but this fidelity is very supple and it should probably not be interpreted as full and complete adherence to a revolutionary ideology.

The inquiry of *Réalités* suggests that, in general, the French worker is reformist, a view which requires almost infinite corrections and nuances. At the same time there is among the workers an extremely widespread feeling of injustice. To the question, "According to what you see, do you have the impression that in the actual state of things there is much injustice?" 63 per cent responded "very much" and only 17 per cent said "not so much." This feeling of injustice is probably too alive and too widespread for any rallying to reformism to appear frankly and openly at the moment. In brief, even those who scarcely believe in the eventuality or the efficacy of the Revolution are not able to renounce frankly this perspective as long as their demands for "justice" are not better satisfied.

From what sources does this sentiment come—that in the actual state of things there is too much injustice? To answer this question, three kinds of research are indicated. It would be necessary first to examine the development of the occupational structure. Certainly the most apparent phenomenon is the development of the *ouvrier spécialisé* (semiskilled worker), whose role, according to Michel Collinet, "is to run an automatic or semi-automatic machine without knowing the machinery or its function in the whole of the manufacture."[61] This role is distinguished from that of the traditional manual laborer by the fact that it demands less expenditure of physical energy; "the work of maintenance, of cleaning, of loading and unloading"[62] is evidently the basis of the activities of control which are exercised on the specialized machine. It is the worker's job to look after the machine and to feed it the pieces to be fabricated. If he is nicely distinguished from the traditional manual laborer, the *ouvrier spécialisé* (O.S.) is no less distinguished from the highly qualified professional of many abilities who constitutes the working force in the traditional handicrafts. The semiskilled worker (O.S.) can only execute a small number of operations, although the mechanics and coppersmiths before 1914 accumulated the most diverse skills. They were, M. Collinet tells us,[63] successively fitters, turners, and mounters. Finally, in the majority of cases, the training of the O.S. is extremely rapid, although the professional undergoes an apprenticeship of several years. The increase in the percentage of the O.S. in the working population evidently varies with the industry. An inquiry of the Minister of Labor of 1948 lists the industries where the O.S. are in the majority: textiles, steel, and machinery. In the building trades and in the clothing industry traditional criteria of qualification have remained and have resisted specialization. Finally, in the chemical industry and food products the manual laborer predominates. The increase of the O.S. is correlated, not only with the decline of manual labor but is also associated with the increase in the number of technicians and engineers.

One aspect of this transformation, probably satisfying, is that the physical effort demanded of the worker tends to be less arduous and perhaps also less intense. His work appears to him less "dirty," less "painful." It seems that in this respect the worker makes a comparison between present and previous conditions and that this comparison is favorable to the present. At least this appears to be indicated by the first results of an investigation now in progress in the Lorraine steel industry. (A similar improvement in conditions also appeared evident to me after visiting some chemical products factories.) But over and against this gain which results from the lightening of physical work, it is necessary to place in balance the monotony which accompanies the majority of the operations to which the O.S. is reduced.

A second source of dissatisfaction for the worker, or at least of uncertainty, is the confusion before machines that become more and more complicated and whose functions remain mysterious to him. It is not only the discomfort that the worker feels at not being able to understand the task which he does, but also the more specific threat of increasingly heavy demands for training. To be a mechanic now, it is necessary to complete one's education. This is a threat resented particularly by old workers who fear not being able to keep up and of finding themselves prematurely retired by the progress of specialization. It can also make younger workers uncomfortable to the extent that the demands of specialization and of occupational training activate ambiguous attitudes in regard to instruction.[64]

Is the advancement of the O.S. accompanied by economic advancement? This question directs attention to the more general problem of workers' pay and how this pay is judged by those concerned. Does it appear satisfying to them or contemptible? We have already reported that 52 per cent of the workers questioned by the I.F.O.P. estimate that their standard of living has not increased since 1950 and that 72 per cent of the whole wage-earning population of Vienne sur le Rhône estimate that their income is insufficient. Wages have apparently remained an almost constant proportion of the national income since 1938. While the belief that workers are becoming pauperized is untenable, it is necessary to point out that the average number of hours of work has been increased since 1939, and, at the same time, the employed labor force has increased, resulting in the almost complete disappearance of unemployment. The above-mentioned constancy of workers' wages as a proportion of the national income does not mean that wages themselves have remained constant. On the contrary, everything points to the belief that the average hourly wage has decreased. Also the worker is obliged to seek supplementary work or to seek work for his wife. Perhaps it would be true to say that workers find their work more and more "useless," even though they have much less difficulty in finding work. But more significant still is the transformation in the structure of the wage. First, the family and social payments (sickness and accident insurance) have come to represent a considerable percentage of workers' incomes. In November 1950, the family allowances alone were equal to the following percentages of wages of the Parisian workers: for two children, 48 per cent for the manual laborer (including the allocation for the housewife) and 33.5 per cent for the skilled worker; for a manual laborer with three children, the same allocations represent 85 per cent of his salary whereas they amount to 59 per cent of the wages of a skilled worker.[65] How much of this social income, paid indirectly and compulsorily, is regarded as regular income by the worker, in view of the fact that the expenses for sickness or accident are contingent? The workers refuse to regard as authentic wages the sums that the statisticians and the businessmen list as part (moreover, an important part) of workers' income. And as these deductions and allocations are pro-levied on the mass of wages, the workers believe their wages are reduced by this much without their recognizing that this income is redistributed to those among them who have families or who have been victims of accident or sickness. French social security, financed by advance levies on wages, does constitute a transfer of revenues, but, within the wage category alone. It diminishes the strictly personal and immediately spendable part of the wage. The wage earner is more or less aware that "he should be able to receive more," while the businessman treats the "social charges" as an element in the cost of labor.

If the proportion of wages in the national income has not changed, if secondly there has been a considerable transfer of income within the wage category, it is certain that some have lost even though others have gained. Let us add that the hierarchy of wages has been greatly flattened so that the distance between the base and the summit of the pyramid is markedly reduced. All the administrative measures taken since 1940 have tried to provide a "vital minimum" without allowing the higher echelon to benefit from the same wage increase. Therefore, the various branches of industry find themselves very diversely affected by the long period of inflation which extended from 1944 to 1952. Textiles, food, more generally the low-wage industries of 1938, find themselves in 1950 revalued upward in relation to the metal industry or to the chemical products industry. Commercial employees and the service workers (Colin Clark's "tertiary occupations") find themselves much less well treated.

The transfer of income within the wage-earning class can be a source of dissatisfaction, not only because it destroys the former relative positions of certain socio-occupational categories, but also because, for certain individuals, it causes an absolute deterioration. A final order of phenomena should be evoked here. This is the delay between the moment when new needs appear and the moment when they are satisfied. Certain consumer's goods are immediately desirable either because a certain prestige is attached to them, or because of their utility. But they are not immediately accessible because of their high initial cost or the cost of their upkeep. The worker is a potential client for these goods—washing machines, autos, motorcycles, or refrigerators—the continued exhibition of which constitutes a source of frustration for him. How much of the enjoyment of this equipment is subjectively devalued because it is displayed on all the markets?

Changes in wage and employment structure are probably at the bottom of the dissatisfaction of the workers. But a last and particularly important point should be touched upon. What chances does a worker have, or believe he has, to rise in the social scale? Regarding this problem of mobility, little information is available. A public opinion poll, published in *Population*[66] by M. Bresard, found that 38 per cent of present-day employees in commerce, 18 per cent of instructors, 25 per cent of post-office employees and 20 per cent of commercial representatives were sons of workers. Among salesmen and artisans, only 13 per cent came from workers' families. The interpretation of these figures is difficult because the category "workers" has not been broken down by our investigator. The distinction between O.S., skilled, and manual workers is not presented in his work, but the results probably refer to skilled workers rather than to manual laborers.[67]

Very probably a good part of the workers in industry are former peasants or, at least, the sons of peasants. The percentage of the active agricultural population continues to drop; it is reasonable to suppose that the manual laborers thus freed are employed in the factories. A fraction remains in the rural zones whenever industries, great consumers of manual labor, are cheaply installed there as in the case of the chemical industry in the department of Oise.

It is difficult to give an idea of the chances of worker promotion. But these chances are probably relatively small. It is not yet possible to examine seriously what the workers think of the chances for promotion offered them in French society. One often hears it said that French society is "hardened" and that in conserving acquired situations, it frustrates all hope of promotion of individuals and groups which ask only to rise. It is true that French economy and demography show either over-all rates of decrease or very small increases. But if one undertakes to determine on a sample, supposedly representative, the occupation of the parents of the subjects interrogated, one observes with Natalie Rogoff[68] that 50 per cent of the French workers, as over against 80 per cent of American workers, skilled and unskilled, come from working-class families. From similar observations, the author concludes that French social mobility is for only two fifths of the workers, as high as it would be if the choice of employment were open; that is, did not depend on the profession of the parents, as over against a proportion of four fifths in the American case.

But this ratio of two to one between the two countries appears fallaciously low. Given the importance of the rural group in the active French population, much less important in America, the presumption appears strong that a large part of the French workers of nonworker origin come from families of small income and low status, just as among American workers of nonworker origin a considerable percentage come from the lower middle class. The rates given by Natalie Rogoff appear to confuse horizontal and vertical mobility, and probably reduce the actual differences in vertical mobility between the two countries. Nevertheless, without proof to the contrary, it should probably be said that the mobility of the French workers is absolutely and relatively low. But should so much be made of this rigidity which is so upsetting to the sociologist and the economist rather than to those who have, perhaps, more fear of change than awareness of suffering from immobility? It is in change where in many cases there lies a risk; this is, in general, perceived with an almost painful intensity. "A bird in the hand is worth two in the bush." Distrust of methods of rationalization has much of its source here among the unionized workers. First, it nourishes the fear that these methods only reinforce "the power of monopolies," but fear of losing a job, mediocre but assured is also very lively. One could find without difficulty an equivalent feeling among their bosses. French social stratification is probably not perceived as "immobile" by either workers or bourgeois. This quality would seem to be perceived more by the salaried employees of industry and by the intelligent conservatives who are recruited from the younger members of the liberal professions.

Apart from immobility or rigidity, however, French society appears basically "unjust" to workers. This feeling of being victims, of being exploited, is probably very intense; does not its intensity neatly explain the spontaneous and constant rejection of all reformism by the workers? The injustice is not perceived in a specific context but generally; it feeds a diffuse distrust. If the employers grant an increase of wages, it is proof that they make scandalous profits. "They enrich themselves at our expense." If they refuse, they are accused of pitiless avarice and hardness. This schema is evidently too simplified. The final word seems to be that all amelioration is attributed to "the efficiency of the labor movement" but never to the understanding of the businessmen. This attitude probably explains why the attempts of certain businessmen who are said to be "broad and intelligent" do not suffice to disarm the prejudices and the hostility of their workers. It is notable for example that even in the enterprises where contracts of the "Renault type" [69] have been concluded, the force of the unions is not at all impaired. Let us note one situation: the C.G.T. is able to afford the luxury of refusing to be a party to a contract while presenting the advantages thus obtained as a victory of "its own protest action." This sensibility to injustice is expressed not only in the fear of being "exploited," of having "to do too much for what one is paid," but also by feelings of resentment toward industrial discipline. The employer not only does not pay, but he is also a brute. Between the two wars, the word used to describe a large automobile factory was "workhouse." No writer better describes the protest and revolt the workers feel before a certain type of industrial work than Simone Weil. In *Experience de la vie d'usine*[70] Simone Weil notes those conditions of the worker's life that appear to him the hardest and the most intolerable: first, "the time clock; the road from his home to the factory is dominated by the fact that it is necessary to arrive before a time mechanically determined." Of servitude to a task and a rhythm over which one has no control, here are the consequences that impress our author: "All the workers in the factory, or nearly all, even those most independent of bearing, have something almost imperceptible in their movement, in their expression, and especially in the set of their lips which implies they are constrained and that they count for nothing." And a little further on: "From the moment one enters to the moment one leaves, one is in the position of *submitting* to orders." It is particularly resented when "a new job is imposed suddenly under the form of an order which it is necessary to obey immediately and without reply." More generally, the worker submits to the most artificial of all conditions "inasmuch as the factory demands that all the senses participate in a universe where nothing recalls nature, where nothing is free, where all is knocked around, knocked hard, and at the same time man is overwhelmed by matter." The most absurd, the worst of all, is seeing "that things play the role of men, men play the role of things."

Weil's book underlines both the sickness of the worker in the "technical milieu" ("sometimes the body is exhausted in the evening when leaving the factory, but thought is always exhausted and this is *more*"), and the rigors of industrial discipline ("even the conditions of work hinder one from movements that should be able to occur without the fear of reprimand, the avid desire to accumulate some *sous*, and, in a certain measure, the taste for a reputation for speed").[71] This analysis, so vigorous, so striking, loses little of its impact from the fact that Simone Weil, despite her experience of factory life, remains an "intellectual" and a "bourgeoise." After all, her remarks are corroborated by the work and observations of a sociologist like Georges Friedmann. Furthermore, there is need for more light on a difficulty which until now does not seem to have much interested French writers: In what measure is this attitude toward the technical environment and industrial discipline more intense among French workers than among the workers of other Western countries—Germans, English, and Americans? Do French employers create a harder and stricter industrial discipline than is known among other people?

This is a question that leads one to ask why the various methods known as "human relations" have been welcomed with such reserve. The distrust of French workers for "paternalism" is explained as arising from their fear of being exploited and manipulated, from their conviction that "good works" mask the least praiseworthy intentions. The first and most difficult task for a specialist in human relations is persuading the skeptical workers that the methods he proposes do not constitute a ruse invented by the bosses. But the latter are almost as skeptical as their workers. The following two fundamental rules of all techniques of authority appear to many French manufacturers as objectives disproportionally and uselessly expensive: (1) to make their subordinates understand their orders, (2) to make themselves likeable to their subordinates. If anyone mentions these two rules, he is likely to be considered naive.

Is the very high level of dissatisfaction manifested in French industry normal? "Things are not so good," that is to say, labor costs too much, morale is bad, expenses are too heavy. This familiar refrain among the heads of industry corresponds to the workers' bitterness that is so tightly linked to a feeling of injustice. It is true that the anthem often concludes with "Let's hope that things don't get worse." This pessimism has many sources, but it is its important consequences that should be emphasized. Despite all the recommendations of industrial counselors, the employer dislikes to delegate his authority—especially when the receiver of this authority has not the same "spirit," the same "traditions," as the delegator. This "spirit," these "traditions," are symbolized and preserved in the professional schools (Polytechnique, Centrale, Arts et Métiers). The boss-owner of a small industry, lacking great technical competence himself, is able to hire as a director an engineer. The latter may in fact run the factory, but the owner, in order to save face, guards his more or less successfully delimited power, the exercise of which may interfere with that of his "director." In the inferior echelons of the industrial hierarchy, similar phenomena can be observed. If the foreman is often in an embarrassing position, it is because the field left to his initiative is too narrow and badly defined.

However difficult to verify, a broad hypothesis may be advanced here, relating the essential weaknesses in French organizations (private or public) to the delegation of authority and the conditions of control. The excessive centralization and concentration, "congestion at the center, paralysis at the extremities," are French maladies which if not well studied are at least frequently pointed out. These symptoms are related to an attitude toward authority that seems to be common among the French and characteristic of French "mentality" or French "culture." Apparently the French imagine that authority is unique and all powerful. That authority results from a precarious equilibrium of activities, that it requires—and at the same time avoids—a clear-cut symbolic expression, are not spontaneous ideas. And confusion takes hold of many compatriots when they discover that the authority they see at the center is not actually to be found there, and is not specifically localizable in any part. One of the most prevalent deceptions that inflict the political regime is that "one does not know, one cannot know who commands." This deception is alive not only among the conservatives or the reactionaries obsessed by the image of the leader. It nourishes also a certain Jacobinism, which—believing that all attempts at reform are frustrated before the "wall of silver" or "the occult power of the capitalists"—calls for a tribune of the people or the dictatorship of the proletariat. One of the paradoxes of the French mentality is that, though unable to support authority without difficulty, it shows a spontaneous tendency to conceive of all social relations in terms of authority. This obsession with power in a society where power is impotent is fascinating.

The scientific study of industrial organizations *a la française* ought to some day or other attract the attention of a sociologist. The book of Henri Fayol, *Theorie de l'Administration Generale et Industrielle,* merits, from this point of view, an attentive examination. Fayolism is distinguished in many ways from Taylorism, and it seems evident that the French engineer gives proof of an intelligence as penetrating as that of his American colleague. But the originality of Fayol, which is characteristic of French mentality, is to have seen that the efficacy of the organization rests principally on the aptitudes of its head. Taylor concentrates his interest on the work place; Fayol on the director. Although his work effectively presents a theory of industrial enterprise, it is a theory written from the perspective of the chief and his strategy while the theory of Taylor rests upon the perspective of the engineer. Some consequences seem to be implicit in this attitude. First, industry is regarded as similar to the organization where the direct influence of the chief is the most evident: the army. The director becomes a kind of general and the foreman a corporal. But to enlarge this first image, a second simile is presented. The enterprise has its objectives and its politics, and the director becomes a kind of statesman, pursuing highly complex plans in secret. These images ennoble the function of the director (in the eyes of those who exercise it). An inquiry by deep interview would perhaps reveal the role these political and military models play in the motivation of the big industrialists. Concerning the elaboration of the administrative structure of the large private enterprises, a historical study would make apparent their dependence upon the methods in use in public administration, both civil and military. But does not the ennoblement of the entrepreneur risk losing specificity? And especially in concentrating the powers of decision in the hands of the chief, does it not exclude all active participation of individuals or of groups whose energy is thus lost to the enterprise? These chiefs, thus compelled to consider themselves as centers of decision, are faced with two kinds of frustration. The chiefs of the top level tend to treat the intermediate echelon as they themselves treat their inferiors. All demands of participation coming from subordinates are regarded by them as insupportable interference: "Why do they mix in it? Why should they occupy themselves with it?"

A study of the relations between the immediately contiguous levels in the administrative hierarchy would doubtlessly clarify and illustrate this point.

French Rates of Growth

Although the picture of French society presented here is still somewhat meager, nevertheless certain traits have been established. On the political scene the stability of ideologies and the fluidity and subtlety of parliamentary intrigue have been observed. Among these maneuvers and the convulsive crises of the type of June 1848, the Paris Commune, or the popular front, it is difficult to find a relationship. Anyone who has been taught to look at French politics in terms of a conflict between a rightist and a leftist ideology—"Resistance and Movement," according to M. Goguel—would expect a steady alternation of two well-organized parties, in and out of office. Obviously, this is not the way things happen in France. Similarly, an observer with a taste for the most polished political maneuvering and for the brilliance of arbitrary solutions, which concern only a small number of specialists, would be well prepared to appreciate the mixed coalitions of French ministers, but quite at sea with the noisy popular explosions.

Should it be concluded that the French political regime is incompre-

491

hensible in itself? There is some truth in this remark, but it can be applied to all political regimes. Nevertheless, the regime of modern France does have a somewhat esoteric tradition which can be understood only by a relatively small number of "practitioners." Moreover, a purely "sociological" explanation does not explain much. The characteristics of French politics do not spring in any clear-cut way from its relation with class. The opposition between bourgeoisie and proletariat is very striking. But to reduce the pair (left-right) to the couplet (bourgeoisie-proletarian) would distort the facts and not advance the analysis very much. In all Western industrial societies a "proletariat" is opposed to a "bourgeoisie," if one understands by the first the group which sells its labor and by the second the group which buys the labor. But this kind of opposition has some highly varied political consequences.

In England it underlies the Conservative-Labour party opposition that dominates a relatively simple social structure. Because the peasant vote does not count for much and the traditional social groups do not resist innovations too stubbornly, the political regime is rather stable. The American case is more complex. Although the Republican party is broadly identified with "business," the Democrats probably do not express the will of the working class as such. The noticeable difference in the French case in relation to both the English and the American examples is that the class opposition accentuated among the French is observed to be at the same time extremely fluid in political maneuvering.

The French situation seems at first to be explicable in simple terms: the extreme "reactionary" right and the extreme "revolutionary" left, by canceling each other, fix the beam of the balance near the center in an ill-defined zone where political competition is above all a network of personal rivalries. A simple view in effect, but rather summary, for one must still explain how the extreme right cancels out the extreme left.

The five million Communist voters weigh more heavily than the four million (more or less) opponents of the parliamentary regime. Moreover, if the first regularly bar the road to the second, the second prevent the first from obtaining power. Is there any explanation for this paradox?

Concerning the fundamental conservatism of the French regime the words of M. Thiers, "The Republic will be conservative or it will not be," have in general been respected. Without doubt inflation and rent control have liquidated a good part of the old fortunes in real estate. The agricultural proprietor has fared better: farm rents—expressed in quintals of wheat, hectolitres of wine, or kilograms of butter—have resisted inflation even if a 1946 law greatly reduced the owner's chance to evict tenant farmers. Wartime scarcities have swelled commercial profits, and the small shopkeepers—who today cry so loudly, and some of whom support M. Poujade—profited and consolidated their traditional position. The peasantry, small business, and the liberal professions surpass in political influence the groups who live directly by industrial activity. France has indeed conserved its traditional face.

M. Goguel opposes a "static" France—south of the Loire—to a "dynamic" France—that of the East and North. The per capita income is higher in the Moselle district than in Aveyron or Lozère. None could say, however, that static France votes for the right and dynamic France for the left, nor vice versa. But, according to M. Goguel, it is necessary to distinguish a "static" right where independents and peasants predominate, a "dynamic" right which prefers "modern" parties: RPF, or MRP, and "old left" where the Radical and Socialist union clearly hinders the Communists, who on the contrary dominate in the regions of the "dynamic" left.

Thus for several years, many of the French have considered their country to be characterized by two traits. First, French society can be described as "static" in a Malthusian sense. Next the French increase, weak though it may be, tends to increase the disparities between the different regions. The North and the East become more and more rich at the same time as the center and the South excluding the Marseilles and Toulouse areas, become impoverished and depopulated.

For more than twenty years, M. Sauvy has called attention to the very diverse and generally ruinous consequences for France of a demographic regression that hinders productivity and leaves to the producers only a feebly increasing income, always less than their anticipations. "The maximum French birth rate was reached in 1814 but the decrease began in 1820. During the nineteenth century the general tendency was the same: decrease of the birth rate, decrease of mortality, and a lengthening of the life span." [72] This reversal in the birth rate also had some important effects upon traditional, pre-Revolutionary family structure. [73] Mr. Gemählhing notes that the reduction of the birth rate in the early nineteenth century was accompanied by an elevation of the marriage rate and a lowering of family fertility. This reduction in the size of the domestic unit has contributed to reducing the bonds of relationship, to modifying the relations between brothers, and to changing the nature of the authority that parents exercise over their children. But to these directly social consequences, perceived in an intuitive manner since they have not been made the object of any methodical study, are added some economic effects that in their turn react indirectly on the social plane.

The French age pyramid shows two anomalies: a heavy percentage of old people, imputable to the demographic stagnation at the end of the nineteenth century and to the drain of World War I, and an increasing percentage of children because of the measures taken since 1939 to encourage the birth rate.

A reduced active population is then charged with the care of two heavy categories of unproductive people. What consequences follow this demographic disequilibrium? M. Sauvy proposes to call the various effects "Malthusian," using this word in its larger sense. "Because of the stagnation of the population and of the change in its age composition, the need for new enterprises is not felt at least in older industries. . . . Next, few affairs are directed by young men. These can only await their turn or enter into the growing civil service and take part in creative movements only at a fairly advanced age; that is to say, at a moment when their spirit of enterprise and of adventure has given place to a desire for tranquility. Because of this, our economic progress is less than among our neighbors goaded by the push of young men and by the necessity of construction." [74] Is not "Malthusian demography" thus naturally prolonged in an "economic Malthusianism"? Too many men, too few jobs, but also surpluses of production; voluntary reduction of births, but also control and destruction of surpluses: wheat and wine, for example. M. Sauvy does not attack only the "Malthusianism" of farmers or even of manufacturers who protect their products by tariffs or by quotas. Traces of it are found in the mentality of unionized workers. In a classical analysis [75] M. Sauvy has shown how the forty-hour law instituted by Blum's government deprived the French economy of the advantages which the devaluation of October 1936 had achieved for it. "A rapid economic recovery . . . has thus been broken by an inopportune Malthusian intervention." [76] But far from "being enlightened by these results, the partisans of the forty-hour week used the reduction of activity as an argument to justify the continuation of the law because of the absence of markets." And M. Sauvy concludes with melancholy, "Malthusianism feeds on itself." [77]

This fear that a growing production will lack markets constitutes what M. Sauvy calls economic Malthusianism. It remains to be seen how this is joined to the attitude toward limiting births. For M. Sauvy they are two sides of the same coin. But there is a second effect of Malthusianism, taken in the largest sense, which at first glance seems inverse to that just analyzed. A general decrease of population, and an insufficient percentage of active persons in an already reduced population, induce a curbing effect. But they also produce tension: competition for reduced markets can be very lively and even, at times, deceitful and cunning. If everything is being used, capital and workers producing at less than maximum efficiency, both can be shifted around in the economy in new combinations and produce more efficiently without suffering the costs of producing at a very high level. Considering the case of newcomers (that is, new entrepreneurs or old entrepreneurs starting a new business), the narrower the market, the heavier are their risks. In both cases, the introduction of new things, whether innovations or simple reconversions, are costlier for a small than for a large market. The result is that competition will be very harsh between "old" and "new," and in this struggle the older firms probably enjoy a considerable advantage. The harshness of the competition is explained by the fact that of the general income of a branch of industry supposed constant, the part diverted to the new competitors diminishes by that much the combined income of the old firms; in brief, that which one firm gains is gained at the loss of another. It is not astonishing that the old firms greet the newcomers with inquietude. They seek aid and protection and the guarantee of their "legitimate" interests. The old and new firms usually reach an agreement on a middling profit that assures to the least productive of the established companies a sufficient margin and guarantees to the new firms, if they are well equipped, some very substantial profits.

Thus the participants divide monopolistic income among themselves according to the degree of constraint that they exercise, one on the other. The economics of distribution could be usefully studied from this perspective. Small businesses protest against the Monoprix and the Prisunix, and seek differential financial treatment from the government; the result is that a new price level is imposed where "everybody is equal again." Furthermore, the old firms occasionally succeed in barring new firms from a market where "all the good places are taken." This very "imperfect" competition is mainly indirect. The victory is not decided by price competition alone, with the most efficient producers underselling their competitors, but often by the skill of those entrepreneurs who are well protected politically;

they are thus able to defend themselves against the too automatic effect of the price mechanism.

It is not unreasonable to impute a large part of whatever French economic backwardness there is to "Malthusianism." The aging of the population evidently curbs the increase of the average per capita income.[78] The stability of the demand for consumers' goods deprives the people of the advantages flowing from a large market. It is less easy to determine which of these two forms of Malthusianism plays the role of cause to the other. In general, it would certainly seem that the decline in demographic advancement since 1830 preceded the symptoms of economic Malthusianism, which became clearly apparent with the strengthening of agricultural protectionism toward the end of the nineteenth century. This hypothesis of a rigid dependence between economic stagnation and demographic regression is not, however, entirely convincing; rather, it seems to obscure some important points. Is it possible that a fear of abundance can be observed even in an epoch when French demography was still expanding? The force of tradition and the corporation rules are first indices of this. The almost constant distrust of French opinion before all varieties of economic liberalism should also be noted. Free exchange has scarcely an advocate here: Bastiat, so popular at the end of the reign of Louis Philippe, has not had, as Cobden did, much influence on the legislation of his country. Protectionism is not a malady of the present age. Méline is not the inventor of the tariff which has continuously sheltered French agriculture behind a great wall. One remembers how little success Turgot had—at the beginning of the reign of Louis XVI—in attempting to liberalize the grain business[79] or dismantle the corporations. And Clapham cites these very significant words of Guizot reported by Levasseur: "I am not one of those who believe that in matters of industry and commerce legitimate interests ought to be lightly exposed to all the vicissitudes of an unbridled foreign competition."[80] A protectionism with "Malthusian" effects is found all through our commercial tradition.

It is not certain that the relation between the Malthusian attitude (taken in a general sense) and French demographic stagnation is a pure and simple causative one. Between these two orders of phenomena there is without doubt a connection; but of what sort? It should be remembered that the demographic regression is for a large part allied with the bloodiness of the Napoleonic wars and the blood-letting of 1914–18. That it depends on historical cataclysms, on the will or even the taste of individuals, are facts little taken into account. But French demographic stagnation is not only accidental; a large part of it obviously results from deliberate abstention from procreation. Demographic analysis is not autonomous. Its explanation ought to have recourse to social-psychological hypotheses. "It is necessary," says M. Sauvy, "to mention the important phenomenon called *social capillarity*. From the day when it appeared possible for each person to raise himself up or to elevate his children to a superior class, the usefulness of reducing the number of children became still more plainly apparent. This social capillarity plays both on the desire for promotion and on the fear of slipping down. The ascending current creates a competition so lively that the parents fear to see their children declassed." Each individual has so much more chance of realizing his ambitions for himself and for his descendants if he reduces the volume of his progeniture. Those individuals or groups who desire social promotion the most ardently are those most susceptible to Malthusian influence; these groups are not in general the most disadvantaged but those who, on the contrary, have assimilated the culturally dominant values. "In regard to equal social conditions, the inequality of the standard of living between those without children and those with a family," estimates M. Sauvy, "is not a subject of controversy." This is why the decrease of the birth rate has a close relationship with the degree of well-being of the population.[81] The rigor of Sauvy's statement, written before the measures to aid births had borne fruit, ought to be softened today. But even today the belief that having children decreases the standard of living, sound or not, is still widely accepted and, consequently, very effective.

French demographic stagnation does not constitute a final and independent datum. It is tied both to the mediocre productivity of our economy and to the estimations of each household regarding its standard of life or its place in the nation. From this point of view it bears witness to the discrepancy between individual ambitions and the opportunities, real or imagined, that French society offers. French "regression" however, is very far from being uniform and continuous. Too general a view neglects a more striking trait of the French: their application and their taste for both industrious and ingenious activity from which springs their remarkable success in certain sectors.

Certain French industries, like automobile and aeronautical construction and the manufacture of rubber, achieved a remarkably high development between 1920 and 1935. Citroën, Michelin, and Renault are "captains of industry" whose ingenuity, application, and spirit of initiative cede nothing to their great foreign competitors of the same period. Since 1945 the reparation of our aeronautical industry and the progress of electronics are equally worthy of being cited. French Malthusianism is not flight before effort or a sort of lazy abstention, but rather a kind of sly and fearful prudence.

French Individualism

These reflections lead one to seek in the French "cultural" tradition the causes of certain of the peculiarities or bizarre traits of French society. The word "culture" is often equivocal. It appears too much like a *deus ex machina* to which are transferred the most varied uses. Nevertheless certain ways (usually unconscious) of being, of thinking, and of feeling, transmitted by education (in the large sense), diffused to all the social groups but more easily discernible in the culturally dominant ones, particularly in some collective work or product, help explain why certain institutions, although common to France and to other Western countries, function differently in France, in a manner known only to that country.

France is a democracy, but obviously French democracy is different from the English or the American type. The French family is monogamous, but not like the English or German family. French businessmen are, like their competitors, subject to certain economic laws. The factors of production are combined as efficiently as possible; they are a cost and return an income. But French entrepreneurs do not direct their business as do Germans or Americans; industrial discipline and the authority of the owner do not have the same meaning in France. It is necessary to try to explain these specific differences, but a purely institutional analysis is not very satisfactory here.

Occupational structure in America differs from that in France; does this difference explain the fact that class struggles have not the same character in America as in France? Yes, in part; for the existence of a well-organized working class, relatively well integrated into the larger American society, means that the relations between employers and wage earners are better defined and more regular. But from another point of view, no; for it appears very difficult to deduce without artifice the "radicalism" of the working class or the stubbornness of the employers from the occupational structure alone. Does governmental instability and indecision spring necessarily from "multipartyism"? Not at all. Without doubt the division of a multiparty parliament does not aid the efficiency or the continuity of French governments; but some nations like Belgium and Holland are governed quite efficiently under multiparty regimes. There is then, indeed, a specific difference, properly French, and this difference can be called cultural, for lack of a better word.

Institutions are ways of acting, or thinking, or feeling, socially defined and sanctioned, which give rise to a rather strict system of rights and obligations about which those concerned have decided opinions. My role of father or of son places obligations upon me vis-à-vis my parents or my descendants, but it also bestows upon me a title of respect, of recognition, and of tenderness. These roles are relatively well defined. My father, old, infirm, and without resources, has the right to expect my aid and assistance. It is the law which obligates me; I owe him food and care and observance of the biblical injunction: "honor thy father and mother." I cannot escape this obligation without encountering sanctions. But its limits are also fixed by custom, by law, and even by ethics. If my father should bear himself in an abusive fashion; if, still in good health, he should demand of me, an adult, that I give him part of my income, I would be right to send him packing, and no one could find fault. That which characterizes "culture" in contrast with "institutions" is the fact that the ways of acting, of thinking, or of feeling, called cultural, are largely unconscious or subconscious. While they also constrain rigorously, we are not aware of the processes of constraint. When I excuse myself from thinking of my mother or my sister in terms that my super-ego judges shocking or displaced, I "rationalize" perhaps some feeling learned in my early childhood. But this "rationalization" is based on a series of arguments solidly interlocked; I *ought* not to do, to say, to think this or that. This excuse is presented to me; it is, at least, partially exterior to me. This exteriority of the institution would appear clearer still if, in place of family roles, we take the example of more commonplace roles that are more obviously exterior to the conscience of the subject. A police rule requires me to cross the street at the white lines. If there are no autos in the vicinity and if the policeman is absent, I violate the rule without remorse. The sign of an institutional constraint, exterior to me, is that I am able to decide if and when I can escape from it. To behave badly toward one's father and mother affects the opinion one has of himself, at least when one is a well-bred man. But we regard much of our conduct impersonally, we treat it as a role or as a task; we do not identify ourselves with it; we do not recoil from it.

Let us suppose now that I read in *La Vie Quotidienne des Aztèques*[82] of Jacques Soustelle the description of the bloody sacrifices offered to their gods by the ancient Mexicans. It would be extremely difficult for me not to feel toward this recital at least surprise, probably horror and disgust. Moreover, I would not say to myself in order to justify these feelings: "A Westerner ought to feel indignation toward human sacrifice." I would feel opposed to the practice, and this feeling would not come to me from outside as a rule that would obligate me; it is in me without my knowing it, so substantially that I must make a determined effort to get rid of it, an effort necessary, moreover, if I wish to understand the motivations of the warlike Aztecs. It is this unconscious or semiconscious character of certain ways of perceiving, of feeling, and of conducting ourselves that cultural analysis must take into consideration. People can agree without too much difficulty that two chambers and ministerial responsibility, the rights of succession, or three weeks of paid vacation constitute more or less characteristic practices of our society. But there is no such agreement about what is beautiful or evil or proper; yet it is on the basis of such judgments that we organize our conduct and our total perception of the world.

Thus culture appears as a residue, both unconscious and present in all institutional ensembles. It is, however, difficult to seize upon and isolate the unconscious or semiconscious motivations which give French institutions their tone and their specific color. They are more apparent in certain social groups than in others. Certain themes of French culture are more clearly discernible, more sharply outlined, among the bourgeois than among the workers. All research of this nature begins by determining what social groups are culturally dominant. America, for example, has developed a culture of the middle classes. But in France a group can be culturally dominant in one area and not at all present in another, particularly in the political area, where, in terms of power, it may occupy only a subordinate position. For example, the tradition of the noble life continues without doubt to be very influential in French society even though the nobility as a social group does not amount to much. The ideal of noble life concerns, even for those who remain faithful to it, only a small sector of social relations; one can hold firmly to values like gentility, courtesy, and honor without hiding from the fact that success in the world of business requires other traits. In brief, these cultural themes are very far from being unified even within the society, both by reason of the diversity of the groups which make up this society and the diversity of activities by which this culture is expressed. The task of analyzing French culture is impractical unless these themes are explained in their more stereotyped forms; that is, as they appear in art, in literature, and in history. It is necessary, however, to remember that cultural themes expressed through those media are products of the imagination, symbols to decipher, not facts of univocal meaning. These data need to be both interpreted and explained. It is necessary to ask what they mean and why such meaning has been attributed to such objects or to such personages. For example: Why is Fabrice del Dongo, Stendahl's hero in *La Chartreuse de Parme,* such an appealing character to the French reader? A second difficulty of this method is that authors are extremely partial witnesses even if they speak about things other than their own small social group.

French culture tends to treat social life as a fundamental but very ambiguous value. It appears in what Sainte-Beuve calls *urbanity.* "To possess urbanity is to possess morals . . . morals not in the sense of austerity . . . but in the antique sense. The hard, rustic, savage and fanatic spirit is excluded from urbanity," and Sainte-Beuve prolongs his commentary by remarking that " it is among women . . . especially those who wrote toward the end of the seventeenth century—that one would find most surely some evidences of this decent intimacy, of this fine mockery and of this ease in expressing everything." [83] The taste for urbanity is incarnated in an institution typically French, or rather, Parisian: the salon. Sainte-Beuve says, "The type of social creation which occurred so often in France and which exercised so real an empire did not rise again after the seventeenth century. . . . The little salon of Madame de Sablé, so intimate, so frequented, and which, in the shadow of the cloister, combines without resorting to it too much, something of the advantages of two worlds, does not appear to me to be the kind of salon that we see in our time." [84] The first characteristic of the salon is that it was a meeting ground and a bond. The people that one met there would otherwise have remained strangers. This trait can be observed at Madame de Sablé's where the great world and the Jansenist intellectuals were brought together. This function of liaison was performed in the eighteenth century by Madame du Deffand or Mademoiselle de Lespinasse, who introduced the philosophers and the Encyclopedists into noble society. Proust shows the same type of thing; the salon of Madame Verdurin related the artistic world to that of the bourgeois.

A second trait of the salon is that it is organized around a woman; to the extent that French society is a society of the salon, it is a feminine society. It is through the salon that the influence of women has penetrated French society. The type of conversation which rules in a salon requires some qualities which, without being exclusively feminine, are at least qualities particularly appreciated by women: "the distinction, the intimacy, the natural," to cite Sainte-Beuve again, and especially, "a great facility in the choice of subjects—readiness."[85] It is not necessary to weary with too much inflexibility; not argument, but diversion is wanted. It is here that the mistress of the house plays a decisive role; she orients the conversation, interrupts the gossip and the "gaffeurs." "Madame Geoffrin," Sainte-Beuve tells us, "watches everything; she presides; moreover, she chides, but with a kind of scolding which is hers only. . . . With a word 'Look, this is enough' she stops conversations at the point where they go astray on hazardous subjects or arouse tempers. They fear her and go to make their uproars elsewhere."[86] Proust describes the same situation in caricature in the person of Verdurin and, in a poetic manner, in the traits of Oriane de Guermantes.

A salon, then, is not only a place where one talks; it is also a stage setting where the mistress of the house, a kind of impresario, produces great men to whom she presents her guests, who have the good grace to admire them. "M. de Chateaubriand," writes Sainte-Beuve, "was the soul of the salon of Madame Récamier. . . . He reigned there and when he was present all related themselves to him; but he was not always there, and even then he had there some place, some degree, some part for each." In the same way Madame Verdurin used to value the "newcomers" like Forcheville, or the "old ones" like Cottard when they remained faithful to her. Swann is "my little Charles" to Madame de Guermantes, and this graciousness of the great lady well pays the bourgeois Jew for twenty years of assiduity.

The mistress of a salon not only regulates social relations by imposing the rules of politeness on those who frequent her house and by instructing in urbanity, courtesy, and good talk; she also profoundly socializes love and teaches men to see in the conquest of certain women the symbol *par excellence* of prestige, the most dazzling achievement of success. The most beautiful triumph of Chateaubriand is the love to which Madame Récamier inspires him; to have succeeded in this liaison, both noble and enigmatic, excites curious comment and fills his contemporaries with admiration and envy. The young ambitious men in the nineteenth-century French novels conform to this stereotype that identifies success with success in love.

502

Balzac[87] portrays the first flights of ambition of Lucien de Rubempré; they are discernible as raptures that turn him toward a society woman approaching forty, Madame de Bargeton. Lucien, son of a druggist of the imperial army, is noticed by the society lady whose wit all Angoulême praises. Madame de Bargeton invites the young man to recite some poetry at her home before the circle of her noble friends: "The excessive beauty of Lucien, his voice, all of him seized Madame de Bargeton. The poet was already the poem. The young man, examined with discreet glances, appeared to this woman in harmony with her reputation. She did not violate any of his ideas about the great lady." Balzac shows us Lucien seduced, not by the beauty of the woman, not by her elegance; it is "the conversation of Madame de Bargeton which intoxicates the poet of Houmeau."[88] And a little farther: "Naïs (Madame de B.) was loved as all young men love the first woman who flatters him, for Naïs prophesied a great future, an immense glory for Lucien."

To be loved by a lovable woman, to be recognized by her, even at the price of a painful effort, such is the first ambition of Julien Sorel, a situation that Stendhal describes in chapters eight and nine of *Le Rouge et le Noir*. Julien, by chance, touches the hand of Madame de Rênal, wife of the Mayor of Verrières in whose house he is the tutor. "This hand is withdrawn very quickly; but Julien thought it was his *duty*[89] to arrange it that this hand should not be withdrawn when he touched it. The idea of a duty to be accomplished and of ridicule or, more, of a *sentiment of inferiority*[90] to be encountered if one did not succeed, spoiled all the pleasure in his heart in this situation. The next evening, after dinner, in the garden as the last stroke of ten o'clock was still sounding, he extended his hand and took that of Madame de Rênal who pulled it away immediately. Julien, not too much aware of what he was doing, seized it anew. Although much upset himself, he was struck by the icy coldness of the hand which he took; he squeezed it with convulsive force; she made a last effort to put him off, finally this hand rested in his. His soul was inundated with happiness, not that he loved Madame de Rênal, but his frightful anxiety had ceased."[91]

It is because love is a trial in which the young man is made to be "recognized" by the woman to whom he addresses his homage and in which she is also the witness before which he plays this difficult part—one says in the language of the theater, the gallery, or the public audience—that Julien writes: "Will I also tremble and be unhappy at the first duel which comes to me?" Thus does love appear as an integrally socialized relation where the partners are no more than figures in a spectacle that they play before others. In Proust, for example, the women are at this point so identified by their roles that the only attitude to hold toward them is one of ceremony and, one could even say, of ritual. For the narrator "to love" Madame de Guermantes recurs as a desire to be "received" at her house, to be seen in her company, to accompany her in society; and the highest recompense to which the young man pretends is for her smile to fall on him from the heights of her box at the opera under the interrogative eye of her cousin, the princess.[92]

Can the aesthetic treatment of women by Proust be explained by the homosexuality of the great writer? If his perversion makes of women a taboo in order to justify not touching them, a complementary tendency can be seen among the most "brilliant" of French women who restrain themselves, seeking to be placed apart, holding themselves for something better. In Proust, Madame de Guermantes is chaste as is Madame Verdurin, more or less. This abstention is not exceptional; indeed, it is more the rule, and it finely explains Sainte-Beuve in relation to Madame Récamier: "She has never loved, loved in passion and flame; but this immense need to love which carries in it all her tender soul is changed for her into an infinite need to please or to be loved." Madame du Deffand, who, before succumbing in her old age to a maternal tenderness for Horace Walpole, wrote to her friend, Madame de Choiseul: "You are indeed experienced but you lack one thing that I hope you never will have; it is the loss of feeling with the pain of not being able to get over it."[93]

This extreme socialization of amorous relations that leads the man to provocation and the woman to coquetry has nowhere been better pointed out than by M. Lévi-Strauss: "Women are symbols which one abuses when when one does not give them the use reserved for symbols, that is, of being *communicated.*"[94] There is, perhaps, no better example of this apparent paradox than the French example. That the possession of women is the symbol of our success, that they constitute, to use the vocabulary of M. Lévi-Strauss, gifts which we exchange with other men both to free ourselves from other men and to obligate them to us; that is to say, in both cases to affirm ourselves vis-à-vis others, all this bears a subtle but radical devaluation of the society. To succeed is to be loved; and social success has scarcely any other meaning among our novelists. "I have known how to make this monster of pride love me," says Julien, regarding Mathilde (to whom he is engaged); "her father cannot live without her or she without me." But this attitude never appears so clearly as when success in love is disjointed from success in the social order. Julien goes to prison after he has tried to assassinate Madame de Rênal; everybody is trying to save him from the scaffold. But he wishes to understand nothing, opposing all Mathilde's plans. Mathilde bores him; he is astonished at himself for not feeling any attraction for her. Stendhal tells us: "He rarely thought of Mademoiselle de la Môle." And a little farther on: "Ambition was dead in his heart; another passion was born there of its ashes; he was filled with remorse at having assassinated Madame de Rênal."[95]

Fabrice in his prison behaves as Julien does. Sanséverina tries to get him to escape for fear of General Conti's poisoning his breakfast. But Fabrice, who has for a long time sorrowed at the dryness of the heart and full of happiness at finally being in love, thinks only of Celia and with difficulty of poisoned chocolate. Thus the Stendhalian hero is torn between love and ambition or, rather, he takes one for the other. He believes himself ambitious when he is only a lover, and his conversion takes place when he discovers in the middle of a melodramatic catastrophe that he does not desire intensely that which he burned to achieve, but that which he sought in tension and effort he has under his hand and at the door. It is thus that Julien and Fabrice find happiness in prison.

The work of Marcel Proust could be interpreted from the same perspective. The snobbism of the narrator proceeds from the same source: it is in the affective order that it is affirmed and tends to compensate for the same difficulties. It opens on a "conversion" or on an analogous "revelation." The world is illusory and we ought to attach other selves to other things. But the pessimism of Proust is much more radical. Affections are as illusory as ambition, and will deceive us as much.

Thus is underlined the ambivalence of French culture before society as a value. It manifests an intense taste for urbanity and for what one can call, in a broad sense, the worldly life; it also perceives its insufficiencies and its limits. In one of the most "civilized" epochs of our history, the flowering of the eighteenth century, Meilhan writes: "In France great passions are as rare as great men." It is this same theme that Stendhal develops: the Italians are capable of passion, the French feel only vanities; social qualities, taste, good sense, moderation are depreciated or at least held suspect, not only because they are niggardly and laughable but also because they render us blind to the beautiful. At the side of the man of good company, French culture makes a place for the dreamer to whom it looks for inspiration: Rousseau, "the solitary walker," Chateaubriand, "the voyager in search of himself," illustrate this tradition. Renan, a Breton, combined in an exceptional manner the taste of the Celt for reverie with good sense. In his *Souvenirs d'y Enfance et de Jeunesse* there is a beautiful episode: "My Uncle Pierre." The mother of the author tells him with much tenderness and sympathy of an uncle, something of a black sheep, the memory of whom other families would have preferred to bury. Speaking of his ancestors, Renan writes, "Not one of these brave people sought, as the Normands say, to make money; they always remained poor. . . . They were not of the bourgeois for they were not jealous of the nobles; they were sailors sufficiently well off to be dependent on no one. What shows their nobility is that whenever they wished to do something which resembled trade they were surely taken in." The Uncle Pierre is one of these sailors: "He was one of God's best creatures," says the mother of Renan, "but one could never keep him from traveling." The uncle is a "pure vagabond and this vagabond is an inspired one . . . if you knew what an imagination he had. . . . There were moments when one word of his would make you swoon with laughter."[96]

Our society, so extremely refined over such a long time, has never entirely believed that social values are absolute values. It has never entirely given up being mystified by "the serious mind." This foundation of individualism manifests itself in distrust of conformism, in praise of passion, and in the exaltation of dreams; but never do we find it so explicit as in the various currents of our tradition that can be described as "radical." This French radicalism appears with the greatest clearness in the social criticism of the eighteenth century. "The world," writes Voltaire, "is a chaos of absurdities and horrors."[97] Voltaire is never completely won over to an order which in his eyes incarnates Absolute Reason. His radicalism, however, is not total. It devalues the present, but it prepares for the future: "If reason, sovereign critic, forces us to recognize that there is no sense in the world as it has been up to now, we can experiment at the same time with the pleasure of a clear conscience in having left this chaos behind, of being able to oppose ourselves to all this absurdity, of being free of prejudices."[98]

For the most complete distrust of the world, the most intransigent absolutism, the most decided refusal of all compromise, it is necessary to search in the Jansenist tradition. The antihumanism of Port Royal has been strongly underlined by Sainte-Beuve. M. Lucien Goldman,[99] in his recent and remarkable works, has called attention to the "tragic" character of Jansenist thought, the most perfect expression of which he finds in the *Pensées* of Pascal and the theater of Racine. M. Goldman reviews the elements of all tragic situations: "An essentially insoluble conflict, resulting in a collision between a world which knows only the relative . . . and a universe dominated by the law of all or nothing." The everyday world is devalued at one blow and forever because it has "been touched by the glance of God. Is the man on whom the glance of God has fallen still able to live?"[100]

The devaluation of the world, perhaps even more radical among French Jansenists than among the Calvinists studied by Max Weber,[101] concerns not only that which is inessential in the world, but man who, his nothingness revealed, discovers his real grandeur in this revelation. "Man," writes Saint-Cyran, "as small as he is, is so large that he cannot, without doing wrong to his greatness, be a servant to any but God alone." The servitude can be accomplished only by suppression and curtailment; "from the separation from and the absence of the world," writes the same Saint-Cyran, "is born the presence and feeling of God."[102] M. Goldman asks, What does "refusal of the world" mean? "To oppose a world made up of fragmentary elements that exclude any strain toward totality, which necessarily becomes a strain toward unifying opposites."[103] A text of Pascal on the "conversion of the sinner" describes with an admirable precision the movements of a soul which, cutting itself off from the world, is seized at the end by a "well-being which cannot be ravished from it as much as it would so desire." He adds, "The first thing that God inspires in the soul that he deigns truly to touch is a knowledge by which the soul considers things and itself in an entirely new fashion." From this feeling of estrangement follow indecision and sickness. "One still finds more bitterness in the exercises of piety than in the vanities of the world. In one way the presence of visible objects touches one more than the hope of the invisible, and in another the solidity of the invisible touches one more than the vanity of the visible. And also the presence of one and the solidity of the others disputes one's affection. The sinner begins to consider as nothing all that which ought to return into the nothing, the sky, the land, his spirit, his body, his parents, his friends, his enemies, his goods, his poverty, disgrace, prosperity, honor, ignominy, esteem, distrust, authority, indigence, health, sickness and even life." But once he has found his creator, "the soul is annihilated in consequence and cannot form an idea of itself sufficiently base . . . it makes new efforts to reduce itself to the last abysses of nothingness."[104] It is indeed the theme of nothingness which prevails in this text. And it is this same devaluation of man in his highest aptitudes that we find in the famous letter of Pascal to Fermat of August 10, 1661: "To speak to you frankly of geometry, I find it the highest exercise of the mind; but at the same time I know it to be so useless that I make little difference between a man who is a geometrist and a skilled artisan."[105]

The pressure of absolute totality then, perceived in complete rigidity, suffices to depreciate radically partial successes and fragmentary knowledge. Outside of God, all is nothing. It is necessary to cite these texts to dissuade the foreign reader from a very common illusion: French culture does not exclusively emphasize moderation, decency, and being well spoken. M. Goldman is right to emphasize the importance of the tragic current in our cultural tradition. The devaluation of the world is one of the most constant tendencies in our moral reflections. It is not necessary to believe that it is observed only among mystics like Pascal. The *Misanthrope* himself is through with everything—except his passion for Célimène, of course. But it is in Voltaire that one finds the most startling expression of French pessimism. It is a "chaos of horrors and absurdities" that Voltaire paints for us in *Candide*. What to do? There is no point in losing time as the simpleton Pangloss does, disputing cause and effect; but let us cultivate our garden. Distrust of the world, one would be tempted to say "the fear before the world," is as much alive in Voltaire as among the "tragic thinkers" of the seventeenth century.

But this revelation that the world is a cipher does not mean for Voltaire that man ought to detach himself from everything. What would remain to him at the end of this extreme detachment? Nothing; less than nothing. What Voltaire objects to in Pascal in his long polemic against the author of the *Pensées*—one of the most instructive polemics on some essential aspects of French culture—is not the dark picture he has painted of man's condition, but in the "crazy" therapy he proposes; that is, to make man more stupid, or to aggravate the evils that he pretends to cure. "I say that this man (according to Pascal, 'so miserable that nothing can console him' of an unhappiness natural to his feeble and mortal condition) would be not only an imbecile useless to society; but I say that this man cannot exist. It is impossible for human nature to remain in this imaginary torpor. It is absurd to think of it; it is mad to pretend it; Man is born for action.

Not to be occupied and not to exist is the same thing for man." In Pascal the depreciation of the world returns man to God. Voltaire tries to make man less foolish so that he will not be content with conditions which he alone can make a little more tolerable. "In seeing the blindness and the misery of man . . . I enter into fright as a man would enter a deserted and frightful island and who awakens without knowing where he is and without having any means of leaving." "For me," responds Voltaire, "when I look at Paris or London I do not see any reason for entering into the despair of which M. Pascal speaks. . . . Why make a horror of our existence? Our existence is not as unhappy as one wishes to make us believe. To regard the universe as a dungeon and all men as criminals about to be executed is a fanatical idea; to believe that the world is a place of delight where one ought to have nothing but pleasure is the dream of a sybarite. To think that the land, the men and the animals are what they ought to be in the order of Providence is, I believe, the thought of a wise man."[106]

If I have spent a great deal of time on this ideological analysis, it is because French individualism can be understood only in this framework. I have already noted the ambivalent attitude of our culture to social values. In part the world exercises on our young people the liveliest seduction; it invites them to sparkle; it makes success desirable; it induces them to confound love and self-love. But this world is also perceived as illusory, an obstacle to the affirmation of Self. This devaluation of the world is allied to Pascal and the Jansenists, to faith in the supernatural. For Voltaire it leads to wise despair. In both cases it constitutes an attitude of recoil, of detachment, and of judgment on the world; it is in this attitude that the roots of French individualism lie. In our tradition society is never adequate to the culture. The French cultural ideal is never incarnated in a given state of our society, still less in a particular group of this society at a given moment of its history. One often says that American culture is a culture of the urban middle classes. At least this is what one reads in the majority of contemporary American sociologists. It is easy to show the profoundly antibourgeois character of French culture. The demonstration can be made without difficulty by examples from our literature.

The traits by which Flaubert designates M. Homais indicate well enough why the "bourgeois" constitute a type antipathetic to our cultural tradition. That which renders M. Homais ridiculous and odious is his invincible seriousness, "a man in green leather slippers, somewhat marked by smallpox, wearing a velvet hat with gold tassels, warmed himself against the chimney. His figure expressed nothing but satisfaction with himself and he had as calm an air in life as the goldfinch suspended over his head in a wicker cage; it was the druggist." [107] "Satisfaction with himself," "calmness in life"—these two traits of the bourgeois in Flaubert are not very distant from those that Sartre attributes in *La Nausée* to the *salauds*. The bourgeois virtues of thrift, of perseverance, of prudence, do not have a good reputation in our literature. They are most often described as niggardly, as derisory, and even as perverse. For M. François Mauriac, attachment to money is the sign of a profound wound of the soul which has denied itself to its God. These virtues are presented favorably only when they are detached from the ends which the bourgeois follow, or where transfigured by a note of asceticism and renunciation: "the humble life of boring and easy work," to quote Voltaire.

It is no more difficult to show that French culture is not identified with any particular group. It is no more "worker" than it is "bourgeois," no more "peasant" than it is "noble." No group has succeeded in incarnating the values that our culture recognizes and consecrates. One could sustain the idea that among all groups it is the virtues and the vices of the bourgeoisie which are most alienated from the ways of acting, of thinking, and of feeling that are sanctioned as ideal by our culture. It is in this sense that our civilization is fundamentally individualist. To say that the French are individualists is not to say that they are asocial. Urbanity is important in our culture; so is family life, where domestic relations are treated with delicacy. The sociability of the Frenchman is manifested by his very lively taste for intimacy. "At home" is not only a zone where strangers have no access. It is a closed world where one can commune with one's self.

To many visitors, the French appear distrustful, very little disposed to receive newcomers into their homes. A long probationary period is required, especially in the provinces, before a new "acquaintance" invites one to dinner or accepts an invitation. The refusal to ally oneself too quickly, no matter with whom, is illustrated by the practice of using the formal "monsieur" or "vous" between people who have known each other for a long time. To call someone by his first name almost constitutes a familiarity. This mistrust or, at least, this reserve, arises not only out of negative attitudes. It envelops a very intense feeling that for each person relations with others constitute a capital without price, and that these relations are moreover valuable only if they are reserved for a small number. A formula of Auguste Comte will enlighten the reader: "No intimacy can be profound without concentration and without perpetuity."[108] What Comte calls the "concentration" of intimacy is another manner of underlining the "small number of elect." To speak of "perpetuity" is to mark well the obligation of fidelity. To these two precepts are reduced the essentials of the obligation of friendship. (The current language makes a distinction between "friends" and "acquaintances." And the formula *cher ami,* exhausted by its indiscreet use in correspondence, appears ridiculous.) The "intimates," that is, the *true* friends, are the small nucleus of persons in the company and under the regard of whom we pass our life. These intimates do not include relations, not even cousins; this can be explained without difficulty, for to his intimates one confides certain things that one is hindered by embarrassment, perhaps even by shame, from confiding to one's wife or one's relatives. By and large our friends are those who have the opportunity of knowing us best, over a long period of time. We are very near to our father and mother for twenty years more or less, after which we detach ourselves. Our wife has not known us as a child or even as an adolescent. Our friends we have known since the time that we were students at the same college. What do we owe to them? What do they owe to us? These reciprocal obligations are not clearly defined. They are not, however, situated either exclusively or principally on an instrumental plane. A friend is not a comrade. He does not expect rights or service from us. It is rather our support, our comprehension, that he wants. Better than our wife, our parents, or our children, he knows how to support us, to take us as we are. To a great extent it is a free relationship that is not sanctioned by any obligation of kinship; friendship allows us to take off the masque, to abandon ourselves without thought of consequences to the deliciousness of being what we are, or rather of being the adolescent we like to be.

French sociability appears to us extremely rich and fine. Few societies attach to social values more of a price than does ours. But few manifest more distrust of the regard of *the society* or even of the regard of the particular groups the ensemble of which constitutes *the society*. It is in this sense that French individuals remain extremely original. To the stereotype that represents the Frenchman as an individualist, one could oppose without difficulty a Frenchman no less conventional but enmeshed in community life. Marc Bloch has discovered in the history of our countryside a very complex past where collective rules held a decisive place. The obligation made to the owner not to enclose his field, to submit to a type and a rhythm of crop rotation, to abandon the "worthless" pasture to the common herd after the fields were reaped, imposes strong fetters on the individualism of our peasants. The Frenchman, then, is not impatient of all collective constraints. In the end to what does his individualism refer? First, a taste for personalized social relations: "Because it was he, because I was I," said Montaigne speaking of his friend, La Boëtie. The same attitude appears in the aversion our culture manifests to anonymity. The reproach of treating men like automatons, of not distinguishing individuals except by numbers, is addressed to "machine civilization" a hundred times by our writers. The reproach is, perhaps, frivolous; it is certainly a banal attack; but even its banality advises us that the fear of depersonalization defines one of the critical zones of French sensibility. M. Smith seeks by all means to convince himself that there is no more honorable, no more pleasant a destiny than that of M. Smith. M. Durand does not accept being other than M. Durand. He holds to his individuality, which his Christian name signifies, to his titles and his states of service, to "his personal situation."

This personalization of social relations explains the persistence among the French of rural and artisan values, and French reserve before "mass production" and the "ready to wear." This distrust ends at the point where the universalism of economic criteria clearly predominates. The taste of the French for particularism should not, however, be exaggerated. The "family character" of French industrial enterprises has often been pointed out. Some journalists have denounced the "bourgeois dynasties," and no doubt the French sense of continuity incarnated in a family resembles a feudal lineage more than the nuclear American family. It appears more clearly among the nobles but is present also among the great bourgeoisie and is well understood among the peasants, for whom the permanence of the family and the name is confounded with the constancy of the patrimony. But even in this case does the family constitute an absolute for its members? This is an embarrassing question on which there is but little information. The family does not appear in our literature as a rigorously closed unity to the maintenance of which its members devote themselves. It appears more as a group from which (and by the aid of which) the individuals of the elite leave. It is David Séchard sacrificing himself for his brother-in-law, Lucien de Rubempré. Balzac tells how the parents and the sisters of Rastignac had for many years endured a thousand privations to take care of him in Paris. Inversely if the father of Julien Sorel is odious, it is because he does not recognize the merit of his son. The criticism of the family, so current in the nineteenth and twentieth centuries, is fed by these two principal themes. M. François Mauriac, in *Genitrix,* describes the more or less subtle tyranny that blind parents exercise over their progeniture, the servitude to which demanding mothers reduce their sons so that love has, so to speak, castrated them. This situation is not at all exceptional, having been the lot of Gide, among others, and probably also of Proust, even though the two mothers were profoundly different. Or again one paints the mediocrity of family life that suffocates young talent under the weight of pitiless obligations. In both cases it is in relation to the individual that the family institution is condemned—or exalted—as in Victor Hugo. It is almost never set up as an end in itself, and we would willingly make the hypothesis that those who have a tendency to treat it as an absolute are "rationalizing" some very personal blocks.

French particularism does not mean at all that there is a tendency to take the small closed unit (domestic or residential) as the reference or the norm for individual behavior. Do the obligations of the family constitute for the majority of the French "the end-all of obligations"? No. Nor are the hypotheses sound that explain the conservatism of our industrialists by the predominance among them of purely dynastic cares. To many American observers French society appears as a juxtaposition of isolated milieus, each in a relationship to the others where the criteria of origin and birth are decisive. Generally, this observation is correct. But it is necessary to make some reservations. First, this fact ought to be related to the relative demographic and economic stagnation of our country. Moreover, the American observer comes from a society where individuals receive their status according to what they *make* rather than what they *are,* and the criterion of personal accomplishment weighs more heavily in their own society than in any other; the French speak, as much as do these Americans, of merit, and equality means for them, at least in one of its facets, that each should be treated according to his aptitudes and not according to his birth. In theory the French are universalists; the law is the same for all; "there are not two weights and two measures." But one perceives very quickly what a troubled seduction privilege exercises on them. "Sure, everybody is equal." However, each person finds himself in "a particular situation," each is "an interesting case" to himself alone, of course. Furthermore, should we pass our time in denouncing the privileges that others abuse while claiming the same for ourselves in guarding our particular interests?

The particularism of the French is striking if one understands by it their impatience before universal law. But this particularism is very far from being a pure individualism. Much more than a rebellion against no matter what universal law, it signifies the distrust of an abstract law; and in this distrust lie many of the roots of French individualism. It is not a question of anarchistic rebellion nor of a fundamental unsociability. Moreover, it is not a question of an exclusive preference for the closed and intimate group (of the family community type), but of a suspicious reserve before attempts to objectify, that is to say, to depersonalize social relations. The Frenchman repudiates economic quantification as much as hierarchical determination of status. He does not take to the idea, either, that a man *is* his bank account or that he should be confounded with his rank in an administrative system. It is in this sense that the French remain invincibly individualistic. That the individual constitutes the absolute value is not so certain; moreover, the question doesn't make much sense. But that which he knows well is that he risks deceiving himself badly and deceiving others if he believes that a concrete society or a particular group in a society should ever be able to incarnate his ideas. It is this constant turn of mind through history that we call French individualism.

French Turbulence and Feelings of Inferiority

Culture analysis explains, at least partially, some traits of French society. It even illuminates some characteristics of our political society. Among the French the strictly social values have assumed such importance that the procedures by which prestige and authority are distributed concentrate and excite the interest and the curiosity of all. One could show, probably without too much difficulty, that ambition among well-endowed French youth aims only incidentally at monetary return. "To make money" is certainly a great preoccupation, but it is also important to be able to spend enough "to keep up one's position." However, a rank of great prestige can be held with relatively little money. An example, relevant here, is furnished by the young people who start out in the top administration: the *Conseil d'État*, or the *Inspection des Finances*. The starting salaries are remarkably low, and the chance of future remuneration modest enough. Nonetheless these posts remain very much in demand, and those who occupy them are clothed in an eminent dignity. The comparison between their salaries and those of their comrades of the same age, less endowed or less ambitious (in the French sense), indicates that some economic sacrifices are made for a brilliant career. A certain affectation of austerity is, indeed, often visible here. Even if the young "inspector" has a private income, a sober manner of life is considered suitable. Luxury would pass for frivolity. The career is of more importance than the possession of wealth or fortune.

Although service to the state has long exercised a fascination on young men of ambition, it does not follow that any employment appears desirable. A post has much more prestige if it places its occupant in close contact with those who make "great decisions" and who "deal with great interests." The court under the old regime, the capital of our days, hold a place in the political order analogous to the salon in the social sphere. One's wits are sharpened there as one's taste is formed by contact with "the great minds." On this spectacle, which is dressed up with anticipations of power, are directed all the cameras. The stage setting was very perceptible at the court of Versailles. In our day it is more confused but also more exacting; our ministers occupy the palaces of our kings. The life of the salon was expressed in an original style that Sainte-Beuve called "urbanity." The court and the ministerial antechamber have also their code that makes an art of intrigue. In both cases the same sociability is found at work, the same French taste for social relations, treated not only in their instrumental meaning but appreciated and savored for themselves as a play both complicated and cautious, the spectacle of which is offered to public attention.

Earlier analysis of the political regime has pointed out the radicalism of the French and the attraction that extreme solutions exercise on them. In this sense, French "reactionaries" are as radical as French "revolutionaries"; the same impatience of compromise among the one as among the other, the same devaluation of present-day society—in one case to the profit of an ideal and future order where man will finally be reconciled with himself, with nature, and with other men; in the second case to a past order where everybody will "know his place" and where all will cooperate in common work. The radical attitude common to the two "extremes" is distrust of all social organization which by its nature falls short of what it should be. Thus can political analysis be illuminated and reinforced by cultural analysis. The taste for intrigue juxtaposed to the distaste for moderate solutions repeats on the political plane the theme of immobilism in convulsion.

Does this cultural analysis suffice to explain the character of French society? This analysis can be reinforced without difficulty by the demographic facts. The insufficient numbers of the active population in the total population constitute for French society a source of tension and discontent. The French birth rate declined toward the middle of the nineteenth century because our society failed to "produce," owing to a natural and permanent dissatisfaction. It is rare when the French are content with their own society. They have a tendency to debase themselves vis-à-vis foreigners. The defeat of 1870 gave Ernest Renan an opportunity to make a rigorous examination of conscience, pitilessly underlining French defects so that German qualities were exalted without reserve. The masochistic explosion that followed the "strange defeat" of 1940 and, again, "the false victory of 1945," is not without precedent. It should be considered in relation to the excessive chauvinism to which the French sometimes abandon themselves. Depreciation of their own most obvious merits, exactly like their transcendent distrust of foreigners, expresses an inability to judge themselves and to pass judgment on their own values. It leads them to form attitudes of suspicion, growing out of profound and intense feelings of inferiority.

This last hypothesis has been advanced with much caution; but have the psychologists and sociologists, who have been so much interested these last years in the "cultural determination of personality," insisted as much as they should on the origin and the results of these feelings of inferiority that press so heavily on the formation of French attitudes toward other people? The thesis of Adler is perhaps relevant in this connection, taken first in a large sense and again in a narrow sense. In the first sense, the original frustration is laid to a peculiarity or to an organic malformation. In the second sense, it is interpreted as the reaction of the subject to a situation of dependence, symbolized by people and/or by norms, i.e., the tasks that adults impose. One would not have too much difficulty in showing how the French system of education ceaselessly creates and renews a situation of inferiority for French children. The children pass their time in classes separated according to how well they do. In the bourgeois families where the career of the son preoccupies the parents very early, marks and grades in composition subject the student to a continual test. It is probable that the French expect a great deal from their children, that they en-

516

tertain hopes for them that often lack both modesty and realism. The children are downgraded by making whatever good opinion they have of themselves depend upon a number of difficult and painful accomplishments. The result is that French children are forced into situations of competition and rivalry too early. But these situations are immediately perceptible as social; that is to say, as institutionally defined. It is not a question of a struggle decided by force or luck. It is not even a question of intrigue or skill, which would permit the more skilled to win easily. It is not a question of play without consequences. No one can remove the rules; neither the students, nor the teacher. And does it not seem in the majority of cases that the comparison between individual accomplishments and the norms set up to classify students are perceived as objective? The French school soon places the child in situations where impersonal norms and the criteria of universal classes predominate. The rigor of this procedure can be tempered only slightly by the tact of the teacher, whose interventions are sometimes readily interpreted as abusive and unjust.

The French school demands much from the child. But it does not seem certain that the status of the child in his family depends narrowly on "his grades at school." The French have a tendency to distinguish—sometimes in too strict a manner—between instruction and education. At the school, impersonal rules reign. At home and during vacation, the child is able to escape their tyranny. Not every "good student" is necessarily the preferred, the darling, of his parents, even when these parents are extremely demanding of scholastic success. A good mark is worth a little more pocket money to a small boy; in brief, it is a precise and measured evidence of satisfaction, but it rarely wins demonstrations of tenderness. To follow M. Parsons, the good student receives some marks (specific) of approbation and some esteem (diffuse); that is, he excites in his parents "affectively neutral" reactions. This is far from what Margaret Mead calls conditional love. Affection and tenderness remain largely independent of scholastic success. The parents are thus led to specialize their roles. The father becomes the model, the incarnation of the universal and objective values that dominate the school. The mother is treated as a symbol of the expressive and particularistic values that dominate at home. This duality seems to characterize the French family. The division between the holders of authority is immediately visible there. The constraint that the father exercises is tempered by the maternal presence.

This tension sometimes results in radically devaluing the outside world;

but, owing to the functional complicity between the father and the mother, it more often produces a characteristic ambivalence toward a society that separates the child from the people he loves but where, if the child founders, he risks the loss of their love. Does French "compensation" thus generally have a diffuse character? And whenever the preponderance of the mother gives an exclusively feminine turn to education, the presence — even mute, indifferent, and effaced — of a father who works outside suffices to recall that there is something beyond domestic intimacy. Even in situations where the father shows himself the most intractable, tears, silence, or reserve on the part of the mother suffice to let it be understood by the guilty one that after all his fault is not without excuse, and it offers considerable tactical possibilities to the rebellious child. The compensating investment is made less on a determinate good than on a certain image of one's self that one expects to hold. It is made less in terms of power and more in terms of honor. It is less a question of having accumulated something than of being and excelling. It is especially a question of retaining an honorable image of one's self. A text of Chateaubriand illuminates this trait. One time when he was a pupil at the college of Dol, Chateaubriand was judged guilty of some peccadillo. " 'Now then,' the prefect said, 'Monsieur, you are going to be whipped!' The idea of being shamed," adds the writer, "had never arisen before in my education. At every age of my life there has never been a punishment that I would not have preferred to the horror of being shamed before a living creature . . . the master made me enter his house and ordered me to submit myself. . . . I represented to him that I was his pupil, his disciple, his child, that he would not wish to dishonor his pupil and shame me before my companions. We concluded a treaty. I agreed to submit to the arbitration of the principal; without giving me the reason, the principal indeed wished to remove from me the punishment that I had protested. When the excellent priest pronounced my acquittal I kissed the sleeve of his robe with such effusion of heart and of recognition that he was hindered from giving me his benediction." [109]

The "fiction" or the "ideal" by which we compensate for our inferiority is most often a certain image of ourselves that we wish to present to others. This image, in order to be favorable, supposes that we attain certain ends. But these ends are generally perceived as relative, that is, as temporary and inadequate. Also, boredom holds in French romanticism the place that irony holds in German romanticism. All appears as vain except a certain persistent will to realize one's self, to affirm one's self — an attitude expressed by two kinds of conduct. For indeed, this seeking engenders the turbulence and the inconstancy, so striking among men of letters whenever they occupy themselves with politics. Chateaubriand is an example of it; a monarchist who helped to overturn the restored monarchy. The political career of M. François Mauriac seems to display similar inconsistencies. Here is a man who exalted the Christian Democrats up to the day when he launched against them the most pitiless prosecution.

The complaisant indulgence with which the French treat those they call the *enfants terribles* should also be pointed out. Elsewhere than among the French one's reputation would be lost for fewer tricks and changes than are granted some of their celebrated men. But this "irresponsibility" is not the only response before the world where all is only vanity. French compensation is not so rigid and compulsive as the Adlerian scheme suggests. There is an extreme suppleness in some of the French responses to difficult situations that awaken feelings of inferiority. It is probable that the threshold of tolerance to chaos, to conflicts, to frustrations of all sorts, is remarkably elevated among the French. Family difficulties that end in divorce among Americans are settled by durable compromises among French people. Many peasant proprietors have recourse to a practice which at first view appears intolerable. The father of the family reserves to himself until the end the disposition of funds (one says "to die the owner"); but he installs in his home his son and sometimes even his son-in-law. Two generations often live on the same income and under the same roof. The most perverse experimenter would not be able to imagine conditions more favorable to the development of conflicts among the generations. As a matter of fact, old and young squabble; mother-in-law and daughter-in-law, son-in-law, brothers-in-law, and sisters-in-law are caught up in a network of recriminations, quarrels, and reconciliations. Each member of the household has some chance, even though for a somewhat short period, to enter into all the possible relations of sympathy and hate. However, this situation is sometimes prolonged for many years, and those concerned end by adjusting to each other in the conviction that they are condemned to live together. If they resign themselves, it is in part because they are unable to do otherwise and also because, in the final analysis, cohabitation suits them well enough. Provisionary situations, but indefinitely provisionary, stamp all arrangements with precariousness; but this day-to-day life has the advantage of reserving the future and, at the same time, giving to the present a sufficiently simple and well-defined image. It is in this sense that the "compromise" in French tradition remains different from the English "compromise." The French are very maladroit at accomplishing efficient compromise; but they content themselves willingly with "a badly tailored situation." The English compromise is a voluntary operation, maturely deliberated. Each participant delimits the margin of concessions that he is willing to accord and the size of the advantages that he hopes to obtain from these concessions. The French repudiate this method. They see in it only weakness. To discuss, for them, is to show that one is right, to impose one's point of view. However, as the compromise constitutes an indispensable procedure in all social life, the French have recourse to it as do others, but without saying so. It is not a question of reflective discussion between two individuals trying to understand each other. It is a question of a tacit accord, one might say shamefaced, that things rest in a state that one will not speak of. Let sleeping dogs lie.

What this analysis shows is the characteristic agility of the French in not letting themselves be "alienated" and in not letting their projects or their products trap or mystify them. Turbulence on the one side, and a nearly unbelievable tolerance of the provisionary and the confused on the other, are evidence that the French do not take social situations seriously. This detachment, this fear of being mystified by the serious, demonstrate the French characteristic of attempting thereby to "compensate" for an inadequacy in meeting critical situations. The tendency toward extremism and the taste for cunning, the fascination with social life and the distrust for its vanities, are explainable perhaps as expressions of a similar attitude regarding the norms to which one feels pledged but which one has not renounced judging.

The insufficiencies of this interpretation are clear. To verify these hypotheses it would be necessary to limit them to one sector and to a very narrow epoch rather than to voyage over several centuries and make arbitrary appeal to such or such text that appears suggestive or important. This method is scarcely rigorous. These hypotheses also concern only social and cultural elites, so that they remain limited in value. The political scene has received most attention. As a result, it has been necessary to forgo many reflections at least as interesting as those presented. Finally, this analysis has probably not accorded to history as much of a place as it deserves. Can many of the peculiarities of French society be explained by our great revolutionary crisis of the eighteenth century? But it is scarcely possible in these few pages to do more than briefly sketch an interpretation of certain hypotheses. If the reader is now convinced of the singularity of French society, if he is now aware that this singularity is explicable if one takes into account certain attitudes and values largely unconscious but constantly observable in the cultural tradition of France, then this effort has accomplished its purpose.

Notes

[1] Paris: Charlot.

[2] English writers, or perhaps French writers struck by the English model, like to insist that there has never been a parliamentary regime without the regular alternation of two large parties succeeding to power. This view is evidently a little too simple. In the nineteenth century, England also knew tripartism whenever the Irish minority sold its support, turn by turn, to the two large traditional parties. Between the two world wars Labour governed only as the head of the Liberal-Labour coalition; finally one can note that the English parties of the nineteenth century were well below the degree of rigid organization that our ignorance or our imagination accords them so lightly. Peel, head of the Tories, obtained the abrogation of the Corn Laws with the help of the Liberals.

[3] Gustave Flaubert, *Oeuvres,* Vol. 1 (Paris: Pléiade, 1936), pp. 368–369.

[4] Described in a text of the philosopher Merleau Ponty on the "moment parfait," *Les Aventures de la Dialectique* (Paris: Gallimard, 1955), pp. 122–123.

[5] Auguste Soulier, *L'Instabilité Ministérielle sous la III° République* (Paris: Recueil Sirey, 1939).

[6] This expression was already in the vocabulary of Guizot.

[7] The word "national" has a very interesting meaning in our political vocabulary. It designates that which is "French" in opposition to that which is "foreign"; that which is authentic in opposition to that which is spurious. The parties of the right like to think of themselves as "national" because they attribute to themselves the exclusive care of French interests (in opposition to the parties of the left, whom they accuse of cosmopolitanism); they affirm that they incarnate the tradition of the "land and the dead," whereas their adversaries are only the "uprooted," the unpatriotic, or foreigners.

[8] Speech of Marshall Pétain, October 30, 1940.

[9] *Sondages, Revue Française de l'Opinion Publique* (Paris, 1952), No. 3, p. 85.

[10] *Ibid.,* p. 15.

[11] "The Communist voters judge that the most important thing in their party is the doctrine (44%), then the program. . . . On the other hand only 10% of the Communists said that the most important thing is the head of the party, although 35% of the RPF voters made this response." (*Ibid.,* p. 53.)

[12] *République des Ducs* (Paris: Grasset, 1932), pp. 179–181.

[13] The law of April 13, 1900, reserved to *auditeurs de 1° classe* (young men who enter the "corps") two thirds of the vacant places for *maîtres des requêtes* (next highest civil service grade). The law of April 10, 1910, raised this proportion to three fourths.

[14] In Max Weber's meaning.

[15] No doubt French diplomacy between 1890 and 1914 can be censured in many respects. It let escape some occasions for an understanding with Germany and often, perhaps, put into effect some large political plans inherited from the monarchy even though the military means at its disposal remained quite inferior to its ambitions. This tragic unadaptability strikes one clearly regarding the year 1906, when, before

the Moroccan adventures of William II, the government of the Republic was obliged to sacrifice Delcassé ("a humiliation without precedent," writes André Tardieu in the *Bulletin de l'Étranger du Temps*). But if French diplomacy of this era is questionable, is it more so than that of England, of Russia, of Austria—or of Germany?

[16] It does not seem to be seriously menaced from within. But a serious political crisis, a "convulsion," can not be excluded as the result of an African failure becoming more probable every day. It is to be expected that the regime will not return to a practice tried by the Third Republic—to appeal to a "great statesman" to whom, for some time, "full powers" are given. Clemenceau in 1917, Poincaré in 1926, both filled this role. But this solution would excite, up to the last minute, an understandable distrust and resistance.

[17] Certain constitutional reforms seem to be unquestionably necessary. The *least* that one should demand, which is probably the *most* that one could obtain from the deputies, is the free and loyal granting of the right of dissolution to the president of the Council. But the efficacy of this measure is certainly small, and it carries some risks.

[18] Let us even add the political elites.

[19] *Revue Socialiste* (June 1946).

[20] *Revue Française de Science Politique III*, Vol. VI, No. 1, pp. 70–95.

[21] See André Siegfried, *Tableau Politique de la France de l'Ouest, sous la III° République* (Paris: A. Colin, 1913).

[22] *Ibid.*

[23] "The Social Democrats in the Elections of 1849," *Revue Française de Science Politique III*, Vol. VI, No. 1, p. 95.

[24] *Institut Français de l'Opinion Publique* (I.F.O.P.), p. 49.

[25] Statistics from the Ministry of the Interior and the I.F.O.P. for the legislative elections of June 1951, cited by J. D. Reynaud and Alain Touraine, "La Representation Politique du Monde Ouvrier," *Cahiers de la Fondation des Sciences Politiques*, No. 74 (Paris: Armand Colin, 1955), p. 33.

[26] *Ibid.*, p. 35.

[27] Maurice Duverger, in preface to *Cahiers de la Fondation des Sciences Politiques*, No. 74 (Paris: Armand Colin, 1955), p. 20.

[28] *Sondages, I.F.O.P.*, in *Réalités* (May 1952), p. 11. If one compares the proportion of Socialist voters in each social category with the percentage of this category in the total population, one observes that this proportion is greater in regard to civil servants (13 to 5 per cent); greater among those who live on interest and among the retired (10 to 6 per cent); and greater among agricultural workers (6 to 3 per cent). The proportion is about equal in regard to workers (21 to 19 per cent) and almost equal among the salaried, those in commerce, those who make up the staffs of industries, and among those in the liberal professions.

[29] *Débats de l'Assemblée Nationale*, cited by G. E. Lavau, "Les Classes Moyennes et la Politique," *Cahiers de la Fondation des Sciences Politiques*, No. 74 (Paris: Armand Colin, 1955), p. 73.

[30] *Ibid.*, p. 63.

[31] Duverger, *op. cit.*, p. 21.

[32] I have been able to observe it myself in a wine-producing region.

[33] There are some communities in the Gironde where large families are observed only among the manual workers or sharecroppers but almost never among the farmowners, especially the very small ones.

[34] P. Gemähling, in Georges Friedman, ed., *Villes et Campagnes* (Paris: Armand Colin, 1952).

[35] Jacques Fauvet, *Cahiers de la Fondation des Sciences Politiques*, No. 74 (Paris: Armand Colin, 1955), p. 156.

[36] *Ibid.*, p. 157.

[37] François Goguel, cited by Fauvet, *op. cit.*, p. 157. The italics are mine.

[38] Fauvet, *op. cit.,* p. 155.

[39] Cf. André Siegfried, *op. cit., passim.*

[40] Name, or mask, which the agricultural pressure groups assume to give themselves a respectable front.

[41] *Sondages, I.F.O.P.,* in *Réalités* (May 1952), p. 39.

[42] Let us remember that this poll was taken in the spring of 1952.

[43] *Réalités* (May 1952), p. 39.

[44] *Ibid.*

[45] The italics are mine.

[46] *Réalités* (May 1952), p. 39.

[47] At the least, 65 per cent among them; *ibid.*

[48] *Ibid.,* p. 407.

[49] Jean de la Bruyère, *Les Caractères* (Paris: Librairie des Bibliophiles, 1872–73), Ch. 5, par. 50

[50] Thus on his visit to the Bishop of Noyon, who was a Clermont-Tonnerre: "All his house was filled with his coat of arms, even on the ceilings and the floors; his insignia of count and peer in all the wainscoting; two large genealogical charts with the title 'Descent of the Very August House of Clermont-Tonnerre from the Emperors of the East and, on the other side, from the Emperors of the West.' "

[51] Jules Vallés, *Jacques Vingtras, l'Enfant* (Paris: Fasquelle, 1944), p. 95.

[52] Nearly 40 per cent of the French population still lives in communities of less than 2,000 inhabitants.

[53] An inquiry of the I.F.O.P. that appeared in *Réalités* (February 1956), pp. 39–49.

[54] See the reports of the *Conseil National du Credit* since 1953.

[55] The fiscal system is also responsible for this.

[56] *Réalités* (February 1956).

[57] *Cahiers de la Fondation Nationale des Sciences Politiques,* No. 71.

[58] *Ibid.,* p. 97.

[59] This restriction has probably had the effect of reducing the percentage of the raise held desirable by the respondents. An increase on the order of 40 per cent would be necessary, the I.F.O.P. says, but what the workers judge possible (without raising prices) is, on the average, about 12 per cent above actual wages. *Réalités* (February 1956), p. 54.

[60] See Edouard Dolléans, *Histoire du Mouvement Ouvrier,* Vol. II, 5th ed. (Paris: Armand Colin, 1953).

[61] Michel Collinet, *Essai sur la Condition Ouvrière, 1900–1950* (Paris: Les Editions Ouvriers, 1951), p. 67

[62] *Ibid.,* p. 65.

[63] *Ibid.,* p. 68.

[64] Both are very much desired and appreciated, and considered as a privilege of the rich and the bosses.

[65] Figures cited by Collinet, *op. cit.,* p. 151.

[66] Marc Brésard, in *Population* (March 1950).

[67] Of which one part is furnished by the Algerians (Kabyles) or by foreigners (Italians in construction; Poles or sons of Poles in the coal and iron mines of the North and East).

[68] "Social Stratification in France and in the United States," in *Class, Status, and Power: a Reader in Social Stratification* (Glencoe, Ill.: The Free Press, 1952), pp. 577–589.

[69] This is a contract signed in September 1955 by the Renault management, which anticipates a raise of wages spread out over several years, sickness insurance not covered by social security, and vacations of from fifteen days to three weeks.

[70] In *La Condition Ouvrière* (Paris: Gallimard, 1951).

[71] *Ibid.,* pp. 243–249; the italics are mine.

[72] Alfred Sauvy, *Richesse et Population* (Paris: Payot, 1943), p. 223.

[73] The family of this period (late eighteenth century) was characterized by a very high rate of fertility, but there existed also a very high percentage of celibates, both male and female. See Gemähling, *op. cit.*

[74] Sauvy, *op. cit.*, p. 146.

[75] *Ibid.*, pp. 155–159.

[76] *Ibid.*, p. 157.

[77] *Ibid.*, p. 158.

[78] If instead of taking the average per capita income, we take the average income accruing to the *active* population, the figures are much more favorable to the French economy.

[79] Henry See, *Histoire Économique de la France,* Vol. I (Paris: Armand Colin, 1948). On corporations, see pp. 342–343; on the grain business, see p. 232.

[80] John H. Clapham, *Economic Development of France and Germany* (Cambridge: Cambridge University Press, 1921), p. 74.

[81] Sauvy, *op. cit.*, pp. 69–76.

[82] Paris: Hachette, 1955.

[83] Article on Madame de Caylus, in *Causeries du Lundi,* Vol. II (Paris: Garnier, 1863), p. 69.

[84] Article on Madame Récamier, in *Causeries du Lundi,* Vol. I, p. 120.

[85] *Ibid.*

[86] *Causeries du Lundi,* Vol. II, p. 217.

[87] *Illusions Perdues,* Vol. V, Part I (Paris: Alexandre Houssiaux, 1869), pp. 40–43.

[88] A bourgeois quarter in Angoulême where Lucien lives, which makes a contrast with the area where the nobility reside.

[89] The italics are in Stendhal's text.

[90] The italics are mine.

[91] *Le Rouge et le Noir* (Paris: Garnier, 1938), Ch. 9, p. 53.

[92] *Le Côte de Guermantes,* Vol. I (Paris: Gallimard, 1920), p. 52.

[93] Sainte-Beuve, *Causeries du Lundi,* Vol. I, p. 416.

[94] *Structures Elémentaries de la Parenté* (Paris: Presses Universitaires de France, 1949), p. 615.

[95] *Le Rouge et le Noir,* pp. 447, 450, 472.

[96] Paris: Calmann-Levy, 1929; pp. 78, 80, 83, 84, 85.

[97] Cited by B. Groethuysen, *Philosophie de la Révolution Française* (Paris: Gallimard, 1956), p. 164.

[98] *Ibid.*, p. 165.

[99] Lucien Goldman, *Le Dieu Caché* (Paris: Gallimard, 1955), and *Racine* (Paris: Editions de l'Arche, 1956).

[100] Goldman, *Le Dieu Caché,* p. 47.

[101] *Ibid.*, p. 17.

[102] *Maximes,* 201 and 263.

[103] Goldman, *Le Dieu Caché,* pp. 66–67.

[104] *Oeuvres* (Paris: Pléiade, 1936), pp. 324–327.

[105] Cited by Goldman, *Le Dieu Caché,* pp. 60–61.

[106] Cited from J. R. Carré, *Réflexions sur l'Anti Pascal de Voltaire* (Paris: Félix Alcan, 1935), pp. 93–94, 104.

[107] Gustave Flaubert, *Madame Bovary,* in *Oeuvres* (Paris: Pléiade, 1936), p. 392.

[108] *Discours sur l'Ensemble du Positivism* (Paris: Société Positiviste Internationale, 1907), Part IV, par. 104, p. 251.

[109] *Memoires d'Outre-Tombe,* Vol. I (Paris: Garnier, 1904), pp. 85–86.

*

Emilio Willems

BRAZIL

*

The Value System

CULTURAL ORIGINS AND CULTURAL UNITY

IT HAS often been stated that contemporary Brazil contains a hybrid people and a hybrid culture, the foundations of which were laid by Portuguese settlers, African slaves, and detribalized native Indians. Although essentially correct, this statement must be qualified insofar as it may convey the false impression that the influence of each of these ethnic groups was felt with equal intensity in all parts of Brazil, or that the cultural contribution of each group was, quantitatively or qualitatively, comparable to those of the others.

To judge from the presence of Indian elements in different parts of contemporary Brazil, it would seem that contact with diverse native societies occurred under conditions which must have varied considerably from one region to another. As may be expected, the Portuguese were most receptive to autochthonous influences wherever they were isolated and the Indian societies had reached a stage of development which made the borrowing of cultural traits profitable. It is not surprising, therefore, that more Indian traits are found in the Amazon Basin than in any other part of Brazil. In the central, eastern, and southern sections of the country the distribution of Indian elements is so irregular and its pattern so poorly known that any generalizing statement is bound to be misleading, except for a few regions which have been adequately covered by students of native cultures.

Of course, the Indian cultures were essentially "rural," and their contributions were likely to disappear where urban civilization developed. They were rural in the specific sense in which self-sufficient, small, isolated and sacred societies are rural. When brought into the orbit of commercial agriculture, their rurality was apt to lose its Indian features to those technical and economic changes which distinguish a society of farmers from a true peasant society.

African influences remained naturally limited to plantation and mining areas. However, for reasons which have not been satisfactorily explained, African influences have persisted in urban rather than rural surroundings. It may well be that the anonymity of the coastal cities, from São Luia do Maranhão down to Porto Alegre, offered the kind of setting in which African cults and African customs could survive, while the social intimacy of small agricultural communities did not provide such opportunities.

In contrast with the local and rather fragmentary nature of Indian and African survivals, Portuguese culture contributed heavily to the basic value system. Although adaptable to the varying conditions of the new country, this system never lost its identity. It provided the binding force which prevented Brazil from becoming merely a physical rather than a cultural concept. Exactly how the cultural unity of those 3,279,799 square miles has been achieved and maintained is still imperfectly known. Historical events and geographical accidents seemed to favor the development of culturally distinct regions which would eventually achieve political emancipation and sovereignty, not unlike those of the Andes and the La Plata area. Indeed, the cultural differentiation of Brazil into distinct areas is an incontrovertible fact. And at times there seemed to be little, if anything, to hold these regional traditions together. Not even political attempts to secede from the commonwealth were lacking during the century following national independence. Yet there were always factors which kept cultural differentiation in accord with the basic design of a common Luso-Brazilian value system. Recent studies of small communities, sometimes thousands of miles apart, once again confirm the existence of such a system, whose main elements bear an astonishing degree of mutual resemblance.

Among the possible answers to the enigma of a unified Brazilian culture, only one can be attributed a major role solidly supported by historical facts, namely internal migration. The extent to which the lower rural classes of Brazil move about, either attracted by better economic opportunities or driven away by periodical droughts, fully justifies the assumption that migration itself has become an integral pattern of lower-class culture in Brazil. Internal migration most effectively mingled people of different races and subcultures, in a virtually continuous process which left hardly any corner of the Brazilian territory untouched. Spontaneous in most of its phases, it created channels of communication and cultural diffusion which did not depend upon the communication system maintained by the urban civilization of the coast. Whatever else may have contributed to create a basic value system and a common political structure, it probably possesses neither the continuity nor the coverage of the population movements which are responsible for the extension and shape of the Brazilian territory.

LANGUAGE, FAMILY, AND RELIGION

In spite of massive miscegenation accompanying and, in part at least, conditioning cultural blending, John Gillin's statement that "Latin American culture is growing toward an integrated configuration more rapidly than is the mestizo race,"[1] applies perhaps to a greater extent to Brazil than to most Spanish-speaking countries of Latin America. The pervasiveness of Portuguese culture is a well-known fact. Its human bearers approach native societies with apparent humility, tolerate their idiosyncrasies, absorb selected customs and techniques, and out of the old and new smoothly create a new design in which the Portuguese elements nevertheless occupy a position of dominance. Not only Brazil, but those parts of West Africa, India, and Southeast Asia which at one time were under Portuguese control bear witness to the almost uncanny persistence of Portuguese culture.

Basic cultural values, whose roots clearly lie in Portugal, are expressed particularly in three institutions: language, family, and religion. The symbolic position of the Portuguese tongue is indicated by the accepted philosophy of linguistic unity. Not only were the native tongues definitely supplanted by Portuguese, even in territories where they seemed solidly rooted in the habits of the people, but also minority languages like German or Italian, introduced and tenaciously held by immigrant groups, stand little chance to survive two or three generations.

The most striking and perhaps the most relevant single aspect of Brazilian culture is the family. Both its internal arrangements and its dominant position in the general social structure provide clues to the understanding of other aspects of the culture. Value-wise the bilateral extended form of the Brazilian family is based on the social recognition of both consanguinity and affinity as factors determining certain reciprocal obligations within a large circle of relatives. In an otherwise individualistic or relatively amorphous social structure, the extended family has developed a strong sense of belonging and cooperativeness among its members. The highly valued self-directedness and self-sufficiency of the personality, although respected within the family, do not interfere with the obligations that one is expected to discharge as a family member. On the contrary, there is a tendency to value the individual person as a member of a given kin group. Thus personal status has traditionally been derived from family status, though within the Luso-Brazilian culture family status is probably less rigid than in the Spanish culture.

The role of religion in the Brazilian value system cannot be assessed by church affiliation. The fact that, in 1950, 93.49 per cent of all Brazilians professed to be Catholics does not have the meaning which similar figures may possess in the United States or Europe. Nor does the assertion that many or perhaps most Brazilians are only nominal Catholics adequately characterize the situation. A large proportion of the people adheres to rather unorthodox forms of Catholicism, yet willingly accepts the role of the Church on occasions such as birth, graduation, marriage, and death. Few persons would pass up an opportunity to get the Church's blessing: "A new home or a new shop is dedicated during an informal religious ceremony. A new car is also taken to the priest, just as practically all cars in Brazil carry on the dashboard a medal of St. Christopher, the protector of travelers; in fact, there is an annual ceremony in the cities, just after the new models have arrived, during which the newly bought cars pass in front of a priest."[2] The discrepancy between religion as practiced and religion as established by the Church is much more pronounced in the rural areas where a rather unorthodox folk Catholicism, more or less at variance with the doctrine of the Church, bears testimony to the genuine religiosity of the people.

RACE ATTITUDES

Tolerance of racial differences constitutes a basic value in Luso-Brazilian culture. In contrast to the United States, Brazil has frequently been referred to as a racial democracy. However, by interpreting race relations merely in terms of absence of prejudice and discrimination one misses the point. The Brazilian race situation is not so much characterized by a relative absence of prejudice, but by the emphatic acceptance of colored races to the closest possible type of association: marriage. During the Middle

Ages the Portuguese had been exposed to long-lasting contacts with the darker-skinned Arabs who ruled the Iberian peninsula from 711 to 1244. "They had brought with them," Donald Pierson reminds us, "a superior culture, were more learned in the arts and sciences. They had become the wealthy class who occupied the towns and lived in the principal castles and on the great estates. Consequently, it came to be considered an honor for Portuguese women to mate with them, and we know that such marriages often occurred even among members of the royal family."[3] It was then, probably, that superior social status was associated with dark skin. Later, during the fifteenth and sixteenth centuries, when the Portuguese engaged in building one of the largest and most complex colonial empires of all times, it became necessary to strengthen the weak demographic structure of Portugal by stimulating intermarriage between Portuguese men and native women. Thus everywhere in the Portuguese empire, in Africa, in Southern and Southeastern Asia, and in Brazil, a mixed population developed which provided the foundations for relative stable political controls.

When the Portuguese started colonizing Brazil they had already learned to consider race mixture as a source of cultural vigor. Actually, there was little need for the official encouragement and recognition which state and church liberally granted to interracial marriages. The doctrine of white supremacy never influenced Portuguese colonial policy to any discernible degree, and in recent decades, when race issues began to worry the West, the practice of miscegenation developed into what may be called a social doctrine of racial blending which is strongly supported by public opinion and law. It is not free, however, as we shall see, from inconsistencies and ambivalence.

The history of race relations in Brazil indicates that racial democracy did not evolve merely out of the practice of miscegenation. The existence of relatively large mixed populations, in all areas of contact between Europeans and colored peoples, proves that miscegenation must be regarded as a world-wide phenomenon from which not even the most fanatical advocates of white supremcy escaped. In most colonial areas, miscegenation encouraged rather than prevented the emergence of a color bar and a caste system. The crucial test is to be seen in the attitudes which develop toward the mixed offspring of illicit unions. If the white father repudiates his responsibilities, and if the children share the social fate of their native mother, or if they are altogether treated as outcasts by whites and natives alike, the prospect of a racial democracy seems dim indeed. The Brazilian father, as a rule, did not disavow his colored children. There is abundant historical evidence that such illegitimate children were cared for, if not at least *de facto* adopted. Together with their legitimate siblings they could expect a formal education and jobs which raised their status far above that of their colored mothers. The considerable number of mulattoes who entered the bureaucracy and the professions during the nineteenth century bear witness to the highly developed sense of paternal responsibility and the strong emotional attachment which Brazilian fathers, especially in the upper classes, felt toward their illegitimate offspring. One may safely assume, therefore, that the roots of racial democracy, as it evolved in Brazil, are firmly attached to the peculiar structure of the Brazilian family.

THE PATTERN OF GOVERNMENT

The political functions of the extended patriarchal family, as it evolved on the plantations of colonial Brazil, made it difficult, if not impossible, to avoid a familialistic political structure. Its consequences may be measured by such traits as patrimonialism, authoritarianism, nepotism, and personalism. The political function of the plantation family owed its importance to the relative weakness of the Portuguese government, to the general insecurity of the country, infested by pirates, hostile Indians and bands of runaway slaves, as well as to the difficulties of organizing a rarified and widely scattered population on a purely territorial basis. There was little security except in the shadow of the plantation, a condition which naturally led to feudal bonds between the owner's family and a variety of people living on or nearby the plantation. Frequent blood feuds among rival families contributed to reinforce the cohesion of the *familia rustica* as feudal law, and history designated the free inhabitants of a territory controlled by a suzerain. Territorial immunity, which had been a privilege of Portuguese aristocracy, although declining at the time when America was discovered, throve in Brazil and was *de facto* still respected in the nineteenth century. "Authorities and police respected the *engenhos* (sugar mills and plantations), which sometimes were sanctuaries for criminals and inaccessible, like sacred taboos; certain arrogant lords did not permit the police to visit their properties even for the most plausible reasons. They regarded it as an insult that required retaliations, no matter how. Even today this prejudice still exists and police visits to the *engenhos* involve real assaults and bring almost always inconveniences."[4]

The political history of Brazil is, to a large extent, a struggle between state and family for political control. If the state eventually won, victory was neither easy nor complete. There are still numerous survivals of family power in rural areas where, not infrequently, local communities are dominated by single kinship groups.

Modeled after the extended patriarchal family, such political structures are based upon the recognition of the discretionary power of a landlord and the almost feudal loyalty of his dependents. Only kinsmen are entrusted with important jobs, and administrative affairs are apt to be conducted according to patrimonialistic rules. There is, above all, no clear distinction between private and public spheres. Fiscal matters are decided as if they were personal matters of the lord, and public servants tend to become his personal servants. Rendering of services and their remuneration are interpreted in personal terms. Functionaries are hired and fired by personal decision of their superiors and for reasons which lie in the personal relations between appointer and appointee. Not responsible to the public, but to their sponsor alone, functionaries tend to regard their jobs as a source of personal revenues.[5] Although in Brazil patrimonialistic procedures and policies were always a matter of usurpation rather than legality, they were frequently anchored in local custom and tenaciously resisted change. Eventually they gave way to modern bureaucratic structures, but residues are still frequently found, especially in local government.

ECONOMIC ENDEAVOR: ADVENTURE AND ROUTINE

Attitudes concerning economic matters have been visibly influenced by the Portuguese heritage of slavery and predatory colonialism on the one hand, and the mirage of inexhaustible potentialities on the other. Whether mercantile interests preceded or followed the colonial expansion of Portugal seems to be a moot question. There are indications, however, that the Portuguese nobility was sensitive to economic success and inclined to recognize its social implications rather than to follow the example of European nobility which stuck rigidly to birthright and caste lines.[6] At any rate, by methodically investing its people and resources in colonial expansion, Portugal struck it rich. The investment paid a hundredfold in Africa, India, and Southeastern Asia. The experiences of at least two centuries taught the Portuguese that bold adventure and relentless gambling on uncertain, but highly promising, prospects yielded far higher returns than the obscure and unrewarding life on the hill farms back home. Under such conditions, it was only to be expected that Portugal would lean heavily on the slave trade and slavery, as it indeed did long before Brazil was even discovered. Farming became the despised occupation of servile labor to which one did not pay more attention than strictly necessary. The plantation system, which the Portuguese erected in Northeastern Brazil, during the second half of the sixteenth century, heavily contributed to reinforce this attitude toward menial work and to develop a preference for white-collar jobs and the professions ("gentleman complex").

It has been argued that the Iberian attitude toward work is deeply rooted in a general repugnance to the cult of labor which is related to Protestant ethics. "Action upon things, upon the material universe, involves submission to an external object, acceptance of a law which is alien to the individual. It is not required by God, it adds nothing to His glory, nor does it exalt our own dignity. On the contrary, one may say that (such action) damages and vilifies it. Menial and mechanical work aims at a good foreign to man, and is designed to achieve the perfection of an object distinct from him."[7]

Whether such untestable but plausible attempts at interpreting incontrovertible facts are correct or not, contempt for menial labor and its association with servile or, at least, lower class status, has been consistently adhered to by the Iberian and Ibero-American peoples, in obvious contrast with Protestant morals and practice.

Now it would most certainly be an oversimplification to equate contempt for menial work merely with preference for leisure. Dignifying as leisure may be in a man's life, it is only so in contrast with work. Yet work must be mental, and it must leave the individual unruffled. There is nothing like the professions and public administration, especially if baited with political prospects, to gratify personal ambitions, to grant respectability, and to bestow a sense of power upon the individual. Within the context of Iberian culture it was particularly the manipulation of the law which came to be regarded as a symbol of social prestige. The *bacharel* (bachelor of law) became one of the leading figures of public life who successfully competed with the rural "aristrocracy" and the military for political control.

The tendency to look upon the menial and technical occupations as a necessary evil led to routinization. Wealth was highly desirable, but not at the cost of steadfast and laborious effort. When toil was inevitable it was left to slaves and peons. The socially approved goal was to become a landowner and to enjoy rapidly acquired wealth in dignified leisure. It has often been noted that the Brazilian economy was of the "boom and bust" type. First sugar cane, then gold and diamond mining, cotton, rubber, and finally cocoa and coffee constitute the "economic cycles" of Brazilian history. They are all characterized by boldness in planning and action, by rapid expansion and ephemeral prosperity that brought fabulous wealth to a few, but left the masses almost unaffected. Until recently little was done to improve production methods or to secure permanent markets.

Improvidence, dissipation, ostentation, gambling, and the predatory use of the land have been pointed out by many Brazilians as major "weaknesses" of what may be called, with some qualifications, national character.[8] Without questioning here the propriety of these terms, it must be admitted that they are consistent with Luso-Brazilian colonial traditions. The speculative booms that characterize the Brazilian economy may be interpreted as a form of gambling, in a wide sense, but gambling itself is firmly entrenched in the institutional structure of Brazilian culture. Gambling, particularly under the form of government-sponsored lottery, must be considered as a major economic pursuit.

INDIVIDUALISM

The well-known cult of the individual personality, which has so often been commented upon with regard to Latin America, permeates like a leitmotif the entire value system. It should be added, however, that it is essentially a cult of the male personality. Brazilian society, like the other societies of Latin America, is, in contrast with the United States, pronouncedly androcentric. The role of the female has traditionally been limited to providing background effects.

In this androcentric society there has been little inclination to do things on behalf of the community or any other group, except kinship groups. Activities that require concerted effort of some continuity were, and still are, difficult to sustain. To make such sweeping statements seems rather hazardous, especially in view of the numerous changes which have taken place in the traditional value system. If the above statement were literally true, Brazil would hardly have developed any of the operative or regulative institutions which rank it among the "advanced" countries of the West.

Yet there are aspects of Brazilian social organization which differ thoroughly from comparable aspects of American society, for example. All forms of spontaneous organization on the community level, which are commonly taken for granted in the United States, are either nonexistent or rather unstable in Brazil. In fact, the difference is so obvious, that the most cursory survey of Brazilian community life is apt to show it clearly. Above all, the numerous civic, educational, religious, and recreational associations characteristic of American communities, simply do not exist, or if they do, their life consists of the sporadic, groping, and halfhearted efforts of a few. Not even those forms of entertainment among neighbors, colleagues, church or club members, which Americans take as a matter of course, are really desired in Brazil. Outside the extended family circle the male rather prefers chance encounters with friends and acquaintances in sidewalk cafés or in the streets. Such encounters are felt to be enjoyable exactly because they do not involve the distasteful obligation to synchronize one's pleasure with the equally disagreeable duties of the housewife to serve dinner and to dress up on a certain day, and at a certain hour. In the same manner, women prefer chance contacts with neighbors and relatives of the same sex. Dinner parties are restricted to one's kinsfolk and a few intimate friends.

Political individualism shows in the considerable fluidity of parties and their membership. The loyalty one may feel toward a political party seldom exceeds the time necessary to conduct an electoral campaign. The parties themselves may be considered as ephemeral groups centered on persons rather than programs.

Historically, political personalism produced the somewhat glamorized figure of the *caudilho* ("leader"), who is commonly believed to be a typical Latin-American phenomenon. There is little doubt that even in recent political history some basic traits of the *caudilho* apply to certain Brazilian politicians who attempted to combine conspiracy and social demagoguery in order to gain office.

REACTIONS TO THE CULTURAL HERITAGE

The Brazilian people may be divided into those who take their cultural heritage for granted and those who show some sort of positive or negative reaction toward that heritage. The first category certainly constitutes the majority. Most of its components are preliterate peasants whose culture is regional rather than national. The other category is predominantly urban, and its components belong to the middle and upper strata. The most remarkable thing about these Brazilians is perhaps the fact that, as one writer once put it, they have turned their back to their own country, and most of their attention is caught by happenings on the other side of the ocean. This attitude of continuously cupping the ear and listening to Europe was very early adopted by educated Brazilians. This "other-directedness" is organically tied in with a deeply critical attitude toward their own culture. A number of historical events may be related to it.

First of all Brazil was discovered, colonized, and controlled by Portugal, a tiny country which early lost its status of a great international power. Its ruthless exploitation of the agricultural and mineral resources of Brazil, combined with an equally ruthless suppression of industrial and intellectual initiatives, eventually led to the political emancipation of the country. Hatred and contempt for the Portuguese survived the war of independence and frequently flared up in riots against Portuguese subjects during the nineteenth century. Many Brazilians felt that colonization by the Portuguese had produced mostly undesirable results, a feeling which has been overcome only in the last two or three decades. And, it was sadly pointed out, the Brazilian Indians ranked among the least developed of all South American natives. To complete this negativistic picture, the African heritage was actually considered as something to be ashamed of. Although widely practiced, race mixture was looked upon by some Brazilians (who frequently were mixed-bloods themselves) as a possible source of cultural inferiority.

At the same time the physical greatness and the almost untapped natural resources of the country inspired ambitions that were not supported by an economic development comparable, for example, to that of the United States.

Disappointment and frustration induced the Brazilians to turn their eyes to the great nations of Europe. France especially seemed to offer everything that Brazil, like most Latin American peoples, ardently desired. Thus political emancipation was immediately followed by organized attempts to develop the fine arts, literature, sciences, and education. Groups of French painters, sculptors, actors, composers, architects and scientists were hired by the imperial government of Brazil, which thus expressed the prevailing belief in the superiority of French culture. This belief came to be so dominant that every single aspect of Brazilian middle- and upper-class culture still bears its marks. For at least a century the members of these classes were educated, to a large extent, by French priests and nuns. They learned to speak and think French; in fact, French became a second mother tongue for many of them. The legal system was based on the Napoleonic Code, and familiarity with French philosophy, French political ideas, poetry, and the novel ranked high among the "polite achievements" of several generations of educated Brazilians.

All this must largely be understood as a reaction against the cultural heritage of the country: Emulation of alien cultures served the function of compensating inferiority feelings. In the Brazilian cities of fifty years ago a way of life had developed which at the present time is felt to be artificial and unrelated to the country, its culture and people. Sporadic outbursts of nationalism, which have become more frequent and perhaps more intensive since 1930, may be interpreted as attempts to revalidate the cultural heritage of Luso-African-Indian origin. The most consequential of these efforts was probably the "rediscovery" and revalidation of the Portuguese-African heritage by men like Gilberto Freyre and his followers.

Although return to the "Brazilian realities" has been preached with great insistence, especially since Alberto Torres published his critical volumes on the political and economic problems of the country, the deep-rooted feeling of cultural inadequacy has not disappeared, and admiration for alien models shifted from France to the United States. Already the first constitution of the Republic (1891) was virtually a duplicate of the American Constitution. In the meanwhile American technology and, more recently, American education, literature, and motion pictures have replaced to a large extent former French models.

The Economic System

BASIC ASPECTS AND HISTORICAL BACKGROUND

The economy of Brazil has traditionally been concerned with gathering, farming, and extraction of mineral resources. As gatherers and farmers the Portuguese owed much to Indian techniques and experiences. Gathering could be taken up without initial capital investment, yet whenever it went beyond the immediate needs of subsistence and involved products which had to be exchanged for food items or currency, its profitableness became automatically dependent on market conditions whose control did not lie in the hands of the gatherers. The great rubber boom which lasted from 1860 to 1910, approximately, constitutes perhaps the most striking example of how industrial development and conditions in the world market, both completely alien to the rubber-producing area, brought sudden "progress" to one of the least developed regions of the world. Under its impact a number of Amazon towns expanded into important

536

centers of commerce and conspicuous consumption. With the end of the rubber boom came depopulation, stagnation, and poverty, and since World War I the Amazon has been living on memories and rather unsuccessful attempts to revive the rubber economy.

The exact number of individuals primarily engaged in gathering activities is almost impossible to determine, but in 1950 their total did not amount to more than perhaps 1 per cent of all persons engaged in some definable economic activities.[9] In some of the northern states, however, gathering ranks high in the economic scale. In the Acre territory and the state of Amazonas, where people engaged in the so-called extractive industries are mostly gatherers, their number exceeds that of any other occupation, and in Pará it ranks second only to agriculture.[10] In southern Brazil, gathering is almost nonexistent, except for a small area where Paraguay tea (*herva mate*) is collected from wild-growing trees.

Inversely, agriculture in any of its widely varying forms, from slash-and-burn agriculture to modern truck farming, appears to be concentrated in the South. As a matter of fact, in 1946 80 per cent of all cultivated land was located in seven southern states, particularly in São Paulo, Minas Gerais and Rio Grande do Sul.[11] The agricultural dominance of the South began with the rapid expansion of coffee cultivation during the second half of the nineteenth century. In previous periods the center of dominance had lain in the northeastern states that controlled first the sugar market and subsequently the cotton market in Europe. The nineteenth and, to a much higher degree, the twentieth century brought an inexorable shift to the South. Environmental conditions, such as the droughts that periodically afflicted the northeastern states, or the favorable climatic and soil conditions of the São Paulo area may be adduced, together with conditions of the world market, as partial explanations of the most far-reaching economic change that ever occurred in Brazilian history.

Some interpreters of economic history have perhaps been misled by certain connotations of the term "cycle," which is frequently used regarding the major phases of Brazilian economy. With the "end" of a "cycle," the production of a particular item may be thought to have virtually vanished from the economic system of the country, while in fact only a monopolistic or at least dominant position in the international market has come to an end. It is true that already by 1655 Brazil's position in the sugar market had been weakened and toward the end of the seventeenth century West-Indian competition had displaced Brazil from its most profitable foreign markets. But the sugar industry never ceased to be a mainstay of the economic structure, especially as the internal market expanded. In 1938, Brazil was the world's third largest producer of sugar. In 1954, 8,451 mills with a total production of 921,670 tons were still located in the traditional sugar area of the Northeast. But in the same year 9,383 mills with a total production of 827,404 tons were found in the four southern states of São Paulo, Paraná, Santa Catarina, and Rio Grande do Sul. São Paulo possessed the largest number of mills (95) with modern equipment and produced far more sugar (184,580 tons) than any other single state, including Pernambuco (590,445 tons).[12] For years a politically inspired quota system, intended to protect the Northeast against southern competition, has contributed to maintaining an unstable equilibrium between Northeast and South.

In a similar fashion, cotton agriculture extended to the South. Extensive migrations from the Northeast to São Paulo secured the necessary labor supply, and by 1935 this state had become one of the principal producers of cotton. Although declining over a number of years, São Paulo's cotton production was in 1954 much higher (205,255 tons) than that of all northeastern states combined.[13]

São Paulo, alone or in combination with other southern states, holds a similar position of predominance as a producer of such vital items as rice, corn, bananas, potatoes, and citrus fruits.

During the last hundred years, however, no agricultural product has played a role comparable to that of coffee in the economic structure of Brazil. Shortly before World War I about 70 per cent of all coffee exports came from Brazil, but high prices encouraged international competition, and soon the government, strongly influenced by the planters, resorted to a series of schemes designed to support world prices. In 1949 the number of coffee trees had declined from approximately three billion to two billion, mainly by placing a prohibitive tax on new plantings. The policy of unilateral action came finally to an end in 1940, when Brazil entered the Inter-American Coffee Agreement which assigned export quotas to the fourteen coffee-producing countries of Latin America. The steady decline in the production of coffee reached its lowest point in 1944 with 686,686 tons. After World War II high prices in the international market stimulated a new expansion and a partial restoration of deteriorated coffee plantations. In 1948 production again exceeded a million tons, a figure which has oscillated little since. São Paulo has continually asserted its place as the largest producer of all Brazilian states.

The livestock and meat industry, which ranks higher in value than any single farm crop, is also concentrated in southern and south-central Brazil. As cattle are produced almost entirely on natural pastures, extensive areas are necessary to supply the most densely populated and urbanized regions of the South. Thus the natural pastures of Rio Grande do Sul, Mato Grosso, and Goiás provide the necessary cheap land which, under present conditions, could hardly be used for agricultural purposes. Again, in 1934 more cattle were slaughtered in São Paulo than in any other state, and the combined figures for São Paulo and Rio Grande do Sul, the second largest meat producer of the country, account for little less than 50 per cent of the total domestic output.[14]

INDUSTRIALIZATION: GENERAL DEVELOPMENT

Together with the historical shift of agricultural dominance from the Northeast to the South, industrialization of the southern states must be considered as a major change in the economic structure of contemporary Brazil.

In 1889, when the Empire came to an end, there were only about 636 industrial establishments, and many of these were small shops operated in the manner of handicrafts. With the beginning of the republican era, industrial activities were taken up with considerable zest, but typically in a speculative, gambling-like fashion. "Fantastic firms rose and fell, going bankrupt with the growing discrediting of their shares. These bankruptcies motivated greater pessimism as to the future of Brazilian industry."[15] Only the adoption of a markedly protectionist policy associated with a successful effort to stem the tide of inflation somewhat restored the confidence in the future of the national industry. There were 1,088 industrial establishments in 1895, a figure which had ascended to 3,250 in 1907, when the first industrial census was carried out. By this time the industrial predominance of the South was already established. São Paulo, the Federal district, and Rio Grande do Sul accounted for 53 per cent of the total output, of which the foodstuff industries represented 26.7 and the textile industry 20.6 per cent.

World War I brought the turning point in the development of a domestic industry. The temporary inability of the industrialized countries to supply the internal consumption of Brazil resulted in a rapid expansion of national production; 5,936 new industrial establishments arose during World War I, and in 1920, there were 13,336 establishments which employed a total of 275,512 workers. During the following decade the growth slowed down, but gained momentum after 1933. At the outbreak of World War II the number of industrial establishments totaled 49,418, with 960,633 employees, out of which 781,185 were workers.

The impact which World War II produced upon the industrialization of Brazil was similar to that of World War I. According to the Industrial Census of 1952, there were 38,793 industrial establishments which employed 1,354,030 persons. Their distribution among the principal branches of industry indicates that the production of textiles absorbed 341,151, or a little over 25 per cent of all industrial employees.

The foodstuff industries ranked next with 192,348, or 14.2 per cent of all employees. A rather comprehensive census category named "transformation of non-metallic minerals" which refers primarily to the cement industry, employed 119,922 persons, or 8.6 per cent of the total. With 111,187 employees, or 8.25 per cent of the total, metallurgy occupied the fifth place. Among the remaining branches only the chemical and the combined clothing and shoe industries employed more than 5 per cent of the entire industrial labor force. Of this force 571,263, or 42.2 per cent, were concentrated in São Paulo, and 781,073, or 57.5 per cent, in the four southernmost states, including São Paulo.[16]

SPECIAL PROBLEMS OF INDUSTRIALIZATION

Industrialization has been delayed by a considerable lag in the production of energy. Almost all accessible coal deposits are located in the three southernmost states of the country, and the quality of Brazilian coal compares rather unfavorably with that of American or European origin. Under the pressure of World War II, coal production increased from 907,224 tons in 1938 to 2,072,881 tons in 1954, the highest figure ever arrived at. In 1953 Brazil produced 2,024,929 tons of coal against 745,889 tons which had to be imported, predominantly from the United States, to supply internal consumption.[17]

Despite steady and considerable progress, the production of electric energy has not kept up with the needs arising from industrialization and urbanization. From 357,203 kilowatts in 1920 the production increased to 747,101 kilowatts in 1930 and to 1,243,877 in 1940. The most impressive increase, however occurred between 1950 and 1954, when the total production soared from 1,882,500 to 2,807,578 kilowatts. Again, most of the production of electric energy is concentrated in the state of São Paulo, where it increased from 564,654 kilowatts in 1940 to 1,127,128 kilowatts in 1954. Despite such efforts, consumption of electricity has at times been rationed in the metropolitan area of São Paulo and some other cities.

If industrialization exempted the Brazilians from importing such items as textiles, shoes, paper, some chemical and pharmaceutical articles, it led, on the other hand, to the import of machinery and certain raw material that were indispensable to the production of those items. Thus, further efforts became necessary to reduce or eliminate such imports. Moreover, steel and cement had to be produced domestically, for both products are indispensable to erect modern factories and residential houses, to build bridges and roads, railways and ports, tools and machinery. By 1926 only 3.3 per cent of all cement consumed in Brazil was of domestic origin. Three years later the proportion of domestic cement had arisen to 15 per cent, and in 1942, again under the pressure of war, 98 per cent of the total consumption was produced in Brazil.[18] Total production ascended from 147,409 tons in 1942 to 2,476,995 tons in 1954. Yet urbanization reached such proportion after World War I, especially with the erection of hundreds of skyscrapers for commercial and residential use in the great metropolitan areas of the country, that import of cement increased to 981,642 tons in 1953.[19] The following years, however, it was down to 332,331 tons, reflecting, in part, the increasing capacity of the domestic cement industry. About one third of the production figure attained in 1954 is to be attributed to São Paulo. In the same year, Rio de Janeiro and São Paulo together produced slightly over 60 per cent of all domestic cement, thus responding to the local needs of the two most urbanized and industrialized areas of the country.[20]

The great wealth of iron ore and the poor grade of coal, separated from each other by a thousand miles and some major topographic obstacles, constitute one of the most harassing economic and technological problems of contemporary Brazil. The first large-scale attempt to solve this ancient impasse and to free the country from the limitations of charcoal-operated furnaces, the steel mill of Volta Redonda was erected. It was an initiative of the federal government, which was able to secure American capital. Its location in the state of Rio de Janeiro was chosen in such a way as to facilitate transportation of iron ore from Minas Gerais and coal from Santa Catarina, and to keep cost at the lowest possible level. Of no lesser significance is the fact that political pressure was not allowed to interfere with its location or operation which was taken up in 1946. In the same year, the domestic production of pig iron went up from 259,909 tons to 370,722. Mainly due to the expanding capacity of Volta Redonda this figure reached 1,088,948 tons in 1954. During the same period (1945–54), the output of steel grew from 205,935 to 1,148,322 tons, while that of rolled plates soared from 165,850 to 970,842 tons.[21] Since 1947 Volta Redonda has been marketing rails, coupling plates, supports, thick and thin plates, hold and cold rolled, along with products of the coking plant and the subproduct factories, such as ammonia sulphate, coke, naphthalene, motor fuel, benzol, toluol, silol, naphtha solvent, coal tar, pitch, and oil.[22]

Domestic demand for steel has kept ahead of domestic production, and high tariff protection has proved unnecessary. Despite an expanding output, imports have remained considerable. In 1954, 562,104 tons of pig iron and steel came from overseas.[23]

Restrained by the high cost of prospecting and a constitutional provision excluding aliens from the exploration of mineral resources (Article 153, Constitution of 1946), the petroleum industry has lagged behind other industrial developments. Oil was found in the state of Bahia where, by 1947, out of 100 wells drilled, 45 were producing oil and 14 gas. Oil production in Bahia expanded from 10,367 tons in 1953 to 119,691 tons in 1954, which represent of course only a small fraction of the domestic demand for oil and oil products. Internal consumption of gasoline and diesel fuel has steadily increased, especially since World War II, a fact which raises the problem of balance of payments. "The situation is particularly critical in the case of petroleum, for in 1947 Brazil used $19 million on this commodity alone; meanwhile its needs for petroleum are growing with the development of industry and the expansion of highway and air travel."[24] In 1947 the total consumption of gasoline went not beyond 1,316,294,000 liters. By 1954 it reached 3,637,917,000 liters, and further increases seem unavoidable. Partial relief is expected from the construction of two refineries where imported crude oil will be processed, thus reducing the deficit of the balance of trade.

The structural significance of the changes which have affected the Brazilian economy during the last half century may be defined as a shift from a one-crop agrarian system to a diversified mixed agrarian-industrial system. A high degree of economic dependence, caused by the fact that almost all manufactured goods had to be imported and paid for by coffee exports, has been attenuated by industrialization and by increased reliance on exportable products other than coffee. It is true that coffee still represents about 50 per cent of the country's total exports, but ever since 1940 its share in the total domestic production amounts to less than 10 per cent.

Although successful in its attempt toward industrialization wherever industrialization promised substantial rewards, Brazil is primarily thought of as an agrarian country which ought to preserve and develop its agricultural resources. If this is to happen, the predatory exploitative techniques of the past must be replaced by such methods as are deemed appropriate to prevent erosion and soil exhaustion. The reserves of virgin land suitable for agricultural exploitation are rapidly coming to an end, a fact which is bound to stimulate the most incisive and far-reaching technological and economic change yet observed in Brazilian history, namely stabilization of agriculture.

DRAWBACKS AND ATTEMPTED SOLUTIONS

If one views industrialization in retrospect as a process of diffusion whereby an extremely intricate complex of machines, skills, and attitudes had to be transferred and adapted to widely varying ecological and social conditions, it would seem that it has been taking place in a rather haphazard and piecemeal fashion, and that some of its phases are badly lagging and threatening the continuity of the whole.

Capital accumulation, for example, has been slow and insufficient to satisfy current needs for credit. Nor has actual capital investment been consistent with recognized long-range needs of the country. The inflation of the Brazilian monetary system, which has disturbed the equilibrium of prices and salaries for several decades, is continuing almost unchecked. Furthermore, there is the often criticized failure of agricultural production to keep up with the demands of a growing population. There is also an insufficiency of skilled labor, whose recruitment and training have failed to keep pace with the rhythm of industrialization. There is an obsolete transportation system which, on the whole, has remained far behind the needs deriving from the continuous expansion of domestic and international markets.

Attempts to solve economic problems by governmental intervention have been frequent and thoroughgoing. There is no field of economic endeavor which has not felt, at one time or another, the effects of bureaucratic action intended to restrict or to encourage. As we shall see in a forthcoming section, the principle of *dirigismo*, as systematic governmental interference in economic matters is sometimes called, appears to be consistent with actual patterns of political behavior, as well as with a number of political doctrines recently imported from Europe.

Haphazard industrialization tends to produce social problems that particularly affect the working masses. The newly created industries had to rely on migrant labor from rural areas chronically afflicted with illiteracy, a low level of living, and endemic diseases. Rural-urban migration naturally transferred these problems to the new industrial centers where poor housing facilities, low wages, and ill-adapted working habits considerably aggravated the already existing problems. In order to promote the well-being of the working masses and to prevent political unrest, the National Confederation of Industries, which somewhat optimistically "seeks to improve the total environment in the whole country, to promote moral and civic betterment and the development of a spirit of solidarity among employees and employers".[25] Since a rise in the real wages of the workers was made particularly difficult by continued inflation, the Social Service of Industry was entrusted with the task to find a suitable solution to the wage predicament.

TOWARD THE WELFARE STATE

Preceding such spontaneous attempts to alleviate the situation of the workers, a certain amount of rather politically inspired social legislation was undertaken, a great deal of which was enacted between 1937 and 1946 and consequently without the sanction of a democratically elected parliament. There was hardly any aspect of labor relations which the government did not attempt to regularize. Old age and accident pensions for employees were established and collective bargaining contracts were recognized by constitutional provisions. The Constitution of 1946 itemizes the improvements which were to be bestowed upon the Brazilian worker. Such benefits as the eight-hour workday, minimum wages, participation in entrepreneurial profits by the workers, severe limitations to the employer's right to fire employees, free medical care and hospitalization, assistance to the unemployed, and the right to strike were made explicit and clearly reflect current European models.

Conciliation and judgment boards as well as arbitration committees for labor disputes were created by law. Most remarkable about these hasty attempts to accomplish in a few years what had taken a century of bitter social conflicts in Europe, is the fact that the working masses of Brazil had little, if any, initiative in the discussion and enactment of the numerous laws designed to protect them. The unions were effects rather than causes of these measures. They too were created by law and remained, at least in many instances, legal fictions.

Among the industrial workers predominate illiterate and ignorant rural migrants who are poorly prepared for concerted political action. Two factors have frequently been adduced to explain these "royal presents" with which the Brazilian workers were showered: demagoguery and the earnest desire to prevent political radicalism. At any rate, demagoguery and Communist infiltration have been successful in awakening a degree of class consciousness and in shaping labor parties, which have developed an increasing amount of political initiative. On the other hand, the employers were forced to give up their laissez-faire attitude and to join in associations whose power has been felt in recent political activities.

Prior to 1930 there were only 36 syndicates, 32 of employees, 3 of employers, and 13 of the liberal professions. In 1954 this number had increased to 2,172, of which 1,254 were syndicates of employers, 816 of employees, and 102 of liberal professions. In 1953, 807,442 employees, 84,146 employers, and 25,550 professionals belonged to syndicates.[26]

Little attempt has been made to measure the effectiveness of the Brazilian unions, yet according to current criticism it seems that legal encouragement is a poor substitute for spontaneous growth, and, frequently, unionized workers have shown no more capacity for utilizing their potential strength than their nonunionized colleagues. In numerous instances it has become rather obvious that syndicates are manipulated by the government and by ephemeral political parties with intentions which bear no relationship to the original objectives of the unions.

THE ROLE OF IMMIGRANTS

Abolition of slavery and the desire to create a population of small landholders, comparable to European peasants, induced Brazil to encourage foreign, particularly European, immigration.

Although intended to benefit the rural areas of the South, immigration had very definite effects upon the urbanization process. Among the 4,611,528 immigrants who entered Brazil between 1884 and 1954, there were many skilled laborers and technicians who contributed heavily to

545

the industrialization of the country. They were also bearers of economic attitudes that were relatively seldom encountered among the old Luso-Brazilian stock. As rural settlers they produced to sell rather than to subsist. As urban dwellers they tended to become entrepreneurs, willing to assume risks and to combine managerial skill with technical know-how.

The beginnings of industrialization are closely associated with Italian and German names. Even today the most important enterprises in São Paulo bear Italian and Syrian names. A sample taken in 1935 showed that out of 717 industrial establishments located in the state of São Paulo, 521 were owned by immigrants or descendants of immigrants.[27] Under the impact of a rapidly growing population and an almost continuous flow of new immigrants, small market places rapidly evolved into commercial and industrial centers of regional dominance. Workshops grew into factories, and retail businesses founded upon rather primitive forms of barter gradually emerged into wholesale establishments. At the same time a concentration of educational, religious, and recreational facilities occurred; and new administrative units were established which led to the integration of areas that hitherto had been almost unnoticed appendages of larger and loosely integrated political units.[28]

In contrast with the deep South, São Paulo found itself in the privileged position to add the entrepreneurship and the skills of its numerous immigrants to the wealth derived from coffee agriculture. Here state revenues were far higher than elsewhere, and during the last quarter of the nineteenth century the state government could afford to spend millions in subsidizing immigration from Europe. Between 1827 and 1939 2,439,490 immigrants entered São Paulo,[29] a figure which pushed this state far ahead of any other state of Brazil. São Paulo's dominant position in the international coffee market also provided the capital necessary to develop a railway system which no other state could possibly attain. Under such favorable conditions it is not surprising that foreign capital invested heavily in the development of the natural and human resources of São Paulo.

GROWTH AND DISTRIBUTION OF POPULATION

The population of Brazil has increased at a rate which appears to be considerably faster than, for example, that of the United States. Between 1900 and 1920 it gained 19 per cent, while that in the United States increased by 39 per cent. During the following two decades the population of Brazil grew by 35 per cent, that of the United States by 27 per cent.[30]

BRAZIL

Between 1940 and 1950 there has been a further gain of 25.99 per cent (from 41,236,315 in 1940 to 51,944,397 in 1950). Although the increase has affected every state of the union, the population has shown a growing tendency to concentrate in the South, a fact which reflects the general shift of economic dominance to this region. Comparison of population figures concerning the years of 1872 and 1950 reveal the changes which took place in the spatial distribution of the population. (See Table 1.)

The position of the South appears to be the more remarkable as its territory represents only 9.69 per cent of the country. A comparison of the

Table 1. Development of Population in the Five Geo-Economic Areas of Brazil

Area	1872		1950	
	Absolute Numbers	Per Cent	Absolute Numbers	Per Cent
North	322,847	3.29	1,883,325	3.58
Northeast	3,093,901	30.60	12,652,624	24.03
East	4,893,661	48.40	19,162,745	36.40
South	1,570,840	15.53	17,183,594	32.64
Central-west	20,812	2.18	1,763,191	3.35
Total	10,112,061	100.00	52,645,479	100.00

Table 2. Population of the South in Brazil

Year	Absolute Numbers	Percentage of National Population
1872............	1,570,840	15.53
1890............	2,815,468	10.64
1900............	4,078,774	23.55
1920............	8,129,335	26.54
1940............	12,915,621	31.32
1950............	17,183,594	32.64

Table 3. Number and Population of Cities with more than 5,000 Inhabitants in 1950

Number of Inhabitants	Number of Cities		Urban Population	
	1940	1950	1940	1950
5 to 10,000..........	165	263	1,136,063	1,834,338
10 to 50,000.........	119	181	2,052,653	3,741,308
50,000 to 100,000......	15	20	995,305	1,401,472
100,000 to 500,000.....	0	1	. . .	522,468
Over 500,000.........	2	2	3,040,482	4,377,647

547

results of six national censuses conveys a more detailed picture of the demography of the South. (See Table 2.)

Although Brazil appears to be one of the less urbanized countries in South America, the population living in communities with 5,000 and more inhabitants, as well as the number of such communities, underwent a remarkable increase. (See Table 3.)

Urbanization of the South is indicated by the fact that in 1950 out of 478 communities (according to census data) with 5,000 and more inhabitants, 198 or 41.4 per cent were situated in São Paulo, Paraná, Santa Catarina, and Rio Grande do Sul. Among these São Paulo ranks in the first place, with 120 or 25.1 per cent of the total.[31] Insofar as the Brazilian cities are to be considered as products of political factors, one may think of Davis' and Casis' characterization of the role of Latin-American capitals: "Since everything, including economic advantage, political patronage, and cultural support revolved about politics, the capitals became the national nerve-centers. It is therefore no accident that in every Latin-American country the largest city is also the capital."[32] This statement calls for qualifications so far as Brazil is concerned. It is true that Brazilian cities in general, and not only the capital, emerged as institutional nerve centers, but they did so in competition with and sometimes in opposition to the latifundia. This process, which began in the eighteenth century, is still continuing in some areas of Brazil.

Furthermore, of all Latin-American countries, Brazil is the least centralized, or, as one may say, the states and *municípios* have been given some leeway to develop their capitals and seats of administration into centers of political patronage and administrative bureaucracy. The union and the states at least have found ways of channelizing their revenues to the capital cities where they are largely translated into acquisitive power of a numerous administrative bureaucracy, and comparatively little is returned to the provincial and rural taxpayers in the way of public services, schools, hospitals, and the like. Between 1935 and 1951, from 42 to 49 per cent of all revenues of the federal government were spent to maintain a large bureaucracy and to pay for personal services. It seems noteworthy that in 1953 out of a total of 180,410 federal employees with civil-servant status, 119,185 or 66.1 per cent were residents of Rio de Janeiro.[33] Also the state capitals have increasingly become concentrations of bureaucrats, composed not only of public servants but also of those employed by the government-controlled institutes of social welfare.

Industrialization has been an additional, though rarely a determinant, factor in urbanization. Southern Brazil, however, possesses a number of small and middle-sized cities whose origin and growth are directly related to the foundation and expansion of industrial enterprises. But in many instances, mainly in the North and East, urbanization is unrelated to industrialization. "Between 1920 and 1940 the population of Brazil increased 36 per cent and the population of the 22 cities for which a 1920 figure is obtainable increased 61 per cent."[34] During the following decade the general population of the country increased by 25.99 per cent, while that of 22 capital cities gained 55.12 per cent. Although these figures suggest that Brazil has not remained exempt from the urbanization tendencies characteristic of Western civilization, it is still of predominantly rural character. According to the census data of 1950 only 22.6 per cent of its population live in communities with 5,000 or more inhabitants. Whatever ecological or social features, besides population figures, are selected as indices of urbanization, there is little doubt that their applicability to many towns of 5,000 or so is extremely limited.

The Political System

HISTORICAL PRECEDENTS

It is generally assumed that through the study of the constitution and other basic laws of a country, one may gain insight into the ways in which it is ruled. The written law is believed to reflect the existing power structure. This assumption, however, is limited by the awareness that there are always unauthorized forces of varying strength which seek to influence political decisions in a fashion which is neither defined nor necessarily approved of by the basic laws of the country.

In Brazil, as in most Latin-American countries, this lack of congruence between the legal and the factual aspects of political organization is so marked that any attempt to understand the latter by a study of the legal institutions alone would be apt to produce a rather distorted picture of the political reality. It has frequently been pointed out that the conflict between political organization as conceived by constitution-markers and as practiced by the people, owes its existence to the fact that the established social order was, and in part still is, incompatible with democratic government.

During the three centuries of colonial history large territories were granted in a feudal fashion, and soon a landed aristocracy developed, which was mainly based upon the exploitation of native or imported labor. In the sugar-plantation area of northeastern Brazil the size of the estates varied from eight to seventy or more square miles, and enslavement of African Negroes and Indians provided cheap and abundant labor. Life was centered in the extended family of the landlord, whose functions went far beyond those of economic control. During the sixteenth century the great landowners became local potentates who ruled over entire regions, maintained a large bodyguard, engaged in private warfare, and even assumed judicial functions. At that time, Portugal, one of the smallest European countries, tried to build one of the largest colonial empires of all times. Its attention and forces were concentrated on Africa, India, and Indonesia, rather than on Brazil.

Thus, political control, which the motherland sought to establish and maintain in her great American colony, was rather weak, especially in the interior portions of the country. Attacks and plunder by hostile Indian tribes, pirates, and runaway Negroes constantly threatened most of the settlements, but little protection could be offered by the colonial government. Small wonder, then, that under these conditions administration of justice was highly precarious. Favored by the vastness of the country and the lack of communications, offenders could easily avoid punishment. If a crime were committed against a member of the landholding upper class and the criminal belonged to a northern family of the same class, a bloody feud might ensue and last for several generations. The colonial history of Brazil is full of family feuds. As a matter of fact, retaliation became an institutionalized procedure maintained by tacit consent and sanctioned by practice. Very soon people learned that compliance with the law carried little, if any, reward, and that breaking the law did not necessarily involve punishment. However, they learned to respect the will of the local potentate, who was able to offer them protection and security which the colonial government failed to provide.

As in Spanish America, the estate was inherited, undivided, by the eldest son. Thus, new grants of land were sought for younger sons. The family was, of course, strongly interested in obtaining grants in the vicinity of the parental estate. In this way large areas were ruled by closely integrated kinship groups under the leadership of the eldest male. These kinship groups, often improperly called "clans," received additional strength from the rather pronounced tendency to choose one's mate from the circle of blood relatives. Uncle-niece, as well as cousin marriages, became extremely frequent in Portuguese America. The political role which these kinship groups have played in Brazil until the present time can hardly be overestimated.

Thus an institutional dualism developed, which has not been completely overcome in all regions of Brazil. On the one hand, there was a semifeudal organization based upon local oligarchies, and, on the other hand, a legal superstructure was erected, first, by the Portuguese crown, later on by the national governments of the country. During the nineteenth century, Brazilian statesmen endeavored to adjust existing power structures to legal constructions borrowed from Europe and North America. In the twentieth century, a change toward the opposite tendency has taken place: The republican governments have been trying to adjust the legal superstructure to the "social reality" of the country.

There are some fundamental facts concerning the political organization of the colonial society which must be kept in mind if an adequate understanding is to be attained. First of all, local self-government was either absent or organized along oligarchic lines. It is true that in contrast with Spanish-American townships, the *vereadores* (councilors) of the Brazilian municipal chambers were elected. Although this seems to be a democratic feature when taken at its face value, the municipal chambers were as solidly controlled by local oligarchies as in Spanish America. The right of voting was limited to the *homens bons*, a small minority consisting of immigrated Portuguese nobles and their descendants, plantation owners, wealthy merchants, and members of the civil and military bureaucracy. Their names were listed in the *Livro de Nobreza* (book of nobility) of the municipal chamber, and no one who had not been included in the book of nobility was allowed to vote or to be voted into office.[35]

It should be added that the municipal chambers were closely controlled by the almost arbitrary powers of the *capitão-mór*, the local representative of the Portuguese crown. Responsible only to the governor and viceroy, the local rule of the *capitão-mór* was often a source of oppression and terror. Thus, it seems important to keep in mind that the colonial heritage of Brazil certainly did not contain, in contrast to British America, the pattern of local self-government. Three hundred years of almost absolute rule implanted not only deep-rooted feudal loyalties but also the apparently contradictory pattern of rebellion and revolution.

Emancipation from Portuguese rule and the erection of a constitutional facade did not bring, as the more idealistic statesmen expected, much change to the existing power structures. Suffrage, which is believed to be the main conquest of the independent peoples of Latin America, came to perform a rather unexpected function instead. Under the previous colonial rule, the power of the oligarchies had been economic rather than political. Now the landed "aristocracy" took over political power, too. Relationships with the laboring class, which had been those of masters and slaves, sometimes characterized by paternalistic benevolence and reciprocal loyalty, now included the obligation of helping the master with the elections. Indeed, this became the main obligation of the peons, the sharecroppers, the tenant farmers, and the entire host of more or less parasitical elements which constituted the masses attached to the big house. Not only their votes were required, but any possible assistance they were able to give. They had to watch and spy on members of the rival group, they formed the armed bodyguard of their masters, they were expected to eliminate political enemies and to retaliate against any attack carried out against members of their own group. Thus, political obligations became definite, and relationships with the local potentates gained in precision. Transfer of the previous feudal loyalties to the new situation was easy and had long-lasting effects. People became accustomed to the idea that the vote did not express political conviction or interests on their side, but merely personal loyalty. One unquestioningly "owed" the vote to one's landlord or political chief. It was merely one more duty added to the previously existing ones.

On the other hand, suffrage was apt to quantify the personal power of the landlord and to provide a legal facade to his political ambitions. He was now a man with seventy, a hundred, or more votes. That meant he alone, or in association with some other groups, would be able to control or upset the local power balance. The votes "belonged" to him, and the voters were "his" men. The main social function of suffrage was that of *preserving the existing power structure*. Within the traditional patterns, suffrage added opportunities for displaying and reinforcing feudal loyalty. At the same time, it reinforced and legalized the political status of the landowner.

Despite all changes that have taken place, this is still the prevalent situation in most rural areas of Brazil. It has often been stated that ignorance, illiteracy, and economic dependence of the rural masses must be considered as the principal causes of their political "inertia." However, it should be emphasized that the pattern of personal loyalty to political leaders cuts across class lines and may be found in urban areas among middle- and upper-class people as well. During electoral campaigns, it is customary to "ask for votes." This request is usually supported by promises and more or less concealed pressure or menaces, according to the local pattern. If the candidate or his electioneers belong to the same kinship group (including ceremonial kinship), the person who is being asked can hardly refuse to "give" his vote. Otherwise, the supreme law of kinship solidarity would be violated. If the candidate is a friend or neighbor, refusal is equally felt to be difficult. Thus, people vote on behalf of kinship, friendship, or "good neighborliness," and political convictions and ideologies have little, if any, bearing upon one's choice. If class difference, though no actual dependence, is involved, a refusal becomes even more improbable, especially if one "owes a favor" to the candidate or his electioneers. It seems amazing to what extent personal loyalties influence political decisions, even under the rule of secret suffrage. It will be seen that recent political changes in the more urbanized and industrialized areas of Brazil must widely be interpreted in terms of an increasing disintegration of the traditional system of primary relationships upon which political organization was based.

POLITICAL CHANGES AND CLASS STRUCTURE

As long as the masses remained in semifeudal relationships to a few oligarchies who alternated in power, substantial changes of the existing political organization could scarcely occur. Attempts toward real democratization were necessarily conditioned on changes in the traditional class structure. As a matter of fact, these changes have actually taken place, not everywhere at the same time, or in the same way, or with the same intensity. But comparison of the present situation with that of half a century ago clearly shows that a new situation has emerged, which is most noticeable in the urbanized and industrialized areas of the South.

During the second half of the nineteenth century, the urban population of the country began to increase at a rate which has accelerated extraordinarily during the last decades. In some cases it has reached a rhythm comparable only to the growth of some North American cities in the late nineteenth century. The main outcome of urbanization lies in the fact that the political leaders have to cope with atomized masses of urban voters who can not be controlled by the paternalistic techniques of the past. And of course, on the national level no candidate can hope to win an election without support of the urban voters.

Since 1930, and especially since 1945, numerous political leaders have

553

realized that these masses of urban voters represent a rapidly growing potentiality that has to be included in political calculations. This realization has led to an apparently contradictory policy: On the one hand, demagoguery shifted in such a way as to make it attractive to the masses of wage earners. On the other hand, the government tried to establish and maintain tight control over the growing labor forces.

Following a trend whose foundations had been laid by the Constitution of 1934, dictator Getulio Vargas tried to build up his New State mainly upon the political support of urban wage earners, and one of the world's most advanced bodies of social legislation was enacted. When the New State was finally overthrown in 1945, his most loyal followers set up a nationwide labor party with a "mildly socialist" program. The dinner pail (*marmita*) became a kind of emblem of the new party, and its members proudly called themselves *marmiteiros* (carriers of dinner pails), in close parallelism with Juan Perón's *descamisados* (shirtless ones). Vargas was worshipped as the "father of the poor" and a national savior. The elections of 1945 already revealed the power of the new party, and in 1950 Vargas' farsighted labor policy paid off, for in spite of his dictatorial past, he was elected president of the Republic. However, more important than Vargas' victory was perhaps the fact that the candidate of the party in power suffered an annihilating defeat, gaining far fewer votes than any other opposition candidate.

If, on the one hand, the benefits of extremely advanced social laws were bestowed upon the masses of wage earners, the groups represented by the government, on the other hand, feared they might be unable to control the forces which they had been fostering. Thus, in order to prevent subversion of the established social order, trade unions were subjected to direct governmental control. The fact that most unions have been willing to accept state tutelage is by no means alien to Brazilian (and Latin-American) political patterns. To North Americans, it may appear strange that nonlabor governments readily embrace socialist tendencies of various brands, directed against the interests that they are supposed to represent. But the predominant pattern of Latin-American demagoguery shows that there is little concern with the idealogical content of political movements. Ambitious leaders are usually apt to embrace, as long and as far as convenient, any ideology, provided that substantial electoral gains are to be expected. This is the familiar pattern of personalism pushed to the uttermost extremes.

Nor is there any inconsistency in the attitude of the unions that accept state tutelage. In view of the feudal and paternalistic regime of the past, one can scarcely expect the masses to be able to carry anything through at their own initiative. On the contrary, there is a strongly pronounced tendency to expect everything from the government. From jobs, stable prices, credit, high wages, security, and transportation, to subsidies for charitable associations and those who wish to conduct carnival masquerades, there is hardly anything for which the government is not expected to provide. Thus, state tutelage for any kind of social institution is undoubtedly consistent with traditional Brazilian culture.

On the other hand, whatever role labor has played in the past decades, today it has become conscious of its political strength, and, in the more industrialized parts of the country it represents, at the time being, a power which has to be taken into account for any political decision of importance.

Another change in the political organization is closely connected with the relatively high rate of social mobility which characterizes rather large sections of Brazil. Italian, Portuguese, German, Japanese, Syrian, and Lebanese immigrants and their descendants—representing economic and political traditions, skills and interests different from those of the landowning native elites—went, to a very great extent, into industry, business, and professional activities. In the more urbanized and industrialized areas, the formerly small middle classes have become much stronger, and a new upper class of wealthy industrialists, bankers, and businessmen emerged who have successfully challenged the political monopoly of the old elites.

To break the sway which the ruling oligarchies held over the masses, such innovations as the secret ballot and the *justiça eleitoral* (electoral justice) were introduced. Voting came to be considered as a duty rather than a right of all citizens, and its extension to women substantially increased the masses of voters. The *justiça eleitoral* exerted the expected effect of giving morality to electoral practices, which prior to 1930 had been reputedly dishonest. Thus a legal basis for mass participation was provided, which offered many advantages to the emerging political elite. Of course, the most effective weapon in the hands of the new leaders—many of whom were branded as "unscrupulous adventurers" by the defeated elites—was the type of social legislation which has already been discussed. It ought to be emphasized that the power of the new elites is structurally and functionally interrelated with the political role of the working masses, but obviously the

555

stability of political interclass relationship rests upon a careful balancing of radicalism and conservativism in national politics.

A socialist labor program would in all likelihood have alienated the sympathies of the industrial middle and upper classes. In order to avoid this dangerous cleavage, the new political elites cautiously limit their anticapitalistic demagoguery to protests and measures taken against the operations of foreign industrial and business groups. In compensation for certain "sacrifices" imposed by the new social legislation upon native and foreign enterprises alike, national capitalism has strongly been supported against foreign capitalism. Compensation has further been provided by sudden changes from radical prolabor and anticapitalistic policies to rather conservative attitudes, indifferent or hostile to labor movements and more friendly with regard to foreign capital.

STATE TUTELAGE

It has been said that state tutelage is consistent with traditional patterns of Brazilian culture. The concept of government as the universal provider has laid solid foundations for state tutelage and state intervention, almost undisturbed by reactions of the kind which the same issue has aroused in the United States and the liberal countries of Europe.

However, there are at least two more independent variables that have probably strengthened the existing tendencies toward state tutelage. Intervention of the government in the economic sphere has been made, to a large extent, in the name of nationalism. The "nationalization" of railroads, power plants, streetcar companies, and airlines, the founding of steel mills and other industries with capital furnished and controlled by the government, the stabilization and control of prices by government agencies, as well as distribution of loans by public financing institutes, have received strong support from public opinion. It is felt to be the government's duty to protect the national economy against misfortunes of all imaginable kinds, especially against the "exploitation of colonial imperialism."

In addition to economic nationalism, there is an extremely pronounced tendency toward bureaucratization, which from the standpoint of sound fiscal policy seems to be out of proportion, at least in comparison with the United States. The main reason probably lies in the fact that the political parties seek to attract voters by generous promises of jobs. At least a certain percentage of promises must be fulfilled if the winning party wishes to survive its term. Since dismissal of civil servants seems to be at variance with the Brazilian concept of humanitarianism, the bureaucratic bodies have shown strongly pronounced symptoms of hypertrophy. This tendency toward bureaucratic expansion, inherent in the electoral mechanism, seems to converge with the extension of state tutelage. Each new government agency serves two purposes: it provides jobs for party members and expands the area of government control.

State tutelage has produced a varying number of institutions that are mostly concerned with economic activities. Labor control and protection have already been mentioned.

The recently eliminated *Departamento Nacional do Cafe* (National Coffee Department), established in 1933, acquired and burnt, during the years of "overproduction," part of the coffee output. This procedure was financed by means of a special tax which the Department levied on exported coffee.

The *Conselho Nacional de Petroleo* (National Petroleum Board), founded in 1938, controls import and export of all petroleum products as well as the exploitation of deposits. Prices of gasoline, kerosene, and mineral oil are dictated by the *Conselho*.

Various control functions are performed by the *Instituto do Açucar e do Alcool* (Institute of Sugar and Alcohol), *Instituto do Cacau* (Institute of Cocoa), *Instituto Nacional do Mate* (National Institute of Mate), *Instituto Nacional do Pinho* (National Institute of Pine Lumber), *Instituto Nacional do Sal* (National Institute of Salt), and the *Conselho Nacional de Immigração e Colonização* (National Board of Immigration and Colonization). In 1941 the Brazilian government and a few semigovernmental institutions subscribed the whole issue of preferred stock of the *Companhia Siderúrgica Nacional* (National Steel Company).

Governmental agencies consistently try to prevent "ruinous" competition among industrial and agricultural producers. Thus minimum prices are established, areas of cultivation are limited, and importation of new machinery is restricted for industries judged to be in overproduction. For example, restrictions have been applied to certain types of machinery in the hat, match, paper, shoe, sugar, and textile industries.

It ought to be emphasized that in many cases these restrictions do not derive from integrated plans intended to establish a "planned economy," but they represent victories of powerful pressure groups. There are rather strong indications that competition, economic and otherwise, has never been fully accepted in Brazil. The concept of free competition as a regulator of economic health does not appeal to Brazilians. If prices go down in a certain branch of economic activity, the producers are likely to put pressure on the government, and a "Commissariat," "Board," "Junta," or "Institute" is established with the ultimate function to eliminate or restrict competition. If the competitors are foreigners, the policy is immediately sanctioned by public opinion. This trend is particularly pronounced in the professions. Alien doctors, lawyers, dentists, engineers and pharmacists are not allowed to compete with natives. Exclusion and discrimination are effective economic weapons.

State tutelage, as it has developed in Latin America, is often interpreted in terms of socialism or fascism. Although certain similarities may be intended and do undoubtedly exist, these words carry Old-World connotations which, to a large extent, fail to apply to Brazil. The following facts militate against such interpretations:

The cornerstone of a socialistic regime is a strongly integrated party with a consistent political philosophy. Despite countless attempts, this type of party has never grown roots in Brazilian culture. The survival of the Communist party is probably due to the steel grip of the Cominform. The restlessness and volubility of the masses have been a matter of constant concern to the Communist leaders.

Although the personalistic features of fascist parties may be more consistent with the political traditions of the continent, fascist discipline, on the other hand, certainly does not appeal to Brazilians. From this standpoint, the *Açao Integralista Brasileira* must be regarded as a significant experiment. Its political doctrine was a congeries of traits mostly borrowed from fascist Italy and Portugal. Attempts were made to achieve a maximum adjustment to Brazilian "reality." The outcome was a political party with far over one million members under the romantic and sentimental leadership of Plinio Salgado. The official doctrine was centered in the concept of the corporate state, and to such an extent permeated with religious ideas that it became almost mystical. Despite the large number of militant members, this counterfeit of European models just lacked the kind of discipline that reduces the individual to an integral part of the mass, and achieves a maximum of cohesion and capacity for concerted action. The *Açao Integralista Brasileira* failed to act when the opportunity for action had come, and when finally revolution was attempted, defection had taken place to such a degree that nothing could be accomplished.

THE STRUCTURE OF BRAZILIAN POLITICAL PARTIES

The traditional party system of Brazil grew out of the semifeudal relationships between the landholding oligarchies and the masses. Most parties have been of the personalistic or "patronage" type, in contrast with doctrinal and class parties. With a few exceptions, the parties have merely sought high political posts for the leaders and administrative jobs for their "staff," without much consideration for political programs and doctrines.

On the whole, party organization is extremely loose, and though wealthier members are expected to contribute funds to sustain electoral campaigns, no dues are levied and no rigid membership rules exist.

Traditionally, the parties moved within a dichotomous system: Originally, a liberal party was opposed to a conservative one. The conservative party centered around the interests of the big landowners, while the liberal parties were mainly supported by the urban middle and upper classes. As the liberal parties opposed the oligarchical rule of the landlords, they were held to be more interested in true democracy. Although in some aspects this historical dichotomy is still visible, many changes took place that have resulted in more complex figurations. Transition from a semifeudal, two-class structure toward a more differentiated, industrialized, and urbanized society has not only produced a larger number of political parties, but a more pronounced instability as well. Almost every electoral campaign produces new parties whose designations usually reflect recent political developments in European countries. "Liberal," "democratic," "socialist," "national," "radical," "conservative," "*frente popular*," and all conceivable combinations of these words have largely been used in recent years, but the actual party programs are very much alike, and the underlying political philosophy is still personalistic.

A really significant change, however, has occurred so far as relationships between political parties and social classes are concerned. The traditional Brazilian parties cut across class lines, which means that each party recruited its members from all the existing classes. This is exactly the type of organization which would be expected from a semifeudal society wherein the lower classes owe allegiance to the landholding elites. With the emergence of labor movements, a structural change of utmost importance began. Instead of being absorbed by the existing parties, as in the United States, the labor movements largely crystallized in labor parties with more or less pronounced socialistic programs. To what extent this development has been determined by competition with rather strong

Communist groups still remains to be investigated. Thus a new type of political party, the class party, emerged, mostly under the impact of ambitious leadership and official demagoguery, but certainly favored by the growing political and economic unrest of the urban masses.

The receptiveness of the urban populations to this kind of party structure is clearly demonstrated by recent Brazilian elections. In 1946, for instance, the largest number of voters was concentrated in two parties, the *Partido Social Democrático* and the *União Democratica Nacional*. Although both parties belonged to the traditional "vertical" type of structure, the propaganda of the PSD was shrewdly directed in such a way that many voters were led to believe in a fundamental class difference between the two parties. The UDN was said to serve the interest of the *granfinos* (slang expression meaning upper-class people), while the PSD was pictured as the people's party. A survey carried out in São Paulo City after the elections showed that in the middle- and upper-class sections of the city, most people had actually voted for the UDN, while the majority of the PSD voters were located in the lower middle- and lower-class sections of the city.

It must be emphasized, however, that the emerging class party still preserves essential features of the patronage party type. Even the Moscow-controlled Communist party, with its rigid discipline, has indulged in compromise with the prevailing personalistic trends in Brazilian political life. The outlawed Communist party, one of the strongest of Latin America, has largely been a one-man show. Its great appeal is mainly based upon the personal prestige of Carlos Luis Prestes, a former army officer with a legendary past and a Caudillo-like personality. His cognomen, *Cavaleiro da Esperança* (Knight of the Hope), as well as the generous amount of hero worship which the masses have paid to him, brings Prestes close to the role of a charismatic leader.

THE CONSTITUTIONAL SETUP

The foremost characteristic of the Brazilian as well as of most Latin-American constitutions is perhaps the concentration of power in the hands of the president. In this particular aspect the legal provisions come close to the actual power structure, despite that fact that the president is elected by the people (for a five-year term). Actually, it is impossible to tell the presidential powers by the existing legal provisions. Customary procedures tend to encroach, with more or less success, upon the constitutional setup, and, as a consequence, the real power of the president is usually greater than the Constitution leads one to believe. This may be considered as a genuine expression of Caudillism, which seems to hold it own despite legal restrictions.

Special mention should be made of those constitutional provisions which limit democracy and positively sanction, at least temporarily, dictatorship. Most of these provisions refer to the *estado de sítio* (state of siege) which allows the president to set aside the guarantees of the Constitution and to run the country in a dictatorial fashion. According to the Constitution of 1946, the state of siege must be limited to certain areas and cannot be decreed more than twice for consecutive periods of thirty days each. The president is obliged to submit the reasons for this measure to the Congress, and Congress is allowed to revoke or to extend the duration of the state of siege.

Even with these limitations, the powers of the president are still extraordinarily great. During the state of siege, he is entitled to force individuals to stay in certain localities, to arrest and to exile persons, although common penitentiaries and unhealthy and uninhabited sites of the country must not be used for the purpose of detention or exile. The president is further allowed to decree censorship upon mail, publicity, radio, and theatres; he may suspend the right of assembly and decree police searches and confiscation in private homes; he is finally entitled to suspend public servants as well as employees of public utility companies and to intervene in the control of these enterprises.

It should be added that the Brazilian Constitution is one of the more moderate documents wherein the powers of the president have been far more restricted than, for example, in Mexico, Argentina, Peru, and Bolivia.

Congress is composed of two chambers, and its members are chosen by the people. Deputies serve four years, senators eight years. So far as electoral procedures are concerned, it should be added that the institution of primary elections is unknown in Brazil. On the whole, the members of a party have little, if any, influence upon the nomination of candidates. As a rule, the parties are run by a small group of leaders who are believed to "control" varying numbers of voters.

So far as electoral participation of the people is concerned significant changes have taken place since 1930. In sharpest contrast with previous practices, all prospective voters were subjected to a careful though cumbersome screening process in order to prevent frauds. When the elections to the *Assembléia Nacional Constituinte* took place in 1933, only 1,466,700 voters had been recruited, but this figure rose to 2,659,171 in 1934 when the new Congress was elected. After a period of dictatorial rule, a new government was chosen in 1945, with an enrollment of 7,459,849 voters. Five years later, the total of enlisted voters came to 11,449,532, and in 1954 it reached 15,104,604 voters.[36]

Voting participation of the enlisted electorate fluctuated between 83.12 per cent in 1945 and 65.21 per cent in 1954. Although the recruitment of voters is still restricted by a literacy test and various ecological factors, an electoral pattern has emerged since 1933 which is a far cry from the way in which political democracy was practiced prior to 1930.

In the political history of Brazil, phases of centralization have alternated with phases of decentralization. The Constitution of 1891 substituted the provinces for autonomous states, each with its own elected governor and legislative body. The state government has preserved the right to levy numerous taxes, and to keep a military police which, in the larger states, more than once played the role of state armies fighting against the federal government. Before the revolution of 1932, the military police of São Paulo were equipped with artillery and even maintained a small air force. The New State again brought tight centralization, which ceased only in 1945. By the Constitution of 1946, however, the military police were incorporated in the national army as auxiliary forces. Federal intervention in state affairs is permitted by the Constitution, but has very seldom been carried out except in dictatorial phases.

The *município* (county) has been given a fairly large degree of autonomy. Mayor and council are elected by the people. The state government is allowed to interfere with county affairs only in case of insolvency. The *município* not only may levy taxes, but the national government is obliged to refund a considerable percentage of certain federal taxes to the local administration. While the *município* is permitted to play a considerable role in school affairs, police and the administration of justice are under the exclusive control of the state government, and the *município* is not permitted to frame its own character.

There is a growing awareness that the *municípios* should be allotted a larger share of autonomy. Although the extent to which the Constitution of 1946 provided for municipal self-government is much more liberal than ever before in the history of the country, the past decade has witnessed an organized movement named *Municipalismo* which seems to reflect the need for further decentralization. *"Municipalismo,"* one of its leaders emphasized, "is an expression of cultural federalism or regionalism which should be one of the objectives of cultural policy and democracy in Brazil. Thus, *Municipalismo* should strive on a plane parallel to that of the educational system, for a change of the pattern of ideas, in such a way as to exalt legitimate local values without lowering the receptivity for alien values which may be adapted to and integrated with local experience, in order to improve the material and cultural standards of its life."[37]

The Structure of the Family

THE STEREOTYPE

Students of Brazilian social history have emphasized the family of the landed upper class to an extent which seems inversely proportional to its numerical importance. So far as the present situation is concerned our own findings strongly suggest that the family of the lower rural class is, in many respects, different from that of all other social classes. Indeed, these differences are more pronounced than most students would expect to find in a social stratum which is supposed to participate in the same general culture.

There is a similar blindness for class differences in numerous travel accounts of Americans and Europeans who wrote on the Latin-American family. As their contacts were usually limited to the middle and upper classes, the family of these strata was held to be the prevailing type. The picture which emerges from these descriptions may be summarized as follows:

Courtship is strictly controlled by the family, which shows a corporative concern for the conduct of its members. The rules of chaperonage prevent young men and women from becoming reasonably well acquainted with each other. After marriage, the role of the dominant and authoritarian father is taken over by the husband. Married women are expected to become devoted mothers and housekeepers rather than companions of their husbands. Watched by zealous parents or jealous spouses, Brazilian women are supposed to adjust themselves to their domestic role and to limit their outdoor activities to worship in church. Men are allowed all the liberties they can possibly desire. The so-called double standard of sex morals makes premarital and adulterous sexual intercourse socially acceptable when practiced by males, but unpardonable and socially stigmatizing when practiced by females. Even distant relatives are united by a strong feeling of solidarity which characterizes the Brazilian family as an extended consanguinity rather than a conjugal group.

There is little doubt that some aspects of this conventional picture have been affected by changes. Of course, changes have occasionally been pointed out, but little is known about their structural and functional relevance. Despite factors like urbanization and industrialization—which are eating away institutional arrangements complementary or peripheral to the family, like courtship and chaperonage, and which have made inroads into the network of intrafamily relationship as well—certain values and attitudes show a surprisingly strong resistance to change.

THE UPPER- AND MIDDLE-CLASS FAMILY

The upper- and middle-class family of Brazil may be interpreted as a dialectic structure based upon asymmetric roles ascribed to males and females. The female role is centered in a cluster of values which may be characterized as a virginity complex. The belief that the virginity of unmarried females ought to be preserved at any cost has so far tenaciously resisted change. Such institutional arrangements as segregation of the sexes, chaperonage, and family-controlled courtship, which are to be regarded as component traits of the virginity complex, have undergone so many changes, at least in the larger cities of Brazil, that the original pattern is hardly recognizable. However, under the somewhat deceiving appearance of changing intersexual relationships and vanishing family controls, the old rule that females should abstain from premarital sexual experiences has been rigidly maintained. Carefully conducted interviews carried out over a period of nearly twelve years showed that even the most liberal-minded men were apt to become suddenly intransigent if asked what they thought of the prospect of marrying somebody with premarital sexual experience. Most men feel they would make fools of themselves if they married a girl who had been "deflowered" by somebody else. There is not the slightest indication that the traditional sanctions against girls who are known to have lost, or are suspected of having lost, their virginity have changed in the social classes under scrutiny. Men either avoid such a marriage or, if they unknowingly marry a deflowered girl, they probably break up the marriage as soon as they find out about the physical condition of the bride. This sanction is supported by a provision of the Civil Code stipulating that in such cases marriage may be adjudged void.[38] Once the chances for marriage have vanished, a woman may choose between the dreaded life of a spinster attached to some relative's household and concubinage or prostitution. Traditionally, there was nothing in between those highly undesirable prospects, but modern city life has produced a wide gamut of intermediate ways in which work and concubinage, or more or less casual erotic adventures, are combined.

An attempt to adjust slowly changing ideas about sex to the iron rule of tradition may be seen in the not infrequent practice of "restoring" virginity by a surgical operation. Thus, at least what may be called the anatomic chance for marriage is thought to have been recovered.

Despite the fact that women may now choose among many different occupational prospects, there are as yet very few career women in Brazil. Those who study or work are apt to regard this as an interlude which by no means is thought of as precluding or even postponing marriage. Consequently, adjustments to changing social conditions are made in such a way as to avoid forms of behavior which might possibly spoil or reduce the chances for marriage. Under the closest scrutiny of an androcentric society, under the pressure of gossip and slanderous interpretation of inadvertent actions, the Brazilian girl is forced to protect her reputation under conditions which make efficient protection increasingly difficult. Small wonder then that wherever women appear in public they tend to stick together, to form at least groups of two or three and to avoid places and hours which may cast suspicion on their behavior. Dating in the American sense of the term, which in Gorer's opinion "is almost by definition promiscuous," has little chance of being adopted by Brazilian girls. To be seen in the company of different men, and under circumstances suggesting intimacy, would be extremely damaging to a girl's reputation.

As it is now practiced in the larger cities of Brazil, dating is rather "monogamous" and noncompetitive. Obviously it does not serve the selective function that has been attributed to it in the United States. The male companion is not supposed to assume definite obligations toward the girl as long as he does not visit her parent's home. Unchaperoned dates of this kind are increasingly tolerated by urban parents, but single dates are still frowned upon and usually concealed from the girl's family. Antagonism and conflict between parents and children are frequently accommodated by gradual and, perhaps, unconscious compliance of the parents, so that in families with a number of female offspring, courtship behavior of the younger daughters follows patterns divergent from those that had been permitted to the elder ones.

It should be added that fathers and brothers have by no means relinquished their traditional role of avengers who are expected to react if the honor of a daughter or a sister has been polluted. Immigration from Portugal, Spain, and southern Italy, where similar patterns exist, has contributed to reinforce attitudes toward female virginity.

To the Brazilian woman, marriage does not mean relief from premarital restrictions. It is probably true that in larger cities married women even lose some of the liberties they may have enjoyed before marriage. The same setup of control and sanctions, which ought to be considered as an integral part of the virginity complex, continues to be operative in the life of a married woman. Exactly as before marriage, her sexual behavior is strictly controlled. She must refrain from anything that, from the standpoint of a jealous husband, may be interpreted as an interference with the sexual monopoly he holds. In other words, she must strictly avoid all those situations in which a man could find opportunity to make advances to her if he wanted to. Such rules of avoidance led to the development of an elaborate social ritual which cannot be discussed here. Sanctions against female unfaithfulness are comparable to those which punish premarital sex experiences. If caught *flagrante delicto* the lovers may be put to death or severely beaten by the enraged husband, who is supposed to fall into an emotional seizure that relieves him of legal responsibility. At any rate, if the wife survives being caught *in flagrante*, actual and legal separation is the almost inevitable consequence. As there is no divorce in Brazil, the woman cannot remarry, but the husband may, without damaging his reputation, take a concubine. A man who does not make use of these radical measures is likely to lose his standing in the male society. The designation *corno manso* (cuckold), one of the worst insults, may be attached to him.

A new pattern is now emerging, which, in the long run, may defeat the principle of indissolubility of the matrimonial bond as stipulated by the Constitution of Brazil. This innovation is called *casamento no Uruguay* (marriage in Uruguay), and is based on the erroneous assumption that in this country legal divorce may be easily obtained by foreigners. Nowadays well-to-do couples who wish to get "remarried" go to Montevideo, and from there they announce their pseudo marriage to relatives and friends. Although there is still much opposition to this kind of "marriage," a steadily increasing number of cases may be observed in which supposedly divorced and remarried couples enjoy a status hardly distinguishable from that of truly married persons.

Up to this point it has already become clear that the role of the Brazilian male is antithetic to that of the female. His is a markedly androcentric society, which encourages almost everything denied to women. The male role is centered in a set of values which may properly be called a virility complex. A young Brazilian is expected to get actively interested in sex at the age of puberty. Even before puberty the average boy becomes used to the sexual bravado of older companions. He learns that regular sexual intercourse is not only believed to be physically healthy, but above all an essential attribute of manhood. There is a generally accepted opinion that early and frequent sexual intercourse is stimulated by peculiar racial qualities and the physiological effects of a tropical climate. This point of view, which is presumed to be scientific, entitles men to feel irresponsible in sex affairs. Marriage is not expected to channelize or to restrict his sexual activities. Normally a male feels free to have intercourse with as many different women as may be available.

Interestingly enough, this pattern has not yet been eradicated or even weakened by the Catholic Church, which of course seeks to substitute the ideal pattern of Christian chastity. Male chastity is not only ridiculed but is also looked upon as possible evidence of impotence. It is not surprising, therefore, that the Brazilian male learns to build up his self-esteem largely in terms of sexual prowess. Erotic adventures obviously perform the function of bolstering up his ego. Obviously, institutionalized prostitution becomes an indispensable corollary to a social order wherein males are encouraged to indulge in promiscuous sexual relationships and respectable females are expected to accept severe restrictions regarding their association with men. An inquiry into prostitution, as practiced in Brazil, would probably show that some of its most peculiar aspects are closely tied in with the two culture complexes under scrutiny. This does not imply that prostitution is more extensively practiced than in other occidental societies. Gorer's statement that in the United States the clients of prostitutes "come predominantly from older men" does not apply to Brazil, where the brothel plays an important role in the sexual initiation (*desemburrar*) of young men.

At first glance it may seem improbable that these antithetic roles, which largely determine husband-wife, father-daughter, and brother-sister relationships, should be integrated into such a closely knit group as the Brazilian family. Actually these roles are adjusted to each other with a minimum of friction or conflict. There is a strict separation between the sex-ridden, overbearing, and irresponsible Brazilian male as he likes to appear to his companions outside his home, and the devoted father and provider as he appears to the members of his family. Typically, Brazilian men have a highly developed sense of honor and respectability with regard to their families, and they endeavor to bring up their children in accordance with the austere rules of tradition. Thus, whatever his conduct outside the family, a Brazilian husband and father is apt to assume his role of guardian of strict morality toward his family. On the other hand, his family, especially his wife, ignores or pretends to ignore his escapades. There is a strong tendency not to take "these things" too seriously as long as they do not interfere with a man's role as provider and father. From numerous inquiries and interviews we gathered that, with relatively few exceptions, unmarried women showed little concern for the occasional unfaithfulness of their future spouses. Most of them did object, however, to their husbands' taking mistresses.

This attitude ought to be interpreted in the light of the different expectations that characterize a woman's approach to marriage and family. Despite the increasing importance of the romantic love pattern, she still seems to be primarily interested in acceding to the desirable status of married woman and mother. This attitude is undoubtedly an integral part of a distinct female culture with its own institutions, emotional patterns, and compensations. Male and female culture, if they are as divergent from each other as in Brazil, prevent the very kind of intimate association between spouses that is usually expected in the United States. In doing so they perform the function of maintaining a cultural and social distance between spouses, the breakdown of which would probably lead to an increase of friction and conflict within the family. It may be said that, other things being equal, domestic consensus could hardly be achieved if male and female members of the Brazilian family did not participate in divergent culture spheres.

Although urbanization and industrialization have so far been unable to change the antithetic positions of the sexes, peripheral changes in the family structure have been numerous. Under increasing economic pressure many middle-class husbands do not object any more to their wives' holding other than teaching jobs, and unmarried daughters are not only allowed, but in most cases are even expected, to work. There is little doubt that these changes relieve fathers and brothers of a great deal of their former controls, but hasty conclusions should not be drawn as to the freedom Brazilian women are supposed to enjoy, or as to their desire to enjoy the degree of freedom which is taken for granted elsewhere.

To what degree is the Brazilian family still an extended family? If the term is taken in the sense of joint residence, it must be said that, except for the *famille-souche* type, the extended family is rapidly disappearing. However, in the sense of solidary groups of related nuclear families residing in the same locality, the extended family is far from being extinct. Despite huge internal migrations and what might be called atomistic aggregation of migrants in urban centers, existing family ties are frequently strong enough to resist even the diluting influences of metropolitan centers like São Paulo and Rio de Janeiro. Residents of São Paulo City who could be interviewed were able to distinguish between thirty and five hundred relatives, a considerable part of whom lived in the same city. It is taken for granted that one may expect protection and aid even from distant "cousins" whom one may never have met before. In the cities of northeastern Brazil, a young relative from the interior may suddenly come to visit his uncle and stay for several years. During that time, the uncle is expected to feed him and take care of his education.

The fact that in southern Brazil hardly anybody would expect this kind of aid from relatives other than his own parents indicates regional differences that are not necessarily those between city and rural areas. However, there are forms of aid and protection that, in any part of Brazil, may reasonably be expected from a relative. Individuals holding an important job are likely to become employment agencies for their kinfolk. Large kinship groups are extremely valuable to those who are running for office; in such cases electoral support is taken for granted.

The Brazilian family, like the family in other Latin-American countries, is "extended" in still another sense. Ceremonial kinship, or godparenthood, actually creates rights and obligations very similar to those which characterize true blood relationships. However, ceremonial kinship does not merely run parallel to consanguine relationship. Parents and godparents assume comparable obligations toward a child as well as toward each other. The ceremonial kinship terms they use in addressing one another (*compadre, comadre*), which have no equivalent in English, do describe a social relationship close to that between siblings. Baptismal cosponsors are not supposed to marry each other, and Brazilian folk beliefs know of drastic supernatural sanctions supposedly inflicted upon those who break this incest taboo.

Kinship solidarity brings us to the question whether the Brazilian family has preserved the multifunctional character which social historians have attributed to it. It seems rather obvious that the functions of mutual aid and protection extended to a far larger number of relatives than, for example, in the family of the United States and northern Europe. On the other hand, the functional significance of the contemporary Brazilian family has certainly shrunk when compared with the traditional plantation family of the early nineteenth century. So far as the present situation is concerned, there seems to be a close correlation between functional significance and the extent to which the structural characteristics of an extended family type have been retained. The aforementioned regional variations also apply to the functional aspects.

THE LOWER-CLASS FAMILY

In the light of the rather limited information available, the structure of the lower-class family seems to be quite different.

There is hardly anything to which the term courtship may properly be applied. After a young man has achieved some understanding with a girl, he seeks to obtain the consent of his prospective father-in-law, which is rarely denied. As there are no property arrangements to be made, marriage follows immediately. Most girls marry at an age which varies between 14 and 17. As to the form of marriage, the church ceremony certainly is the preferential pattern; but in localities that are seldom visited by Catholic priests, people are quite tolerant with regard to common-law marriages. Civil marriage, however, is not only expensive but meaningless as well. This attitude toward civil marriage has doubtlessly historical roots. During the Empire (1822–89) the religious marriage ceremony performed in a Catholic church by an ordained priest was not only legally recognized but also the only form of marriage with religious and legal effects. Separation of church and state led to a distinct, civil marriage procedure. Since then, the religious marriage ceremony has been regarded as the act by which social and supernatural sanctions may be obtained, while the civil procedure has been accepted as an indispensable legal formality, chiefly by the middle and upper classes. To lower-class rural people, however, who do not have to worry about property and inheritance, the civil procedure adds nothing to the religious sanction, except fees.

Recently, separation between civil and ecclesiastical marriage has been somewhat reduced by a law providing for ecclesiastical marriage with legal effects. Prior to the church ceremony a legal document may be obtained which states that the marriage will be performed in such and such a church by such and such a priest. Otherwise the separation persists. Children whose parents are not married according to canon law are illegitimate in the eyes of the Church. And those whose parents are married only according to canon law are illegitimate so far as the legal authorities are concerned. Thus official data on illegitimacy are misleading. However, by legally recognizing their "illegitimate" offspring, parents are allowed to equalize the status of their children with those born out of a legal marriage.

Among the rural and urban lower classes there seems to be no perceptible discrimination between sexually inexperienced women and those who have previously indulged in sexual intercourse. Thus female virginity is not regarded as a prerequisite for a stable union, and consequently the rules of chaperonage and segregation of sexes are far less elaborate.

Jealousy and violent retaliation following female unfaithfulness are relatively nonexistent. A different concept of personal and family honor sharply contrasts with the pattern predominant in other classes.

Marriage is relatively unstable. The initiative in breaking up matrimonial ties is often taken by the woman who, as a rule, does not find it particularly difficult to associate with another man. Larger kinship groups, aside from the extended family, are not felt to be a particularly desirable pattern. Especially in the coastal community there is little of the solidarity that characterized the upper-class family described above.

These facts suggest that the lower-class family of rural Brazil lacks most of the characteristics that are of structural and functional significance in the middle and upper classes. The looseness of its structure is probably conditioned by the fact that there is no easily distinguishable cultural focus in the corresponding class culture. The middle- and upper-class family grew strong on the plantation, the development and defense of which have been that family's main concern. But there was nothing for the peon family to concentrate upon—no property, no specific institutions of any kind that might have acted as centers of a more integrated family structure. The absence of a definite culture focus is reflected by an astonishing degree of aimless shifting in space, which in turn reinforces the existing instability. These people sometimes remind the observer of detribalized Indians whose life has lost its *raison d'être*.

CHILD TRAINING

By European standards parents are overindulgent toward their infant children, and there is hardly any attempt to enforce a rigid discipline. Usually infant training follows the patterns of traditional lore rather than the standards of modern psychology and medicine. Parents seeking advice of social workers and physicians still constitute a small minority. In fact, where scientific facilities are available, it has been rather a problem to induce the parents to utilize them.

The tightly knit extended family of the upper strata must of course be considered as a far more effective training agency than the somewhat amorphous, loosely integrated family of the lower classes. In the middle and upper classes the child is not only trained *by* the family but also predominantly *for* the family. Very early it receives the indelible family stamp and learns to think in terms of family relationships. That particular way of life, which has been named youth culture, and which consists of a peculiar mixture of irresponsible play and responsible learning, must still be considered largely as a privilege of the middle and upper strata. In the lower classes, however, emphasis is laid on early breadwinning, and youth culture remains conspicuously absent, especially among the rural populations where the social status of the youth, boy or girl, is measured by his or her capacity of performing the normal task of an adult.

THE BRAZILIAN AND THE AMERICAN FAMILY

Some of the structural differences between the American and the Brazilian family do not need to be pointed out, especially those that refer to the antithetic positions of spouses. The structural isolation of the nuclear family in the United States contrasts with the structural integration of the nuclear family in Brazil, but increasing ecological isolation of the Brazilian nuclear family may eventually lead toward structural and functional isolation.

From the standpoint of the individual, structural integration of course means that one is never drastically separated from his family of orientation. Loyalty to one's spouse does not necessarily precede the loyalty that one owes to his family of orientation. The present phase of transition is reflected by a great deal of compromise and conflict. In many cases we found that mother-daughter relationships were emotionally more gratifying to young women than the relationships with their husbands.

Furthermore, emphasis on family ties is reflected by the Brazilian law of inheritance. There is no complete testamentary freedom as in the United States. By law, descendants or ascendants inherit half of the property.[39] Talcott Parsons' statement as to the "relative weakness of pressure to leave all or even most property to kin" ought to be inverted with regard to Brazil.[40]

As in the United States, the family is a multilineal structure, but in contrast to the United States, inheritance of the family name is not patrilineal in Brazil. As a rule, a child is given the names of his father and mother, and in traditional-minded upper-class families the names of maternal grandparents may be added to one's family name.

Finally, a major difference bears upon the position of the family in the sociocultural system of the two countries. The Brazilian system, as that of Latin America in general, is largely family-ridden. There is probably not a single major institution in Brazil that is not to a considerable extent controlled or deflected by family interests. It is true that in areas of heavy foreign immigration, the position of family oligarchies was not strong enough to prevent the rise of a new economic and political elite, but it also is true that the new elite has adopted the same patterns of familism and nepotism that characterized the traditional power structure.

Religious Institutions

BASIC HISTORICAL FACTS

Colonial Brazil was characterized by an intimate union of state and Catholic Church. The colonization of the country went forward without the colonizers being particularly concerned with racial unity or racial purity. Throughout practically the entire sixteenth century the gates were open to all foreigners; the only thing that mattered to the colonial authorities was that the newcomers be unquestionably of the Catholic religion. A friar was put aboard every entering ship "to examine the conscience, faith, and religion" of the new arrivals. The "danger" lay not in the possibility that the foreigner was unhygienic or diseased, but in the possibility of his being a "heretic" non-Catholic. Religious unity was maintained throughout the entire colonial period, and it served the interests of national unity to an extent not approached in other parts of America.

The Constitution of 1824, establishing an independent constitutional monarchy, made specific provisions for the unity of state and church, and Catholicism remained the sole religion of the state. Restrictions against non-Catholics, however, became less severe, and a few Protestant churches were established, especially in the southern states among recent immigrants.

The union of church and state resulted in a considerable mingling of

political and religious functions: bishops and priests became leading statesmen, liberal and revolutionary priests became active in sporadic attempts
to change the existing order, and both regular and monastic clergymen, still
the principal factors in the intellectual life of the nation, actively participated in all the manifestations of political and social life. This close relationship between church and state inevitably led to a competition between
the two powers which, in the latter half of the nineteenth century, developed into open conflict, as the state moved to assume more and more
powers which the church leaders felt were rightfully in their domain.

During and even before independence the Brazilian clergymen were
often quick to leave their own natural field of action and to enter worldly
affairs alien to the ministry. Contributing to this tendency was the general
scarcity of well-educated men outside the Catholic clergy. The churchmen
weakened their position as religious leaders by becoming recruiters for the
various political parties, and ended by losing much of their prestige and
compromising the authority of the church leaders. Politics, on the other
hand, tended to intrude into the affairs of the Church, disturbing the harmony between the two powers and weakening the authority of the church
leaders over the mass of the priests. The power of the crown to create jobs
(patronage) tended to reduce the Church itself into an instrument of
politics.

In his analysis of the developing conflict between the Church and the
state, Fernando de Azevedo puts considerable emphasis upon the role of
Freemasonry in that struggle. Secret societies of Freemasons had begun to
spring up in Brazil in the early nineteenth century. Some of the most eminent men of the times, including many prominent clergymen, became members. "There was no Masonic Lodge in which there did not figure side by
side with civilians, fighting for the same ideals, participating in their rites
and activities, some liberal wearers of the cassock."[41] Prominent among
the aims of Masonry were political goals, including the abolition of the
monarchy and the establishing of a republic in Brazil and the abolition of
slavery. During the third quarter of the nineteenth century the leading
bishops of Brazil became increasingly concerned over the part which
churchmen under their nominal if not actual authority were playing in the
Masonic lodges. It was about this time that it became evident that one of
the goals of Masonry was the juridical separation of the religious and the
civil powers. It was from this situation that developed the most bitter
struggle between the Church and the state in Brazil's history. The peak of

574

this struggle, which lasted roughly from 1872 to 1875, was characterized by the bishops' attempts to retain their authority over the priests, which was being threatened by the political influences of the Masonic lodges and the civil authorities. The immediate cause of the crisis came when the bishops made it known that they would inflict severe sanctions upon members of the clergy who refused to resign from the Masonic lodges. The state forbade the bishops to exercise such sanctions against churchmen who refused to leave Masonry. The bishops ignored this demand which they considered undue political interference in their sphere of action. The state counteracted by trying, convicting, and imprisoning two of the church leaders. After this, until the two powers were finally separated, the civil power tended to absorb more and more of the functions of ecclesiastical authority by constant incursions into the realm of spiritual matters.

The religious question, which caused considerable bitterness in the latter part of the century, showed clearly the disadvantages of the union between church and state and prepared the way for the separation of the two powers. Separation was finally achieved with the Republican Constitution of 1891, which also guaranteed the principle of freedom of worship and belief.

While the new Constitution brought about open competition between the Catholic Church and various Protestant sects, it improved the situation of the Church by freeing it from dependence upon the state.

Azevedo speaks of the "Religious Renaissance" of the Catholic Church in Brazil in the second quarter of the twentieth century. The development of new religious associations of students and workmen and the active participation of Catholics in campaigns against the legalization of divorce and in favor of religious education in the public schools figure among the elements in the "renaissance" of the Church.

Throughout the Republican era, anticlericalism became rampant among political leaders, many of whom had been educated in religious schools. These leaders tried to apply the spirit as well as the letter of separation between church and state. However, the Church remained so closely tied up with so many phases of national life that even the most anticlerical politicians had to establish a *modus vivendi* with it. In recent years the militant anticlericalism of the early Republicans has subsided and relations between the Church and the state have become more cordial.

The Church has entered the national political arena only when issues it considered vital were at stake. Such was the case when it was proposed that divorce be legalized in Brazil, twice, in 1934 and again in 1946, a divorce bill was presented to Congress. On each occasion it was believed that the bill would gain sufficient votes to become law. Each time, however, the Church mobilized all its power and influence in vehement opposition to the proposed bill, secured advertisements in daily newspapers and radio time to present its case. When it became clear that the Church would not waver in its position, many congressmen who had prepared to vote for the bill reversed their votes for fear of adverse political repercussions among the voters. On both occasions the bill was defeated.

The Constitution of 1946 declares that freedom of conscience and belief are inviolable. Religious freedom is secured for all, unless its practice is "against the public order or morality." No one is to be deprived of his rights because of his religious, philosophical, or political convictions. As in the previous Republican constitutions, no church is granted special privileges. The rather peaceful development of Protestantism in Brazil indicated that the text of the Constitution indeed reflects a degree of tolerance which one seeks in vain in some other Latin-American countries.

THE NATURE OF BRAZILIAN CATHOLICISM

Gilberto Freyre emphasizes his belief that with the ascetic, orthodox Catholicism known elsewhere in Europe, Portugal could hardly have forged her enormous empire. He gives credit to "the warming and voluptuous contact with the Moors" and to pagan survivals as factors which caused Catholicism in Portugal and Spain to evolve differently from the way it did in other parts of Europe.[42] It might be added at this point that it was those very special features of Catholicism peculiar to the Iberian Peninsula which so appealed to the millions of Africans and Indians in Portuguese America and made their acceptance of Catholicism a much simpler process.

The missionaries obtained their greatest successes on the mystic, devotional, and festive side of the Catholic religion. The Indians were Christianized through music, liturgy, processions, feasts, religious dances, the adoration of relics and saints' statues, and the decorative chains, ribbons, and rosaries worn by the faithful. All these elements, while they served the cause of gaining acceptance of Christianity, tended to be reinterpreted by the Indians and Negro slaves in the light of their own beliefs.

A large proportion of the Brazilian people are still conditioned by a religious system which represents a blending of the already heterogeneous

European heritage, the religious system of Africa, and certain traits derived from Indian cultures.

The numerical importance of those who conform closely in religious beliefs and practices to orthodox Catholicism is relatively small. Padre Pascoal Lacroix, who believes that the shortage of clergymen is the foremost problem of Brazil, states that it "is the opinion of many priests that in our country the general average of true Catholics does not exceed ten percent." This authority believes that the remainder of Brazilians—the other 90 per cent—consists of a "great number of neo-pagans, many spiritualists," some Protestants, and many "who are Catholics in name and by baptism, who do not practice the religion, not from wickedness, but from habit, ignorance, and prejudice."[43]

The great number of religious holidays in Brazil is a feature which impresses itself upon all visitors. Most of these holidays, commemorating the lives of various saints, are celebrated in the form of public feasts at which fireworks, the ringing of bells, the adornment of churches, dramatic and musical performances, religious processions, and the distribution of food are predominant elements.

Annual pilgrimages to the many shrines which dot Brazil, some of them extremely favored, reach amazing proportions. Devotees of all social classes, but chiefly the poorer ones, flock to the shrines from all directions. They expect deliverance from the troubles or maladies from which they suffer, or they come to fulfill promises they may have made to particular saints in order to obtain their aid. The saints themselves are humanized to an extent that would appear blasphemous to most American Catholics. Some saints are endowed with human failings as well as with human virtues, and they are supposed to react to reward and punishment inflicted by humans.

The role of the *irmandades*, or religious brotherhoods, can hardly be overrated. They must be given credit for a good deal of what was accomplished in the field of social security, including old age and sickness benefits for their members. Some of these so-called "third orders" limited their membership to the most aristocratic of white planters while others received only mulattoes or Negroes as members. Some were composed strictly of Negroes, and these held St. Benedict, the Negro saint, as their patron. Since many wealthy men in the colonial days left their wealth to the *irmandades*, some of them were able to establish hospitals and orphanages and to build churches. In the early days of Brazil these organizations performed many such valuable functions—functions that were carried out by the state in other parts of Latin America. The *irmandades* remain important to the present day in Brazil.

In 1953 there were 18,434 Catholic associations, mostly of the *irmandade* type, in Brazil with a total of 3,569,862 members.[44]

The lack of priests is usually considered as the greatest weakness of the Catholic Church. It was stated in 1939 that there were only 4,700 priests in the whole of Brazil and, of these, only 2,200 belonged to the regular ordained priesthood.[45] This makes an average of only one priest for every 20,000 inhabitants. In 1939 a Catholic leaflet, *Escola Apostolica Cristo-Rey*, commenting on these statistics, stated: "At least two-thirds of our Brazil may never become Catholic if the number of the clergy is not increased."[46]

In 1953, the number of Catholic parish priests had risen to 7,031. On the basis of an estimated 55,772,000 inhabitants, there is now one priest for every 7,932 inhabitants. However, the distribution of parish priests appears to be extremely unequal. Thus the state of Maranhão with 1,583,248 (1950) inhabitants possessed only 99 parish priests, while Santa Catarina with a population of 1,560,502 counted on 333 priests.

BRAZILIAN PROTESTANTISM

According to the national census of 1940, 1,074,857 or 2.6 per cent of the 41,236,315 inhabitants of Brazil were Protestants.[47] In 1950 the number of Protestants had increased to 1,741,430 or 3.3 per cent of a total population of 51,397,000, out of which 48,558,854, or 93.5 per cent declared themselves to be Catholic.[48] No reliable breakdown of these figures is available, but it ought to be borne in mind that Brazilian Protestants belong to a wide variety of denominations. There are Methodists, Adventists, Presbyterians, Baptists, Congregationalists, Episcopalians, Pentecostals, Christian Scientists, The Assembly of God, various Lutheran groups different from and competing with German Lutherans, as well as an impressive number of rather fluctuating denominations reflecting native dissensions from larger groups.

All these groups, except the German Lutherans, are proselytical, and a large percentage, probably the majority of those who professed to be Protestants, were converted to the new creed during their lifetime. Conversion, however, constitutes to most a sharp break with traditions both sacred and secular. It means repudiation of the saints and all practices by which saintly

help had been secured. Many congregations adhere to the brand of Fundamentalism that was introduced during the nineteenth century, mostly by
American missionaries. Thus, religious prohibitions are strict and numerous, including those against drinking, smoking, gambling, dancing, exposure of the body, attending theatrical performances, using cosmetics, as
well as emphasis on chastity and matrimonial fidelity. The sum of these
sinful activities is encompassed by the concept of *mundanism* (world-
liness), an expression which denotes a series of tight controls over Protestants, but which conveys no definite meaning to Brazilians in general.

The controls that the average Protestant congregations succeeded in
establishing over its members are probably tighter than those found in most
Catholic parishes. Moreover, such controls affect the relative position of
the family within the congregation. The traditional supremacy of the family
group seems to have been relinquished by the Protestants, while at the
same time the family has reached a higher degree of internal cohesion.
Attempts to eliminate the so-called double standard of sex morals has
changed sex mores with visible repercussions upon husband-wife relationships. Economic behavior has been found to differ from that of non-
Protestants insofar as Protestants do not participate, as producers, distributors, and consumers, in some major economic pursuits that are taken
for granted by the larger society.

Within both the lower and the lower middle classes where the new creed
has found most of its adherents, Protestants tend to be more literate and
to have a broader outlook upon life than non-Protestants.

The Educational System

Education in the narrow sense of formal instruction, both general and
specialized, presents two major problems in contemporary Brazil. There
is, first of all, the problem of illiteracy, which periodically arouses public
opinion and engenders governmental and private action characterized by
widely varying degrees of efficacy. Eradication of illiteracy appears to be
difficult, not only because of the scarcity of financial means, the shortage
of teachers, or the extreme dispersion of the rural population, but primarily
because different sections of Brazilian society represent different phases of
cultural development. Indeed, so different are these phases that the technologically most advanced sectors of industrialized urban society cannot
be thought of without the type of specialized instruction which is found in
similar sectors of the United States or Europe. But there is also a relatively

large proportion of rural Brazilians whose situation concerning the school is comparable to that of those highland communities of Guatemala where, according to Redfield, "abolition of schools would leave the culture much as it is."[49] Likewise, there are communities in Brazil where the school, if it exists at all, has not really come to fill a gap because there was no gap to fill.

It is probably a prejudice of urban man that a need for the three R's must exist merely because of the fact that a particular group of people live within a given national territory, or because the school is considered as the universal panacea for all forms of "underdevelopment," whether or not this is felt by the people involved. Actually, however, there seem to be a number of communities where the type of education provided for by the grade school has no definite place within the context of the local culture. Children may go to school for a few years, they may acquire the rudiments of reading and writing, yet as they probably will not find either need or encouragement to apply their knowledge, they are apt to lose it and to slide back into the state of illiteracy or semiliteracy. Whatever occasional need there may be for the three R's is easily fulfilled by a few semiprofessionals in these arts. The fact that formal education seems to perform no function in many rural communities means that they are preliterate rather than illiterate. Their development into actual literacy, however, can not be accomplished by the school alone. Indeed, the school appears to be only part of a more complex process by which the community is gradually integrated into an ecological and economic system of a different order. Only if and when the continuance of a local sociocultural system has come to depend on formal instruction, may the school, in any of its forms, be regarded as an integral part of that system.

Frequently, however, integration is a matter of degree, and between the functionless and the integrated school there are those situations in which the school performs a very definite function that is neither intended nor desired. It has often been pointed out that, in many rural areas and small towns, the school prepares people to leave for the industrial centers of the country. On numerous occasions it was learned that particular communities expressed the desire to obtain schools or to improve the existing ones in order to get better paying jobs in the cities for their children. But within the context of Brazilian local cultures, the creation or improvement of educational facilities is no simple matter.

The main differences between the educational system of Brazil and that of the United States lies in the fact that the Brazilian system is relatively centralized while that of the United States is highly decentralized. Community initiative resulting in spontaneous and concerted action of those members of the local citizenry who are willing to take responsibilities in organizing and maintaining local school systems appears to be rare in Brazil; in fact it is only found among minority groups of recent European or Asiatic extraction.

Private initiative in the realm of education, however, is rather frequent in Brazil because commercial profit may be obtained by founding schools. The tendency to organize schools as business enterprises is particularly strong in the larger cities, where the government has been unable to meet the need for formal education. As may be expected, this development has frequently been criticized for being incompatible with the recognized necessity of attaining higher standards of scholarship.

There are also hundreds of schools maintained by religious orders and congregations, mainly of the Roman Catholic Church. While the public school system is coeducational, the sexes are separated in the Catholic schools, which in many respects are comparable to those of the United States.

In spite of the fact that considerable efforts have been made to increase the number of schools, illiteracy is still high and probably will remain so for a long time to come. According to the Census of 1950, 51.65 per cent of all inhabitants 10 or more years old could neither read nor write. The lowest illiteracy rates were recorded in Rio Grande do Sul, 34.17 per cent in 1950. São Paulo and Santa Catarina followed with 34.63 and 35.80 per cent. In the northern and northeastern states, however, illiteracy was much higher, reaching 74.78 per cent in Maranhão and 74.41 per cent in Piauí. Cities are invariably better off than the small areas. In the capitals of Rio Grande do Sul and São Paulo, illiteracy had been reduced to 15.41 and 15.60 per cent in 1950. And in the larger cities of the North and Northeast it varied between 30 and 40 per cent.[50]

The expansion of the educational system is characterized by a general increase in the enrollment, the number of schools and the teaching personnel. There were 95,533 school units available in 1953 against 46,583 in 1940. The total enrollment of 3,732,878 in 1940 went up to 6,777,254 in 1953, and the number of teachers rose from 115,836 in 1940 to 238,307 in 1953. If the efficiency of an educational system can be measured, to some degree, by the number of students who concluded the course in which they had been enrolled, the Brazilian system has obviously been lagging behind its established objectives. The percentage of students who terminated their studies went down from 11.59 in 1940 to 11.11 per cent in 1953.

The second major problem the Brazilian educational system has been faced with may be seen in the need to adapt its methods and contents to the requirements of a technological and scientific civilization, which Brazilian society has chosen to adopt. This choice, which has to a considerable extent been determined by the cultural evolution of the Western world, implies a reorientation of the traditional value system. Brazilian culture is of the humanistic-literary type, which predominates in the so-called Latin countries. High value is placed on the manipulation of the language, on correct and esthetically satisfactory verbalization, on elocution and eloquence.

It is probably true that verbalization of both the emotional and the cognitive content of the culture is equally encouraged by Brazilian society. In the realm of the emotional this becomes especially manifest in sacred and "social" oratory as practiced, for example, from the pulpit and during electoral campaigns. Verbalization of the cognitive values appears to be concentrated on juridical rhetoric, on the manipulation of legal concepts, and on dialectical skill. Traditionally, law, letters, and the priesthood were the only dignifying professions for the members of the leisure class. In sharpest possible contrast with the pragmatic and scientific values of the Anglo-Saxon culture, there was little attempt to encourage the learning of the sciences, scientific research, or the application of scientific knowledge to technical problems. Until the turn of the century, schools of sciences and engineering were extremely rare, and their standards did not compare favorably with similar American and European institutions. Despite the fact that medicine came to be included among the prestige-carrying professions, schools of medicine remained few, and numerous Brazilians preferred to acquire their medical training abroad.

The past three or four decades have brought a prodigious multiplication of secondary and higher institutions of learning. Statistics for 1953 are set forth in Table 4.

Until 1930 there were no colleges for the training of high school teachers. In 1953, 281 such colleges had been established, but the number of students who obtain degrees from such schools has remained too small to supply all high schools with trained personnel, especially in the sciences. A change in value orientation is indicated, to some extent, by the number

Table 4. Secondary and Higher Institutions of Learning in Brazil in 1953

	Number	Enrollment	Teachers
High schools	2,434	512,455	34,620
Schools of agriculture	92	5,840	1,121
Industrial schools	416	19,074	6,266
Schools of business	864	99,367	9,575
Schools of arts	714	23,567	2,533
Normal schools for grade school teachers	1,059	62,158	10,153
Higher institutions of learning	516	56,091	9,240

of high school students who prefer scientific courses to the humanities. Against the 66,985 who, in 1953, had been enrolled in the scientific "cycle," there were only 10,947 enrolled in the humanistic "cycle."[51]

The proliferation of scientific courses on the secondary and college level can not be taken at face value. Although most of the newly founded schools profess strictly professional objectives, they lack trained instructors. Moreover, instruction in the sciences is severely impaired by the lack of adequate laboratory facilities and the deep-rooted tendency of many instructors to limit teaching to the verbal communication of knowledge. The students are led to memorize their biology, chemistry, and physics rather than to practice them in the laboratory. Opportunities for experiments and research are rare, and the students are easily induced to accept temporary results as irrevocable truths. Exceptions from the rule are found only in a limited number of institutions in southern and southeastern Brazil, whose standards of scholarship and research compare favorably with those of the United States and Europe.

During the past three decades the Brazilian educational system has gone through a series of changes that were perhaps not always induced by real needs and whose inadequacy has often been subjected to severe criticism, but which may be regarded as a manifestation of the rapid change of the culture in general. Some such changes were carried out under the pressure of circumstances that the existing school system proved unable to cope with. The most remarkable of these changes may be seen in the National Service of Industrial Apprenticeship, in whose day and night courses approximately 40,000 industrial workers learn 43 different trades.

Recreational and Artistic Life

Certain peculiarities of Brazilian social structure and cultural development are reflected in the forms of recreation that the people habitually engage in. Earlier stages of recreational life are still to be found in the rural areas and small towns where relaxation and diversion are not sharply differentiated from work and duty. Clock-measured working hours as well as high-geared productivity are still unusual, and minor forms of recreation such as gossiping, joking, singing, and drinking are frequently interwoven with work. The great festivals of the year are primarily occasions for discharging religious obligations, although they provide, of course, highly enjoyable forms of diversion and entertainment. To the extent that secularization of rural culture has taken place, the merely recreational aspects of numerous major and minor feasts have developed at the expense of the religious ones, especially under the impact of commercialization, which tends to convey an autonomous meaning of fun-making and amusement to institutions fundamentally intended to be sacred. Thus the dissociation of sacred and secular brought about some of the major developments of urban recreation, especially the seasonal cycle of winter festivals (Saint John, Saint Peter, Saint Antony), the *Kermesses* (patron saints' days) and Christmas.

In traditional Brazilian society only the upper classes had adopted recreational patterns similar to those of Europe. The habit of distinguishing periods of respite to be spent in resort towns chosen in accordance with seasonal conditions was alien to the bulk of Brazilian society. Yet, here again, urbanization and diffusion of European patterns, mediated to a large extent by economically successful immigrants, produced some major changes. At least in the larger cities of southern and southeastern Brazil, the concept of the vacation as a period during which the individual should be freed from his occupational obligations, and which should be spent in a pleasurable and relaxing environment, has been widely accepted by all social classes. As a matter of fact, by stipulating that all employees, whether urban or rural, have a right to a paid vacation every year, the Brazilian Labor Code somewhat forced the process of cultural diffusion which would have reached the lower urban classes anyway. Vacations were not unusual even before social laws were enacted, and now some employers maintain hotels in seaside and mountain resorts where their employees may spend their annual vacation at little cost.

As recreational habits spread, the number of health resorts increased, obviously more so in the southern and southeastern regions than in the northern and central sections of the country. Following European patterns some have acquired a reputation for their invigorating mountain air, others for their mineral waters. And near the larger cities the beaches are dotted with summer houses and hotels, where people have become accustomed to spent week-ends and vacation periods.

There are four highly commercialized forms of entertainment limited to urban life, which have quite drastically changed a number of social customs: moving pictures, soccer, radio, and, more recently, television. With the exception of television, all are accessible to all social classes. Their mass appeal can be estimated by the number of soccer stadiums and motion picture theaters. In 1954 there were 2,953 motion picture theaters seating 1,573,113 persons in the entire country. Out of these, 792 with a seating capacity of 553,654 were located in the state of São Paulo.[52] During the same year the 3,721 pictures approved by the National Bureau of Censorship drew an audience of 279,350,000.[53]

Although no figures are available on either soccer or radio, the role of soccer as a form of mass entertainment can be estimated by such facts as the growing capacity of city stadia, some of which seat up to 200,000 persons; the nonseasonal character of the game, which draws huge audiences during the entire year; concentration of all important games on Sunday afternoons when people find time to attend; and the development of a wide "fringe" of related phenomena, such as extremely widespread though illegal betting, extensive reporting by papers, some of them being almost entirely devoted to soccer, the role of professional soccer, the amount of capital invested in players and games, and so forth.

Motion picture theaters and soccer games have probably contributed more to relieve Brazilian women from the traditional confinement to domestic pleasures than any other single factor. Motion pictures and soccer games are held to be compatible with the canons of respectability that regulate public appearances of "serious" women.

Women of dubious reputation, however, play a dominant role in the ways in which Brazilian males go about their less conventional forms of entertainment. They are mostly centered in sex, as made available in *cabarés* (night clubs) and bordellos of various types. Life in an upper middle-class bordello, as a gathering place of friends and distinguished by an atmosphere of restraint and quiet elegance, has been described by H. Tavares de Sá.[54]

The other markedly androcentric type of diversion is gambling. Although most forms of gambling arc unlawful, they are practiced in the safe retreat of respectable clubs. As a rule, such clubs were founded to offer various kinds of entertainment to the families of the male members. In fact, however, such activities are limited to a few parties that may take place on such occasions as Mardi Gras or Saint John's day, while the remaining days of the year are devoted to nightly gambling sessions.

Enjoyment of works of art may be regarded as a form of relaxation. So far as folk arts are concerned—especially music, poetry, dancing, and dramatic performances—their recreational function in the rural cultures of Brazil can hardly be overestimated. There is a surprising wealth of musical and poetic creations that have fully preserved the anonymity and spontaneousness of genuine folk art. The deep interest in musical and rhythmic expression has survived among the urban population, and the strong demand for such creations is currently satisfied by popular composers and poets whose ranks are currently replenished with young talent from the lower classes.

However, the more sophisticated forms of art appeal only to a relatively small section of the people. There seems to be a rather obvious discrepancy between artistic creativeness, namely in the realm of literature, painting and music, and the number of people prepared to enjoy "high-brow" poetry, novels, symphonies, chamber music, paintings, and sculpture. As a matter of fact, even the editions of best sellers of high literary quality rarely exceed a few thousand copies. Yet, on the whole, the situation has changed considerably in the last forty years. With the gradual improvement of the educational system and the rise of the middle classes, a taste for the fine arts has ceased to be a monopoly of a small crust of upper-class intellectuals. Concerts and art exhibits now draw large audiences, and such events as the foundation of a museum for modern art in São Paulo, with its astonishing collection of truly representative paintings and sculptures, may be interpreted as a promising indication of future developments.

Institutional Integration

If Brazilian culture is viewed as a historical process, its institutional framework may be said to have developed out of the dichotomy, family-state. There was the extended, multifunctional, patriarchal family of the landed upper class, which grew strong on the latifundia and firmly encroached on practically all institutional aspects of colonial society. At first the state was clearly in a position of defense against the tentacles of the *familia rustica*. But gradually, perhaps from the eighteenth century on, its power grew; yet its position remained weak until the hold of the family was definitely broken during the second half of the nineteenth century, and its residues receded to local levels.

During the colonial period the Roman Catholic Church leaned heavily on both state and extended family. Chapel and priest were dependent on the big plantation house. The authority of the priest, often a son or nephew of the owner, was derived from that of the *paterfamilias*. On the other hand, the patronage system tied the Church to the state. This somewhat contradictory role became feasible by a *de facto* widening of the realm of priestly autonomy at the local level. As the power of the landed family decayed and that of the state grew, the Church was thrown into the orbit of the latter, yet both associations damaged its reputation and reduced its actual hold over the people. Eventually, with the advent of the Republic, the ties with the state were severed, and the Church passed through a phase of reorganization that tended to restore the equilibrium in its relationships to other institutions.

While the plantation economy of the Northeast was structurally tied in with the extended family, a gradually emerging urban economy representing financial and business interests of immigrated Portuguese appeared to be allied to the state. However, the fact that Brazil remained an agrarian country, that all material wealth continued to be produced on the land, and that its producers remained in the rural areas, prevented the early cities of Brazil from becoming more than slow-paced, semirural towns. The decisive change was accomplished by industrializing a number of cities and by urbanizing initial centers of industrial production. For the first time the cities were in a position to compete successfully with the rural areas for people. Eventually the cities grew much faster than the population in general, and the socioeconomic preponderance of modern urban civilization was established. This process must be regarded, to a very large extent, as an acculturation of alien knowledge, techniques, attitudes, and practices to the social conditions and economic potentialities of the country. As it proceeded, the economic dominance shifted definitely to southern and southeastern Brazil. Under its impact the educational institutions entered a phase of change from humanistic-literary emphasis toward a technological and scientific orientation.

In preindustrial Brazil political power was monopolized by a landed "aristocracy" with intellectual overtones. Imported political doctrines were useful ideological trappings, but failed to produce significant changes in the traditional power structure. Far-reaching structural changes, however, occurred under the impact of industrialization and urbanization. In the emerging class system, the urban masses and the new middle classes participated increasingly in political decisions that were opposed to the political designs and claims of the old elite. Unable to control the masses by the traditional electoral techniques, the old elite lost its dominant position to new political leaders who explored the economic situation of the underprivileged classes.

Institutional integration at the national level has been delayed by two facts. The most important is the ecological isolation of a large proportion of the rural population that lives in local subsistence economies, barely touched by the political, economic, and educational institutions of the nation. The second fact lies in the steadily growing socioeconomic and political dominance of southern Brazil. In the long run the national political institutions are hardly in a position to compensate for the effects of such ecological disequilibriums, either with public works or with production quotas designed to prevent the Northeast from dropping out of the internal competition for markets.

Notes

[1] John Gillin, "Modern Latin American Cultures," *Social Forces,* Vol. 25 (1946–47), pp. 243–248.

[2] H. Tavares de Sá, *The Brazilians, People of Tomorrow* (New York: The John Day Company, 1947), pp. 13–14.

[3] Donald Pierson, *Negroes in Brazil: A Study of Race Contact at Bahia* (Chicago: University of Chicago Press, 1942), pp. 116–117.

[4] Julio Belo, *Memórias de um senhor de engenho* (Rio de Janeiro: José Olímpio, 1938), p. 183.

[5] Max Weber, *Wirtschaft und Gesellschaft,* Vol. I (Tübingen: J. P. Mohr, 1926), pp. 650 ff.

[6] Sérgio Buarque de Holanda, *Raizes do Brasil,* 2d ed. (Rio de Janeiro: José Olímpio, 1948), pp. 22 ff.

[7] *Ibid.,* p. 28.

[8] Alfonso Arinos de Mello Franco, *Conceito de Civilização Brasileira* (São Paulo: Companhia Editora Nacional, 1936), p. 158.

[9] Conselho Nacional de Estatística. Serviço Nacional de Recenseamento, *VI Recenseamento do Brasil. Censo Demográfico. Estados Unidos do Brasil. Seleção dos Principais Dados* (Rio de Janeiro: Serviço Gráfico do Instituto Brasileiro de Geografia e Estatística, 1953), p. 9.

[10] *Ibid.,* pp. 36, 38, 42.

[11] Reynold E. Carlson, "The Bases of Brazil's Economy," in T. Lynn Smith and Alexander Marchant, eds., *Brazil, Portrait of Half a Continent* (New York: The Dryden Press, 1951), p. 250.

[12] Conselho Nacional de Estatística, *Anuário Estatístico do Brasil, 1955,* Ano XVI (Rio de Janeiro: Serviço Gráfico IBGE, 1955), p. 180. Hereafter referred to as *Anuário, 1955*

[13] *Ibid.,* p. 107

[14] *Ibid.*, p. 170.

[15] Dorival Teixeira Vieira, "The Industrialization of Brazil," in Smith and Marchant, *op. cit.*, p. 248.

[16] *Anuário, 1955*, p. 139.

[17] *Ibid.*, p. 302.

[18] Vieira, *op. cit.*, p. 259.

[19] *Anuário, 1955*, p. 154.

[20] *Ibid.*

[21] *Ibid.*, p. 155.

[22] Vieira, *op. cit.*, p. 261.

[23] *Anuário, 1955*, pp. 300, 316–317.

[24] Carlson, *op cit.*, p. 258.

[25] Vieira, *op. cit.*, p. 263.

[26] *Anuário, 1955*, p. 417.

[27] Emilio Willems, "Immigrants and Their Assimilation in Brazil," in Smith and Marchant, *op. cit.*, p. 224.

[28] *Ibid.*, p. 215.

[29] *Boletim do Serviço de Imigração e Colonização*, No. 2 (São Paulo: Secretaria da Agricultura, Industria e Comércio, 1940), p. 145.

[30] T. Lynn Smith, "The People and Their Characteristics," in Smith and Marchant, *op. cit.*, p. 162.

[31] *Anuário, 1955*, pp. 51–54.

[32] Ana Casis and Kingsley Davis, "Urbanization in Latin America," in Olen E. Leonard and Charles P. Loomis, eds., *Latin America: Organization and Institutions* (East Lansing: Michigan State College Press, 1953), p. 152.

[33] *Anuário, 1955*, pp. 517, 536.

[34] Halbert L. Dunn, *et al.*, "Demographic Status of South America," *Annals of the American Academy of Political and Social Science*, 237 (1945), p. 25.

[35] Oliveira Vianna, *Instituições políticas Brasileiras*, 2 vols., (Rio de Janeiro: José Olímpio, 1949), Vol. I, p. 146.

[36] *Anuário, 1955*, p. 611.

[37] Romulo de Almeida, "Problemas estruturais do município," *Revista Brasileira do Município*, Ano III (1950), p. 512.

[38] *Código Civil Brasileiro*, 218, 219, IV.

[39] *Ibid.*, Article 1721.

[40] Talcott Parsons, *Essays in Sociological Theory* (Glencoe, Ill.: The Free Press, 1949), p. 238.

[41] Fernando de Azevedo, *Brazilian Culture, An Introduction to the Study of Culture in Brazil*, translation by William Rex Crawford (New York: Macmillan, 1950), p. 152.

[42] Gilberto Freyre, *The Masters and the Slaves, A Study in the Development of Brazilian Civilization*, translation by Samuel Putnam (New York: Knopf, 1946), p. 259.

[43] T. Lynn Smith, *Brazil: People and Institutions* (Baton Rouge: University of Louisiana Press, 1947), p. 707.

[44] *Anuário, 1955*, p. 500.

[45] Smith, *Brazil: People and Institutions, op. cit.*, p. 688.

[46] E. N. Long, "To Read the Gospel in Brazilian Schools," *The Christian Century*, 56 (1939), p. 1178.

[47] *Anuário, 1949*, p. 30.

[48] *Censo Demográfico, 1953, op. cit.*, p. 6.

[49] Robert Redfield, "Culture and Education in the Midwestern Highlands of Guatemala," *American Journal of Sociology*, 48 (1943), p. 641.

[50] *Anuário, 1955*, p. 429.

[51] *Ibid.*, p. 451.

[52] *Ibid.,* p. 487.
[53] *Ibid.,* p. 488.
[54] H. Tavares de Sá, *op. cit.,* pp. 17–18.

Supplementary References

Almeida, Vicente Unzer de, and Octavio Teixeira Mendes Sobrinho, *Migração Rural-Urbana* (São Paulo: Secretaria da Agricultura do Estado de São Paulo, 1951)

Azevedo, Fernando de, *Canaviais e engenhos na vida política do Brasil* (Rio de Janeiro: Instituto do Açúcar e do Alcool, 1948).

Bastide, Roger, "Religion and the Church in Brazil," in T. Lynn Smith and Alexander Marchant, eds., *Brazil, Portrait of Half a Continent* (New York: The Dryden Press, 1951).

Braga, Erasmo, and Kenneth G. Grubb, *The Republic of Brazil: A Survey of the Religious Situation* (London and New York: World Dominion Press, 1932).

Calogeras, J. P., *History of Brazil,* translation with additional material by P. A. Martin (Chapel Hill: University of North Carolina Press, 1939).

Cunha, Euclydes da, *Rebellion in the Backlands,* translated from the Portuguese by Samuel Putnam (Chicago: University of Chicago Press, 1944).

Davis, Kingsley, "Political Ambivalence in Latin America," *Journal of Legal and Political Sociology,* Vol. I (1942).

De Jong, Jr., Gerrit, "Brazilian Music and Art," in T. Lynn Smith and Alexander Marchant, eds., *Brazil, Portrait of Half a Continent* (New York: The Dryden Press, 1951).

Freyre, Gilberto, *Sobrados e Mucambos: Decadência do patriarcado rural do Brasil* (São Paulo: Companhia Editora Nacional, 1936).

————, *Brazil, An Interpretation* (New York: Knopf, 1948).

Gillin, John, "Mestizo America," in Ralph Linton, ed., *Most of the World* (New York: Columbia University Press, 1949).

Hill, Lawrence Francis, ed., *Brazil* (Berkeley: University of California Press, 1947).

Institute of Inter-American Affairs. Foreign Operation Administration, *Joint Brazil-United States Economic Development Commission* (Washington, D.C.: U.S. Government Printing Office, 1954).

James, Preston E., *Latin America* (New York: The Odyssey Press, 1942).

Kuznets, Simon Smith, Wilbert E. Moore, and Joseph J. Spengler, *Economic Growth: Brazil, India, Japan* (Durham, N.C.: Duke University Press, 1955).

Leão, A. Carneiro, "The Evolution of Education in Brazil," in T. Lynn Smith and Alexander Marchant, eds., *Brazil, Portrait of Half a Continent* (New York: The Dryden Press, 1951).

Mecham, Lloyd, *Church and State in Latin America* (Chapel Hill: University of North Carolina Press, 1934).

Nash, Roy, *The Conquest of Brazil* (New York: Harcourt, 1926).

Normano, J. F., *Brazil: A Study of Economic Types* (Chapel Hill: University of North Carolina Press, 1935).

Pierson, Donald, "Racial and Cultural Contacts in Brazil: Present State of Research in This Field," *Handbook of Latin American Studies,* No. 6 (1940) (Cambridge: Harvard University Press, 1941).

————, *Cruz das Almas: A Brazilian Village* (Washington, D.C.: Smithsonian Institution, Institute of Social Anthropology, Publication No. 12, 1951).

————, "The Family in Brazil," *Marriage and Family Living,* Vol. XVI (1954).

Pierson, W. W., ed., "Pathology of Latin American Democracy," *The American Political Science Review,* Vol. XLIV (1950).

Pinto, Luis A. Costa, *Lutas de Famílias no Brasil* (São Paulo: Companhia Editora Nacional, 1947).

BRAZIL

Putnam, Samuel, *Marvelous Journey: Four Centuries of Brazilian Literature* (New York: Knopf, 1948).

Ramos, Arthur, *The Negro in Brazil* (Washington, D.C.: The Associated Publishers, Inc., 1939)

Ribeiro, René, "On the *Amaziado* Relationship and Other Problems of the Family in Recife (Brazil)," *American Sociological Review*, Vol. X (1945).

Rios, José Arthur, "The Cities of Brazil," in T. Lynn Smith and Alexander Marchant, eds., *Brazil, Portrait of Half a Continent* (New York: The Dryden Press, 1951).

Simonson, Roberto C., *História Economica do Brasil*, 2 vols., (São Paulo: Companhia Editora Nacional, 1937).

Sodré, Nelson Werneck, *Oeste* (Rio de Janeiro: José Olímpio, 1941).

Tavares Lira, A., *Organização política e administrativa do Brasil* (São Paulo: Companhia Editora Nacional, 1941).

Troncoso, Moises Poblete, "The Social Content of Latin American Constitutions," *Social Forces*, Vol. 21 (1942).

Wagley, Charles, "Regionalism and Cultural Unity in Brazil," *Social Forces*, Vol. 26 (1948).

————, "Brazil," in Ralph Linton, ed., *Most of the World* (New York: Columbia University Press, 1949).

————, "The Indian Heritage of Brazil," in T. Lynn Smith and Alexander Marchant, eds., *Brazil, Portrait of Half a Continent* (New York: The Dryden Press, 1951)

————, Bulhões, Octavio de, Stanley J. Stein, and Carleton Sprague Smith, *Four Papers Presented in the Institute for Brazilian Studies* (Nashville: Vanderbilt University Press, 1952).

Willems, Emilio, "Race Attitudes in Brazil," *The American Journal of Sociology*, Vol. LIV (1949).

————, "Caboclo Cultures of Southern Brazil," in Sol Tax, ed., *Acculturation in the Americas*, Vol. II. Proceedings of the 29th International Congress of Americanists (Chicago: University of Chicago Press, 1952).

————, "Protestantism as a Factor of Culture Change in Brazil," *Economic Development and Cultural Change*, Vol. III (1955).

Wythe, George, *Brazil, An Expanding Economy* (New York: Twentieth Century Fund, 1949).

*

Jessie Bernard

THE UNITED STATES

*

Freedom and Equality in a Context of Abundance

IN THE eighteenth century a handful of French sociologists—or philosophers as they were then called—viewed the debacle of the feudal system,
quarried the past in order to interpret the present, invoked the newly
emerging scientific viewpoint, and came up with a set of concepts and
ideas that shook the world when they became articulated and popularized
as the theoretical core of the French Revolution. Among such concepts,
for example, were freedom and equality. And the history of all the advanced nations of the world in the nineteenth and twentieth centuries
might well be written in terms of the way each of them coped with the
impact of these ideas. Each met the challenge in a characteristic manner,
determined in large part by its own history.

American institutions, because they lacked a feudal background, were
peculiarly susceptible to influence by the new currents of thought. Indeed,
the American Revolution matured in the theoretical atmosphere of the
French Enlightenment. The ideals of freedom and equality, reinforced by
the British concept of the role of law and by the continuing influence of
the frontier, became embedded in the very framework of the new republic.
Colonial America in the seventeenth century had revealed no such preoccupation with the ideals of freedom and equality, however much the
conditions of living tended in their direction. The Pilgrims had come to
New England for freedom of worship for themselves; but it had not necessarily been a principle that applied to everyone else, as their own theocratic
policies soon revealed. Nor was the ideal of freedom a value for the great
colonial planters of the South. But the ideals of freedom and equality did
become sacred values after the establishment of the Republic—not, to be

sure, for everyone—and American institutions have been struggling with them ever since.[1] For one who has not actually canvassed the literature it is almost impossible to appreciate to what an extent a preoccupation with freedom and equality characterizes American society, as a preoccupation with grace and salvation characterized an earlier civilization. American institutions cannot be understood, as commentators and observers have noted for almost two centuries, except in terms of a straining toward the implementation of the ideals of freedom and equality.

But the conditions under which the struggle for freedom and equality has taken place have varied enormously during the last century and three quarters. And the context in which it occurs today is unique—not only in American history, but in human history as well—the context, that is, of abundance. The transition from an economy of scarcity to an era of abundance has caught us quite unprepared. Ethical codes, standards, and psychological orientations have all grown up in response to living conditions in an economy of scarcity. They are not always relevant guides in a time of abundance. The problems of freedom and equality are themselves altered. The implications of abundance are therefore of fundamental importance in any analysis of American institutions at mid-century.

ABUNDANCE

Almost fifty years ago an economist, Simon N. Patten, pointed out that an era of abundance was about to replace an era of scarcity. By mid-century this prediction was in the process of realization: productivity had increased at an average rate of about 2 per cent per year; living standards had just about doubled between 1900 and 1950.[2] The rate of increase was accelerative, so that for the decades of the second half of the century an increase of from 3 to 5 per cent per year was anticipated.

Abundance implies a wholly new orientation for institutional behavior. Historians began to trace the influence of economic abundance on American character, showing how it affected all aspects of social life and personality.[3] Economists began to ponder Keynes' concept of "relentless consumption." Social psychologists began to explore the changes in the character of the American people and sociologists the changes in social structure which abundance—with its emphasis on consumption as contrasted to work—produced.[4] Political scientists began to trace the impact of abundance on class alignments.[5] Advanced church leaders were among the first to see the moral and ethical implications of this abundance.[6] In brief, all institutions—family, school, leisure-time activities, government, industry, the church—reflect this change in orientation. Old concepts like "thrift," "saving," "hard work," and "industriousness" lose their former significance. Institutions have to be revamped to cope with the problems of abundance.

The newness of an economy of abundance reveals itself in the difficulty Americans experience in trying to convey its significance to citizens of other countries. There is really no way to communicate it except by participation. Americans usually fall back on reference to the millions of automobiles which travel over thousands of miles of paved highways; to the millions of homes outfitted with electric refrigerators, food freezers, electric stoves, television sets, garbage disposal units, dish washers, appliances of all kinds; to the chic and glamour of the women, among whom it is difficult to distinguish the stenographer from the debutante; to the tables groaning with so much food that overweight has become a major health hazard; to the figures showing enormous consumption of tobacco and alcoholic beverages; to the burgeoning recreation industry, including travel, commercialized amusements like motion pictures, and other mass media.

Reference to these indexes of abundance out of context sounds invidious. To outsiders it is often offensive, as though Americans were showing off or bragging. Not understanding the signficance of these indexes (any more than the American), the outsider may only smile—knowingly or contemptuously or disgustedly, according to his point of view—at the "materialism" of Americans. Out of context wealth implies its opposite, deprivation. But to the American, reference to abundance is not invidious; he speaks of it simply as a fact, not gloatingly, as it so often sounds, or materialistically.

For actually all these statistics of productivity, which sound so materialistic, are indexes of something more profound and meaningful. The exuberant productivity of the American economy means a great deal more than mere technical efficiency. It is, in the last analysis, as important spiritually as materially. It releases the individual from the degradation of exhausting labor; it makes possible a generous, outgoing personality. It means, most significantly, that the existence of Haves does not imply the existence of Have-Nots. It means that people do not need to eye one another suspiciously or enviously; there is enough for all. They do not have to play their cards close to their chests. When one man drives a Rolls-Royce and the other man must trudge on foot, the differences between them are qualitative; when one drives a Lincoln and the other drives a Ford, the differences are only quantitative.

No one would dream of claiming that Americans have learned how to use their abundance in the wisest and most creative manner possible. There is no model for them to imitate anywhere in the world today, or even in history. The aristocratic European pattern will not serve. It created a model for a small leisure class and produced some very fine flowers—the patron of the arts and sciences, the gentleman scholar, the amateur scientist—as well as wastrels and destroyers; but it has nothing to offer on a scale commensurate with the needs of the American economy.

Throughout the discussion in this chapter the implications of abundance will have to be dealt with, since, as pointed out above, economic life, political life, family life, education, leisure—all reflect the problems which it creates.

FREEDOM

With respect to freedom the questions have always had to be raised: freedom for whom? freedom for what? or even, freedom against whom or what?

Originally freedom meant, almost exclusively, political freedom for a limited group. For nations it meant freedom for self-determination, freedom from imperialistic exploitation. For individuals it meant freedom of speech, of assembly, of the press, of religion, or from unwarranted search and seizure. Such freedom from oppression by either the federal or the state governments in the United States may never be complete; eternal vigilance may be required to maintain it. But the principle has been isolated and accepted, and embodied in basic political documents. It is not necessarily a *fait accompli*, now and forever; new threats are always arising. But Americans know more or less what the problems are, and they have at least tentative ways or models or tools for dealing with them. The same might be said of the concept of freedom as extended in the nineteenth century to include economic as well as political freedom from oppression or exploitation by industry, including freedom for Negroes, for women, and even for children.

But there are as yet no models for dealing with the problems of freedom posed in the twentieth century by the impact of industrialization on human nature, the problems, for example, of psychological freedom for spontaneous action,[7] freedom from the pressures of conformity, freedom for autonomy.[8] Many people feel we must cope with still other forms of exploitation, if not oppression, from those in control of mass media, from propagandists of one kind or another who have at their disposal a veritable science of control—which in the hands of our opponents we label "brainwashing." Freedom of research is also a new problem at mid-century; academic freedom takes on new aspects when it must cope with security risks. Not so much political and economic freedom, in brief, as the far subtler kinds of mental and spiritual freedom pose the most serious problems in America today.

The picture, then, is one of constant change, of fighting now in one sector, now in another. No sooner does one battle seem to be won than a new front threatens. American institutions have never been able to settle down into a fixed stability, assured that now freedom had been achieved once and for all. American institutions are by no means perfected for handling all the new threats to freedom, especially the psychological ones.

There are, however, two kinds of freedom—freedom from the past and freedom from locale—which are so characteristic of American institutions and which have so thoroughly pervaded their functioning that commentators on American life invariably take note of them.

Although the examination, interpretation, analysis, writing, and teaching of history have become almost a major industry in the United States, the imprint of the past is not deep. In the first place, physical reminders of the past do not long remain in America. The concept of obsolescence— itself a construct of an economy of abundance—which has, in effect, institutionalized change, leads men to tear down the old to make way for the new, even though the old is still in good repair. A modern American city is always in the process of being torn down and rebuilt. Except in New England and parts of the Old South and the Southwest, there are few if any visible signs of the past. Wherever the physical plants of the past remain in use—as in prisons, jails, asylums for children or the mentally ill, and hospitals of one kind or another—they are looked upon with disfavor; they impede the implementation of new ideas; they embalm the past.

All this is in decided contrast to Europe, where every place one turns one sees visible reminders of the past. Even more significant, perhaps, is a strong impression that what remains of the past in Europe are its glories; that only the best has survived, in the form of cathedrals, palaces, castles, and art treasures. The squalor, the poverty, and the degradation have long since passed into merciful oblivion. One does not see the wretched hovels from which the masons went forth to work on the Gothic arches; one sees only the majesty and the grandeur of the stones they shaped and placed. One does not see the misery of the serfs; one sees only the wonders of the tapestries that covered the lord's castle walls. Bcause of these constant physical reminders of his heritage, to the cultivated European the past means something quite different from what it means to the American. A large part of his time as a schoolboy was invested in mastering it. His schooling had the effect, if not the intention, of humbling him before the past. Every new generation, vis-à-vis an accumulation of centuries of grandeur, finds itself inferior. The greatest things have already been done, the greatest thoughts have already been thought, the greatest music already played, the greatest poetry already sung. To many cultivated Europeans anything that happened after, say 1914, is relatively unimportant, not worth study, something transient and incidental. They have devoted so large a part of their own lives to imbibing the past, they have such a vested interest in it, that a lack of appreciation of it seems like a reflection on them. The American student's characteristic preface to his remarks—"it seems to me"—is irrelevant to the European. It makes no difference how it seems to the student. He is insignificant; the classics, history, the past, these alone are important.

Freedom from locale, which has left an equally powerful impress on American institutions, is revealed in the tremendous amount of spatial mobility that characterizes the American population. Only a small proportion live and die where they were born. They move from country to city, from city to city, from state to state, from region to region. And this frequent severance of local ties tends to weaken the impact of institutions, of status patterns. Freedom from local ties thus implies also freedom from control by institutional pressures. It may mean, as some students feel, greater control by relatively temporary group associates. The newcomer must prove his conservatism, must conform, must prove that he is like others. He must re-establish his status every time he moves. He is expected, in effect, to declare and act in the manner in which he wishes to be treated. This implies a high degree of vertical mobility.

The movements of population vary from time to time. In the nineteenth century the movements were prevailingly westward. In the twentieth century there have been important movements northward; there have also been movements away from the middle states toward both the East and the West. There has been, as everywhere, a consistent movement from farms to cities. But in the middle of the twentieth century one of the most characteristic patterns of movement has been away from the centers of old cities out to the suburbs and even beyond, to rural but nonfarming areas. A whole new set of institutions is evolving around the resultant new suburban style of living.

Much of this freedom from the past and from locale is both a cause and an effect of modern technology. It is freedom from the past which makes Americans so receptive to technological changes, and it is these changes, in turn, which sever the ties with the past. The essence of institutions is stability; institutions persist, and they incorporate ways of doing things which come down from the past. But American institutions can be understood only in terms of change. The one characteristic most commonly attributed to Americans has always been, and still is, change—"excitement," it used to be called—movement, restlessness, rootlessness. To European observers in the nineteenth century, reared as they had been in a relatively stable, slow-moving society, this constant change—of residence, work, or status—seemed dangerous. To many modern Americans its absence would seem dangerous, a sign of inflexibility, stratification, and stagnation.

The most important institutional changes stem primarily from technological changes. And one of the most revolutionary things that has happened to American institutions in the twentieth century is the institutionalization of such changes by means of scientific research. Vast and increasing sums of money are allocated by government, industry, schools, and foundations for the express function of revealing trends, illuminating needs, inducing change. Business and advertising, with their concept of obsolescence—already referred to—have made change a regular, some think indispensable, part of American life. It is this constant, or rather, accelerative change which gives the impression of speed and breathless tempo in American institutions, and which makes the past, even the immediate past, seem so remote.

EQUALITY

Equality is a relative concept. De Tocqueville, measuring American society against a European (that is, aristocratic) standard, found equality everywhere in the United States,[9] even at a time when great inequalities were institutionalized in slavery; but twentieth-century researchers, measuring American society against its ideal, find inequalities everywhere.

One kind of equality which is characteristic of American institutions might be called psychological rather than material, subjective rather than objective. It is a feeling, an emotion, or an attitude. American institutions make people feel themselves to be the equal of anyone and everyone.[10] This feeling is fostered, at least in part, by the fact that as a member of an audience or public, as consumer or as voter, as target for advertising or propaganda, the American is accustomed to being constantly catered to, coaxed, cajoled, wooed, courted, and competed for. He has something—a consumer dollar and a vote—which powerful interest groups want. They must win him over; therefore he is made to feel important. A sure-fire campaigning technique is the so-called folksy touch; the great must appear to be humble and no better than anyone else. Public-relations counsels make their clients—even glamorous motion-picture stars—appear just like anyone else.

As a corollary of the equality ideal there have arisen conventions so strict as to amount almost to mores. No one in public life is permitted to "look down" on his inferiors. Even the social worker must deal with her clients as a friend, certainly not condescendingly or patronizingly as a superior. Anyone may be contemptuous or act superior to his equals, but no one may similarly treat his inferiors. The wealthy may not publicly condescend to the poor; the powerful may not "push people around." Power must be exercised with humility, even apologetically. Hauteur provokes guffaws rather than obeisance. The professor has no special privileges; the boss stands in line in the cafeteria. The fiction must be maintained that all persons actually are equal. Children must be "consulted" in making rules for their discipline; workers must "participate" in decision-making; all must share in policy determination. A great scandal was precipitated at mid-century when a Cabinet member spoke contemptuously of the unemployed. There is a great cult of the underdog.

Americans accept with complacency specific inequalities in many areas of personality, but not a generalized or implicitly inherent inferiority. They cheerfully grant that some people have more money than others, more ability in specific areas, more ambition, more talent, more speed, more skill, and more knowledge. Some are admittedly better baseball players, athletes, readers, and writers than others. They grant all these specific inequalities, yet they resist to the utmost any implication of general or inherent superiority in the sense that some people *are* better than others. A score of specific superiorities will not necessarily add up to a total superiority. Parents will accept a classification of students on the basis of reading ability; they will admit that their child cannot read as well as some other child. But they resist any classification on the basis of any criterion which implies that one child *is* better than another.

In spite of the institutionalization of the value "equality," there is nevertheless a considerable public sharing of feelings of inferiority. For when the voter or consumer silences his radio or television set, puts down the magazine advertisements, turns from the dazzling flattery beamed at him as a member of a voting or buying public and attempts to interact with his "superiors" as a lone individual, he finds a different situation. When he wishes to talk personally to the leader or the star he finds himself being firmly, albeit graciously, turned away. The top people who were so ingratiating to him as part of a public or audience are not available to him as an individual. He has high status primarily in his role as buyer or voter, not as an individual.

DISCREPANCY BETWEEN THEORY AND PRACTICE

To note that freedom and equality have been deep-seated American values does not, of course, mean that they have always been successfully incorporated in the functioning of American institutions. As we have noted, there have always had to be struggles to extend and to implement them. One of the most interesting developments in institutional analysis among American sociologists in the last two decades has been the emphasis, as though it were a new and shocking discovery, on the discrepancy between the professed values of American society and actual practice.[11] There has been an almost compulsive drive to rub our noses in the discrepancy between our ideals and our practices. It received its first major recognition at the turn of the century in the work of a group of journalists —known as the muckrakers—who made us inescapably aware of it. It was stated by social scientists in the form of the so-called J-curve of institutional or conformity behavior. One sociologist spoke long ago of what he called our "schizoid" culture.[12]

It is only, however, since Myrdal made his famous analysis of what he called the American dilemma that it has become fashionable to point out the failure of American institutions to live up to American ideals. Nowadays most people distinguish between the theoretical and the operational mores in any society, between the professed ideals and the practiced ones, the dream and the reality. There are varying conceptualizations of this discrepancy—latent patterns,[13] for example, and community dissociation.[14]

Perhaps no society functions according to the theory it professes, but only in America does such nonconformity of practice to theory seem to occasion so much comment. Nowhere is it so self-conscious; nowhere does it seem to present such a problem; nowhere is there so much determined effort to do something about it on the part of voluntary organizations. The important point seems to be that the values are actually used as a measure of performance; they are thus used as weapons by groups fighting to realize them; accordingly, they have power even when they do not prevail.

Sometimes the discrepancy between theory and practice is due to the fact that it takes a long time for practice to catch up with theory. At any one historical moment of time the conditions of living create a hiatus between theory and practice; fifty or a hundred years later the hiatus may be closed, but meanwhile a new one has opened up and yawns ominously. A condition of inequality and lack of freedom may continue for a long time before successful efforts are made to redress it.[15] The existence at any one time, therefore, of inequalities and restraints on freedom in American institutions does not mean that the ideals of freedom and equality are empty words or hypocritical cant; it means, more likely, that movements to destroy the inequalities and restraints have not yet arisen. The chances are that they soon will.

THE CONFLICT BETWEEN FREEDOM AND EQUALITY

The implementation of the values freedom and equality runs headlong into a number of dilemmas. Not only is there the discrepancy between theory and practice just noted, but sometimes there is also a discrepancy between these two values themselves. Can we have both? Or is there a dilemma inherent in the relationship between them?

Competition, for example, is based on the premise of inequality in the competing units.[16] The winner is necessarily superior. What, if anything, should be done about that? Freedom, in the sense of absence of control, allows natural inequalities to emerge; and often these inequalities destroy freedom for the inferior. Free competition may mean that the smaller, the weaker, the less powerful cease to be free. What should be done when free competition leads to the elimination of competitors, or to excessive power and dominance by a few? Without some kind of regulation, the weaker group is rendered exploitable by the stronger. How much regulation should there be? When does regulation become oppression? How much regulation is compatible with freedom? In the realm of conflict as well as of competition, unregulated freedom has been found to mean freedom for only the successful. Actually, therefore, in order to approximate equality, in both competition and conflict situations, some restrictions on freedom have been found necessary.

Legal institutions in the United States reflect a constant struggle to preserve or impose freedom on one set of interest groups even at the expense of another. Thus, for example, laws are passed to protect competitors from one another—to equalize them—at the expense of the strong competitor. The efficient businessman is not free to price his products competitively; that would be "unfair competition." The union protects workers from competition among themselves; it equalizes pay for the same job, regardless of quality of work, and thus deprives the superior worker of a certain amount of freedom. Compulsory school laws attempt to equalize at least educational opportunity. Numerous laws regulate political competition—elections—in order to prevent gross inequalities. In areas of conflict also, laws attempt to equalize conditions at the expense of freedom. Thus laws are passed to protect consumers when a seller's market prevails, and to protect producers when a buyer's market exists. Laws are made and interpreted in favor of "capital" or management when it is felt that their interests must be favored as compared with those of labor; then laws are made and interpreted in favor of workers in order to equalize their position vis-à-vis management. In the middle of the twentieth century an effort is being made to redress the balance, so equality now means restrictions on the freedom of unions. Laws are made restricting the freedom of the majority group in industry, education, and politics in order to give more freedom to minority groups—especially Negroes—and so it goes. The continuing and never-ending effort to balance freedom and equality among all the numerous parties to competition and conflict in a complex society is a fundamental key to understanding American institutions.

THE CONFLICT OF FREEDOM AND EQUALITY WITH OTHER VALUES

The values freedom and equality often conflict not only with one another but also with other cherished values. Freedom, for example, may conflict with security; equality, with family values. The second third of the twentieth century saw the emergence of a demand for security even if it meant losing a certain amount of freedom; the great depression of the 1930s revealed to millions the price that had to be paid for freedom, and they came to doubt the desirability of a kind of freedom which meant unemployment, hunger, and cold. Equally serious perhaps is the conflict between the values which center in the family and the values of equality of opportunity. A child's life chances are closely related to his class background as determined by his family. The tremendous preoccupation with problems of stratification among American sociologists attests to the difficulties Americans experience in swallowing the contradiction between family values and the ideal of equality.

So much by way of introduction. The strategy of this discussion is to view American institutions, at mid-century, as engaged in a continuing attempt, more or less successful, to realize in a unique context of abundance the ideals of freedom and equality for different segments of the population, in different areas, and in response to different threats.

Industrial and Economic Institutions

The logic of Adam Smith's *Wealth of Nations*, written at the threshold of the technological changes we call the First Industrial Revolution, was indisputable for the kind of production then current. Smith prescribed the allocation of scarce factors of production for the maximization of output. Although never completely implemented, this theory served as an ideal for many decades. Efforts were made to shape economic institutions to fit it. Refined and elaborated by later thinkers, it was, par excellence, the political economy for an era of scarcity.

But modern industry, it has become evident, operates according to laws quite different from those of the eighteenth and nineteenth centuries. The laws governing productivity today are technological rather than personal or individual. The great productivity of the modern individual American worker is not based on his superior talent or skill or industry as compared with individual workers of former times; it is based, rather, on the superior tools he works with and the superior management—especially technical staff work—that organizes production.

Nor do the old economic theories of distribution hold for an age of abundance. If the returns of modern industry were distributed according to nineteenth-century concepts, or in terms of individual initiative, the production machine would stall and grind to a stop, for the major returns really belong to the owners of capital and to management. And automation, which we shall discuss below, will in time reduce the worker's contribution even more.[17] Yet the worker must be paid more and more as his distinctive contribution becomes less and less. Otherwise there would not be a market large enough to absorb the goods being produced. One of the great problems at mid-century is that of finding some face-saving formula according to which the worker will be paid in spite of a declining relative contribution. Even today much of modern productivity is virtually given away to the worker under a thin guise of wages in the form of feather-bedding, made work, and similar devices.

As the worker becomes decreasingly important as a producer, he becomes increasingly important as a consumer. As productivity increases—at the estimated rate of 3 to 5 per cent per year at mid-century—the problem becomes one of channeling goods and services to the widest possible consumer public. In classical economics the consumer was king, in the sense that by "voting" for certain goods and services through his purchases he decided how the factors of production should be allocated. The consumer is still king, but in a different sense. The functioning of the economy depends on his being able to consume the goods that are produced, whatever they may be.

One of the great fears of the nineteenth century was the so-called *leveling-down* effect of democratic institutions. Whether or not such a leveling down has occurred in other areas—education, taste, or art—need not concern us here. At this point we are interested primarily in the great *leveling up* which has accompanied or resulted from abundance in occupation and in income distribution. Little by little, though perhaps at an increasing rate, modern technology is obliterating the unskilled worker—the man at the bottom who contributes mainly muscle—and is upgrading the whole economy occupationally; the welfare state and union pressure are tending to equalize incomes; and mass markets are tending to equalize consumption habits.

OCCUPATIONAL UPGRADING

One of the most spectacular trends in the occupational composition of the working force in the twentieth century has been the decline in the proportion engaged in agricultural pursuits—including forestry and fishing—from 53.5 per cent in 1870 to only 13.7 per cent in the middle of the twentieth century.[18] The rural style of living, the values, and the point of view which characterize people who live on farms and which once were typical of American institutions, have now come to characterize only a relatively small proportion of all Americans. And as modern technology improves channels of communication, even this declining proportion of the population becomes increasingly urban in its thinking and orientation. The farmer is a minority group, fighting with other interest groups for control of power.

Professionals have increased threefold since 1870. In that year they constituted 2.6 per cent of the working force; by mid-century, 7.5 per cent.[19] By far the largest part of this increase came from the emergence of wholly new professions which did not even exist until the twentieth century. Thus if we compare the increase between 1870 and 1940 in the traditional professions—those including doctors, lawyers, clergymen, artists, teachers, professors, and musicians—with the increase in engineering and technical professions, we find that although the first increased by 571 per cent, the latter increased by 4,889 per cent.[20] Many men who would once have worked with hammers and saws now work with test tubes and electronic instruments.

Other white-collar and service workers have increased more than twofold, from 17.8 per cent of the working force in 1870 to 37.6 per cent at mid-century.[21] A large part of this increase reflects the influx of women into the labor force as office workers and sales persons. But much of it is due to young men who, a generation or two ago, would have been wearing overalls and carrying a lunch box, but who now wear business clothes and carry a brief case. Many of these clerical jobs are not much better than factory jobs, but they carry with them a different orientation and standard of living. At the lowest level the white-collar workers are inferior in pay to the manual worker; they are, in effect, a "proletariat in street clothes." At the upper levels, however, they may be technicians of the highest order. On the whole, the members of this great new white-collar class are better educated — in the sense of having attended school longer — than their forebears.

These white-collar and professional people, including a large number in the proliferating new professions—in engineering, in management, in personnel services, in counseling—constitute a new middle class; the bourgeois or old middle class of independent businessmen and property owners has shrunk to minor significance. In 1950 only 10.3 per cent of those employed in nonagricultural industries were self-employed, and many of these were owners of small shops,[22] *petit* rather than *haute bourgeoisie.*

Of major significance for the social order is the gradual reduction of the lowest rungs of the industrial hierarchy. We seem to be moving toward the virtual abolition of the "toiling masses," toward the creation of a society in which a middle-class orientation is typical. The unskilled manual worker is becoming an anachronism. In the first half of the twentieth century the proportion of workers who were semiskilled increased; the proportion who were unskilled decreased.

The old question which used to be raised in discussions of democratic institutions—"but who will do the dirty work?"—is being answered by the machine. So far, so good. But in the middle of the twentieth century a Second Industrial Revolution, automation, so called, ushered in a substitution of machines not only for manual labor but also for many of the higher level kinds of work as well. The feed-back principle makes it possible for machines to check errors more accurately even than human beings; it renders machines sensitive to deviations and able to correct them. The giant computing machines do the work of thousands of even high-grade clerical workers.

At mid-century there were already plants run automatically, especially in the oil industry; parts of the automobile industry had similarly been reduced to automatic production and other plants were also experimenting in this direction.[23] Thus not only the manual worker but also the skilled and even the white-collar worker were each in the process of becoming an anachronism. One technologist was quoted as saying that every human being in a factory was an engineering defect which must ultimately be corrected; ideally the factory should be wholly automatic, the only personnel being a small complement of engineers and scientists.

The use of fissionable material for power, along with automation, is part of the Second Industrial Revolution. It will enormously increase the sources of power; it was almost cheap enough at mid-century to be competitive with conventional power sources in some parts of the world.

What will become of the worker when the machine takes away his job? In the past this question has been answered by the absorption of workers in new industries. New jobs have been created as old ones have disappeared. So far the process of automation has followed the old pattern; the increased requirements of firms which have installed automatic equipment have absorbed the workers whose jobs have been eliminated. But there is no assurance that this trend can continue indefinitely. In the past, leisure was the privilege of a relatively few at the top of the social structure; in the future will a job rather than leisure be the privilege of a relatively few at the top?

The problem, as we saw above, is essentially one of finding a technique for distributing the goods which the productivity of modern industry makes possible. Labor leaders were fully cognizant of the sinister implications of the Second Industrial Revolution. Their strategy was not—as was that of the workers in the early nineteenth century—to fight the machine, but to see that the costs of automation were shared and not charged exclusively to the worker in the form of unemployment or underemployment. As a first step they proposed the so-called guaranteed annual wage, "to achieve increases in and an improved distribution of purchasing power in order to balance ability to consume with ability to produce; and to safeguard against hardship those directly affected by the march of the new technology."[24]

A second way to meet the new Industrial Revolution is a shorter work-week with the same or even higher pay. There was at mid-century talk of a four-day week; it was predicted for a decade later. An even greater increase in service occupations and the professions is suggested—more counselors, more entertainers, more copy writers. Increased waste by accelerating the rate of obsolescence has also been proposed to stimulate people to discard their equipment often and replace it with newer models. More sinister is the siphoning off of huge chunks of production for military matériel, and the withdrawing of large numbers of workers temporarily from the working force for military service. Sharing American goods with other peoples is another way to cope with abundance; but even this demands taking care not to demoralize world markets.

INCOME DISTRIBUTION AND LEVELING UP

The drastic use of the income tax and social security laws, together with strong pressure from unions, has had a tendency, students of the subject believe, toward equalization of income distribution. Low income, which used to be related primarily to unemployment or to underemployment, at least in "normal" or husband-wife families, seems to be associated increasingly with disturbance in the family make-up or with age. A comparison of the composition of low-income families in 1939 and 1947, for example, revealed the differences shown in the accompanying tabulation.[25] "Low income," concludes another student, today "is thus not so much a matter of rates of pay for work as it is the system of support of those unable to work and the amount of income provided by social-security programs."[26] If people are poor it is not usually because the breadwinner is underpaid; it is more likely because there is no breadwinner or because he is old or ill.

	Percentage of Units with Income	
	Under $500 in 1939	Under $1,500 in 1947
All	100	100
Unrelated individuals	17	25
Husband-wife families	68	58
Women living alone or as heads of families	20	30

The trends toward equalization of income by region, occupation, and race have been summarized as follows:

. . . unless there were countervailing tendencies among other groups, incomes in general have tended to become somewhat more equal. . . . From 1929 and 1939 to 1949 the per capita income of the low-income regions had increased by a greater percentage than that of the high-income regions, and . . . the most noticeable shift in the distribution of population among regions had been the expansion of the region which in 1949 had the highest per capita income. . . . Also . . . net migration from 1940 to 1950 was clearly away from low-income and to high-income regions. . . . Further . . . from 1939 to 1949, wage-or-salary income increased by a greater percentage for low-paid than for high-paid occupations, and . . . the number of workers in the high-paid occupations had increased by a greater percentage than in low-paid occupations. In addition, available data indicate that from 1939 to 1949 the average income of nonwhites had increased at a somewhat greater rate than that of the whites. Since the whole is the sum of the parts, there is reason to believe that incomes in general have been becoming somewhat more equal.[27]

THE SOCIAL STRUCTURE OF INDUSTRY

The social organization within American industry has undergone great changes in the twentieth century. In the nineteenth century the top positions in industry were filled by a bold, reckless, adventurous type of man with an almost piratical point of view. Such men were, in fact, sometimes referred to as robber barons. They built huge industrial structures—sometimes called empires—and ruled them in a feudal manner, as though they were private property. They identified themselves with their industries and resisted all efforts at outside control. In the later years of the nineteenth century and the beginning of the twentieth the great corporations came into the hands not of the industrialists who had created them but of financiers who manipulated them. Industries became the pawns of bankers. These two types—industry builders and financial manipulators—came to be stereotyped as "capitalists," and throughout the world they were caricatured in all their predatory ruthlessness.

At the bottom of these great enterprises were the masses of unskilled workers, in large measure foreign born and therefore easily exploitable. The relations between employer and employee were harsh and hostile. The concept "toiling masses" had some validity, particularly with reference to the large industries; in the smaller organizations the relationships were likely to be personal and even friendly.

Both of these concepts—"capitalist" and "toiling masses"—have become anachronistic in the twentieth century. In the modern corporation ownership and management have been divorced. Management has been taken over by a more or less professional class which is quite different in background and orientation from the old-fashioned "capitalist" who had built the industry or manipulated or even undermined it by exploitation. The new professional manager is an educated man; his motivations are likely to be different from either the original builder or the financial exploiter. His main obligation is still to make a profit for his stockholders—the Supreme Court said so in 1916—but he also feels obligations to the consuming public or customers and to his working force. An equally striking change has taken place at the other end of the industrial structure. The immigrant generation eventually died off, and after 1924 the recruitment rate became so low as to be negligible. The children of the immigrants went to school. They achieved political power and the know-how to use it. In the 1930s they elected an administration which gave them the right to organize into unions. In addition, as we just saw, technological changes gradually reduced the lowest unskilled jobs and upgraded everyone else. Analysts of American society no longer find such concepts as "capital" and "labor" useful; instead, they speak of management and manpower resources. Workers are no longer viewed as "factors of production," but as human resources which must be husbanded and developed.

OCCUPATIONAL MOBILITY

The enormous amount of study of the American economy to determine whether vertical mobility—or its converse, stratification—is increasing or decreasing has resulted largely in equivocal findings. At mid-century the conclusion seemed warranted that the relative fluidity, or perhaps we should say permeability, of the economy varied from time to time, but not necessarily in a one-way direction. In the 1930s, when much of the research data on mobility was gathered, there may have been a relatively great amount of rigidity in the economy; earlier and later, however, the rigidity relaxed, making room for more flexibility. In brief, stratification has not been a permanent feature of American society. There are no institutionalized barriers to upward mobility; there are only periods of retardation in mobility due to the functioning of the economy itself.

So far as individuals are concerned, workers tend to end their working careers in occupations higher than those they began in; there are, for example, many more who rise from laboring to business and professional occupations than who decline thence to the laboring class.[28] The relative mobility which prevails in a society is, however, apparently more closely related to its technology than to its historical tradition. Thus, for example, one study which compared occupational mobility in the United States and France found that although mobility was greater in the first—67.5 per cent as compared with 48.3 per cent—both showed a great deal of mobility in spite of the feudal tradition in the one and the frontier tradition in the other.[29]

And of course all interpretations of occupational mobility must be made with the fact in mind that the whole economy is being upgraded. More and more personnel are required at the higher levels; less and less, at the lower.

FREEDOM AND EQUALITY VERSUS BUREAUCRACY

The increasing size of industrial units has posed problems of freedom and equality to personnel within the corporation which are sometimes subsumed under the rubric of "bureaucracy."

The hierarchical principle or "chain-of-command" theory of organization, if not inevitable, seems historically to have been the almost universal recourse of large organizations.[30] It is simple, easy to grasp, and looks fine on wall charts. It has had such widespread adoption that it has all but inhibited even the exploration of other principles of organization.

But hierarchical organization or bureaucracy is antithetical to American ideals. Its rigid system of inferiors and superiors does not sit well with people accustomed to the theory of freedom and equality. So long as the American working force consisted largely of immigrant workers there was little resistance to bureaucracy. But in the second quarter of the twentieth century, when the labor force was made up primarily of native workers, it began to appear that the old principles of organization would have to be modified. Bureaucracy began to be a subject of detailed scientific analysis by social scientists. The so-called human-relations-in-industry movement began; it was both an index of and contributor to a quiet revolution in industrial organization.

The types of motivation in the plant which had seemed to succeed with workers in the nineteenth and early twentieth centuries were no longer usable in the second quarter of the twentieth century. In an age of scarcity it had been possible to discipline the worker because discipline was inherent in the process of production; if the individual worker was not efficient, if he did not work hard, there was a decline in the total product. But in an economy where productivity snowballs according to laws of its own, with relatively little regard to the old laws of individual industry, and becomes increasingly independent of the workers who man the machines and increasingly dependent on the laboratory scientist, the technician, and the engineers who invent and design; in an economy where, as we saw above, men must be paid in order to buy, old motivational patterns break down. Even if technological changes had not been so drastic, changes in the working population would have demanded new organizational patterns in industry as the sons of immigrants brought their point of view with them to the plant. The old "straw boss" who could order men around would not be tolerated. Power has to be exercised tactfully, and the illusion has to be created and maintained that decisions are not handed down from the top but cooperatively arrived at. The worker, no longer an independent self-directed, self-employed craftsman or businessman, has to feel nevertheless that he is more than a cog in a machine. The principles of the human-relations-in-industry school of industrial relations attempt to restore to workers the sense of personal worth which is inherent in the concepts of freedom and equality. Policy decisions must be explained and interpreted rather than simply announced. The worker must not be permitted to feel that he is being manipulated or "pushed around." Departments are to be assigned tasks, but are themselves to work out ways of performing them. Less, not more specialization; more, not less diversification; flexibility rather than rigidity; decentralization rather than centralization — these seemed to be the goals, however far from implementation, toward which industrial-plant organization was tending at mid-century.

There was opposition on the part of union leaders to the human-relations-in-industry approach on the ground, in part, that it was not genuinely democratic; that it was paternalistic, designed primarily to increase productivity rather than to practice democratic methods; and that it was, in effect, designed to win the loyalty of workers to the employer rather than to the union.

AGRICULTURE

Because agriculture is the major industry in most nations throughout the world, it is in this area that American achievements are probably best appreciated.[31] There is no peasant class as Europe knows it, with a culture of its own, custom-bound and backward-looking.

Almost three-fourths of all American farms, at mid-century, are operated by owners or part-owners. A little less than a third are operated by tenants, while not even 1 per cent are operated by a hired manager. Tenancy is of four major kinds: cash tenants pay cash rent for the use of land; share-cash tenants pay part of the rent with a share of the product and the rest in cash; share tenants pay a share of the product for rent; and the sharecropper is a share tenant to whom the landlord furnishes all the equipment. The first of these forms of tenancy is most common in the Northeast and Far West; the second in the Middle West; the third in the Great Plains; and the last in the South. The sharecropper is the poorest agricultural worker; his standard of living is low. He is, fortunately, becoming an anachronism as the South becomes increasingly industrialized and its agriculture modernized.

The commonest size of farm is between 70 and 140 acres. But both very large or so-called factory farms and very small or part-time farms are increasing in number. The first are farms of thousands of acres, run like factories by corporations, raising great commercial crops like fruit, onions, lettuce, and similar truck products. The second are small acreages owned by workers who supplement their incomes by other jobs.

The family farm is still typical, although the factory farm is probably also characteristically American. On two fifths of all farms the work is done by family members; on another two fifths, farm workers are hired for help from one to seventy-five days per year. Thus farming is still—in spite of the inroads of factory farming—one industry which is organized on a family basis.

The productivity of American farmers has become legendary throughout the world, and it is increasing. Not only the use of machinery but also the application of all kinds of science have upped the productivity of American agriculture until methods have to be devised to brake it. The approach is dynamic rather than static. For example, the shape and size of animals as well as of plants are viewed as amenable to change. If small turkeys with much breast meat are desired in the market, turkeys are bred to these specifications. The natural laying capacity of hens is not accepted fatalistically; it is stretched by the use of electricity and feeding. New uses for agricultural products are always being sought. A new profession—the county agent—has arisen to teach farmers how to incorporate the newest scientific findings in their operations; and a corresponding profession teaches farm women how to process foods for family nutrition.

The productivity of agriculture has released a large number of workers who have migrated to urban communities. Migration from rural areas has also raised perplexing problems with respect to the position of agriculture in the total economy. Because the system of representation in legislative bodies gives undue weight to rural areas, even when their populations decline in relation to urban expansion, farmers—both in the several states and in the nation as a whole—exert a disproportionate influence on policy.[32]

Farmers for the most part enjoy a high standard of living. Almost all of them now have electricity and radios; most of them have automobiles and all-weather roads; about half have telephones and running water. About three fourths of farm children fourteen to seventeen years of age remain in school. Health standards are also improving, as reflected in the large proportion of babies in farm areas—about three fourths—born in hospitals.

Countervailing Power

Economic institutions are technological, as they refer primarily to industry and production; but they are also political, as they refer to policy with respect to control. Indeed, the scientific study of such institutions was called political economy throughout the nineteenth century. Transitional, therefore, to the following discussion of political institutions is a brief statement with respect to American policy vis-à-vis economic institutions.

One of the first results of the earlier technological revolution in industry was the change it brought in economic organization. The family ceased to be the chief organizational unit of production except in agriculture, and the corporation emerged as seemingly the most suitable way to organize production.[33] A characteristic pattern of industrial growth in the United States has been something like this: As a new industry emerges, a fairly large number of people and firms enter it. After a while the grueling competition weeds out many of them until finally, by one means or another—

consolidations, mergers, elimination, absorption[34] — only a relatively small number remain; the Big Three, for example, or the Big Five, or the Big Four. These giants come to control the industry. A certain number of smaller independent firms remain either to supply local markets or to perform specialized functions, or to take care of special markets. But they are nevertheless controlled by the behavior of the Big N in their industry. This has been the story in oil, sugar, whisky, rubber, automobiles, chemicals, steel, motion pictures, radio, television, air conditioning, and electronics. Free competition seems to run this inevitable course, ultimately converging in a fairly small number of giant competitors.

In Europe the tendency in the past has been not to fight these trends. When large units were formed and decided to cooperate in so-called cartels rather than to compete they were protected, not prosecuted. In the United States, in order to promote free competition, two quite different paths have been followed. One was in the direction of laws forbidding monopoly — so-called fair trade laws — and the other of protecting the less efficient competitor.

In spite of the early antimonopoly laws the trend toward the concentration of economic power continued, almost unabated. But the expected results predicted by economists did not materialize. The remarkable performance of the American economy in the forties and fifties led one economist to reappraise the theory on which antimonopoly policy was based. He found that in spite of concentration of power, wages increased and prices declined rather than, as expected, the other way around. He concluded that there was, in the American system, a principle operating which tended to mitigate the evils inherent in too great concentration of economic power, namely the principle of countervailing power.[35] It states that in the American economy, when primary power becomes too great there is a tendency for checks to emerge in the form of countervailing power which insists on sharing the primary power.

Labor unions illustrate the action of this principle. In the nineteenth century freedom for the enterpriser came to mean lack of freedom for the worker. The courts said that the worker was "free" to bargain and contract his services, but that he could not be fettered by collective contracts. By insisting on the worker's freedom of contract, the courts had effectively shorn him of his freedom. It was not until the second third of the twentieth century that the right to organize became fully guaranteed by law. The National Labor Relations Act required employers to bargain collectively with representatives of their workers. It attempted to equalize the bargaining power of worker and management. It was a case of countervailance in that the worker, through his union, was attempting to share the original power.

Consumers also exert a countervailing influence. Today management must appease not only the worker but also the consumer, and no longer has the power to distribute profits to shareholders as it wills. Reduced prices as well as high wages are demanded. Consumers are by no means as well organized as workers, nor do they share original power to the same extent. Nevertheless, they constitute a form of countervailing power.[36]

Political Institutions

Americans have been called politically naive. In the ideological sphere and in the Marxist sense of preoccupation with theory this is doubtless true. But in the practical operation of political machinery they are extremely mature as measured by the stability of their government. The formal structure of American political institutions has remained essentially unchanged since the adoption of the Constitution, with the exception of the addition of a number of amendments to the federal Constitution and occasional revisions of state constitutions and local charters. This formal structure can be found in the constitutions of the federal government and the several states, in official documents—treaties, proclamations, executive orders, administrative rulings—and in court decisions.

Within this stable framework, however, numerous revolutions—taking many forms—have occurred by way of court decisions; by way of party organization; by way of constitutional amendment; and by way of planned legislation or administrative procedure. The decades have flowed through the constitutional framework, leaving it outwardly or formally unchanged but inwardly or functionally transformed. Our concern here will not be with documentary exegesis, but with the actual functioning of political institutions as they faced the problems of mid-century, with how they attempted to meet the challenges of freedom and equality in a setting of abundance.

THE EXECUTIVE BRANCH AS A CONGERIES
OF CONFLICTING AGENCIES

The theory of government as an impartial umpire, as a disinterested above-the-battle spectator and policeman concerned only with enforcing rules of fair play, does not fit the facts of American political life. Neither, however, does the concept of a ruling class, in the sense of a class which can impose its will upon the government. There are as many ruling classes as there are interest groups being served by executive agencies. For the executive branch of the United States government might well be analyzed, figuratively, as a vast geological formation which shows, level by level, the history of the conflicts of interest or veto groups which have deposited their residues there. It consists of layers of some 2100 agencies set up at different times to administer laws in favor now of one group, now of another. As each party or coalition of interest groups has achieved power — or countervailing power — it has set up by law permanent agencies to safeguard its interests.

The history of this vast wilderness of agencies, then, reflects the history of countervailing power. The one thing which has characterized American political institutions is that whenever any interest group seems to be getting too much power, the voters will turn against it or it will evoke countervailance. Americans do not want any single interest to get too strong, be it church, unions, corporations, or political parties.

As a result, the executive branch of the government is a wilderness of agencies, sometimes in conflict with one another. A commission challenges a lower court; a board sues a commission; or a bureau hales a board into court.[37] Labor, management, consumers, producers, minority groups, competitors, all seek protection against the exertion of power by others through governmental agencies established in their behalf.

The executive branch of the government may also be at odds with the legislative branch, for it sometimes happens that the Congress is controlled by a party different from the president's. The repercussions are particularly serious in the area of international relations. American political institutions have not been well adapted to the conduct of international affairs. They are entrusted to the Chief Executive, but all commitments must be approved by the Senate. If the Senate is under the control of an opposition party or a segment of the party hostile to the Executive's program, a deadlock may ensue.[38] Some people feel that American political institutions are inadequate for the tasks imposed by world leadership.

Furthermore, American representatives dealing with representatives of other nations are handicapped because they cannot commit their government to any long-time policy or course of action. Foreign negotiators are fearful that any negotiation with the Executive of the United States may be undone at the next election.[39] There is confusion also in the relationship of treaties to congressional statutes, and apprehension whether a treaty may abrogate certain provisions of the Constitution. Recurring efforts to restrict the executive branch in negotiating with foreign powers have so far not met with success.[40]

THE INDEPENDENT JUDICIARY

Nowhere is the constantly changing nature of the concept of freedom in America more clearly illustrated than in the opinions and decisions of the Supreme Court. A large proportion of the cases argued before this tribunal deal with civil rights, and the interpretations have tended—especially in the second third of the century—constantly toward expanding the rights of individuals, members of minority groups, and, in general, the underdog.

By means of a brilliant stroke of judicial reasoning, the first chief justice of the Supreme Court, John Marshall, established the principle—in the famous case of *Marbury v. Madison*—that the Supreme Court could declare actions of the Congress unconstitutional and therefore void. Sometimes in American history the Supreme Court, being appointed and therefore far removed from the average citizen, has been more conservative than the Congress, which, being elected, must be responsive to the electorate; but on occasion the Court has been more liberal.

The first ten amendments of the American Constitution protect citizens against invasion of their rights by the federal government; the fourteenth amendment protects them against invasion by the several state governments. And increasingly the tendency is to protect individuals against invasion of their rights by other individuals and groups, as well as by governments. As former President Truman once said, "The extension of civil rights today means, not protection of the people *against* the Government, but protection of the people *by* the Government."[41] The new governmental protection is increasingly against the violation of rights by other individuals or groups. The effect is to deprive some segments of the population of certain kinds of rights or freedom and to bestow new kinds of rights or freedom on other segments.

Thus, for example, in the second third of the twentieth century the Supreme Court found that property owners were not free to use the courts to enforce the so-called restrictive covenants not to sell or rent to Negroes or other minority groups (1948). They were free to make such covenants, but not to enforce them in court. Similarly, employers in many states were not free to discriminate against workers on the basis of nationality, color, or religion. In 1954 the Supreme Court found that local school boards were not free to segregate Negro children, and denied the boards the right to deprive these children of "equal protection of the law."[42]

We have here illustrated the basic principle of countervailance, or checks and balances, which is so characteristic of American institutions. There is a great expansion in freedom for certain elements of the population, gained by curtailing the freedom of certain other elements. The Supreme Court, removed from the necessity of answering to a constituency, watches the balance and tosses a weight, now on one side, now on the other.

POLITICAL PARTIES

The American Constitution makes no provision for political parties, or "factions," as they were originally called. The hope was that the nation would function without them. It was soon found, however, that the Constitution could not be implemented without some form of organization willing to assume the responsibility of selecting and backing candidates. Thus as early as the administration of John Adams, political parties began to emerge; today they are an integral part of the government.

American political parties are wholly improbable, illogical, and theoretically nonsensible. Their major virtue is the necessity they place upon conflicting groups to come to terms with one another. For each party is itself in effect a coalition of disparate and often conflicting interest groups. The bargaining and concessions and compromises go on within the party rather than in public, for the party must present a united front, especially during campaigns. So long as a party can accommodate these conflicting elements and thus achieve a working equilibrium, it can retain its hold on power. Only when a party fails in this constant effort at equilibration does the opposing party succeed in deposing it.

Historically the Republican party has consisted of eastern industrial interests and midwestern agrarian interests; the Democratic party, once primarily representative of southern agrarian interests, came in the second third of the twentieth century to include the urban working classes also. By and large, the people with higher incomes, more education, and native parentage have tended to be Republican; those with lower incomes, less education, and foreign background, Democratic. At mid-century, however, many changes were in process. The South was becoming industrialized, for one thing, and its interests correspondingly different. Farmers were forsaking their traditional ties with the Republican party. Even more significant, the urban workers were changing their allegiances.

The impact of upgrading the whole economy by technological advance, the creation of a large new-style middle class—not of petty bourgeois property owners but of white-collar, especially clerical workers—was compounded because it coincided with demographic—ethnic and racial—changes also. The lowest classes, which were slowly being eliminated from the industrial structure, were also for the most part immigrants with a variety of ethnic backgrounds. Their children rose in the economic ladder, and it was they who came to political power and contributed the great dynamic force in the so-called Roosevelt Revolution. The New Deal, which their power effectuated, represented a fundamental change in direction for political and economic life. The old idea of *laissez faire* went by the boards. It became an accepted fact that government must step in to protect human beings when great catastrophes strike.

But once these governmental welfare programs became an established part of government, the question arose—even for those who had benefited from them—how far should political control be permitted over economic life? Those who had profited from the new institutions did not necessarily wish the trend toward more government to continue. They had been boosted in status from Have-Nots to Haves. Millions of voters were being pulled in different directions by divided emotions and shifting fears.[43]

Although conflicting points of view with respect to the limits of government constituted perhaps the sharpest political issue between parties at mid-century, the actual trend of government policy seemed to be inexorably in the direction of widened activities. Welfare activities were extended under Republican as well as under Democratic administrations, more slowly perhaps, more frugally perhaps, more cautiously perhaps, but no less inevitably for that.

CENTRALIZATION

Even in areas where there was consensus with respect to governmental functions there was growing confusion with respect to which of the several levels of government should perform certain functions. Welfare activities had long been recognized as obligations of the local government; in the nineteenth century state governments had taken over some. At mid-century many formerly local or state activities were being performed by the federal government. In other areas as well, there were continuing and perennial issues arising between so-called states' rights and the powers of the federal government. The most salient illustration of this historical issue at mid-century was the reaction of several southern states to the Supreme Court decision, in May 1954, on the segregation of Negroes in elementary schools.

INSTITUTIONAL ASPECTS OF PUBLIC OPINION

The term "public opinion" has both a static and a dynamic aspect.[44] In its static aspect it refers to the totality of mores, attitudes, beliefs, and values which are taken for granted. There is only one—and, therefore, in effect, no—opinion about them. The intuitive political leader knows these values so intimately that he rejects anything which would go counter to them; hence they do not become issues. In its dynamic aspect, however, public opinion refers to controversial issues. Here there is a choice; people may be pro or con, and different points of view emerge.

Because institutional or static public opinion in the United States opposes aggressive war, it is difficult to convince Americans of the need to go to war. War must always be presented to the American public as either defensive or preventive, taking account of the fact that institutional public opinion favors democracy, wishes to share American blessings with less favored nations, opposes concentration of power, and tends to side with the underdog.[45]

Our discussion of the institutional structure of the dynamic or controversial aspect of public opinion will be deferred to a later section, since it refers to nonpolitical as well as to political issues. But one more point should be made here. Foreign observers have commented on the manifest preoccupation of Americans with the attitude or opinion of others toward them. They have made much of the assumption that Americans want everyone to "love" them.[46] The implication is that Americans are, in this respect, big babies, unable to bear disapproval. As a matter of fact, the preoccupation of Americans with the attitudes and opinions of other nations reflects their reliance on social and psychological controls rather than on physical force. Nations which rely on force do not have to worry so much about whether or not they are approved.

THE COMMUNIST THREAT AS A TEST OF AMERICAN
POLITICAL INSTITUTIONS

American political institutions have had to pass many serious tests— slavery, for example, and the assimilation of immigrants of diverse ethnic backgrounds, the rise of great corporations, two world wars, and the great depression of the 1930s. The question has always been, can they pass this test, can they pass that one? Are they flexible enough to meet this assault or that attack? Can they adjust to this new situation or to that? Can they protect themselves against this blow or that thrust? At mid-century the most serious test of American political institutions was that posed by the threat of communism.

First, on the domestic scene. American political institutions were not designed to protect themselves against the kinds of conspiratorial attack which communists have made on them. A conspiratorial tradition being lacking, the assumption has always been, as Jefferson and Holmes believed, that in the free market place of ideas, American principles and ideologies could win in competition with all comers. Since provision was made for revolution by means of constitutional channels, it was believed that there would be no reason to resort to extra-constitutional revolutions for the overthrow of the government. Revolution could take place within the framework of the Constitution itself, as, indeed, it did, during the nineteenth and twentieth centuries.[47]

But the theory of American political institutions made no provision for an organization which assumed the façade of a political party and yet functioned as the agent of a hostile foreign power with the avowed aim of destroying them. Boring from within, Trojan-horse tactics, conspiratorial organization, plots designed in a foreign capital—all with the protection of guaranteed civil rights—were baffling problems. The question seemed to be: do our principles of freedom require us to permit people who do not believe in them to take advantage nevertheless of the protection offered under these principles while seeking to destroy them?

The Communist party in the United States (and also in Great Britain) was, in contrast to that in France and Italy, largely made up of deviant personalities. The children of immigrants or immigrants themselves were more likely than others to find solace and comfort in the party.[48] The Communist party seemed, therefore, to be foreign. When, in addition, it was found to be under the direction of foreign—that is, Kremlin—leadership, the reaction was sharp. Although the extent of this reaction has been exaggerated,[49] it is true that nationalists, isolationists, anti-intellectualists, reactionaries,[50] fear-ridden personalities of all kinds, along with ordinary, everyday loyal Americans began to think up ways and means for coping with this unprecedented problem of a disciplined, highly organized corps, obedient to a foreign power, dedicated to destroying the American system.

It was generally agreed that the threat was serious and that American political institutions had to be protected against it. There were differences of opinion on the best way to achieve this end. Some believed that there were adequate criminal laws available for prosecuting Communists when they were proved guilty of violating them, that meanwhile they should be safeguarded in their civil rights. Others believed that they should be restrained by special laws and, if necessary, deprived of the protection of the Bill of Rights. The excesses of congressional investigating committees in violating the civil rights of witnesses, in stimulating "informing," and in spreading the fear of noncomformity led, at mid-century, to a number of suggestions for reforming this old political institution.[51]

On the international scene, the communist threat was also a test of American political institutions. The expansion of activities which it entailed in many parts of the world was extremely uncongenial to many Americans. The responsibilities of power were not, as they were in the era of colonial empires, compensated for by large returns. Not only did the United States receive no economic returns from the responsibilities she had to assume, but she had to spend a great deal in the process of discharging them. It was not profitable—as it had been to the British Empire, for example—to be guardian of the free world. On the contrary, it was so costly that a large measure of political power at home was exerted in attempting to divert these costs from one group to another in the form of tax exemptions or penalties, protection, subsidies, and similar devices.[52]

The fight against communism confronted American political institutions with still another unaccustomed problem. It was a strange thing for Americans to find, for example, that the domestic policies of foreign nations had become a matter of immediate concern to them. Of grave consequence was the fact that the working classes in France and Italy were virtually cut off from access to power because this meant that they were at the disposal of the Communist party which could hold these nations in a state of virtual siege.[53]

Serious as was the test of American political institutions, implicit in the communist threat at mid-century, few people doubted that they would pass it. New security measures might have to be imposed, the old assurance in the inevitable triumph of democratic principles might be shaken, but most Americans felt convinced that some solution would be forthcoming which would protect against subversion without sacrificing the most basic American political institutions—the freedoms guaranteed by the Bill of Rights.

Family Institutions

The problems of freedom and equality in a setting of abundance have been no less perplexing in the area of family relations than in economic and political relations. The technological revolution has freed many women from domesticity, many children from parents. Modern machinery tends to equalize the sexes so far as production is concerned; a woman with a machine is the equivalent of a man. Skill and speed, not sheer muscular power, are important. Childbearing and child rearing take a decreasing proportion of a woman's life, another equalizing influence between the sexes. The family is involved in problems of economic and political equality as well as of interpersonal equality, as the Marxists so cogently point out.

LEGAL ASPECTS OF THE FAMILY AS AN INSTITUTION

So far as the legal aspects of the American family are concerned there is a fairly high degree of stability. There are fifty-three separate jurisdictions—the forty-eight states, the District of Columbia, Alaska, the Hawaiian Islands, Puerto Rico, and the Virgin Islands—enforcing their many separate legal provisions for marriage, family relations, and divorce. Most of them are very conservative; a great deal of pressure is usually required to bring about innovations.

The most striking legislative trends concerning marriage in the recent past have been toward increasing restrictions and qualifications. For example, all but eighteen states have now passed laws requiring a waiting period, ranging from one to five days before issuance of the license (twenty-six states), or from seventy-two hours to five days after issuance of the license (two states), or three days before and twenty-four hours after issuance of the license (one state). And since 1938 all but twelve states have passed laws requiring physical examinations and blood tests for both applicants. There is also a trend away from recognition of so-called common-law marriages; only twenty-one states recognize them if contracted later than a specified date.

With respect to family obligations, once the marriage has taken place, the trend is in the direction of equalizing duties and responsibilities between husband and wife. However, the equalization is usually not complete. Thus, although a husband is required to support his wife even if she has independent means, a wife is not obligated to support her husband unless he is unable to do so. Alimony, as distinguished from support of children, is tending to disappear except in cases of older wives who would not be able to support themselves.

The legal responsibility of parents for the welfare of their minor children continues. But the responsibility of adult children for the care of their aged parents—taken for granted in the extended family, or in the rural family, and in all families a generation or two ago—is in a transitional phase. The American family as a demographic unit has changed so radically in the twentieth century that legal institutions have not yet had a chance to catch up with the changes. These demographic changes—summarized herewith (see Table 1)—have placed particularly difficult strains on the institutional patterns with respect to the care of aged parents. When one parent dies before the youngest child marries, it is not too difficult for the unmarried child to assume responsibility for the care of the surviving parent. But when a parent dies some fourteen years after the last child has established a separate home of his own and assumed family obligations, care of the survivor may impose a hardship. Life patterns have been laid down; family income has, in effect, been committed; emotional independence from parents has been achieved. If the surviving parent is taken into the home all these facts may combine to produce very difficult problems. In some instances taking in the surviving parent may mean a

Table 1. Median Age of Husband and Wife at Each Stage of the Family Cycle, for the United States in 1950, 1940, and 1890

Stage	Median Age of Husband			Median Age of Wife		
	1950	1940	1890	1950	1940	1890
First marriage	22.8	24.3	26.1	20.1	21.6	22.0
Birth of first child		25.3	27.1		22.6	23.0
Birth of last child	28.8	29.9	36.0	26.1	27.2	31.9
Marriage of first child		48.3	51.1		45.6	47.0
Marriage of last child	50.3	52.8	59.4	47.6	50.1	55.3
Death of spouse	64.1	63.6	57.4	61.2	60.9	53.3
Death of husband, if last	71.6	69.7	66.4			
Death of wife, if last				77.2	73.5	67.7

Source: Paul C. Glick, "The Family Cycle," *American Sociological Review* (February 1947), p. 165; "The Life Cycle of the Family," *Marriage and Family Living*, 17 (February 1955), p. 4.

sacrifice in plans on the part of the children; there may be a conflict between the passing and the rising generations.

These changes have not as yet been reflected in the laws of all states. In some jurisdictions adult children may still be held legally responsible for the care of their parents; in others, however, they may not. Those who are nearest to the problem, namely social workers administering old age assistance laws, tend to oppose legal sanctions imposed on adults to care for their parents. The argument is that if adults wish to support their parents, they will do so without legal compulsion. If they do not wish to, the invoking of legal sanctions will embitter the family relationship for both generations. And if a choice must be made by a man and wife between parents and children, social workers argue, it is better for them to invest in their children and seek outside assistance for the aged. Fortunately this issue is finding a solution in the growing number of older persons who profit by the Old Age and Survivors' Benefits provisions of the Social Security Act. Fewer older people are dependent on assistance than on insurance benefits, and the number is expected to decline markedly.

There is a trend toward greater legal control over both adoption procedures and the means of ameliorating the status of the illegitimate child. Some observers feel that adoption has become far too difficult, tending to worsen rather than improve the position of the child. And in an increasing number of jurisdictions no reference is made to illegitimacy on the birth certificate.

There are three kinds of provision for the legal dissolution of marital ties: annulment, limited divorce, and full divorce. Annulment erases the marriage from the records; to all purposes, it never occurred. The woman resumes her maiden name; no legal obligations of any kind remain. The grounds for annulment are usually any cause which would have rendered the marriage illegal to begin with, such as one or both parties not having reached the age of consent, deceit or fraud, false pretenses, and previous, undissolved marriage. Legal separation, or limited divorce, frees the spouses from having to live with one another, but they are not free to remarry, nor is the husband relieved of his legal obligation to support his family. Absolute divorce frees both parties from marital obligations except those imposed by the court with respect to care of children and, in certain cases, alimony.

The grounds for legal divorce have not changed markedly in the last several generations. Proved adultery is a universal basis for divorce; desertion, cruelty, and alcoholism are widely accepted as grounds. Conviction of a felony, neglect to provide support, and insanity are grounds in more than half of the jurisdictions. Although incompatibility has been admitted as a ground for divorce in only two jurisdictions—Alaska and the Virgin Islands—actually the provision for divorce on the basis of separation in nineteen jurisdictions or of absence in six, is almost tantamount to admission of such a ground, even though the procedural requirements specifying the length of absence or separation may run as high as seven years. The indeterminate but undoubtedly large proportion of divorces involving collusion are also, in effect, divorce by mutual consent or for incompatibility.

For the most part, however, the theory of the law remains that one party comes to court with "clean hands," that is, "innocent," while the other one is "guilty" on legal grounds. The theory is that the "innocent" party asks for the divorce and the "guilty" party fights it. If both parties admit that they want the divorce, in most jurisdictions they cannot have it.

There is a movement on the part of professional persons most closely informed on the problem— social workers, marriage counselors, lawyers, judges, students of the family—to revamp the legal institutions of divorce to bring them more closely into line with current practice. The hope is that a therapeutic rather than a punitive approach may be worked out which will transform the proceedings from one in which the two parties vie with one another in degrading their former partners into one in which the approach is that of healing a sick relationship. Accordingly, people seeking a divorce would be referred to a professional counselor who would make a thorough and sympathetic study of the situation, work therapeutically with all parties concerned, and attempt to salvage the relationship. If he succeeded, the parties could withdraw their application for divorce. If he did not, his review of the case would form the basis of recommendations to the judge with respect to legal divorce. The proceedings would be dignified and quiet; there would be a minimum of dirty linen washed in public. An atmosphere of good will, conducive to working out the best solution for all parties concerned, would be sought rather than one of bitterness, acrimony, and hostility, as at the present time.

There is much resistance to such efforts, especially on the part of conservative lawyers and church people. The lawyers fear the discretion permitted to judges in the kind of court and proceedings contemplated, and church people feel that any move to make divorce less punitive than it now is would only tend to encourage it.

626

CRESCIVE FAMILY INSTITUTIONS

In contrast to the relatively slow rate of change in the legal aspects of family institutions is the rapid rate of change in the crescive aspects—in customs, conventions, collective attitudes, and mores, for example. We shall here consider only a small number of such changes, namely, in mating customs, customary age at marriage, customary number of children, customs and attitudes with respect to working wives and mothers, and attitudes and standards of parent-child relationships.

Mate Selection. It has never been customary in the United States for parents to select mates for their children. Nor has it ever been customary to select mates primarily for utilitarian or family reasons. The ideal has been one of freedom of choice. Young people have sought and found their own mates.

At mid-century this process of mate selection begins fairly early, in a characteristic institution known as dating. Boys and girls from about the ages of 12, 13, or 14 begin to associate or "go out" with one another in a fairly stylized manner, and dating continues throughout adolescence. They go to moving pictures, youth canteens, school parties and dances, picnics, record sessions, basketball games, and corner drugstores ("coke dates"), they go swimming and skating—all these either with one another alone or with others of their age in a group. There is no serious intent involved for the most part. It may happen that this youthful dating in some cases leads to a lasting relationship, but if so, this result is extraneous, not inherent in the process. Dating is ostensibly a form of play, and functionally it is an educational experience. Something analogous to dating is not unknown in preliterate societies, but dating as it is practiced in the United States is unique among advanced countries. The amount of freedom permitted to young people seems almost frightening to foreign observers.

Not all youngsters, however, succeed in dating. The practice is strongly competitive; often it becomes a race for status rather than basically a learning process. Prestige comes to inhere in dating certain girls or boys, regardless of whether or not one likes them. A small number of boys and girls become the object of much competition while others are left with no dates at all. The institution of dating has become so widely accepted that some schools make an effort to help all young people achieve some success in it.

For some youngsters the problem of possible competitive failure is solved by "going steady." An understanding is reached that neither person will "go out" with anyone else; this understanding is respected by others, so that each one is sure of a partner for parties, games, and the like. The reverse side of the shield, however, is that the experience of each is limited and that the relationship may be difficult to break. In the United States, unlike some European nations, parents wish their children to go out with a large number of partners, not just a few. They feel that in this way there is less danger of choosing a partner merely because no other opportunity has offered itself.

Theoretically, dating leads to courtship, the latter being a more serious phase of the former. It is doubtful, however, if there is much "courtship" in the United States. Nor is there such a thing as a formal declaration of intentions or even, for that matter, a formal proposal of marriage in many cases. The whole relationship between young people is so open, so candid, so free, so informal, that there is often no need for a formal proposal. Both young persons know when the relationship has reached the point where marriage is being considered. The proposal is, in effect, merely the articulation of a *fait accompli*.[54] If one party does not wish to enter marriage the relationship is broken off before a proposal is made. It is considered unethical for a young woman to "lead a man on" if she is not interested in marrying him.

The old custom of asking a father for his daughter's "hand" in marriage has virtually disappeared. Usually the young people announce to their parents that they are planning to be married. Ordinarily there is nothing surprising in this announcement, however, since the parents have probably known the situation for some time. The fact that they have little to do with the selection of their children's mates is a matter of pride for some parents, of frustration for others.

There are few formalities. No business arrangements are involved. There is no dowry. The young woman brings only her trousseau and the gifts which friends have "showered" upon her before marriage and those which others have given as wedding presents. She may have a "hope chest" in which for some years she has been accumulating household textiles and equipment, but this is by no means universal or expected. Wedding presents may in some cases amount to a sizable endowment, ranging up into thousands of dollars' worth of silver, china, glass, and electrical equipment.

Formal weddings, when they occur, have become so complicated that piloting brides through them has become a major profession. In large cities there are women who specialize in directing the arrangements for weddings. (There are even books and periodicals devoted to the subject.)

Honeymoons—lavish or modest, according to wishes or means—are also customary.

Customary Age at Marriage. One of the most striking trends in American family life today is the increasing youth of those who marry. The average age of men at marriage was 26.1 in 1890 and of women, 22.0; in 1950 the ages were 22.8 and 20.1 for men and women respectively. This relative youthfulness at marriage means that a larger proportion of the population is married in the United States than in most advanced countries of the world.

It means a great deal more also. It reflects, for example, a totally different conception of the nature and obligations of marriage. It used to be expected that when young people got married they would establish a household and that the young husband would assume full responsibility for its upkeep. Young people did not get married until they were in a position to set themselves up in housekeeping on a fairly high level. The young man was supposed to be vocationally settled, ready to assume the responsibility of family life in terms of income and occupational maturity. He was expected to have either a substantial amount of property or a good, secure income. The young woman was supposed to be equipped to run a complex domestic establishment. At the present time such demands are not made; such expectations do not exist. It is not at all unusual for young people to marry even before the man has completed his professional education; it is often taken for granted that the young wife will help support the family for several years. The setting up of a formal household is no longer expected of all young married persons. A small apartment with a minimum of— often makeshift—equipment, some of which they may themselves make or receive as wedding presents, is all that is expected. There is no loss of status in being "poor," that is, in not being able to live at a high level of consumption. These young people may even boast of their ability to manage on very little. American mechanical talent and manual skills are enlisted for making things which would once have been hired. Young people may even build their homes with their own hands.

Number of Children. The American family at mid-century seemed to be reversing itself with respect to the customary number of children. The birth rate which had been declining ever since records became available— with fluctuations owing to war, prosperity, and depressions—turned upward in the 1940s. For a long time demographers doubted the genuineness of this upturn. They explained it in terms of prosperity, delayed marriages from depression years, anticipated marriages because of military service, the result of the baby boom after World War I, and the increasing incidence of marriage, particularly early marriage. They finally came to accept the increase as real. There were more third, fourth, and even fifth babies than there had been in the twenties and thirties, although not, of course, more than there had been in an earlier period.

The increase in the birth rate at mid-century reflected a changed attitude toward having children. Motion picture actresses who never before would publicize their motherhood now gloried in it and exploited it. Fashion magazines showed styles designed for pregnant women, exhibited by beautiful models during their own pregnancies. Millions of people watched a glamorous television star play the part of a pregnant woman during her own pregnancy, even up to the point of delivery. Maternity, in brief, came to be looked upon as fashionable, even glamorous. There was, however, little likelihood that the really large family would return.

Working Wives and Mothers. Another spectacular aspect of mid-century family life in the United States was the large number and percentage of working wives. Conditions of full employment in the economy lured women into the labor market before marriage; after marriage but before children were born; and then again as the last child entered school when the mother was still, on the average, only thirty-three years old.[55] While her children are of preschool age the modern young American mother is perhaps the hardest worked person in the population. But once the children enter nursery school or school, the amount of work required to run a modern home is greatly reduced by the large number of frozen and prepared foods available and by the automatic appliances which cut down the amount of time required, as well as the amount of effort invested in ordinary housework.[56]

Sex Mores. Sexual mores have changed at a rapid rate in the twentieth century. Perhaps the most obvious change is reflected in the openness with which sex is discussed. Sex is now talked about unabashedly, with a candor which would have been shocking forty or fifty years ago.

The mores still forbid sex relations outside of marriage, but a large amount of nonconformity exists, both before and after marriage.[57] Because of the moralistic outlook of most Americans, extramarital relationships are less likely to be accepted and condoned than in many other advanced countries.

Prostitution is not legalized; but in many cities it is under police surveillance. As an institution, however, it is on the decline. The "call girl" and the nonprofessionally promiscuous have largely taken the place of the old-time prostitute.

Parent-Child Relationships. It was once taken for granted that parents knew more than their children; they had lived longer and accumulated more experience; they therefore had better judgment and knew the answers to life problems; their authority was based on a logical as well as on a moral or customary rationale. This conviction gave self-confidence to parents and security to children. Until well into the nineteenth century the above picture was doubtless correct for most people.

But for millions of Americans it was never true. The children of immigrants, for example, could look down on their parents because they represented a strange and foreign civilization; they were not American. Their experience was of little if any value to their children, who consequently had no confidence in their parents' approach to life. The children turned elsewhere for guidance and came to look down on their Old World parents. The same—if to a less exaggerated extent—was true of the millions of farm children who came to cities, or children of parents who had themselves come recently from rural areas. The answers to life problems which rural parents offered to city children did not seem adequate. The urban child could feel superior to his rural parents. And now an analogous situation has befallen other parents, neither recently immigrants from abroad nor from the farm. Each generation goes to school longer and therefore ends up with more years of formal schooling so that it can look with condescension upon its predecessors. Whole generations are being occupationally upgraded by modern technology; sons of manual laborers who would formerly have themselves become manual laborers now become white-collar workers, and then, too, can feel superior to their fathers. If there is no other basis for feeling superior, they can base their condescending attitude on the fact that they have television; their fathers did not. The rate of change is now so rapid that parents seem almost to come from a different culture. The generation of parents who came of age before World War I grew up in a world that bears little resemblance to the world of today. And their children, those who became adults in the twenties, never achieved self-confidence; they possess little authority; they are often unable to cope with their own children. The insouciance of the twenties, the disillusionment of the thirties, the series of moral shocks of the forties, have in effect unnerved many parents of contemporary young people. The

631

mores supporting parental, especially paternal, authority have therefore been in process of erosion for a long time. The decline in parental authority reflects one inequality which, as we saw above, is looked upon with almost universal equanimity in the United States, indeed, with complacence and satisfaction; namely, the superiority of the present over the past.[58]

From the point of view of the parent's relationships with the child, especially in infancy, there has been a series of interesting changes in customary patterns, as reflected in manuals on child care. At one time, for example training was rigid and rigorous; discipline was emphasized; thumb-sucking and masturbation were viewed as dangerous and to be suppressed at all costs. Later on the approach became softened, although rigid schedules were still advocated. In the thirties and forties, however, a more permissive point of view came to the fore; the infant was allowed to set his own eating and sleeping rhythms. Great emphasis came to be placed on the importance of affection between parents and children.[59]

The results of the new approach, as they reveal themselves in the personalities of children, cannot yet be assessed. It will take some time before this more liberal and permissive attitude becomes incorporated by the institutions of the family on a broad enough scale to show results. It does appear, however, that the children of mid-century America have great aplomb; they show little of the shyness and timidity in the presence of adults which used to be common in children. They are accustomed to being consulted; they offer suggestions freely. They are rarely embarrassed when they are the center of adult attention. They seem to be at home in their world. When the American family is functioning normally it seems to produce a self-reliant, independent, confident child.

MALFUNCTIONING OF AMERICAN FAMILY INSTITUTIONS

But institutions never operate perfectly, nor is their impact always the same. It is probably easier for things to go wrong in the functioning of American institutions than in those of other societies because of the rapid rate of change which characterizes them. The freedom which we have been tracing through American institutions means freedom to make mistakes, freedom to be wrong, and mistakes often occur. The young woman selects —freely—a mate who turns out to be a wrong partner for her. The cost of such a mistake is greater perhaps in the context of the American family than in that of other forms of family organization, since there are few if any compensatory supports to keep the marriage from failing. The large family, property interests, and community props would all tend to mitigate the failure of interpersonal relationships in some societies. In the United States, however, the family does not have these supporting props to the same extent. Marriage and family relationships have relatively little support from law, custom, collective attitudes, and mores; there is almost complete dependence on love and affection and compatibility to maintain stability. Not duty but love is relied upon. Alone, isolated, dependent on the affection they feel for one another, surrounded by an atmosphere which emphasizes the importance of love, and therefore feeling more cheated than ever by comparison with a high standard, marriage partners may be severely tried when there is a defect in their relationship. And the damage may reflect itself both in the parents and in the children. The divorce rate in the United States has shown a long-time upward trend, modified by wars, depressions, and prosperity, and reaching an all-time high in 1946 when many of the hasty war marriages were dissolved. Since that time there has been a steady decline in the divorce rate,[60] but no one expects a return to the low rate of the early years of the century.

Family malfunctioning—including both desertion and divorce—tends to occur more frequently in the lower socioeconomic classes. As more and more families achieve middle-class status it is possible that family stability will improve also. Greater stability may come also from the efforts now being made to prepare young people for the hazards of family life as institutionalized in the United States.

EDUCATION FOR FAMILY LIVING

One of the most characteristically American ways—in process of institutionalization—of dealing with the problems of modern family life is exemplified by the movement known as family-life education which has burgeoned in the last two decades. It takes the form of courses, in secondary schools and colleges, dealing with the problems of family living. These courses try to instill into the students an orientation toward family life which is based on understanding and appreciation rather than on rigid role conceptions. They are, in effect, creating new role conceptions. Boys and young men are taught that helping with home chores and child care is not a violation of masculinity; girls and young women are coached in the problems involved in the equivocal nature of the feminine role in contemporary culture.[61] A permissive approach to parent and child tends to be fostered. Emphasis is placed on the importance of affectionate relationships both between parents and between parents and children; "romantic love" is underplayed. The results of this movement as these relationships reveal themselves in family life cannot yet be evaluated.

American Schools at Mid-Century

The school is one of the great institutional attempts to equalize opportunity in the United States, to clear a channel for upward mobility. This attempt has been one of the most difficult assignments that any institution was ever called upon to carry out. For what, exactly, constitutes equal opportunity? The school, for example, finds that it must cope with many kinds of inequality, namely, in the family background, talents, and abilities of the pupils. Does identical schooling, then, constitute equality? If not, what, exactly, does? Is vocational training "equal" to classical education? Does free education for all tend to level down achievement and reduce standards? These are among the problems which the ideal of equality poses.

Problems of freedom also plague the school system at all levels. Should anyone be free to establish schools? Is it good policy to force boys and girls at the ages of 15, 16, or 17 to remain in school if they have little aptitude for or interest in schooling? Why keep them isolated from a functional role in community life when that is what they really need? Does compulsory school attendance actually do these young people harm? Does it not also harm the school, rendering it a mere custodial institution, keeping young adults out of the labor market but at the same time damaging them as human beings?[62]

Problems of freedom become even more difficult when they arise in connection with the relations between school personnel — administrators especially — and parents or community leaders. Who should decide educational policy? How much of education is a strictly technical and professional concern and therefore safely consigned to the hands of the educators, and how much is general and civic? Should the school people make all the decisions about what should be taught? Or should parents also be considered? At mid-century this was one of the most serious problems of all, for unlike parents of children in European schools, the parents of children in American schools take an active role in dealing with school problems, especially through the so-called parent-teacher associations. How much control should they exercise? How much freedom should the teachers have?

Europeans frequently ask visitors from the United States about their schools at home, and it is difficult to convey to them the impossibility of talking about American schools as though they were a simple, homogeneous phenomenon. The range of variation is so great that almost anything one says about American schools is probably true of some of them. Although the United States shares with all other advanced nations a belief in the necessity for universal compulsory elementary education, it differs from many of them with respect to control and administration.[63] It resembles England more than France, in that control and administration are decentralized rather than centralized. This principle of local control is basic; it is felt that a decentralized system—even with all its admittedly numerous defects—is safer from capture by interest groups than a centralized system.

ELEMENTARY SCHOOLS

Until recently there was no question that elementary public school education was a function of the local community. State governments might regulate standards for buildings, equipment, attendance, length of school year, qualifications and salaries of teachers; but curriculums, courses of study, internal school administration, and everything pertaining to the school itself has been under the control of local elected school boards. This decentralization has made for flexibility, experimentation, and adjustment to local needs. It has kept the school close to the people. It has encouraged parent participation in the affairs of the school.

But it has also had its adverse effects. It has meant, for example, that poor communities have had poor schools; it has placed the school at the mercy of conflicting ideologies in the local community; it has placed the teacher at a disadvantage, robbing him of much of the status which should inhere to his profession. Instead of being viewed as a professional, with a specialized contribution to make, he—more especially she—has often been viewed as an employee. Humiliating restrictions have been imposed on the woman schoolteacher, robbing her of self-respect in many cases. Local property holders, finally, have sometimes evaluated school programs not in terms of their educational functions but in terms of their costs. The school tax is a large item in the tax program of most communities. If there are many property owners who do not have children in the schools they may begrudge expenditures beyond a bare minimum. Expenditures for new buildings, equipment, and salaries must pass the scrutiny of many taxpayers. Few school administrators dare to defy the prejudices of their boards and community. Often attacks on the schools are made not to correct defects and flaws, but primarily to save taxes.

Until the twentieth century parents knew quite well what they wanted the elementary schools to do. They wanted the schools to teach their children how to read, write, spell, and do the simple arithmetic required for ordinary living. A little geography and American history they could also see use for. They believed that the reading should be moral primarily, and some didactic poetry was found acceptable. Other skills the child would learn by living. Book learning was important but nonetheless incidental to other considerations. It provided necessary tools but it was not the core of education. Parents in rural areas hired a young man or woman for a few winter months to give their children the elementary tools for living. In many urban areas English was a foreign language, so some emphasis had to be given to teaching it, especially along the eastern seaboard. The elementary school was functional in the sense that what it taught could be directly related to the needs which everyone felt had to be met. The "little red schoolhouse," as the one-room building which housed all the children of the community was called, in which one teacher taught all the children, has only recently become a thing of the past. It had been almost a family affair; its teacher lived with the families, and the course of study —as well as the administration of the school—was a matter of community concern. Weekly programs, at which the children performed, displayed to parents what the school was doing for their children.

In the twentieth century, however, new complexities in administrative organization have tended to alienate schools from family and community. A case in point is the trend toward the consolidation of school districts so that several together can pool their resources and offer better facilities than each alone could provide. This means that children travel a greater distance to get to school than formerly; sometimes they spend an hour or more in the bus each day. Consolidation means also that the school is less intimately tied up with the family and the small local community. In the larger cities as well, schools have become huge institutions, out of touch with the families of the children. As schools become larger and move farther away from the parents there sometimes arises a feeling of estrangement, and even of hostility, between the elementary school and the family. In the middle of the twentieth century the public schools were the center of a raging debate and, in some cases, the object of serious attack. But first a word about the secondary school.

THE SECONDARY SCHOOLS

The secondary school was at first a private academy or college preparatory school for children fourteen to eighteen years of age. The classics and
mathematics, along with religion, constituted the backbone of the curriculum, a course of study designed for a relatively small elite. Most people did
not want these subjects taught their children because there was no functional tie between them and the workaday world they lived in. The classical
curriculum of the nineteenth century was an upper-middle-class prerogative; it was associated with high social status; it looked to the past. In the
old academy a teacher faced a classroom of students who, although they
may have resisted his efforts to inculcate abstract and difficult subjects,
nevertheless shared his belief in their value. Students and parents alike
took for granted the value of Latin, mathematics, and grammar; to them,
the curriculum seemed functional.

Provision for public school education at the secondary level became
legalized through the so-called Kalamazoo case in 1874. At first the public
high school was much like the old private academy; its function was conceived in about the same terms, that is, the preparation of an elite for profession or college. It was, in effect, the poor boy's academy, offering him
the same courses as those the privileged boy enjoyed. A high school di-
ploma stamped its recipient as an educated person.

It began to be evident in the twentieth century, however, that the public
high school was not the same as the old private academy. The course of
study was gradually expanded to meet the needs of more and more students with more and more diversified requirements. The curriculum became increasingly proliferated. Today the public high school offers a wide
variety of subjects; in addition, vocational high schools have also greatly
increased in number.

THE GREAT DEBATE OF THE MID-CENTURY

Once the schools had become divorced from parents, they were allowed
to feel their way toward solutions of the problems forced upon them by
the tremendous number of students coming to them. The parents paid
relatively little attention to what was going on. And the schools, facing
problems never faced by schools anywhere before, tried heroically to find
the answers. They found many answers in the work of John Dewey, whose
philosophy of learning by doing offered some guidance in the chaos, especially his idea that learning was effective only when it was functional, when

the child could see that he needed what he was learning. Motivation by fear was frowned upon; spontaneity rather than rote-learning was to be encouraged. Intellectual discipline was valued for its own sake, while drill and memorization were discounted.

High school teachers, faced with students to whom the classical subjects were alien, foreign, irrelevant to the life they lived and no longer considered useful by their parents, made a virtue of necessity. They gave up the old curriculum and substituted courses that they could hope to teach. The ancient world, the medieval world, and the pre-Columbian world seemed to bear no relation to the world the students lived in. The spotlight of history seemed to be playing on a new stage, where the past was of only tangential significance.

There is no reason to believe that the new approach was evolved as a deliberate attack on the old type of school. If it had been possible to teach abstract mathematics, literature, history, and foreign languages—including Latin—to all public school children, there is no doubt at all that teachers would have been willing to do so. Since it was not possible, however, a new program, less demanding intellectually, was substituted. Teachers could not perform superhuman feats of pedagogy, even with all the new techniques at their disposal. They could teach no more than their students had been processed to value or were capable of learning. It is a question whether many parents would, in fact, have been willing to continue to require the classical and traditional subjects in tax-supported schools.

The great controversy at mid-century was between ideologies which, for lack of better names, we may call Traditional and Progressive. In general the Traditionalists lean toward the European concept of education. On the one hand, they believe that the aim of education should be primarily intellectual, to produce intelligent individuals; that emphasis should be on individual achievement; that recognition should be given to the bright student; that rigorous discipline should be maintained; that standards should be high. They allege that the lax procedures current in many schools turn out practically illiterate graduates who have neither habits of intellectual discipline nor specific knowledge. The Progressives, on the other hand, lay great emphasis on the relationships within the group; they aim to help the child learn to work with other people; they minimize competitive strivings and would keep children within their chronological peer group regardless of their academic achievement; they put little emphasis on drill and hold that learning is a by-product of active participation in stimulating projects.

Emphasis is on cooperation rather than competition; accordingly, report cards do not tell parents how well their children are doing with reference to an objective standard, or where they stand on a scale, but merely make general statements which, the Traditionalists claim, are not illuminating.

The emphasis on ability to work in groups has been derisively labeled "groupism." It has implications which disturb thoughtful observers of the American school, even those who are not Traditionalists. In the nineteenth century solitude was considered a good thing. Essays were written that enlarged upon its beauties. Thoreau, the archetype of nonconformity, glorified it in his description of life at Walden Pond. In the twentieth century a quite opposite point of view has emerged. The child who enjoys being by himself—who is not working or playing in a group—is suspect. "Adjusting to group living" or "group-mindedness" has become almost a fetish.

The implications are rather fundamental. The person who engages in group activities must submit himself to the discipline of the group. The group holds the person to certain standards, sometimes higher, sometimes lower than those he would have adopted for himself. Conformity is sometimes achieved at the expense of creativity or spontaneity, the person being held in line by all the interpersonal controls which groups exert. The costs of nonconformity include deprivation of the benefits the group has accustomed its members to expect. However, the person who has never submitted to the group cannot be as easily punished by it. There are many people who have great misgivings about the "groupist" tendencies in modern education whether they are the cause or the result of modern living conditions.

WHO MAY ESTABLISH SCHOOLS?

The question whether private—especially parochial—schools should be allowed to operate alongside state-supported public schools has been answered by the Supreme Court, which declared unconstitutional a statute in Oregon that forbade private schools. Although public school education is viewed as a basic function of the state, it is not therefore conceived as a monopolistic right. Private schools are permitted, but they are not supported. In recent years, attendance at private schools has increased more rapidly than attendance at public schools.[64]

Even though private groups may establish schools, should they be entirely free from supervision? What rights and privileges do they have? What access to taxes? This last question poses special difficulties in connection with the effort of the Catholic hierarchy to secure tax support for at least some of the activities of Catholic schools.[65]

COLLEGES AND UNIVERSITIES

The first colleges, like the first academies, were private institutions. But in 1862 the Morrill Act was passed by the national Congress. This act allocated public lands to the states for the establishment and support of institutions of higher learning. These publicly supported schools—sixty-nine in number—have become the so-called land-grant colleges. They were designed to offer technical and agricultural training as cheaply as possible without neglecting the liberal arts. Most of the great universities of the Middle West include land-grant colleges in their organization. Of fairly recent origin is the municipally supported junior college, offering two years of education beyond high school.

There are about 1900 institutions of higher learning in the United States,[66] varying widely in size and standards, as well as in prestige. It is therefore as impossible to generalize about colleges and universities as about lower schools. At one extreme are the "Ivy League" institutions, including Harvard, Yale, Columbia, and Princeton, and other great institutions such as the University of Chicago. These are among the great universities of the world, ranking with the best of the European universities. At the other extreme are small liberal arts colleges, precarious and insecure, under the necessity of competing for and catering to students and therefore unable to maintain good standards.

Unlike some of the great European universities which are autonomous, self-governing bodies, colleges and universities in the United States are usually administered by boards of trustees, appointed or elected. In some cases alumni are also represented. These board members are rarely professional educators or themselves professors. They are likely to be successful business and professional men. Sometimes they bring to their position of board member the point of view of an employer, and they tend to look upon the faculty as hired men or employees. So long as they limit their activities to the care of the financial resources of the institution there is not likely to be any difficulty. It is only when they attempt to control educational policy or to lay down rules for faculty members that problems are likely to arise. At mid-century the issues were likely to center in loyalty oaths and academic freedom in relation to teaching about communism.

In smaller institutions the president must spend a great deal of time soliciting funds. He tends to become sensitive to the wishes and points of view of potential donors. He is likely to take the side of donors in any conflict with his faculty. The result may be an intimidated staff, emasculated so far as creative thinking is concerned.

At mid-century, when the insecure position of the private colleges and universities vis-à-vis the tax-supported schools became evident, industrial leaders soon realized that they had a stake in preserving these institutions. A strong movement arose for the support of these schools by industry, either directly or by way of generous scholarship programs.

Too Many Educated? By the second third of the twentieth century the colleges and universities were being subjected to the same kinds of strains which the high schools had experienced in the first third; not only an increasing number, but also an increasing proportion of young people were going to college. At the beginning of the century, about 1 in 24 persons of college age went to college; at mid-century, 1 in 4. Furthermore, by mid-century 15 per cent of all adults had attended college. According to recent estimates, by 1970 college enrollments will be twice those of 1954.

The increasing number of young persons attending college not only raises problems regarding the quality of the education which is offered, the pressure for equipment and personnel, and the influence on the cultural level generally, but also directs attention to the political implications of having on hand an educated "proletariat" in case of an extended and severe depression. Many people, alarmed by this contingency, ask the inevitable questions, How much education? How many educated?

In the minds of some people there is a haunting fear of educating too many people. The case of Germany is pointed to as a horrible example; allegedly, it was an educated proletariat which found Hitler's leadership congenial. There a large number of highly educated young people could find no place to exercise their talents; precisely because of their training they became the more dangerous when they succumbed to Hitler's promises. If we educate more people than we can find room for in our economy at the higher levels—especially in view of the Second Industrial Revolution, in which intellectual tasks as well as manual jobs are being taken over by machines—is there not the possibility of incurring a real danger?

The danger is doubtless real in a relatively static society where there are only a limited number of positions available for educated people. Even in the United States, as late as 1949, one student documented this fear in an analysis of the job market for college graduates.[67] He found that a "proletariat of the A.B." was emerging, and anticipated that by 1969 there would be two or three college graduates for every job commensurate with their training. Of the ten to fifteen million college graduates in 1969 that he foresaw, a large proportion would not be able to enter occupations of their choice. He warned that unless some action were taken, American institutions would be burdened by a frustrated intelligentsia and faced with all the sinister implications inherent to political and social tensions. He proposed that education be viewed not necessarily as an open sesame to professional advancement but as part of the enrichment of life; he also proposed that measures be taken to seek out talent wherever it was found and, if necessary, to subsidize it even at the expense of squeezing out more privileged but less talented persons from the institutions of higher learning.

In partial contrast, so far as policy is concerned, was the point of view of the President's Commission on Higher Education, which in a report in 1947[68] expressed the hope that college enrollments could be expanded to include one third of those of college age, since at least that many people have sufficient ability to profit from such education. Like the author of the study just cited, the authors of this report felt that, if necessary, talented people should be actively sought out and subsidized.

The seeming contradiction between the fear expressed by the first study and the hope expressed by the second has been reconciled by pointing out that the one envisaged higher education in terms of professional training, the other as preparation, primarily for enlightened citizenship.

Yet even in terms of professional training the problem at mid-century was one of preparing enough people for jobs rather than one of finding jobs for trained people. A careful survey of America's resources of specialized talent, for example, found that, at least for the foreseeable future, concern about a surplus of highly trained persons was not justified.[69] On the contrary, it reported a deficit in many key professions. Furthermore, many persons who attend college in the United States, unlike those in other advanced countries, do not plan to enter the high-prestige occupations. They are not frustrated intellectuals, however. They become farmers, businessmen, schoolteachers, journalists, librarians, county agents, pharmacists, and morticians. And even with the rapidly increasing number of college graduates, there are not enough of them to fill the demand for the best ones. The relationship between anticipated supply of graduates from 1953 to 1957 and demand in certain fields of specialization has been summarized as follows: [70]

Field	Demand	Supply
Natural sciences . .	High	Inadequate
Psychology	Increasing	Inadequate
Social sciences . . .	Increasing	Moderate shortage at top; adequate at lower levels
Humanities	Increasing	Inadequate at top; adequate at lower levels
Engineering	High	Inadequate
Applied biology . .	Variable	Adequate in agriculture and forestry; inadequate in home economics
Health fields	High	Inadequate
Business	High	Will attract from other fields
Schoolteaching . .	High	Very inadequate
College teaching . .	Increasing	Inadequate
Law, ministry . . .	Moderate	Adequate
Social work	Variable	Variable
Other professions .	Variable	Variable

Far from being alarmed at a shortage of jobs, thoughtful persons at mid-century were more disturbed by a shortage of personnel, especially in the engineering and scientific professions. It was pointed out that Russia was training many more persons in these fields than the United States, and plans were made for increasing the supply of students in these areas.[71] The danger of an American "proletariat of the A.B. degree" now seemed remote.

IMPLICATIONS: LEVELING DOWN OR LEVELING UP?

The arguments against the American school system in the great debate of the mid-century instill a feeling that the system surely must be a colossal failure; illiteracy must surely be on the increase; Americans must be rapidly deteriorating. The fact that they continue to man a complex social structure with success seems to prove nothing at all.

It is certainly true that an attempt to evaluate the American school system from the point of view of a curator of the past, taking the training of a gentlemanly leisure class for a measure, will place American education far below the older standards. Apart from many notable exceptions, American schools do not compare favorably with those of Europe; it is often pointed out as a deficiency that American students are allowed to graduate from high school without having to acquire as much academic information as their European counterparts.

But as one perceptive European observer has pointed out, to judge

American education in terms of formal instruction alone is to misunderstand completely the function of the American school.[72] To judge American schools by European standards is to ignore the profound difference in function and objective. The tremendous achievement which Americans have been able to show has been the reward, in fact, of their ability to organize and work together in contributing to a group enterprise. They learn early how to work in groups; how to divide and share work; how to select leaders; how to function on committees. They are given practice in making decisions; they learn how policies are threshed out; they learn how to make use of all kinds of talents. Rather than the acquisition of factual knowledge, these educational experiences are emphasized in the schools.[73]

Both the European and the American school show paradoxical patterns of conformity and individuality. The European emphasis is upon acquisition of facts, "training the mind," conformity to certain fixed standards. Yet the students themselves are "rugged individualists" in the sense that they are all competing against—and aiming to surpass—one another. It is difficult, for example, to imagine the concept of "the gentleman's grade" in a French university, where a man's future career may hinge upon his examination grades. Every man is out for himself; a lifetime career may be at stake. In the United States, on the other hand, academic discipline is more lenient; it does not emphasize memorization or the acquisition of facts; it does not attempt to standardize the student.

The tone of European schools, as pointed out earlier in this discussion, is distinguished by a sense of humility in the face of the past. The student is required to accept; he is not called upon to react. He is expected to admire; not to judge. His opinions are of no significance; to declare them would be only presumptuous.

Individual by individual, it is undoubtedly true that the graduates of the average American secondary school emerge with less factual information than the graduates of a European secondary school. But they have in large measure the one thing they most need, experience and training in organization, both formal and informal. Skill in organization makes up for academic deficiencies. Organization makes it possible to discover the usefulness of people of relatively little talent and training, and it gives greater leverage to the brains of the top men. American schools, concludes the observer referred to above, are designed to let students instruct one another in how to live in America.

There is great concern that the influx of students from lower and lower socioeconomic backgrounds has lowered academic standards all along the line. It is argued that there has been a great leveling down. There is, however, no unequivocal proof of falling standards.[74] The good students can probably still get training as good as any ever before offered. American scholarship and scientific achievement equal those of any other country. It might even be cogently argued that there has been, rather, a leveling upwards. We now expect many, if not most, professions to reach the same level of academic achievement as that formerly required in only the traditional learned fields. We expect farmers, foresters, pharmacists, engineers, and people in other professions to live up to standards formerly reserved for an intellectual elite. The agonized consternation displayed by professors—especially, perhaps, in the land-grant colleges—at the inability of their students to write clearly and forcefully or to master abstract materials may be an index not of low standards, as it is usually interpreted, but an index of high standards because never before have such talents been demanded of so many different professions.

The curriculum of American schools is always being subjected to close scrutiny. As contrasted with European schools a great deal of the past has been jettisoned, in the feeling that there is so much of the present to be known that the past must be sacrificed. The accelerative growth of culture means that many choices must be made with respect to what should be preserved and what should be discarded. In making such choices American schools tend always to lean toward what is current; European schools tend to cling to the heritage of the past. American civilization is so complex that to understand it requires more of the student's time than is needed by European students to understand their own civilizations.

Religious Institutions

The most striking characteristic of ecclesiastical institutions in the United States is their separation from the state. Europeans often express great astonishment when they hear that there is no tax support for any church or for any church activity. The complete separation of church and state is almost unique. The only support churches receive is the remission of taxes on their property. The employment of chaplains in the military forces is not interpreted as support of any church but as a necessary service to military personnel; some services to parochial school children are also tax supported in some states on the same grounds.

THE PROTESTANT CHURCHES

Protestant, Catholic, and Jewish institutions have all undergone transformations in the process of accommodating themselves to the conditions of life in America. The Protestant churches in colonial times, for example, were theocratic in their thinking; the Episcopalian and Presbyterian churches were hierarchical in organization and tended to be aristocratic in orientation. In the nineteenth century, churches that preached a more democratic gospel and followed their members to the frontier—the Methodists, for example—grew much more rapidly than the older sects. A dynamic and strongly evangelical tone came to characterize these frontier denominations. In the twentieth century the great sectarian groups have become institutionalized and conservative; but new religious sects are constantly arising. Some achieve the stability and status of denominations; others remain sectarian groups, following charismatic leaders and dependent on the personality of these leaders for their continuance.

The nineteenth and early twentieth centuries were essentially centrifugal in tendency, and witnessed the splitting off of separatist groups. The second quarter of the twentieth century has been marked by a strong ecumenical movement toward uniting the several major denominations. So far, the movement has succeeded in uniting the northern and southern branches of the Methodist Church; but it is still far from having achieved union for all major Protestant denominations. There is, nevertheless, a great deal of cooperation among the several denominations in the National Council of the Churches of Christ in the United States, especially with respect to social and ethical questions.

PROBLEMS OF ETHNIC GROUPS

The several ethnic groups have also had to adjust their religious institutions to life conditions in America. The typical pattern for recent immigrants may be illustrated by an ethnic group bringing to America its European-trained religious leaders, whether priests or rabbis. In their own ethnic communities these immigrants tried to re-establish, as best they could, the community pattern of the Old World. The priest was a strongly conservative force, likely to resist the so-called Americanization of his parishioners because all too often this meant the throwing off of religious as well as other Old World traits. To the immigrant generation and to their children, the Catholic religion was inextricably tied up with their ethnic background. They thought of their religion as Polish, or Hungarian, or Italian, as a nationality trait. In attempting to become "American" they often rejected their religion as well as their ethnic background. They were ashamed of it because in their minds it was associated with being a Dago, a Wop, or a Polack. In the second quarter of the twentieth century, however, the younger members of the ethnic groups had come to separate the distinctively ethnic component of their religion from the distinctively religious component. They were learning how to be Catholic, or Jewish, in an American way. Thus both Catholicism and Judaism were in process of becoming Americanized. People were learning that the Old World adhesions—which had embarrassed and disconcerted them—were not intrinsic parts of their faiths. Thus American Catholicism and American Judaism at the present time have become the leading branches of the Catholic and Jewish faiths in the world today.

THE CATHOLIC CHURCH

The adjustment of the Catholic Church to the American scene has not been easy, for in many ways there are fundamental conflicts between the ideology of the Catholic Church and the ideology of American institutions. The Catholic Church, for example, does not officially believe in religious freedom or toleration; it believes it should be supported by taxes; it believes it should have charge of elementary instruction; it does not accept the doctrine of separation of church and state except as an expedient. These are contrary to basic American principles. The Church has come to terms with the American problem by concluding that where it is not a majority religion it must—as a matter of expedience if not of principle—accept the separation of church and state. Some Catholic leaders anticipate, however, that if the Catholic population should outstrip the non-Catholic,[75] it might in time, as a majority group, legislate Catholic principles into practice.

Within the Catholic Church several ethnic groups contend for control. Because the Irish Catholics were the earliest Catholic immigrants on a large scale, they have for many years occupied the strategic position of power in the hierarchy. The increased militancy of the Catholic Church in recent years has been explained by one student of the subject as the result—at least partly—of the expansion of the Irish and German middle and upper class.[76] During the 1930s, however, the supremacy of the Irish was challenged by Catholics of Italian and Polish backgrounds, children of the immigrants who had come earlier in the century. These children had

647

been exposed to American education, even high school and college in many cases; they had benefited from the New Deal; they were part of the new middle class. As such they were formidable competitors for power not only in political organizations and in the civil service, but in the Church as well.[77]

The increased militancy of the Church at mid-century has also been attributed to the rise of Soviet Russia as a threat to world peace. The opposition of the Catholic Church to communism has been a great asset to it.[78]

So far the Catholic Church in America has not produced scholars of the caliber of European Catholic scholars. There is far less urbanity in American Catholic scholarship than in European; there are no American Maritains or Dawsons. Some American Catholics attribute their cultural backwardness to the narrowing influence of the Irish leadership; some attribute it to the strong censorship exercised over the thinking of Catholics; some attribute it to the humble immigrant origin of so many leaders who, because of their background, lack a tradition of culture and scholarship; some, to the lack of a secure, unchallenged position which would relieve leaders from the necessity of protecting themselves and free them for creative work.

AMERICAN JUDAISM

Jews in America also show ethnic cleavages. Of the earliest Jewish immigrants, who came in the middle of the seventeenth century, a few were Spanish; the others, mainly German.[79] By the time immigrants from eastern Europe began to come—in the late nineteenth and early twentieth century—the German Jews were well established; they no longer lived in ghettos; they had become indistinguishable from the native population, not only in speech, dress, and manner of living, but in style of worship as well. In their religious practices they were Reform, that is, they had given up many of the medieval adhesions of their faith and stripped it down to basic principles. The first quarter of the twentieth century was a time of ferment and uncertainty as Jews from east European ghettos came and settled in the large cities in ghettos of their own. The children of these immigrants—like the children of Catholic immigrants—tended to throw over a good deal of their religion as they discarded the ghetto communal life of their parents. Some of these children, attempting to find a place where they could feel at home, became atheistic and embraced secular religions like socialism and even communism.[80] Some turned to Reform

Judaism. Still others, however, attempted to Americanize the practice of their faith without going so far in a nonliturgical direction as had the Reform Jews. A so-called Conservative Synagogue emerged; it discarded the distinctively Old World adhesions of Judaism which had grown up in European ghettos, but it was not so stripped of tradition as the Reform Temple. At mid-century, therefore, there were three major groups among Jews, namely: Orthodox Jews, who retained a great deal of the Old World pattern of worship and belief; Conservative Jews, who had discarded much of the Old World pattern and Americanized the rest; and Reform Jews, who, although less liturgical than either of the other two, were, like members of all kinds of churches, Christian as well as Jewish, turning to greater emphasis on liturgy.

The rise to power of Hitler, and his wholesale liquidation of Jews in Germany, had a shocking impact on Jews in America. It checked the drift away from orthodoxy; it re-established a feeling of unity in the face of outer threats; it stimulated support of Zionism and later of Israel. At mid-century, indeed, a large proportion of the support for the state of Israel came from the contributions of American Jews, and the policy of the American government in the Middle East was allegedly influenced by the ties of American Jews with the new state.

Protestants, Catholics, and Jews all act as pressure or veto groups on the political stage. Each group attempts to exert its power in the making of policy. This use of political pressure is not interpreted as a violation of the principle of separation of church and state; however, such intervention in public affairs by religious groups sometimes leads to conflict.[81]

Social Work

In the nineteenth century technology introduced the means of a vast increase in wealth but at the same time brought unparalleled poverty to all industrialized societies. In the United States this problem was aggravated by the presence of large numbers of immigrants who were greatly disadvantaged because of their strangeness in the new environment. So far as legislative programs for dealing with poverty were concerned, the United States tended to lag behind other advanced nations. Germany and Great Britain, for example, instituted social security programs long before the United States; even at mid-century there remained in the United States a hard core of opposition to the so-called welfare state. Americans had long relied upon traditionally private voluntary organizations rather than the government to perform philanthropic functions.

For one of the most characteristic patterns in America has been the purposive instituting of behavior quite outside the legal framework, and independent of custom or tradition. The practice of setting up voluntary organizations for the accomplishment of specific goals has been commented on by foreign observers since the time of De Tocqueville. These organizations have been of many kinds, but we limit ourselves here to those primarily concerned with welfare or humanitarian activities.

For a century, social work—originally "charity" and later "philanthropy"—had developed as a privately supported profession, originally dependent in the main upon wealthy donors. As voluntary organizations, private social work agencies developed high standards of professional competency. Realizing that standardized procedures are often inadequate, they worked out the characteristic individualized approach known as "case work," which tailors its methods to meet the specific problems of each case. The relationship between social worker and client is viewed not as that of a superior telling an inferior what to do, but as an interaction between them to help the client in solving his own problems. The term "case work" is usually taken over into foreign languages without attempting a translation, for there has been nothing like it in most societies. The theory of human values on which it is based is directly opposed to that on which the old-time "poor law" was based.

The conflicting points of view between voluntary and public agencies became increasingly focal as the twentieth century wore on. Efforts to obtain public funds for mothers' pensions and assistance for the aged began fairly early, but it was not until the second third of the century—during the great depression—that the revolutionary change took place. At first efforts were made to meet the catastrophe with old tools; private agencies did what they could. The inadequacy of their resources, philosophy, and methods soon became obvious. A new approach, based on a new theory of modern society, was gradually worked out and embodied in the Social Security Act of 1935. It recognized that two different kinds of problems were involved and that two radically different approaches were demanded. On the one hand were the problems that befell wholly normal people for reasons beyond their control, such as unemployment, death of a wage earner, accident, illness, or catastrophe. On the other hand were the problems of people who, because of physical, emotional, or mental handicaps, could not compete with normal people and were regarded as "incompetents." Institutional patterns for dealing with problems of the first type, at least, were worked out during the second third of the century; the mid-century saw these patterns in the process of expansion.[82]

With the assumption by the state of so many social work functions, private agencies have been faced with the problem of working out their niche in the total structure. They have tended to assume responsibility for exploring new areas, piloting new programs, working out new techniques. They tend to work more intensively on a counseling basis, aiming at emotional re-education rather than budgetary relief, using relief as only one tool in a therapeutic kit. They tend also to serve on a fee basis, meeting the needs of middle-class clients who can pay for help.

BROTHERHOOD AS GENEROUS GIVING

The values freedom and equality which we have emphasized in our discussion are hard and unsentimental in nature; they are fighting words. They are inextricably involved in conflict and competition. Freedom implies an exploiter, a master, a power—personal or impersonal—which is oppressing people or holding them down or limiting their choices. Equality implies some harnessing of competition, which is based on inequalities. But there was another term in the Enlightenment's trinity of values— brotherhood—which is in quite a different category. Brotherhood is an affective concept, emotional, sentimental even, if you will. It implies a way of thinking and feeling about one's fellow men. It is in no sense a necessary corollary to freedom or equality.

Brotherhood may be viewed in two contexts, namely that of generous giving and that of ethnic relationships. Although, as Bryce pointed out, brotherhood in the first sense has long characterized American institutions, the goal of brotherhood in the sense of racial and ethnic integration has had a long and difficult history in most American communities. The lack of success in realizing the brotherhood ideal has had profound repercussions on American institutions, permeating political and industrial institutions, and reflecting itself in church and school, recreation and housing. At this point, however, we limit ourselves to brotherhood in the sense of generosity.

PATTERNS OF GIVING

The age-old pattern of giving through the church has prevailed in the United States for generations. Many humanitarian and social work activities are still supported by church contributions. The large number of Catholic, Jewish, and Protestant welfare agencies further illustrate the pattern. The sources of their funds include the gifts of generous donors, bequests of many kinds, and regular contributions as well as the proceeds of benefit activities. A large part of the activities of women in church organizations consists of fund-raising projects of one kind or another.

The concept of stewardship has activated wealthy families in the United States to a much larger extent than in most advanced nations. Many wealthy families have felt obligated to use their wealth for the benefit of the community. Libraries, art galleries, schools, colleges, and universities have long been the recipients of grants from private fortunes, as well as the more usual philanthropic agencies. Even organizations of debutantes like the Junior League feel they must contribute to community welfare agencies.

In the twentieth century a characteristic pattern of giving developed in the form of privately endowed foundations. These foundations were established originally to institutionalize and professionalize giving. They were part and parcel of the American economy long before the income-tax laws made them an acceptable way to escape taxation. These great fortunes, administered by professional persons with the sole purpose of doing good, have been likened to the old institution of patronage which used to characterize the nobility. The difference lies in the highly organized, impersonal, bureaucratic nature of the foundations, contrasted with the personal, almost intimate, basis of patronage by the nobility. Among the great early foundations were the Rockefeller, the Carnegie, and the Russell Sage, originally concerned with public health, world peace, and community welfare. What began as muckraking in the first decade of the century —the Pittsburgh Survey of the Russell Sage Foundation, for example—became social science research later on. Toward the middle of the century, tax exemptions on funds contributed to these foundations had the effect of greatly proliferating them; there were literally thousands of them, large and small, devoted to a myriad of welfare, scientific, and cultural ends.

Equally characteristic is another pattern of giving, this time drawing upon people at large and institutionalized in the so-called community chests. Once each year a week is devoted to the highly publicized Red Feather drive, during which people tax themselves—voluntarily, in the sense that it is nonpolitical—for the support of social work agencies in their communities.[83] The national Red Cross conducts similar drives. Recently this "drive" pattern of giving has also been enlisted to raise funds to finance medical research. There are national associations whose primary function is the raising of funds for research in poliomyelitis, heart ailments, multiple sclerosis, muscular dystrophy, cancer, tuberculosis, arthritis, and even mental retardation.

The Physical Structure of American Communities

Although American cities were spared destruction by war in recent years, they are nevertheless in a constant process of being torn down and rebuilt. At mid-century most American cities barely resemble the way they looked even as recently as twenty-five years ago. In the nineteenth century, American cities just grew; as communities, they were unplanned and plainly showed their deficiencies. The ideology of "rugged individualism" revealed itself in a highly exploitative use of the land. Sites—waterfronts, for example—which in Paris, Rome, or London were reserved for community pleasure and enjoyment, were turned over to heavy industry; factories and mills besmirched the air and polluted the waters. Individual plots of land were covered with buildings, leaving little or no room for air or recreation. No provision was made for play space for children. There were few restrictions on what individuals could do with their land. In all of these respects American cities were no different from most nineteenth-century industrial cities. At that time people simply had not yet learned how to live in cities. The old industrial cities of England or the Ruhr Valley showed essentially the same pattern. But in Europe, where there was a precedent for greater control over individual behavior, it was easier to institute city planning and to enforce regulations for the benefit of the community even at the expense of the individual.

In the twentieth century, however, even American cities realized that they could not continue their uncharted course and began to set up plans for their future development. Zoning ordinances were passed, attempting to regulate the use of land. Improved housing standards were enacted. Areas were cleared to serve as "lung blocks" or breathing spaces. Parks and playgrounds were set aside for children and adults, and even for the elderly. Greater attention was devoted to the architecture of public buildings. Skyscrapers were required to terrace their upper stories in order to permit light in the canyons below. Cities made determined attempts to clear the air and clean the streets. (Although Americans are, as a whole, outstandingly concerned with bodily cleanliness, they are notably deficient in concern for the cleanliness of their city streets; litter is a perennial problem in most large cities.) The twentieth century also made clear that slums and blighted areas were a luxury that cities could no longer afford; they cost more than they paid in taxes. Chicago, after creating miles of magnificent waterfront boulevard, turned its attention to the acres of slums behind that glittering façade. Although American cities in the twentieth century had not yet achieved the beauty of a Paris or a Rome, they were on their way. They were beginning to realize that unregulated, unplanned, individualistic city growth was impossible; in the end everyone paid for the mistakes of anyone.

But perhaps the greatest force for change in the structure of American cities was the widespread use of the automobile. The old urban pattern included a central business district where large department stores, recreation and amusement facilities, banks, and various light industries were concentrated. People from all parts of the city used to go "downtown" to do their major shopping where a greater variety and choice in merchandise was available. But as automobile traffic increased without adequate provision for parking and the narrow streets choked movement, it became more and more inconvenient to shop "downtown."

The automobile also stimulated another spectacular change in American communities, a movement out to the suburbs. In the past, comfortably situated city families had tended to gravitate to newer areas, leaving the older sections to newcomers, to immigrants from the Old World or migrants from the rural areas. These older areas were usually near the industrial or business districts; they were areas of social disorganization, with high rates in physical and mental illness as well as in delinquency. There were ethnic islands and Black Belts in these areas, cut off from the main current of community life. *Anomie* was common. Because rents were cheap, they were usually the first station for newcomers to the city. But as these newcomers got their bearings and learned their way around in their new setting, they tended to move out into more desirable areas. In the past they tended to displace other groups in better areas of the city. But at midcentury all classes and ethnic groups were fleeing the heart of the city and setting up new communities in the suburbs.

Suburban developments grew up almost overnight. The political, economic, and social implications of these changes in the physical structure of the community were profound. Political parties had to adjust their programs to a new geographical distribution of voters.[84] The old urban areas lost tax revenues, yet had to continue to supply services to an increasing number of people. The shopping centers established in the new suburbs have large parking areas and therefore attract customers away from the old urban centers; large department stores establish branches in the new communities, and other shops—so-called discount outlets—are able to undersell other retailers because of their lower rents and freedom from delivery and other service expenses. Churches desert the cities and migrate to the suburbs. Schools in some areas have room to spare; in others there is overcrowding. American institutions at mid-century were in the throes of adjusting to the many problems posed by these new patterns of community structure.

ETHNIC STRUCTURE

But not everyone, of course, moves out of the city; many of the old problems remain. Among these is the problem of relations among the several different ethnic and racial groups. And just as the physical structure of the community became a matter of public concern late in the nineteenth century, the ethnic structure has become a matter of public concern in the twentieth. In 1943 Chicago and Detroit established municipal intergroup agencies charged with the function of reducing intergroup tensions. Ten years later there were twenty-five such agencies; in addition, almost fifty cities had mayor's committees or civil unity councils performing essentially the same functions; and twenty-six other cities had commissions charged with enforcing or promoting fair employment practices.[85] These agencies are staffed with professional persons who have their own professional organization, formed in 1947. Their work has been described as follows:[86]

The ameliorative tension control programs had been augmented not only with educational programs designed to change attitudes—mass media materials having been widely introduced along with the earlier good-will type programs—but now included specific group involvement programs aimed at changing community living patterns. The earlier concern with the impact of certain public services on intergroup relations, such as police and recreation, led directly to the goal of eliminating all forms of discrimination and segregation in all of the services flowing from government. The municipal intergroup relations agency undertook to review Civil Service procedures, school employment patterns, health service practices, as well as the operation of public housing programs under municipal control, among many other phases of municipal activity.

In addition, programs frequently were devised to implement civil rights laws and licensing controls in the area of public accommodation. Discriminatory policies and practices by quasi-public agencies, such as those supported by Community Chests, were reviewed and programs were devised aimed at the elimination of such practices in these agencies. The expansion of equal employment opportunities and opportunities in the private housing market and the elimination generally of racial, religious, and ethnic discrimination became increasingly basic to the municipal intergroup relations agency program.

While not all the agencies have undertaken all these kinds of programs at the same time or in the same way, there has emerged a clear concept that the sanction of government must be shifted from the support of racial, religious, or ethnic discrimination and segregation wherever it exists, toward the positive support of democratic community living patterns. The existence of an agency within the framework of government itself, with the purpose of advancing such democratic patterns, has come to be regarded in many quarters as basic to government's proper discharge of its responsibilities. In this respect, then, the emergence of the municipal intergroup agency marks one of the major gains of the present civil rights movement.

. . . Today, in nearly all the cities where municipal intergroup relations agencies exist, a close working relationship has been established between the private civic groups and the governmental agencies.

These agencies are increasingly entrusted with administrative authority to enforce fair employment legislation. They have important advisory and coordinating functions, working with both governmental and private agencies.

These new ethnic-relations institutions have been the outgrowth, in part, of years of intensive research on the part of American social scientists. For at least half a century the immigrant and the Negro have been a matter of close scientific scrutiny; always the problem has been viewed in terms of the American ideal. Facts which in a less idealistic society would have been suppressed or hidden from public view have been exposed and widely publicized. Muckrakers have pointed their fingers at communities which exploited minority groups. A disapproving public opinion has been instituted. Race and ethnic relations in the United States have thus been in the public eye for many years; failures to improve these relations have been used as propaganda weapons by the enemies of ethnic groups. But the most important aspect of the situation has almost been overlooked, namely that there has been a steady progress toward improvement in ethnic and race relations. Americans are far ahead of most other parts of the world which have similar problems. Even the South is far ahead of South Africa. And it is a matter of interest to note that people in other societies, confronted with problems similar to those of the United States, behave little, if any, better than Americans,[87] and in many cases, worse. Indeed, the history of ethnic minorities in Europe is a far sadder record than that of ethnic minorities in the United States. There is nothing in American history to compare with the massacres and suppression of ethnic minorities in Europe from St. Bartholomew's Day to Buchenwald. It is in no sense to excuse riots in the United States if we point out that they never exceeded in virulence or extent the pogroms of the old regime in Russia or the systematic extinction of Jews by Hitler.

STATUS STRUCTURE

The criteria of status may be classified for our purposes here into three categories, namely: (1) those related to institutionalized rank and family or lineage; (2) those related to work or production, including industry, government, church, or profession; and (3) those related to consumption or styles of living, entertaining, and "social life" in the narrow sense of "society."

Institutionalized Rank and Family. Today no more than when Lord Bryce was observing the American scene are there institutionalized ranks in American society. Today, as then, "the idea of a regular 'rule of precedence' displeases the Americans, and one finds them [still] slow to believe that the existence of such a rule in England entitling the youthful daughter of a baronet, for instance, to go first out of the room at a dinner party on the host's arm, although there may be present married ladies both older and of some personal distinction, is not felt as a mortification by the latter. . . . That an obscure earl should take precedence of a prime minister who happens to be a commoner shocks Americans out of measure."[88]

Much less than in the nineteenth century is a family a source of social distinction at mid-century. In some New England communities and in some old communities of the South, "family" or "lineage" may be made much of; but in most American communities pretensions to status based on lineage are viewed indulgently rather than obsequiously by most people. The trends away from family-based status noted by Bryce have become even more marked in the twentieth century. When a large proportion of the population were immigrants, it meant something to be American-born or of native parentage; but as an increasing proportion of the population is native-born and live and think like other native-born persons, "family" is harder and harder to enforce as a basis for status. Furthermore, as we pointed out earlier, the great mobility of Americans tends to weaken the status-giving importance of "family." Outsiders or newcomers are less likely to be impressed by "old families" than are those who were born and reared in the community.

Production- or Occupation-Related Areas of Status. When Bryce was observing the American scene, great industrial wealth was a source of high status.[89] But despite the importance attached to wealth, Bryce continued, in and of itself it was less important so far as status was concerned than it was in England, for in England, rank, with the accompanying status, could be bought, whereas in the United States it could not. In America, he observed, if a man's "private character be bad, if he be mean, or openly immoral, or personally vulgar, or dishonest, the best society will keep its doors closed against him."[90] The kind of status described by Bryce as inherent in great industrial leaders seems at mid-century to be accorded to great figures in the world of consumption—moving picture stars, great athletes, great baseball players, great entertainers.[91]

In any hierarchical structure, status is accorded to the positions in accordance with the levels they occupy. This is as true in the United States as in Europe, including the U.S.S.R. In general, status is measured in terms of privileges and prerogatives, and is proportional to the amount of power exercised.

No more than in Bryce's nineteenth century is intellectual attainment today the basis for high status until—as he pointed out—it becomes eminent. Men like Einstein achieve high status, as do winners of Nobel awards. But the scholars and scientists in the universities, while given theoretical recognition, do not enjoy high status in the sense that streets are named after them—as in European and Latin American countries—or that they are deferred to. They wait in line like everyone else.[92]

Consumption-Related Areas of Status: "Leveling Up and Leveling Down." There is still another kind of status based on how people live, on consumption patterns. Bryce, who described the situation as it existed in New England in the nineteenth century, predicted that status based on exclusiveness would tend to spread to all parts of the country.[93] Actually, the reverse has tended to occur. "Society," in this sense, is becoming an anachronism in most American communities in the twentieth century, a tendency seemingly inevitable whenever abundance supersedes scarcity.

The tremendous growth and spread of high consumption standards tended to erase many of the older differences in living styles. The decline in a servant class made it difficult to maintain large domestic establishments on the lavish scale of earlier years. The consumption antics of the old high-status classes became matters of quaint historic interest; the public gaze had, in effect, inhibited them.[94] It was increasingly difficult to be exclusive when fewer and fewer people were striving to be included and when such social pretensions were either ignored or provoked public criticism.

The psychology of consumption in an age of abundance differs from that in an age of scarcity. The use of excessive consumption to maintain invidious status distinctions becomes anachronistic. Kings, prelates, and nobility have, from time immemorial, used lavish display as a technique for dazzling and, in effect, cowing the masses. The wealthy in the past similarly practiced conspicuous consumption to that end. One American social scientist traced consumption patterns in the leisure class back to symbols of exploitation; the canons and standards of taste were devised to demonstrate that the leisure class did not have to work; it exploited others to do its work.[95] In the United States this function of conspicuous display was performed vicariously by women.

By mid-century, however, the old patterns had suffered attrition. The economics of abundance rendered the invidious use of consumption anachronistic, for there can be little invidious distinction in consumption when it is important that everyone consume. One may still achieve a measure of invidious distinction by driving a Cadillac rather than a Plymouth; but there is no distinction in merely owning a car.[96]

The picture of a small group at the top enjoying luxuries denied to the large masses below them is unrealistic in an economy organized like that in the United States.[97] The luxuries of the people at the top depend on a wide distribution of goods beneath them. They cannot have Cadillacs unless the masses can and do buy Plymouths; they cannot have 27-inch color television sets unless the masses have at least table models; they cannot have their custom-built modern homes unless millions of people have prefabricated or pre-cut houses.[98]

Even in the areas where status distinctions have traditionally existed or exist today, the kinds of behavior institutionalized for superior and inferior have not involved servility on one side or hauteur on the other. The only place where the servility pattern has characterized status relationships has been in the more isolated or backward southern communities where Negro-white relations have been of this nature. But elsewhere it has been strikingly absent as an institutionalized phenomenon. Its absence has, for over

659

a century, been frequently noticed by foreign observers.[99] Even deference as an institutionalized pattern is not common, an omission that has also been widely commented upon as illustrating the lack of manners in Americans. European immigrants used to come with habits of deferring to their "superiors" as they had done at home, only to discard them soon after becoming "Americanized."

The occupational upgrading of the economy, the trend toward the equalization of income, the increase in the average amount of education, the gradual disappearance of ethnic differences, and the rise in consumption standards have had the effect of increasing middle-class patterns of thinking. Most people think of themselves as middle class. This middle-class point of view has had the effect, as we pointed out above, of decelerating the impetus of labor unions, of rendering many workers conservative politically, and of giving a middle-class stamp to the arts. Such qualitatively different classes as "nobility," "bourgeoisie," "proletariat," and "peasant" have no more reality in the United States than such other nineteenth-century European classes as "capitalist" and "toiling masses."[100] The trend in the United States is toward a large congeries of middle classes, with only vestigial classes above and below them.[101]

The Structure of the American Mind

Observers of American institutions have, at least since Bryce's great classic, recognized the basic function performed by public opinion. We spoke earlier of its static aspects in connection with political institutions. At this point a brief statement with respect to the more dynamic aspects of this great force seems in order.

Although there is a legitimate sense in which we may speak of *the* American public, actually there are literally scores of American publics— financial, consuming or buying, motion-picture, sports, radio, television, photography, high-fidelity, hot-rod, churchgoing, gardening, fashion, do-it-yourself, jazz, traveling, camping, hunting-and-fishing, skiing, and so on. And even within each of these specialized publics there are subpublics, so that a motion-picture star speaks of his public, or a ball player of his. Some publics are local; others extend beyond local limits. Some publics are latent or potential and have to be created or set up. There was, for example, no adolescent public until it was created by such magazines as *Seventeen*; no horror-story-reading public until magazines catering to this taste were published.

So far as the informational content of the "American mind" is concerned, we should distinguish several levels. At the lowest level, aside from the limited personal observation which individuals make in the course of their day-by-day living and the gossip and talk they engage in, the chief sources of information about the outside world come from the local newspaper or radio or television report. The emphasis here is almost wholly personal. The conception of what constitutes news is quite different from that, let us say, in the U.S.S.R. Anything unusual that happens to people—whether it is good or bad—is news. No matter how much it reflects on American institutions, it is freely published, it is not suppressed. The news, therefore, is about the doings and activities of individuals or groups of individuals. News is about people.

Personality journalism also characterizes the national news weeklies. Abstract forces and trends, reported through their impact on people, are rendered colorful by being related to how they affect John Doe and his family.

For the most part news is reported objectively and without evaluation. It reflects a kind of journalism not commonly found on the Continent, where newspapers are often party organs. Although most American newspapers are either Democratic or Republican in editorial policy, there is a powerful tradition that the news itself should be presented objectively, unslanted. There is also a powerful tradition of freedom of the press, jealously guarded by professional newsmen; the least infringement of this right is attacked as censorship and strongly resisted. It was once feared that large advertisers could influence newspaper policy; but most advertisers prefer to avoid the adverse publicity which such attempts at control might harvest. More serious is the trend toward monopoly in the dispensing of news. It is expensive to establish a newspaper; in many cities there is only one. It is feared that the concentration of news into so few channels will have a distorting effect, and that not enough differing points of view will be made available for the public to base its opinion on.

News is not self-interpreting; it has to be commented upon and analyzed. There is, therefore, a second layer in the news-opinion structure which consists of editorial writers, news commentators, and columnists. They have daily or weekly channels in newspapers or on the air through which they tell their readers, listeners, or viewers what to think about the factual news which the lowest layer of reporters has gathered and presented. This level in the opinion structure ranges from dignified, high-caliber, thoughtful analyses to bigoted, emotional, prejudiced harangues. European read-ers are familiar with this type of writing; some of their newspapers consist almost wholly of this kind of editorializing, even in news columns.

The monthly and quarterly press attempts to tell the reader what is happening, not in terms of personalities but in terms of social forces. The men who engage in this kind of writing do a more basic type of research than do the newspaper reporters, making use of social science research, government reports, official documents, interviews with leading men in many fields, and a host of other sources. They attempt to put all the pieces of the jigsaw together. In the popular magazines, this kind of writing—the article—has now surpassed the leisurely literary essay, and even fiction, in popularity.

The number and complexity of issues facing people today are unprec-edented. They cannot possibly keep abreast of all of them. What happens is that people select the issues that arise in their own publics and ignore—are apathetic about—the others. It often takes a great effort to "rouse the public" to issues that are not of immediate concern to its members.

Since in a democracy the vote of even the most uninformed person has the same weight as that of the most informed, misgivings are sometimes expressed about the ability of modern governments to govern effec-tively.[102] On the other hand, one student of public-opinion polls con-cludes that the public is often ahead of its leaders.[103]

It is of great importance for government to know what is actually going on in the "American mind." A similar need has arisen in connection with industries which cater to the public, especially in advertising and market-ing. There has developed a highly complex technique for studying public opinion, based on social psychology, sociology, political science, eco-nomics, and statistics. Polling, community surveying, analysis of the con-tents of mass media, and other experimental techniques have been insti-tutionalized on a high level of competency. Some of this dredging of the American mind is on a fairly superficial level, but, there is also research of high-grade quality, done by social scientists, perhaps under such govern-mental auspices as the Department of Agriculture, the Bureau of Labor Statistics, the Census Bureau, or independently in the universities.

It is, of course, only a stone's throw from measuring public opinion to attempting to manipulate and control it. The implications for freedom of the emerging science of control are profound. In the early years of the science of advertising, use was made of such relatively simple psychological laws as those of suggestion, of color, of perception. Research eventually moved out of the laboratory into the field; simple polling techniques were added to test the success of various methods. At the present time even psychiatry is being requisitioned to help probe unconscious motives in buying, to discover how to appeal to unconscious fears and wishes.[104] Sociology is also being applied to show how group relationships may be exploited for marketing purposes.[105]

An extremely serious problem is posed by the emergence of this science of control, or "brain-washing," as it is called in the hands of one's enemies. How much freedom is possible for those at whom these controls are beamed? Do the mass media produce a "mass man," anonymous, suggestible, gullible, pitiable, contemptible, unanchored, alienated from his fellows, individuated—that is, severed and isolated, but not individualized —cut off from stable group moorings that used to protect him? Is he thereby made ready to attach himself, willy-nilly, to any leader or slogan that is properly presented to him? Is he left without self-determination, oriented to the mass media rather than to his fellows, a passive spectator distracted by empty amusements, a nonentity to be manipulated at will by those with scientific know-how? The spectacle of a population made up of such robot-like individuals is dispiriting. Scientific control may be more humane than control by violence; but is it less dangerous?

One social scientist has said that "the power to control individual human behavior and the exercise of such power are incompatible with human freedom. By recognizing that circumstance, by voluntarily tying our own hands and laying a solemn injunction upon our ardent imaginations, we become able to use the control that science has given us to set future generations free."[106] This seems like a counsel of perfection, and correct as it undoubtedly is, we may not have to rely on it. For whatever may be the situation with respect to control in totalitarian societies,[107] the situation in the United States does not seem too sinister.

The mass man may, in fact, be an illusion, an artifact resulting from the conditions of communication through the mass media. The man to whom the advertising or the propaganda is beamed cannot answer back immediately. Actually, however, the seemingly passive, powerless public may be seething with resentment. The public fights back, but it operates slowly. It takes some time before it bestirs itself, but finally it acts. Then, much to his surprise, the manipulator finds himself confronted with an enraged consumers' reform movement. Although the public may be described as readily subjected to exploitative manipulation, it is perhaps equally accurate to picture the "mass man" as the one holding the whip and making the would-be manipulators jump through the hoop. The "mass man" must be constantly wooed by new techniques.[108] When he ceases to respond to a certain appeal it must be discarded and another substituted for it. The illusion of power entertained by the manipulators results from their concentrating on successes and discounting their failures.

Cultural Institutions: Leisure and Taste in a Middle-Class Society

To many nineteenth-century observers the United States was merely a backward Europe. No powerful privileged class had as yet arisen to supply aristocratic models of refinement and culture. Given time, the inference was, such an aristocracy would emerge. Without such an upper class there could be no culture at all; no alternative possibility ever occurred to these early observers and critics. The "certain condescension in foreigners" which Lowell commented on was posited on the theory that all culture had to be aristocratic to be recognized as culture in the first place.

The United States was, in fact, a cultural dependency of Europe throughout the nineteenth century. There was, to be sure, an indigenous folk culture—oral and aural—on the frontier. There were ballads, square dances, singing schools; there were lyceums and chautauquas. But this was not the sort of thing one showed company; one did not apologize for it, of course, but it was not in the grand tradition.

As it turned out, however, the United States was not merely a backward Europe destined in time to fit the aristocratic model. It proved to be something new and radically different. Leisure was not to become a privilege limited to a small class that could specialize in taste. With abundance and its emphasis on consumption, leisure and taste became mass phenomena.

In the twentieth century, therefore, especially in the second quarter, Americans began to throw off the thralldom of European tradition. Painters, writers, and musicians began to see the potentialities of their native background and created an idiom of their own. American artists were becoming emancipated from their former colonial attitude toward European culture. They were more self-confident about their own contributions, about characteristically American art forms. Accustomed to the old colonial attitude, some European observers were surprised to find Americans engaged in creating their own culture with more or less unconcern for

664

European models, not even looking at them over their shoulders as they worked, not asking for approval from their erstwhile teachers. In many areas America has, so to speak, seized the initiative.

LEISURE

Leisure-time activities are a major industry in the United States. Travel, sports, and entertainment are big business. History offers no guidance in solving the problems of leisure in an economy of abundance. In no other age but the present could the *hoi polloi* command the services of artists for their leisure-time enjoyment. In the seventeenth, eighteenth, and nineteenth centuries, as we saw above, Europe created an aristocratic pattern for the consumption of leisure which, at its best, was admirable and beautiful. The gentleman scholar, the patron of the arts, and the amateur scientist were the beneficiaries and guardians of wealth, and they took their cultural responsibilities seriously; the creative tradition was strong. Mass leisure, however, as known today, is a quite different phenomenon.

When leisure first became an item of mass consumption the tendency in the United States was toward heavy patronage of the so-called spectator sports and passive forms of recreation, such as motion pictures. The burgeoning do-it-yourself movement at mid-century suggests, however, that as the amount of leisure increases further, it tends to be invested in more active and creative channels. People buy power tools and machinery. They build their own homes, make furniture, and take up gardening. They assemble high-fidelity record-playing machines; they reassemble automobiles, substituting different parts for standard ones. They sail boats; they organize bands and orchestras for fun; they square dance; they put on plays. In brief, the passive, spectator phase of leisure-time consumption may be only an initial and transitory stage in which leisure is still not great in proportion to work. It is conceivable that as the amount of time required for work decreases, leisure-time activities will tend to become more active and creative.

Americans do not buy and read books to the extent that citizens of other advanced nations do.[109] This fact has been attributed to the rapid tempo of business life, to the nonintellectual tone of the country-club set, and to the competition of radio, television, and automobile for the reader's time. Nonreading habits, it is also alleged, result from the use of books written solely as texts in college teaching and the "corrupting" influence of the misapplication of John Dewey's theories of education.[110]

Although Americans are not book-buying readers, they are avid magazine readers. The mass periodicals carry a surprising amount of quality writing. *Life Magazine*, for example, published Churchill's *The Second World War*, Hemingway's *The Old Man and the Sea*, and Charles Beard's *The Republic*, among other outstanding classics. The recent rise to popularity of the cheap paper-bound book—some 250 million a year—has increased the number of people buying and reading books. Many of the titles are reprints; many of them are detective, western, horror, or sex novels; but many of them are books of the highest quality.[111]

A common observation by foreign observers is the lack of good talk or conversation in the United States. The European custom of sitting around a table and engaging in intellectual give-and-take is not characteristic of Americans. Ordinary nonoccupational conversation is likely to be devoted to automobiles, television sets, electrical appliances, and the like. Students do have their so-called bull sessions, which resemble European conversation, but for the most part such spontaneous interplay is not common. There is, however, a substitute in the form of study groups, workshops, round tables, town halls, forums, buzz sessions, question periods after lectures, discussion groups, and conferences of one sort or another where people come together primarily to talk with each other in a serious but friendly way.

TASTE

Aristocratic taste operated on a small scale; it emphasized the precious, the contrived, and the subtle.[112] Beauty inhered in the exquisitely wrought, in qualities that took years of culturing to achieve and to appreciate. Such cultivated taste is likely to be traditional and conservative, to lean heavily on the past, to find its standards in the classics. Much time is involved in training and acquirement; taste is therefore a prerogative of only the leisured class and a form of the "conspicuous consumption" which Veblen analyzed. It is probably not indefinitely extendible because it is so far removed from actual popular standards. The fact that so many people wear business clothes and speak with fairly correct grammar can be misleading when we come to evaluate popular culture. Because they look so much like the classes that formerly had exclusive access to culture, we expect them to have cultivated tastes. We hold up highly cultivated standards in music, in appreciation of the fine arts, in all areas of taste. Contemplation of the actual popular standards is therefore likely to cause some revulsion.

666

Radio, television, books, magazines, motion pictures, and records reveal a lamentably dismal vulgarity if judged by traditional or classical norms. If the people who enjoy these forms of popular art wore overalls and spoke with identifying mannerisms, there might be less concern. High standards of taste would not be expected of them.

There are doubtless as many people with highly cultivated taste in America as in most advanced countries, as the number of symphony orchestras, quality records, and high-caliber books suggests. The difference is that in other countries popular forms of art do not characterize the culture; in America they do. We do not think of British culture, for example, in terms of its music-hall artists, or of French culture in terms of its café singing and dancing. There is no reason to suppose, however, that, given a choice, the British would not choose the same kind of radio and television programs that Americans choose. Indeed, the fact that American popular art finds a world-wide acceptance, being welcomed wherever it is allowed to penetrate, suggests that there is nothing unique or characteristically debased about American taste. American motion pictures, jazz records, and comics have universal appeal. As a matter of fact, the popular singers, dancers, comedians, clowns, actors, and other entertainers seem to be interchangeable among all the advanced nations. In the field of taste, it might be said that the "dictatorship of the proletariat" is stronger in the United States than anywhere else—certainly stronger than in Russia. The man with the consumer dollar sets the standards of popular taste.

An interesting paradox marks popular taste in America. On the one hand, popular art as purveyed by the mass media, especially by the national magazines, radio, television programs, and motion pictures, is peopled by a cheerful, even childish, population which loves games, action, prizes, jazz; it loves to laugh condescendingly at amiable people who make absurd mistakes. It wants a happy ending. The effect is often distracting rather than recreative.

On the other hand, there is great preoccupation with violence. This in itself is not distinctive; the mind of the folk everywhere reveals the same preoccupation. Fairy tales are full of it, as are legends, ballads, and folk tales. Dragons must be slain; deaths must be avenged; children are spirited away or kidnapped; animals eat human beings; and so on. There is doubtless a valid psychological explanation for this interest in violence, and there is nothing inherently morbid or pathological about it. One British analyst, indeed, sees violence as a protest of modern man against enforced conformity, against lack of appreciation.[113]

American popular art, however, has elaborated the theme of violence to such an extent that many people have become alarmed by it. Scores of murders take place on television screens every day; radio programs abound with them. So-called comic strips and books depict murder as an everyday occurrence. Motion pictures have several genres—the western, the detective story, the horror story, the war story—centering in killing.

It is not the violence per se that alarms people; it is the attitude toward it which seems sinister. There is violence for its own sake, even sadistic violence. There is a tendency, as in the fabulously popular creation of Mickey Spillane, Mike Hammer, to justify the use of violence outside the law, to allow people to decide for themselves when and where they may use it.[114] This is one of the darker aspects of American taste in mid-century, and its implications are searchingly explored by thoughtful observers in many professions.

In the effort to spread the enjoyment of aesthetic satisfactions as widely as possible, the precious, the exquisite, and the subtle tend to be sacrificed. But glamour tends to be heavily emphasized. Certainly, glamour plays an important role in any society. One of the commonest adverse criticisms made of communistic countries is that the life they offer is drab, dreary, without éclat. Even Russia has found it necessary to introduce touches of glamour in the form of cosmetics and fashionable clothing, as well as in ballet and music. In the United States glamour has been institutionalized to a high degree. It is big business. Cosmetics, beauty parlors, advertisements, fashion, household equipment, automobiles, and travel are all part of the enormous effort to glamorize life for the man on the street, his wife, and his children. Observers have long pointed out the egalitarian impact of mass clothing. The design which is created by the *haut couturier* for the aristocrat is reproduced for mass production and is soon commonplace. Automobiles are designed to appeal to women in beauty as well as to men in performance. Color is introduced everywhere. Gaiety is looked for as well as utility. Glamour is as regular a part of life as eating; and if her sink full of dishes looks discouragingly unglamorous to the housewife, all she has to do is turn on the television set and be reassured that if she is using So-and-So's detergent, her hands may be as beautiful as those of the lovely girl demonstrating the product on the screen.

This brief overview of American institutions can give only the most superficial conception of the complexity of American society. It is full of all the contradictions which communists insist must presage the downfall of capitalistic economies. And yet it is perhaps precisely because of these contradictions that American society is so strong and so stable. The tough balance which they strike makes for strength rather than for weakness.

And, finally, it should be pointed out that the problems of working out its destiny, in an era of abundance, which beset the United States at mid-century are unique only in the sense that these problems have not yet arisen in other societies. But if industrialization there runs a similar course, the same problems will doubtless occur among them also. The most important conclusion one can draw from the nature of American institutions at mid-century is this: that the road to the "classless society" need not be sought through a transitional "dictatorship of the proletariat"; the expansion of the middle class, especially by the leveling up in income, occupation, education, and consumption, which the abundance of modern technology makes possible, leads as near to that goal as the nature of social organization permits.

Notes

[1] The ideals of freedom and equality are only two of many American values about which I might have chosen to integrate my discussion. Many students, native and foreign, have attempted to formulate the animating genius of American institutions. Henry Steele Commager, for example, tells us that there were several thousand foreign commentators alone, over a century and a half, who attempted to describe American institutions; see H. S. Commager (ed.), *America in Perspective* (New York: Mentor edition), p. x. In addition, hundreds of social scientists in the United States devote their whole lives to researching and interpreting them. The list of values which have been delineated by them is indeed long; for example, monogamous marriage, freedom, acquisitiveness, democracy, education, monotheistic religion, science, associational activity, disregard of law, direct action, local government, practicality, prosperity, material well-being, patriotism, uniformity, conformity, personal achievement, success, activity, work, moral orientation, progress, material comfort, equality, external conformity, secular rationality, nationalism-patriotism, individual personality, and racism. See Robin M. Williams, Jr., *American Society* (New York: Knopf, 1951), pp. 390ff. Other attempts to distill the essence of American institutions have been made by modern anthropologists, including Margaret Mead, *And Keep Your Powder Dry* (New York: Morrow, 1942); Geoffrey Gorer, *American People* (New York: Norton, 1948); and Clyde Kluckhohn, *Mirror for Man* (New York: McGraw, 1949). I have selected only two of these values—freedom and equality—not only because space is limited, but also because selection and emphasis focus discussion of a topic—American institutions—which might otherwise become unmanageable.

[2] W. F. Ogburn, "Technology and the Standard of Living in the United States," *American Journal of Sociology*, 60 (January 1955), 380–388. For more detailed documentation of the trend toward abundance, see Jessie Bernard, *Social Problems: Stress, Role, and Status in a Context of Abundance* (New York: Dryden Press, 1957), Chapter 1.

[3] David M. Potter, *People of Plenty, Economic Abundance and the American Character* (Chicago: University of Chicago Press, 1954).

[4] David Riesman's *The Lonely Crowd* (New Haven, Conn.: Yale University Press, 1950) analyzes the changing American character structure in terms of its emphasis on consumption rather than, as formerly, on work.

[5] Samuel Lubell, *The Future of American Politics* (New York: Harper, 1950).

[6] In 1947 the Department of the Church and Economic Life was formed in the Federal Council of Churches (which became, in 1950, the National Council of the Churches of Christ in the U.S.A.) to undertake a series of studies, financed by the Rockefeller Foundation, on some of the basic ethical problems of a business society. Among the six volumes published in this series was one by Elizabeth E. Hoyt and collaborators, on *American Income and Its Use* (New York: Harper, 1954), in which the implications of abundance are dealt with in some detail. All six studies have been summarized in a small volume by M. W. Childs and Douglass Cater, called *Ethics in a Business Society* (New York: Mentor, 1954).

[7] Erich Fromm, *Escape from Freedom* (New York: Farrar and Rinehart, 1941).

[8] David Riesman, *op. cit.*

[9] See H. S. Commager, *op. cit.*, pp.38 ff.

[10] Nothing about America excited more comment by foreign observers in the nineteenth century than this sense of equality. To those accustomed to receiving deference in Europe, it was often distasteful; to those who came as immigrants, it was exhilarating. (*Ibid.*)

[11] Although the ideals of freedom and equality are always recognized as basic values in American institutions, sociologists in the United States do not often talk in terms of such concepts. They look like shibboleths and are usually shunned as glittering generalities. American sociologists are likely to speak, instead, of their opposites, namely, control or regulation, and stratification. Control and stratification have become almost an obsession with American sociologists. One great justification for the study of sociology is that it would provide a basis for the control of social life. A tremendous research literature has developed on the techniques of control. Only rarely has anyone pointed out the contradiction between this control orientation in research and the ideal of freedom. In the area of stratification, however, there has been a great to-do about the lack of correspondence between the ideal of equality and the facts of inequality.

[12] Read Bain, "Our Schizoid Culture," *Sociology and Social Research*, 19 (January 1935), 266–276.

[13] F. S. Chapin, *Contemporary American Institutions* (New York: Harper, 1935), pp. 45–47, *passim*.

[14] Jessie Bernard, *American Community Behavior* (New York: Dryden Press, 1949), Chapter 22.

[15] The period between the first agitation for redress and its final achievement, however approximate, has been labeled a "cultural lag." The theory states that a harmonious integration among the parts of a social system is the normal situation; if a disorganizing factor occurs, usually an invention or technological advance, one aspect of the society or institutional integration gets out of kilter, and until the other institutions "catch up" there will be maladjustment and dislocation, manifested in the form of social problems. The facts which this theory attempts to explain are certainly correct. Changes do not occur at the same rate in all aspects of a society's institutional structure. But the implications of the lag theory do not square with the facts. It assumes "the common welfare as the goal of common effort" (*Recent Social Trends in the United States* (New York: McGraw, 1933), Vol. I, p. xv). Actually, the realignment, the balancing, must be a deliberate and conscious effort on the part of the victims of change or of others in their behalf. The lag theory is correct if interpreted as follows: a new invention or technological change tends to upset an existing equilibrium so that inequalities are created if they did not already exist, or

exaggerated if they did, or reversed. The interest group which feels itself disadvantaged by the change then attempts to equalize its position, even at the expense of the freedom of the other party.

[16] Jessie Bernard, *op. cit.,* Chapter 5.

[17] One commentator points out that in time the average man will have little if anything in the way of industrial contribution worth paying for. See Norbert Wiener, *The Human Use of Human Beings* (Boston: Houghton, 1950).

[18] A. J. Jaffe and Charles D. Stewart, *Manpower Resources and Utilization* (New York: Wiley, 1951), p. 192.

[19] *Ibid.*

[20] *Ibid.,* p. 196.

[21] *Ibid.,* p. 192.

[22] *Ibid.,* p. 143.

[23] John I. Snyder, Jr., "The American Factory and Automation," *Saturday Review* (January 22, 1955); see also *New York Times* editorial (December 7, 1954), and news item in the same issue, p. 17.

[24] Nat Weinberg, "Labor on the Hook," *Saturday Review* (January 22, 1955), p. 38. This article suggests that in addition to stabilizing employment, the effect of the guaranteed annual wage, according to its proponents, would be (1) to humanize the process of technological change; (2) to minimize layoffs; (3) to maintain living standards of displaced workers up to a year; (4) to encourage retraining of displaced workers for new jobs; (5) to encourage efforts to discover or develop alternative employment for displaced workers; and (6) to encourage reduced prices.

[25] Herman P. Miller, "Factors Related to Recent Changes in Income Distribution in the United States," *Review of Economics and Statistics,* 33 (August 1951), p. 218.

[26] Margaret Reid, "Changing Income Patterns," in Elizabeth E. Hoyt and collaborators, *op. cit.,* p. 128.

[27] *Ibid.,* pp. 233–234.

[28] A. J. Jaffe and R. O. Carleton, *Occupational Mobility in the United States, 1930–1950* (New York: King's Crown Press, 1954), p. 52.

[29] Natalie Rogoff, "Social Stratification in France and in the United States," *American Journal of Sociology,* 58 (January 1953), p. 356.

[30] It is, of course, basic to most military organizations and inherent in totalitarian systems.

[31] Even Russia has held up American agriculture as a model for imitation.

[32] The reapportionment of representation, which the Constitution prescribes every decade, does not take place. The theory for flouting this provision is that the rural vote constitutes a conservative force and should therefore be protected.

[33] Other ways to organize production besides family and corporation are (1) individual enterprise, (2) cooperative organizations, and (3) governmental agencies.

[34] There have been three great eras of mergers or consolidations in American history: the late nineteenth century, the 1920s, and the 1950s. The first resulted in the great trust era, which aroused so much public hostility that it was braked by the Sherman Anti-Trust Act of 1890. In 1914 the Clayton Act was passed, attempting to strengthen antitrust legislation.

[35] John Kenneth Galbraith, *American Capitalism, The Concept of Countervailing Power* (Boston: Houghton, 1952).

[36] In the nineteenth century it began to be clear that if the producer and seller were to be free to do whatever they pleased, consumers were in danger of being victimized. A great consumers' movement, led by the Central Federation of Women's Clubs, resulted in laws for the protection of consumers; a second great consumers' movement in the 1920s extended legislation protecting consumers. The need to protect consumers and buyers is not, of course, peculiar to the American economy. One student canvassed the history of British legislation and emerged with a devastating indictment of business methods as reflected in it. From at least the thirteenth century

on, fraud, deceit, and adulteration have been the subject of strict legislation. See Gustavus Myers, *America Strikes Back* (New York: Washburn, 1935).

[37] The Hoover Committee, for example, revealed in 1954 that there were then in process many lawsuits in which one agency of the government was suing another. See *Newsweek* (October 18, 1954), p. 30.

[38] In addition to the checks and balances built into the American government by the Constitution, others have grown up. For example, because rural votes tend to predominate in the election of the Congress and urban votes tend to elect presidents — a result of the electoral system — there is a rural-urban conflict of interests reflected in the conflict between these two branches of government. By and large the rural vote has tended to be more "isolationist" than the urban, especially as regards Europe. See Samuel Lubell, *op. cit.*, p. 250.

[39] As a matter of fact, however, the history of American foreign policy has shown remarkable independence of the party in power.

[40] Note, especially, the perennially proposed Bricker amendment.

[41] Address at the Lincoln Memorial, June 29, 1947.

[42] The complex constitutional problems involved in this case had been foreshadowed earlier. In two cases — *Classic* (1941) and *Screws* (1945) — it was recognized that the national government had the authority to safeguard the fundamental civil rights of suffrage and due process by policing the actions both of private persons and of state and local public officers. But the problems of policing the actions of local school boards by the national government were of another order of magnitude.

[43] Samuel Lubell, *op. cit.*, p. 261.

[44] Wilhelm Bauer, "Public Opinion," *Encyclopaedia of the Social Sciences* (New York: Macmillan, 1934), Vol. 12, p. 670.

[45] Hadley Cantril (ed.), *Public Opinion, 1935–1946* (Princeton, N.J.: Princeton University Press, 1951); George Gallup and S. F. Roe, *The Pulse of Democracy* (New York: Simon and Schuster, 1940).

[46] Geoffrey Gorer, *op. cit.*

[47] The Jacksonian Revolution, for example, and the Roosevelt Revolution were more than mere figures of speech. They were fundamental reorientations in philosophy and policy.

[48] Gabriel Almond, *The Appeals of Communism* (Princeton, N.J.: Princeton University Press, 1954).

[49] As shown, for example, by Samuel Stouffer in *Communism, Conformity, and Civil Liberties* (New York: Doubleday, 1955).

[50] The Communists, trained in exploiting grievances wherever they were found, were on the side of the underdog in most cases. That their motives were Machiavellian and exploitative was beside the point. The reactionary could label as "communistic" any movement which Communists had supported, no matter how clearly in line with American traditions it was, especially in the area of civil rights.

[51] Two scholarly studies of the congressional investigating committees, one from 1938 to 1944 and one from 1945 to 1950, came to the conclusion that they should be abolished since the international threat from communism could best be dealt with by the Foreign Relations and Armed Services committees, and the internal threat by the Judiciary committees. See Father August Raymond Ogden, *The Dies Committee, A Study of the Special House Committee for the Investigation of Un-American Activities, 1938–1944* (Washington, D.C.: Catholic University Press, 1943); and Robert K. Carr, *The House Committee on Un-American Activities, 1945–1950* (Ithaca, N.Y.: Cornell University Press, 1952).

[52] Samuel Lubell, *op. cit.*, p. 243.

[53] Gabriel Almond, *op. cit.*

[54] The sketch of dating in the text refers primarily to middle-class children. At lower socioeconomic levels ethnic differences reflecting Old World ideologies may persist, as in the case of some Italian families who tend to shield their daughters

from unchaperoned contacts with men. Or dating may, among children of immigrants, take on a wholly unromantic cast. See, for example, Arnold W. Green, "The 'Cult of Personality' and Sexual Relations," *Psychiatry: Journal of the Biology and Pathology of Interpersonal Relations,* 4 (August 1941), pp. 344–348.

[55] Joseph I. McConnell and Janet M. Hooks, in Elizabeth F. Hoyt and collaborators, *op. cit.,* p. 240.

[56] *Ibid.,* p. 239. The popular European stereotype of the American housewife feeding her family entirely out of cans implies that the diet must be inferior. Less value is placed on a large investment of time in cooking in the United States, it is true; but the nutritional value of frozen and precooked foods is usually equal to foods prepared in a more traditional manner.

[57] This fact has been documented by many studies, the most extensive and famous of which are those by A. C. Kinsey and his associates.

[58] The shock to parent-child relationships produced by technological change is by no means restricted to the United States. It is found all over the world in varying degree, especially in underdeveloped areas. See, for example, Margaret Mead (ed.), *Cultural Patterns and Technical Change* (New York: Mentor, 1955).

[59] Martha Wolfenstein, "Trends in Infant Care," *American Journal of Orthopsychiatry,* 33 (1953), pp. 120–130.

[60] This decline in the divorce rate since 1946 in spite of prosperity, which usually increases it, is probably related to the decline in the marriage rate, itself a reflection of a small generation of marriageable age, the generation born during the depression in the 1930s.

[61] Mirra Komarowsky, *Women in the Modern World, Their Education and Their Dilemmas* (Boston: Little, 1953).

[62] It is argued, for example, that for those without academic inclinations, the school is a constant reminder of inferiority. Hostility is generated which may become extremely destructive.

[63] For example, although compulsory attendance at school is accepted as a principle, the stringency of the laws and the rigor with which they are enforced vary from state to state, and even from community to community.

[64] Attendance at private schools was reported to have increased 49 per cent between 1946 and 1954; at public schools, 20 per cent. See *Time Magazine* (January 31, 1955), p. 67.

[65] For a brief summary of state laws with respect to tax support of parochial schools, see Jessie Bernard, *American Community Behavior, op. cit.,* pp. 442–443.

[66] *Statistics of Land-Grant Colleges and Universities* (U.S. Department of Health, Education, and Welfare, Bulletin No. 8, p. iii, Washington, D.C., 1954).

[67] Seymour Harris, *The Market for College Graduates* (Cambridge, Mass.: Harvard University Press, 1949).

[68] *Higher Education for American Democracy* (Washington, D.C., 1947).

[69] Dael Wolfle, director, Commission on Human Resources and Advanced Training, *America's Resources of Specialized Talent* (New York: Harper, 1954).

[70] *Ibid.,* p. 77.

[71] Some of the shortage in personnel at mid-century was the result of the low birth rate in the 1930s during the depression years. Many of the young people who should have been entering the professions in the 1950s had never been born. A great new wave of young people was anticipated for the 1960s. These were the babies born in the great upsurge in the birth rate of the 1940s.

[72] Denis W. Brogan, "A Cambridge Professor Celebrates the American Public School," in H. S. Commager, *op. cit.,* pp. 213–223.

[73] A European schoolboy was once asked why he did not attend discussion groups at the local *Amerika Haus,* where he could learn about the problems of boys in other countries. He replied that he had too much homework to do; he didn't have time for such activities. The implication was that they were trivial, not important, at least not

as important as book learning. In the United States the opposite point of view would tend to prevail; participation in discussion groups is considered of equal importance to book learning.

[74] Comparisons of the achievement of students in the schools today with that of students of the past are equivocal. In some respects modern students are superior; in others, they are not. For a summary of half a dozen such comparisons see "Which is Better—the Old or the New?" *Saturday Review* (September 11, 1954), p. 19.

[75] The Catholic population is reported to have increased 50.7 per cent between 1929 and 1952; eighteen large Protestant denominations increased 42.7 per cent in the same period.

[76] Samuel Lubell, *op. cit.*, p. 223.

[77] *Ibid.*

[78] One student notes, however, that it has tended to force an irreconcilable we/they choice which may not always be wise. See *ibid.*, p. 223.

[79] There were individual immigrants as early as the seventeenth century, but not in large enough numbers to set up communities.

[80] Gabriel Almond, *op. cit.*

[81] Some of the issues are divorce legislation; legalization of contraceptive information; use of tax funds for parochial schools; legalization of gambling, especially the game of bingo by which some Catholic churches raise money; censorship; Sabbath observance.

[82] The needy aged were provided for by the Old Age Assistance program; disadvantaged children were provided for by the Aid to Dependent Children program and by the Maternal and Child Health programs; two insurance programs were also set up, one for retirement and one for unemployment. There is as yet no federal provision for general assistance, although there is such provision in most states. The feeling is strong that health is a public concern and that there should be federal help in this area; by mid-century, however, there was as yet no public health insurance program. The most disadvantaged children are those of (a) broken families and of (b) families where the breadwinner is ill, or of (c) large families with only one breadwinner. The Social Security Act of 1935 attempted to help in the first two kinds of cases. All states except Nevada now cooperate with the federal government in programs of aid to such dependent children. In 1952 about one and a half million children were receiving aid in almost 600,000 families. The average amount paid ranged from $26 per month in Mississippi to $121 in Idaho, averaging $81 per family for all states and territories. Almost half of these children were in families in which the father had deserted the family or had not married the mother or was not in the home for some other reason; only about one fifth needed aid because of the actual death of the father. A considerable proportion of the need resulted from some disability of the father. No claim is made that the assistance is adequate; nine tenths of the families had incomes of less than $2,000 even with help. Yet a survey of the operation of the program from 1936 on shows that in general the aims of the program—to furnish economic support needed for health and development, to secure an education, and to share in community life—have been at least partly achieved for the estimated six million children helped. See Joseph L. McConnell and Janet M. Hooks, *op. cit.*, pp. 250–255.

[83] At mid-century community chest drives were finding it difficult to achieve their goals in many communities. Searching questions were being asked about the whole structure of voluntary agencies. Instead of surveying community needs and finding the most effective way to meet them, administrators had to appease the vested interests of private agencies, even those not making a basic contribution.

[84] "To map the growth of almost any of our larger cities since the turn of the century is to map this upward, outward push of the masses toward the greener suburbs, propelling the older residents before them. And the story of the Democratic party in the big cities is really the story of the social and political revolution which

marched along with this exodus from the slums. The exodus was not accomplished in a single, mass evacuation, but through successive moves, from one neighborhood to the next. Each new neighborhood represented a higher rung on the social and economic ladder. And as they climbed, the masses were transformed." See Samuel Lubell, *op. cit.*, p. 60.

[85] National Association of Intergroup Relations Officials, *NAIRO Reporter* (January 1954).

[86] *Ibid.*

[87] Note, for example, the reactions of England toward the influx of Negro workers from British Guinea and Jamaica, or that of the French toward the Arabs in Algeria.

[88] Lord James Bryce, *The American Commonwealth* (New York: Macmillan, 1891), p. 618.

[89] *Ibid.*, p. 619.

[90] *Ibid.*, p. 620.

[91] This change in popular interest from heroes in the world of production to those in the world of consumption was documented by a study of popular magazines in the twentieth century. See Leo Lowenthal, "Biographies in Popular Magazines," in P. F. Lazarsfeld and Frank Stanton (eds.), *Radio Research 1942–1943* (New York: Duell, Sloan, and Pearce, 1943), pp. 507–520.

[92] It was reported in the press that a number of German scientists who had been imported into the United States left as soon as they could because they felt they were not accorded the status they deserved and were accustomed to receiving in Germany.

[93] Lord James Bryce, *op. cit.*, p. 623.

[94] Popular descriptions of lavish balls and parties often exposed them as vulgar displays, lacking imagination or taste. See Ferdinand Lundberg, *America's Sixty Families* (New York: Vanguard Press, 1937) and Cleveland Amory, *The Last Resorts* (New York: Harper, 1952).

[95] Thorstein Veblen, *The Theory of the Leisure Class* (New York: Macmillan, 1898).

[96] By mid-century a kind of reverse snobbism deterred some people from driving Cadillacs; they drove Ford station wagons instead.

[97] It is still accurate, according to observers, in the U.S.S.R.

[98] That the above situation is not uniquely American but inherent in mass production in a nontotalitarian economy is shown by the fact that at mid-century it was found emerging in England also. On the Continent, as well, the idea of a mass market was beginning to influence industrial organization.

[99] Sometimes the foreign observer was sympathetic with the absence of this kind of status relationship, as Bryce, for example, was (*op. cit.*, pp. 622–623). Sometimes, however, he resented the "off-handedness of the servant, the rudeness and shortness of the shop girl, the boorishness of the casual employee, the unconcern of the official, the familiarity of the colored porter on the railways . . . the vanishing of those amenities which had their foundation in the realization of superiority on the one hand, of inferiority on the other." See Frederick C. de Sumichrast, *Americans and the Britons* (New York: Appleton, 1914), pp. 3, 8, 22.

[100] A large corporation may have more owners than employees.

[101] Increasingly the "lower class" consists of people who are somehow or other handicapped — widowed mothers and their children, the aged, the defective, or the ill — rather than of normal people in the working force.

[102] Walter Lippmann, *Public Philosophy* (Boston: Atlantic Monthly Press, 1955).

[103] George Gallup, *op. cit.* The impact of public opinion on foreign policy is not always enlightened, however. See Thomas A. Bailey, *The Man on the Street* (New York: Macmillan, 1948).

[104] Lydia Strong, "They're Selling Your Unconscious," *Saturday Review* (November 13, 1954), pp. 11–12, 60ff.

[105] William H. Whyte, Jr., "The Web of Word of Mouth," *Fortune Magazine,* 50 (November 1954), pp. 140–143, 204ff.

[106] Margaret Mead, *And Keep Your Powder Dry* (New York: Morrow, 1942), p. 192.

[107] See, for example, Czeslaw Milosz, *The Captive Mind* (New York: Knopf, 1953).

[108] The resort to probing the unconscious, referred to above, resulted from the fact that less than 30 per cent of the public believe most of the advertising they read. See Lydia Strong, *op. cit.,* p. 60.

[109] "The Common Reader's Choice," in the London *Times Literary Supplement,* Friday, September 17, 1954, p. lvi. George Gallup found, as a result of a two-year survey of reading habits, that the typical Englishman reads nearly three times as many books as the typical American; that if the United States had as many book-shops per capita as Denmark there would be 23,000 of them instead of only 1,450.

[110] *Ibid.*

[111] *Ibid.*

[112] Alexis de Tocqueville, in H. S. Commager (ed.), *op. cit.,* p. 41.

[113] J. Bronowski, "The Face of Violence," *The Nation,* 180 (January 29, 1955), pp. 93–96.

[114] Christopher LaFarge, "Mickey Spillane and His Bloody Hammer," *Saturday Review* (November 6, 1954), pp. 11–12, 54ff.

Index

INDEX

*

Displaced persons: Finland, 200–1, 214

Divorce: United Kingdom, 112–14; Australia, 163–64; Finland, 222; Poland, 263–65; Yugoslavia, 317; Greece, 380; Brazil, 566, 576; USA, 625–26, 632–33

Dreyfus affair, 451, 458

Drinking: United Kingdom, 86, 127; Australia, 180–81; Greece, 373; Brazil, 584–8

Duclos, Jacques, 467

Durkheim, Emile, 14, 16, 17, 17–18, 34–35, 93

Duverger, Maurice, 466

Economic controls: United Kingdom, 69, 75–79; Australia, 146, 150–52, 157; Finland, 205–6; Greece, 379; Brazil, 557–58

Economic institutions: United Kingdom, 65–86; Australia, 149–56; Finland, 197–209; Poland, 253–61; Yugoslavia, 293–309; Greece, 335–46; Israel, 403–16; Brazil, 536–49; USA, 603–13. *See also* Agriculture and forestry; Collective farms; Commerce; Cooperatives; Economic controls; Economic planning; Employers' associations; Employment; Entrepreneurship; Foreign trade; Handicraft; Income; Industrialization; Industry; Labor relations; Labor unions; Management; Mechanization; Merchant shipping; Monopoly; Occupations; Private enterprise; Public ownership; Social security; Social services; Socialism; Taxes; Wages; Welfare state; Women, employment of

Economic planning: Poland, 253, 256–57, 261; Three Year Plan . . . Poland, 256; Six Year Plan . . . Poland, 256; Five Year Plan . . . Yugoslavia, 292–93, 295, 328

Education:

United Kingdom, 121–25; education and social status, 56–58, 121; Education Act of 1944, 57, 121, 123; primary and secondary schools, 121–25; vocational training, 122, 124–25; adult education, 123, 125; higher education, 123–25

Australia, 169–73; home training, 166; primary and secondary schools, 169–72; parochial schools, 171–72, 174; higher education, 172–73; adult education, 178–79

Finland, 222–25; primary and secondary schools, 222–24; double-track system

discussed, 223–24; Swedish schools, 224; vocational education, 224, 225; adult education, 225

Poland, 266–69; ideological education, 266–67; primary and secondary schools, 267; vocational education, 267–68; higher education, 268

Yugoslavia, 320–24; history of education, 282; ideological education, 317, 318; primary and secondary schools, 320–22; vocational education, 321–22; higher education, 323–24

Greece, 363–69, 380; history of education, 363–66; higher education, 364–65; vocational education, 364–65; teachers, 365–67, 367–68; private schools, 365, 368; primary and secondary schools, 367–68

Brazil, 579–83; eradication of illiteracy, 579–80; private schools, 581; parochial schools, 581; adaptation to technological civilization, 582; higher education, 582–83

USA, 634–45; local school boards, 635; primary and secondary schools, 635–37; the great debate, 637–39; parochial schools, 640; higher education, 640–43; evaluation of education, 643–45

Education Act of 1944: United Kingdom, 57, 64, 121, 123

Einstein, Albert, 658

Electric power: Finland, 205; Greece, 338

Elizabeth II: Queen of England, 94; Queen of Australia, 158

Emigration: from United Kingdom, 48

Employers' associations: Australia, 155; Finland, 208–9

Employment: United Kingdom, 65–66; Australia, 152; Finland, 199; Yugoslavia, 293–94; of immigrants Israel, 392

Entertainment. *See* Leisure-time activities

Entrepreneurs: Israel, 409–11, 413, 416

Episcopal Church: Brazil, 578; USA, 646. *See also* Church of England

Equalitarian social attitudes: working class, Australia, 144

Equality: USA, 592–93, 598–600, 600–2, 634

Establishment for Social Insurance: Yugoslavia, 307

Ethnic composition: Australia, 137–38; Brazil, 525–27

Ethnic relations: Australia, 138–40,

681